Feasting on the Word

Editorial Board

Feasting on the Word

Preaching the
Revised Common Lectionary

Year C, Volume 4

DAVID L. BARTLETT and BARBARA BROWN TAYLOR

General Editors

WESTMINSTER
JOHN KNOX PRESS
LOUISVILLE · KENTUCKY

Book design by Drew Stevens
Cover design by Lisa Buckley

First edition
Published by Westminster John Knox Press
Louisville, Kentucky

This book is printed on acid-free paper that meets the American National Standards Institute Z39.48 standard. ∞

PRINTED IN THE UNITED STATES OF AMERICA

10 11 12 13 14 15 16 17 18 19 — 10 9 8 7 6 5 4 3 2 1

Library of Congress Cataloging-in-Publication Data

Feasting on the Word : preaching the revised common lectionary / David L. Bartlett and Barbara Brown Taylor, general editors.
     p. cm.
  Includes index.
  ISBN 978-0-664-23103-3 (v. 8 alk. paper)
  ISBN 978-0-664-23102-6 (v. 7 alk. paper)
  ISBN 978-0-664-23101-9 (v. 6 alk. paper)
  ISBN 978-0-664-23100-2 (v. 5 alk. paper)
  ISBN 978-0-664-23099-9 (v. 4 alk. paper)
  ISBN 978-0-664-23098-2 (v. 3 alk. paper)
  ISBN 978-0-664-23097-5 (v. 2 alk. paper)
  ISBN 978-0-664-23096-8 (v. 1 alk. paper)
  1. Lectionary preaching.   2. Common lectionary (1992)   I. Bartlett, David Lyon, 1941–
II. Taylor, Barbara Brown.
  BV4235.L43F43 2008
  251'.6—dc22

                              2007047534

Contents

Publisher's Note

Feasting on the Word: Preaching the Revised Common Lectionary is an ambitious project that is offered to the Christian church as a resource for preaching and teaching.

The uniqueness of this approach in providing four perspectives on each preaching occasion from the Revised Common Lectionary sets this work apart from other lectionary materials. The theological, pastoral, exegetical, and homiletical dimensions of each biblical passage are explored with the hope that preachers will find much to inform and stimulate their preparations for preaching from this rich "feast" of materials.

This work could not have been undertaken without the deep commitments of those who have devoted countless hours to working on these tasks. Westminster John Knox Press would like to acknowledge the magnificent work of our general editors, David L. Bartlett and Barbara Brown Taylor. They are both gifted preachers with passionate concerns for the quality of preaching. They are also wonderful colleagues who embraced this huge task with vigor, excellence, and unfailing good humor. Our debt of gratitude to Barbara and David is great.

The fine support staff, project manager Joan Murchison and compiler Mary Lynn Darden, enabled all the thousands of "pieces" of the project to come together and form this impressive series. Without their strong competence and abiding persistence, these volumes could not have emerged.

The volume editors for this series are to be thanked as well. They used their superb skills as pastors and professors and ministers to work with writers and help craft their valuable insights into the highly useful entries that comprise this work.

The hundreds of writers who shared their expertise and insights to make this series possible are ones who deserve deep thanks indeed. They come from wide varieties of ministries, but they have given their labors to provide a gift to benefit the whole church and to enrich preaching in our time.

Westminster John Knox would also like to express our appreciation to Columbia Theological Seminary for strong cooperation in enabling this work to begin and proceed. Dean of Faculty and Executive Vice President D. Cameron Murchison welcomed the project from the start and drew together everything we needed. His continuing efforts have been very valuable. Former President Laura S. Mendenhall provided splendid help as well. She made seminary resources and personnel available and encouraged us in this partnership with enthusiasm and all good grace. We thank her and look forward to working with Columbia's new president, Stephen Hayner.

It is a joy for Westminster John Knox Press to present *Feasting on the Word: Preaching the Revised Common Lectionary* to the church, its preachers, and its teachers. We believe rich resources can assist the church's ministries as the Word is proclaimed. We believe the varieties of insights found in these pages will nourish preachers who will "feast on the Word" and who will share its blessings with those who hear.

Westminster John Knox Press

Series Introduction

A preacher's work is never done. Teaching, offering pastoral care, leading worship, and administering congregational life are only a few of the responsibilities that can turn preaching into just one more task of pastoral ministry. Yet the Sunday sermon is how the preacher ministers to most of the people most of the time. The majority of those who listen are not in crisis. They live such busy lives that few take part in the church's educational programs. They wish they had more time to reflect on their faith, but they do not. Whether the sermon is five minutes long or forty-five, it is the congregation's one opportunity to hear directly from their pastor about what life in Christ means and why it matters.

Feasting on the Word offers pastors focused resources for sermon preparation, written by companions on the way. With four different essays on each of the four biblical texts assigned by the Revised Common Lectionary, this series offers preachers sixteen different ways into the proclamation of God's Word on any given occasion. For each reading, preachers will find brief essays on the exegetical, theological, homiletical, and pastoral challenges of the text. The page layout is unusual. By setting the biblical passage at the top of the page and placing the essays beneath it, we mean to suggest the interdependence of the four approaches without granting priority to any one of them. Some readers may decide to focus on the Gospel passage, for instance, by reading all four essays provided for that text. Others may decide to look for connections between the Hebrew Bible, Psalm, Gospel, and Epistle texts by reading the theological essays on each one.

Wherever they begin, preachers will find what they need in a single volume produced by writers from a wide variety of disciplines and religious traditions. These authors teach in colleges and seminaries. They lead congregations. They write scholarly books as well as columns for the local newspaper. They oversee denominations. In all of these capacities and more, they serve God's Word, joining the preacher in the ongoing challenge of bringing that Word to life.

We offer this print resource for the mainline church in full recognition that we do so in the digital age of the emerging church. Like our page layout, this decision honors the authority of the biblical text, which thrives on the page as well as in the ear. While the twelve volumes of this series follow the pattern of the Revised Common Lectionary, each volume contains an index of biblical passages so that all preachers may make full use of its contents.

We also recognize that this new series appears in a post-9/11, post-Katrina world. For this reason, we provide no shortcuts for those committed to the proclamation of God's Word. Among preachers, there are books known as "Monday books" because they need to be read thoughtfully at least a week ahead of time. There are also "Saturday books," so called because they supply sermon ideas on short notice. The books in this series are not Saturday books. Our aim is to help preachers go deeper, not faster, in a world that is in need of saving words.

A series of this scope calls forth the gifts of a great many people. We are grateful first of all to the staff of Westminster John Knox Press: Don McKim, Jon Berquist, and Jack Keller, who conceived this project; David Dobson, who worked diligently to bring the project to completion, with publisher Marc Lewis's strong support; and Julie Tonini, who has painstakingly guided each volume through the production process. We thank Laura Mendenhall, former President of Columbia Theological Seminary, and Columbia's Dean, Cameron Murchison, who made our participation in this work possible. Our editorial board is a hardworking board, without whose patient labor and good humor this series would not exist. From the start, Joan Murchison has been the brains of the operation, managing details of epic proportions with great human kindness. Mary Lynn Darden, Dilu Nicholas, Megan Hackler, and John Shillingburg have supported both her and us with their administrative skills.

We have been honored to work with a multitude of gifted thinkers, writers, and editors. We present these essays as their offering—and ours—to the blessed ministry of preaching.

David L. Bartlett
Barbara Brown Taylor

A Note about the Lectionary

Feasting on the Word follows the Revised Common Lectionary (RCL) as developed by the Consultation on Common Texts, an ecumenical consultation of liturgical scholars and denominational representatives from the United States and Canada. The RCL provides a collection of readings from Scripture to be used during worship in a schedule that follows the seasons of the church year. In addition, it provides for a uniform set of readings to be used across denominations or other church bodies.

The RCL provides a reading from the Old Testament, a Psalm response to that reading, a Gospel, and an Epistle for each preaching occasion of the year. It is presented in a three-year cycle, with each year centered around one of the Synoptic Gospels. Year A is the year of Matthew, Year B is the year of Mark, and Year C is the year of Luke. John is read each year, especially during Advent, Lent, and Easter.

The RCL offers two tracks of Old Testament texts for the Season after Pentecost or Ordinary Time: a semicontinuous track, which moves through stories and characters in the Old Testament, and a complementary track, which ties the Old Testament texts to the theme of the Gospel texts for that day. Some denominational traditions favor one over the other. For instance, Presbyterians and Methodists generally follow the semicontinuous track, while Lutherans and Episcopalians generally follow the complementary track.

The print volumes of *Feasting on the Word* follow the complementary track for Year A, are split between the complementary and semicontinuous tracks for Year B, and cover the semicontinuous stream for Year C. Essays on the Old Testament lections for the Season after Pentecost that are not covered in the print volumes will be available on the *Feasting on the Word* Web site, www.feastingontheword.net.

For more information about the Revised Common Lectionary, visit the official RCL Web site at http://lectionary.library.vanderbilt.edu/ or see *The Revised Common Lectionary: The Consultation on Common Texts* (Nashville: Abingdon Press, 1992).

Feasting on the Word

PROPER 17 (SUNDAY BETWEEN AUGUST 28 AND SEPTEMBER 3 INCLUSIVE)

Jeremiah 2:4-13

⁴Hear the word of the LORD, O house of Jacob, and all the families of the house
of Israel. ⁵Thus says the LORD:
What wrong did your ancestors find in me
    that they went far from me,
and went after worthless things, and became worthless themselves?
⁶They did not say, "Where is the LORD
    who brought us up from the land of Egypt,
who led us in the wilderness,
    in a land of deserts and pits,
    in a land of drought and deep darkness,
    in a land that no one passes through,
    where no one lives?"
⁷I brought you into a plentiful land
    to eat its fruits and its good things.
But when you entered you defiled my land,
    and made my heritage an abomination.
⁸The priests did not say, "Where is the LORD?"
    Those who handle the law did not know me;

Theological Perspective

When our children were little, we enjoyed vacations at the beach. For many years, though, our son did not like the ocean itself. He feared the water's rush. It could knock you down and get in your eyes, he said. It could carry you away and, besides, there might even be sharks.

He preferred to play in what we called the "baby pools," puddles carved and filled by receding tides. Some of them were not so very small, either—up a ways from the surf, where the water was ocean, of course, but manageable and still. He splashed and played, made castles on the puddle's shore. Eventually, however, the water went away, soaked back into the sand. When it did, we sometimes tried to make baby pools—dug holes and ferried buckets of ocean water to fill them, but that did not work at all. Soon he learned that the only lasting water was the real water. Yes, it was dangerous, but that is where the wonder was too.

It is a parable, of course, bemusing and even pastoral. A similar image of "living water" and "managed water" is used in our text for today, but there is nothing pastoral about it. Nor is the prophet bemused. Jeremiah stands aghast on God's behalf, expresses God's utter incredulity that the chosen people have chosen against the Almighty, who brought them out of Egypt and through the

Pastoral Perspective

It is hard to hear indictment. We do not want to hear it; we would rather not. It is not a channel where parishioners choose to linger, nor will we find it cross-stitched and hanging in congregational homes. Even while the contemporary hearing community may be deflecting its confrontation by presuming this word is about an ancient time and another place, its truth resonates with our own waywardness and lifestyle until, at some level, hearers are aware that it is truth about their stories as well. These words become uncomfortably revealing for the congregation. They have about them the ring of a parent full of righteous indignation upbraiding wayward children. This paraphrased line particularly sounds parentally proverbial: "People who pursue worthless things become worthless themselves" (v. 5).

The prophet may command, "Hear the word of the LORD, . . . house, . . . families" (v. 4), but the pastor can help listeners hear by acknowledging that this may not be comfortable, and that may well be because we are hearing its truth. This work is something like that of a choir director teaching a chorus a difficult and unfamiliar piece, but one which is substantive and powerful. Part of the work for the pastor is helping the people to sit in the presence of this uncomfortable word until they begin to hear it.

the rulers transgressed against me;
the prophets prophesied by Baal,
and went after things that do not profit.

⁹Therefore once more I accuse you,
says the LORD,
and I accuse your children's children.
¹⁰Cross to the coasts of Cyprus and look,
send to Kedar and examine with care;
see if there has ever been such a thing.
¹¹Has a nation changed its gods,
even though they are no gods?
But my people have changed their glory
for something that does not profit.
¹²Be appalled, O heavens, at this,
be shocked, be utterly desolate,
says the LORD,
¹³for my people have committed two evils:
they have forsaken me,
the fountain of living water,
and dug out cisterns for themselves,
cracked cisterns
that can hold no water.

Exegetical Perspective

This section is part of a longer address by Jeremiah that stretches from 2:1 to 4:4, but it may well be considered the heart of the matter, for these verses constitute the announcement of a covenant lawsuit. Jeremiah, speaking for the Lord, indicts and judges Israel for breaking the covenant. This reference to a legal proceeding is a common device among the eighth-century prophets (e.g., Isa. 5:1–7; Mic. 6:1–8), and Jeremiah thus stands in a long tradition of formalized patterns of prophetic speech.

This passage probably comes from the earliest period of Jeremiah's ministry, following his call in 626 BCE. This period included the efforts of Josiah to expand his kingdom northward but is prior to the reforms of Josiah launched in 621 BCE, after the discovery of the scroll of what was probably the book of Deuteronomy in the temple under repairs. This earliest period includes Jeremiah's strong opposition to idolatry, a major theme of this passage.

God's indictment against Israel begins with a poignant question, "What wrong did your ancestors find in me?" (v. 5a). The implied answer is "Nothing." This implied claim of divine innocence is backed up by a historical retrospective recalling the wonders of exodus deliverance and protection through the perils of the wilderness (v. 6). Finally, God brought them into the land and gave them the

Homiletical Perspective

Texts like this one present special challenges for preachers, since they assume the backdrop of the Sinai covenant—a theme unfamiliar to some congregations. A first step for preaching, then, may be to sketch this covenant background. Israel and its God are partners in a type of covenant common in the ancient world, bound together by a web of mutual promises. Israel, however, has defaulted on its obligations, and in this text the divine Partner's dismay pours forth in language full of pathos—part legal argument, part lovers' quarrel. Unless things change quickly, political and economic consequences will bear down on the nation with terrible force.

Clearly, a Christian congregation is not a nation among other nations. Hastily drawn parallels with the North American situation may be misleading. At the same time, this text and others like it in Jeremiah present a good opportunity for preacher and congregation to consider together how Christian readers of such texts may discern a lively word for their own time, taking seriously the historical, cultural, and political distance that separates ancient nation and contemporary congregation. Resonances with our own experience emerge when we recognize that Christians, like the ancient Israelites, understand themselves as claimed by a gracious God. Considered through that lens, this text offers at least two strong themes for preaching.

Jeremiah 2:4-13

Theological Perspective

wilderness. Nowhere else in all the world has a nation "changed its gods, even though they are no gods."

The setting of Jeremiah 2:4–13 is that of a courtroom—a familiar image in the prophetic literature. God routinely brings suit against wayward Israel (and their leaders). Of particular interest here is how the Almighty not only prosecutes the people of the current generation but names as coconspirators even the ancestors who first left Egyptian captivity (and presumably all generations since). By means of Jeremiah's intense interrogations God also indicts priests, prophets, and kings. Ironically, tragically, these "leaders" have been installed by God both to mediate the divine presence and to lead God's people in pursuit of their sacred purpose. Like blind guides they have led them only astray. As the ancestors ceased seeking after God's will (v. 5), so have recent generations of priests (v. 8); and Jeremiah, himself of priestly lineage, seems to have been especially sensitive to this irony. No one, it appears, follows God's ways or even attempts to discern what those ways might be.

Jeremiah appeals to water as an image to seal the Almighty's indictment. It is customary for the prophetic imagination to interpret the commonplace, of course—and no image Jeremiah could have marshaled would have been so obviously powerful or telling. God's providing water in the desert for the parched and bitter refugees was a part of the collective consciousness. Too, Jerusalem and surrounding precincts were long familiar with seasonal dramas related to water supply. "Normal" droughts could mean an immediate and grave danger. With the installation of aqueducts, leaders imagined they had, through engineering, "solved" the problem—but that self-congratulation was only hubris. The constellation of these factors would enrich the simple image of living water and cisterns even without the Babylonian threat.

As it is, Jeremiah writes just before the destruction of Jerusalem. The chosen people's rejection of God has come to full term, and utter annihilation is upon them. The people question why it has come to this—although in truth they do not want to hear or know the answer. Jeremiah quotes the Almighty's indictment of the chosen people:

My people have committed two evils:
They have forsaken me, the fountain of living water,
And [they have] dug out cisterns for themselves,
    Cracked cisterns that can hold no water.

(2:13)

Pastoral Perspective

Helping the congregation to examine the form of the presentation and the tone of the text may well help them get close enough to recognize its connection with their lives. Verses 5–9 contain a pattern of rebuke that parishioners may well have used in their own family arguments. "What did I do wrong? Why didn't you? I initiated positively, but you, you responded negatively! You failed to do the positives, and you implemented the negatives, there, there, and there as well. You are responsible for this, and it has consequences!" Where have these cadences from Jeremiah already been heard in parishioners' lives, or where may they be repeated in their homes? Are listeners thinking, "This sounds like my parent," or "This sounds like my spouse," or "This sounds like me"? How might that familiarity affect their hearing of the Scripture? "Therefore once more I accuse you, says the LORD, and I accuse your children's children" (v. 9).

In the ears of the congregation these words can sound appropriately like a courtroom prosecutor. What is that experience like for a congregation that may well contain prosecutors and defendants, the indicted and judges, both vocationally and personally? The pastor can help discernment by slowing down the hearing of the text, acknowledging the variety of feelings evoked, and encouraging the congregants not to flee, but to find the courage, community, and trust to remain in the presence of the indictment.

Jeremiah reports that the Lord accuses the people of a foolish wastefulness: "I brought you into a plentiful land to eat its fruits and its good things. But when you entered you defiled my land, and made my heritage an abomination" (v. 7). "My people have changed their glory for something that does not profit" (v. 11). The relevance of this connection for contemporary people leaps off the Internet news and cable channel. The ecological crisis and the addiction to consumption are a cause of anxiety for many congregations. Pastorally, this ancient text brings into clearer focus the connection between this contemporary behavior and faithfulness. We can paraphrase the text: "This foolish wastefulness is sin. It is a refusal to live out God's intentions for our lives. This is not what the Creator intends for the creatures to do with creation."

What is truly an abomination to the Lord? What in our behaviors is an abomination to the Lord? We tend to look for "abomination" in our neighbor's behaviors or in foreign behavior. The speck in our neighbor's eye keeps us from seeing the beam in our own. The pastor may lift up the text here that points

plenty they now enjoy (v. 7a). Within the context of indictment God pleads the divine case as a gracious and saving God.

By contrast, Israel is described as choosing what is "worthless" and becoming worthless themselves (v. 5b). This is clearly a reference to idols, frequently referred to in Jeremiah as "worthless things" (e.g., 16:19–20). In turning to idols, Israel has defiled God's gift of the land and made it an "abomination" (v. 7).

The overall theme of this lawsuit against Israel is that the people have given up a God whose saving grace has been demonstrated in favor of loyalties that are false, worthless—in a word, ineffective. Such loyalties do not profit; they do not work. The word translated "profit" in verses 8 and 11 is used by the prophets almost entirely to describe the negative effect of false gods and false loyalties (e.g., Egypt in Isa. 30:5). The Hebrew word is *ya'al*, a play on the word "Baal." Baal equals no profit; *ba'al* is no *ya'al*.

Those who should have guarded the covenant tradition, condemned idolatry, remembered the story of God's graciousness, and kept the law have failed God and the people. Jeremiah leaves no one out. All categories of leadership are condemned as going after "things that do not profit": priests, teachers of the law, rulers, and prophets (v. 8). These are all the formal leadership roles in ancient Jerusalem. Priests fail to ask, "Where is the LORD?" Priests are the leaders who mediate between God and the people, so if the Lord has failed the people, priests should cry out in appeal to the Lord. The tradition of the laments in the Psalms shows this dynamic at work; but this has not happened.

Those who teach the law, perhaps scribes or sages, are accused of not knowing the Lord. The theme of the "knowledge of the Lord" is a major one in Hosea, who is often cited as an influence on the early Jeremiah. To know the Lord is not just to have conceptual, cognitive data about God. It is to be in relationship. In Hebrew "to know" implies participation in that which is known; so "to know the Lord" is to participate in the life of God. Those who were to teach this have failed to do so.

Rulers have transgressed. Jeremiah later has much to say about transgressing rulers, as Josiah's death ushers in a series of self-serving kings. Even in this early time, Josiah has yet to hear the scroll and confess that he is far from covenant obedience.

Finally, prophets—Jeremiah's counterparts—have abandoned their primary loyalty in favor of the popular cult of Baal and in so doing have chosen "no profit," worthlessness.

One central claim of this text is that the stories we remember and tell in worship matter. From its beginnings, the nation of Israel knew itself as a people delivered from the grip of bondage by mighty, saving acts of God. Now that story is no longer told, contends Jeremiah. Even the priests have forgotten. One of the chief reasons Israel and Judah have drifted into their present spiritual malaise is that they have failed at decisive moments to remember and practice the great narrative of their origins, the story of deliverance from slavery in Egypt.

Christians, too, understand who they are by telling a story of the gracious, mighty acts of God. We know ourselves as a people delivered through grace out of darkness into light, out of bondage into freedom. Baptism and the Table of the Lord compress that saving story into an economy of words and eloquent action. If we cease to tell, enact, and live by that saving story, other narratives will rush in to take its place. A widespread Western cultural story insists that we *are* what we *possess*. It is a false story—as is another that says the wealthy can enrich themselves endlessly at the expense of the poor, without consequence. Shaped by such stories, our lives no longer bear the distinguishing Christian markers of profound trust in God and generosity toward neighbor and stranger in Christ's name.

Our great Christian narrative of origins claims that our lives and all it takes to sustain them are gracious divine gifts—not rights or achievements—received at the hand of a God who loves all and wills the well-being of every person. A person or community that remembers its story as a story of grace is delivered from the bondage of anxious self-aggrandizement. Held in the grace of God, we do not need to finesse our way out of crisis through compromise or sell our birthright for short-term gains (vv. 6–8). We can attend to the well-being of others, knowing we are held in good hands.

A second theme that plays throughout these verses is the contrast between life that is worthy or worthwhile and life that is "worthless" (empty or vain). The term "worthless" occurs three times, in verses 5, 8, and 11. Israel, contends the divine covenant Partner, has become "worthless" (v. 5) by taking its cues from pagan neighbors rather than the covenantal code. Israel has exchanged the practices that construct a God-given life of true worth for a flimsy structure of short-sighted political alliances and religious compromises.

Parallels with contemporary experience are not far away. Human beings are as prone as ever to cast a

Jeremiah 2:4-13

Theological Perspective

The people of Jerusalem are dying of thirst—and the truth beneath those verses is both literal and spiritual. The Babylonians have laid siege to the city, or soon will, the great and relentless army from the north surrounding the holy city, cutting off both aid and supplies. The city's water is almost gone. While there was water in abundance when the aqueducts still worked, that flow of running water has been stopped, and the city's great cisterns are by now cracked and leaky. The people's water is running out. Get it?

For Jeremiah, though, the sad truth is not just the literal fact. For Jeremiah, the people's deathly thirst is a parable of a spiritual crisis. They have long since turned from the deep well of God's goodness and have, instead, tried to quench their deepest thirst with the thinnest of tonics, with leaky pots full of maggoty gruel: elixirs of gold; drafts of pagan alliances; double shots of worldly power and bloody militarism; cauldrons of boiling idolatries, poisonous leaders, false prophets, and unrepentant kings. Like saline for a people adrift at sea, these brews only intensify their thirst.

Long ago, God provided fresh water for the Israelites in the wilderness. Jeremiah will later say that even in this present wilderness God can again supply the people with water—which is to say, God is yet able to deliver this generation and its leaders from what seems a hopeless situation. God is still Israel's deliverer, or may be; but the prophet is not hopeful, if only because the people and leaders refuse to ask God for help. God, consequently, does not give it. Even if God were to provide instruction, the people and their leaders would refuse to obey— as it was in the beginning, is now, and ever shall be. So it is that God's desperate people have left to them only a memory of moisture.

The theological irony at the heart of Jeremiah is shown in sharp relief: the chosen of God have chosen other gods, have shunned God's purposes, even if it meant shunning God's provision. Now whatever provision they have made for themselves is at an end. They desire less than the Almighty, and that, Jeremiah says, is exactly what they have: gods who are no gods, who cannot hear or answer prayer, who cannot save them, now that calamity is upon them.

THOMAS R. STEAGALD

Pastoral Perspective

us toward our own "foolish wastefulness" as an "abomination."

"My people have changed their glory for something that does not profit" (v. 11). What does profit us, and what does make us appear glorious before God? Reflection on the experience of their lives will help parishioners to discern what has been rewarding and what has been empty. Culture has actively worked to persuade people to accept as rewarding things that are not a part of God's heritage of blessing. The pastor may use this text to help people define what profits them, and what does not profit them, by remembering what has been a part of their heritage of blessing from God. Our confusion about what is actually rewarding has become so profound that we have become idolatrous. We make into gods things that are not God or God's blessing to us. "Has a nation changed its gods, even though they are no gods?" (v. 11). The notion of "profit" is a tight knot in the modern mind, and this indictment text can serve as helpful sharp tool in unwinding it.

Being "appalled" and "shocked" and "desolate" (v. 12) are appropriate emotions for people who have been so foolishly wasteful with such an extravagant blessing. It is a familiar human pattern. It is like Esau's selling his birthright for a bowl of porridge. It is a familiar enough pattern that its familiarity adds to the credibility of the indictment. Like a physician diagnosing pneumonia, we should learn to recognize the symptoms. When we are spiritually thirsty and empty of rewarding purpose, it is very likely that we have abandoned the gifts that really give life and have embraced an ineffective substitute. "They have forsaken me, the fountain of living water, and dug out cisterns for themselves, cracked cisterns that can hold no water" (v. 13).

Pastorally, facing the relevance of this text and the losses it points toward means then dealing with the accompanying grief of acknowledgment. Are there pastoral or worship resources for grief work that help the congregation in the hearing of this text? What pastoral resources of reconciliation and restoration, such as services of prayer and healing, will help the congregation be blessed by the hearing of this text?

JOHN T. DEBEVOISE

Exegetical Perspective

The word "therefore" in prophetic speeches usually signals statements of judgment and penalty, but in this passage there is an immediate statement that God accuses both the present generation and the children to come; that is, they have incurred the wrath of God. However, God's anger seems to boil over again. God asks in puzzlement if anyone has gone to the farthest places (Cyprus and Kedar) and seen people who abandoned a God who served them graciously to serve a loyalty that brings no profit (vv. 10–11). God thinks the heavens should be shocked at this.

The closing images in these verses focus on water (v. 13), a crucial resource in the ancient world. Nothing could be of greater value in the geography of Jerusalem than fresh water. To refer to the Lord as a "fountain of living water" is instantly to communicate value almost beyond measure. Water is literally a source of life. The prophet suggests that the Lord is the source of such living water for Israel. To choose the Lord is to choose that which endures, renews, gives of itself; this is the opposite of choosing "no profit." The people who focus on immediate material life alone are tempted to think that Baal and his storms give life to the earth, but the prophet suggests that Baal's water is not reliable, and relying on Baal is too narrow and materialistic an understanding of life. Baal is like a cistern, the source of water when we have no source of fresh water, the stagnant water of last resort, which brings only the most limited life and, in any case, does not last. Cisterns notoriously become cracked, and the water leaks away. A cistern does not endure; Baal does not endure.

The idolatry Jeremiah indicts is focused less on false objects than on false hopes. In turn, these false hopes are based on forgetfulness. We have forgotten the stories of what God has done. We do not hear God's poignant plea to remember the history of divine grace we have inherited. We are lured by the new because we have forgotten the power and wonder of the past. For that forgetfulness we stand, along with ancient Judah, as those hearing the covenant lawsuit fully indicted.

BRUCE C. BIRCH

Homiletical Perspective

calculating eye toward their neighbors, eager to appropriate whatever tastes and trends seem to prevail among those whose power they envy—the rich, the successful, the influential. Change and chance happen to all, and all too quickly the possessions and social capital on which we have counted for self-worth and substance can slip from our grasp. Even leaning too heavily for a sense of worth on a successful career or a bond with a beloved person (partner or spouse or even children) can prove to be a dangerously brittle foundation for life. To find the truly worthy life, we may need to stop asking, "What will the neighbors think?" or even "How can I make myself indispensable (to an organization or a person)?" and ask instead, "What does God want to do in and through me for the sake of the world?"

We have said that this text needs to be read with care. The new community God has created is the church, not a chosen nation. However, there is undeniably a message here for those in positions of political power. Human beings cannot secure their own lives, individually or corporately. Consistently placing global economic and military domination ahead of the needs of the poor at home and abroad is, ultimately, a "leaky cistern" (v. 13) and no substitute for embracing the ways of the life-giving God. Only when we align our choices, individually and corporately, with the concerns of God in the world will our lives make sense and make a difference.

One attraction of the self-devised cisterns we construct to sustain our lives is that we feel we can control them. Living in active relationship with the life-giving God of the Scriptures brings obligations: the patient work of worship and prayer, acting compassionately, and working for justice. It is when we participate in the redemptive work of God—keeping promises, welcoming strangers, forgiving debts—that we drink from the fountain of the living God and discover a quality of life both sustaining and sustainable.

SALLY A. BROWN

Psalm 81:1, 10-16

¹Sing aloud to God our strength;
     shout for joy to the God of Jacob.
. . . .
¹⁰"I am the LORD your God,
     who brought you up out of the land of Egypt.
     Open your mouth wide and I will fill it.

¹¹"But my people did not listen to my voice;
     Israel would not submit to me.
¹²So I gave them over to their stubborn hearts,
     to follow their own counsels.
¹³O that my people would listen to me,
     that Israel would walk in my ways!
¹⁴Then I would quickly subdue their enemies,
     and turn my hand against their foes.
¹⁵Those who hate the LORD would cringe before him,
     and their doom would last forever.
¹⁶I would feed you with the finest of the wheat,
     and with honey from the rock I would satisfy you."

Theological Perspective

This text centers theologically on the relationship between God and God's people. It opens on a note of celebration for "the God of Jacob," in whom the people find their strength. The lectionary selection, however, focuses not on what has gone right in this relationship, but on what has gone wrong. Instead of listening and submitting to the divine will, the people have determined that they know better. As a result, the God who would be their strength—who would fight their enemies for them—has instead given them over to their own stubborn self-certainty. By implication, then, the people suffer—deservedly—at the hand of their enemies.

The passage encapsulates a theological perspective that runs through the Old Testament, particularly in the Deuteronomistic history and the book of Proverbs (although it is contested by Job and Ecclesiastes/Qoheleth): bad things happen to bad people. The triumph of one's enemies is a sure sign of one's infidelity to God. The trials brought on by political or military defeat are the divine hand chastening the people and reorienting them toward their God who, as Psalm 81 reminds its readers, brought them out of Egypt (thus constituting them as a people in the first place).

Within Christian theological tradition, this text calls to mind the doctrine of divine providence, with its echoes of traditional notions of original sin.

Pastoral Perspective

One of the enduring bits of wisdom that has helped shape my life came when my mother struggled with her mother's dementia. As my grandmother aged, her usual sweet self became demanding, even unreasonable. One day Mother said to me, "I am just going to have to make decisions about Mom as though her best self were still in control."

In this psalm, we hear an affirmation of God's best self: "Sing aloud to God our strength. . . . I am the LORD your God, who brought you up out of the land of Egypt" (vv. 1, 10a). We also hear a lament over Israel's worst self: "But my people did not listen to my voice; Israel would not submit to me" (v. 11).

In the midst of the dialogue, we catch glimpses of the "shadow" side of God: "So I gave them over to their stubborn hearts, to follow their own counsels" (v. 12).

As we listen to the psalmist, we need also to listen to ourselves. When we feel alienated from other people or from God, complex feelings, mixed memories, and conflicting emotions often dominate. External events and internal realities can skew our perspective. The gifted scholar Walter Brueggemann often reminds us in his books and lectures that in our journey of faith we can be "oriented" and "disoriented." Psalm 81 reflects orientation and disorientation, the same feelings or attitude my mother

Exegetical Perspective

This psalm calls people to sing in praise of God. The history of Israel impinges upon the tune and lyrics of this song. Singing is more than performed emotion; praise requires an understanding of the relationship between the singer and God.

Singing to God. The beginning of the psalm instructs the hearer or reader to sing praise to "God our strength" and to "shout for joy to the God of Jacob" (v. 1). In verses 2–3, the instrumentation becomes more specific: this is a song for voice, tambourine, harp, and trumpet. The song also has a time. This is a song for the new moon and the full moon, as God decreed in the days of Joseph (vv. 4–5). The psalm does not call for spontaneous, individual singing. This music is a group activity, involving many instruments and people praising God together. The music of praise occurs at regular intervals, already scheduled with a pattern set down in ancient days, before the people had even arrived in the land they called Israel. Although the lectionary selection does not include these verses, this context is necessary for understanding the type of worship occurring here. Worship provides a rhythm to life, a musical beat that began in past centuries and moves down through history to include these psalmists and, through the text, even readers today.

Homiletical Perspective

Facing Psalm 81 in the context of this week's lectionary selections, preachers encounter an opportunity either to complement a richly set table of texts for Sunday nurture or to select this particular one and prepare it as the main course for this week's Sabbath meal. The most difficult task may be choosing how to proceed, a dilemma many hosts face when anticipating special guests whom they wish to welcome with gratitude and care.

The heart of this psalm beats in the change of perspective that occurs following the opening stanza's call to worship. As the second stanza opens, the human partner singing this psalm adopts the point of view of God addressing the people, reminding them that they have been the object of divine compassion and the recipient of divine deliverance. Moreover, he confronts the people's failure to live up to expectations that have accompanied this divine embrace of their lives. The move is a bold shift, but one that temple worshipers understood and valued, knowing that the cantor (or singer) did not presume to take God's place. Rather, like the people, the cantor was assuming a representative role.

According to the Talmud, this psalm was set aside for weekly and annual use in the temple liturgies. Each fifth day, this psalm and its message would be

Psalm 81:1, 10-16

Theological Perspective

Providence and original sin have deep and intertwined roots in the theology of Augustine of Hippo (354–430 CE), articulated in his masterwork, *The City of God*.[1] Augustine's classic formulation of the divine-human relationship posited God as sovereign—firmly in control of all that happens. Human beings are both the crown of the created order and the cause of its undoing. That evil exists is the result of humanity's refusal to stay in its place of subordination to God. Augustine reads Genesis 2:4–3:24 as the story of humanity's precipitate "fall" into sin. Although ensconced in a veritable paradise where all their needs are met and desires satisfied, Adam and Eve turn away from God and toward themselves in the secret places of their hearts. Indulging their newfound pride, they willfully throw off the yoke of obedience to God.

As a result, according to Augustine, the good gifts that come with being human (free will and intelligence, especially) are corrupted. As John Calvin put it, their descendants are born into a state of total depravity. Only a dim shadow of humanity's original goodness and beauty remains—enough to call to mind what is lost in Adam and what will be redeemed (for the elect, at least) by Christ. This strand of Christian tradition parallels its Hebrew antecedent in theological perspective: bad things happen to bad people. All that human beings experience as suffering is deserved because it is the result of original sin.

The harshness of this perspective has, of course, come in for criticism from its very inception; but one can acknowledge a certain wisdom in it without endorsing some of its more problematic claims (including its basis in a certain biblical literalism). Certainly those who hold this text sacred would want to affirm that their strength lies in God and not in themselves. Faithful people aim to follow the divine will, to listen to the divine voice. Discerning that voice and thus living out that will, however, prove very difficult in practice. Human beings are gifted by God with intelligence and autonomy, with the ability to remember the past, analyze the present, project into the future, and to act on our analyses and projections; but our intelligence is not omniscience. We misread our present and our predictions fail. Often we either fail to anticipate or deliberately ignore the likely outcome of our actions. Our autonomy meets its limits in other individuals as well as

Pastoral Perspective

affirmed as she acknowledged that my aging grandmother had a "best self" and a "worst self."[1]

To live in the world and to live with a Christlike faith is to live with the tension created by having a "best self" and a "worst self," a tension created by internal realities and external events that cause orientation and disorientation. Through this tension we can lose sight of God's "best self" and focus on God's shadow self rather than God's faithfulness.

Therefore, these verses from Psalm 81 provide important clues for a mature faith. Mature faith rises out of sacred memory. The capacity to recall times when we have been oriented—or times when those we have known and respected have been oriented— becomes a witness in times of disorientation. The psalmist can recall the exodus and its central role in the life of the nation Israel; my mother could recall years of love and respect which she defined as my grandmother's "best self." Mature faith also recognizes the reality of evil: defiant spirits, stubborn hearts, and a refusal to live in ways of faithful love and service to God or to the people of God. In those hard, disoriented times, mature faith longs for orientation, a return to the old ways:

> O that my people would listen to me,
> that Israel would walk in my ways!
> Then I would quickly subdue their enemies,
> and turn my hand against their foes.
> Those who hate the LORD would cringe before him,
> and their doom would last forever.
>
> (vv. 13–15)

Such a longing is not what happens, however; the treasured ways of old do not return. Instead, a new reality, a new normal occurs; a new creation comes forth, a creation wiser in the ways of faith and wiser in the ways of life. Brueggemann calls this spiritual move "reorientation."

Reorientation is another word for resurrection life. When the old ways are gone, destroyed, never to return, the promise of faith is that God can bring forth new life. The Old Testament does not speak as much about resurrection as the New; however, the Old Testament community of faith has a resurrection hope. That community knows God's power to put a new song on their lips, a new hope in their hearts.

While lamenting stubborn hearts and deaf ears, the psalmist remains confident that the God whom

---

1. Augustine of Hippo, *The City of God*, trans. Henry Bettenson (New York: Pelican, 1972; reissued with new introduction by Penguin Classics, 2003).

1. See Brueggemann's *The Message of the Psalms* (Minneapolis: Augsburg, 1984) for full discussion of this insight into Psalms.

Out of Egypt. This psalm's call to singing grounds itself in a character from the book of Genesis. Joseph's older brothers sold him, and he became a slave in Egypt (Gen. 39:1). He was then imprisoned on false charges (Gen. 39–40). In jail, Joseph became known as an interpreter of dreams. When Pharaoh, the ruler of Egypt, learned of Joseph's skill and found himself in need of it, Pharaoh not only sent for Joseph (Gen. 41:14) but established him as second-in-charge of all Egypt (Gen. 41:41–44). From this administrative position, Joseph was able to manage the empire's food supply in ways that would bring salvation to both Egypt and the Hebrew people in times of severe food shortage. The book of Exodus tells of later days, after Joseph's death, when a new Pharaoh treated the Hebrews harshly and enslaved them (Exod. 1:8).

Reflecting back on this history, the psalm calls for praise because God heard the Hebrews' cry and responded with rescue (vv. 6–7; Exod. 2:23; 3:7). This psalm is not only a reminiscence of salvation. The lyrics recall the people's testing (v. 7) and admonition (v. 8). The people are tempted to worship other gods, but God commands them to avoid those other gods because there is only one God who brought them out of Egypt.

Stubborn Hearts. The lectionary passage resumes with the assertion that God is the one who brought the people out of Egypt (v. 10), who rescued them from oppression and slavery. The people, however, have been stubborn. They have not listened to God (v. 11). They have sought other gods. They have listened to their own human wisdom (v. 12). As a result, the people's lives are not at all as God wants them to be. The people have made enemies who hate God and oppose God's people (v. 14). This is not what God wants. God wishes that it were all different (v. 13), that the people would follow God's chosen path for their lives and behave as God would have them do. If the people follow God, there will be an end to the enmity and hatred that divides God's people from their opponents.

Traditionally, this passage has been translated in terms of God's subduing Israel's enemies and turning God's hand against Israel's foes (v. 14), with the result that the enemies cringe before God in recognition of their doom (v. 15). This is not the only way to translate this passage, which is more complex than it may seem. It could be possible to translate these verses as:

sung to those worshiping at the temple[1] and in its precincts. Yearly, most likely during the fall pilgrimage festival of Sukkot, the same psalm would be used to remind the people of God's anguished concern for their welfare and fidelity, recalling their root experience of liberation and their subsequent struggle in the wilderness.

One could call this a Shema with anguish. The psalmist has dared to give voice both to the embrace and call of Israel and to God's anguish regarding Israel's response to that summoning relationship. The Shema, of course, is the summoning reminder of Deuteronomy 6:4: "Hear, O Israel: the LORD is our God, the LORD alone." The Shema, the heartbeat of daily Jewish prayer, has distinguished the practice of faithful Jews as they begin and end every day with its words. To call this psalm a Shema with anguish is to dare to imagine God's side of the Shema's call to fidelity and responsibility, God's side of that hope for Israel. God's side of that desire for relationship. God's anguish for God's people.

Even so, the regular use of this psalm in the temple liturgy captures something more. Liturgical repetition signals a nation or community that remembers past mistakes and anticipates continuing failures even if they are yet to happen. That is, a people committing itself to this kind of liturgical action is submitting itself to divine judgment for unfaithful behavior even before it occurs. Ever after, the people of this community intend to be reminded of the flawed character of the relationship from which they draw their identity. They will limp, self-consciously, as Israel (Gen. 32:31).

The people being confronted by the psalm's pleading summons have chosen to ritualize (sacramentalize, if we do not misuse such a term) this sung memory of chastened responsibility. As a result, the psalm and its ritualization express the people's doubly representative role in creation—not simply the life of covenantal responsibility they are called to lead, but also the difficulties of living out that responsibility. In other words, it appears that they have taken their representative role as a way of identifying fully with the world they share with others and of taking responsibility for the summons that is their charge as God's people in that world.

Preachers may want to ponder how to explore this dimension of the text with their congregations. It would be a misuse of this psalm to preach it as a simple condemnation of Israel's stubborn infidelity.

1. *Tamid* 7:4.

Psalm 81:1, 10-16

Theological Perspective

natural and social forces. Like our mythical foreparents in Augustine's rendering, we supplant the divine will with our will; we conflate our own wisdom with divine wisdom. Like them, we fail to realize our folly until it is too late.

Thus the reading serves as a cautionary tale that reminds us of our hubristic tendencies—which can afflict nations, denominations, and congregations, as well as individuals—and recalls the faithful to an original humility. This is not an easy lesson to learn, and it is one that bears special poignancy at this time of year. Hurricane Katrina struck the Gulf Coast on August 29, 2005. In the wake of the storm's devastation, certain high-profile preachers were quick to read that disaster as a sign of divine punishment on New Orleans for its sexual excesses (signified by Mardi Gras and the gay pride parade). They warned that the disaster was just a shot across America's bow. However, those who suffered most were not the ostensible objects of divine wrath identified by these self-proclaimed prophets, but the poor and elderly (overwhelmingly people of color) who had no way to flee a drowning city.[2] Moreover, the catastrophe itself resulted as much from decades of human hubris, neglect, and environmental exploitation as from what insurers call "an act of God."

Discerning the divine voice and the divine will, then, requires something other than self-righteously pointing fingers at others; it requires looking more deeply into ourselves. Here, the insights of Reinhold Niebuhr, Martin Luther King Jr., and liberation theology can be helpful. All found inspiration in the Hebrew prophets and in Jesus' ministry, particularly as it is described in Luke's Gospel. All discern God's will as a call to justice, a justice ultimately rooted in this text's opening verse: the recognition that strength lies not in human might, but in God. In the words of the prophet Micah, "What does the LORD require of you but to do justice, and to love kindness, and to walk humbly with your God?" (Mic. 6:8).

ELLEN T. ARMOUR

Pastoral Perspective

Israel remembers and reveres will not give up and stands ready to bless people with finest wheat and honey from the rock. "Honey from the rock" (v. 16) is a mixed allusion, referring to Moses's bringing forth water from the rock (Exod. 17:6) and to the gift of honey in the promised land (Exod. 3:8 ff.). New Testament synonyms for the images of the finest of the wheat and honey from the rock are captured in words such as amazing "grace" or the promised "kingdom of God." Amazing grace is that gift from God that has power to reorient our lives as we live in the holy tension between orientation and disorientation. The grace of God rises in times when we and our world are rebuked, disoriented. Something in life goes awry; we become confused, scared, angry, disappointed. God seems to have disappeared, yet we go forward to discover that in the midst of confusion, mysterious turns of events occur. We receive more than we deserve. That experience becomes the foundation of reorientation, resurrection orientation. By grace, we capture a vision of God's "new normal," God's promised rule, or the kingdom of God—a vision symbolized by the finest of the wheat and honey from the rock.

Psalm 81 likely refers to a time of national political crisis; a time of national disorientation. In this pastoral reflection, I have used the psalm to remember a time of personal disorientation. Scripture has the power to speak in both dimensions: the public and the personal, the communal and the private. When our church, our nation, or our world appears to have abandoned God, we see our collective "worst self." We long for our community to return to the ways of God. Going back to the old way is rarely possible, however—or even desirable. A new normal, a resurrection life, will have to emerge. Our hope will be in God's love for the church, the nation, the world—not just for me or my family. Insights that strengthen faith in the personal realm can become a means of affirming God's grace amid crises in larger spheres of communal life. In those moments, ancient words of Scripture combined with personal experience give us hope that God will feed us and all of creation with the finest of the wheat and honey from the rock.

ARTHUR (ART) ROSS III

---

2. For a powerful critique of such claims, see Michael Eric Dyson, *Come Hell or High Water: Hurricane Katrina and the Color of Disaster* (New York: Basic Civitas Books, 2007).

"I wish that my people would listen to me,
that Israel would walk in my paths.
Quickly I would make their enemies humble;
I would reach out my hand to their opponents.
Those who had hated YHWH would change their
  selves toward God,
and God would be with them forever."
                              (vv. 13–15, my trans.)

This suggested translation is not certain, but the difference between this translation and the NRSV highlights some ambiguities involved in any translation of these verses. It is not clear that God is standing ready to punish and destroy. Instead, God may desire that Israel change its ways into moral godly paths, so that they no longer antagonize others. Further, God may be promising that if the people act rightly, God could quickly get the enemies of Israel and the haters of God to change their minds and their actions, when God extends a saving hand to them as well. Israel and its enemies could then live together forever with God.

In either translation, the psalm points to a time of unity with God's presence, and this miracle of salvation begins with the Israelites' return to God and their practice of God's principles for their lives.

Finest Wheat and Honey from the Rock. The psalm ends with God's promise to feed the people with the finest wheat and to satisfy them with honey from a rock (v. 16). The NRSV translates "I would feed you," whereas the Hebrew literally should be rendered "I will feed them," as if God is feeding finest wheat to the people who hated God in verse 15. The promises of God are many and the abundance of God's provision is never to be underestimated, even after God's people have failed to follow God. A return to God's paths and priorities will begin a remarkable restoration and nourishment. This is why the people should sing for joy (v. 1). This joyous praise is not a self-congratulatory worship that celebrates human worthiness. God commands worship that is regular and frequent, bringing together many people and instruments in common accord, where all can reflect on how we have left God's path and how rich life could be if only we would listen again to the God who has saved us in the past.

                              JON L. BERQUIST

For congregations needing to face negative attitudes toward Jews in general, or difficulties recognizing the good news contained in the Hebrew Scriptures, this text could offer helpful guidance. Taking time to ponder a people that has placed difficult memory at the heart of its weekly life of worship is a sobering reminder of their wisdom and humility as a people, a trait rare in any time, and one that bears witness to a people at home in its own skin, willing to resist pride and complacency alike.

In the case of parishioners who struggle with their own stumbling walk with God, or a church agonizing over its failures to be as responsible as it would like to be, this text offers a glimpse of God as an anguished parent pleading with imperfect children to be more responsible—or as a parent or loving friend or family member who is practicing tough love in order to guide someone special into facing the need for help and change. In either of these cases, the way into the psalm is the recognition of the relationship that provides the context of either the anguish or the tough love that might be offered. Parents of teens learning to drive or finding other ways to explore their emergence into near-adulthood will know this precarious journey of parenthood well—both its anguish and its love.

In the end, facing Psalm 81 will mean confronting both the text and its contexts, what scholars call the worlds behind the text as well as in front of it. In many ways, the world behind the text may be seen as the social world that surrounds it, extending it not only to those who encountered it then but to us as well. These contexts are important. They are the compositional and liturgical settings from another time as well as the circumstances and needs of contemporary Christian communities that worship with this historic, Jewish prayer song. If the psalm and its contexts were "sacramental" (i.e., representatively embodying the Holy) for Jews, what might they be for contemporary Christian congregations? Offering this text as the main course in the Sunday feast could be quite a meal.

                              HENRY F. KNIGHT

Hebrews 13:1-8, 15-16

¹Let mutual love continue. ²Do not neglect to show hospitality to strangers, for by doing that some have entertained angels without knowing it. ³Remember those who are in prison, as though you were in prison with them; those who are being tortured, as though you yourselves were being tortured. ⁴Let marriage be held in honor by all, and let the marriage bed be kept undefiled; for God will judge fornicators and adulterers. ⁵Keep your lives free from the love of money, and be content with what you have; for he has said, "I will never leave you or forsake you." ⁶So we can say with confidence,

"The Lord is my helper;
I will not be afraid.
What can anyone do to me?"

⁷Remember your leaders, those who spoke the word of God to you; consider the outcome of their way of life, and imitate their faith. ⁸Jesus Christ is the same yesterday and today and forever. . . .
¹⁵Through him, then, let us continually offer a sacrifice of praise to God, that is, the fruit of lips that confess his name. ¹⁶Do not neglect to do good and to share what you have, for such sacrifices are pleasing to God.

Theological Perspective

There is nothing on earth quite like a North American religious congregation. American congregations are centers of worship and the arts related to worship, such as music and drama. They are community centers. They serve many as extended families. For many, they are the first priority for free time apart from family or work. The churches of childhood show up in our fondest dreams.

American congregations can also be maelstroms of contentiousness. Your stomach can clench in knots as you turn into the church parking lot. A radio preacher was once heard to cry, "When the devil fell out of Heaven, he landed in the choir loft!" Many a finance committee could go the choir one better. Indeed, the natural tendency to think of church as "family" risks importing into the sanctuary all the strife we fled when we left home.

Contentiousness, however, *is* energy, energy that can readily be transmuted into adoration of God, loving respect for one another, and service to the needy world. Far better to be contentious than to be inert. So even the energies that make our churches sometimes painful to occupy are usually signs of life.

If we want to move more centrally into the zone of the actual will of God for our congregations, the passage we consider from Hebrews 13 offers much that is vitally essential for making the transition

Pastoral Perspective

With chapter 13, the author of Hebrews is summing up. It begins, "Let mutual love continue," and then offers some closing thoughts about what mutual love means. First of all, it is not about loving only family and friends already in the community: "Do not neglect to show hospitality to strangers, for by doing that some have entertained angels without knowing it" (v. 2). The writer is singing a refrain that echoes countless biblical passages, beginning with Abraham and Sarah's showing hospitality to strangers by the oaks of Mamre, strangers who turn out to be messengers of God with news so unbelievably good that Sarah can only laugh (Gen. 18).

Despite this recurring biblical theme, most of us are hesitant or outright resistant to living this out. We not only usually fear the stranger, but we teach our children to beware of strangers. Although this is a sad testimony to the reality of child predators, to continue as adults always to be suspicious and wary of strangers is to miss messengers from God (and maybe even Christ himself, according to Matt. 25:31–46).

When thinking about this text, the preacher might decide that verse 8 is a good place to end. Although it is often worth paying attention to passages the lectionary skips over, in this case it is easy to see why verses 9–14 are omitted. A pastoral word

Exegetical Perspective

The Revised Common Lectionary's final installment in Hebrews (late first century CE) consists of short admonitions drawn from the concluding chapter. They cover an array of matters basic to Christian living: mutual love, hospitality, solidarity with prisoners, sexual morality, wealth, community leaders, and generosity.

Two of the admonitions are introduced by the phrase "do not neglect" (vv. 2 and 16) and two by the word "remember" (vv. 3 and 7); most are given a brief rationale, and a few echo the main body of Hebrews. By and large they are, like much early Christian paraenesis, a potpourri of freestanding, undeveloped exhortations. While they promote social cohesion, their cumulative impact has more to do with their sheer number than with a unifying theme.

Mutual Love and Hospitality (vv. 1–2). Mutual love, a virtue extolled in early Christian circles (Rom. 12:9–10; 1 Thess. 4:9; 1 Pet. 1:22; 2 Pet. 1:7), refers not to broad-based love of humanity but to community-based love of believers for believers. Such love entails willing the good of others in the group and involves doing (see Heb. 10:24) as much as feeling. Hebrews 6:10 had already acknowledged "the love that you showed for his name in serving the saints, as you still do." So the admonition in 13:1, prompted perhaps

Homiletical Perspective

A lawyer once asked Jesus what he should do to inherit eternal life. "Eternal life" then did not mean life that just went on and on. It meant life that really mattered and so endured. It was the life of the new age—living by God's ways. As the lawyer summed it up, it was to love God with everything one has and to love one's neighbor as oneself. Jesus responded with the story of the good Samaritan: "Go and do likewise" (Luke 10:25–37).

Most people want to live such a life and to be good persons. Today's passage sums it up too: "Do not neglect to do good and to share what you have, for such sacrifices are pleasing to God" (v. 16). The Letter to the Hebrews also spells it out, offering a short catechism of what it means to do and to be good.

One does not do good by oneself but in "mutual love"—in the sharing and mutual support of love. A certain purity of life is important. Marriage is to be honored. This virtue is set in context. It is one important part of being able to love and share with others, because that is difficult to do if one's need for sexual relationship and gratification is out of control. Self-control is one of the vital gifts of the Spirit (Gal. 5:23) for the sake of others.

Learning to be free from the love of money also enables one "to do good and to share what you have"

Hebrews 13:1-8, 15-16

Theological Perspective

from inertness to contentiousness to being the very front porch of God's kingdom.

What are those vital elements? There are three. The first and most basic is found in verse 15: "Through him, then, let us continually offer a sacrifice of praise to God, that is, the fruit of lips that confess his name." *Worship*, in effect. When the New Testament churches think of worship, they do not contemplate a headlong rush from pages 355 to 366 in some worship manual within the statutory one-hour slot, offering the worshipers all the spiritual scenery of a subway ride. No. Look at how they describe it: "a sacrifice of praise to God." They are describing happy effort. The work of actually praising God and meaning it is transformative; it changes us.

Here is how it works. You come to resemble what you admire. People who admire money get green and crinkly. People who admire computers grow user-unfriendly. People who admire youth get juvenile. People who actively and deliberately admire Jesus Christ come to resemble him as he actually was and remains today, unchanged from age to age: generous, merry, tender, fierce, courageous, somewhat mischievous, fully open to others after his self is sorted out. Real worship is the engine of personal transformation. Congregations that craft their worship out of love for our Lord more than out of love of respectability are well on their way to kingdom-level vitality.

The second element in becoming a vital congregation is *fellowship*. "Let mutual love continue" (Heb. 13:1). Souls that emerge from a worship service in which people actively admire and praise our Lord are in a somewhat fluid, molten state. The issue then is, how will my molten soul "set up"? Will I rush back into my normal routine, to be shaped once again by the world's mold? Will I sit docilely in some class where a teacher or pastor tells me exactly what to believe and practice and exactly how to do it? That would be like pouring my molten soul into somebody else's ice tray—and calling it "growth"! Far better to gaze around the coffee hour for eyes equally ablaze and forge relationships with them, letting my self-in-transformation be shaped in our mutual discovery of Jesus' high adventure.

The third element of congregational vitality is *ministry*. By ministry the New Testament rarely means what we would call "church work." You can do church work without prayer. Try "remembering" (that used to mean visiting and feeding) those in prison and those being tortured—I will bet you

Pastoral Perspective

on this text is challenging enough without trying to tackle the connection between animal sacrifice and Jesus' death, so the jump to verses 15–16 with their references to the meaning of sacrifice from the prior texts seems a bit disjointed.

The passage as suggested by the lectionary offers an opportunity for us and our congregations to reflect upon times we have been blessed by showing hospitality to strangers. Some years ago, I was traveling alone and passed a hitchhiker. My first impulse is to pass hitchhikers by, and putting biblical mandates aside, I would not want to advise anyone else to do otherwise. That day, though, something in the face of the old man with his thumb out made me pause. Perhaps it was his snaggletoothed grin or the way he happily waved as I passed. In any case, I found myself hitting the brakes and pulling over. I watched in the rearview mirror as he moved toward my car, hurriedly, despite a prominent limp.

In a moment, he crawled in the seat beside me, shook my hand, and said exuberantly, "Thank you for the ride, young man. My name's Henry." Henry was quite a talker, or perhaps he had just not had a chance to talk in a while. He ended up telling me a lot of his life story and was interested in mine as well, not hesitating to ask questions that many might consider too personal from a stranger. He was retired and did not own a car. One of his children was in the hospital several hundred miles away, and he was going to make a hospital visit. I told him I was going only about half the way before I would turn and go in another direction.

At one point, he began talking about a place he liked to eat near where I would leave him. Thinking he was going to ask for money, I was considering how much to give him when he pulled out the most ragged billfold I had ever seen. He searched through it and said, "I think I've got enough here and would like to buy us both a supper."

I laughed and said, "No, no, I can buy my own supper. In fact, I can buy yours if you like."

"Nope," he replied, "you've done enough already giving me a ride this far."

We ate a great little meal at a roadside diner where the waitress knew his name, and I left him there to continue his journey and my own. Later, I suspected I had entertained one of God's angels without knowing it.

The writer of Hebrews goes on to mention another unlikely place to entertain angels without knowing it (and again echoes Jesus' words in Matthew 25), with those in prison. It is a challenging

by the fact that some members are neglecting to meet together (10:25), is that this mutual love "continue."

Hospitality (v. 2) is one way, obviously enough, in which this love becomes concrete. Travelers of many sorts—itinerant preachers, letter carriers, Christians on nonchurch business, migrants, and others—were crucial to the spread of early Christianity and the sense that otherwise-isolated communities had of belonging to a much larger whole. Given the dangers and rigors of travel in the ancient world, these visitors needed secure lodging, food, and whatever encouragement their hosts could provide. Even those without letters of recommendation, it seems, were to be received on trust. A tall order! It is not surprising, then, that the author strengthens the injunction that hospitality not be neglected by grounding it in biblical precedent: in providing for strangers "some" have entertained angels (divine emissaries) unknowingly. The allusion is presumably to Abraham and Sarah, who entertained three "men" who turned out to have supernatural qualities (Gen. 18:1–15), though Lot, Gideon, and Manoah may also be in view (Gen. 19:1–14; Judg. 6:11–24 and 13:3–23). How does this precedent function? It seems to promise more encounters of this kind and perhaps to warn that their significance is easily overlooked.

Prisoners and Victims of Torture (v. 3). In the first instance, these people are to be kept in mind through the full force and focus of the imagination: "as though you were in prison with them," "as though you yourselves were in the(ir) body." (The paraphrase in the NRSV, "as though you yourselves were being tortured," eviscerates the image.) It is as if empathy can partially mitigate the isolation and degradation of people so powerless and easily abused. Beyond that, remembering them almost certainly entails visiting them and providing for their emotional and material needs—something encouraged and reported in Matthew 25:36, 43; 2 Timothy 1:16–17; 4:9–13; Philemon 10–11, 23–24 (cf. Acts 28:16, 30). The addressees had already "partnered" with the persecuted and imprisoned; indeed some had suffered persecution and imprisonment themselves (Heb. 10:32–34). So once again the author is not advocating that a new ministry be initiated but that an old one be sustained.

Hebrews 13:3 does not prohibit torture; it deals only with pastoral care. That reflects the social reality of the time. Early Christians had no power to set or modify state policy. As their status changed, many

(v. 16). Few persons want to think that they love money, but greed born from anxieties and the lure of the power that money offers over the time and efforts of others are powerful forces. It takes love's discipline to serve and worship God rather than mammon (see Luke 16:13).

No Christian manages to live the good life 100 percent. Wanting to lead such a life is, however, on the way to being ready to offer hospitality to strangers in the manner the Good Samaritan did to the injured man. One is reminded of Jesus' admonition to "invite the poor, the crippled, the lame and the blind" to lunch or dinner (Luke 14:12–14). Indeed, the Bible is replete with reminders to care for the poor, widows, orphans, and strangers in our midst. This is not the easy or even natural thing to do. I mostly want to entertain "relatives or rich [or at least reasonably well-to-do] neighbors" (Luke 14:12). Perhaps in our time we see again how hard it can be to offer hospitality to migrant people "in your midst." Being able to offer hospitality to strangers comes from a new kind of reaching out in love. This is empathetic love that also enables one to put oneself in the shoes of those in prison and to *feel in one's own body* what it is like for another to be tortured (v. 3). In a time when torture can be rationalized and nearly two million American brothers and sisters are shut away in our rather grim penal system, one realizes painfully what an adventure of love it is to try to participate fully in the good life—to participate in eternal life and to act as the Good Samaritan and Jesus did.

Then it is well nigh impossible not to hear Jesus' counsel to his followers: "I was hungry and you gave me food, I was thirsty and you gave me something to drink, *I was a stranger and you welcomed me*, I was naked and you gave me clothing, I was sick and you took care of me, *I was in prison and you visited me*" (Matt. 25:35–36; emphasis added). For Christians, "doing good" means to follow in the way of Jesus and to emulate those who have sought to do so beforehand—"those who spoke the word of God to you" (Heb. 13:7). Disciples can imitate their faith as well, while it is Jesus who was and is their chief model for learning the love of God and others. He is the centerpiece for faith and love because his words of service and love were matched by the good that he did. He came "not to be served but to serve" (Mark 10:45), and he walked the talk. He not only spoke the words of God; he enacted them and is the Word of God. He is, in the imagery with which this letter begins, "the reflection of God's glory and the exact

Hebrews 13:1-8, 15-16

Theological Perspective

cannot do *that* without prayer. The prayer will not be some rote, feelingless formula; it will be more like "*Help!*" God tends to prefer that kind of prayer, you will discover. You will notice that the most robust ministries, both within and outside the church building, grow spontaneously out of the new relationships forged between worship-molten souls.

These three elements occur in this Hebrews passage in close proximity. That suggests they must not be separated. If we allow them to delaminate from one another, what would be the result? *Worship* that does not melt the soul and lead to deepened relationships with fellow servants of our Lord becomes a fussy curatorship of moribund customs. It becomes a cause of strife and contentiousness rather than a fresh way of addressing our love to God. *Fellowship* that does not grow out of spirited worship and point into courageous ministry becomes boozy, gossipy, and, as this passage warns, potentially adulterous. Cliques in a congregation are fine, provided they are nexuses of positive energy, but disconnected from worship or ministry, they are a circle of wagons on the congregation's prairie. *Ministry* that does not grow out of worship-forged friendships becomes proprietary and sour, something to fight others about, rather than something to offer to them. If the payoff for ministry is not the love of God and your fellow ministers, it will decay into prestige maintenance.

Suppose your congregation, or any other, were to face into and lay claim to the energies with which we have voiced contentious discontent, asking God's forgiveness only for its target, not for its voltage and amperage? Suppose we were to direct that same energy into passionately adoring Jesus Christ in church? Suppose we applied the judgment that formerly shaped our gossip into appreciating the excellence of potential friends in the congregation? Suppose those energies made us brave in the face of the world's many needs?

Just imagine it. There would be no institution quite like *that* church anywhere in the world—not even in America.

GRAY TEMPLE

Pastoral Perspective

word to remember those in prison, "as though you were in prison with them," and even more demanding to remember "those who are being tortured, as though you yourselves were being tortured." Wow! If we took this passage seriously, we would all be joining organizations that would help us identify in an empathic way with victims of torture, whether in Guantánamo Bay or Beijing. The pastoral word may have to be a prophetic word today.

Then the text shifts, presenting a big challenge for pastors. After making sure that the community shows mutual love for strangers, even those in prison, including those being tortured, the writer turns attention homeward. Clarence Jordan, who offered a radical model of strangers finding reconciliation in the segregated South by establishing Koinonia Farms, has a great paraphrase of verses 4–5: "In every way consider marriage a precious thing, don't let sexual intercourse be perverted. For God will pass judgment on those who go around tomcatting and having illicit relationships. Don't let the desire for money dominate your life. Make do with what's on hand, for [God] has said, 'Never will I abandon you or run off and leave you.'"[1]

Infidelity and love of money are impediments to making mutual love the hallmark of the Christian community. The author then reminds the community to remember those leaders who model mutual love and closes this section with the reassurance that the best model for mutual love is Jesus Christ himself, who "is the same yesterday and today and forever." To which we can say, Amen.

LANNY PETERS

---

1. Clarence Jordan, *The Cotton Patch Version of Hebrews and the General Epistles* (New York: Association Press, 1973), 41.

later Christians would come to condemn torture in any and all circumstances. Although the admonition in this verse provides no direct warrant for an all-out ban, it is so emphatically centered on solidarity with the oppressed as to be congruent with one.

Sexual Morality and Wealth (vv. 4–6 and 15–16). Exhortations to chastity and warnings against the love of money are staples of first-century Christian instruction on personal morality. We find the former in 1 Corinthians 5:1–13; Ephesians 5:3–5; 1 Thessalonians 4:3–7; and the latter in Matthew 6:19–21, 24–34; Luke 12:22–34; 1 Timothy 6:10; James 5:1–5, where they are developed in various ways. Here in Hebrews 13 the exhortation to chastity is grounded in the prospect of divine judgment (v. 4b), and the warning against avarice in the promise of divine assistance (v. 5b). To emphasize the promise of assistance, which avarice in effect denies, the author appends two scriptural citations: (a) "I [God] will never leave you or forsake you," an allusion to Deuteronomy 31:6, 8 and Joshua 1:5, and (b) "The Lord is my helper; I will not be afraid. What can anyone do to me?" Psalm 118:6 as rendered by the LXX. Given this tremendous trust in the ability of God to provide and the ability of believers to be content with what they have, which flows from such trust (v. 5a), it is fitting that our reading concludes with an injunction to be generous (v. 16). Sharing and other good works are framed as "sacrifices pleasing to God" (cf. Rom. 12:1–2; Phil. 2:17; 1 Pet. 2:5).

Community Leaders and Christ (vv. 7, 8). Throughout our passage the author speaks with striking confidence. This confidence is based in part on the knowledge that this community has been blessed with leaders whose conduct and faith are worthy of imitation (v. 7). In referring to the "outcome of their way of life" the author may have in mind the founding fathers who have died, or it may be that these leaders are the same as those who are presently to be obeyed (v. 17). In either case, they rank with the exemplary "cloud of witnesses" of earlier times whose faithful persistence inspires now (Heb. 11). The author's confidence derives above all from Christ. His "sameness" (v. 8; cf. 1:12), his unshakable reliability, no matter the circumstance or passage of time, is the ground of Christian hope and endurance.

DAVID R. ADAMS

imprint of God's very being" (Heb 1:3). Thus is he "the same yesterday and today and forever" (13:8). Jesus will not now or ever leave or forsake his followers (13:5). As we try to live the life that matters now and so endures as eternal life, and as we endeavor to be disciples who "do good and share what you have," we are able to say with confidence:

> The Lord is my helper;
> I will not be afraid.
> (v. 6; cf. Ps. 118:6)

C. S. Lewis once keenly observed that, while Christians may think what they most want is to possess life's beauty, this is not their deepest hope. The most ardent hope and desire is to share in the beauty—to participate in the beauty and goodness of life.[1] "This is my commandment," Jesus told his disciples, "that you love one another as I have loved you" (John 15:12). The poet George Herbert had in mind the sharing of life's goodness and love when he observed, "There is no greater sign of holiness than the procuring and rejoicing in another's good."[2] Here surely is life's greatest challenge and adventure into which this passage of Scripture invites us: "to do good and to share what you have, for such sacrifices are pleasing to God" (v. 16).

FREDERICK BORSCH

1. C. S. Lewis, *The Weight of Glory and Other Addresses* (New York: Macmillan, 1949), 12–13.
2. *George Herbert: The Country Parson and the Temple*, ed. John N. Wall Jr. (New York: Paulist, 1981), 63.

Luke 14:1, 7-14

¹On one occasion when Jesus was going to the house of a leader of the Pharisees to eat a meal on the sabbath, they were watching him closely. . . .

⁷When he noticed how the guests chose the places of honor, he told them a parable. ⁸"When you are invited by someone to a wedding banquet, do not sit down at the place of honor, in case someone more distinguished than you has been invited by your host; ⁹and the host who invited both of you may come and say to you, 'Give this person your place,' and then in disgrace you would start to take the lowest place. ¹⁰But when you are invited, go and sit down at the lowest place, so that when your host comes, he may say to you, 'Friend, move up higher'; then you will be honored in the presence of all who sit at the table with you. ¹¹For all who exalt themselves will be humbled, and those who humble themselves will be exalted."

¹²He said also to the one who had invited him, "When you give a luncheon or a dinner, do not invite your friends or your brothers or your relatives or rich neighbors, in case they may invite you in return, and you would be repaid. ¹³But when you give a banquet, invite the poor, the crippled, the lame, and the blind. ¹⁴And you will be blessed, because they cannot repay you, for you will be repaid at the resurrection of the righteous."

Theological Perspective

"Chile, I just want to be a blessing. That's all I want for my life, is to be a blessing to others." I remember my grandmother saying this many times as I was growing up. In my first memory of hearing it, around the age of three, I did not have a clue what she meant or what a blessing was. I could tell that it was a good thing and a Christian thing, but beyond that I was caught in a childhood mystery of faith. As I grew older, the notion of blessing began to take on helpful contours and became understandable. Blessing was something that Jesus, God, and the Holy Spirit did on a regular basis to good little girls and boys. We had to mind our elders, work hard in school, share our toys, and learn to pray really hard for our families, for others, and for ourselves. If we did all these things, then we would receive whatever we asked for—this was blessing.

However, this worked only for a time, because life became more complicated, and I learned in Sunday school one morning that sometimes the answer from God was a "No" rather than a "Yes." This, too, made sense over time, because I could, on occasion, ask for more than was realistic or reasonable—like a pony when we lived in urban areas or that the president (who I thought was all powerful, but not to be confused with God) simply declare an end to racist behavior and thereby settle the race problem in the United States.

Pastoral Perspective

In this passage, Jesus heals a desperately ill man and shares table fellowship in the home of a ruler of the Pharisees. Both his gift of medical healing and his personal response to hospitality in the home of a Pharisee leader deepen Luke's theme of conflict developed during Jesus' journey toward Jerusalem (Luke 9:51–19:44).

This is the fourth Sabbath controversy of Jesus (Luke 6:1–5; 6:6–11; 13:10–17). The Pharisees have hated him for his claim of lordship over Sabbath activities. In the first instance (Luke 6:1–13, with parallels in Mark 2:23–3:6 and Matt. 12:1–14), Jesus and his disciples pluck grain, and the Pharisees accuse them of violating the prohibition of work on the Sabbath. Jesus counters with the version of the Sabbath command in Deuteronomy 5:13–15, which prescribes observance that honors the exodus gift of freedom from slavery in Egypt. In the view of Sabbath as the celebration of freedom for slaves, the Gospel of Luke shows that Jesus offers liberation from the diseases that destroy fullness of human life.

In addition to healing, Jesus joins a leader of the Pharisees, who are holding Jesus under surveillance (14:1). In his response to the leader's offer of hospitality, Jesus, even though he is the object of their hostility, is unexpectedly free for table fellowship with one Pharisee who is strangely attracted to him.

Exegetical Perspective

The Jesus of Luke's Gospel is certainly preoccupied with eating. Not only does he imply that some think he is a glutton and drunkard (7:34, following Matt. 11:19); there are in Luke more references to eating, banquets, tables, and reclining at tables than in any of the other Gospels.[1] The *trapeza* or table (or a verbal concept implying sitting or reclining around the table) suggests that this is one of our Lord's key loci for teaching (22:24–30), reproving (11:37–41), and encountering those who are marginalized (7:39); the table even serves as a focal site for some of his parables (16:21). That the table is a principal site for fellowship and discourse for Luke's Jesus should not escape notice.

In this passage, we are again at table, but this time at a *gamos*, or a "wedding feast." The communal meal has increased in size in this pericope, incorporating many more people and necessarily requiring an enhanced sense of decorum. Thus, we could assume that the instructions given here are the basis for the subsequent fellowship of this nascent Christian community, for whom communal meals are among the principal bases of their common worship experiences. Import is attributed to these instructions

1. Robert J. Karris, *Luke: Artist and Theologian: Luke's Passion Account as Literature* (New York: Paulist, 1985), 47.

Homiletical Perspective

A friend once observed that, in her experience, those who most need to hear a word of grace are more likely to hear a word of judgment, and those who might benefit from hearing a word of judgment are more likely to hear only grace! Humility is certainly a virtue, but exhortations to be humble can be dangerous to those who already have little sense of their own worth.

A congregation sent letters to all the members when the annual stewardship drive fell short of the goal. While not apparently moving everyone who received it, a member confined to a nursing home took the appeal to heart. In tears, she confided her distress to her pastor, dismayed and ashamed because her small income was not sufficient to respond to the church's need.

Reading and preaching this text about taking the "lowest place" carries with it certain risks. Those who are already in that place might hear it as a demand to empty themselves more than they already have. Of course, on the other hand, some may hear the passage as a formula for their own advancement. They may position themselves to compete with others in a race for the "lowest place," hoping to win the prize awarded to the humblest of all!

Context is everything. Jesus tells the story in a setting where he has noticed "how the guests chose the

Luke 14:1, 7-14

Theological Perspective

Blessing became more complex, more elusive, and more special; as I grew into young adulthood, I became aware of the high demand my grandmother was placing on her life and witness. Being a blessing is not easy, but trying to jump-start it by scurrying into spaces and places we think will shower us with blessings or display the blessings we have received or perceive we have received is much easier. In all these cases, the deep theological meaning of blessing is lost, as Jesus is doing more than giving a biblical-world Miss Manners lesson. He is highlighting the ways in which the realm of God establishes its own social and spiritual order; trying to presume a place in that order is unwise and perhaps even unfaithful.

As helpful background, this passage relies on some knowledge of Palestinian wedding feasts, in which the male guests recline on couches, with the center couch being the place of honor, its inhabitants chosen according to wealth, power, or office. If a more prominent man arrives late, as is often the case, someone of lesser rank is asked to move to a less prestigious location. Jesus is offering sound practical advice to choose the lowest place so that you can be invited up, but he is also pointing to something deeper and richer.

The realm of God is also about how God offers an invitation in our lives to receive a genuine blessing when we learn that it is crassly unfaithful to store up spiritual brownie points to note our goodness and then make it worse by ostentatious displays of that goodness. Receiving a blessing that invites us to grow into a deeper relationship with God is not something we can work our way into through acts designed to display our worth. No. God asks us to live into our createdness through our everyday acts toward each other and in and through our relationship with God and creation. Jesus wants us to understand that our all-too-human drive to seek the best seat in the house or at the party will not mark genuine participation in God's mercy or love.

Jesus is not done, however, for he has words of wisdom, warning, and blessing as well for the host who may be falling victim to a bout of elitism by thinking that inviting those who can return his invitation is a sign of faithful witness. This is akin to arranging the deck chairs on a sinking ship—nothing is gained and time grows shorter. Jesus is clear who should be invited: people who are the very fabric of God's realm—the poor, the crippled, the lame, and the blind. For Jesus, extending genuine hospitality to the least of these through acts of unselfish hospitality and kindness can wash God's blessing over

Pastoral Perspective

Jesus shows his own Sabbath lordship and freedom to sit at table, sharing bread and cup.

Luke deepens this irony through Jesus' teaching. Jesus borrows from "The Wisdom of Solomon" (Prov. 25:6–7) and tells the hustling guests to follow the traditional wisdom guiding proper etiquette in the royal court or at a meal in the presence of an aristocratic host. The guests should not rush to the head of the dining room, but sit in a humbler location, on the happy chance they should be invited closer to the attractive host. With further daring, Jesus reminds the host not to invite those who can repay him, but rather to invite the poor, the crippled, the lame, and the blind, who can offer nothing in return.

The reward for this curious obedience may be claimed in the resurrection of the righteous, in which all social boundaries and unjust divisions in the human community are judged. This inversion, embodied in Jesus' own sharing of someone's hospitality, is wisdom's vindication "by all her children" (Luke 5:29–32; 7:33–35). Luke inverts the traditional etiquette of the banquet; he elevates the lowliest to the new royal welcome in the kingdom of God and urges the social climbers to become the lowliest, on the chance they might be invited higher up!

Jesus' healing and practice of table fellowship become metaphors of the kingdom of God, where they "will come from east and west, from north and south, and will eat in the kingdom of God" (Luke 13:29; cf. Ps. 107:3). His example and teaching thus confirm the main emphasis in Luke, as in the songs of Mary (1:46–55) and of Zechariah (1:68–79), in the Sermon on the Plain (6:20–49), and throughout the Gospel. Jesus' pastoral ministry exemplifies the foundation of the pastoral service we are to offer as the people of God.

Karl Barth offers us for our pastoral work an interpretation of this kind of hospitality in fellowship (koinōnia) as one of the many forms of the ministry of the Christian community.[1] When the community acts to establish fellowship, it witnesses to God's fellowship established in Jesus Christ, both between the whole world and God and among human beings. God in Jesus Christ joins with humankind. God establishes this fellowship between us and Jesus Christ. The Lord calls the community of God's people to bear witness to the fellowship between God and humanity by establishing fellowship between

---

1. Karl Barth, *The Doctrine of Reconciliation* (*Church Dogmatics* IV/3, second part), trans. G. W. Bromiley (Edinburgh: T. & T. Clark, 1962), 898–901.

by placing them in the mouth of the Savior himself. But there is more going on here.

Verses 7–11 provide the context for instructions against hubris when coming together for a wedding feast. Noting the human tendency for self-aggrandizement prevalent on the occasion of social meetings (frankly, we all tend to prefer the "best seats in the house" when we are out), Jesus provides a set of guidelines to counter this tendency. Thus, he says, instead of assuming the privilege of place and being humiliated in a vainglorious grab for status, forgo this presumption of privilege and assume a humble posture. The ones doing this may be pleasantly surprised to find that the host will, in turn, find them worthy and then elevate them in the sight of all.

The nature of the instruction that Jesus gives is reminiscent of the Hebrew wisdom tradition. Wisdom literature captures the pedagogical lessons passed from one generation to another about how gracefully and prudently to negotiate the seemingly mundane details of life. In this instance, Jesus' instructions provide guidance to those who would share a common table, discouraging the presumption of privilege and encouraging a humbler tack. Similar lessons are found in the Hebrew wisdom traditions. In Proverbs, for example, there are numerous aphorisms prohibiting arrogance (6:17; 8:13; 16:5; 16:18–19; 21:4; 30:13) or championing humility (15:33). Each of these aphorisms reflects the gist of Jesus' instruction in Luke 14:7–11. There are also a number of proverbs addressing table etiquette, including Proverbs 23:1–3, dealing with etiquette at a ruler's table, and 23:6–8; 23:20–21; and 23:30–35, all of which focus on other aspects of behavior to be avoided while at table. Perhaps the proverb that most closely resembles Jesus' teaching in Luke 14:7–11 is Proverbs 25:6–7: "Do not put yourself forward in the king's presence or stand in the place of the great; for it is better to be told, 'Come up here,' than to be put lower in the presence of a noble."

The similarity of content, details, and form between this proverb and Jesus' words could lead one to suspect the dependence of the latter on the former and suggest that Jesus' instruction is itself from Wisdom literature concerned with mundane matters. This also seems to fit the context, for verse 1 sets this narrative at a Sabbath feast in the home of a leading Pharisee, and verse 7 declares that Jesus' words are uttered in response to guests' choosing "places of honor" on this occasion. Hence, we could assume that Jesus seeks to put down arrogance and

places of honor" (v. 7). The ethical admonition to underestimate oneself, rather than overestimate, while poison to some, is potent medicine for those too impressed by their own resumés. We may find it difficult to assess exactly where we fit in the pecking order, but Jesus' story tells the truth: God's point of view matters more than our own, and more than the assessment of those in a position to turn the spotlight on us or away from us.

As church officers were receiving a group of new members, they went around the circle introducing themselves. One officer, an academic scientist who had helped to identify sites for the first moon landings, introduced himself: "I'm a teacher." True as it was, he left it to others to discover, or not, what he had left unsaid.

As useful as this text can be as a form of ethical injunction—either to introduce a little humility where humility is scarce, or to shape a community's values—it appears also to make a theological point. How can one read verse 11 without being reminded of Philippians 2:6–11, that early hymn or affirmation of faith that celebrates Jesus? "He humbled himself. . . . Therefore God also highly exalted him." In his life, death, and resurrection Jesus embodied what he taught; and he taught what he embodied.

One is struck, in singing or saying the Apostles' Creed, that the creed jumps directly from "born of the Virgin Mary" to "suffered under Pontius Pilate." Jesus' whole life is somehow hidden in the comma between one phrase and the next. No mention is made of his parables, his sermons, his instructions to his disciples. There are no exhortations in the creed, to humility or any other virtue. Is this an unfortunate omission? Could it be that all the teachings are made manifest in the cross and the resurrection? "Those who humble themselves will be exalted." If a contrast is needed to make the point, one might look at those persons of power whose names are handed down to us in the Gospel: Pilate, Caesar, Herod, Caiaphas. Those who are powerful, according to the conventional measurements of power, exhibit no hesitation about occupying the places of honor. How have things worked out for them? "For all who exalt themselves will be humbled" (v. 11).

As if learning humility were not difficult enough, Jesus adds a second admonition to those gathered for the Sabbath meal. When you give a party, do not invite someone in expectation that your guest can pay you back. "Invite the poor, the crippled, the lame, and the blind" (v. 13). Is this meant to be a literal command, an obligatory protocol to anyone

Luke 14:1, 7-14

Theological Perspective

us and give us a sense of the great blessing that is to come in the resurrection.

Being a blessing is even more challenging and grace-filled. Theologically, my grandmother was pointing to the power of righteousness in the Christian journey. As you explore this passage in relation to your congregation, there is much to mine for how we seek blessings, rather than how we try to live our lives as a blessing. Righteousness or right living encourages us to live our lives with honesty as we seek justice and sound moral principles and behaviors in the context of a community or the variety of communities to which we belong. My grandmother understood well the importance of covenanting within a community as a tangible witness to God's salvific acts in history. Being a blessing, living righteousness in our daily lives, draws us into relationship with those who have less than we do, yet are the true representatives of God's countless blessings in our lives and in the lives of others.

As you think through the various ways that you can help hearers of the word be in touch with deeper and more challenging meanings of blessing, what ways can you encourage those hearers to live into the covenant God has made with us? This covenant is the foundation of the blessing that frames righteous living. How can you encourage them, as well as yourself, to live justly with those who represent the coming-but-not-yet realm of God as we live our lives framed with mercy? How can you encourage them to be a blessing to those whose lives they touch?

EMILIE M. TOWNES

Pastoral Perspective

human beings. Barth unpacks the concept with four dimensions:

1. as the community reaches out to all nations, it offers unity among peoples that overcomes national, ethnic, and linguistic barriers in our world;
2. in its attitude toward racial differences, the church refuses to accept either the legitimacy or necessity of dividing up the community into "special white, black and brown congregations";[2]
3. responding to the plurality of human cultures, the ministry of the people of God brings different people together to overcome cultural differences, rather than to sanctify or bless cultural differences; and
4. in its pastoral work the Christian community sets aside class distinctions in society between rich and poor.

Barth says the community of God's people, the church, "would be mortally sick if it were to identify itself with a class, or its concerns with the interests, its faith with the ideology, or its ethos with the morality of such a class."[3] Barth's pastoral theology offers us the Christian practices of hospitality and welcome to heal national, ethnic, racial, cultural, and class divisions in the world. In the reflections of this great theologian, hospitality and fellowship become central to the church's ministry.

Luke gives beautiful testimony to this barrier-breaking hospitality in the account of the journey of Mary and Joseph from Nazareth to Bethlehem, where she gives birth and lays Jesus in a manger "because there was no place for them in the inn" (2:1–7). The birth of Jesus thus breaches the blockade of welcome for the babe at the inn and embodies royal David's line in an unexpected way. The hospitality of the manger becomes a paradigm for Luke's particular emphasis on the welcome of the stranger and the communion at table that breaks down the barriers at the borders to human community and overcomes the constrictive exclusions of fear and loathing in the world.

CHARLES E. RAYNAL

2. Ibid., 899.
3. Ibid., 900.

generally enhance the dynamics at common meals; but there may be more at stake.

In 22:30, the *trapeza* or table is revisited as a metaphor for a communal fellowship space in the reign of God. Likewise, the table is spiritualized in 24:30, as actions at this location reveal the identity of the resurrected Messiah. Because the progression of table imagery in Luke transforms this mundane meal site into a symbol of life in God's reign, Jesus' instruction may have greater implications as well. Initially we can understand this as reproof for the Pharisees, who presume privilege in relation to God, suggesting that it is only the grace of the Divine Host that conveys the "higher" seat at the Lord's banquet; their presumption of priority does not make them favorites at God's table. Further, it serves to dissuade Christians from all presumptions of privilege, noting the vanity of self-aggrandizement in the kingdom, for we are all "seated" according to our Host's will.

Verses 7–11 bear witness to the nature of life under God's reign, where presumptions of privilege—not only those of individuals, but those of groups, things like "race," ethnicity, class, gender, nationality, and native tongue—do not "distinguish" us; but if we allow them to define us, they will certainly "disgrace" us. These aspects of our identity that would have us assume the right to the higher seats of honor are deemed void of meaning, for it is not we who determine worth at God's table. In our collective life in Christ, may we always remember his words in verse 11: "All who exalt themselves will be humbled, and those who humble themselves will be exalted."

Verses 12–14 also continue this counterintuitive message, telling us that our own tables should be surrounded by strangers, who are the "poor, the crippled, the lame, and the blind," in essence. We should populate our tables with those who are at the greatest social disadvantage. Although this instruction is patently this-worldly in its orientation, it says something about the nature of God's reign as well; it lets the hearer know that the attributes ascribing favor in this world are not the same as those that do so at the coming feast. Those viewed as lower are to be treated with greater respect, to receive greater favor, and to enjoy places of honor in our own lives!

RODNEY S. SADLER JR.

who ever thinks of entertaining guests? It can be literal enough, perhaps, in that it is meant at least to turn us toward the hurting, the struggling, and the vulnerable in every dimension of our lives, not excluding the festive times, so that they are never out of sight, out of mind. This teaching may also be intended to form communal values that celebrate self-giving rather than calculating what one is likely to get in return for a good deed.

This saying of Jesus says less about manners than about Jesus' own ministry. He turns himself toward "the poor, the crippled, the lame, and the blind." He shares the table with those from whom folks with conventional values turn away. From one society to another, and from one era to another, there seem to be different lists of those from whom respectable people expect to turn aside. Jesus' challenge reaches across boundaries of place and time, calling us to be more aware of those from whom we are inclined to avert our eyes, and to follow him rather than those who baptize common prejudices as virtues. We who "have been baptized into Christ Jesus" (Rom. 6:3) are called to conform to him and to his ways. To live into our baptism is to be ever mindful of those who are typically left out. ("Do not be conformed to this world" [Rom. 12:2].)

Jesus' second saying, like the first, has a theological as well as an ethical dimension. The word "banquet" provides a clue. In the New Testament, a banquet is a symbol of the reign of God, the kingdom of heaven. "Blessed are those who are invited to the marriage supper of the Lamb" (Rev. 19:9). The Lord's Supper serves as a foretaste of the wedding banquet when "people will come from east and west, from north and south, and will eat in the kingdom of God" (Luke 13:29). The host will be the One who has already invited those who do not take an invitation for granted, including the ones who are typically uninvited.

RONALD P. BYARS

Jeremiah 18:1-11

[1]The word that came to Jeremiah from the LORD: [2]"Come, go down to the potter's house, and there I will let you hear my words." [3]So I went down to the potter's house, and there he was working at his wheel. [4]The vessel he was making of clay was spoiled in the potter's hand, and he reworked it into another vessel, as seemed good to him.

[5]Then the word of the LORD came to me: [6]Can I not do with you, O house of Israel, just as this potter has done? says the LORD. Just like the clay in the potter's hand, so are you in my hand, O house of Israel. [7]At one moment I may declare concerning a nation or a kingdom, that I will pluck up and break down and destroy it, [8]but if that nation, concerning which I have spoken, turns from its evil, I will change my mind about the disaster that I intended to bring on it. [9]And at another moment I may declare concerning a nation or a kingdom that I will build and plant it, [10]but if it does evil in my sight, not listening to my voice, then I will change my mind about the good that I had intended to do to it. [11]Now, therefore, say to the people of Judah and the inhabitants of Jerusalem: Thus says the LORD: Look, I am a potter shaping evil against you and devising a plan against you. Turn now, all of you from your evil way, and amend your ways and your doings.

Theological Perspective

Søren Kierkegaard, characterizing the champions of immanence and transcendence, famously noted four basic differences between "the genius" and "the apostle." In sum, the genius's gift is inherent "in and of itself," then the apostle—and the apostle's proclamation—has import and significance only by virtue of "divine authority."[1]

Kierkegaard's argument runs basically along these lines. First, the genius is a singularly "gifted" individual whose aptitudes seek expression and carry their own authority. The apostle, however, is not so much apt as "called," whose life and preaching do not voice giftedness but a "given" word. Second, if the genius explores or attempts to discover what is "new," the apostle stewards truths passed from generation to generation. Apostles, it could be said, never have an original thought. Third, with time the insights of the genius become conventional wisdom. The apostolic message, however, remains a kind of foolishness. Fourth, while both geniuses and apostles work more or less in solitude, the actual labor of the former remains an essentially solitary venture, while the apostle both labors in and speaks to a community of faith.

Pastoral Perspective

There is a powerful impetus in this text to change one's behaviors, to repent; and the impetus is that if the people do not change their behaviors, then the Lord will simply smash down and remake them, like an artist working with clay. One way the church has dealt with the challenging call to change leveraged by the frightening threat of destruction in the text is to focus on the metaphor of a potter. Pottery has been the dominant image the church has taken from this passage, and many Western Christians will hear the text through the filter of the hymns and songs about potters and clay engraved on their hearts. The initial work of the pastor may well be here to separate the songs from the text in the congregation's mind, so that the text can be heard on its own.

People love this image of "the potter." Potters are gentle people, are they not? Are they not artists who are sensitive souls constitutionally averse to violence? Not in this text. Think of the violent artistry of the band Smashing Pumpkins. Remember that Vincent van Gogh cut his ear off. Picture the clay animation character flattened by a steamroller. "The vessel he was making of clay was spoiled in the potter's hand, and he reworked it into another vessel" (v. 4). "Thus says the LORD: Look, I am a potter shaping evil against you and devising a plan against you" (v. 11). The pastor will have the work of conductor as

---

1. Søren Kierkegaard, *Without Authority: Kierkegaard's Writings, XVIII*, trans. Howard V. Hong and Edna H. Hong (Princeton, NJ: Princeton University Press, 1997), 91–108.

Exegetical Perspective

The image of the potter in this passage, one of the best-known passages in Jeremiah, raises one of the most important theological issues in Scripture: the tension between divine sovereignty and human freedom. Do our actions as human beings really have any effect on what God decides to do? Are we as individuals and communities locked into a course of events that God has already determined?

The context for Jeremiah's preaching in this text is probably a time in his ministry when he has been forced to resume his preaching after the death of Josiah, the great covenant reformer. The king who eventually comes to the throne is Jehoiakim, a self-serving puppet of Egyptian power, who has no intention of continuing Josiah's covenant reforms. Jeremiah resumes the preaching he had suspended during the time of Josiah's reforms, to warn of the danger of disregarding Judah's covenant commitment. God's judgment can sweep them away and, indeed, in Jeremiah's lifetime, through the power of Babylon, Judah is swept away into exile. At this point in his ministry, however, a key question is whether God's plan of judgment (v. 11) is fixed and inevitable or can be averted.

The passage opens with a command to Jeremiah to go to a potter's house, where the word of the Lord will come to him (vv. 1–2). What follows is a

Homiletical Perspective

Preachers can bring to life the theologically rich metaphor at the heart of this text by beginning as Jeremiah does, sketching with spare, bold lines the potter bent to the wheel, clay spattered from head to foot, sensitive hands pressing and shaping the spinning clay to draw forth something useful and beautiful.

The hymn text that petitions, "Mold me and make me / after thy will,"[1] envisions the divine-human relationship strictly on the individual level. However, the covenant framework at work in the background of text after text in Jeremiah also governs the metaphor here. Legitimate though it may be to imagine God's shaping our individual lives, Jeremiah here is addressing primarily the life of the called community, not the individual. God means to shape the *community of faith* in its collective social, religious, and political life to serve divine purposes. The most faithful preaching and hearing of the text will emerge when preachers attend to this primarily communal level of textual address, and only secondarily to the implications for individual lives of faith.

One preaching approach will be simply to let the dynamism of the metaphor open up fresh theological insights about the interplay of the ongoing,

1. Adelaide A. Pollard, "Have Thine Own Way, Lord!" (1907).

Jeremiah 18:1-11

Theological Perspective

These distinctions can provide interesting background for consideration of Jeremiah 18:1–11. Jeremiah is called to his life's work; he is a steward of the tradition; he is considered foolish; he is lonely within his community (one might easily substitute "prophet" for Kierkegaard's "apostle" and start preaching!).

Like other true prophets, Jeremiah's call is rooted in Israel's constitution and purpose. The prophet's message has for its headwaters the living God, and for its streambed the long history of the chosen people. As the prophet recalls, explores, reiterates the tradition handed down from generation to generation, the prophet's words will seem "familiar" to the people who hear them—they are not unmindful of the stories. Still, the true prophet's word is invariably greeted with skepticism and is regarded as foolishness, whether political or military, religious or ethical.

The prophet knows, however—and better than the community chooses to remember—that God's word first formed and ultimately liberated the descendants of Abraham and Sarah, that God constituted and covenanted with Israel to make it a holy nation and distinct people. The historical, divine initiatives—blessing, provision, protection—prescribe for Israel corresponding temporal expectations: worship, justice, and obedience. Over and over the prophets are called to remind the people of both past mercies and deliverance—precisely to summon Israel back to thanksgiving and service.

Therefore, while prophecy can be iconoclastic (and there are some who define prophecy always and only in just such terms), a prophet's preaching may also be constitutive. Indeed, God, via the prophet, may "pluck up and break down," especially when the culture to which the prophet speaks has deviated from the purposes for which God established it. That said, the prophet's appointed work may be to "build and plant," to summon the nation, the culture, the people to return to its essential theological identity. In such an instance, the prophet's words may be nationalistic but they are not propaganda (that particular idolatry characterizes the preaching of the false prophets). In either case the import and significance of the word is its divine investiture, and in both cases the prophets understand their work to be service to and for the community.

This communal aspect proves crucial when we turn to the imagery of "the potter and clay." In short, what is the clay? In Christian worship the metaphor is most often employed more or less *privately*, as a hymnic prayer for personal transformation

Pastoral Perspective

people examine this text, and the journey likely will travel from an assumption of pleasant compliance to a frightening awareness of impending disaster.

Pastors can expect that congregations, once they hear the text, will naturally move to wonder if current events in their lives are signs of God's similar movement today, God's call to them to change their behaviors. In the call for Judah to change, parishioners will look for their own call to change (although sometimes protective avoidance takes the form of seeing more clearly where we believe our neighbor should change). The text evokes the work of discernment for the people: "Is the Lord threatening to reshape us?" "Where are we being called to change, and how quickly?" Pastors might help the congregation encountering the text by asking, "Where in your own story has God used events to reshape you?" "What stories from the life of the larger church lift up faithful narratives of people who changed their behaviors in the face of crisis, and reported the crisis as God's impetus to change?" "What role does crisis play in conversion?" Despite Romans 9:20, with its allusion to Isaiah 29:16, the people will ask themselves, and the pastor, "Why has God made me like this?"

This text may well be troubling for parishioners, because it raises for them the notion of God's changing God's mind ("I will change my mind about the good that I had intended to do to it," Jer. 18:10), and similarly because of the way the language of the text seems to speak of the Lord's planning evil toward the people ("Thus says the LORD: Look, I am a potter shaping evil against you and devising a plan against you," v. 11). Both of these characterizations may well conflict with the deep convictions of parishioners about the character of God, and some of those convictions will come from the good theological grounding of their faith traditions. "Does God change God's mind?" and "Does God bring evil?" are pastoral questions and will be intertwined with parishioners' individual stories. People particularly struggle with the worry that painful things they experience are punishments from God.

Pastors can anticipate that authentic hearing of this text (as opposed to singing gentle songs about compliant pottery) will raise those questions. What experiences are an inducement to necessary and faithful change, and what experiences are a sad reality of living in a broken world? This is the work of prayerful discernment, pastorally done in corporate worship and small groups as well as in the pastor's study and in private devotion.

straightforward description of the potter at his craft. Anyone who has observed a potter at work knows that working the clay is demanding and time-consuming. The vessel the potter intends frequently grows misshapen in his hands as too much or too little pressure is exerted, or a wall of the vessel becomes too thin, or an intended shape does not develop as planned. When this happens, the potter collapses the vessel, compresses the clay, and begins again.

Jeremiah observes this process at work (vv. 3–4), and the word of the Lord comes to him, making the work of the potter into a metaphor for the way God works with communities and nation. In God's metaphorical teaching, God's people Judah takes the role of the clay, and God is the divine potter. Judah is the only portion of God's covenant people remaining, so it is referred to here as the house of Israel (v. 6), that is, God's covenant people. Implied in this address are all of the commitments and obligations that come with covenant relationship, from Sinai to the present. Also implied is the care and love that God has committed to Israel.

Jeremiah's lesson from God begins with the negative side of the metaphor. God, as divine potter, can shape, destroy, and shape again. In this lesson, however, God emphasizes that the divine will may be to "pluck up and break down and destroy" a nation (v. 7). This is within God's power, and God can will it.

This language is not unfamiliar to readers of Jeremiah. When Jeremiah is called as a youth to become God's prophet, he is commissioned to speak words God has placed in his mouth "to pluck up and to pull down, to destroy and to overthrow" (1:10). Jeremiah is reminded that the word of God's judgment was a part of his commission from the beginning, and God can collapse the vessel of Israel if its shape is not what God intended as covenant partner.

In the same moment, God declares that "if that nation . . . turns from its evil, I will change my mind" (18:8). This may well be a surprising statement, to Jeremiah and to us. We are not accustomed to thinking of God as changing the divine mind. We are prone to think of God determining the course of the future and staying fixed upon that course. Can God's "plan" (an idea mentioned in v. 11) be changeable? Perhaps equally surprising is the notion that human actions might play a role in changing God's mind. If a nation judged by God turns from evil, then disaster can be averted. God's judgment is not fixed in some deterministic way. God responds to repentance. The Hebrew verb "to turn" is used to mean "to repent" in the Bible.

creative work of God in human affairs and a congregation's common life. First, like the potter intent on drawing a useful vessel from the clay, God is *deeply invested in our common life*. The potter does not work aimlessly, nor does God. Every turn of the wheel matters. God means to shape us for purposes that often exceed our vision and imagination, and which most certainly exceed our typical preoccupations with congregational maintenance. Second, the relationship between potter and clay, divine artisan and called community, is *robustly dynamic*. As a potter is not indifferent to the condition of the clay, so God is not indifferent to the way our collective life is taking shape. The text is ambiguous in verse 4; what is the source of the flaw in the clay? The language implies that *this* clay can actively resist the hand of the potter! In our common life, too, we can choose to align ourselves with God's redemptive purposes or pursue self-interested agendas.

Third, there is a point in the process of raising a pot from the wheel *when its future shape is set*. For communities of faith, too, there are watershed moments when the community faces choices that will have a profound impact on its future: the choice to retain an aging urban property or to move to greener pastures in the suburbs, the choice to call a pastor who breaks the mold of congregational expectation in some significant way or to call a more traditional pastor. A preacher might explore with her congregation turning points in the congregation's history, or those of the wider denomination or world church, when the destiny of church and society has turned on critical, precedent-setting choices made by people of faith. The pressing decisions that face every local congregation take on new import when seen in light of such decisive moments of the past.

Grappling with the unavoidable note of judgment in this text is also worthy of a sermon. Every potter exercises constant judgment about the condition of the clay and the shape of the emerging work, and responds accordingly. She may moisten the mix, press deeply here, shape quickly there. For a time, the clay is pliable; the piece can be mended or recentered as needed. Sometimes a flaw in the clay itself or a problem with its emerging shape is beyond fixing, leaving the potter no choice but to scrape the piece off the wheel and start again. God is determined, out of love for the world, to shape communities whose distinctive ways of worship and life bear witness to the redemptive purposes of God. When they do not, the text tells us, communities can be broken down

Jeremiah 18:1-11

Theological Perspective

(presumably accomplished in solitude). Jeremiah has in mind something different, something far more comprehensive. God remains the potter, of course, but the clay is neither individual persons nor even the nation (as in Isa. 64:8). Instead, the clay is God's will and purposes.

Jeremiah is directed to a potter's house. What Jeremiah "sees" there allows him to "hear" the words of God. The scene is pedestrian enough: a potter working at the wheel. Whatever piece the potter has intended to make has spoiled in his hand. The clay on the wheel remains malleable, though, so the potter reforms the now formless mass into something else again, "as it seemed good" to the potter to do (v. 4).

The power of the image is in its interpretation, of course, a deep theological significance imputed to the image by "divine authority" (the image itself is akin to Kierkegaard's "apostle"). In all such images— whether water, figs, a man and his sons, or a woman and her housework—commonplace realities gather and convey extraordinary and even revolutionary truths. When preaching interprets these images only (or primarily) individualistically, both the image and the preaching are diminished

Pablo Picasso once suggested that "art is a lie that helps us see the truth."[2] As God explicates this scene, we have a variation on Picasso's dictum. Specifically, what Jeremiah sees at the potter's house is the "truth" that helps Israel (and us) see the "lie" of immutability, at least as it often has been preached. Yes, God is the same yesterday, today, and forever, as the writer of Hebrews says of Jesus (Heb. 13:8); the same cannot be said, however, of all God's plans and actions.

In sum, the reshaping of the ruined clay reveals the malleability of God's will: "If that nation, concerning which I have spoken, turns from its evil, I will change my mind" (Jer. 18:8). Positively, the evil God intended is reshaped into blessing. One is reminded of Hosea, how God turns from justifiable anger to compassion (although in that case not on account of *Israel's* repentance but rather when God recalls that *as* God, the Almighty is as free to act with compassion as with wrath). One thinks also of Jonah and the repentance of the Ninevites. God in turn repents of the already-planned destruction of the city (in all of Jonah, only the prophet does not repent!). Conversely, God reminds Judah (and others) that blessing is not an entitlement but always a gift.

THOMAS R. STEAGALD

Pastoral Perspective

The metaphors in the text are so powerfully engaging that we can analyze them and focus on the nature of clay and the character of God, and thus be distracted from the central message: change your behaviors. "Turn now, all of you from your evil way, and amend your ways and your doings" (v. 11). For Judah and for the church comes the honest imperative: change your behaviors, "your ways and your doings," your patterns and your actions that are not a part of God's intentions for your lives. Matthew recalls that Jesus came preaching, "Repent, for the kingdom of heaven has come near" (Matt. 4:17). At the beginning of Jesus' gospel is the imperative to change our ways, and the impetus is also the approach of the Divine. Both Mathew and Jeremiah contain the notion that an impetus is necessary to our change.

The pastoral opportunity is to lift up for the people the call to change and the opportunity to change and the impetus to change that God supplies. In the New Testament, this impetus comes in Christ. In Jeremiah 18, "disaster" might be the mechanism for reshaping the people (v. 8), but there is never a report that the Lord will reshape the people into something other than what the potter, the creator, intends. When "reshaping" comes, it will be the means for recreating the people into what God desires and plans. Jeremiah calls the people toward change, but the change is the change into God's design and order. The opportunity to repent, to change, is an opportunity for faithfulness. It should be a source of pastoral comfort for the people that the changes into which God is calling them are a part of God's intention and order, standing over and against the chaos and disorder of disaster. The New Testament promise is that ultimately God, the potter, will reshape us. It will look not like disaster but like resurrection. "We will not all die, but we will all be changed. . . . For this perishable body must put on imperishability, and this mortal body must put on immortality" (1 Cor. 15:51, 53).

JOHN T. DEBEVOISE

2. Pablo Picasso, cited in John Horgan, *The End of Science: Facing the Limits of Knowledge in the Twilight of the Scientific Age* (New York: Broadway Books, 1997), 231.

Exegetical Perspective

God's word using the potter metaphor goes on. In verse 9 God refers to the divine intention to "build and plant" a nation or kingdom. God as potter may intend to shape and guide to full life the people created by divine guidance. This once again goes back to Jeremiah's call as a youth. He was commissioned not only to bring God's word of judgment, but also to announce God's intent "to build and to plant" (1:10). God's divine will can be to create and guide to fulfillment the life of a people linked to God in covenant partnership.

Now God's metaphor announces that even a people God intended to plant and to build can suffer the fate of the misshapen pot on the potter's wheel "if it does evil in my sight, not listening to my voice" (18:10). Evil is defined in terms of disobedience to the covenant. Covenant relationship is conditional. It can be broken. The vessel begun by the potter can be destroyed. Once again the prophet states flatly in the voice of God's word, "I will change my mind about the good that I had intended to do" (v. 10b). Covenant relationship is not an unconditional guarantee for good.

In verse 11 Jeremiah comes to the harsh conclusion of this metaphor and the word of the Lord it speaks to Judah. God can have a change of mind. Like the creation of the potter, whatever was originally intended, good or ill, can be altered if the vessel is not being shaped as God intended. Now Jeremiah says bluntly that the Lord is shaping evil against Judah and Jerusalem. For all the covenant history between them, God has now determined to destroy the vessel and begin again. However, the last half of this verse (v. 11b) suggests that turning (repentance) is still possible. Evil ways can be left behind and the people can "amend your ways and your doings." One of the great teachings of this text is that the "plan" of God is not a fixed, deterministic course of events. God's plan takes into account obedience and disobedience, sin and repentance.

BRUCE C. BIRCH

Homiletical Perspective

(vv. 4, 7–10). It is an inconvenient but necessary truth for every community of faith to face.

Preaching this text as if the choices we make in our common life do not matter, or as if there will never be a day of reckoning, would be to suppress the many-sided, if uncomfortable, truth the metaphor tells. Being honest about the note of judgment does not mean that there is no room here for hope. The strong verbs of the call narrative of Jeremiah 1 resonate in the background here; and while they include "to pluck up and to pull down, to destroy and to overthrow," they also include "to build and to plant" (Jer. 1:10). The discarded clay of a misshapen vessel can be remixed and worked into a new shape (18:4), and God can raise out of the ruins of a community's self-indulgence or indifference a new faithfulness and a new usefulness (see v. 4b; cf. Jer. 31:31ff). Conviction can lead to repentance expressed in action: practicing forgiveness, breaking silence about matters of justice, placing compassion ahead of self-interest. The divine potter hovers over us, shaping and reshaping us for our high calling as vessels of divine love and justice.

Clay work is messy, as those who have tried their hand at the potter's wheel know. We clay-footed bearers of the divine image can expect to get our hands dirty, run some risks, and—on occasion—face failure as we respond to the Potter's hand and bear witness to God's redemptive aims in the world. Recognizing that participating in the creative work of God is always messy and risky can be a help to congregations in the in-between time of interim ministry or congregational conflict over worship or the overall ministry direction of the church.

At the end of the day, a potter steps away from the wheel covered with the stuff of her art, spattered head to foot with clay. Jeremiah invites us to envision God up to the elbows in our making and remaking. Metaphors can be pushed too far, to be sure—but surely there is a legitimate hint here of the God who *becomes* clay, that the beloved clay itself might express the potter's own heart and will.

SALLY A. BROWN

Psalm 139:1-6, 13-18

¹O LORD, you have searched me and known me.
²You know when I sit down and when I rise up;
    you discern my thoughts from far away.
³You search out my path and my lying down,
    and are acquainted with all my ways.
⁴Even before a word is on my tongue,
    O LORD, you know it completely.
⁵You hem me in, behind and before,
    and lay your hand upon me.
⁶Such knowledge is too wonderful for me;
    it is so high that I cannot attain it.

....

¹³For it was you who formed my inward parts;
    you knit me together in my mother's womb.

Theological Perspective

Today's reading speaks out of a deeply intimate sense of an individual's relationship to God. On the one hand, the psalm articulates a profound awareness of being surrounded by the divine presence at all times and in all places. God anticipates where the psalmist is going and what the psalmist will say. God knows individuals better than they know themselves, the psalmist suggests. This is not just a parlor trick on God's part. This kind of intimacy arises from God's role as creator. In verse 13–14, the psalmist speaks in poetic terms of knowing oneself to be God's creature: "You knit me together in my mother's womb. I praise you, for I am . . . wonderfully made."

The passage invites readers to consider afresh the relationship between what theologians speak of as divine transcendence (God's distinction from the world) and divine immanence (God's intimate connection to it) through the traditional claims that God knows all (omniscience) and that God created all. Holding transcendence and immanence together is not always easy. Contemporary theologian Sallie McFague has argued that much of the theological tradition we have inherited has sacrificed a sense of God's connection to the world in favor of an emphasis on God's rule over (and thus distance from) the

Pastoral Perspective

Dawn breaks over Port-au-Prince, Haiti, said to be the poorest country in the Western Hemisphere. Two weeks earlier, troublemakers filled the streets, smashing thousands of windows, overturning countless garbage cans, looting stores. Food prices were going up; incomes were going down. People were angry. Today, however, all is back to normal—normal chaos, normal poverty and exploitation, normal crowded streets.

First light gleams behind the mountains, the air is cool, roosters are crowing, shoeshine men are ringing their bells, donkeys are braying. Jumbled homes, built almost on top of one another, and women going to the well for water create a vision of first-century Palestine, a land of unstable, often violent political forces; a land of poverty and faith; a land of hunger and hope.

This pastoral reflection on Psalm 139 began on such a morning in Haiti. The words spoke with power, a power different from what would have been possible at home.

Imagine various settings in which the psalm has been heard or will be heard: in a hospital room, before surgery, following a death, or as a mother holds a newborn child; in a prison cell; at the beach on vacation; on a rooftop as morning comes to

¹⁴I praise you, for I am fearfully and wonderfully made.
   Wonderful are your works;
   that I know very well.
¹⁵ My frame was not hidden from you,
   when I was being made in secret,
      intricately woven in the depths of the earth.
¹⁶Your eyes beheld my unformed substance.
   In your book were written
      all the days that were formed for me,
      when none of them as yet existed.
¹⁷How weighty to me are your thoughts, O God!
   How vast is the sum of them!
¹⁸I try to count them—they are more than the sand;
   I come to the end—I am still with you.

Exegetical Perspective

Whereas many psalms depict God's saving activity in Israel's past or in the observable reality of the person praying, Psalm 139 points beyond the pale of the visible into the microscopic, the infernal, the lofty, and the cosmic, striving to describe a God who remains firmly beyond words or comprehension.

God Searches. The psalm begins with an amazing image of God as the seeker. God searches (v. 1; see also v. 23). God's search is thorough and relentless. God follows everywhere we go. Whatever we do, God keeps looking for us, watching for us and observing us.

God not only is looking for something; God exudes knowledge. God knows all sorts of things, including private moments of past, present, and potential future (vv. 2–5). Every time I stand up or sit down, God knows. When I travel by day and sleep by night, God is watching. God knows what I am thinking (v. 2), even before I say it (v. 4).

The scope of God's search and knowledge is clearly personal and intimate. Unlike other Old Testament passages (e.g., Job 38–39) that emphasize God's cosmic and divine knowledge, God in this psalm knows a single person, the unnamed speaker of the psalm. God's knowledge is immediately around this person, with every movement of the

Homiletical Perspective

Like their parishioners, preachers face a choice as to how they view the intimate knowledge God has of human beings. That choice is reflected in how they approach and treat this psalm. They can view it as a searching examination of sinful and disobedient creatures by an omniscient creator from whom none can escape, or they can approach the psalm as an occasion to explore the intimate knowing that arises between Creator and creature when each is wholly and thoroughly attentive to the other.

The significance of this choice is reflected in the initial verses of Psalm 139. The psalmist and those who worship with this psalm declare, in direct relationship to the One who has made them, "You have searched me and known me. You know when I sit down and when I rise up; you discern my thoughts from far away" (vv. 1–2). The knowing is past and ongoing; intimate and unlimited. There is no hiding from it. Is that knowledge to be feared or embraced? If the unguarded knowing that mirrors the relational familiarity of the most intimate relationships is a clue, then this confession is an expression of the deepest trust one can give another. If that knowing is only the searching evaluation of an omniscient judge, then the relationship is characterized by the surrender of power and responsibility. Reading this

Psalm 139:1-6, 13-18

Theological Perspective

world.[1] Hymns and liturgies speak of God as king and lord.

As comforting as these images are, conceiving God predominantly in those terms tempts Christians to sit back passively and wait for God to work out God's will—in this world or the next. This, McFague argues, is a dangerous posture in view of the realities of nuclear proliferation and a global environmental crisis—problems that require our active participation if they are to be resolved. She proposes instead an expansion of the Christian imagination, a theological agenda that resonates in many ways with this psalm.

All language for God falls short of the mark, McFague reminds us. As the author of this psalm acknowledges, it is impossible for humans to grasp the mind of God. Theologians from Augustine to Thomas Aquinas to Paul Tillich and Karl Barth have long recognized this fact. The abstract language of transcendence, immanence, and omniscience (along with their colleague, omnipotence [all powerful]) was developed by theologians to attempt to capture this reality. Even *that* language falls short. As Aquinas argued, while we rightly claim that God knows all, we cannot give that claim any content because our finite minds cannot know what it would be like to know *all*.[2] In the same vein, the psalmist here describes the vastness and weightiness of the contents of the divine mind as exceeding our finite minds' accounting (vv. 17–18). This psalm also witnesses to the fact that experiencing divine love, care, and mystery compels us to attempt the impossible—to speak of God. So we do.

McFague's interest is not in highly conceptual language, but in the images or metaphors we use to speak of God. Because we understand God as relational, we tend to draw on human relationships to image God, she notes. Metaphorical language, though, is just as limited as conceptual language is in its ability to capture the divine essence. Images and metaphors do not name God in any literal sense, but express our experience of and beliefs about God. God *is* not literally a king, but speaking of God *as* king reflects the Christian claim that, as creator, God is the source of cosmic order.

Against this theological backdrop, some of the imagery that the psalmist uses in verses 13–15 is particularly striking. We have long been accustomed to

1. See especially Sallie McFague, *Metaphorical Theology: Models of God in Religious Language* (Philadelphia: Augsburg Fortress, 1982) and *Models of God: Theology for an Ecological, Nuclear Age* (Philadelphia: Augsburg Fortress, 1987).
2. Thomas Aquinas, *Summa theologica* 1-1, q.13, a.1.

Pastoral Perspective

Haiti. Imagine and listen as the psalmist shares the conviction that God knows us, *wherever* we may be. That conviction is the heart of biblical revelation. God searches us, sees us as we are, where we are. God accepts us. Acceptance, however, is not the same as approval; grace, the grace of God, bridges the gap between God's acceptance and God's judgment.

Haiti came into being through the slave trade. Haiti became a free nation before slavery ended in the United States. Freedom for slaves in Haiti stirred up fear in our own nation. Fear led our nation to abandon Haiti for years. Remember that sad truth and ask, What does it mean to be known by God? What does it mean to be searched by God, to realize God is "acquainted with all [our] ways" (v. 3), personally and as a nation? Such questions help us see the gap between God's acceptance of us and God's judgment, a divide that only grace can bridge. Such awareness "hems us in," even as it becomes "too wonderful" for us to grasp. Such awareness becomes the "hand" of God "upon us" (v. 5).

The power of Psalm 139 is its honesty. The psalm is like a mirror revealing us as we are: "fearfully and wonderfully made" (v. 14). We are fearfully made because God has created us and not we ourselves. We are finite, limited; that knowledge stirs up fear. We have the capacity to make choices, but we cannot choose the consequences of our choices; that knowledge stirs up fear. We can imagine life in which sin is not present, but we discover we are powerless to achieve that vision. The gap between what we can envision for ourselves and reality creates fear. Consequences of the slave trade in Haiti and in our own nation—poverty, chaos, violence—are tragic reminders of that truth.

We are fearfully made, and we are wonderfully made: we have unique capacity for wonder, prayer, song, friendship, love, and redemption. Morning worship at the guest house where we stay in Haiti is a reminder of that truth. As first light fills the sky, a bell rings. I leave my rooftop perch for the chapel, joining about twenty boys and young men who live in the home. All have come as orphans or children rescued from abuse. They begin each day with psalms, prayer, and song, followed by shared embraces. Then they are off to do assigned chores, share breakfast, and attend school. I have been coming to this home for eight years. I have watched as shared worship, shared support, shared education, and shared friendship give these boys and young men a life beyond anything they could otherwise have imagined. In a country that reveals all that

person's body, every thought of the person's mind, every habit and quirk. Nothing in our lives is off limits for God's knowledge. Secrets are impossible. Our privacy means nothing to God. Not only does God watch, but God also reaches and touches us (v. 5). Personal space shrinks with God's observation and vanishes to zero with God's hand upon us.

God Surrounds. It is not enough that God knows, and that God's knowledge of us is intimate, personal, and invasive. God surrounds (vv. 7–10). The lectionary selection does not include this passage of the psalm, which verges on the claustrophobic. It begins with a question: "Where can I go from [God's] spirit?" (v. 7). God is present in heaven, earth, and Sheol (v. 8); God is present in the farthest west and east (v. 9). Not even night can hide one from God (vv. 11–12). In all these places, stretched as far away as one could possibly conceive, God is present. God surrounds the person praying this psalm. Just as in verse 5, God hems us in, present on every side imaginable.

God Whom We Cannot Comprehend. We cannot understand God (v. 6). What God knows is more than we can know, or could ever possibly learn. Likewise, we cannot understand how big God is, how many places God can be and already has been, or how God stretches from past to future. To call God omnipresent or omniscient cannot do justice to the vastness of God's reality. The reality is even more daunting; we cannot know how big God is. We have neither words nor concepts for such size. This knowledge, even though we can never attain it, is so big and so high, so weighty, that it threatens to crush us.

God Who Forms Us. God is not only a pervasive observer; verse 13 makes a further claim, that God formed us. Not only does God surround us and confound our knowledge, but God is intimately involved in our very existence. God shaped us, inside and out (v. 13). Although our bodies were made in secret, God knows it; God was there; God did it (vv. 14–16). The psalm asserts once that this happened "in my mother's womb" (v. 13) and once "in the depths of the earth" (v. 15), as if our bodies were constructed far underground. In either case, God made our bodies in secret, known only to God, in some unknown and inaccessible place. The point of this passage, however, is neither the location of such construction nor the immense knowledge that God's making us necessitates. The psalm emphasizes that God created us, that God shaped and formed us, that God not

psalm in the context of Deuteronomy 30 offers an orienting perspective. Moses admonishes his people that as God's people they are called to choose between life and death, blessing and curse, as partners in God's creation. Even, and especially, in their difficult journey through the wilderness, this choice points the way forward. The relational knowing of Psalm 139 is to be embraced and explored as one follows that path. It is, to use another biblical phrase, the psalmist's *hineni*—declaring, "Here I am. You know me. That is good and right, and it is the basis of my own knowing."

Approaching the psalm in this fashion recognizes it to be a trusted companion—a text taken to heart and committed to deep memory. Such a text beckons like an old friend. On the long passage through the wilderness, it stands like a familiar and oft-visited way station, a place of refuge and renewal on the difficult way. Those who have known its nurturing shelter can welcome other travelers, inviting them to join them and spend time in its domain.

That invitation can be shared in several ways— devotionally, in study groups, in worship as an act of praise, or through sermons that seek to explain or embody the knowing that is acknowledged and confessed in this psalm. When preachers choose to focus on this text for a sermon, or a series of sermons, they face a decision about rhetorical strategies. Should the sermon address the text didactically, explaining what it is and what it is not, what it does and what it does not do, or should the sermon seek to embody something of the prayerful knowing to which the psalm bears witness?

Approaching the text as a way station or inn for travelers on the covenantal path of faith allows us to do both, to teach and to worship. The metaphor invites an imaginative encounter with the psalm that allows us to represent our relationship to it and the way it can be inhabited through study as well as prayer. The preacher-as-host attends the text as an innkeeper tends his or her lodge, preparing the rooms, greeting the guests, and offering them shelter and nurture during their retreat from the journey.

Many of those who seek shelter in this place are returning guests who want the comfort of a trusted room that has welcomed them in previous visits. The preacher/host of this inn, however, knows that this house of hospitality is richer than the one room its visitors may know well. His or her task may be to introduce these guests to the abundance of its accommodations, sharing not just *one* room that is distinguished by wonder, for example, but many

Psalm 139:1-6, 13-18

Theological Perspective

speaking of God as father, but here the psalmist moves toward more maternal imagery. The psalmist does not claim that God *is* literally his or her mother, but the depth of the relationship with God draws the writer to image God *as* maternal—as intimately involved in the process of gestation. Indeed, the cosmos itself is imaged as womblike, as the psalmist goes on to speak of "being made in secret, intricately woven in the depths of the earth" (v. 15).

This language succeeds admirably in conveying both God's transcendence of the finite and God's immanence within it. On the one hand, imagining God involved in gestation (whether in the womb or in the depths of the earth) knits the finite with the infinite, to extend the psalmist's metaphor. The difference between God and the world, the finite and the infinite, is clearly maintained. One is creator and the other created; one knows all from the start, the other comes to its limited knowledge only as it moves along life's journey.

The physicality of this imagery is critical to its theological richness. The connection between God and God's creation is imaged here through physical action (knitting, weaving) that results in the creation of a new physical entity: a human being. In marveling at being "fearfully and wonderfully made" (v. 14), the psalmist echoes the refrain repeated throughout the account of creation in Genesis 1: "It is good." In focusing on the goodness of embodied creation, this psalm offers a refreshing counterpoint to any tendency within Christianity to focus on souls rather than bodies. It places care for our physical needs and for our material world squarely at the center of divine concern. If these things matter to God, then they must matter to Christians. In (re)orienting us, the psalm reaffirms the value of exercising the theological imagination in praise of the Divine.

ELLEN T. ARMOUR

Pastoral Perspective

creates fear in human life, I have seen shared faith and friendship create wondrous joy and hope.

Bill Nathan first came to the home at the age of eight; he is now twenty-four and the resident director. Muscular, calm, athletic, and artistic, Bill leads morning worship. I have known Bill for almost a decade. When we visit, he quietly shares his trust that God directs the path of his life, that God is acquainted with all his ways. Bill was born in the mountain city of Hinche; his father died first, then his mother. He was sent to live with a woman who beat him and turned him into her personal servant. Roman Catholic nuns rescued him and sent him to the home in Port-au-Prince.

Before her death, his mother shared her strong faith with her son. Her conviction that "God is good" shaped Bill's faith and became an anchor for his life. Over the years, visitors to the home recognized his gifts as a drummer and his intelligence as a maturing man. Bill has now performed in North Carolina, New York City, Brazil, Zambia, and Canada, where he performed for the pope on his visit. Bill knows fear, and Bill knows wonder.

Bill can help us hear the closing words of the psalm. Bill lives in a land of poverty and instability; he is surrounded by victims of tragedy and cruelty. Nevertheless Bill can praise God, confident that God has knit his life together, woven in the depths of the earth. Bill is convinced that God's eyes beheld his unformed substance, that God's thoughts for him are greater than the sand on the Haitian beaches, and that at the end—whatever the end may be— God will still be with him. Bill becomes a witness, a witness to peace-filled faith.

Worship is over; the boys scatter. I return to the rooftop. The sun is now above the mountains. A new day has arrived, a day in which we are called to go forward, trusting the God who has searched us and known us, the God we praise, for our God knows that we are fearfully and wonderfully made.

ARTHUR (ART) ROSS III

only knows us but takes responsibility for who we are. Likewise, God shapes both our beginnings and also our endings, as well as every day in between (vv. 16, 18). Debates over nature versus nurture have no place here; God surrounds them both, shaping us from the start, in each day of life, and to the end.

God Who Is Ever Present. Beyond thought, there is still God. God is always present, wherever we are, whatever we think, whatever we do (v. 18). God's presence is never passive; God is always actively involved in our formation, maturation, and disposition. God is always with us. Whether or not this seemed claustrophobic or invasive in the earlier verses, the psalm echoes that God is with us—always a promise, even if God's presence frightens us or requires more of us than we would wish to allow.

The lectionary does not include the ending of this psalm, perhaps shying away from the disturbing rejection of enemies in verses 19–22; we nevertheless cannot understand where this psalm would take the reader unless we consider the final two verses:

> Search me, O God, and know my heart;
>   test me and know my thoughts.
> See if there is any wicked way in me,
>   and lead me in the way everlasting
>   (vv. 23–24)

Thus the psalm moves toward this conclusion in which the person praying does not just affirm God's searching and knowing, but invites God to do all of this. God's intimate exploration of our lives is not simply a neutral fact of life; it is what we most need and most deeply desire. We need God's knowledge of us, so that God can show us ourselves as we truly are. As the psalm ends, it voices a plea: Please, God, show me myself, and lead me in your way. God knows our ways already (v. 3), but here we pray that God can show us *God's* way, which is everlasting. This psalm, so often understood to be a philosophical or scientific statement, is in the end a call to morality, and to the following in God's ways that we have learned to call discipleship.

JON L. BERQUIST

rooms, each capturing that attitude in different ways. For example, several of the rooms might emphasize the intimacy of knowing and being known by the Holy One of all creation, developing implications for how one might live out of that sense of partnership with the creator of the universe.

The rooms abound, of course. Some may be set aside for quiet reflection, where guests can ponder more deeply the words and phrases, twists and turns that distinguish the hermeneutical structure built by this text. Some may choose to offer a vantage point to ponder how the psalm expresses God's abiding care for all creation. Such a choice, however, leads to reflection on verses 11 and 12, even though they are not designated for inclusion in the lectionary passage. They are essential for understanding the overall meaning of the psalm and clearly influence how one experiences this psalm. A close reading of those verses could lead a twenty-first-century Christian to ask, How might confidence in God's abiding presence be affirmed in the face of the twelve-year night of the Holocaust?

Letting that night interrogate this text, and letting this text declare that God is present even in the face of that darkness, may yield a more sophisticated way of thinking about God's ways with an often cruel world. For example, the intimate relationship to which this psalm points does not require the interventionist logic of a God who controls and interrupts history—though one might bring such a perspective to this text. Instead, one might ponder God's ongoing venture of creation as the act of a divine host welcoming life in all its forms, even those that rebel and reject the very gift that makes life possible. In this case, God's dynamic hospitality to life would be seen as a vulnerable venture of choosing life with all its relational possibilities, a divine embrace of life that accepts all the risks and possibilities of relationship. A gifted preacher has the opportunity to help his or her parishioners consider the profound implications of this psalm and its relevance for challenging times.

HENRY F. KNIGHT

Philemon 1-21

[1]Paul, a prisoner of Christ Jesus, and Timothy our brother,
To Philemon our dear friend and co-worker, [2]to Apphia our sister, to Archippus our fellow soldier, and to the church in your house:
[3]Grace to you and peace from God our Father and the Lord Jesus Christ.

[4]When I remember you in my prayers, I always thank my God [5]because I hear of your love for all the saints and your faith toward the Lord Jesus. [6]I pray that the sharing of your faith may become effective when you perceive all the good that we may do for Christ. [7]I have indeed received much joy and encouragement from your love, because the hearts of the saints have been refreshed through you, my brother.

[8]For this reason, though I am bold enough in Christ to command you to do your duty, [9]yet I would rather appeal to you on the basis of love—and I, Paul, do this as an old man, and now also as a prisoner of Christ Jesus. [10]I am appealing to you for my child, Onesimus, whose father I have become during my

Theological Perspective

What a wonderful letter! Despite its brevity, this letter is the most human in the Christian Scriptures. The opening salutation combines the Hellenic ("Grace") and Hebraic ("Peace") with suave urbanity. We find a witty play on words nobody translates well: the name Onesimus means "useful" in Greek, although Onesimus had scarcely been useful to his master. The writer's tact in asking as a favor what he asks could otherwise bespeak a cultural refinement rare in the New Testament.

Forget for a moment who wrote it, and you would go to a lot of trouble to meet its author. Ah, but there *is* the trouble. Paul of Tarsus wrote it. This letter permits us to do two things: first, to rescue Paul from the terrible press he has received during the last century or so; second, to bring one of his profoundest—and most confrontational—ethical teachings to light.

To the first task: reclaiming Paul. Paul, a misogynistic moralist, whom all the dourest preachers most enjoy slapping us with whenever they assume we are enjoying ourselves? Paul, who insisted that no work of ours counts before God, right? (Generations of Christians have sweated through midnight bedsheets worried that their strenuously contrived "faith" might prove to be a "work.") Was this not the man who wanted women to wear veils in church, who

Pastoral Perspective

The letter to Philemon is a model of pastoral care: loving, thoughtful, diplomatic, and carefully theological. The situation is delicate, and Paul the pastor stands between two parishioners who are at serious odds, asking them not only to be reconciled to each other but also to model the new life in Christ to which the entire church is called.

Philemon is a wealthy man. He owns a slave (v. 16) and is master of a house large enough to accommodate a church (v. 2). He, his wife Apphia, and Archippus are the leaders of this congregation (vv. 1–2), and the entire community is invited to listen in as the apostle makes his request (v. 2). What has Onesimus done to Philemon? Did he simply run away? Verse 18 mentions both "injustice" (NRSV "wronged") and "debt" (NRSV "owes . . . anything"); did Onesimus steal something from his master? Paul says only that Onesimus has found his way to Paul, who is in prison (v. 1), and has become a Christian through the agency of Paul's ministry (v. 10), even as Philemon himself once did (v. 19).

The letter begins, as all Paul's letters do, with a greeting from God (v. 3) that reminds Paul's listeners that he speaks not on his own authority but as an agent of the Lord Jesus Christ. This is surely Paul's most personal letter, although it is just as apostolic and ecclesial as the others. Following the salutation

imprisonment. [11]Formerly he was useless to you, but now he is indeed useful both to you and to me. [12]I am sending him, that is, my own heart, back to you. [13]I wanted to keep him with me, so that he might be of service to me in your place during my imprisonment for the gospel; [14]but I preferred to do nothing without your consent, in order that your good deed might be voluntary and not something forced. [15]Perhaps this is the reason he was separated from you for a while, so that you might have him back forever, [16]no longer as a slave but more than a slave, a beloved brother—especially to me but how much more to you, both in the flesh and in the Lord.

[17]So if you consider me your partner, welcome him as you would welcome me. [18]If he has wronged you in any way, or owes you anything, charge that to my account. [19]I, Paul, am writing this with my own hand: I will repay it. I say nothing about your owing me even your own self. [20]Yes, brother, let me have this benefit from you in the Lord! Refresh my heart in Christ. [21]Confident of your obedience, I am writing to you, knowing that you will do even more than I say.

Exegetical Perspective

The brevity, subtlety, and topicality of Philemon have conspired to make it the most neglected of Paul's letters, despite its rhetorical riches and personal warmth. To retrieve it for the church as anything more than an epistolary artifact requires attention to what we can say about it with certainty, what remains uncertain or unknown, and what in our own culture is analogous to the circumstances under which it was produced.

The broad outlines of the situation and Paul's response are clear enough. Onesimus, a slave, has run away from his master, Philemon, a convert of Paul's, and absconded with funds or property of some sort. He has made his way to Paul, who is in prison. In that unlikely setting Paul has converted Onesimus as well. Now Paul composes a letter on Onesimus's behalf, attempting to persuade Philemon to take his slave back as a brother in Christ, and promising to make restitution for anything Onesimus has stolen.

Among the uncertainties and unknowns are the place of Paul's imprisonment (maybe Ephesus, but possibly Rome or even Caesarea), the date of the letter (ca. 56 or 62 CE), and the precise circumstances under which Onesimus made his way to Paul. The most significant uncertainty is the scope of Paul's intent. What does he mean when he expresses the

Homiletical Perspective

This is a good story. It is a personal story involving a web of friends and relatively new disciples of the Lord Jesus. Good stories make one think of other stories.

Many a preacher will want to retell this story of Paul, Onesimus, Philemon, and their friends; but, like many good stories, this one has its uncertainties, gaps, and opportunities for reading between the lines that call for imagination and empathy.

Here is what the story could look like.

Paul, who has earlier visited the Asia Minor city of Colossae and helped to form the house church there (v. 2), is now under a kind of house arrest in Rome (or possibly Ephesus). A young man named Onesimus has run away from Colossae and has come to be helpful (his name means "useful" or "beneficial") to Paul in his imprisonment. Paul has strengthened Onesimus's fledgling Christian faith, and a close bond—like that of a father to a son—has grown between them. While recognizing that Onesimus is still indebted to Philemon or in some way estranged from him, Paul gives thanks for Philemon's Christian love and faith and appeals to him—not on the basis of duty but of love—to take Onesimus back. He asks that he do so, not only without any punishment to him, but as a "beloved brother . . . in the Lord" (v. 16), as "the faithful beloved brother, who is one of you" (Col. 4:9).

Philemon 1-21

Theological Perspective

could not stand the thought of a woman in the pulpit or at the altar or in a classroom of mixed adults? Paul, whom clergy now mention only with the qualification, "And *we all know about Paul!*"—accompanied by wriggling eyebrows?

This letter's charm invites us to reconsider Paul's personality. When he reminds the Galatians of how much they loved him, it is possible he does not exaggerate (Gal. 4:14–15). His friendships with the upwards of thirty people he greets in Romans 16, a third of whom are women, may be honestly earned.

Paul needs his lawyer in the room when we read him. He has been at the mercy of casual, careless readers for more than a century—uptight moralists who assume he is the same as they are and supercilious progressives who have not read him attentively.

If you complain about what appear to be his moral rules, his lawyer would reply that rules bore Paul too—his real interest is in experimenting with a new freedom of the will, once the Spirit has released us from our compulsions. He might remind you that the sin Paul mentions most is greed, not anything sensual.

Is he a neurotic misogynist? Then we would have to explain why he asks a woman "yoke-mate" (NRSV "companion") to use her influence to compose an argument between two church women in Philippi (Phil. 4:2–4). What he does *not* say is, "Tell those women to shut up!" On the other hand Paul *does* say, "[In Christ] there is no longer male and female" (Gal. 3:28). Few of us bother to notice that Paul's first letter to Corinth replies to a stupid letter they have written to him (1 Cor. 7:1), that it is a party in Corinth, not Paul himself, that wants to veil women, or that *they*, not Paul, want to hush women in church. The human warmth of Philemon could spur a reconsideration of this great saint's personal manner.

More deeply, this letter illustrates that Paul actually lives and practices a very deep ethical principle that he shares with our Lord: the principle of non-dominance. Culturally and linguistically Jesus and Paul are very different men, yet each teaches and embodies a refusal to dominate other people—even when they can easily do so—and a casual disregard for others' attempts to dominate them.

In this letter, Paul openly declines to dominate Philemon (vv. 8–9) although, as he tells the latter, he well could do so. Verses 15 and 16 dare to contemplate a wealthy Hellenistic Christian's receiving one who has been a disobedient slave as a spiritual equal, as a brother, trusting Philemon not to fall back into

Pastoral Perspective

is a thanksgiving in which Paul speaks directly to his reason for writing. Philemon's love and faith are well known among Christians (vv. 4–5), and the apostle prays that the partnership of Philemon's faith (v. 6; NRSV "sharing") might become still more well known among believers. Paul asks no small favor from Philemon in order to make effective that "knowledge of the good" (v. 6). He calls him to manumit a slave and forgive a debt, two things that could cause a wealthy man in antiquity to lose face.

Paul says he makes an appeal rather than a command (vv. 8–9) because of his love for Philemon. His repeated references to his own imprisonment (vv. 1, 9, 10, 13, 23) serve to remind Philemon of the cost of Christian discipleship; he asks no more of Philemon than Christ asks of all believers. He also piles up images of the relationship he and Philemon share. They are coworkers (v. 1) and partners (vv. 6, 17) in the gospel; Philemon is both Paul's brother (vv. 7, 20) and his son (v. 10). Philemon has hosted not only the church but the apostle as well (v. 7) and will soon have the opportunity again to show hospitality (v. 22). The metaphors of the household dominate in this letter. The apostle writes not only as a brother, but as the old person in the family (v. 9), a reminder that he was in Christ before Philemon was and thus has the superior family status and the right to ask what he does.

Peace between Philemon and Onesimus requires that the former receive the latter "no longer as a slave but . . . a beloved brother" now that both are Christians (v. 16). This is not simply metaphorical kinship, but emphatically social, because it is "both in the flesh and in the Lord" (v. 16), and Onesimus therefore now merits the same welcome in Philemon's home that Paul enjoys. It is considered extremely shameful in antiquity to enslave one's brother; so to call Onesimus a brother "in the flesh" forbids Philemon to hold him in bondage. Paul calls Philemon to renounce his privilege and be willing to suffer loss, both socially and economically. This is at the heart of Paul's ethical teaching: elsewhere he says, "Let each of you look not to your own interests, but to the interests of others. Let the same mind be in you that was in Christ Jesus" (Phil. 2:4–5). To give up his rights to collect a debt and punish a slave, Philemon must imitate Christ's own willingness to give up his "equality with God" (Phil. 2:6). It is also to imitate the apostle, who renounces his rights for the sake of the gospel that gives him those rights in the first place (1 Cor. 9:1–23).

How might contemporary Christians listen to the apostle along with the church that meets in

hope that Philemon will receive Onesimus "no longer as a slave but more than a slave, a beloved brother" (v. 16) and when he expresses his confidence that Philemon "will do even more than I say" (v. 21)? Is Paul suggesting that Onesimus be recognized as an evangelist, or that he be manumitted, or that he be returned in order to continue to aid Paul in prison—or perhaps all three? We have tantalizing hints but nothing more.

However broad Paul's objective may be, there is no guarantee that even his basic request, "welcome him as you would welcome me" (v. 17), will be heeded. The matter is grave. Can Philemon be expected to receive his slave without inflicting the punishment to which he is legally entitled? The matter is also unprecedented. Can Philemon be expected to trust a runaway whose conversion may be nothing more than a tactic of convenience?

Given the delicacy of the situation and the magnitude of the request, Paul is by turns tactful and forceful. On the one hand, he frames the letter as an "appeal" (vv. 9–10) and emphasizes his desire for Philemon's voluntary consent (v. 14). On the other hand, he commences the body of the letter by asserting his boldness to "command" Philemon (v. 8)—although he will refrain from doing that!—and concludes by affirming his confidence in Philemon's "obedience" (v. 21). In a declaration of apostolic authority reminiscent of 1 Corinthians (esp. 4:14–15), he reminds Philemon that he owes his "own self" to Paul. This is presumably a reference to Philemon's conversion—a matter about which Paul says he will "say nothing," but, in so saying, he speaks to even greater effect, one of the letter's many fine rhetorical touches (v. 19).

Even the opening salutation adds to the force of Paul's appeal. The salutation (vv. 1–3), unlike the rest of the letter, which is addressed to Philemon alone, includes all those in the church who assemble in Philemon's house and mentions Timothy, Paul's associate. The implication is that the issue at hand is not merely one of private judgment but one of communal concern. As an exercise in diplomacy, the letter is adroit and disarming from start to finish. We can only marvel at Paul's skill.

Still, the letter is more than a diplomatic coup. It is an expression of genuine fondness for Philemon and genuine appreciation for the mutual bonds of faith that make this intervention possible. As in 1 Thessalonians and Philippians, terms of endearment abound. Philemon is Paul's "dear . . . coworker," "partner," and "brother" (vv. 2, 17, 20). Philemon's

Tychicus, another "beloved brother" (Col. 4:7–9), carries the letter to Philemon, and perhaps another to the church at Colossae, and brings Onesimus along with him. With him, too, come other news and encouragement from Paul and several of his companions to the new Christian friends in Colossae. Aristarchus, Demas, Luke, Archippus, and Epaphras are other brethren and disciples mentioned in both letters, and there is also the sister Apphia (Phlm. 2). Would it not be interesting to hear the story from the perspective of "our beloved fellow servant" Epaphras, "faithful servant of Christ" and "fellow prisoner in Christ Jesus" (Col 1:7–8; 4:12; Phlm. 23)? It sounds as though Epaphras, likely also imprisoned with Paul, has come to know both Paul and Onesimus well. Evidently he comes from the area of Colossae. He "is one of you" and has "worked hard for you" and also in the neighboring Lycus valley cities of Laodicea and Hierapolis. Moreover, "he is always wrestling in his prayers on your behalf" (Col. 4:12–13). Maybe it is Epaphras who instigates and helps Paul write his letter on behalf of Onesimus. Surely Tychicus will also bring with him news and encouragement from Epaphras. What other thoughts and prayers might Epaphras have for Philemon and, for that matter, Onesimus and Paul as well?

Later interpreters have accused Paul of being manipulative with his flattery regarding Philemon's faith and love. Paul also adds his hope (a kind of mild threat?) to come for a visit ("prepare a guest room for me," v. 22)—a wish he was probably never able to fulfill. He has been criticized too for being too accepting of the institution of slavery, if that is, indeed, Onesimus's condition (see Col. 3:22–4:1); yet the driving force behind the letter is Paul's desire for reconciling love in a new community of siblinglike relationships. "In the Lord" or "in Christ" (a favorite expression of Paul's) there is no longer special status—up or down, older or younger, slave or free, male or female (Gal. 3:28)—for all are beloved brothers and sisters in the love of God in the Lord Christ Jesus.

We do not know how the story ends. It might make one recall the story of a father's attempt to reconcile back into a family the wastrel, prodigal son and his self-righteous brother. "All these years I have been working like a slave for you," complains the elder brother to his father. We do not know how that story (Luke 15:11–32) ends either. Does the elder sibling finally come in and join the party, reconciled to his brother again? Does he stay outside pouting, insisting on his legal and moral rights? At the conclusion of

Philemon 1-21

Theological Perspective

the reigning patterns of prestige, discrimination, and violence that structure everyday life in those days.

This teaching of Paul and of our Lord is so radical that the church at large has as yet refused to pay it any attention. We routinely regard power structures in the church as normal and worry about matters of authority as though God does. Both Paul and our Lord do not. They are braver than we.

This letter offers three of Paul's challenges to us.

First, as mentioned, Paul challenges us to a novel twofold way of relating to people. He counsels us never to try to dominate another person. Even riskier, he counsels us to pay no attention to their attempts to dominate us. Can you feel a trace of the inner freedom involved?

Second, Paul's trust in God is so deep that he is able to discern the love of God in every circumstance, no matter how contrary—even in imprisonment, from which he writes as calmly as from a hotel penthouse. Imagine for a moment revisiting the catalog of *your* ills and misfortunes and discovering a loving gift concealed within each. That may sound Pollyannaish to you, but it is the discovered wisdom of humanity's most courageous teachers.

Third, Paul challenges Philemon to allow the Holy Spirit to take up residence within him and start moving the furniture. He trusts his friend to quit worrying about respectability, in favor of what is just and right. That Spirit heightens our native abilities in ways that feel at once both natural and preternatural, always generously on behalf of others.

None of that is for sissies.

It is way past time for conservative Christians to recognize Paul's profound challenge to our jejune moralizings aimed at other people. He would have none of it. It is also way past time for progressive Christians to recognize that Paul is far out ahead of us—and is not only braver than we are but more loving. Paul is God's gift to us. It is time we make his acquaintance and risk taking him up on his dares. The little letter to Philemon is a fine entrée.

GRAY TEMPLE

Pastoral Perspective

Philemon's house? The distinction we make between charity and justice—on the one hand, meeting people's needs and, on the other hand, changing structures that make and keep people in need—means we respond first to the fact that Paul nowhere condemns the institution of human chattel slavery. Such an ethical distinction seems not to be on Paul's radar screen, although it is imperative to us. Some have suggested that the nearness of Christ's return in glory makes such political and social action as opposing slavery unimportant to Paul. The revelation of Christ crucified and raised, however, means that Paul is convinced that God is indeed overturning social structures, although that revolution takes place in the church rather than in the world. It would fall to later generations of the church, after it had become a majority force in some cultures, to draw the conclusion that slavery is inimical to Christian faith.

More immediately, there are untold instances of conflict between church members—or between different communities of Christians—that mirror Philemon's conflict with Onesimus. People wrong one another and owe one another, whether or not the institution of slavery blots the relationship. Although Paul does not address the economic and social system that permits one man to possess another, he speaks of both men as Christian brothers and calls the stronger to release the weaker. This preference for the weak over the strong runs throughout the Bible, not only in Philemon. So also, Paul prevails on Philemon to honor the bonds that Christ has formed between him and Onesimus. The language of brotherhood and sisterhood to describe the church results from Paul's use of the metaphor of adoption to describe baptism, which makes Philemon and Onesimus brothers (Rom. 8:15, 23; Gal. 4:5; cf. Eph. 1:5). Paul's letter to Philemon reminds us that we are not to use language of sisterhood and brotherhood lightly in our churches. The terms represent real and deep family ties; and as with every family, those ties always have profound and sometimes profoundly difficult consequences.

E. ELIZABETH JOHNSON

love and faith are singled out in the thanksgiving (vv. 4–7), a section of Paul's letters that typically commends the recipient and introduces a major concern. In this case Paul states his gratitude for Philemon's love, which has "refreshed" the hearts of the saints through some unspecified generosity or kindness. This love is a source of comfort and joy for Paul (v. 7). It engenders the expectation that Philemon will "refresh my heart in Christ" (v. 20) by receiving Onesimus who, in a stunning image, is depicted as "my own heart" (v. 12). Much of the letter is an appeal to and celebration of the affections.

What are we to make of Philemon, so intensely personal as it is, yet so accepting of an institution, slavery, that we now find universally repugnant? For all his pastoral sensitivity, Paul is at pains, when all is said and done, to observe Roman law. He is returning the runaway—not harboring him or protesting the system—and emphatically promising "in my own hand" (vv. 18–19) to make good on any losses the slave owner has incurred.

One function Philemon serves, precisely because of its historical setting, is to remind us that the church's social teaching has changed over time. Whether it be slavery, usury, or the status of women, the church's approach to social issues has evolved with great struggle and sometimes shifted dramatically. Just a century and a half ago North American Christians were still torn over slavery. It is instructive and sobering to read the chapter "The Dilemma of Slavery" in E. Brooks Holifield's magisterial study *Theology in America,* which outlines how the Bible was invoked by proslavery and antislavery advocates:

> The debate over slavery would introduce American readers to critical questions about history, doctrinal development, and hermeneutics. It compelled some theologians to recognize that they had to choose between biblical literalism and a form of interpretation that took into account historical criticism, the social and cultural context of the biblical writings, diversity and development within the canon, and the force of presuppositions in biblical scholarship.[1]

It all seems so obvious in hindsight, yet the very same challenges confront us in the controversy over homosexuality today.

DAVID R. ADAMS

that story, the question is put to the hearer of the narrative. So is it for Philemon. What would we do in similar circumstances?

One might think of another story involving a runaway slave and a letter, the letter Huck Finn plans to send to Miss Watson—the letter that would turn in Jim who has run away when he learns that he might be sold downriver and separated forever from his wife and children. The law and the mores of the time tell Huck what he ought to do: he should restore Jim to his rightful owner. Huck even feels better after he drafts the letter to Miss Watson—until he begins thinking about all he has been through with Jim, how Jim has cared for him and become a friend and like the kindly father Huck has never had. Huck then tears the letter up.

Imagine an illegal immigrant today. Say that it is José trying to earn money for his family back in Guatemala, or Rosa, now the single mother of children born in this country, but who herself entered the country illegally. There are reasons for laws dealing with illegal immigrants, and Christians are meant to be law-abiding citizens, yet, before all else, the immigrant is a sister or brother in the love of God. Gospel teaching and baptismal vows call Christians to respect the dignity of every human being. Imagine receiving a letter—one Christian community to another—commending reconciliation and care for Rosa.

So the story does go on, giving added significance to Paul's concluding words and prayer in his letter to Philemon: "The grace of the Lord Jesus Christ be with your spirit."

FREDERICK BORSCH

---

1. E. Brooks Holifield, *Theology in America: Christian Thought from the Age of the Puritans to the Civil War* (New Haven, CT: Yale University Press, 2005), 494–95.

Luke 14:25-33

[25]Now large crowds were traveling with him; and he turned and said to them, [26]"Whoever comes to me and does not hate father and mother, wife and children, brothers and sisters, yes, and even life itself, cannot be my disciple. [27]Whoever does not carry the cross and follow me cannot be my disciple. [28]For which of you, intending to build a tower, does not first sit down and estimate the cost, to see whether he has enough to complete it? [29]Otherwise, when he has laid a foundation and is not able to finish, all who see it will begin to ridicule him, [30]saying, 'This fellow began to build and was not able to finish.' [31]Or what king, going out to wage war against another king, will not sit down first and consider whether he is able with ten thousand to oppose the one who comes against him with twenty thousand? [32]If he cannot, then, while the other is still far away, he sends a delegation and asks for the terms of peace. [33]So therefore, none of you can become my disciple if you do not give up all your possessions."

Theological Perspective

Faithful discipleship is definitely not for the faint of heart. We are somewhat prepared for this continuation of Luke 14, however, if we have been reading closely the passage from last week with its stress on blessing and righteous living by making the guests and hosts of a wedding banquet the poster children for how *not* to behave in the realm of God in the face of the resurrection. Between the passages for this week and last, there is the parable of the great supper with the feast being held for the poor, the crippled, the lame, and the blind from near and far. The stakes rise throughout this chapter as it becomes clearer what is at stake when one says that he or she wishes to follow Jesus. Hence, Jesus uses strong language to spell out the high cost of discipleship—it must be total dedication that moves from wish to careful deliberation and decision making. It cannot be done on impulse, because Jesus knows that the cross looms ever before his followers. As preacher, you must remind the hearers of the word that the cross also emerges before us.

At this juncture, some may be tempted to say, "Bonhoeffer, Dietrich. *The Cost of Discipleship*. Read. Discussion series begins next week." This would be good for a lively Christian religious education series, but the sermon demands something different and can be used, perhaps, as the prelude or epilogue to

Pastoral Perspective

How do the people of God choose discipleship, and what does it look like when they choose it? The question is nowhere as vivid as in Jesus' teaching about accepting all of the consequences of coming to him and following him. Three times in this passage, Jesus says that without definite decision, a person cannot be his disciple. First, he requires a person to hate parents, spouse, children, siblings, and even one's own life. Second, he commands carrying the cross and following him. Third, he demands the giving up of all possessions. Even if we soften his word "hate," Jesus still leaves us with his requirement that we make family ties and normal self-preservation subordinate to following him. The pastoral work of the Christian community involves a clear and frank acknowledgment of the great challenge, the fearsome requirements of becoming and doing what Jesus expects of us.

John Calvin's teaching on the Christian life provides a classical resource that we can use as a way to come to terms with the call of Christ to Christian obedience today.[1] To the pastors whom he was teaching, the reformer offered a way of understanding the Christian life that was liberating for many.

---

1. John Calvin, *Institutes of the Christian Religion*, ed. John T. McNeill (Philadelphia: Westminster Press, 1960), 1:684–719.

Exegetical Perspective

This is a complex pericope that requires the hearers both to count the cost of discipleship, to ensure that they can "afford" to follow Jesus, and to remember that the cost could include all your family (v. 26) and "all your possessions" (v. 33). We find here a preliminary qualification for discipleship: Jesus boldly declares that we should not even begin this journey unless we are willing to go all the way!

Jesus says, "Whoever comes to me and does not hate father and mother, wife and children, brothers and sisters, yes, and even life itself, cannot be my disciple" (v. 26). How is that for "family values"? There is an impressive list of people dear to us by virtue of their kinship that we are commanded to *miseo* or "hate" in this pericope. Why does Jesus the Christ, the personification and embodiment of love, here call for his followers to hate their nearest kin and even their own lives? This is a difficult passage to read because it asks—no, demands—that we push away those whom we are most inclined to embrace. In our nation, which celebrates "family values" and elevates this commonplace virtue to a principal position superior even to patriotism, this is an uncomfortable word.

In light of Jesus' previous instructions in Luke, this word should not strike us as a bolt from the blue. After all. it resonates with Jesus' instruction in 12:51–53, where he exclaims, "Do you think that I

Homiletical Perspective

Just when Jesus seems all about healings and invitations to dinner, he stuns with words that shock in their directness. The word "hate" punctures pious romanticism. Does discipleship really require one to "hate" parents, spouse, children, siblings, even one's own life? "Hate" may be hyperbole, but it does not underestimate potential costs of discipleship. Life meets almost everyone with choices that are emotionally costly. In ordinary circumstances, it mostly works out. However, when Jesus uses the word "hate" in the same sentence with parent, spouse, child, he raises the ante. He is not speaking about cold abstractions.

We can love more than one person, one congregation, one circle of friends at a time. There is enough for parent, spouse, children, siblings, even ourselves, and it all balances out well enough; but sometimes it does not balance. A father becomes ill and dependent on his son; duty may require some sacrifice of attention or resources, and what ordinarily would go to spouse or child is diverted to parent. A mother with three children finds her time and energy consumed by the needs of a severely autistic child; what belongs to the other two has been nearly used up. The rural physician finds that needy patients consume time she needs to devote to her marriage. Conflicts of loyalty can be heartrending.

Luke 14:25-33

Theological Perspective

such a series. In exploring the theological meaning and importance of the cost of discipleship, it is important to stress the notion of cost along with discipleship. This term for "cost" appears only once in the New Testament, and it is in this passage. Cost is what we give up to acquire, accomplish, maintain, or produce something. It involves a measure of sacrifice and perhaps loss or penalty in gaining something. Cost requires effort and resources.

When coupled with discipleship and accepting and spreading the good news of Jesus Christ, one can see the power of Jesus' call in this passage and the commitment it demands of us as hearers and doers of the word. Discipleship, we must remember, is a process. This takes time and involves both false starts and modest successes, as we grow in our faith journeys to live into the fullness of our humanity and dare to begin to live the holiness that resides in each of us. As disciples, we learn to face life's challenges and joys with a spirit of love, hope, faith, and peace that leads us to an ever deeper spirituality and life of prophetic witness.

For example, rather than accept the slow pace and often inept attempts of the federal government to aid in the rebuilding of New Orleans and the Gulf Coast after Hurricane Katrina in 2005, many people of faith have traveled to the area—often repeatedly—to help rebuild, using whatever skills they have. This is the church coming alive in its discipleship as people of faith spread the good news through their active witness in helping those who have been and continue to be brutalized by poorly constructed levees and abject neglect.

In the process of becoming living disciples, we must, as Jesus states, also learn to give up all of our possessions—our need to acquire, our yearning for success, our petty jealousies, our denigrating stereotypes of others, our prejudices and hatreds, and more—and follow the way of Jesus, as we place ourselves on an ever-treading potter's wheel to examine our thoughts, words, and actions. These possessions keep us further and further away from the Christlike walk to which Jesus invites us in discipleship.

Here the preacher may want to think through the various ways he or she has observed this in their congregation or in people's life circumstances in general. This can include exploring how overwork can become an addiction that keeps us from nurturing our relationships with our families, friends, and God. Overwork itself becomes a possession that we can hoard through rationalizations such as, "I promise that after I am done with this project, I will not

Pastoral Perspective

He chose Jesus' teaching of his disciples after Simon Peter made his confession of faith (Mark 8:34; Matt. 16:24; Luke 9:23) and applied it to Luke's text for today. For Calvin, the Christian life should be understood from four implications of Jesus' teaching: (1) *self-denial*, (2) *cross bearing*, (3) *meditation on eternal life*, and (4) the *proper use of the gifts of God in daily life*. With pastoral imagination and careful interpretation, we can use these implications for preaching, teaching, and pastoral care in the congregation today.

1. *Self-denial* in Calvin's interpretation does not mean the embrace or enjoyment of self-destructive tendencies. Uriah Heep in Charles Dickens's *David Copperfield* (1868) would be a disgusting example of a person who relishes self-destructive practices, other-destructive practices, and proud humility. For Calvin, on the other hand, self-denial is the way Jesus offers us freedom from selfishness and the "deadly pestilence of love of strife and love of self." Denial of self is the escape from selfishness. Self-denial is the gift Christ gives us that enables us to dedicate ourselves to God and to seek the things which "are of the Lord's will."[2] The person who fails to deny herself is not able to love God or neighbor, but self-denial leads to the very positive affirmation of the power of love in human relationships of God and neighbor.

2. *Cross bearing* is for us the dimension of self-denial that enables us to face suffering. To bear our cross means to obey God even in our pain and loss, in facing the tragedies, trials, and griefs of life. The image of the cross of Christ appeals to the Christian imagination to elicit our patience in bearing pain. Calvin teaches that the cross of Christ is healing medicine for the diseases and injuries of life, punishment and correction for our mistakes in life, and, above all, comfort when we are persecuted because we stand with God's justice. So the cross of Christ brings us cheer, honesty to acknowledge our hurt, and a freedom from bitterness.

3. *Meditation on eternal life* engages us to contemplate the mystery and cherish a sense of wonder about the promise for human beings in the resurrection of Jesus from the dead. Calvin inherited and embraced the language of contemplative medieval piety, which included the rhetoric of "contempt" for the body as the "prison house of the soul." This kind of piety was one of the ingredients in the thinking of other reformers, like Desiderius Erasmus (1469?–1536) and Ignatius of Loyola (1495?–1556).

2. Ibid., 694, 698.

have come to bring peace to the earth? No, I tell you, but rather division!" The divisions he then describes are in the most significant institution in the lives of his audience, the household. He speaks of a household divided between father and son, daughter and mother, mother-in-law and daughter-in-law. The instrumental bonds that form the basis of their communal lives and social order will be rent asunder by the radical faith that Jesus proclaims. This is not a faith comfortable with familiar patterns of "family values," for it requires a commitment from its adherents, from us, that surpasses even that which we have for those most dear to us.

Similar themes are found earlier in Luke's Gospel. In 14:12 he admonishes his host, a leader of the Pharisees (14:1), not to invite his "brothers" and "relatives" to banquets; instead he should invite the "poor, the crippled, the lame, and the blind." According to Luke's Gospel, family is reconfigured by this new faith. Both this instruction and that in our focal pericope presume the one found in 8:19–21; when sought by his mother and siblings, Jesus redefines family, not as those with whom we share bloodlines, but as those who "hear the word of God and do it" (8:21). Discipleship moves us beyond comfortable kinship ties to forge new relationships among those commonly committed to Christ, who become to us new family.

A final instructive message on family is found in chapter 18. In the aftermath of Jesus' visit with "a certain ruler" (18:18) who seeks knowledge about eternal life, Jesus tells those that have given up "wife or brothers or parents or children, for the sake of the kingdom of God" (18:29) that they will receive "very much more in this age, and in the age to come eternal life" (18:30). There is much at stake in this reconfiguration, but faithful disciples should be assured that their sacrifice will be rewarded by more of what they lost (for a similar message, see Job 1:13–22 and 42:10–17) and also with "eternal life."

A further difficulty in this pericope attends to Jesus' demand that a disciple would "carry the cross and follow" him (14:27). As such, this instruction is reminiscent of 9:23, where Jesus instructs would-be followers to "deny themselves and take up their cross daily," then sets this in the context of losing their lives for his sake. What a harsh word this is for the contemporary Christian community, for we know where Jesus' way leads. This is a word of obligation to a church obsessed with grace; worse, it is obligation with consequence, for those who refuse the cross are deemed unworthy of discipleship.

It is not only family members who compete for our affection and dutiful attention. Along with family, one loves the city, the patria, the flag, the church, the Lord. Usually one can keep various loyalties and obligations in balance, but sometimes interests come into conflict. Should one salute the flag and keep the mouth shut? Salute the flag and, when required by a conscience shaped by Lord and church, name the sins? Conform to an ecclesiastical rule or question it?

Not everyone is called to be a disciple. Discipleship goes a step further than being a responsible human being. Although discipleship is not always in conflict with other allegiances, sometimes it is, turning us upstream against the ordinary flow of loyalties to the point of reordering duties and affections that might normally claim first place. Jesus does not say it will not hurt. "Whoever does not carry the cross . . ." (v. 27). When loyalties compete, they need to be sorted out according to some priority. For those who hear a call to discipleship, Jesus himself becomes the sorting principle. The embodiment of self-offering love, of mercy and compassion, is our "true north."

Verses 28–32 offer examples of situations that require seriously calculating the costs of undertaking a project that will be costly, whether to the treasury or to the heart. Advance warning: discipleship adds to ordinary life another potential conflict of loyalties. Do not claim not to have read the fine print! Our baptism is the fine print written in water. We are baptized into Christ's death, "so that, just as Christ was raised from the dead by the glory of the Father, so we too might walk in newness of life" (Rom. 6:4).

Every baptismal occasion testifies that all the baptized share in Christ's cross as well as his resurrection. At the font the church rehearses its vocation. The community is called to inhabit that vocation and teach it and model it even to the very young. The journey starts here, and the hard choices will be shaped by the waters where Christ claimed us.

Luke's text begins with hard words and ends with hard words: "None of you can become my disciple if you do not give up all your possessions" (v. 33). Luke tells us that Jesus is speaking to "large crowds." Is Jesus trying to winnow the circle of people who have become attached to him and his cause, warning away those who cannot bear the heat? Is he trying to toughen the resolve of those who would stick with him? Are his words meant to be literal instructions for those few who would accompany him through the coming conflict? Are they meant equally literally for us?

Maybe. The possibility should at least be carefully pondered. One might understand this challenge as

Luke 14:25-33

Theological Perspective

take on so much anymore." This passage from Luke gives the preacher a potent opportunity to invite folks to step back and engage in that deep process of reflection that discipleship demands of us, to explore whether we are being followers and doers of the word or if we are measuring our lives by human yardsticks.

At the heart of discipleship is transformation. The cost of discipleship is not just becoming accumulators of new information about life and living it fully, or changing our behavior in regard to Jesus' teachings. The cost is engaging in a profoundly radical shift toward the ethics of Jesus with every fiber of our beings. There is no driftwood in discipleship, as we are called to live lives of complete devotion to God. Jesus reminds us in today's passage from Luke that following him means that we cannot be shallow or uncommitted believers—the adjectives simply do not fit the noun.

As part of this transformation, the cost of discipleship means entering into an intimate relationship with God in Christ that teaches us that obedience to God is not blind. It is a thought-probing and deliberative process in which we grow in our ability to ask the tough questions about life and living, not only of God but also of ourselves. This intimate relationship invites us to mature in our faith. Yes, the cost of discipleship also includes salvation—a theme that runs throughout the Lukan passages of the last three weeks. It is important to weave this into the message of today's passage, as well, as the passage can appear harsh and unforgiving in ways that keep contemporary people from being able to engage its message and its invitation to transform their lives. Here the preacher may want to engage Bonhoeffer's poignant words: "The call to discipleship is a gift of grace and that call is inseparable from grace."[1]

EMILIE M. TOWNES

Pastoral Perspective

Although this rhetoric of piety is sometimes objectionable to us, Calvin's pastoral commitment was to offer the people of God in their meditation on eternal life a critical perspective on physical death and also on the acquisitive and material desires of life, by comparing them with the greater fulfillment in the life to come through the power of the resurrection of Jesus Christ.

4. When Calvin interprets Jesus' call to self-denial and cross bearing, he finds reliable foundation for our *proper use of the gifts of God in daily life.* Scripture teaches us "the right use of earthly benefits,"[3] both things of necessity (needs) and things of delight (pleasures). Calvin counsels a simplicity of life in which we understand ourselves to be on an earthly pilgrimage toward home. We become free from both undue severity and from excessive indulgence; neither asceticism nor libertinism should mark the Christian life. He offers four guiding rules for this balance in life: (a) we should indulge ourselves as little as possible; (b) if we have small resources, we ought to do without things patiently; (c) we must understand that God entrusts all things to us for an accountable stewardship; (d) in all of life's actions we should look to our calling from God.

Can the Christian community offer an interpretation of the cost of discipleship for daily life that is plausible and freeing for the people of God today? How would Calvin's advocacy of freedom from selfishness, commitment to love, honest facing of suffering, and the faithful stewardship of creation and its gifts sound to people inside and outside the churches? The housing and economic crises; the damage to the earth by the burning of fossil fuels; and the hunger, poverty, and pandemics suffered by people in all parts of the world are certainly calling us in the church to give Jesus' call to costly discipleship a new lease on life.

CHARLES E. RAYNAL

---

1. Dietrich Bonhoeffer, *The Cost of Discipleship* (New York: Macmillan, 1963), 55.

3. Ibid., 719.

Exegetical Perspective

The message is clear: discipleship costs. In fact, it will cost us everything (see also 12:33–34)! The potent words of a sermon I heard preached in a big-steeple church in Charlotte, North Carolina, a few years back emphasize this lesson. The pastor, preaching to a church of the affluent and influential, offered the challenge of discipleship to his comfortable congregation, then told them, "If you cannot heed this call, then you ought to renounce your baptism." Contextually the message was poignant, because the upper-middle-class (and upper-class) church members were reminded that this faith should cost them something dear. The pastor's exhortation shook all of us in the congregation that day, because it made us all cognizant of the deeds that being part of the reign of God necessitates that we perform, and of how our lack of action is tantamount to forgoing our faith.

Approaching this passage, the reader should be aware of the unusually high number of negative particles used in this brief pericope. O, so many ways to say no! There is at least one negative particle or adverb in each verse of this pericope from verse 27 to verse 33, and in some (vv. 27, 28, 29, 33) there are two. The repetition of these negative particles and adverbs serves to emphasize the inability of the subject faithfully to follow Jesus, should she or he fail to "count the cost." Again, there is a pragmatism to Jesus' instruction, as he lets his disciples know that the road he is walking is *not* without its sacrifices; to follow Jesus is *not* without its heavy demands; to carry the cross is *not* without its tangible consequences. We must be willing to endure these consequences if we ever hope to experience the promised rewards of following Jesus' way.

RODNEY S. SADLER JR.

Homiletical Perspective

literal and even life-saving wisdom for anyone who has become consumed with possessions. Sometimes the health of the soul may require a radical divestiture.

However, maybe it should not always be understood as a literal command. If my spouse and I own a home jointly, should I insist on giving it away as a demonstration of spiritual athleticism, even though she is reluctant? Should I transfer ownership to her, so that loss of the liquidated assets will not deprive her (or me) of a home? Would it be just and honorable to give away all possessions if it should mean becoming a ward of the state or a beggar on the street? One can pose all sorts of objections to deliberately becoming dependent on the mercy (and pocketbook) of others when it is possible to provide for oneself.

It seems important to take Jesus' exhortation with utter seriousness, recognizing that, for most of us, it poses a problem that needs to be thought through. Certainly it means at least that disciples should travel lightly, not unduly encumbered by acquiring, hoarding, or guarding one's possessions against the other in her/his need. Certainly it must also mean that, when interests come into conflict, discipleship takes precedence over security.

Working out our discipleship in terms not only of what we give away, but also what we keep for ourselves, is no small issue. What we own can come to own us, posing a serious threat to our spiritual welfare. Because we are so heavily invested in decisions we have already made, most of us are not in the best position to assess our situations impartially. Can the church as a community of mutual admonition and encouragement become a forum in which we can help each other to work out the implications of discipleship in the specific contexts of our own situations? Is this best done in a pastoral-care setting? In small groups in which there has grown to be a high level of trust? By confiding in a spiritual director? How seriously should one take the call to discipleship?

RONALD P. BYARS

PROPER 19 (SUNDAY BETWEEN SEPTEMBER 11 AND SEPTEMBER 17 INCLUSIVE)

Jeremiah 4:11-12, 22-28

¹¹At that time it will be said to this people and to Jerusalem: A hot wind comes from me out of the bare heights in the desert toward my poor people, not to winnow or cleanse— ¹²a wind too strong for that. Now it is I who speak in judgment against them.

. . . .

²²"For my people are foolish,
   they do not know me;
they are stupid children,
   they have no understanding.
They are skilled in doing evil,
   but do not know how to do good."

²³I looked on the earth, and lo, it was waste and void;
   and to the heavens, and they had no light.

Theological Perspective

This lament of Jeremiah is part of the larger unit that describes the foe from the north, the Babylonian threat looming on the horizon. From the privileged location of North America, it can be difficult to resonate with the ubiquitous threat of an empire. The Babylonian threat was real in the sixth century CE; one can but ask what the analogous threats are in the twenty-first. Verses 5–8 are a warning poem. There are two prose seams, verses 9–10 and 11–12. The prose seam sets up the poetic warning that follows (vv. 13–21). The summarizing question "how long?" (v. 21) sets up the transition to the next section. Verse 21 brings the reader back to that question. What do you know? The section is inundated with references to a kind of foolishness that is seldom spelled out. When we move to verse 22, we have a parallel foolish (my people) and stupid (these children).

A key metaphor in the passage is the "hot wind/spirit" from the barren wilderness way. The target of this wind is "my poor people" (v. 11). The Hebrew term *bat ʿammi* is rendered multiple ways in the NRSV: "my beloved people" (Isa. 22:4), "wound of my people" (Jer. 8:11), "my sinful people" (Jer. 9:7), "daughter of my people" (Jer. 14:17) "destruction of my people" (Lam. 3:48), "my people" (Lam. 4:3, 6, 10). However, the most frequent NRSV rendering of this term is "my poor people" (Jer. 4:11;

Pastoral Perspective

Two of the prophet Jeremiah's contributions to the history of the tradition especially stand out. One is the bringing forth of the new covenant between YHWH and the people of Israel. The other is his fidelity to God in the face of great odds. For more than forty years Jeremiah prophesied about repentance and the importance of restoring the original intent of the Mosaic covenant. His prophecies provide insights into the history of the Hebrew people, the land of Israel, cultic rites and rituals, and his own faithfulness to YHWH. However, in the end, it was not YHWH's will that the Mosaic covenant be restored. Instead, YHWH put into place a new covenant. "But this is the covenant that I will make with the house of Israel after those days, says the LORD: I will put my law within them, and I will write it on their hearts; and I will be their God, and they shall be my people" (Jer. 31:33).

The new covenant was put in place when Judah and Jerusalem were defeated by Babylon. Jeremiah proclaimed the unwelcome news that Babylon was an instrument of YHWH. He framed the destruction of the old covenant in religious terms and explained that the house of Israel was no longer dependent on geography, cultic practices, and tribal traditions. Instead, there was to be a new covenant, lived out in those whose hearts responded to the reality that

²⁴I looked on the mountains, and lo, they were quaking,
and all the hills moved to and fro.
²⁵I looked, and lo, there was no one at all,
and all the birds of the air had fled.
²⁶I looked, and lo, the fruitful land was a desert,
and all its cities were laid in ruins
before the Lord, before his fierce anger.
²⁷For thus says the Lord: The whole land shall be a desolation; yet I will not
make a full end.
²⁸Because of this the earth shall mourn,
and the heavens above grow black;
for I have spoken, I have purposed;
I have not relented nor will I turn back.

Exegetical Perspective

The early prophecies of Jeremiah were especially prophecies of denunciation and condemnation of the people of Judah (e.g., see the OT reading for Proper 17, Jer. 2:4–13, discussed in pp. 2–7), along with warnings about forthcoming attacks by an unspecified foe from the north (see 4:5–8; 5:15–17; 6:22–23). This week's readings likely represent prophecies that Jeremiah uttered first during the earlier years of his prophetic ministry and then reproclaimed at some later date as the prophesied foe became more obviously embodied in the Babylonian invader that eventually destroyed Jerusalem and exiled the people of Judah.

This selection includes texts that critical analysis would attribute to at least three different provenances. Verses 11–12, though not belonging to the unit which begins in verse 23, describe the same type of total, undiscriminating disaster as verses 23–26. The "hot wind" coming upon the people is the sirocco, a devastating wind that can reach hurricane speeds, bringing dry and dusty conditions. This wind, as verse 11 notes, is not the kind that provides the beneficent effect of winnowing chaff from seed. The sirocco devastates without discrimination. This wind, which God affirms comes "from me" (v. 11), represents the divine judgment, which ravages leader and people, rich and poor, just and unjust alike. This

Homiletical Perspective

This passage begins with an image that is surely transcultural, although it probably has more of an immediacy within an agricultural or pastoral society. We still are likely to ask, "Which way is the wind blowing?" We will anticipate a difficult encounter by saying that there are storm warnings up. We may still sing: "The answer, my friend, is blowing in the wind, the answer is blowing in the wind,"[1] but it is different from living in a situation where the separation of grain from chaff could be dependent on or aided by a familiar breeze. It is different from living in an environment where there are desert sandstorms of such intensity that the sand blots out the light of the sun at midday and the particles that are carried along insinuate themselves into every opening.

It is within such a context that the prophet announces God's judgment upon Israel as if it were a desert wind that will make the land uninhabitable, unable to sustain human life. In fact, as we shall note later, the prophet in essaying the impact and experience of God's judgment will record a series of images and references that can be summarized as the repeal of the creation.

The word "for" begins verse 22, announcing the divine assessment on the spiritual condition of the

---

1. Bob Dylan, "Blowin' in the Wind," in *Freewheelin' Bob Dylan* (New York: Columbia Studios, 1963).

Jeremiah 4:11-12, 22-28

Theological Perspective

6:26; 8:19, 21, 22; 9:1). The location of these occurrences in lament material, despite multiple renderings of the Hebrew phrase into English, accents the vulnerability of the people. The phrase is a genitive that functions appositively, "my fair people."[1]

The vulnerability connoted by the term "my poor people/my fair people" very clearly does not extinguish the culpability outlined in the recurring call for repentance (7:3; 26:13). In other words, vulnerability does not go bail for culpability. God voices a concern for these culpable and vulnerable people, namely, the coming onslaught.

The nature of the hot wind is intense. The intensity determines the use and nature of the wind. The wind has been used for centuries. One purpose of the wind was for winnowing, that is, to separate the wheat grains from the chaff. A breeze can also clean. However, there are winds that are so intense that they no longer function for human purposes of winnowing or cleaning. Some winds scatter but do not winnow, even though the same verb is used here.

The metaphor of winnowing continues to dominate the term. The language occurs again in Jeremiah 15:7 and 51:2, where the deportation models a type of winnowing. The writer plays on the semantic range of the term, which can denote scattering or winnowing. The positive and negative elements of the word come together and shape the understanding in this passage. The task for a person in the midst of personal or political turmoil is to determine whether the events of Israel are a scattering or a winnowing. The difference between scattering and winnowing is the difference between having and not having meaning, having and not having purpose. The purpose of the sirocco is not winnowing. This hot wind is filled with curse and disaster.[2]

One can almost feel the divine frustration. God's own people are foolish and stupid; they neither know nor understand (4:22). The shift to Wisdom language reminiscent of Proverbs points to the role of character and virtue as central to the message of Jeremiah and the pathos of God depicted in the book. The call to repentance was real. However, a deontological, rules-based model wrongly construes the rules as the central focus. The people's inability to follow the rules is not the core problem, but a symptom of a deep and abiding spiritual stupidity and ignorance. In order to draw out the poignancy of the situation, the writer makes clear that in true

Pastoral Perspective

YHWH's law was part of their very beings. Babylon may have defeated a political system that had religious roots, but Babylon did not disable the vitality of YHWH and YHWH's constancy with YHWH's people.

Jeremiah's other great contribution was his ability to report YHWH's words and his own reflections in a seamless flow. This grants readers a view of Jeremiah as an individual that is unprecedented in prophetic literature. His writings provide insights into a spiritual journey that is timeless in its fidelity to the human situation. His poetry invites us to participate in the interior reality of a soul in the midst of existential travail.

Today we might say that his work to accommodate the shift from the Mosaic covenant to the new covenant entailed the collapse of one worldview and the construction of another. This process entailed the demolishing of assumptions about how the world works and the integration of new ideas into already existing patterns of thought and behavior. Jeremiah's work to understand what YHWH was doing in the world provides useful insights into the sorts of pastoral care that would be helpful for those who are experiencing the pain and anxiety of such a transition.

In the reading from chapter 4, Jeremiah is a young prophet, and it is early in his ministry. Jeremiah reports that YHWH's fierce anger will be like a hot wind scorching all that lies before it—people, flora and fauna, even cities. YHWH brings such destruction upon his people because they are not only foolish in ignoring the tenets of the Mosaic covenant, but also willfully ignorant of what is required of them.

Jeremiah describes in detail how he reacts to this threat. He sees the earth as desolate, barren, stripped of its ability to bring forth sustenance for the people. Even the sun has been affected and cannot shine. Neither human nor animal life animates the landscape. The cities are reduced to rubble. This is YHWH's doing. YHWH and the people of Israel have a two-way covenant, and if Israel does not honor its side of it, there are consequences.

YHWH, however, stops short of saying that everything will be totally destroyed. What does it mean that YHWH will not make a "full end"? It is easy to read this early passage as if it were a forecast of the new covenant in Jeremiah 31.

At this time, however, it is doubtful that Jeremiah would have understood that to be YHWH's meaning. When in his ministry would Jeremiah have

---

1. William L. Holladay, *Jeremiah 1*, Hermeneia (Philadelphia: Fortress Press, 1986), 156.
2. Ibid.

undiscriminating judgment represents the reverse of God's gifts of sun and rain, which, as Jesus says, do not discriminate between the evil and the good, the righteous and the unrighteous (Matt. 5:45).

Within verse 11 the people of Judah are referred to in one place impersonally as "this people" and in another with the endearing term "my daughter, my people."[1] Does this reflect an ambivalence within God's heart as YHWH tries to establish an impersonal distance from "this people" and yet returns to the more affectionate term, even while announcing "judgment" (Heb. *mishpatîm*) against them?

Verse 22 utilizes language common in the Wisdom tradition of Israel to express the astonishing folly of YHWH's people. In another of Jeremiah's oracles we learn that his fellow citizens and leaders prided themselves on their "wisdom" (Heb. *hᵃkamîm*), their pride seemingly based on their possession of and familiarity with YHWH's law (8:8–9). But at 4:22 the Lord parodies the supposed wisdom of "my people" by affirming that they are indeed "skilled" (Heb. *hᵃkamîm*)—in doing evil. They do not know (Heb. *yadaᶜ*) either God or the good (cf. similar sentiments in Isa. 1:3; Hos. 4:1). That the Judeans are "fools" is exemplified by behaviors cited in other early prophecies of Jeremiah: ingratitude (2:5–8, 20–21; 3:19–20), unresponsiveness to discipline and warnings (2:30–32; 5:3; 6:16–17), hypocrisy (3:4–5), and seeking other saviors (2:17–19, 26–28). As one of the programmatic words of the book of Proverbs declares, "The fear of the LORD is the beginning of *knowledge*; *fools* despise wisdom and instruction" (Prov. 1:7; emphasis added).

Verses 23–26 constitute the centerpiece of this week's lection. Jeremiah describes visions of the world's devolution to chaos like that before creation. The dire condition of Judah's shallow religion and the fierce anger of YHWH called for extravagant language, which is a precursor to the horrific visions of apocalyptic literature. Part of the rhetorical power of this passage derives from the repeated "I looked [Heb. *raᵓîtî*] . . . and lo . . ." The prophet finds the horror so spellbinding that he cannot take his eyes off it—fixed in terror at what he sees.

Jeremiah's vision reveals a ghastly undoing of God's creative labor. Genesis 1:2 contains the only other OT occurrence of the phrase *tohu wa-bohu*, which NRSV translates in Jeremiah 4:23 as "waste and void" (in Gen. 1:2 NRSV has "a formless void";

people that has resulted in God's acting in judgment. God seems to issue a report card. The people are "stupid"; they are "foolish"; they "do not know how to do good." This may at first sound pedantic or overly intellectual. It may sound superficial. To many, it may sound off the mark. We live in a period when we rightly try not to be narrowly judgmental about the mental capacities of students. We rightly understand that the intellectual capacities of individuals are no necessary index of their capacity for good, for growth, and for love. So this verse may sound both shrill and inaccurate.

Psalm 14 and Psalm 53 use much the same language and provide insight into what God is saying through Jeremiah. In both of the psalms, the "fool" is the individual who says in word or in deed, "There is no God [Pss. 14:1; 53:1]; I belong to myself; I am accountable only to myself for my behavior." It is a practical worship of the self as the sole reference point for one's existence. Thus power dynamics trump the demands of justice in the exercise of relationships. Personal needs, desires, and goals take precedence over respect for equity within the community.

As Psalm 14 makes clear, accountability before God is a matter of being measured against the actions of God's sovereign love in creating a community in time, one that reflects and responds to God's character as just and faithful. Accountability is human stewardship of the gift of that love and its goals within the community.

Perhaps there is a secondary manner in which one can be "foolish." To say that there is no God—specifically, this God, the covenant God of the exodus and Sinai and David—is to live as if there is no hope, there is no grace. To fail or refuse to remember, to hope, and to obey is to be "stupid." In the way Israel has compromised its worship of God, Jeremiah sees the root of its failure to remember gratefully and also loyally who created the nation as a people. The people collectively have regressed into a state of spiritual adolescence; they are "stupid children" (v. 22).

The depth of the calamity that is coming upon Israel is so catastrophic, from the perspective of God's original intention for the community, that Jeremiah envisions it as comparable to a repeal of the creation. Verses 23 through 26 all begin with the phrase: "I looked . . . and lo . . ." The very first of these parallels the beginning of the Genesis account of the first act of creation. The earth is a formless void; there is darkness! It is as if the desert wind of God's judgment (Jer. 4:11) is a counterpart to the "wind from God" (Gen. 1:2) that brought form to the

1. This is the translation of *bat-ᶜammi* (a term analogous to *bat-ziyyon*, "Daughter Zion," as in 6:2) proposed by John Bright, *Jeremiah*, Anchor Bible 21 (Garden City, NJ: Doubleday, 1964). NRSV translates "my poor people." Some translators would use "my dear people."

Jeremiah 4:11-12, 22-28

Theological Perspective

wisdom's absence the people have developed wisdom and skill in doing evil.

Amid these poems of chapter 4 we have a poetic vision report that describes the return to a primeval state. First, there is waste and void without light (vv. 23–27). Then comes a common metaphor in prophetic speech, the destabilization of the hills and the mountains in an earthquakelike situation. The third element describes a depopulated world absent humans and birds; clearly here birds represent all wildlife. The fourth and final vision is the devastation of the arable land and the destruction of the cities. The creation (Gen 1:2) and the salvation history that established the nation have been effectively undone by the absence of character and virtue in Judah.

The "for"—the Hebrew term *kî*—sets up the observation about the lack of character and virtue in the land, using the metaphor of foolishness and stupidity (v. 22). Now there is another "for"—once again the Hebrew term *kî*. God pronounces the devastation of the whole world (v. 27). Furthermore, the second part of the verse implies that only God could remedy this situation and God chooses not to fix it. The NRSV translation "yet I will not make a full end" depicts a near miss. The translation by William Holladay, "none of it will I remake," strikes me as more compelling.[3] That is to say, it fits the tone of the present passage.

Therefore, "the earth shall mourn" (Jer. 4:28; 12:4; Hos. 4:3). The covenant has cosmic consequences for these writers. The divine speech has two elements, the first part positive, speaking and deciding. The second element is unapologetic and unrelenting. It is poignant, if not ironic, that God petitions the people to repent and turn, but now in this early chapter voices an unwillingness to change course,. The people refuse to change course because they fundamentally do not understand that they need to change. God, in the face of the people's failure of character and virtue, chooses not to rescue them from their own consequent demise.

STEPHEN BRECK REID

Pastoral Perspective

understood that YHWH intended to abandon as useless the Mosaic covenant and replace it with a new one? It must have been all but unthinkable the first time such a thought occurred to him. He must have felt that he was threatened by total annihilation, as if he had peered into the abyss of absolute nothingness or encountered a spiritual black hole.

Throughout his prophecies Jeremiah grieves, recoils in shock, experiences horror, and is plunged into doubt of both himself and YHWH as he wrestles with the insights YHWH presents to him. He asks searching questions of YHWH about the consequences of what he is given to say. He lives with pain, without companionship, and with no assurance that things will get better. He portrays a soul in torment, the sort of torment mystics have described as the "dark night of the soul."

Many people today are in the process of reconstituting the values and expectations that are no longer sufficient to their social, cultural, or economic realities. A divorce makes it necessary for a young mother to put her children in day care and return to the workforce; being injured in war makes it impossible for a young man to pursue a career in marine conservation; the price of gas puts an independent trucker out of business. When people have been forced by circumstances outside their own control to consider alternative views, they often are unable to conceive of anything that might take the place of the ideas they assumed were eternal. If those ideas are not true, they can see only that their interior landscapes are laid waste, utterly barren and without hope of restoration.

Jeremiah speaks their language. He does not sugarcoat how difficult his adjustments were or promise that all will be well. His message is that God is ever present and that people are equipped not only to survive change and disruption but also to thrive in ways not known ahead of time. Jeremiah's ability to portray pain, emptiness, and abandonment and yet remain in faithful relationship to God is a powerful message of persistence and hope to people who suffer.

SHARON PEEBLES BURCH

---

3. Ibid., 143–44, 167.

NIV translates "formless and empty" in both passages). In Genesis 1, God's word was responsible for the conquest of that precreation chaos; now the return to chaos is attributed to the divine word (v. 28). Verses 22–28 leave no doubt that, from the prophetic perspective, this is all the Lord's doing. Second Isaiah, prophesying at a time not much later than that of Jeremiah, has YHWH declaring, "I form the light and create darkness, I bring prosperity and create disaster; I, the Lord, do all these things" (Isa. 45:7 NIV) We hear from these prophets a radical monotheism; there is no resort to a theodicy that would ascribe darkness and chaos to some other power or deity.

The traditions now found in the book of Jeremiah represent the result of an extended history of transmission and reinterpretation by successive generations. Verse 27 is commonly adjudged as an addition by a later hand, attenuating the strong sense of disaster announced by verses 23–26. The common explanation is that verse 27 was added by an editor aware that the people of Judah did survive the tragedy of 586 BCE.[2] However, taking the text as literarily whole as it stands, we have a witness to an ambivalence in the heart of God which is not unprecedented in the Hebrew Scriptures. It is as if God walks up to the abyss and then pauses, unwilling to proceed with utter destruction of the creation. We find a similar tension within the divine heart reflected in Hosea 11:1–7, juxtaposed with Hosea 11:8–9 (see also the comments about v. 11 in the third paragraph of this commentary).

This passage should not be construed as a conditional threat, a summons to repentance in the hope that disaster might be forestalled or prevented. The placement of verse 28 following this ameliorating statement in verse 27 reinforces the basic message that disaster is inevitable. However, as other texts in Jeremiah—especially in chapters 30–33—proclaim, the people will find grace beyond that disaster.

GEORGE W. RAMSEY

creation. The result will be manifest in the instability of the land (Jer. 4:24), the absence of sound and song (v. 25), and the absence of habitation and community as well as the fruition of the land that is necessary to sustain life (v. 26). The behavior of Israel, its leaders and people, amounts to a rejection of the generous purposes and character of God in creating the world and then Israel itself. Therefore, the judgment upon Israel being played out on the stage of history will be experienced as if the creation were disorganizing, even disappearing: "The earth shall mourn, and the heavens above grow black" (v. 28).

If God punctuates the Genesis account of the creation with the occasional, "It is good," here one can almost hear Jeremiah murmuring, "It is bad," as he canvasses the devastation of the creation and the deterioration of Israel's behavior.

In our era, Jeremiah's images and visions may seem less like metaphors and more like predictions of the outcome of political, international, and technological folly. Nuclear war or accident, global warming, the disappearance of biodiversity, demands on the water and food resources of the earth are challenging crises; their possible results strikingly resemble the images that haunted Jeremiah's spirit.

Verse 27 is obviously a prose insertion into the poetry surrounding it. Whoever's thought it was, whoever inserted it, it acts like a catch of the heart. Is judgment the end? Is the end the end? The answer is a paradox if not a contradiction: "Yet I will not make a full end." God's very judgment is an act of engagement with and not abandonment of Israel and all of history. Judgment and truth are the preconditions and prologue for God's new creation.

DWIGHT M. LUNDGREN

---

2. See, for example, Robert Carroll, *Jeremiah*, Old Testament Library (Philadelphia: Westminster Press, 1986), 170–71.

Psalm 14

¹Fools say in their hearts, "There is no God."
  They are corrupt, they do abominable deeds;
  there is no one who does good.

²The LORD looks down from heaven on humankind
  to see if there are any who are wise,
  who seek after God.

³They have all gone astray, they are all alike perverse;
  there is no one who does good,
  no, not one.

Theological Perspective

This psalm is nearly identical to Psalm 53 and so its themes are doubly expressed in the Psalter. It is a conglomerate of several psalm types, resembling a lament, but also incorporating aspects of Wisdom and prophetic themes (vv. 1, 2, 5–6). Psalm 14 uses the personal Hebrew term for "God" (YHWH) while Psalm 53 uses the generic term "God" (*Elohim*).

Three elements constitute the psalm: (1) a lament for the total corruption of humans (vv. 1–3); (2) the rebuke and threat of punishment (v. 4–6); and (3) a hope for restoration (v. 7).

Human Corruption. "Fools say in their hearts, 'There is no God'" (v. 1) is a famous expression, usually associated with atheism. Those concerned with humanity's rejection of belief in God or a "supreme being" often appeal to this verse to indicate that nonbelief in God is "foolish."

In the Old Testament, the fool is not only one with no sense, but also the one who resolutely rejects the highest "wisdom" of all, which is the fear and obedience of God. The fool is the one who disregards God, convinced that God does not matter in life. Fools have thus closed their minds to God and to all God's instructions—not defining God as nonexistent, but shutting God out from their life.

Pastoral Perspective

"Fools say in their hearts, 'There is no God'" (v. 1). Whether or not worshipers can readily identify the canonical location of this phrase, it is surely familiar to many. Familiarity, however, often leads to misinterpreting the verse as a defense against atheism. "Only the foolish fail to see the clear evidence of God's existence in nature, Scripture, or loving human relationships," goes the argument. Interpreted in this way, secularism or intellectual atheism is regarded as the chief threat to Christian faith and practice. The pastoral application of this text becomes apologetic: believers and unbelievers alike must be convinced that there are rational, intellectually credible grounds for believing in the existence of God.

There is great rhetorical power in this first verse, and preachers may be tempted to take on the philosophical reductionism of someone like physicist Richard Dawkins, the early-twenty-first-century champion of intellectual atheism. However, as J. Clinton McCann points out, foolishness in this instance is more a moral assessment than an intellectual one; Psalm 14 addresses "practical atheism" rather than "philosophical atheism."[1] The remainder of the psalm clearly interprets the nature of the fools' behavior: they

1. J. Clinton McCann Jr., "The Book of Psalms," in *The New Interpreter's Bible*, vol. 4, ed. Leander Keck (Nashville: Abingdon Press, 1996), 729.

[4]Have they no knowledge, all the evildoers
   who eat up my people as they eat bread,
   and do not call upon the LORD?

[5]There they shall be in great terror,
   for God is with the company of the righteous.
[6]You would confound the plans of the poor,
   but the LORD is their refuge.

[7]O that deliverance for Israel would come from Zion!
   When the LORD restores the fortunes of his people,
   Jacob will rejoice; Israel will be glad.

Exegetical Perspective

Historical Context. Several commentators place this psalm in the postexilic period. This tumultuous time could well have given rise to the "practical atheism" of verse 1, the sense that God's presence is not efficacious or relevant.[1] This historical verdict sits uneasily with the psalm's Davidic attribution in the superscription, not printed above. Although only 73 of the 150 psalms in the Psalter bear David's superscription, in later Judaism and among early Christians the entire Psalter was attributed to David. According to a second-century-CE rabbinical tradition, the legendary king would arise from his slumbers in the middle of the night, when a soft breeze made the strings of his harp vibrate, to compose psalms until dawn. Despite the hold David had over the popular imagination of later periods, many of the psalms reflect historical situations and theological themes quite different from those of the tenth century BCE, when David lived. Several seem thematically related to the prophets Isaiah and Jeremiah, and a few make explicit mention of the exile (Ps. 137) and the return (Ps. 126).[2] For all these reasons we are convinced

Homiletical Perspective

Psalm 14 is composed of meditation and lament, prayer and celebration. The preacher taking up this text will want to reflect that multiplicity of genres and moods.

The psalm begins with a brief meditation on the mentality and the mendacity of the fool (v. 1). Most who hear this psalm read out on a September Sunday morning in your sanctuary or meeting room will be unfamiliar with the idea that the word "fool" is a moral and spiritual category in ancient Wisdom literature. The preacher of this text may want to examine foolishness as a behavioral practice, in contrast to foolishness as a moral and spiritual state. The foolish behavior of individuals frequently has negative consequences for the responsible person or persons. Moral foolishness, however, impacts whole groups of people, even nations, in negative ways. That fact is the concern of this psalmist.

The lament is best seen in the all-inclusive nature of the psalmist's language. Repeated use of words like "no one" and "all" (vv. 1, 3, 4) speaks to the emotional state of both the author and those who sang this song with him: "they are all alike perverse," "they have all gone astray," "there is no one who does good." While these phrases might be an overstatement of the actual situation at the time, the emotion behind them is exasperation bordering on despair. It

1. A. A. Anderson, *The Book of Psalms*, vol. 1, *Introduction and Psalms 1–72*, in Ronald E. Clemens and Matthew Black, gen. ed., The New Century Bible (Paulton Somerset, England: Marshall, Morgan, & Parnell, 1972), 131. See Pss. 10:4 and 73:11; see also Jer. 5:12; Zeph. 1:12; and Rom. 1:28.
2. Samuel Terrien, *The Psalms: Strophic Structure and Theological Commentary* (Grand Rapids: Eerdmans, 2003), 10.

Psalm 14

Theological Perspective

Biblically, this contrasts with the "wise," who listen to and obey God. "Fools" has a collective sense here; this rejection of the knowledge of God perverts the whole orientation and fabric of life itself (Rom. 1:18–32 chronicles this dynamic). The strongest possible terms are used to describe this condition of being "corrupt" and doing "abominable deeds" (v. 1). God looks at humankind to see if there are any who are "wise" and finds that "they have all gone astray," are "perverse," and that "there is no one who does good, no, not one" (vv. 2–3). Paul indicates this applies to both Jews and Gentiles (Rom. 3:9–12).

The people of Israel, for the psalmist, should be the "wise" and should follow God instead of being "fools." The Bible does not really worry about trying to "prove" the "existence" of God. Genesis 1:1 begins by assuming there is a God! The Scriptures are concerned most with those who want to shut themselves off from the reality of God and live without regard to God's will or ways. Karl Barth saw this as the root of a major form of sin, the sin of sloth. God is "revealed" to humanity; but humans "will not accept the fact in practice." This is "wicked ignorance of God."[1] For Barth, "sin in the form of sloth crystallizes in the rejection of the man Jesus."[2] When we reject the way and wisdom of Jesus Christ, we act as "fools," denying the reality of God and thus living in corruption and sinfulness. It is not only sinful "deeds" that show this "going astray" from God; it is also our whole life direction where we may even misapply our intellectual powers to justify our rejection of God's revelation and claims upon our lives. So human corruption is very real; and it is real when we—even when we think we are "wise" or claim to live that way, even in the church—deny the divine direction, summons, and claim upon us that comes to us from God in Jesus Christ.

Threat of Punishment. Human rejection of God's ways evokes the threat of punishment, according to the psalmist. Amazingly, the people of God who should know better—do not; and thus they are rebuked (v. 4) and threatened with God's punishment. This is directed to the people of Israel, to "my people."

Actions have consequences. Lives lived in rejecting the realities of God's will and ways without calling upon the Lord will lead to "terror" and calamity. This is a certainty to which the psalmist points.

Pastoral Perspective

"are corrupt" (v. 1b), they "eat up my people" (v. 4), and they "confound the plans of the poor" (v. 6). The psalmist vividly condemns wealthy elites who exploit the poor.

Seen in this light, their folly, according to the psalmist, is that they deny God's concern for those whom they exploit. They believe they can act with impunity because "there is no God" to hold them accountable for their corruption or to defend the interests of the oppressed. Thus, the primary interpretive and pastoral concern here must shift from intellectual debates about God's existence to real-life questions of oppression and resistance. As J. David Pleins asserts, the chief theological question in this text is "justice, not belief, the chief error is oppression, not secularism," and the folly the psalmist attacks is "the folly of the social injustice that cuts the oppressor off from God."[2]

This leads to a reconsideration of the pastoral dimensions of this text. Psalm 14 has traditionally been categorized as a psalm of communal lament. Pleins places it in a block of material he names "prophetic oracles of judgment," in which the psalmist cries out for God to judge the world's injustice. For many preachers and worship leaders, these scholarly categorizations might not suggest Psalm 14 as a resource for deeply sensitive pastoral application. As indicated above, the interpretive context of Psalm 14 directly addresses this fallacy and suggests some promising possibilities for pastorally prophetic witness within the church's worship.

Willingness to confront injustice and oppression is a prominent dimension of the Christian ministry. Ministries of care work with persons and communities to change exploitative behavior; to effect healing, restoration, and reconciliation; and even to demand restitution when appropriate. A psalm like this, calling as it does for God's judgment on the way things are, will be received as good news by a host of people who gather for Christian worship week after week. For those who suffer at the hand of an abusive spouse, for those whose dignity is diminished by racism, for those who have suffered sexual harassment or other indignities in their workplace, there is assurance that God is the refuge for those who suffer, even if their tormentors would attempt to "confound" God's plans. Hearing or even praying the words of Psalm 14 gives voice to those who experience cruel or repressive relationships or circumstances as they call for God's justice in the world.

---

1. Karl Barth, *Church Dogmatics*, IV/2, ed. G. W. Bromiley and Thomas F. Torrance, trans. G. W. Bromiley (repr., Edinburgh: T. & T. Clark, 1967), 415.
2. Ibid., 406.

2. J. David Pleins, *The Psalms: Songs of Tragedy, Hope, and Justice* (Maryknoll, NY: Orbis, 1993), 173. The quote in the next paragraph is from p. 175.

that many of the psalms date from a date far later than that of the celebrated king.

Rhetorical Form. Rhetorical classification is not easy with Psalm 14. Is it a lament, a Wisdom psalm, or a prophetic oracle? Perhaps the best answer is "all of the above." Claus Westermann covers two categories when he classifies this as a Wisdom psalm, but sees in it a lament that sings the future negative fate of the wicked. Structures vary, he says, but in each he discerns three characteristic motifs: (a) a description of the evildoer, (b) the fate of the evildoer, and (c) in contrast, the fate of the pious.[3] Other scholars emphasize the similarities of this psalm's themes and language to the prophets (see Jer. 5:1–2, 8:6–7; Isa. 59:4–8; 64:7; and Hos. 4:1–3).

Key Terms in the Passage. The fool, or the *nabal*, in verse 1 is not the simpleton or the gullible fool of Proverbs 1:4, but the fool whose mind is hardened to God and not open to instruction. The *nabal* is like the people mentioned in Isaiah 32:6 who "speak folly," whose "minds plot iniquity," who "practice ungodliness" and "utter error concerning the Lord." The fool is one of those impious people who scoff and revile God's name (Ps. 74:18).

The statement, "There is no God," in verse 1 is a statement of practical atheism. It does not refute God's existence; it dismisses God's relevance. "There is no" occurs twice in the first verse of the psalm: "There is no God" and "there is no one who does good." The two are connected. Human beings cease to do good when they discount the presence of God. The final phrase at the end of verse 3, "no, not one," puts the exclamation point on the connection between disrespect for God and injustice done to others. The fool is one who lives on the assumption that God does not matter. God is nowhere to be found, but is instead far off and uninvolved or powerless or unwilling to prevail against the wicked. The fool believes that there is no punishment for the wicked and no help for the oppressed.

This assumption must have been very real in Israel. The wicked found themselves able to carry out their oppression of the poor without negative consequences to themselves. Here we see a lament element of Psalm 14, which, like Psalm 10, expresses despair in the face of injustice.

is quite likely that public policy and social practice were married in the heart of the fool. Consequently the masses of people were "eaten up" (v. 4) and the poor victims of various forms of injustice (v. 6). It is not uncommon for people of all descriptions in America, and indeed in the world, to feel powerless in the face of apparently unjust, unfair, or downright ineffective policy decisions made by those who are supposed to represent them.

We might assume that the whole of Psalm 14 is directed to God in the context of a worshiping community. In that sense it may be categorized as prayer rather than prophetic speech. Prayer is perhaps the safest of all forms of public speech when "nations conspire" and fools "take counsel together against the Lord and his anointed" (Ps. 2:1–2).

The political tenor of this psalm gives the sense that there was an imbalance of power within empire and that God was not pleased with what God saw (v. 2). Given that power differential, offering a prayer both put the whole case before God and provided those who offered it, or heard it offered, some clarity about the ultimate power broker. Here, then, we have the use of a liturgical category for spiritual, social, and political purposes. Prayer becomes a way of recognizing and announcing God's presence as both judge (v. 2) and deliverer (v. 7b). Prayer therefore is not simply some form of request; it is also a form of proclamation. It is a means of declaring God's presence and God's purpose when neither seems to be apparent.

The recognition and subsequent declaration of God's presence and purpose in the midst of a seemingly hopeless situation supply the motive for celebration and hope. Deliverance is not just possible, but probable, precisely because a just God will not tolerate injustice forever. The psalmist therefore uses the last few words of his prayer to predict the rejoicing of Jacob and the joy of Israel (v. 7).

Several homiletical themes emerge in Psalm 14. One alluded to earlier in this essay is the contrast between foolish behavior and moral foolishness. The former has to do with dull-headed silliness, the latter with spiritual darkness. The former may have immediate though temporary consequences; the later has long-term and eternal ones. One exhibiting foolish behavior may or may not be in covenant relationship with God. One who is morally foolish, however, is definitely not in covenant relationship with God.

It is always a good idea for a preacher to focus on God. In this psalm, God "looks down from heaven on humankind" (v. 2), "is with the company of the

---

3. Claus Westermann, *Praise and Lament in the Psalms* (Atlanta: John Knox Press, 1965), 192.

Psalm 14

Theological Perspective

"The company of the righteous" or the godly Israelites, those who do what God desires, are consoled in the midst of this corruptedness by God's being "with" them (v. 5). "God is with" has a theological meaning in the Scriptures beyond simply the "presence" of God—wonderful as that is. It also means that God is "on the side of" or "in favor of" or "for" the people (see Rom. 8:31 and Luther's *Deus pro nobis*). As surely as punishment is a threat for the "fools," so God's actions are "for" and "on behalf of" those who truly seek to "live rightly" in the eyes of God. While evildoers will seek to bring anguish to the poor, God will protect them and save them from danger. This highlighting of a way in which a disregard for God expresses itself—in the defeating and humiliation of poor people—focuses on those whose welfare is of special concern for God, and should be of special concern to the "righteous" as well.

Hope for Restoration. In the midst of "corrupt" persons who disregard God, the "righteous" pray for deliverances and restoration of "the fortunes" ("salvation") of Israel (v. 7). This deliverance will come "from Zion," meaning from God, who lives on Zion. Hope is fixed on God for the restoration of righteousness, the end of perversity, and "victory" in the world. This accords with the pervasive theological recognition throughout the Bible that "salvation" is from God, comes as a gift to the people, and causes the people to rejoice. The resolution of the psalmist is to depend on God, even in the midst of all corruption and calamities. Calvin said that while God may leave us for a time and we languish, we should not be weary or lose courage, so that while our troubles continue, "the most effectual solace we can have is often to return to the exercise of prayer."[3] Hope for the future and the future reign of God is grounded in God's work, when all "foolishness" will cease and the pervasive presence of God will feature all persons "rejoicing" and being "glad" (v. 7).

DONALD K. MCKIM

Pastoral Perspective

According to Patrick Miller, this psalm reflects significant questions in the psalmist's community about the presence and ability of God to respond to situations of human suffering, questions that resonate with contemporary fear and uncertainty about God's ability to make a difference in a world of pain and inequity.[3] Nevertheless, the psalmist confidently asserts the promise that God will restore to wholeness those who suffer, while those who refuse to acknowledge God's sovereignty will quake with terror when they realize their errors.

Of course, those who oppress and exploit are also found gathered in Christian churches each week. Psalm 14 assures the abusive spouse, the domineering employer, and the unscrupulous business person of God's concern for their victims, challenging them to transform their behavior. The preacher or liturgist might creatively employ this text to confront comfortable North American Christians about their complicity in the exploitation of low-wage workers in South Asia, the abuse and monopolization of earth's natural resources, and indifference to crushing poverty and disease in the underdeveloped world.

There is an eschatological dimension to the text in its promise that God cares about the plight of God's suffering children, despite what the foolish exploiter might assume. It assures the church and the world that God is working to right these wrongs. It invites God's people to be transformed to participate in such healing work. This is a deeply pastoral concern; as Pleins reminds us, the folly of injustice cuts *the oppressor* off from communion with God. Pastoral leaders must help their congregations find ways to express appropriate remorse and move toward more justly ordered relationships. This text can help us, pastors and congregations, to leave behind our own versions of practical atheism.

In short, to function pastorally involves working toward the healing of human relationships and the full flourishing of creation. Ordinary time focuses attention on the everyday practice of Christian discipleship. Psalm 14 can help Christians confront, renounce, and transform the ways we are complicit in unjust behaviors, close to home and around the globe, as part of the ongoing work of discipleship.

TIMOTHY HESSEL-ROBINSON

---

3. John Calvin, *Commentary on Psalms*, 14:7.

3. Patrick D. Miller Jr., *Interpreting the Psalms* (Philadelphia: Fortress Press, 1986), 97–99.

Exegetical Perspective

Evildoers in verse 4 are probably those Israelites who have no regard for the welfare of the weaker members of the community.

"My people," referred to in verse 4, is described as "the righteous" and "the poor" in verses 5–6.

"They eat up my people as they eat bread" (v. 4) declares that to the wicked the oppression of their fellow human beings is as commonplace as the eating of bread.

"The LORD is their refuge" (v. 6) has the connotation of safekeeping and being watched over. Verse 5 tells us that "God is with the company of the righteous," and Psalm 1:6 asserts that "the LORD watches over the way of the righteous."

Verse 7 concludes the psalm with a reference to Mount Zion, the source of blessing to Israel, a place from which the people believed God's presence emanated. This final verse may be a later addition to the psalm, reinterpreted and applied to a new situation to make it truly a national lament. The emphasis here seems to be that help can be expected only from YHWH, but that it can be expected.

Preaching Themes. Psalm 14 is very much in the spirit of the book of Proverbs and Israel's conventional Wisdom teachings in its emphasis on the eventual well-being of the wise, contrasted with the destruction of the fool. It is foolish, according to Psalm 14, to discount the presence and power of God, just because appearances seem to belie them. The wise person trusts in God's promises. As preachers, we need to find a nonliteral way to convey the assurance of God's presence (v. 5), God's protection (v. 6), and God's deliverance (v. 7). We need to affirm these realities in the face of the injustice, misfortune, and death that are part of the lives we live and observe others living.

ALYCE M. MCKENZIE

Homiletical Perspective

righteous" (v. 5), is a "refuge" for the poor (v. 6), and "restores the fortunes of his people" (v. 7b). Regardless of the homiletical theme addressed, the preacher will want to attend to the theology embedded in the text. God is present and active in every instance where a direct reference to God is made. Clearly the psalmist wanted to send the message that God, though seemingly absent in the face of injustice, is powerfully present and active on behalf of the people of God.

Preachers accustomed to doing a good deal of teaching in their sermons will perhaps choose to pull from Psalm 53, which is almost identical to Psalm 14. Differences between the two emerge at verse 5. Where Psalm 14 proclaims God's presence with the righteous (v. 5) and concern for the poor (v. 6), Psalm 53 continues with the theme of terror (v. 5b) and promises God's awful judgment of the ungodly. Another significant difference between the two psalms is that Psalm 14 uses YHWH in reference to God while Psalm 53 uses Elohim.

Finally, there is a strong justice theme in this psalm. The prayerful lament emerges out of a circumstance of injustice. Here injustice is connected to foolishness, which is moral and spiritual separation from God. Women and the poor of all descriptions, third-world peoples and descendants of Africans, people burdened with chronic diseases of various sorts, and recent immigrants in every period of American history are among those who experience or have experienced various forms of injustice in the Christian West. Psalm 14 declares the justice and deliverance of God for those who suffer or who are forced to struggle against the foolishness of the foolish.

MARK A. LOMAX

1 Timothy 1:12-17

¹²I am grateful to Christ Jesus our Lord, who has strengthened me, because he judged me faithful and appointed me to his service, ¹³even though I was formerly a blasphemer, a persecutor, and a man of violence. But I received mercy because I had acted ignorantly in unbelief, ¹⁴and the grace of our Lord overflowed for me with the faith and love that are in Christ Jesus. ¹⁵The saying is sure and worthy of full acceptance, that Christ Jesus came into the world to save sinners—of whom I am the foremost. ¹⁶But for that very reason I received mercy, so that in me, as the foremost, Jesus Christ might display the utmost patience, making me an example to those who would come to believe in him for eternal life. ¹⁷To the King of the ages, immortal, invisible, the only God, be honor and glory forever and ever. Amen.

Theological Perspective

This text expresses gratitude for the mercy of God that saves sinners. In the history of Protestantism, Martin Luther (1483–1546) is called to mind because of his similar emphasis upon the mercy of God in the face of human sinfulness. In his early years, Luther was ridden with anxiety because he believed that he could not live up to God's righteous standards. Then, as he studied the Scriptures, he realized that the righteousness of God was not a standard to which he must attain, but rather a *gift* from God: a mercy by which persons are passively made righteous through the righteousness of Christ. It is a mercy in which "the faith and the love that are in Christ Jesus" (v. 14) have a twofold effect: first, revealing the depth of sin, which Luther interpreted as the human arrogance that attempts to justify oneself before God, and second, setting the human right before God through the righteousness of Christ, who acts, loves, and believes on our behalf.

To illustrate, Luther portrayed a courtroom drama in which the human person stands before God the judge. In this scene, the human, who has attempted to attain his own salvation, meets his undoing. God reveals both the impotence and pride of the sinner. Instead of punishing the sinner, God extends mercy, declaring the arrogant sinner righteous in the righteousness of Christ.

Pastoral Perspective

"Paul, an apostle of Christ Jesus, . . . To Timothy, my loyal child: . . . " (I Tim. 1:1–2). First Timothy is a letter from a mentor to a cherished mentee, from a father figure to a "son of the heart," from an older pastor at the brink of retirement to a young pastor just beginning ministry. However, this Pastoral Epistle was not included in the canon just to aid those in the professional ministry, but for the edification of the entire body of Christ. Who are the Pauls and Timothys of the twenty-first-century church?

When I consider the Timothys of my local congregation, I see the young adults heading out into "real life," to college or graduate school, or into the workforce. The next generation of the church? Perhaps. The twenty-first-century Timothys of my acquaintance have been raised in a mainline congregation deeply committed to the expression of faith through social justice and intellectual inquiry. They have been taught to question and discern what they believe for themselves, and to "be the change you want to see in the world."[1] They believe deeply in the inclusion and acceptance of all people, all ages, genders, sexual orientations, abilities, and races. They are alternately passionate about changing their world and paralyzed

1. ThinkExist.com, http://thinkexist.com/quotation/be_the_change_you_want_to_see_in_the_world/148490.html

Exegetical Perspective

Of Paul's seven undisputed letters, five—Romans, 1 Corinthians, 1 Thessalonians, Philippians, and Philemon—contain, between the salutation and the body, an expression of gratitude to God. This structure follows the typical pattern of Hellenistic/Roman letters, which included a brief prayer or thanksgiving after the salutation. (In Galatians, the thanksgiving section is absent, likely because the apostle was so upset with the Galatian churches that he did not pause to offer thanks. In 2 Corinthians, a benediction occurs in the location where Paul's thanksgiving customarily appears.)

Several features of this thanksgiving in 1 Timothy, however, are different from the ones in Paul's undisputed letters. Most noticeably, in Paul's undisputed letters, he gives thanks for the persons to whom the letters are addressed, specifically expressing gratitude for their faithfulness, support, and exemplary behavior; in 1 Timothy, gratitude is offered for what Christ has done for Paul. In the undisputed letters, thanksgiving is directed to God; in 1 Timothy, "Christ Jesus our Lord" is the recipient of gratitude. Even the vocabulary for expressing gratitude is different. Paul's usual style is to say, "I give thanks" (*eucharistō*), whereas the wording in 1 Timothy 1:12 is "I am grateful" (literally, "I have gratitude," *charin echō*). These significant variations lend support to the widely held view that the Pastorals

Homiletical Perspective

If Paul[1] were a guest on one of the tell-all talk shows on television today, the crooked life to which he confesses here would not spike the ratings. The "fornicators" and "sodomites" he mentions earlier (v. 10) make for spicier tabloid fodder. Sex and sin sell— but *blasphemy*?

Paul persecuted Christians, and tradition has him holding the coats of those in the mob that stoned poor Stephen (Acts 7:58), but we reelect people who vote for war. We probably would not dare hold the coats of people actively committing known sin (would we?); but our sins of omission are glaring. When did we last pray for refugees targeted in the latest genocide? Many who suffer on the other side of the globe are "out of sight, out of mind."

Shame on us.

Like it or not—and the "worst of sinners" line can get tiring—Paul's past sin is central to his testimony. His emphasizing how far he fell, in order to illustrate how low a gracious God would stoop to pick him up, may feel a little forced, but he is sticking to it. This is Paul.

Perhaps we are a bit dulled to the before/after lives of the John Newtons (writer of "Amazing Grace")

1. Whoever authored the Pastoral Epistles took on the literary persona of Paul. This essay will therefore code the author as "Paul."

1 Timothy 1:12-17

Theological Perspective

In recent decades, feminist theologians have revisited this conception of God's mercy toward human arrogance, which has dominated Reformed thought. Women like Valerie Saiving and Serene Jones argue that such a construct of sin as pride "misses the mark" of women's lives and experiences. Saiving explains:

> The temptations of woman *as woman* are not the same as the temptations of man *as man*, and the specifically feminine forms of sin . . . have a quality which can never be encompassed by such terms as "pride" and "will to power." They are better suggested by such terms as triviality, distractibility, and diffuseness; lack of an organizing center or focus; dependence on others for one's self-definition; tolerance at the expense of standards of excellence . . . in short, underdevelopment or negation of the Self.[1]

Likewise, Jones argues that most women's lives are characterized, not by a boastful presumption to righteous actions, but by the opposite: by an inadequate sense of personal agency and by a dissipated experience of the self, which is further undone by the crucifying wrath of God. In other words, God's merciful revelation of hubris in Luther's courtroom drama not only fails to reveal the sin of a woman, but actually "recapitulates the very dynamics of her oppression."[2] Such an emasculating mercy is no mercy at all for those whose selfhood is characterized by self-negation. *So in their efforts to become active agents of their existence, are women then forced to reject the mercy of God?*

This passage in 1 Timothy reinforces the dilemma of interpreting salvation with a masculine paradigm. In verse 13, Paul expresses his gratitude that he has been transformed from an agent acting against God and neighbor ("a blasphemer, a persecutor, and a man of violence") to a passive agent who "received mercy." While one can understand that Paul experienced salvation as a move from active violence to passive acceptance, does this paradigm relate to the persecuted and the violated? For many persons, such as battered women, passive receptivity is the very means of their destruction. Does this passage contain resources for the one out of four American women who are experiencing domestic abuse or the one out of five girls who are the victims of sexual violence?[3]

1. Valerie Saiving, "The Human Situation: A Feminine View," in *Womanspirit Rising*, ed. Carol P. Christ and Judith Plaskow (San Francisco: Harper & Row, 1979), 25–42.
2. Joy Ann McDougall, *Christian Century*, July 26, 2005, 23.
3. García-Moreno et al., *WHO Multi-Country Study on Women's Health and Domestic Violence against Women* (Geneva: WHO, 2005), xiii. http://www.who.int/gender/violence/who_multicountry_study/Introduction-Chapter1-Chapter2.pdf.

Pastoral Perspective

with anger and fear about the world they are inheriting from their parents and grandparents.

Though these twenty-first-century Timothys may have heard all their lives that "Christ Jesus came into the world to save sinners," the saying is not "sure and full of worthy acceptance" in the frantic post-9/11 world in which they live. They live in a pluralistic religious world where claims of exclusive paths to God cause strife or oppression at the very least and terrorism at the extreme. They are searching for a living relationship with a living God who is also the God of their Jewish, Muslim, Buddhist, Hindu, Wiccan, or New Thought/New Age neighbor, not to mention the huge variety of Christian neighbors. They are suspicious of orthodox Christian theology and the authority of Scripture, suspicious of "churchy" words such as "sin," "sinner," and "salvation."

In the letter of 1 Timothy, a first-century Paul charges a first-century Timothy with a life of discipleship by sharing his personal relationship with the mystery of God in Christ Jesus. In what is quite literally a letter of pastoral care, Paul shares with his younger friend intimate revelations and confessions of faith and gives practical advice. Can the Pauls of our time share intimately with the Timothys their confessions of faith, their personal relationships with God, their questions and doubts, as well as affirmations and celebrations? Honest, raw sharing must build the base for communication with twenty-first-century Timothys. They have no patience for platitudes and warmed-over theological sentiments. They want to know if there is substance behind the ancient language of the church.

The Pauls of the twenty-first century are being invited to reexamine the language of Christian faith, not to dispose of it, but revitalize it, to reframe it for twenty-first-century ears. For example, after a discussion of the parables of the Mustard Seed and the Yeast in Matthew, a young man asked his pastor to explain the kingdom/realm of God in "plain language" and not in "church words." Haltingly, she began picturing the organic unfolding of creation and all that is in it, including human beings, as a part of the Divine, as a revelation of the Divine, as the continuing work of the Divine. "Oh," he replied, "The Oneness of all things. The way we are all connected energetically. I get it." Of course the pastor's description only touched the surface of a discussion on God's realm, but she had gained his attention and sparked his imagination.

Twenty-first-century Timothys long for personal *experiences* of the mystery of life and the animating

belong to the category of deuteropauline literature, rather than being letters actually written by Paul.

Even though the style of the thanksgiving varies from Paul's normal practice, the biographical information contained in the thanksgiving is generally consistent with Paul's own statements in Galatians and 1 Corinthians, as well as the reports of his activities in the book of Acts (8:1–3; 9:1–2). Paul described his earlier life as one in which he "was violently persecuting the church of God and was trying to destroy it" (Gal. 1:13). He saw himself as "the least of the apostles, unfit to be called an apostle, because I persecuted the church of God" (1 Cor. 15:9; cf. Phil. 3:6). The vocabulary of this passage in 1 Timothy even heightens the contrast between Paul's life before and after his life-changing experience relative to the undisputed letters, which do not use the terms "blasphemer" or "man of violence" (1 Tim. 1:13) in describing his earlier attacks on the church. (The phrase in Gal. 1:13 that is translated in the NRSV as "violently persecuting the church" actually reads "persecuting the church to the extreme.")

The intent of this section is not to provide biographical information about Paul's life but to establish a stark contrast between the "before and after" Pauls. Just as Paul's life before Christ is portrayed in extreme terms, so also is his life after Christ—"the grace of our Lord overflowed for me" (v. 14), that is, grace was "superabundantly present." Paul the persecutor became Paul the apostle, set apart for service by the abounding grace of Christ. This contrast serves to illustrate the depth of the mercy of Christ. The grace and love of Christ are so great that even the worst of sinners—of whom Paul is put forth as the prime example—can be redeemed and transformed by the love of Christ.

The expression in verse 15, "the saying is sure," appears four other times in the Pastorals (1 Tim. 3:1; 4:9; 2 Tim. 2:11; Titus 3:8), where it is used to draw attention to and affirm the truthfulness of what precedes or follows it. Here it introduces the affirmation "that Christ Jesus came into the world to save sinners," which was likely a creedal statement belonging to early Christian tradition.

Reflection on the depth of Christ's mercy leads to an exuberant outburst of praise in the form of a doxology in verse 17: "To the King of the ages, immortal, invisible, the only God, be honor and glory forever and ever. Amen."[1] Although no similar

---

1. The version of this doxology familiar through the opening words of the hymn by Walter Chalmers Smith, "Immortal, Invisible, God Only Wise," is indebted to a textual variant, represented in some manuscripts that were perhaps influenced by Rom. 16:27, where the phrase "to the only wise God" appears. The KJV accepts the longer reading here.

who once traded slaves but turned out rosy in the end. Perhaps we are standoffish like the prodigal son's elder brother (Luke 15:11–32): suspicious and polluted with more than a tinge of envy. Whatever the reason, our neighbor's news that he has seen the light elicits more queasy stomach than glad heart.

Shame on us, again.

The preacher with less-jaded congregants can get away with pushing this angle unabashedly. Otherwise, she should tread carefully, but tread she *must*. While there may be unmarked mines, unpacking Paul's "testimonial" bears sweet fruit for a hungry flock. As Paul does not mind being a fool for Christ (1 Cor. 4:10), neither should preachers and teachers as they explore this text.

Two things are worth noting. First, Paul's testimony is personal. He was blinded and shattered on the way to Damascus (Acts 9:1–18; Gal. 1:13–24). His world was turned upside down, and he is going to tell us about it. This appeals to Generation Xers and the millennials, who are said to value personal experience *first*. The life of the mind is *not* the suit with which they lead. An emotional connection grabs them first; then the intellectual exercise afterward continues to feed them. Both are important, but notice the order.

Testimony is the heartbeat of a person's story. It is about as close to an experience as one can get without actually having it. Paul's story was well known long before it appeared in this letter to Timothy. He likely tells it again because he knows it stirs folk, and he hopes it would lead others "to believe in [Jesus] for eternal life" (v. 16). Perhaps we have a testimonial to share, or someone in our flock does. Now might be the time.

If a safer distance is preferred, the teacher may share stories from memoirs and biography here, people who have been grabbed by the gospel and lived to tell about it. Barbara Brown Taylor's *Leaving Church* would cause a lot of head nodding in agreement during worship at a presbytery meeting. Anne Lamott's *Traveling Mercies* gets single mothers stirring in the amen corner. Frederick Buechner's autobiography, and Reinhold Niebuhr's *Leaves from the Notebook of a Tamed Cynic* would hit the head of the homiletical nail for many parishioners wary of the faith, but compelled by it nevertheless.

Examples from fiction and film also abound. There is the sad story of Elphaba, the so-called Wicked Witch of the West, who, knowing she is different, sings, "Hands touch, eyes meet / Sudden silence, sudden heat / Hearts leap in a giddy whirl /

1 Timothy 1:12-17

Theological Perspective

While the passage is certainly dominated by the Lutheran paradigm, I suggest that it also points toward two revelations of God's mercy for women. First, God's mercy overflows with faith and love in Christ Jesus (v. 14). Such salvific faith and love is demonstrated toward women in Christ's encounter with the woman caught in the act of adultery (John 8:1–11). Rather than punishing her, Jesus exposed the sin of the society that sought to destroy her. He saved her from death and dissipated the condemnation of others. In addition, he expressed faith that she would become the agent of her own action by saying, "Go your way, and from now on do not sin again" (v. 11). The same faith and love in Christ, which called Paul to become a passive recipient of his salvation, called this woman to personal agency, to recreate herself in light of God's mercy.

Second, in this passage the mercy of God exposes Paul's ignorance and unbelief (1 Tim. 1:13). The unbelief, he explains, gave rise to a violence that he directed outward. In this passage he implicitly condemns such violence by attributing it to his sinful nature (v. 15). By implication, God's mercy in Christ also condemns the violence of the persecutor. In addition, it exposes and condemns the unbelief of the oppressed, which often expresses itself as a violence directed inward. This violence against the self may have a variety of expressions for women, from active or passive self-destructive patterns (such as accepting abuse) to dissipating the self for others.

In Luke 10:38–42 Martha dissipated herself when she accepted her social role as hostess and denied her true need. Christ exposed her unbelief as it was expressed in her worry and distraction and challenged her to choose "the better part," even when it defied social norms. In a manner similar to Paul, Christ called Martha to bring an end to her activity. Her activity, unlike Paul's, was an act of violence against herself, a denial of her need, for the sake of the "other." In this manner, the critiques of modern feminist theologies challenge the reader to reflect more broadly on the mercy of God as experienced by men and by women as they encounter Christ.

STEPHANIE MAR SMITH

Pastoral Perspective

force that they hope lies behind the workings of the creation. If the church can offer them these experiences, they may decide that "church" is a viable institution for their world, not a relic from Christianity's bygone glory days. These Timothys search for wholeness of body, mind, and soul and wholeness of creation. It is this wholeness that is salvation to them. They understand sin as disconnection from wholeness, from the Oneness of the universe, for it means disconnection from their very selves. They have been raised to understand the web of life as it is seen in family systems, ecological systems, and quantum physics. Tearing the web, denying its existence, this is sin. While they reverence the connectivity of the universe, they are caught up in and wounded by its brokenness as easily as older generations. They seek ways to be part of the healing process.

How might worship based on the saying in 1 Timothy 1:15, "Christ Jesus came into the world to save sinners," invite young adults into the mystery of Christ? Could the energy field discussion of quantum physics be used analogously to open up the concept of the animating, regenerating presence of God in Christ in the world? Could this discussion be embodied in the sacraments of Communion and baptism? Does the New Testament understanding of sin as missing the mark relate to sin as tearing the fabric of creation's connectivity? Could the ancient liturgical practice of confession be reworked as a healing practice for restoring connection? How can God's story of salvation through the life, death, and resurrection of Jesus the Christ be told so as to resonate with the notion of salvation as the restoration of wholeness in the creation?

Our challenge as twenty-first-century Pauls, our charge as the older generation which mentors them, is to listen carefully to our Timothys so that together we can participate in experiencing God in Christ Jesus. Our Timothys invite us onto unknown paths of worship planning, where the Spirit leads to us to reframe our "churchy" language and to engage in liturgical experience that may be beyond language.

JANE ANNE FERGUSON

doxology appears in Paul's undisputed letters, the doxology is consistent with Paul's theology. In Romans, using the same vocabulary that appears here, Paul refers to God as being immortal (1:23) and his "eternal power and divine nature" as being invisible (1:20). Perhaps surprisingly, Paul never applies the title "king" to God, but he does mention on several occasions the kingdom of God (Rom. 14:17; 1 Cor. 4:20; 6:9, 10; 15:24, 50; Gal. 5:21; 1 Thess. 2:12 ["his kingdom"]). The phrase "King of the ages" probably reflects Jewish prayer language (see Jer. 10:10; Tobit 13:6, 10; Sirach 36:22). Doxologies normally consist of three elements: a reference to God, an ascription of eternal glory, and an "amen." All three elements are present here, with the first element greatly expanded.

Doxologies, likely a common part of the worship experience of Judaism and early Christianity, appear in several New Testament letters (see Rom. 11:36; 16:25–27; Gal. 1:5; Eph. 3:21; Phil. 4:20; 1 Tim. 6:16; 2 Tim. 4:18), where they usually conclude a section of text. They belong to the category of performative speech; that is, they are not just making a statement about God or inviting others to praise God. Rather, the utterance of a doxology is itself an act of praising God. The "amen" that concludes the doxology is evidence of the liturgical nature of the doxology. In Jewish and Christian worship, worshipers responded to prayers, blessings, and doxologies with their "amen" as a way of affirming and joining with what had been said. Since letters written to early Christian communities were intended to be read aloud as the community gathered in worship, perhaps the doxologies in New Testament letters were concluded by congregations joining in the "amen" as the letters were read to them.

Whether written by Paul or by someone reflecting appreciatively on the Pauline tradition, this thanksgiving overflows with gratitude, written from the perspective of someone who not only has been given an unmerited second chance, but also has been called to serve in a special way.

MITCHELL G. REDDISH

He could be that boy, / But I'm not that girl."[2] She is beautiful, but her skin is green in Stephen Schwartz's play *Wicked*. Plopped like a stone in the twelfth seat in row F, we see ourselves up on that stage, quivering.

In a like way, Paul welcomes us into his heart through its broken places and fervently hopes that we see something of ourselves in desperate need of God's grace through Christ. He is drawing not only from his own experience; he is leaning on promises that precede him. This is a second thing worth noting. "The saying is sure and worthy of full acceptance, that Christ Jesus came into the world to save sinners" (v. 15). That is church lingo, perhaps an early theological formulation. Paul is quoting in order to give nod to what the wider church has been saying. His story fits God's desire for everyone's salvation.

The preacher will want to hold in tension the personal nature of Paul's testimonial, on the one hand, and the tradition of the saints who preceded and surround him, on the other. Each serves as context for the other. So, we tell our tale *in light of* Scripture, never without it. Our personal story needs to find meaning within the larger communal story of God's people. We take the clothes of the faith and try to wear them in such a way that they do not make our hips look big. Our story and the Apostles' Creed. Paul's story of sin and the Theological Declaration of Barmen. All are *testimony* to the grace of God in Christ.

This is a way of saying we need each other (and the convictions of those who proceed us) because we often get it wrong. "God is love," we rightly affirm, and "love is blind. Stevie Wonder is blind. God is Stevie Wonder." It started out making sense!

Barbara Brown Taylor has said that if it has not been said before, then we likely are wrong to say it now, because we preach and teach from a tradition.[3] Certainly, she was quoting someone else.

What *Paul* says means nothing without what *God* said first in Jesus Christ.

WILLIAM P. "MATT" MATTHEWS

2. Stephen Schwartz, "I'm Not That Girl," *Wicked* (Decca Broadway, Universal Classics Group, 2003).
3. Barbara Brown Taylor, "Do This and You Will Live" (lecture, Festival of Homiletics, Peachtree United Methodist Church, Atlanta, GA, May 15, 2006).

Luke 15:1-10

¹Now all the tax collectors and sinners were coming near to listen to him. ²And the Pharisees and the scribes were grumbling and saying, "This fellow welcomes sinners and eats with them."

³So he told them this parable: ⁴"Which one of you, having a hundred sheep and losing one of them, does not leave the ninety-nine in the wilderness and go after the one that is lost until he finds it? ⁵When he has found it, he lays it on his shoulders and rejoices. ⁶And when he comes home, he calls together his friends and neighbors, saying to them, 'Rejoice with me, for I have found my sheep that was lost.' ⁷Just so, I tell you, there will be more joy in heaven over one sinner who repents than over ninety-nine righteous persons who need no repentance.

⁸"Or what woman having ten silver coins, if she loses one of them, does not light a lamp, sweep the house, and search carefully until she finds it? ⁹When she has found it, she calls together her friends and neighbors, saying, 'Rejoice with me, for I have found the coin that I had lost.' ¹⁰Just so, I tell you, there is joy in the presence of the angels of God over one sinner who repents."

Theological Perspective

A *New York Times* travel article on pubs in Oxford commented that "a good pub is a ready made party, a home away from home, a club anyone can join."[1] One can imagine the Jesus of Luke 15 sitting in such a pub, eating and drinking with "anyone," to the chagrin of the proper and the pure. To be more specific, in Luke 15 Jesus is eating and drinking with "tax collectors and sinners" while the "Pharisees and the scribes" are grumbling about the company he keeps (that is, the company he "seeks out," *prosdechomai*; NRSV "welcomes," v. 2). In response to this muttering, Jesus tells a series of "lost and found" parables that have to do with homes and parties and letting anyone in. The theological issues here circle around soteriology and ecclesiology—who is in and who is out, who is lost and who is found, what does it mean to be saved by Christ, and what does it mean to be the community of Christ today?

Earlier in Luke, Jesus says, "Search, and you will find" (11:9), and one might be tempted to read these parables as emphasizing the same point—that we are saved by finding what we seek. We might imagine ourselves as the shepherd looking for the sheep or as the woman looking for the coin. We might imagine

1. Henry Shukman, "A Pub Crawl through the Centuries," *New York Times*, April 13, 2008; online: www.travel.nytimes.com.

Pastoral Perspective

This couplet of parables introduces teachings of Jesus regarding the nature of God, particularly God's nature to forgive and restore God's people. The parables repeat throughout what forgiveness is like in terms of things lost and things found. Jesus challenges the hearers to consider what it means to be community and what boundaries, if any, community has. In so doing, he invites us to consider what God is like by considering our own experience. This is the power of the parable.

The crowds are pressing in around Jesus to hear his teachings. All manner of people make up this community. They gather around Jesus for a variety of reasons: the disciples to receive instruction; the Pharisees and Sadducees to keep tabs on Jesus' radical teachings; and the people who do not really belong anywhere because they have lived so much of life on so many fringes. They are described as the tax collectors and sinners, which mean that they are the people no one else wants to hang around with, for fear that the reprehensible reputations of the one would implicate the good reputations of the other. Somehow these outsiders have crowded into the community as well. This was a group of strange bedfellows, hardly a dinner list that anyone of any salt would put together. Here they are, eating with Jesus. If you are, after all, known by the company

Exegetical Perspective

At Luke 9:51 the reader is told that Jesus "set his face to go to Jerusalem." On this journey from Caesarea Philippi in the north to Jerusalem in the south, Jesus instructs his disciples about what it means to be a disciple. Seventy of them are sent on a special mission, carrying with them no belongings. They go "like lambs into the midst of wolves" (10:3), but return with joy, because even the demons are subject to them. Repeatedly, throughout this section, Jesus speaks about money and its dangers, about the demand for repentance, and about the costliness of following Jesus. Frequently Jesus eats with Pharisees and with scribes, and on one occasion he confronts the guests and the host with their need for humility and hospitality, especially with regard to the marginalized and weak people of the town (14:7–14). On one occasion Jesus eats with tax collectors and sinners.

Now Jesus' association with the tax collectors and sinners offends the Pharisees and scribes, especially since the sinners are "hearing" Jesus. "Hearing" for Luke is a sign of repentance and conversion (see Luke 5:1, 15; 6:17–18, 27, 47, 49). Like the prophet Jonah in the Hebrew Scriptures (Jonah 4:1–5), the Pharisees and scribes do not take kindly to the possible repentance of those who lie outside their definition of the redeemable. So the Pharisees and scribes "grumble" (NIV "muttered," v. 2), reminiscent of

Homiletical Perspective

Familiar stories are often the most challenging to preach. The quest to find a new angle, a fresh insight, and a relevant message from a well-known parable is ever before the conscientious interpreter of the word. However, a closer look at the occasion Luke supplies for these parables may help. The two stories were a direct response to a criticism from the religious insiders surrounding Jesus. Their grumbling was provoked by the radical hospitality they were witnessing. This promiscuous meal sharing by the rabbi offended their sensibilities. After all, they were the ones who were intimately acquainted with the rules, the ones who drew the boundaries, the ones who enforced the holiness codes of clean and unclean.

The parables are given to those religious insiders, just as they are given to us. We are placed in their company by the very nature of our work. As preachers, we are religious insiders, along with our leaders and our church members. Often this parable unfolds in a way that emphasizes the redemption of the "lost," but it is the "already found" that the parable is meant to bring to repentance.

Out of a multitude of ways to preach these oft-told twin parables, four themes are offered here to help congregations mine the treasure.

Luke 15:1-10

Theological Perspective

that these parables encourage our searching, so that we might find what we have lost. The parables in fact do something else. They make us, the sinners, not the searchers but the lost object, lost not in the subjective sense of not knowing where we are (though that may be part of it), but in the objective sense of having become the object of another's search. That is, we are lost *to* someone, who is, we are assured, seeking us.

In an Easter sermon in 1620, Lancelot Andrewes said of Christ, "He is found of them that seeke Him not, but of them that seeke Him never but found."[2] The peculiar twists and turns in this sentence can leave a reader spinning, with expectations twice thwarted. First, we read "He is found of them that seeke Him" and assume that we have, indeed, a reaffirmation of "search, and you will find" from Luke 11. But the "not" at the end of the phrase catches us off guard, and, like a good parable, it disorients us, because we expect to be affirmed in our search, to receive the object we seek (presumably Christ himself) as a reward for our efforts. Christ is found, however, by those who seek him *not*. Andrewes's text continues, "But of them that seeke Him never . . ." and of course at this point, following the logic of the "but," we assume that those who seek him will never find him—an alarming thought, but one that seems to follow from the logic of the sentence to this point. Again we are taken up short: "never *but* found." So we come to rest, letting the sense of Andrewes's sentence sink in. Like the sheep and the coin, we are found—and found in a way that is not dependent on our seeking but only on our being sought. The good news is just that—we are sought, and more, we have always already been found (lest the gift be confused for a prize).

The human role in this drama is the role of the lost object, a role that could be construed as passivity. This would be a mistake. The human role here is neither passive nor active. Rather, there is a kind of "middle voice" at work, an open and active receptivity that turns to the finder ("repents," v. 10) but does not do the finding. The text seems to invite an attentiveness to the voice of the one who calls, a working out of our own salvation that is at the same time the relinquishing of our working, since it is God working within us (as in Phil. 2:12). Our seeking is but our willingness to be found.

What if it is precisely our faith that we have lost? Do we not sometimes find ourselves in the place of

2. Lancelot Andrewes, *XCVI Sermons*, 3rd ed. (London: Richard Badger, 1635), 538; cited in Stanley Fish, *Is There a Text in This Class? The Authority of Interpretive Communities* (Cambridge, MA, and London: Harvard University Press, 1980), 184.

Pastoral Perspective

you keep, Jesus has completely thrown the community into a panic.

The side conversations begin immediately, and so the Jesus community begins to crack. The whispering starts, "Who invited them? Why would Jesus embrace this woman, this man? Does he not know who they are, what they do for a living? Who is this Jesus? He talks of godly things on the one hand, and yet he eats with them on the other."

Perceiving the questions, Jesus begins to address the growing division in the crowd by talking about the nature of God in terms they can understand. He approaches it on economic terms, talking about things that they value. He wants them to think about what is most important to them. For example, the shepherd values the health and the safety of his flock, his source of income; the woman values the hard-earned money she has scraped and saved to feed her family; the parent values the happiness and well-being of his or her children. Think of that thing most precious in your life and what it would be like to lose it, whether through carelessness, or intent, or theft. Something on which you place extreme value goes missing. You would be devastated. Not that you cannot continue; you can. People adapt—but life is incomplete. Part of the whole is missing.

God is like the shepherd who values each sheep in the flock, like the woman who accounts for every silver coin in the purse. God treasures every child of the family. When one goes missing, God goes into search mode. God's nature is love, and love looks like one who goes out tirelessly searching, because the one who is lost is so lost that she cannot find her way back home.

Woven in with the nature of God is the nature of the one who is lost. A lost sheep that is able to bleat out in distress often will not do so, out of fear. Instead it will curl up and lie down in the wild brush, hiding from predators. It is so fearful in its seclusion that it cannot help in its own rescue. The sheep is immobilized, so the shepherd must bear its full weight to bring it home. Similarly, the lost coin, an inanimate object, is unable to call out or shine brightly to bring attention to itself. Its rescue is totally dependent upon the woman's diligence.

Jesus elucidates this point with another parable about a father with two sons (15:11–32). The younger son, after wasting his life and sinking as low as he can go, resolves to return to his father. He rehearses an apology but does not get to use it. His father is way ahead of him. His father has been watching out for him since he left. How easily the

Exegetical Perspective

Israel's grumbling and complaining against Moses and Aaron during the wilderness wanderings.

Here in chapter 15, in response to the persistent complaints of the Pharisees and scribes, Jesus tells three stories that serve to critique the inhospitable character of the Jews. Two of these stories comprise our lesson for today. (The third story, about the loving father and his two sons, i.e., Luke 15:11–32, is in the assigned lection for the Fourth Sunday in Lent.) The first story in Luke is paralleled by a similar story in Mathew's Gospel (18:12–14), which is set in the context of settling disputes within the church.

The first two stories in Luke can be superimposed on the same outline:

> Which man/ woman . . . having 100 sheep/10 coins, if he/she loses one . . . does not leave/sweep . . . go after/and seek . . . until he/she finds it? When he/she has found it . . . he/she calls together his/her friends and neighbors, saying, "Rejoice with me, for I have found my sheep/the coin . . . which was/I had lost." Just so, I tell you, there will be more joy/is joy in heaven/before the angels of God over one sinner who repents.[1]

The first story begins with the query, "Which one of you, having a hundred sheep and losing one of them, does not leave the ninety-nine in the wilderness and go after the one that is lost until he finds it?" It is a question that orients by disorienting. What about the ninety-nine that are left in the wilderness, we ask? Were they left unattended? Nothing is said about their care. The narrative of the story focuses solely on the lone lost sheep and the shepherd, who goes after the lost one until it is found, and who lays it on his shoulders and comes home rejoicing and calling in his neighbors for a party to celebrate the one who was lost and now is found.

The second story depicts a woman who, having lost one of her treasured silver coins, lights a lamp and sweeps her house carefully until she finds the lost coin. She is overjoyed and calls her friends to celebrate the finding of the lost coin. No doubt her coin was a drachma, worth the price of a sheep or one-fifth the price of an ox. She has thus invested a great deal in the party she has thrown for her friends. No other parable in the New Testament presents a woman as a metaphor or allegory for God. This would shock and surprise the audience, since God is depicted as a searching woman, who rejoices over finding her lost coin.

Homiletical Perspective

The Threat of Coming Near. "The tax collectors and sinners were coming near" (v. 1)—that is when the threat begins. They were approaching the inner circle and thereby usurping the place of the religious insiders. We can easily feel displaced from our positions of "nearness." Our power is diminished, and our safety feels threatened. This is not lost on Jesus, the masterful storyteller, for he reminds the insiders that those whom he seeks are already near. They are in the flock, they are as near as your sheep; they are in the house, as near to you as the coins you clasp in your hands. They are already near, our friend from Nazareth tells us; so do not be threatened that I share a meal with them as I share it with you. The intimacy of breaking bread is simply a tangible act of this nearness.

Religious insiders can still be easily threatened in the sharing of a meal. Many churches put conditions on the Communion table. In fact, in one church, people wearing rainbow sashes, indicating their solidarity with LGBT people, were refused Communion. A person who was offered Communion took his wafer and began to break it into pieces to share it with those who had been denied and deemed unworthy. The church officials, the religious insiders, called the police. How do we react when our nearness is threatened?

Difference between Welcoming and Saving. No one would dispute that at the core of each parable is a story of searching and finding; but what is the search for? The search is for something specific in each case: a wandering lamb, a lost coin. The joyful finding of the wandering one could be a comforting message to those who have wandered afar, who feel lost and outside of the care and even the reach of God. This may be a perfect occasion to preach about the long, loving reach of God. The God who will travel into the thicket to pull you out, the God who crawls into the hole you have dug for yourself and lifts you up and out. Is it a search to save or a search to welcome? It is one thing to "save" and another to "welcome." Religious insiders are often more comfortable with saving the lost than welcoming those whom they perceive to be lost. Saving is about power, whereas welcoming is about intimacy. Saving is primarily focused on the individual, whereas welcoming is focused on the community.

The Diligent Search and the Joyful Find. There could be an emphasis on the diligence that the search often requires. The diligence of going the extra mile, going into the dark places, or the hard work of sweeping

---

1. David Tiede, *Luke* (Minneapolis: Augsburg, 1988), 274.

Luke 15:1-10

Theological Perspective

the seeker, not exactly seeking God, but seeking the faith that has become lost to us? What is it to "lose faith" but to lose the conviction that one has been found, to begin to wonder whether one is sought at all—whether there is in fact a shepherd or a peasant woman tracking us down? To those whose lost object is faith itself, these parables whisper that losing faith—that is, becoming like the tax collector and sinner rather than the Pharisee and scribe—is to have wandered into the place where one can be found.

If for the sinners and tax collectors, doubters and skeptics, these parables are about being found, for the Pharisees and scribes they are stories about learning to rejoice. The parables of the lost sheep and the lost coin both end by calling together friends and neighbors to join in the celebration. Indeed, the movement of joy pulses outward from the one to the many, from the earth to the heavens. The party takes on a cosmic scale. Rejoicing itself seems to be the *telos* of these stories, the goal toward which they move beyond the penultimate moment of finding. So salvation consists not purely or even primarily in rescue, but in being drawn into the eternal celebration. For the Pharisees (and for every critical, nay-saying voice in the church) the question becomes, "Who are you ready to party with?" If the answer is "We don't party," or "We don't party with them," then those righteous ones will have ceded to the pub the role of parable of the kingdom.

SCOTT BADER-SAYE

Pastoral Perspective

children of God wander away and become lost, so filled with regret they are unable to undo their mistakes. There seems no possible hope for reconciliation. They cannot retrace their steps or make it right. Jesus assures that God is a step ahead. Home is already waiting. Love's door is open.

Joan Osbourne sang words that express the longing of the Lost to be found: "What if God was one of us . . . trying to make his way home."[1] The murmurings of the Pharisees and scribes would judge Jesus by the company he kept, implying that the one who shows hospitality to the sinner is himself a sinner. The sinner would see things differently. Jesus understands the struggle with being lost, the emptiness of being separated, and the struggle to return. Jesus does not turn away from the sinners, but toward the lost, to make a place for them, to welcome them home.

Jesus understands that those on the fringe of the community are integral to what the community in all its fullness should be. Until they return, the community is incomplete. The parables are about a hospitality that seeks to forgive and restore.

These parables call the community to open its doors and rejoice. This call is repeated again and again. Sinners and tax collectors gather at the table with the Christ? Rejoice! Laugh! Be glad! They have returned home and now sit in the presence of God. The sheep who wandered off from the rest of the flock, lost in the thicket, is now safe and sound! Hallelujah! Worry no more! The coin that fell through the cracks was easily forgotten but is blessedly retrieved. We can feast! Hope is restored!

When one in our community goes missing, we are all affected. When one is restored, we are all better off for it. That is how it is in the household of God.

HELEN MONTGOMERY DEBEVOISE

1. Joan Osbourne, "One of Us," 1996, from the album *Relish*.

Exegetical Perspective

Jesus shared with the Pharisees and scribes a common attitude toward the tax collectors and sinners, namely, that the tax collectors and sinners were lost. However, these parables point out a sharp difference between Jesus, on the one hand, and the Pharisees and scribes, on the other, with regard to God's searching out and finding the lost. The point of the stories is twofold, emphasizing the compassionate concern of a searching God (note the frequent use of the word "lost" in these two parables) and heaven's glad delight over discovery, when one sinner, either tax collector or Pharisee, comes to faith.

In fact, the themes of joy and celebration are paramount in both stories. Each story ends with a statement that there will be joy in heaven over one sinner who repents (vv. 7, 10). Neither a sheep nor a coin can repent. The issue of the two parables, therefore, is not to call sinners to repentance, but to invite the righteous to join the celebration. "Whether one will join the celebration is all-important, because it reveals whether one's relationships are based on merit or on mercy. Those who find God's mercy offensive cannot celebrate with the angels when a sinner repents. Thus they exclude themselves from God's grace."[2] The Pharisees and the scribes put themselves outside the circle of divine grace by the way in which they grumble at Jesus' fellowship with tax collectors and sinners. There is no joy or celebration, no partying or delight, among the Pharisees and scribes. Even though invited to the reception given in behalf of the joyous shepherd/woman, they cannot bring themselves to come; thereby, like the elder brother (15:25–32), they are exposed.

CHARLES B. COUSAR

Homiletical Perspective

clean and sweeping out old notions of humanity, of worthiness, and of righteousness. This kind of search and sweeping would indeed be a grand repentance, for the true nature of repentance is not to feel bad but to change one's mind. An attentive and careful search for those who have remained outside would be a profound paradigm shift in thinking about who is welcome and who is not. This diligence and hard work is to be done joyfully, not grudgingly. Every aspect of the story is laced with joy. As Jesus told the story, he must have been exhibiting that joy, or rejoicing as he invited the audience in. Jesus not only emphasizes joy; he expects *rejoicing*, an expression of the true joy when all are included.

Who Is the Sinner? Who are the sinners? The turn of the phrase at the end of the parables provides a final twist. The sinners in this story are the ones who need repentance, the ones who need their minds changed. God rejoices when the religious insiders (in all of us) change their minds about who is in and who is out. The rejoicing happens when community is complete and there is no such category as the *one* and the *ninety-nine*. True repentance happens when our minds are changed to such a degree that we cannot see a community as whole until all are included and none are "lost."

The wise teacher even attempted to change people's mind about God. He used an image of God as masculine in the shepherd and as feminine in the woman sweeping the house. By using two different parables he made sure no one was left out, not even a feminine God.

As storytellers ourselves, we must be equally attentive to our nuances in unveiling the layers of these parables and in drawing people in. We can invite the twists and turns of the truth to surprise us and lead us to a mind change, a heart change. Still, some of the truth will remain hidden, to be discovered only in a thorough search or in a sweeping clean.

G. PENNY NIXON

---

2. R. Alan Culpepper, "Luke," in Leander Keck, ed., *The New Interpreter's Bible* (Nashville: Abingdon Press, 1995), 9:298.

Jeremiah 8:18–9:1

¹⁸My joy is gone, grief is upon me,
  my heart is sick.
¹⁹Hark, the cry of my poor people
  from far and wide in the land:
"Is the LORD not in Zion?
  Is her King not in her?"
("Why have they provoked me to anger with their images,
  with their foreign idols?")
²⁰"The harvest is past, the summer is ended,
  and we are not saved."

Theological Perspective

This lament of Jeremiah over Judah captures the prophet's pathos with intensity similar to the narratives like Jeremiah 32:1–44. The rhythms of the poetry keep pace with the anguish of God and the human community of Jerusalem. The poem obfuscates who is the speaker, YHWH or Jeremiah, for they share the strong pathos that comes with the people's failings and plight.

Every generation can hear the lament of Jeremiah with new ears, because demoralization and suffering span the centuries and cultures. Similarly, the life of a prophet is difficult at all times, and it was a burdensome ministry for Jeremiah. He was probably the butt of jokes. The first three measures of this song or poem set the tone: "My joy is gone, grief is upon me, my heart is sick" (8:18).

On the one hand, the lament is from the people, God's beloved vulnerable people far and wide in the land. Once again Jeremiah refers to "my poor people" (8:19), which probably functions as a term of endearment. We can think of the term being inclusive, hence the language "far and wide in the land" (8:19a). In one respect determining how pervasive the lament is, at the same time it brings a level of inclusiveness. On the other hand, it is not clear who raises the questions of verse 19b. This section calls into doubt the theological and political framework

Pastoral Perspective

When Jeremiah was a young man and Josiah was king of the land of Israel, Assyria waned in power and left Israel on its own for a while. One of Josiah's first acts was to rebuild the temple, something that stirred up the nationalism repressed during the Assyrian occupation. Josiah, aided by the discovery of a version of Deuteronomy unearthed during the reconstruction of the temple, then launched a program of religious reform that was far reaching and effective. He rid the countryside of the shrines that honored Assyrian deities and rooted out remnants of pagan worship. He closed shrines and places of local worship and invited the clergy from outlying areas to Jerusalem to practice in the temple. By recentering religious and cultic practices in the temple in Jerusalem, he greatly increased the influence of the temple in cultic worship and the lives of everyday people.

Of course there were unintended consequences. It is easy to suspect that clergy that came into Jerusalem from outlying areas needed to be shown the ropes, introduced to how it was done in the big city, a process that all but guaranteed them second-class status in the temple hierarchy. Then, more than likely, rules were enacted to prevent the most blatant abuses. That made the game shift to how to give the appearance of observing the rules but not make any changes in how things were done. Anyone with

> [21]For the hurt of my poor people I am hurt,
>   I mourn, and dismay has taken hold of me.
>
> [22]Is there no balm in Gilead?
>   Is there no physician there?
>   Why then has the health of my poor people
>   not been restored?
> [9:1]O that my head were a spring of water,
>   and my eyes a fountain of tears,
>   so that I might weep day and night
>   for the slain of my poor people!

Exegetical Perspective

Jeremiah is often labeled "the weeping prophet," and there is no passage that warrants that label for him better than this one. Today's lection from Jeremiah is taken from a portion of the prophetic book that deals with the unrepentant and incorrigible people of Judah and God's wrathful reaction. Jeremiah has denounced the confidence the people of Judah have put in the temple and sacrificial rituals automatically to save them (7:8–15), regardless of their provoking YHWH to anger by their idols, and despite the Lord's repeated sending of prophets to warn them (7:16–26). In the face of such abominations (7:30), God promises to bring an end to mirth and gladness (7:34). In their perpetual and unrepented backsliding, the people have shown themselves to be more foolish than the birds (8:4–7). Possession of and familiarity with the law of the Lord is not the equivalent of wisdom (8:8–13). The doom that is coming is portrayed with images of poisoned water, devouring attackers on snorting horses, and snakes (8:14–17).

There seems to be a change of personae at several points: in verses 18–19a the speaker laments the plight of "my daughter, my people";[1] verse 19b quotes the cry of this people, raising plaintive questions that

1. My preferred translation of Heb. *bat-ʿammi*. NRSV reads "my poor people." See comments about this translation in the discussion of Jer. 4:11, 50–55.

Homiletical Perspective

If one has had any exposure at all to the American church tradition, it is impossible to approach this passage without hearing the African American spiritual "There Is a Balm in Gilead" echoing in one's mind, if not also upon one's lips. The song is a powerful as well as poignant reminder of how Scripture can come alive, how it can be appropriated in a deeply immediate manner that does not merely instruct but sustains and empowers. Of course, it is sung as a gift, as an act of encouragement to someone else whose momentary assessment of their life and faith leaves them feeling broken or inadequate.

However, the powerful reflection on this passage that the old spiritual provides can also limit other directions and questions to which the prophet's words may take us. It is not an act of ingratitude to make the effort to "hear" this text anew, listening for it to address today's conditions with the same Spirit-given power that gave rise to the treasured spiritual.

The question about the "balm in Gilead" (v. 22) is a rhetorical question, used to explore and emphasize the depth of the spiritual and moral crisis that afflicts the people of Israel. A balm in Gilead was a commercial and medicinal reality of that area. In Genesis 37:25 we are told that the caravan of Ishmaelites that were traveling from Gilead to Egypt were carrying, among other items, "gum, balm, and

Jeremiah 8:18–9:1

Theological Perspective

that presumes God is in Zion and the king in Jerusalem. The Christian church engages the world beyond its walls. What happens in the context of the world and its politics and economies shapes us.

The next question ("Why have they provoked me?" v. 19c) makes it clearer that God is the speaker. The community ethos of idolatry creates a divine pathos. Idolatry functions as the evidence that relationship between God and the community has been lost. The relational bond is now so deteriorated that repentance becomes impossible. With this in mind, lament becomes a natural response to the disaster on the horizon. Idolatry generates its own disaster.

Modern idolatry is a slippery item for today's preacher. The category "my poor people" might help identify the divine and human experience of injustice. What are the parallel idolatries of our time, hurtful evidences of the distance between God and human communities? One example may be the scourge of twenty-first-century slavery and genocide, which both give evidence of that distance and wound God's "poor people."

The writer makes the point that the time has come and gone. Harvest and summer would have been good times for salvation, but it did not come (8:20). The tone of repentance we heard earlier in the book is gone. The gospel singer Rev. James Cleveland sings a song that is not politically correct, "It's going to be too late." This idea that it is too late for redemption, for a miracle, for something, is one of the most difficult messages for the North American reader to hear. North American optimism rehearses a metanarrative that presumes there is always a second chance for a happy ending. Harvest and summer would have been good times for salvation, but it did not come. Jeremiah argues that the brokenness is now very much with us.

Despite this strong metanarrative, sometimes reality breaks through. In Sam's family it was Christmas. Sam's dad was an active alcoholic. This day was no different. So almost every Christmas, right after the children's toys were opened, Sam's dad accidentally broke his favorite new toy, not two hours old. In that house the kids learned that toys were always broken. You learned that you could have fun with broken toys. Too late—already brokenness is too much with us for any credible denial.

Verse 21a works in multiple voices. If the prophet is the speaker, then one might surmise that when the people languish, the prophet cannot thrive. If the speaker in verse 21 is God, then could one argue that when the people languish, God cannot thrive? The

Pastoral Perspective

experience with life in typical churches probably would be able to imagine what it was like.

To make matters worse, Josiah was killed in battle and Jehoiakim became king. Jehoiakim did not value the reforms Josiah had initiated, and his lackadaisical approach may have made things worse.

These verses from chapters 8 and 9 are YHWH's lament for the people who are feeling deserted by their God. It is their own behavior that has them trapped, but as anyone who has taken part in a 12-step recovery program can attest, it is hard to identify the rationalizations and excuses that perpetuate destructive habits. Wanting to change destructive behavior does not always produce the means to do so. YHWH hears their desperation and their panic and mourns for them in their agony. YHWH must have abandoned them, they reason, or they would not feel such despair. YHWH asks, "Is there no balm in Gilead? Is there no physician there?" (8:22).

The law in these verses is on stone tablets, not as yet on the hearts of the people. One of the functions of the clergy, the "physicians," was to make sure that the cultic worship practices were observed, sacrifices offered, and tithes paid. Clergy were central to the adjudication process when the law was violated. The people of Israel were charged with examining their own hearts and removing from them any traces of apostasy they found there, but they also were to be taught and guided with regard to their cultic practices.

Because the clergy had abrogated their responsibility, because they were involved in the administration of "cheap grace," the people had no one to tell them the truth. There was no physician available to them. It was as if Gilead, the one region in the land of Israel famous for the balm that closes wounds and keeps them from suppurating, had none for its own people. The temple, with its responsibility for upholding the covenant, was the one place where the people of God were told the unvarnished truth about their behavior and the consequences of their self-interest. Because the temple did not do this, it had failed the people—there was no balm in Gilead that could save the sin-sick soul.

If the cultic practices that anchored the original covenant no longer made a difference to people, if the clergy who presided over the sacrifices and offerings were no longer themselves faithful to the covenant as it was originally conceived, what must it have meant for the nation of Israel? Jeremiah says that if these vital elements no longer effectively instruct or guide and support people who seek to observe the rites and rituals, attitudes and behaviors that represented how

seem to be rhetorical; in verse 19 we hear yet a third voice, obviously that of the Lord ("Why have they provoked *me?*"). Verse 20 apparently uses a proverb to voice the people's sense of hopelessness. The remainder of the passage from verse 21 seems to return again to the speaker of verses 18–19a, referring several more times to "my daughter, my people." Considerable debate exists as to the identity of the speaker(s) in Jeremiah 8:18–9:1. Is it the prophet himself, whose joy has gone (v. 18) and who is pained by the cry and hurt of "my daughter, my people " (8:21–9:1)? Is the prophet assuming the role of personified Jerusalem, who mourns for her inhabitants? Could Jeremiah be speaking for God, whose heart is sick? The preacher's approach to this text will vary somewhat according to which understanding is adopted.

Since it is customarily YHWH who refers to the nation of Israel or Judah as ʿammî, "my people" (e.g., 2:13, 31; 6:14; 7:12) the use of bat-ʿammî is a reason to think that the Lord is speaking through Jeremiah, taking into the divine heart the angst and the hurt of the people of Judah.[2] Alternatively, if one should follow the interpretation that Jeremiah assumes throughout the guise of the city of Jerusalem,[3] the prophet's identification with his people and their city will govern the exposition and application of the text.

Probably the most theologically fruitful interpretation of this passage is one that understands Jeremiah as empathizing with both God and the people. Jeremiah likely felt himself in a very real sense to be caught in the middle between his role as God's spokesperson and the role of the prophets to which less attention is commonly given, namely, that of intercessor for his people (cf. Isa. 37:1–4; Jer. 27:18; Amos 7:2, 5). To identify simultaneously with the betrayed God and the sinful people was a burden under which Jeremiah labored. We can glimpse the strain of this dual role in the so-called confessions of Jeremiah (e.g., 15:15–18; 17:14–18; 18:19–23).

Today's passage amounts to a disputation concerning the correct interpretation of events in Jerusalem and Judah. The immediate literary context, which evinces a military threat (8:14–17), prompts strong consideration that the approach of the foe from the north is what triggers the cry of the people. The sense of the rhetorical questions in verse 19 seems to be that the Judeans find the threat to

2. This is the interpretation adopted by Kathleen O'Connor in her commentary on Jeremiah in the *Oxford Bible Commentary*, ed. John Barton and John Muddiman (Oxford: Oxford University Press, 2001), 497.
3. So Robert P. Carroll, *Jeremiah: A Commentary*, Old Testament Library (Philadelphia: Westminster Press, 1986), 285–86.

resin." The implication of Jeremiah's rhetorical question is that the disease infecting the life of the people is more devastatingly chronic and morbid than can be remedied by physical means. It is a disease of the spirit, the psyche, the soul, and the will.

Perhaps symptoms of medical distress suggested the image to Jeremiah, but his diagnosis was both broader and deeper. It was broader in the sense that it was a diagnosis not of individuals suffering from a pathological condition but of the community as a whole: "Why then has the health of my poor people not been restored?" (v. 22b). Actually, later in Jeremiah 9:3 (beyond the boundary of this lection), he says that "they have grown strong in the land for falsehood, and not for truth." They are proving false about one another and, just as importantly, with one another. Jeremiah is fierce about the religious declension and waywardness of the people and about the foolish political moves of the leaders; but he is equally exercised by the behavior that has destroyed communal integrity.

We may joke and be cynical about leaders who say in so many ways, "I feel your pain," but what is dramatically true of this prophet is that he does feel the pain and extremity of those before whom he is called to be God's witness. "For the hurt of my poor people I am hurt, I mourn, and dismay has taken hold of me" (8:21). The whole passage illuminates the relationship between personal lament and intercession. The drama of the prophetic words of Jeremiah has bequeathed to our language the word "jeremiad," referring to any strong judgmental and uncompromising indictment of a situation or person.

Too often these statements—whether from politicians, pundits, professors, or preachers—sound dismissive and demonizing of those about whom they are addressed. Their very stridency often suggests that the individuals about whom they speak have become mere targets rather than people. In contrast, Jeremiah's words, as severe as they can be, as unpopular as they were, are expressions of lament that make them an act of intercession for the covenant community. This lament encompasses Jeremiah, the people, and those who are responsible for the integrity and vitality of the community. Jeremiah never separates himself from the entire community he is called to address.

There is a deeper mystery about intercession that is suggested by Jeremiah's identification with his community in lamentation. He experiences within his spirit not only the actual distress that has come upon the people; more importantly, he is burdened

Jeremiah 8:18—9:1

Theological Perspective

brokenness of the people is our brokenness. The hurt heals, only to leave a visible and visceral scar. This is a brokenness from which one never fully recovers. When we separate ourselves from God, we are broken, hence brokenness. God through the prophet expresses a profound solidarity with the beloved, poor people. After the statement of solidarity, the speaker returns to the language of mourning found in chapter 4. Now, in addition to the mourning, dismay has taken hold (8:21b).

The prophet asks whether there is a balm in Gilead, a place known for the tree that made a soothing ointment, a balm. The Gospel of John makes the point that God has not left us bereft of hope (see, for instance, John 14:18–20). The old gospel song begins with this Jeremiah text but answers the question affirmatively: "There is a balm in Gilead." All of these things would encourage one to construe this as a rhetorical question, with "yes" as the appropriate answer. However, the prophet seems not to think so, and you and I have our doubts. In fact, to some degree, we must recognize that when our reading completely takes away the brokenness this passage describes then our interpretation robs the passage of its poignant power. North American interpreters in particular must be careful at this point. There is no balm in Gilead to undo the near genocide of Native peoples in Canada and the United States. There is no healing from the Holocaust, ethnic cleansing in eastern Europe and Africa, to name but a few tragedies.

Because there is no easy answer, no cheap grace for the healing of God's poor people, Jeremiah ends the lament with a cry. He pines for more capacity to grieve on behalf of the slain. The ethos of idolatry set in motion the expression of pathos, divine and prophetic, set forth in this chapter. Jeremiah bids today's reader to pause for a moment and observe God's grief and God's love for the poor people of God.

STEPHEN BRECK REID

Pastoral Perspective

the covenant shaped their lives, YHWH will abandon that covenant and replace it with a new one.

People today are no less lost than they were at the time of Jeremiah, and many times their quandary is precisely the same. Self-interest blinds people to the harm done to others. Greed flourishes because insecurity reigns. Fear drives people into rigid defensive postures. No one recognizes her or his own role in turning away from God toward preliminary concerns, the "foreign idols" that have replaced their Deity.

However, someone is responsible for interrupting their misapprehensions, someone has to be able to explain why they are unable to receive from their false gods the comfort, healing, and peace of mind that come from God. What has happened to those who are charged with transmission of the sacred to the lost and bewildered populace that so yearns for God?

Jeremiah's questions are as pertinent to today's church as they were the day they were first recorded. How do the rites and rituals of the church mediate the sacred to the people that it serves? What makes the church meaningful in contemporary society? How does the church teach people about the way God makes and keeps human life human? How can clergy guide people in their decision-making processes so that the principles and precepts of Christian teachings are included? When a critique of a behavior, way of thinking, or decision is necessary, how can clergy make an effective correction?

Often congregations desire justification of what they are currently doing. When they decide to support a mission project and provide money and prayers for it, they expect unconditioned praise. Unwelcome is the voice of the pastor who suggests that the project may not be the best choice for the recipients, or that needs in the church's neighborhood are equally grave but remain unaddressed. The "false prophets" who uphold the status quo often are better heard than the prophets who hold congregations to account. The question remains, "Are there no physicians here?"

SHARON PEEBLES BURCH

Exegetical Perspective

their city hard to fathom in light of their theology. Their cry questions the reliability of their religious traditions, which celebrate King YHWH's presence in Zion and YHWH's defense of Jerusalem (Pss. 48; 102:12–17; 149:2).

The Lord's retort, "Why have they provoked me?" interrupts the people's shallow musings. The people of Judah had been forgetful of YHWH (2:5–8, 31), presumptuous about YHWH's care or indulgence (3:4–5; 5:12), and/or heedless of the divine warnings (6:17). Jeremiah 8:15 suggests that the false prophets of "peace" had beguiled the people into expecting that all is well (cf. also 6:13–14). The Lord *is* in Zion—with implications quite different from the people's expectations. The tradition expresses a sound theology, but the people have bought into a gospel of "cheap grace," expecting God's protection and deliverance, at no cost to the recipients.

The people seem to resume their lamenting in verse 20 as if the word about their provocations of God had not even been uttered! The content of verse 20 is likely a proverb current in Jeremiah's day that would be used by those who in despair concluded that they had reached the point at which no satisfactory deliverance is possible for them.

When Jeremiah speaks of the "hurt" that he suffers from the "hurt" of the people (8:21), the Hebrew term ("brokenness," NASB) is one used of the breaking of pottery. It is a hurt that cries out for healing (see v. 22), and from the time of Moses the Israelites had celebrated YHWH as the one who could heal (see Exod. 15:26). Jeremiah himself had preached that the Lord promised to heal the faithlessness of the people who would return (3:22); but too often the people looked to the theological snake oil of those who "have healed the wound of my people lightly, saying, 'Peace, peace,' when there is no peace" (6:14; 8:11 RSV). The "weeping prophet" longs for his head and eyes to produce enough tears adequately to express his (and God's) grief over this circumstance.

GEORGE W. RAMSEY

Homiletical Perspective

by their refusal of insight, recognition, contrition, and repentance. In this action of his spirit, he takes their sins upon himself lamenting *on behalf of* and *in the place of* the community. The pitch of his untiring distress at Israel's situation within the world and before God manifests the act in which the acknowledgment of God's right in judging is and can be the only source for Israel's salvation and healing. Jeremiah's suffering "embodies" this. It is not inappropriate to ponder the possibility that Jeremiah's suffering is a sign of how God suffers at the refusal of the people to acknowledge their dereliction and disloyalty. In this, the words and life of this prophet begin to prepare us to understand a life that in its sorrow and "acquaintance with grief" (Isa. 53:3 RSV) both judges and reclaims the world as God's own.

Being prophetic is a matter of speaking truth to power, but it is much more than that. It is also a matter of speaking truth to suffering, to weakness, to laziness, and to failure to take responsibility. The list does not stop there. Of course, it is also a "speaking" that involves acting and engaging those with whom one is in contention. In fact, it speaks and acts truth as an act of solidarity with the adversaries or the recipients of the indictment. We have seen unforgettable examples of this in our times. On the world stage, there are Nelson Mandela and Desmond Tutu and the many they represent in the story of South Africa's journey out of apartheid. They "proclaimed" that apartheid was both a social and spiritual wrong. They also spoke and acted, in the face of cruel and ferocious opposition, out of a hope for a future that included both the victim and victimizer. Their actions and suffering enacted a hope that required both "truth and reconciliation."

DWIGHT M. LUNDGREN

Psalm 79:1-9

¹O God, the nations have come into your inheritance;
    they have defiled your holy temple;
    they have laid Jerusalem in ruins.
²They have given the bodies of your servants
    to the birds of the air for food,
    the flesh of your faithful to the wild animals of the earth.
³They have poured out their blood like water
    all around Jerusalem,
    and there was no one to bury them.
⁴We have become a taunt to our neighbors,
    mocked and derided by those around us.

⁵How long, O Lᴏʀᴅ? Will you be angry forever?
    Will your jealous wrath burn like fire?

Theological Perspective

This psalm is often called a "national lament," in which full expression to God is given by the psalmist on behalf of the nation in the face of some national calamity. It has traditionally been associated with the destruction of Jerusalem and the desecration of the temple, which rank in the annals of the Jewish people as disasters par excellence. The events were remembered on various occasions.

Beyond the specific historical contexts, whatever they may be, the psalm is a deep expression of prayer in the midst of devastation, when an "enemy" has wreaked destruction and the hardest of harms has to be endured. The psalm describes the desolation (vv. 1–4) and then breaks into a prayer for forgiveness and help (vv. 5–9).

Desolation and Destruction. The descriptions of the results of the terror visited by the "nations" (v. 1; RSV, "heathen") upon Israel are among the most devastating that can be imagined for the nation in covenant relationship with God. When the psalmist speaks of invading God's "inheritance"—which usually means God's people but here means the land (Jerusalem and the temple)—the emphasis is on the fact that this is God's possession (v. 1). This makes the defiling all the worse, since this is an affront to God. God's city and God's temple have been laid in

Pastoral Perspective

One of the lectionary's great gifts is that it sometimes leads Christian congregations into places they would rather not venture in their worship—places where opportunities for profound transformation often await. Psalm 79 is a communal lament arising from Israel's historical experience of Babylonian invasion and devastation.

On its surface, the psalm may seem light-years removed from the everyday experiences of most North American Christians, presenting the preacher or worship leader with such challenges to make pastoral connections that they may choose simply to ignore this lection. Avoidance is a common practice with lament psalms. Lament psalms are practically absent from Protestant worship, even though they make up approximately one-third of the Psalter. A cursory examination of popular publications for worship leaders or lists of the most commonly used contemporary worship songs turns up a great deal of emphasis on celebration and joyful praise. Church publicity often leaves the impression that the Sunday morning liturgical experience requires a polite posture and an attitude of cheerful contentment. What kind of response might a congregation receive if it advertised a 10:30 a.m. Lament Service each week?

However, a little reflection can unearth multiple contexts in which laments like Psalm 79 might

⁶Pour out your anger on the nations
    that do not know you,
and on the kingdoms
    that do not call on your name.
⁷For they have devoured Jacob
    and laid waste his habitation.

⁸Do not remember against us the iniquities of our ancestors;
    let your compassion come speedily to meet us,
    for we are brought very low.
⁹Help us, O God of our salvation,
    for the glory of your name;
deliver us, and forgive our sins,
    for your name's sake.

Exegetical Perspective

This psalm is a national lament concerning the havoc brought by foreign invaders to Jerusalem. The specific cause of its lament was probably the destruction of Jerusalem and its temple in 587 BCE by the Babylonians.[1] In just the first three verses, the psalm vividly describes three horrors: invaders have defiled the temple, laid Jerusalem in ruins, and left the bodies of the dead in the open with "no one to bury them."[2] If the lament was initially specific, though, later it was probably sung out on certain days of fasting to help Israel mourn other national devastations (see Zech. 7:2–7; 8:18–19).[3]

Formally, Psalm 79 follows the general pattern of laments, especially resembling Psalms 44 and 74. There are three sections. The first section (vv. 1–4) consists of a lamentation over the ruin wrought by an enemy. The second section (vv. 5–12) is the psalmist's prayer on behalf of the afflicted nation. The third section (v. 13) is an expression of the people's faith in God.

---

1. If this is true, the "kingdoms that do not call on your name" (v. 6) are probably the Edomites, the Ammonites, and the Moabites (Mitchell Dahood, *Psalms 51–100*, Anchor Bible [Garden City, NY: Doubleday, 1968], 251).
2. The proper interment of the dead was vitally important to ancient Near Eastern people. The inability to bury slain fellow Israelites was a crushing tragedy that apparently lingered in the national memory (Dahood, 251).
3. E.g., 1 Maccabees applies Ps. 79:2–3 to the slaughter of sixty pious Jews in Jerusalem during the Maccabean wars of the second century BCE (Dahood, 250).

Homiletical Perspective

People and communities who have been traumatized by nonsensical, brutal violence might find the sentiments expressed in Psalm 79 familiar. This psalm communicates a feeling of violation so deep that the very breach itself has spiritual implications. Indeed, some of those who experienced it cried out to God with penetrating theological questions like, "How long, O LORD? Will you be angry forever? Will your jealous wrath burn like fire?" (v. 5). Interestingly enough, these questions point not to the possibility of divine injustice, but to the failures of God's people to live in obedience to God's covenant stipulations. The violence experienced by the nation is perceived as divine punishment.

The psalmist—and ostensibly those who sang this song in worship—was just as concerned about YHWH's reputation as she or he was about the violence visited upon YHWH's people. It was YHWH's inheritance and holy temple that were breached and defiled (v. 1); and it was YHWH's servants (v. 2) who were devoured by scavengers and left unburied (v. 3). Such a perspective might be difficult for contemporary congregations to hear, since it is rare for preachers and congregants in America to link covenantal theology to global politics and military action.

This psalm compels the contemporary reader to stretch beyond personal considerations and ask

Psalm 79:1-9

Theological Perspective

ruins. A worse fate could not be imagined. John Calvin called it a "hideous overthrow."[1]

Compounding this is the leaving of the corpses of the dead Israelites unburied, a final indignity and disgrace (vv. 2–3). The resulting damage leaves Israel to be taunted and mocked by the surrounding nations, which do not worship the God of Israel (v. 4).

We may try to lift the experience of the psalmist with national destruction into our own times and own nations when we think of attacks by terrorists, most drastically, the attack of September 11, 2001. However, our contexts are different. For the psalmist, this destruction is the worst imaginable: desolation and destruction of all that was most central to the life of the nation and to the outward symbols of the nation's relationship to God. The city and the temple were emblematic of God's presence to the people; now both of these are in ruins.

So we find here a theological issue: whether and how God's presence with the people can be maintained when the outward expressions of this relationship have been destroyed.

How Long, O Lord? This psalm, then, is an honest expression for the times in life when our "foundations" seem destroyed. God had chosen the people of Israel for an "inheritance," and now they are left desolate. It is not a far stretch to apply this to personal circumstances in times of tragedy and sorrow. Devastation can take a number of forms, and it is part of human life to experience desolations that can feel as though they will leave us completely destroyed. The theological problem is heightened for Christians when we feel as though God has not helped us, has "permitted" these evils to come upon us. Perhaps these experiences will attack the very foundations of our Christian faith. When we look to God to provide for our safety and comfort, and these are attacked, our faith itself may be shaken.

The psalmist's honest expression is given voice in the cry "How long, O LORD?" This is a prayer that is also on the lips of the pious. "Will you be angry forever?" (v. 5) We feel God has deserted us or handed us over to destruction, so it is natural also to pray that God will vindicate: "Pour out your anger on the nations" (v. 6).

Prayer for Forgiveness and Help. In the face of all this, there is only one way open, theologically speaking: One must pray for forgiveness and help.

1. John Calvin, *Commentary on Psalms*, 79:1.

Pastoral Perspective

appropriately be employed. For instance, the descriptions of carnage in verses 1–3 are as graphic as any media reports of what was happening at the World Trade Center on September 11, 2001: "They have laid Jerusalem in ruins. They have given the bodies of your servants to the birds of the air for food. . . . They have poured out their blood like water all around." These powerful images evoke the horror and heartache experienced in such moments, not only in North America but around the world.

Consider a congregation beset by sudden tragedy: the death of several youth group members in a van accident; disease claiming the life of a young, vibrant congregational leader; or a clergy sexual abuse scandal, to name some not entirely uncommon examples. Expressions such as "Let your compassion come speedily to meet us, for we are brought very low" (v. 8) or "We have become a taunt to our neighbors, mocked and derided by those around us" (v. 4) might seem very appropriate for congregations facing such devastating and disorienting circumstances.

This text raises theodicy questions, which are the most deeply pastoral of all: Where is God when humans suffer? Does God hear and care? Is God impotent to respond after all? These questions dwell in the hearts and minds of many who gather for worship in Christian congregations week after week. Where do they find opportunities to voice these concerns? What resources do churches offer to assist them in interpreting life's tragic circumstances in order to live genuinely, not trivially, into Christian hope?

News media reports indicated that in the days and weeks after September 11, 2001, North American churches were packed with worshipers who came to express their awful distress and confounding questions. In many cases, they had no idea where to begin or how to articulate their deep bewilderment. J. David Pleins says that in contexts of profound social disruption, when the circumstances threaten to close off communication between the people and God, the communal lament psalms may help worshiping communities to open a dialogue with God in the midst of despair and rage. If, as Pleins says, the communal lament psalms are "conceived of as discussions between the community and God," then they can help the community in its disorientation and fear to "breach the wall of silence that suffering can build between God and God's people."[1]

Walter Brueggemann makes three observations about communal laments like Psalm 79. First, the laments show Israel "giving authentic expression [to]

Exegetical Perspective

The psalm features several main themes. The theme of taunts (vv. 4, 12) runs like an undercurrent throughout and may well have been the motivation for its authorship. The first three verses articulate the physical violence done to the people. Verse 4 lifts up the experience of taunting as an additional source of their suffering, a literal adding of insult to injury. One's reputation in the community was greatly valued in the honor and shame cultures of the day. Says Proverbs 3:35, "The wise will inherit honor, but stubborn fools, disgrace." To be taunted in that social context was the emotional equivalent of physical torture.

The question "how long?" is a frequent expression of lament in the Psalter, but it is one that contains a kernel of faith. "How long?" can refer to God's actions or the people's sufferings. How long is God going to take to deliver the people? (6:3); how long is God going to forget God's people? (13:1); how long are they going to have to bear pain in their souls? (13:2); how long is God going to look on without acting? (35:17); how long are their foes going to scoff? (74:10); how long is God going to be angry with the people's prayers? (80:4); how long is God going to show partiality to the wicked? (82:2); how long is God going to hide and be angry? (89:46); how long are the people going to be taunted? (89:50); how long are the wicked going to exult? (94:3). Throughout this litany, psalmists assume help will come; they just want to know why it is taking so long.

The psalmist's pleadings take other forms, too. Verse 8, which the NRSV translates "Do not remember against us," could also be rendered "Do not record it to our debit" or "Do not act upon." The psalmist is pleading with God to meet the people with compassion, not to sever his relationship with them. In verse 9 the psalmist asks God to forgive the people's sins with two appeals to the divine honor, "for the glory of your name," and "for your name's sake."

There the lectionary text concludes, leaving out verses 10–13 of the psalm. Left out is the psalmist's plea to God to stop the oppression and avenge the wrongs done to the people. The psalmist expresses once again the pain of being taunted (vv. 10, 12), reminds God of the groans of the prisoners (v. 11), and asks that the people be avenged in some dramatic, public way (v. 12).

The psalmist wants God to feel the anger he feels at being taunted and to take action to avenge the wrong. Insults and blasphemies from neighboring peoples were apparently a frequent trial endured by Israel (see Ps. 89:50–51). In Psalm 79:12 the psalmist asks God to "return sevenfold into the bosom of our

Homiletical Perspective

herself or himself questions about the spiritual commitments and connections of the community and the nation. Are there indeed consequences for nations who claim to love and follow YHWH in Jesus' name but whose public policies and global practices fail to reflect the standards of the divine-human covenant? Another way of approaching the theology embedded in this psalm would be to ask oneself whether it remains tenable. Do we, as God's covenant people, still believe that national calamity of whatever sort is tied to human behavior, that indeed there is a covenant between God and people that can be violated through chronic disobedience?

The psalm also stretches the preacher's and congregation's customary emotional range. The imagery in Psalm 79 is horrific, but it is not unfamiliar. Most people see such images on the nightly news, at movie theaters, and even in their own living rooms. Notwithstanding those facts, a preacher may decide that the images communicated in Psalm 79 are too gory for Sunday services, although it is the images that make this lamenting prayer so poignant. The blood drying in the streets, the sight and stench of decaying bodies, the whirring and buzzing of flies, are the real-life stuff of communal sorrow. They are also the stuff so many people on the planet have experienced—especially, in the modern world, people of color.

The psalm takes a surprising turn in verses 6 and 7 when the writer-worshiper asks YHWH to turn the divine anger on the unbelieving "nations" because of what they have done to the people of YHWH. Christians who have internalized the Golden Rule ("You shall love your neighbor as [you love] yourself," Mark 12:31) and the standard for forgiveness found in the Sermon on the Mount ("If you forgive others their trespasses, your heavenly Father will also forgive you," Matt. 6:14) will find the vengeful sentiments expressed in these verses difficult to accept as Scripture. The preacher may wish to ask openly whether such prayer is exemplary, whether it rightly reflects God's character, whether God would hear such brutally honest prayers.

The remainder of the psalm is a powerful mixture of petition and confession. The theme of revenge continues to emerge (vv. 10, 12), so there is no escaping the fact that the writer saw God as a God of vengeance and that the *lex talionis* (law of retaliation)—"eye for eye, tooth for tooth" (Exod. 21:24; Lev. 24:20; Deut. 19:21)—was an acceptable social and spiritual standard. Notwithstanding, the fervency of the confessions and petitions is potent. The preacher would want to capture the emotions that

Psalm 79:1-9

Theological Perspective

The psalmist acknowledges that sin has been part of the nation's experience. There are "the iniquities of our ancestors" (v. 8). The psalmist prays not to be held to account for these, but they are confessed. They are confessed, and God's compassion is sought (cf. Ps. 51:1).

The prayer for forgiveness is our first theological response in the midst of the devastations that can engulf us. We do not look for a direct "causality" between our sin and destructive things that happen outside our control. The relationship between "bad things" and "good people" is one we all recognize— "bad things" may happen to people who do not explicitly "cause" them by some direct sinful action. So we turn away from this type of retributive theology.

At the same time, human sin is part of the human story, even for Christians. When we face difficulties, even of great proportions, we do confess our sin and plead for God's compassion. This is our only hope. We do not "deserve" the compassion, and confessing our sins does not "entitle" us to it; but we honestly admit before God our sinfulness, and because of our faith, we dare to pray, "Let your compassion come speedily to meet us" (v. 8).

From this confession of sin, we ask, "Help us, O God of our salvation, for the glory of your name; deliver us, and forgive our sins, for your name's sake" (v. 9). The people of Israel pray to be saved for the glory of God's name, which is at stake in their obvious and public humiliation. There are, then, two related foci to the prayer: God's reputation and Israel's health. The psalmist knows salvation and deliverance are found only in the God who has saved and who will save. The only plea is for God's glory. Calvin makes the theological point that "sinners are not reconciled to God by satisfactions or by the merit of good works, but by a free and an unmerited forgiveness."[2]

At times when all foundations seem destroyed, we are left to trust only in God's compassion, forgiveness, and salvation. We abandon all attempts at self-help and cast ourselves totally on the God who saves us.

DONALD K. MCKIM

Pastoral Perspective

the real experiences of life," affirming the appropriateness, even the necessity, for contemporary worshipers to remain in the real world, rather than to withdraw into some otherworldly "religious" realm where all is sweetness and light. Second, passages like Psalm 79 show that Israel affirmed life in all its contingency, regarding the tragic *and* the joyful as occasions to sort out their faith. This may include questioning God's power or fidelity, but it also presents opportunities to express their expectations of God *to* God while attempting to reformulate their understandings of how God works in the world.

Finally, the lament psalms show that biblical faith is dialogic. That is, the psalmist expresses Israel's intention to deal with life's hurt, betrayal, and pain in God's presence: "Israel knows that one need not fake it or be polite or pretend in the divine presence, nor need one face the hurts alone."[2] The interpreter may need to confront the idea, assumed by many Christians and affirmed in the psalm, that God is responsible for the evils that beset God's creation. Nevertheless, as Brueggemann states, the accusatory tone of many lament psalms does not obscure the fact that such strenuous lamentation is an "act of faith."[3] Psalm 79 ultimately expresses the expectation that God will respond to human suffering compassionately, righting the wrongs that have been suffered.

Worship does not always need to make a congregation "feel good." The pastoral goal in the face of profound social disruption should be to give voice to the community's deep sense of loss, despair, and disorientation. Beyond those moments of extraordinary social and communal crisis, however, many gathered for worship every Sunday experience crises of health, conscience, and faith. The glibness of much contemporary North American worship strikes these strugglers as shallow and inauthentic, straining as it does to nurture elation, no matter what the circumstance. Joy, exuberant thanksgiving, and firm assurances of God's sovereignty are all appropriate in worship, certainly; but the lament psalms should not be passed over lightly; they offer Christian communities resources to enter into the depths of human experience, and opportunities for profound transformation.

TIMOTHY HESSEL-ROBINSON

---

2. John Calvin, *Commentary on Psalms*, 79:9.

1. J. David Pleins, *The Psalms: Songs of Tragedy, Justice, and Hope* (Maryknoll, NY: Orbis Books, 1993), 38–39.
2. Walter Brueggemann, *The Psalms and the Life of Faith*, ed. Patrick D. Miller (Minneapolis: Fortress Press, 1995), 67–68.
3. Ibid., 76.

neighbors the taunts with which they taunted you, O Lord!" This reference to the fold in the outer garment that overhangs the girdle and served as a pocket is intimate and conveys the psalmist's desire that the enemy experience the pain of being taunted very close to home. The psalm closes with the promise that, if these conditions are met, the people will praise God now and in the future (v. 13).

The lectionary's cut of this passage denies the preacher a few crucial homiletical moves. One is to show respect for the deep pain that motivates a psalm like this. A second is to consider the theological conviction on which this psalm is built: that when we suffer, it is God's punishment for our sins. A third is to help the congregation imagine a positive response to this painful situation. That involves setting the psalm in its canonical context in the Psalter and beyond. That involves reflecting on what this psalm implies about the character of God and what the Psalter teaches us about who God is and how God encourages us to pray in times of deep lament. That involves asserting our freedom to express our anguish and our anger in the context of God's forgiveness and faithfulness.

Preachers will want to extend this reading and open themselves and their congregations to the full scope of the psalm. The lectionary amputates a beautiful and important limb when it cuts off this psalm at verse 9. They say that when you have a limb amputated, you still feel its pain. We need to probe that pain to preach this psalm.

ALYCE M. MCKENZIE

lay in back of those elements of the psalm. "Make Afghanistan into a parking lot! Blast away!" These vengeful words were heard even in churches around New York City in the weeks after 9/11. Memory of recent events has yielded a kind of pathos that can be captured only by lament. Underneath the lament is an earnest desire for YHWH's vindication, the people's deliverance, and the utter destruction of the enemy. There is also a feeling of powerlessness.

The powerlessness felt by the writer, and perhaps the worshipers, also results in hope rather than despair, because there is still faith in YHWH's capacity to bring victory out of defeat. The evidence for this assertion is found in verse 13. The psalm concludes on a note of praise, but this praise is conditional. If God punishes the perpetrators of violence, then the people will praise God.

This psalm possesses powerful preaching potential during times of national or even regional violence and tragedy, when people are prone to call God's power and presence into question. The psalmist is attempting to interpret the national experience of violent invasion theologically and simultaneously asserting that the people of YHWH, not YHWH, were responsible for the tragedy—hence the confessional nature of the psalm.

Psalm 79 also teaches the community of faith how to keep faith during times of inexplicable violence and turmoil. YHWH can be trusted to do what YHWH does—judge the wicked, forgive the sinner, deliver the faithful. YHWH is worthy of praise for acts of justice, mercy, and goodness.

Finally, the most powerful witness of Psalm 79 is the writer's defense of and concern for YHWH's integrity. Such an effort and attitude exemplify a deep and abiding love and commitment to YHWH that is rare to this day. The danger here, however, is that the desire for vengeance is coupled with love of YHWH. An enduring thirst for vengeance does not reflect the God we see in the words of Isaiah or of Jesus. Perhaps the best sermons on Psalm 79 will allow the honest imprecations of its author and the gathered community to be an honest first stage to the longer divine process of transformation.

MARK A. LOMAX

1 Timothy 2:1-7

¹First of all, then, I urge that supplications, prayers, intercessions, and thanksgivings be made for everyone, ²for kings and all who are in high positions, so that we may lead a quiet and peaceable life in all godliness and dignity. ³This is right and is acceptable in the sight of God our Savior, ⁴who desires everyone to be saved and to come to the knowledge of the truth. ⁵For

there is one God;
  there is also one mediator between God and humankind,
  Christ Jesus, himself human,
⁶ who gave himself a ransom for all

—this was attested at the right time. ⁷For this I was appointed a herald and an apostle (I am telling the truth, I am not lying), a teacher of the Gentiles in faith and truth.

Theological Perspective

In this passage, Paul used the repeated Greek phrase that is translated "everyone" to emphasize the universal nature of the Christian faith. This reflection will examine Paul's three uses of this phrase to address two issues: (1) prayer and (2) salvation.

Prayer and Intercession. In verse 1, Paul uses the phrase "for everyone" (*hyper pantōn anthrōpōn*, Gk. v. 2) to describe who should be the focus of Timothy's prayers and intercessions. In verses 3–4, Paul explains that Timothy should pray for everyone so that he might mirror God's own desires for humankind. Thus, Paul first articulates prayer as an act of participation with the salvific will of God on behalf of all persons.

Second, this passage points us toward the theological basis for prayer and intercession: the mediation of Christ. The word "intercession," *deēseis*, is derived from a verb with the meaning "to have the good fortune to be admitted to an audience [with a king]."[1] Verse 5 spells out the basis for this good fortune: "there is also one mediator between God and humankind, Christ Jesus." James Torrance and Hans Urs von Balthasar both point out the centrality of

Pastoral Perspective

"I pledge allegiance to the flag of the United States of America and to the republic for which it stands, one nation under God, indivisible, with liberty and justice for all." Americans say these words often without thinking. "With liberty and justice for *all*." The writer of 1 Timothy exhorts Timothy to lead his community in praying for *all*. Pray for *all*, even *all* in authority, for God wants to save *all* and Christ Jesus gave himself as a ransom for *all*.

The Christian community of Timothy's time was persecuted for proclaiming the new revelation of God in Christ Jesus. They were not an accepted part of the social fabric in Gentile or Jewish communities. How much easier it would have been, under the threat of persecution, to withdraw from society to live a "quiet and peaceable" life! Yet they desired the opposite. They wanted to live fully within their world in order to fulfill the proclamation of God's radical desire of salvation for *all* and Christ Jesus' accomplishment of that salvation through giving himself as ransom for *all*.

Pragmatically, praying for good government may have helped them survive, by promoting acceptance of Christianity as part of the social fabric. With acceptance, the Christian community could prosper and flourish within the security of "quiet and peaceable" living. They would have the stability to live in

---

1. Fritz Rienecker and Cleon Rogers, *Linguistic Key to the Greek New Testament* (Grand Rapids: Zondervan, 1980), 618.

Exegetical Perspective

After presenting Paul in the previous verses as an example of faithful service, the author turns to give instructions concerning prayer. The earlier verses about Paul serve to underline the apostolic authority for these instructions, which are part of a larger collection of advice in the main body of the letter. Cast in the form of pastoral advice to Timothy, these exhortations function as a manual of order for the church, covering such topics as guidelines for how men and women should pray (and the role of women in the church), qualifications for bishops and deacons, and advice for widows, elders, and slaves.

The instructions in 2:1–7 stress the universality or inclusiveness of Christian prayer. Readers are exhorted to pray "for everyone," including "all who are in high positions," because God desires to save "everyone" and Christ gave himself a ransom "for all." Some interpreters have suggested that this emphasis on inclusiveness reflects an intentional corrective to gnostic attitudes that one should pray for only certain people (those in possession of special knowledge, or "gnosis"); others have proposed that the author was exhorting the readers to pray for individuals in their community who were teaching false doctrines and encouraging errant lifestyles.

Regardless of the precipitating factors, the author rightly recognizes that Christian compassion,

Homiletical Perspective

Good grief! Not another sermon on prayer! Last year, preacher, in your nine-part series on the Lord's Prayer, you examined prayer from every angle and said that Jesus' word on the subject is the best word. Now, these words to Timothy. *Tell me, at least, that this is not going to be a series!*

Could that be one of the barriers to a text like this for our attentive flock? Our congregations know they should pray, they are *for* prayer, and many actually spend a lot of time doing it. Their eyelids get heavy, however, when you announce *another* sermon or class on prayer. There is great pressure for the preacher/teacher to overcome the "been-there, done-that" look on her parishioners' faces.

Paul seems sympathetic. Paul may have known that Timothy had gotten a lot of previous instruction about prayer; so he goes easy on him. He cuts to the chase, which may give us a clue for our sermon. Pray often. Pray for everybody. Prayer is good. Prayer pleases God. Paul does not tell Timothy how to do it or describe its mechanics, or even show off with a polished example. Like the athletic shoe commercial, he simply underscores the need for Timothy to *just do it.*

Paul approaches the topic more like plumber than poet. He is looking to get the job done, making practical connections so that Timothy's ministry will not get clogged by less essential things. What is essential

1 Timothy 2:1-7

Theological Perspective

Christ's mediation in the movement of prayer.[2] Prayer is not something we perform in our own autonomous will. Rather, like intercession, prayer is an act resulting from the good fortune that Christ intercedes on our behalf (Heb. 6:20; 7:25–28; 8:1–6).

Third, prayer turns people from anger and argument (v. 8) to leading quiet and peaceable lives (v. 2) that witness to God's salvation. In summary, this passage describes prayer and intercession as (a) participation in God's providential care "for everyone," (b) acts made possible by the mediation of Christ, and (c) a transforming reality for those who pray.

Providence and Salvation. Paul uses the phrase "everyone" a second time in verse 4, when explaining that his former instruction to pray for everyone is right because God desires that all persons (*pantas anthrōpous*)] receive salvation and come to knowledge of truth. God's plan for universal salvation seems to be further expounded in the third "everyone" of verse 6, in which Paul says that Christ gave himself as a ransom on behalf of all persons (*hyper pantōn*). While verse 4 emphasizes God's *desire* to save all persons, verse 6 points to the *accomplishment* of that will through the work of Christ. In the history of the church, these verses have raised an important question relating to God's salvific will of God: *Who are the recipients of God's salvation?* We will highlight two debates that have been significant for modern Protestants.

First, the question of God's salvific will was central to the conflicts between the strict Calvinists and the Arminians that took place in seventeenth-century Holland. The strict Calvinists argued that God, by divine decree, elected some persons for salvation and some for reprobation. They also argued for limited atonement: "it was the will of God, that Christ by the blood of the cross . . . should effectually redeem . . . all those, and only those, who were from eternity chosen."[3] So how could they explain the verses in this passage? John Calvin himself interpreted the *pantas anthrōpous* to be "classes of men, not men as individuals." In other words, he said that God desires the salvation of men from all classes, from rulers to peasants. Unfortunately, there is little textual evidence for this interpretation, but by holding to it,

Pastoral Perspective

"godliness and dignity" (v. 2), which would empower their proclamation of God's love for all. Theologically, they would be strengthened in their faith by learning to pray even for those who persecuted them. As John Chrysostom wrote just a few centuries later, "No one can feel hatred towards those for whom he prays."[1]

In contrast to our early Christian ancestors, Christians today have been part of the fabric of Western society for centuries. Some have suggested that the majority of American Christians have lived "a quiet and peaceable life" for way too long, and that if we truly wanted to live in "godliness and dignity," we would be turning society upside down with the values of radical love and liberation that Jesus preached, rather than living "peaceably." However we might interpret the call to live in "godliness and dignity," 1 Timothy's urging to pray for *all* calls our congregations out of their provincialism and isolation. It calls our congregations to consider the radical implications of sharing God's desire for the salvation of *all*.

James Dunn writes that the

> universalism [of 1 Timothy] inevitably involves a fair degree of openness to the other and acceptance of the other in terms broader than one's own. . . . Any theological system that turns its back on universalism . . . postulates either a less generous God or a less omnipotent God than I Timothy envisions.[2]

The act of imagining that generous, omnipotent God will expand, enlarge, and transform our parishioners' image of God. This God is more challenging than the reassuring, safe, shoulder-to-cry-on God they may come seeking each Sunday. This can be a God of controversy and confrontation. This God stretches us beyond our comfort zones and calls us to love in surprising situations.

This God calls conservative evangelicals to pray for their liberal brothers and sisters and vice versa! Democrats in our congregations are called to pray for Republicans! Those who are upset about change in the church they have loved and served for years are called to pray for those who find the new pastor's leadership cutting edge and prophetic. Those who are champing at the bit to sell the church building

2. James Torrance, *Worship, Community and the Triune God of Grace* (Downers Grove, IL: InterVarsity Press, 1996), 43–67; Hans Urs von Balthasar, *Prayer* (San Francisco: Ignatius Press, 1955), 51–66.

3. From the Canons of Dort, English text found in R. L. Ferm, ed., *Readings in the History of Christian Thought* (New York: Holt, Rinehart & Winston, 1964), 402. The Calvin quote following is from *Institutes of the Christian Religion*, ed. John McNeill (Philadelphia: Westminster Press, 1960), 3.24.16.

1. Thomas C. Oden, *First and Second Timothy and Titus*, Interpretation series (Louisville, KY: John Knox Press, 1989), 90.

2. James D. G. Dunn, "I Timothy 2:1–7, God's Concern Is for Everyone," in *New Interpreter's Bible*, vol. 11, ed. Leander Keck (Nashville: Abingdon Press, 2000), 799–800.

especially as expressed in prayer, should know no bounds. In encouraging prayer, the author uses four different words: "supplications, prayers, intercessions, and thanksgivings." Whereas the terms are not exact synonyms, no distinction among the terms should be forced. The writer has piled term upon term as a way of emphasizing the breadth of Christian prayer.

As a specific example of the comprehensiveness of Christian prayer, the writer exhorts the readers to include the emperor and other political authorities ("kings and all who are in high positions," v. 2) in their prayers. Prayer *for* the emperor is different from prayer *to* the emperor, the latter a practice affiliated with the imperial cult. The Jews had made this distinction as well, offering sacrifices in the temple in Jerusalem on behalf of the emperor, but not to the emperor. If 1 Timothy was indeed directed to the Christian community in Ephesus (as implied in 1:3), this instruction would be particularly appropriate, because the imperial cult was especially strong in Ephesus, which contained several temples to Rome and the emperors.

Christians then (as well as now) faced a major dilemma: to what extent could they be involved in the culture and society to which they belonged without compromising their Christian faith? According to the author of Revelation, any participation in the imperial cult was unacceptable for Christians, an attitude that could be described as "Christ against culture," to use the well-known category of the twentieth-century theologian and ethicist H. Richard Niebuhr. The author of Revelation portrayed the emperor as the epitome of evil, the great beast that was to be resisted at all costs. The author of 1 Timothy, however, takes a less rigid, more accommodating position, exhorting Christians to pray for their rulers, including the emperor. Throughout the Pastoral Epistles, the writer is concerned with adapting Christian ideals to the larger society. The rules for Christian behavior, family life, and even conduct of church leaders are couched in terminology that endorses certain cultural values and norms.

The stated reason why Christians should pray for their rulers is practical: "that we may lead a quiet and peaceable life in all godliness and dignity" (v. 2). Godliness (*eusebeia*) and dignity (*semnotēs*), terms used frequently in the Pastorals, occur rarely in the remainder of the New Testament. Godliness (or piety) is a common component of inscriptions and virtue lists from the Hellenistic/Roman world. For the author of the Pastorals, godliness involved appropriate honor or reverence for God that was

is not prayer, per se, but the kerygma: the One God revealed by the Only Christ (who was truly human and, yes, who prayed), who wants a broken, estranged humankind to be mended with the truth of divine shalom (v. 5).

Prayer is not at the center of things . . . but it gets us there. Prayer is a connection to the heart of our calling as a "preacher and an apostle of the good news" (v. 7 CEV). This is not a bad reminder from a veteran teacher to a newcomer pastor like Timothy.

So, Timothy, pray!

Pray with gratitude. "Tell God how thankful you are for [everyone]" (v. 2 CEV).

John Buchanan once wrote in the *Christian Century* a tribute to the Russian cellist Mstislav Rostropovich.[1] Buchanan admired Rostropovich's courage. In 1970 Rostropovich expressed his support for artistic freedom and human rights in a letter to *Pravda*, the state-run newspaper of the Soviet Union. In response, the Soviets stripped him and his wife of citizenship.

Buchanan saw Rostropovich play a Dvorak cello concerto in Chicago. As the last note faded, the audience sat mesmerized. Rostropovich did an extraordinary thing: he stood up and kissed his cello. The audience erupted. Then he hugged and kissed the surprised conductor. Then he hugged and kissed the entire cello section before moving on to the violins. He hugged and kissed most of the orchestra.

Gratitude.

What if we prayed for others like that?

If we prayed like that, might our prayer-grounded lives better reflect the image of Christ? Might the sometimes-ashen words of gratitude we use in our stiff praying for others, even enemies, blossom into the lilt of song, the vital flesh of action? Might a modicum of our selfishness melt to communal concern? Might we turn away, however slightly, from our penchant for self-reliance (a mirage), toward new submission to the one who "gave himself to rescue all of us" (v. 5 CEV)? To pray like this lessens the space for hubris in the heart of the one who prays and widens its capacity for humility.

Timothy, as a busy pastor, would need such transformation. Our crazy-busy congregations could use this transformative word too. They, no less than Timothy, bear this gospel of grace and, with us, need all the help they can get.

Herein lies a bridge to understanding the text. Since our flocks need so much help (and most of them know it), there is ample cause to pray. The

---

1. John Buchanan, "Bravo!" *Christian Century*, July 10, 2007.

1 Timothy 2:1-7

Theological Perspective

Calvin could uphold the effectiveness of God's will to save the elect while arguing that God does not save all people.

Over against this predestinatarian view, Jacobus Arminius placed an emphasis upon the divine foreknowledge of those who would believe and those who would not. For Arminians, while God makes salvation possible for all people, he elects for salvation only those who he knows will believe in Christ. Thus, both views uphold the effectiveness of God's will to save those whom God elects, and both deny that God saves all people.

In the modern era, the debates surrounding the question "Who are the recipients of God's salvation?" have shifted, away from concerns about predestination, toward the question of universalism. There are now three broad perspectives on universal salvation: exclusivism, inclusivism, and pluralism. Exclusivists believe that both truth and salvation are located exclusively in Christianity. Inclusivists affirm that, while Christianity is the one true religion, it is possible for persons to reap the benefits of that religion without explicit knowledge of its truth. In other words, they hold that the gospel is objectively true and salvation comes through the Christian God, who works through all religions to draw persons to himself, in Christ and through the Spirit. Pluralists argue that truth about God or the ultimate reality can be found in all religions and that all religions provide roads to salvation in their own ways.

While this passage could be used to support the exclusivist and inclusivist interpretations of Christian salvation, its focus on Christ as the sole mediator does not reflect a pluralist perspective. In the history of the church, the exclusivist interpretation has predominated. For instance, in the debates between the Calvinists and Arminians, neither side even questioned the final damnation of the reprobate. Yet passages such as this one in 1 Timothy (cf. Rom. 11:32 and 2 Pet. 3:9) raise anew the question for Christians: Will God's desire to save all persons in Christ ultimately be fulfilled?

STEPHANIE MAR SMITH

Pastoral Perspective

and move to a new location are called to pray for those do not think it prudent even to initiate a building campaign at this time! Not only are these people called to pray for one another, but their prayers will hopefully lead them, as Chrysostom noted, to love one another.

This is just within our own churches. Our parishioners will be called by the God of 1 Timothy to love and to pray for those outside churches as well, those who are radically different themselves and those who may frighten them. It is not easy to pray for the terrorist who plots against our country or the rapist who assaulted a loved one, but if we are fervent in our prayers we will be called to see that person as a child of God, a person created in God's own image just as we are, a person God desires to save. Our prayers will change us.

A pastoral challenge will be to preach this text to those in our congregations who have suffered harm from their authorities—even the ones in their churches. Some will not feel free to forgive, much less to pray for those who have harmed them. The preacher will gain credibility by acknowledging these harms, but need not exempt anyone from the exhortation of the passage.

In fact, those who do not respond miss brilliant opportunities for growth, because our prayers for all people can lead us to new teachers in the faith. We will discover that those whom our society pushes to the side because of age, race, gender, sexual orientation, disability, homelessness, or undocumented legal status have a great deal to teach us about the true nature of salvation. Their lived experiences of discrimination, persecution, and even oppression teach them about God's grace and mercy, salvation and justice in pivotal ways that those of us who live in the more central spaces of Christianity and culture need to hear. Their stories call us to consider salvation as a journey toward wholeness through the experience of knowing God, rather than the assumption of correct doctrine, catechism, or intellectual belief. They can teach us how living into our country's pledge to provide "liberty and justice for *all*" may or may not coincide with God's desire for salvation for *all* through Christ Jesus.

JANE ANNE FERGUSON

Exegetical Perspective

evident in one's lifestyle. *Semnotēs* is close in meaning to *eusebeia*. It denotes serious and proper behavior that gains respect from others. Their prayers for the emperor and other authorities were not for the salvation of the rulers, but for proper governance that would result in a safe and peaceful environment and allow them to live faithfully before God and the world.

The justification for inclusiveness in prayer is that it is pleasing to "God our Savior" (v. 3). The title "Savior," applied to either God or Christ twelve times in the Pastorals, appears in the Old Testament as a title for God. The author of the Pastorals may have emphasized the title as a polemic against its use for the Roman emperor. God alone—not the emperor—deserves to be called "Savior." The text proclaims unequivocally the universalism at the heart of God, who desires "everyone to be saved and to come to the knowledge of the truth" (v. 4). The latter phrase occurs several times in the Pastorals as a synonym for correct Christian doctrine and lifestyle.

Verses 5 and 6 have the ring of a liturgical fragment that the author borrows and introduces here to support his claim for the universality of God's salvation (and thus the universality of Christian prayer). Since there is only one God, salvation is available to all people through that God, mediated through Christ Jesus. Only here and in Hebrews (8:6; 9:15; 12:24) is the term "mediator" used for Christ. The text emphasizes the humanity of Christ ("Christ Jesus, himself human," v. 5), even more so in the Greek text where *anthrōpos* ("human" or "person") precedes "Christ Jesus," perhaps as a corrective to the docetic strand of Gnosticism that claimed that Jesus only appeared to be human, or possibly as a challenge to the imperial cult with its view of the emperor as a divine figure who mediated salvation to the empire.

As the mediator of God's salvation, Christ "gave himself a ransom for all" (v. 6). In this expression, which is a variant of the words of Jesus in Mark 10:45, the emphasis is on the universal work of Christ, whose accomplishment as mediator was for the benefit of all humanity, not only for a select few. Paul himself is an example of that inclusiveness of God, for he "was appointed a herald and an apostle . . . , a teacher of the *Gentiles*" (v. 7; emphasis added).

MITCHELL G. REDDISH

Homiletical Perspective

Heidelberg Catechism asks in question 118: "What has God commanded us to ask of him [in prayer]?" Answer: "All things necessary for soul and body . . ." This is *such* a relief!

So we pray, and this prayer-borne transformation is part and parcel of discipleship. If we miss it, we run the risk of missing everything else. Harry Emerson Fosdick was at his lyric best with this contribution to the church's hymnbook ("God of Grace and God of Glory"). It smells of incense, sounds like angel wings, and reads like prayer: "Cure thy children's warring madness; bend our pride to thy control; shame our wanton, selfish gladness, rich in things and poor in soul. Grant us wisdom, grant us courage, lest we miss thy kingdom's goal."

There is another barrier between this text and our flock. When Paul invites Timothy to give thanks for "everyone," there is a presumption that there is something in "everyone" for which to be thankful in the first place. Not everyone believes this is true. In a world of mean-spirited, us-them, simplistic right-wrong thinking, our flock needs reminding that "everyone" for whom we pray is worthy of God's help and blessing and, likewise, our prayers for them are decidedly worth our breath.

Jesus came as rescue/ransom for everyone, not just the tithing do-gooders in our church. We pray for everyone and seek God's blessing for everyone, just as "God wants everyone to be saved and to know the whole truth" (v. 4 CEV).

James would later write, "Therefore confess your sins to one another, and pray for one another, so that you may be healed" (Jas. 5:16 NRSV). Paul would say, "Amen." That is why, when he wrote Timothy, he made prayer a *first-of-all* matter. Our administrative contributions to the capital campaign committee, our visitation of the flock, even our hours of lesson planning and sermon preparation, will add up to little without the anchor that a life of praying for others provides.

WILLIAM P. "MATT" MATTHEWS

Luke 16:1-13

¹Then Jesus said to the disciples, "There was a rich man who had a manager, and charges were brought to him that this man was squandering his property. ²So he summoned him and said to him, 'What is this that I hear about you? Give me an accounting of your management, because you cannot be my manager any longer.' ³Then the manager said to himself, 'What will I do, now that my master is taking the position away from me? I am not strong enough to dig, and I am ashamed to beg. ⁴I have decided what to do so that, when I am dismissed as manager, people may welcome me into their homes.' ⁵So, summoning his master's debtors one by one, he asked the first, 'How much do you owe my master?' ⁶He answered, 'A hundred jugs of olive oil.' He said to him, 'Take your bill, sit down quickly, and make it fifty.' ⁷Then he asked another, 'And how much do you owe?' He replied, 'A hundred containers of wheat.' He said to him, 'Take

Theological Perspective

The parable of the dishonest steward poses significant theological challenges, not the least of which is the apparent injunction to imitate the unrighteous behavior of the main character (v. 9). Further, a cluster of exegetical problems complicates any plain sense reading of the text. The parable itself seems to end at verse 8a with the master, surprisingly, commending the steward for his shrewd, though dishonest, behavior. This is followed in verse 8b by a gloss on the story, likely a separate saying linked by the catchword "shrewd," which is, in turn, followed by an admonition to do what the unjust steward did. The text takes another turn in verses 10–12, where the command to renounce the dishonest practices of the steward cancels out the previous injunction to imitate him. The final moral of the story appears in verse 13, which seems less a commentary on the parable than a general warning about the danger of money as a rival to God.

We might explain the tensions in the passage by imagining Luke sitting down at his Gospel writer's desk with his big pile of sayings-of-Jesus note cards, adding one maxim after another to the parable, based on loose thematic or simply semantic connections to money and responsibility. Each of the layers of 16:1–13 can be explained in this way. However, even after the redaction-critical maneuvering is

Pastoral Perspective

The strength of parable as a mode of teaching is that it is the people's story. A parable is a grassroots lesson connecting the ordinariness of life with the extraordinary nature of God. Parables are usually gifts of clear insight into God's choices for our lives. However, this parable is difficult to read and difficult to preach. The reader is oftentimes left to struggle for meaning, just as the preacher struggles to interpret. Both end up frustrated.

Why would Jesus make an example for godly living so unsavory? The parable presents as the model for our faith someone whose life is the complete opposite of everything Christ ever taught. Jesus weaves a story in which the main character is a shyster—a lazy, conniving, self-centered manager of someone else's treasure. He is out for personal gain, to save his own skin. We listeners lean forward to the end because we want to see this scoundrel get what is coming to him, and when the master finally speaks, we are shocked.

While it is a compelling story, the ending is anything but satisfying, because instead of being defeated, this scoundrel triumphs. His plan succeeds. His former boss, the one whose estate he has previously mismanaged, now praises him for being ingenious. The reader sighs in disbelief that the manager does not get his due. The lesson is lost. Adding to the

your bill and make it eighty.' [8]And his master commended the dishonest manager because he had acted shrewdly; for the children of this age are more shrewd in dealing with their own generation than are the children of light. [9]And I tell you, make friends for yourselves by means of dishonest wealth so that when it is gone, they may welcome you into the eternal homes.

[10]"Whoever is faithful in a very little is faithful also in much; and whoever is dishonest in a very little is dishonest also in much. [11]If then you have not been faithful with the dishonest wealth, who will entrust to you the true riches? [12]And if you have not been faithful with what belongs to another, who will give you what is your own? [13]No slave can serve two masters; for a slave will either hate the one and love the other, or be devoted to the one and despise the other. You cannot serve God and wealth."

Exegetical Perspective

None of the parables of Jesus has baffled interpreters quite like the story of the dishonest steward (or is he better labeled "the shrewd manager" or "the prudent treasurer"?). The story is clearly set in a context in which wealth is of paramount importance. Luke 16 begins with an acknowledgment of a rich man whose manager was accused of "squandering his property" (v. 1). The disciples are warned that they cannot "serve God and wealth" (v. 13). In the midst of the chapter we are told of "the Pharisees, who were lovers of money" (v. 14) and who sneered at Jesus. The chapter closes with the parable of the Rich Man and Lazarus (vv. 19–31). So the topic clearly has to do with money,

A wealthy man had a financial manager, who was "squandering" (or was he "mismanaging"?) his resources. When it became obvious that he would lose his job, he said to himself, "I am not strong enough to dig for a living, and I am too ashamed to beg." Clearly a shrewd character, he called in two men, who owed his master olive oil and wheat, and asked each of them to reduce the amount owed the master. Whether the two men had their customary cut reduced, or simply had lowered the amount owed the master, is impossible to tell. In either case, they would have to repay less, and thus the manager had successfully placed them in his debt. Of course, the time of reckoning came when the wealthy man

Homiletical Perspective

Most likely, there are as many perspectives and interpretations of this parable as there are readers. It is no exaggeration to say that the parable's meaning has stumped even the best and most creative interpreters of Scripture. Perhaps we could decipher Jesus' intent if we were able to hear the tone in his voice, to see the look in his eyes, or to experience the reality of his hearers' everyday life.

Rather than be tangled in this parable with all the possible meanings and their competing validity, the preaching moment might prove most powerful by preacher's taking a creative line of interpretation and developing the story from that angle. Here are three lenses through which to view the parable for potential development.

True Dishonesty. Because of the appearance of the phrase in verse 8, the traditional title given to this parable is "the dishonest manager." However, when Jesus talks about dishonesty here, he may be doing so tongue in cheek. We know that there were two classes of people in Jesus' time and, hence, in the crowd: the very rich and the very poor. The poor were always at the mercy of the rich landlords who demanded the lion's share of their crops and the Roman government who exacted exorbitant taxes from them at every turn.

Luke 16:1-13

Theological Perspective

complete, we are still left to wrestle theologically with the final form of the text, inhabited as it is by unlikable characters and an overabundance of interpretive glosses.

The parable shows obvious parallels to the story of the prodigal son that immediately precedes it. In both parables a subordinate (child/steward) who "squanders" (15:13; 16:1) the goods of a superior (father/rich man) is, in the end, received back and celebrated/commended. This formal similarity, however, masks very important thematic differences. The steward, unlike the son, is not penitent; and the rich man, unlike the father, does not forgive the squandering but rather commends the steward's shrewdness. As a morality play the prodigal son works well, while the dishonest steward leaves us wondering whether any of the characters should even be commended, much less imitated.

Perhaps the key is that, unlike the prodigal son story and more like the parable of the rich fool, this parable actually encourages the dissipating of mammon ("dishonest wealth"). Indeed, after being released for squandering the master's money, the steward goes on to squander more. He disseminates the master's investment portfolio in order to protect his own future and secure a "home." Like the rich fool (12:13–21), he trusts in wealth to shelter his own uncertain future. Through his gifts to the debtors, he seeks, not to free them of debt, but rather to indebt them to him in the form of a return gift. Like so many of our own gifts, the gift of the steward disappears in a social network of self-promotion where gift giving functions to situate oneself as a benefactor to whom a return of gratitude is owed.

The first twist in the story comes when the master does not condemn but rather praises the steward for these actions. The greater twist, though, comes when Jesus praises the man and commends our imitation (v. 9). But what exactly in the unjust steward are we, the hearers, to imitate?

The clue comes in the final phrase of verse 9, "welcome you into the eternal homes." The NRSV translation of this final word, *skēnas* ("tents"), as "homes" unfortunately covers over a key element in the story. The translation is obviously meant to parallel the "homes" (*oikous*) that the steward seeks in verse 4. The parable, however, turns precisely on the fact that Jesus does *not* promise "homes" but "tents." Jesus does not promise to provide what the unjust steward sought, the stable abode of those who have possessions and security. Rather, Jesus promises the unstable abode of the wanderer, the refugee, and the

Pastoral Perspective

insult, there is still one last surprise. The parable ends by saying: The scoundrel gets it. Believers do not.

Is there anything redemptive or redeemable about this parable?

On another occasion Jesus tells a parable that highlights the positive nature of a person of questionable character. In Luke 11:5–13, Jesus tells the parable of a man who went to his neighbor late at night to ask for bread to feed unexpected guests and was received less than hospitably. Persistent knocking roused the grouchy neighbor, but not without his noting that he had been tremendously inconvenienced. "How much more," then, Jesus says, "will the heavenly Father give . . . to those who ask him?" (11:13). In Luke 18:1–8 Jesus tells of an unjust judge, "who neither feared God nor had respect for people" and closes with another "How much more . . . ?" He seems willing to let parabolic stand-ins for God be unsavory sorts in order to make a point.

This "how much more . . . " comparison appears again in Luke 16, where this manager, this person of questionable character, understood something that "children of light" have had difficulty grasping: dishonest or not, this man understood how to use what was entrusted to him to serve a larger goal. Believers, take note. How much more, then, must the children of God understand the riches entrusted to their care?

With the end in mind, the manager redeemed whatever he could about his present situation. He understood that, in order to be where he wanted to be in the future, how he handled today counted.

Solomon wrote in his proverbs: "Where there is no vision, the people perish" (Prov. 29:18 KJV). The parable of the manager speaks especially to Christians or communities who have lost the vision of the larger picture. Who are the people of God? What have they been called to do? When we have no idea where we are going, the treasures in front of us are hardly treasures at all; they are simply things, things that have no larger value beyond my own need for them. These things too easily become objects to be used, misused, and manipulated.

Here is a slightly different way to read the text: Among those in the crowd to whom Jesus addresses this parable are the Pharisees, whom Luke's narrator characterizes as "lovers of money" (v. 14). Leaders of the chosen people, keepers of the treasures of God, they were like the dishonest steward. They had lost their vision of who God had called them to be. They had traded their call to be God's people to become servant of the treasures of the present day. Controlled by wealth, by money, even complacency, they

discovered what his manager had done and, in a shocking dramatic climax, commended him for it.

Jesus then applied the lesson for his disciples, claiming that children of this world deal more shrewdly with their generation than the children of light with theirs. Then he, ironically, concluded by urging the hearers to make friends for themselves by means of dishonest wealth, so that when it is gone, they may welcome you into "the eternal homes" (v. 9).

The problem is, What has the manager been up to, and what has he done to earn the praise of the master? (The parable apparently ends at v. 9.) Was he a shrewd character, who was bilking his master by reducing the amount of interest on loans his master had made? In doing so, he could have reduced the size of the indebtedness by excluding the interest, forbidden by Deuteronomy 23:19–20. If so, he could have been acting righteously as well as shrewdly. Or could the manager have acted wisely in reducing the indebtedness by the amount that he would have made? Thus he could have forfeited his commission but in the process saved his own face and gained the favor of the debtors. Each of these two options makes it easier to grasp the commendation of the master (v. 8), especially if the parable ends at verse 9, and the advice to the children of light (vv. 8–13) continues the warning about wealth.

The concluding sayings of Jesus in verses 10–13 underscore the relationship between the material possessions one has and what one does with them. Faithfulness and responsibility are the qualities specified. Ironically Jesus asks, How will friends made from dishonest wealth be able to welcome them into the "eternal homes"? "You cannot serve God and wealth" (v. 13).

The third option, that the manager simply acted dishonestly with regard to his master and cut down on the indebtedness of those who owed money to feather his own cap, makes more sense of the details of the story, but makes it difficult to understand why the manager was commended by his master. Why then was the "dishonest manager" commended for acting shrewdly (v. 8), and made an example for the "children of light"? One of the two earlier options makes more sense.

We acknowledge that the manager responded to a crisis appropriate to his circumstances. As Johnson argues, "In other words, the manager is praised for having the qualities of a manager! It is this quality of responsiveness rather than the possible morality of the action that is the object of praise."[1] The cleverness

The property owner in the parable accuses his manager of wrongdoing on mere hearsay. So, knowing he is to be fired, the manager acts "dishonestly" by reducing the debts owed to the landowner. By describing this situation, maybe Jesus is pointing to the harsh reality that there is no way to be honest in a system that is already excessively unjust and dishonest. The telling of the parable may in itself be a shrewd way to unveil the gross dishonesty of a system that cheats and robs the poor daily. The manager acted shrewdly by exhibiting sharp judgment of a system that would otherwise have left him out in the cold. His master praises him not for his dishonesty, but for his shrewdness. Jesus' comment in verse 9 about dishonest wealth is clearly directed at those who are wealthy, for the manager in the story received no monetary gain from his dishonest actions. There is a contemporary and direct correlation to the kind of dishonest wealth and its subsequent oppression of the poor in which many of us are complicit in our own society. Perhaps we could reflect on the ethically disadvantaged in our society and the societies of a small globe and how our own economic systems often make an ethical life difficult, if not impossible, for some people.

The Master's Tools. Audre Lorde has a famous essay in her book *Sister Outsider* titled "The Master's Tools Will Never Dismantle the Master's House."[1] While she was talking primarily about the role of women in society and the inseparable relationship of the personal and the political, her axiom is pertinent here. The manager forgives the magnitude of the debts by reducing them, an action that would be unthinkable to the landlord. In a sense, the manager is not only watching out for his own life and his family's life, but he is also at the same time dismantling the landlord's system of gaining wealth. By reducing debts he may indeed be exposing the unfairness of the existing payment structure. He uses ethically questionable methods to help break down a system built to incur debts by reducing the debts and making allies for himself. He separates himself from a system of repression by cleverly undoing the system in a Robin Hood–like fashion.

Many of Jesus' parables are spoken to help portray the kind of life and relationships characterized in the realm of God. In that realm, the "tools" of oppressive systems are rendered ineffective and

---

1. Luke Timothy Johnson, *The Literary Function of Possessions in Luke–Acts*, SBL Dissertation Series (Missoula, MT: Scholars Press, 1977), 245.

1. Audre Lorde, *Sister Outsider: Essay and Speeches* (Trumansburg, NY: Crossing Press, 1984), 110.

Luke 16:1-13

Theological Perspective

pilgrim, whose mobility requires the dispossession of goods.

Perhaps the Jesus who told this parable calls us to dissipate wealth as the steward did, but in order to be dispossessed of the desire that our gifting produce the benefit of indebting others to us—indeed, to be dispossessed of the illusion that wealth gives us security and stability. Only as we are freed by our holy squandering are we made able to live the pilgrim life of those nomads who have relinquished the possessions that possess them. As Walter Brueggemann notes, one of the central insights of the gospel is the paradox that "letting go is to have and keeping is the way to lose."[1] This parable, in a roundabout way, brings us back to this insight and so reinforces the words of Luke 12:32: "Do not be afraid, little flock, for it is your Father's good pleasure to give you the kingdom." In light of this reading, the call to be "faithful" in 16:10–12 is precisely the call to have faith in the one who provides—enough faith to relinquish our grip on the wealth we think will protect us in order to receive the "true riches" (16:11) of the "unfailing treasure in heaven" (12:33).

If we read this way, the problem with the unjust steward is not that he "gifted" his master's debtors (even his master commends him for this), but that his gifting was poisoned by the ulterior motive of receiving something back from those to whom he gave. Jesus encourages his listeners to imitate the man's scattering of wealth in order to receive the gift that is beyond return and outside any economy of exchange—an "eternal" tenting in which one is received not into a settled domain but into a triune life that is eternally on the move.

SCOTT BADER-SAYE

Pastoral Perspective

had blended into society and lost their vision. To these Jesus says, to paraphrase verse 13, "You can either serve this present age and love its treasures, or you can love God and serve him in this present age. But you cannot do both. One leads to death. The other leads to life."

However we interpret the role of the unjust steward, children who walk in the light of the Lord, understand this: We not only are entrusted with the vision of the kingdom of heaven; we are given the treasures of the King! Even in the present age, with the imperfect treasures of this world, we are stewards of God. However we use what we have before us, we should use these gifts in light of our eternal relationship with God.

The parable warns that the children have lost that eternal perspective of who God is and who we are in relationship to God. Too easily we separate life as it is now from life in the future kingdom. Not long ago, we shouted, "He is alive!" but already we are whispering our faith because we do not quite believe it anymore.

Somewhere in the middle of our journey we stopped living for Christ. We stopped believing that Jesus died and was resurrected and that life was made new. Somewhere along the way it became easy to serve all those pressing demands: of people, of schedule, of money. Somewhere along the way, the vision for God's call became cloudy and muddled. We stopped hearing God's voice and joined the crazy survivor-takes-all mentality. Somewhere along the way, the challenges seemed so much bigger than the answers. So we huddled in an effort to save whatever was left and forgot about living for something greater. We buried our treasures.

This is the crisis that Jesus addresses in his parable. The children of light have lost the vision for God. It is easy to grow complacent about responsibilities God gives us. The parable is a call to reclaim who we are and to renew our vision today for the kingdom of God beyond us and among us.

HELEN MONTGOMERY DEBEVOISE

---

1. Walter Brueggemann, *The Land* (Philadelphia: Fortress Press, 1977), 183.

the children of light are to develop is precisely that they confront and contend with the issues of their own generation, particularly in the matter of material goods. The people of "this age" are cleverer with respect to the crises facing them than are the children of light with respect to "what is prized" by them (v. 15). It is not clear what specific behaviors Luke's Jesus had in mind here. Was it the kind of community of goods the earliest Christian community of Acts would embody (2:42–47)? The Jesus of Luke 16 did not specify. What he did instead was reiterate a truth from Israel's history: God knows the hearts of God's people, and what humans prize has become "an abomination in the sight of God" (v. 15).

Verse 13 puts the issue in plain view: "No slave can serve two masters; for a slave will either hate the one and love the other, or be devoted to the one and despise the other. You cannot serve God and wealth." Greed has quickly turned into idolatry, with the result that the basic confession of Israel has been broken (see Exod. 20:1–3; Deut. 6:4–9). A god other than YHWH has become the object of Israel's affection. Mammon is served rather than the God who led them out of Egypt.

Luke 16:1–13 is one of the great exegetical mountains of Scripture. This bewildering parable and the positive use Jesus makes of its shifty protagonist may never be satisfactorily solved until faith is made sight. In the meantime, perhaps the best we can hope is that our joining the quest for a solution, the grappling of God's people with even the difficult parts of God's book, produces a weary but earnest friendship among the children of light in this generation.

CHARLES B. COUSAR

turned upside down. In the realm of God, debts are forgiven and indentured servants set free. This parable may have been a precursor to Jesus' teachings on the year of jubilee, when the economic playing field is leveled and inequalities are erased. How this happens is not with the Master's tools, not by the ways of the world, or even by the methods of capitalism, but rather, by the new ways of the realm of God that Jesus preached about consistently.

Resources and Relationships. One final way to approach this parable is to reflect on the connection between resources and relationships. In the parable we are given an insight into the manager's motivation. His goal is to make friends so that when unemployed, someone will take him in. Christine Pohl, in an essay titled "Profit and Loss," makes a revealing point about how the parable uncovers the pervasiveness of our love of money. She contends that "Jesus does not commend the manager's practices, but rather his insight into the connection between resources and relationships. When we consider our wealth and economic practices—even the means we employ to accomplish good ends—as peripheral to the kingdom, we are ignoring Jesus' warning that it is impossible to serve God and mammon."[2]

If we embrace this creative interpretation, the manager's insight brings into sharp relief our own connections between resources and relationships. What means do we employ to accomplish good ends? What are our motivations behind the relationships we forge, and how are those relationships economically determined? Perhaps more searing questions are, how are our relationships shaped by class issues, and what must happen in our own lives for us to offer solidarity with the "least of these" (Matt. 25:40, 45) that Jesus so often mentions?

Serving God means that loving people is always the bottom line. So Jesus' closing words, whether or not these words were part of the original parable, are certainly an apt summation of what Jesus is so ardently and adamantly trying to get across: you cannot serve God and wealth (v. 13).

G. PENNY NIXON

2. Christine Pohl, "Profit and Loss," *Christian Century*, August 29–September 5, 2001, 13.

Jeremiah 32:1–3a, 6–15

[1]The word that came to Jeremiah from the LORD in the tenth year of King Zedekiah of Judah, which was the eighteenth year of Nebuchadrezzar. [2]At that time the army of the king of Babylon was besieging Jerusalem, and the prophet Jeremiah was confined in the court of the guard that was in the palace of the king of Judah, [3]where King Zedekiah of Judah had confined him. . . .

[6]Jeremiah said, The word of the LORD came to me: [7]Hanamel son of your uncle Shallum is going to come to you and say, "Buy my field that is at Anathoth, for the right of redemption by purchase is yours." [8]Then my cousin Hanamel came to me in the court of the guard, in accordance with the word of the LORD, and said to me, "Buy my field that is at Anathoth in the land of Benjamin, for the right of possession and redemption is yours; buy it for yourself." Then I knew that this was the word of the LORD.

Theological Perspective

During the biblical period, land could mean the difference between life and death. The agrarian type of society structured its culture to prize land theologically. The legal system sought to protect land for the family. Of course, over twenty-five hundred years this agrarian society has given way to the postindustrial information society. Nonetheless, in our day we still prize space, if not land. Sometimes it is measured not in acres but in square feet. How much we prize land or space depends on the historical contexts and theological constructs. As anyone who has rented an apartment or bought a home knows, real estate transactions depend on knowing the value of the property based on the location and the situation. Once one knows the value, it is a matter of choosing. This passage invites the reader to a life that values human agency amid God's mission.

Jeremiah 32 is a story of prophetic symbolic action. Jeremiah bought a field. That was a simple act. What made it prophetic was its location and situation. Jeremiah's field was located in the city of Jerusalem, and Jeremiah bought it while the Babylonian army was threatening the city of Jerusalem. They encircled the city. However, the city was not the only thing that was encircled; Jeremiah was confined in an enclosure. So much of the transaction had to take place through proxy.

Pastoral Perspective

These verses from chapter 32 relate the details surrounding Jeremiah's purchase of land in his hometown of Anathoth. On the surface, this is a most peculiar transaction. Jerusalem is under siege, and Jeremiah has already stated that Jerusalem will fall to Babylon and that King Zedekiah and the people of Jerusalem will be exiled. Also, Jeremiah is in prison, because, as part of his pronouncement that Babylon is serving YHWH's purpose, he declared that the appropriate response to the siege is to lay down arms and surrender. At a time of war, suggestions like that are regarded as seditious, and the person who makes them is called a traitor. It is hardly a propitious moment to be paying good money for land that is in the process of being conquered.

A second level of reality appears in these verses, however. Jeremiah has delivered the oracle that tells the people of Israel that a new covenant is replacing the Mosaic covenant under which the nation has been operating.[1] For Jeremiah, the new covenant means that the people of Israel are no longer identified by geography, cultic practices, and tribal traditions, but are bound together by the recognition that YHWH's law is part of their very being. Their com-

---

1. "But this is the covenant that I will make with the house of Israel after those days, says the LORD: I will put my law within them, and I will write it on their hearts; and I will be their God, and they shall be my people" (Jer. 31:33).

⁹And I bought the field at Anathoth from my cousin Hanamel, and weighed out the money to him, seventeen shekels of silver. ¹⁰I signed the deed, sealed it, got witnesses, and weighed the money on scales. ¹¹Then I took the sealed deed of purchase, containing the terms and conditions, and the open copy; ¹²and I gave the deed of purchase to Baruch son of Neriah son of Mahseiah, in the presence of my cousin Hanamel, in the presence of the witnesses who signed the deed of purchase, and in the presence of all the Judeans who were sitting in the court of the guard. ¹³In their presence I charged Baruch, saying, ¹⁴Thus says the LORD of hosts, the God of Israel: Take these deeds, both this sealed deed of purchase and this open deed, and put them in an earthenware jar, in order that they may last for a long time. ¹⁵For thus says the LORD of hosts, the God of Israel: Houses and fields and vineyards shall again be bought in this land.

Exegetical Perspective

When Jeremiah received his prophetic call from the Lord, he was commissioned to proclaim a double message: "to pluck up and pull down . . . [and] . . . to build and to plant" (Jer. 1:10). His prophetic mission was to speak forth God's words both of judgment and of promise and hope. Surely there were times when Jeremiah wondered when—if ever—God would give him a message of hope to preach. "Whenever I speak, I must cry out, . . . 'Violence and destruction!'" (Jer. 20:8). The majority of Jeremiah's words consisted of denunciation for Judah's sins and the attendant prophecies of judgment against the people and the nation.

Jeremiah always seemed to be "swimming against the stream." Most of his prophecies of judgment were delivered at times when the people of Judah felt themselves secure from any adverse judgment of the Lord (e.g., Jer. 3:4–5; 5:12; 7:8–10), and at many of those times there were other prophets, preaching comforting words of assurance and hopefulness (see Jer. 23:16–17; 27–28). When finally Jeremiah's message of imminent disaster proved true with the attack of the army from Babylon (Jer. 32:2; cf. 2 Kgs. 25:1–21), Jeremiah's words of hope (found esp. in chaps. 30–33) began to issue forth—words from God that clashed with all appearances.

Homiletical Perspective

With all the passion and pain that informs the prophecies of Jeremiah and the drama of his personal story as a prophet to Israel, it would be easy to forget or ignore the place of Baruch in all of this. This passage, however, although it is ostensibly about an important prophetic "act" on the part of Jeremiah, calls attention to the place of Baruch in the story. This invites us to heed the place and role of those who, like Baruch, are called to "keep" the story and guard the hope. What does it mean to be a servant of the prophetic word?

There cannot be a Jeremiah without a Baruch. There could not be a Paul, by his own word, were it not for most of all of those named in the sixteenth chapter of Romans, to say nothing of individuals like Epaphroditus (Phil. 2:25). Too often in its history, the people of God have not availed themselves of the example of these figures. Whom do we know who was named after Baruch, instead of Jeremiah, or after Obadiah, the civil servant who kept Elijah going in more ways than one?

Baruch is Jeremiah's scribe. In this particular episode, a number of images suggest that Baruch represents, not only the importance of a network of people for the manifestation of God's word and work, but also the response to and the responsibility for that word and work. Baruch's "calling" is to be a

Jeremiah 32:1-3a, 6-15

Theological Perspective

This is not the first or last time Scripture records a significant real-estate transaction. Abraham bought land for a burial place for Sarah (Gen. 23). Boaz redeemed a field (Ruth 4). King Ahab and his queen Jezebel botched the acquisition of a vineyard owned by Naboth the Jezreelite (1 Kgs. 21). Tragic real-estate transactions occur in the New Testament as well. When Judas returned the thirty pieces of silver to the chief priests and elders, they knew the "blood money" would pollute the treasury, so they purchased the potter's field for the burial of aliens (Matt. 27:3–10). When Ananias and Sapphira sold property and underreported their earnings, things did not go well for them (Acts 5:1–11)! Real-estate transactions described in the Bible seem never to be neutral. They advance either a blessing or a curse.

Jeremiah bought a field. His purchase came in what we might call a depressed real-estate market. Recently there had been a drop in the stock market, and on the television commentators wondered if this would be the end of the bull market and everyone would move to selling instead of buying. In the middle of a military siege, Jeremiah gives us meticulous details of the sale. The act is not contrarian just to be different, but Jeremiah does hope it will grab attention.

The transaction is not private and solitary, but public and collaborative. Prophetic symbolic actions provide a model of public theology, because they are public and collaborative. Among Jeremiah's people, this transaction required Hanamel, Jeremiah's cousin, and Baruch, Jeremiah's secretary. The transaction also had wider air time because it required Judeans sitting in the court of the guard. Their presence ensured whispers and rumor about the crazy prophet who was buying bad titles. These Judeans also made this symbolic action one that required collaboration, even if many of the players were unaware that they were part of a prophetic symbolic action. The role of the Judeans points to the public nature of the transaction. Symbolic action here takes place in public. Prophetic action often requires a community of faith to witness it and absorb its symbolism. This is public. The deed is publically filed as well as privately kept by the prophet. The real-estate transaction is public, collaborative, and political; that is to say, it has an impact on developing land and communities from ancient times.

The use of royal land grants for various purposes goes back to ancient times. These became important tools in the colonization of the Americas by Europeans. The United States also used real estate to shape the political landscape. According to the

Pastoral Perspective

munity is now composed of individuals who band together to worship God, strengthen their commitments to live according to the will of God, and celebrate the commonalities created by their dedication to YHWH and the things of God.

For Jeremiah, therefore, while the destruction of Jerusalem and the exile of the people may mean the end of the nation of Israel as it was once identified, it does not mean that YHWH has abandoned YHWH's people or lessened in any way YHWH's connection to them. The people of YHWH are an identified group just as much as they were under the old covenant, and they will thrive—they will till the soil, marry and bear children, worship God and celebrate together, just as they did in the past.

The opportunity to buy the land comes from his family. According to a provision in Leviticus, land could not be sold outside the family, if such a sale would affect the family's ability to sustain itself. Jeremiah is the next of kin with the right of redemption by purchase, and the provisions of the Mosaic covenant have led his cousin to offer the land to Jeremiah. Likewise, the entire transaction—the establishment of the price to be paid, the weighing of the money to pay for it, the form of the deed on which the transfer of the land is recorded, the number of witnesses required to attest to the legality of the sale—is handled as dictated under the terms of the old covenant.

Throughout these verses, Jeremiah emphasizes that he is responding to the will of YHWH. Redeeming this land is not an act of foolish hope or the ability to ignore the obvious. Rather, it is the enactment of faith in the future and in the promise of YHWH to fulfill the covenant between YHWH and YHWH's people. Jeremiah acts on the promise that despite the current siege and defeat of Jerusalem and Judah, houses and fields and vineyards will again be bought in that land.

The language of Paul Tillich may help us to understand the pastoral importance of this passage. For Tillich, a theologian who wrote in the mid-twentieth century about issues of faith, certainty, and doubt, Jeremiah's willingness to invest in land at the very moment that Babylon had Jerusalem under siege would be evidence of the "courage to be."[2]

In the course of his ministry, Jeremiah comes face to face with despair, agony, doubt, and meaninglessness. He questions YHWH, wrestles with what YHWH presents to him, experiences pain and

2. Paul Tillich, *The Courage to Be* (New York: Yale University Press, 1952), 172 ff.

Exegetical Perspective

The passage under study here is the one passage in Jeremiah's Book of Consolation (chaps. 30–33) which is given a clear date (32:1–2). The tenth year of Zedekiah's reign was 587/586 BCE, ten years after the first Babylonian defeat of Jerusalem and the carrying off of one group of exiles (2 Kgs. 24:10–17). Now the army of Babylon has again besieged the city of Jerusalem, and Jeremiah has been imprisoned, under suspicion of being a traitor (see Jer. 37:11–16; 38:28). In today's passage we can be instructed that, in contrast to the prophet imprisoned and the king and people caught in a fateful situation of siege, God's word is free (cf. 2 Tim. 2:9).[1]

The omission from the lectionary text of King Zedekiah's question to Jeremiah in verses 3–5 may seem reasonable. Some commentators note that it appears to be awkward in this place, since there seems to be no direct response or reference to the king's question by Jeremiah. The king, who has incarcerated the prophet, asks Jeremiah why he is prophesying that the Lord pronounces disaster for the city and the king.

The text as it stands suggests that Jeremiah's response to the king's question was . . . a recounting of a real-estate transaction in which Jeremiah became involved! This would not seem a logical reply to the king's query. The transaction itself seems to fly in the face of all reason, given the situation described in Jeremiah's prophesying (vv. 3–5). Taking the sequence of the narrative at face value, the prophet's response to the king may be construed as saying that his own personal experience with God's word has persuaded him of the dependability of any word from the Lord, including the prophecy of Babylonian victory in verses 3–5.

Jeremiah's response to the king affirms the reliability of the word of the Lord in predicting the appearance of Jeremiah's cousin Hanamel (vv. 6–7) with the request that Jeremiah execute the responsibility of a near kinsman ("redeemer") to bail a relative out of financial difficulty, the details of which are undisclosed. The Hebrew law in which this procedure of redemption is rooted appears in Leviticus 25:25–28. Just as the Lord has told Jeremiah, Hanamel appears and makes said request. The coincidence of God's word and the event that transpired persuaded Jeremiah: "Then I knew that this was the word of the LORD" (v. 8).

Jeremiah proceeds to execute, with witnesses and a public record, a detailed property transaction that

1. Cf. John Calvin, *Commentaries on Jeremiah and Lamentations*, trans. John Owens (Grand Rapids: Eerdmans, 1950), 4:152–58.

Homiletical Perspective

witness to the word and work of God and a trustee in time of that multifaceted divine act as it enacts itself through Jeremiah.

All of this is suggested by the rhetorical force and focus of verses 13 through 15. Jeremiah in more than one way "charged" Baruch to be a witness to what transpired in the purchase of the property. He was to be trustee of the deed, the document, and the hope, which is grounded in the promise: "For thus says the LORD of hosts, the God of Israel" (v. 15). Faith is daily life lived in an eschatological dimension. How crazy, how nonsensical, this whole transaction must have seemed to everyone, including, perhaps, to Baruch! "How did I get into this? You want me to do what?"

This is not a request; it is a "charge." What Baruch is called to do is as important, as solemn, as what Jeremiah has just done. The preservation of the deeds is his human responsibility in time that punctuates God's sovereign word as a judgment and a promise. "Houses and fields and vineyards shall again be bought in this land" (v. 15).

The venue for the preservation of the deeds is the life of Baruch; the instrumentality is an earthenware jar. To the ear we are not too far away from Paul's confession: "But we have this treasure in clay jars" (2 Cor. 4:7). We should certainly not forget the drama of the eighteenth chapter of Jeremiah, the vision that arises out of the work within the potter's house. There the quality and dependability of the vessel upon which the potter is working becomes the image of the integrity of the life of God's people. The virtue of a vessel is determined by what it can hold. How useful is it? How secure is it for what it must carry and preserve? Baruch is called upon to be trustworthy in the choice of the earthenware jar and its custody.

Throughout his prophetic career, Jeremiah is called upon to be a "visionary," to hear the word of God by first visually attending to what is transpiring before him. The attention to all of the details of the transaction in which Jeremiah purchases this land suggests that those who will "hear" the words of the record will perhaps then "see" beyond the immediate scene into the hope of God's sovereign loving possession of Israel. Literally captive to the whim, waywardness, and fear of those who will not abide his word, Jeremiah redeems by purchase (vv. 8, 9) a portion of the land, representative of the whole, and then entrusts to Baruch both the recording of the event and the legal, required documentation of the acquisition that actually participates in the act of purchase. Baruch becomes part of the prophetic act and an emblem of the prophetic hope.

Jeremiah 32:1-3a, 6-15

Theological Perspective

Homestead Act of 1862, every person would receive 160 acres and a mule if they stayed on the land and improved it over the course of five years. This legislation was an attempt to populate the land of the Louisiana Purchase, but it symbolically offered hope in the midst of a Civil War and in the first months after the Emancipation Proclamation.

Jeremiah's purchase of the land near Anathoth parallels his instruction to the deportees in Babylon to buy land, build houses, and so forth (Jer. 29:4–7). We see here the domestic and foreign or global mission at work in Jeremiah's prophetic ministry. Jeremiah assures Israel that they will one day buy and sell houses in their dear homeland again. At the same time he encourages them to see God as near and active, even in the present circumstances of their exile. The work of their own rebuilding would happen both in exile and in Jerusalem.

Two of the key verbs in this story are "buy" and "redeem." Here the purchase is synonymous with the redemption. On the one hand, the purchase models that "houses and fields and vineyards shall again be bought in this land" (v. 15b). On the other hand, it is more than a coincidence that the redemption of land by a relative is part of the purchase process. This piece models what God is doing in the redemption of exilic Judah.

While the many laments of Jeremiah arise from disaster and call the people to contemplation, the story of Jeremiah 32:1–3a, 6–15 challenges exiled peoples to imagine hopeful action. This story reminds us that God's grace occurs in unusual places and in sometimes contrarian forms. What will the congregation's hopeful act be today? Will it be material and prophetic—a land buy and a development project in inner-city Detroit? Will the investment be more social—churches building special education programs for kids who seem destined to fail, or addiction-recovery programs for lives that seem to have no future? Whatever the form, the faithful reader of Jeremiah is called to find analogies of collaborative, inspired, public, prophetic actions that speak the hope of redemption in unpromising places and times.

STEPHEN BRECK REID

Pastoral Perspective

torment in the face of Israel's behavior and its limitations. He does all he can to let the people of Israel know what is required of them to restore harmony with YHWH.

Throughout his struggles, the power that animates him is the creative and sustaining hand of YHWH. He knows YHWH is present and working in the world. This certainty that human beings, even in all their limitations, participate as integral parts of something that transcends them utterly, Tillich calls "faith." This is not faith in the sense of declaring to be true something that cannot be proved through the physical senses. Rather, it is the recognition that meaninglessness ("non-being" in Tillich's terms), while not to be dismissed, lacks the power creatively to engage a situation, and so cannot obliterate the power of "being."

Tillich would also point out that YHWH was Jeremiah's "ultimate concern," which "demands the total surrender of him [or her] who accepts this claim, and . . . promises total fulfillment even if all other claims have to be subjected to it or rejected in its name."[3] In some ways, the Mosaic covenant had replaced YHWH as ancient Israel's ultimate concern. The covenant itself was only a "preliminary concern," and as such was unable to provide the fulfillment of the spiritual, aesthetic, and creative aspects of human life.

By purchasing the land in the midst of Jerusalem's destruction by Babylon and while he was imprisoned, Jeremiah defines what it means to have faith in YHWH's future. He attests to his conviction that YHWH is present even in catastrophe. He declares that meaninglessness or nonbeing will not triumph. To the multitudes of our parishioners who suffer from hopelessness and despair of unexpected setbacks, Jeremiah underscores that, out of the chaos of change, YHWH's promises will be fulfilled. Jeremiah bet his bottom dollar on it—he went ahead and purchased a field right in the middle of the turmoil!

SHARON PEEBLES BURCH

---

3. Paul Tillich, *Dynamics of Faith* (New York: Harper & Row, 1957), 1.

Exegetical Perspective

surely seems the height of folly, given the imminent takeover of the land by the Babylonians—which Jeremiah himself has just foretold! The record of the commercial transaction, sealed and deposited in a jar, represents God's word of hope for the Hebrew community—a treasure literally in an earthen vessel (cf. 2 Cor. 4:7). Jeremiah puts his money where his mouth is. This event attests that God's law about the inalienability of the land (cf. Lev. 25:23–24) will be preserved.

Jeremiah's symbolic act of redemption subsequently finds an echo during the exile, when Second Isaiah adopts as his favorite descriptor of YHWH the one who will "redeem" God's people from their exilic plight (Isa. 41:14; 43:1, 14, and passim).

Just as the prophetic word that upset King Zedekiah declared that God would "attend to" the exiled Zedekiah at some unspecified time in the future (v. 5), Jeremiah declares the Lord's word that at some unspecified time "houses and fields and vineyards shall again be bought" in the land of Judah (v. 15). In neither of these events is God's word bound to any human timetable.

Jeremiah, in previous preaching, had warned the people of Judah to expect an exile of considerable duration (Jer. 27:16–22), and the prophet also sent a letter to those who had been carried off into exile ten years earlier, urging them to plan on a settled existence in the exile city to which they had been transplanted (Jer. 29:1–9). However, the future for God's people will be in the land of Judah and Jerusalem. The "again" of this declaration (v. 15, Heb. ʿod) is the same motif found in nearby passages such as Jeremiah 31:2–6, where Jeremiah speaks of the people of the northern kingdom surviving the punishing sword and finding in the wilderness the grace of the Lord, who declared, "Again (ʿod) I will build you . . . again you shall plant vineyards on the mountains of Samaria" (31:4, 5). In Jeremiah 31:23 we find the promise that "once more (ʿod) they shall use these words in the land of Judah and in its towns when I restore their fortunes: 'The Lord bless you, O abode of righteousness, O holy hill!'"

GEORGE W. RAMSEY

Homiletical Perspective

"You will be my witnesses," says Jesus to unsure apostles (Acts 1:8). As was noted above, "we have this treasure in clay jars" (2 Cor. 4:7). Obviously Paul uses this image primarily to draw a comparison between the power, grandeur, and worth of the gospel reality, on the one hand, and the limitations, trials, and frailties of the apostolic company, on the other. The comparison clarifies that the message of the gospel and the accomplishments of the apostolic mission are not attributable to any cleverness, sophistication, or innate gift. It also means that being engaged in this witness does not offer any dispensation from the vicissitudes of life or the hostilities of adversaries.

In this case, the vitality of the "treasure," its power, and its promise shine through and are therefore enhanced by the mundane quality of the vessel. Think again of Jeremiah's visit to the potter's workshop. For Paul, the potter is working from the inside of the vessel outward, shaping it by its content: the revelation of God's reconciling love in Christ. The vessel holds and is shaped by a treasure that transcends it. Here especially is where Baruch can guide the church. He must choose a dependable "jar"; he must be a faithful trustee. He is "charged." God's sovereign, judging promise to Israel has chosen him, but not for his own personal sake. "Houses and fields and vineyards shall again be bought." The "earthen vessel" of the community of faith in Jesus Christ does not exist for itself. It is a trustee of a promise: a community that includes the wandering, wondering, and waywardness of the human story will one day experience a coming home to itself and to its God.

DWIGHT M. LUNDGREN

Psalm 91:1-6, 14-16

¹You who live in the shelter of the Most High,
    who abide in the shadow of the Almighty,
²will say to the Lord, "My refuge and my fortress;
    my God, in whom I trust."
³For he will deliver you from the snare of the fowler
    and from the deadly pestilence;
⁴he will cover you with his pinions,
    and under his wings you will find refuge;
    his faithfulness is a shield and buckler.
⁵You will not fear the terror of the night,
    or the arrow that flies by day,

Theological Perspective

This psalm is a beloved statement of the believer's security and protection by a faithful God. There are no specific events that give rise to the psalm. It is an expression of the experience of the faithful Israelite who lives "in the shelter of the Most High" and abides "in the shadow of the Almighty" (v. 1).

The lectionary passage can be seen as presenting three theological realities in relation to the work and character of God.

Security in God. The psalmist refers to God as "my refuge and my fortress; my God, in whom I trust" (v. 2). This is an expression of personal experience, supplementing the more general statement in verse 1, while giving voice to the same general truth: the believer's security is in God. Here now is "the God of personal experience." Calvin indicated that this statement by a believer is "very necessary in one who would be a teacher; for we cannot communicate true knowledge unless we deliver it not merely with the lips, but as something which God has revealed to our own hearts."[1]

A further expression of this thought is in the images of the following verse: deliverance from "the

---

1. John Calvin, *Commentary on Psalms*, 91:1. Quote in next paragraph is from *Commentary on Psalms*, 91:4.

Pastoral Perspective

One of the primary reasons people participate in worship is to find and nurture a felt sense of God's presence. Psalm 91, a "psalm of trust," assures worshipers that God is present in the midst of danger, difficulty, and disappointment. It promises that God acts decisively to protect those "who live in the shelter of the Most High" (v. 1). Scholars have proposed several originating circumstances for this psalm. It could be the testimony of someone who has found refuge in the temple from persecutors (cf. 1 Kgs. 1:49–53), the thankful utterance of someone who has recovered from illness, part of a purification ritual, or even a liturgy used by a king before battle.

The number of possible origins and uses for the psalm suggests a wide range of potential contemporary applications. The psalm's imagery, language, and cadence resonate with those who find themselves dealing with fear, anxiety, pain, or some other significant challenge. Verses 3 through 6 vividly rehearse a litany of terrifying circumstances: "the snare of the fowler . . . the deadly pestilence," "the terror of the night . . . the arrow that flies by day," and "the pestilence that stalks in darkness . . . the destruction that wastes at noonday."

The psalmist's language is evocative, even alarming, and it takes only a little imagination to produce a litany of equivalently frightening circumstances for

> [6]or the pestilence that stalks in darkness,
> or the destruction that wastes at noonday.
> . . . .
> [14]Those who love me, I will deliver;
> I will protect those who know my name.
> [15]When they call to me, I will answer them;
> I will be with them in trouble,
> I will rescue them and honor them.
> [16]With long life I will satisfy them,
> and show them my salvation.

Exegetical Perspective

Historical and Literary Context. This psalm affirms the nation's faith in YHWH's power and willingness to protect the faithful. The psalm may have been written to honor a king or warrior who has escaped death, but still faces danger. Some scholars classify it as a "royal psalm," composed in honor of the king (see also Pss. 57, 58, 61:2–6, and 86).

Six times the psalmist expresses his conviction that God will deliver. The promise takes several poetic forms: the Most High will deliver (v. 3); overshadow the king or warrior with wings, like a mother bird (v. 4); and shield him on the battlefield (v. 7). No epidemic shall come near him (v. 10); angels will bear him up on their hands (v. 12); and he will travel untouched by animals and monsters (v. 13).

These six assertions of God's deliverance are complemented by three descriptions of the psalmist's faithfulness and three promises of God's salvation in the final three verses of the psalm. The king or warrior in the psalm cleaves to God with passionate love (v. 14a), knows the meaning of God's name (v. 14b), and invokes God (v. 15a). From God's side, God rescues him (v. 15c), honors him (v. 15c), and shows him the meaning of salvation (v. 16b).[1]

1. Samuel Terrien, *The Psalms: Strophic Structure and Theological Commentary* (Grand Rapids: Eerdmans, 2003), 652.

Homiletical Perspective

The core message of Psalm 91 is that God protects those who dwell or live in God's presence. Preachers and pastors will probably want to explore what it means to live (v. 1a) or abide (v. 1b) in the "shelter" (v. 1a) or "shadow" (v. 1b) of God. The words "live" and "abide," "shelter" and "shadow" have different meanings that could be explored and exploited homiletically. There appears to be a deepening of the relationship as one moves from the first to the second clause of the verse. The concept of protection may be fruitful too. Does it include immunity to disaster? illness? heartbreak?

The kind of intimacy that makes the dialogue between "the Most High" and the suppliant possible is found in the proximity indicated by the phrases "live in the shelter of" and "abide in the shadow of" the Deity. Indeed, the remainder of the psalm builds on the relationship implied in the first verse, because it is that closeness that evokes the bold assertion, "My refuge and my fortress; my God, in whom I trust" (v. 2). Though four names of the Deity are used in the first two verses, it would probably be a mistake to read too much into the differences. They are worth noting, however.

It is likely that a priest first uttered the words of verses 1 and 2 to a member of the covenant community enduring tough times. In the space of one short

Psalm 91:1-6, 14-16

Theological Perspective

snare of the fowler and from the deadly pestilence" (v. 3). The former refers to a bird catcher's trap and could be translated as meaning "hidden traps," while "deadly pestilence" can mean "deadly diseases." These are the more concrete expressions of how security in God is enacted. In the midst of the "unknowns" in life ("hidden traps"), as well as threats to health and to life itself, our security is in the God who covers us ("pinions" and "wings," v. 4) as a bird covers its young under its wings. This is an expression of "the singularly tender care with which God watches over our safety."

Faithfulness of God. In this same verse 4, the psalmist comments on God's faithfulness as being a "shield and buckler." The shield is large enough to cover the whole body (see Ps. 5:12), while "buckler" is a small shield carried in the hand or worn on the arm for protection (see Ps. 35:2). The sense here is that God is faithful and will protect you like a shield.

The psalmist grounds our security and protection in God's faithfulness, an aspect of the person or character of God. "Faithfulness" in the Old Testament context refers to God's keeping the divine promises. This faithfulness is the source of security. The God who "shelters" and "delivers" can be depended upon to do so because of God's fidelity to covenant promises. God will not desert the people of God in times of need. As a "shield and buckler," God will "come between" us and our enemies to provide security, because this is what God promises in the covenants that bind the psalmist—and the whole nation of Israel—to God.

No other source for security can be so trustworthy as finding our safety in the character of the God who is able to provide for our needs and intends to do so, as expressed in the covenant relationship. This provides grounds for an ultimate rather than a temporary security, since God's faithfulness can be depended upon through all the vicissitudes of life. The psalmist goes on to indicate that the terrors of the night and the arrows of the day and the "plagues that strike in the dark" (v. 6 TEV) or the "evils that kill in daylight" (v. 6 TEV) will not cause us to fear. There is an "absolute safety" (Calvin) in the face of all life's dangers, because God is our help and God is faithful.

Protection by God. Similar themes are captured in the final three verses of the psalm (vv. 14–16), where protection by God is again grounded in divine promises: God delivers those who love God and protects those who "know my name" (v. 14). When believers call on

Pastoral Perspective

a contemporary congregation. Terrorism, war, disease, poverty, economic recession, global climate change, broken relationships, sexual violence: these terrifying realities are in the headlines and on the minds and in the experiences of those who gather in worship seeking assurance of God's presence.

Just as remarkable as the vivid evocation of danger and fear is the psalmist's testimony of assurance that God is present and active regardless of circumstances. The psalmist's confidence in God's presence and protection is resolute, even matter of fact. The hymns sometimes called "psalms of trust" articulate a spiritual quest to find comfort, meaning, and hope by trusting God in the face of suffering. They instill a sense of confidence and courage so that speaker and hearer alike can resist being crushed by grief or fear. However, like the lament psalms, these passages do not offer painless or undemanding resolutions to life's intractable difficulties. J. David Pleins observes that whereas lament psalms juxtapose divine absence and silence with human suffering, the trust psalms point to the hidden yet deeply felt sense of divine presence *in the midst of* human anguish and anxiety. In doing so they evoke in worshipers a desire to trust in God, a sense of assurance that God is ever present, ever watchful.[1]

Further, as McCann points out, the Hebrew verb translated "love" in verse 14 conveys a sense of "being connected with" God intimately. While the English translation of this verse can be construed as promoting a quid pro quo arrangement wherein God's protection is a reward for following God, according to McCann, the verse suggests that "relation to God *is* deliverance—it is life."[2] This suggests that the point of seeking God is not to avoid suffering or hardship; rather, God is constantly available, sustaining those who will discern God's presence.

Christian history abounds with testimony to this sense of divine presence in the midst of suffering. For instance, the early-third-century martyr Felicitas connected her pending martyrdom with the possibility of mystical union with Jesus: "Another will be in me who will suffer for me, because I am to suffer for Him." The medieval English theologian Julian of Norwich, whose life was marked by illness almost to the point of death, repeatedly affirmed God's presence in her anguish. Julian reported that at one

---

1. J. David Pleins, *The Psalms: Songs of Tragedy, Hope, and Justice* (Maryknoll, NY: Orbis Books, 1993), 45–50. Pleins quote in final paragraph is from p. 46.
2. J. Clinton McCann, "The Psalms," in *The New Interpreter's Bible,* ed. Leander E. Keck (Nashville: Abingdon Press, 1996), 4:1048. Our discussion of the originating circumstances for the psalm depends in part on McCann's work.

Exegetical Perspective

Rhetorical Form. The purpose of the psalm seems to be to arouse courage by strengthening faith. The psalmist seeks to thank the monarch or leader and strengthen his determination to fight on behalf of the people. Like Psalm 15 and 24, Psalm 91 may be an entrance liturgy, addressed to those admitted into the temple. As such, it would be addressed to pilgrims needing divine help. The psalm would encourage them to trust in YHWH and thereby to find blessing and promise.[2]

The lectionary omits verses 7–13, two of which (vv. 11–12) are quoted by Satan in the temptation narratives of Matthew and Luke. Their omission sets aside an important canonical connection, a reference that is important to Christian preaching on this Old Testament text. It also excises a graphic portrayal of God's salvation in battle and angelic protection from mishap and danger. Bypassing verses that offer assurances belied by our life experiences probably makes it easier to preach on this psalm. At the same time, struggling with such passages is an important part of preaching the good news. Our calling is to place biblical texts in conversation with our people's lives. The canonical context is crucial to that dialogue.

Key Terms. The psalm begins with these words: "You who live in the shelter of the Most High, who abide in the shadow of the Almighty." "The shadow of the Almighty" is a figure of speech that refers to the protection of YHWH (see Pss. 17:8 and 36:7). The Almighty (El Shaddai) is an ancient divine title that appears elsewhere in the Psalter only in Psalm 68:14. It contains the ideas of God as refuge (61:3) and fortress (18:2).

Verse 3 specifies the kinds of threats against which God protects the faithful. "The snare of the fowler" refers to humanly produced threats or evils, rather than natural disasters. The "deadly pestilence" can also be rendered "the destructive word." The thought may be of false accusations and treacherous plots.

Verse 4 assures worshipers that God will cover them "with his pinions." The metaphor is of God as an eagle protecting its young. Bird metaphors also occur in Deuteronomy 32:11, Isaiah 31:5, Matthew 23:37, and Luke 13:34.

Verse 5 assures the worshipers that they need not fear "the terror of the night" or "the arrow that flies by day." Midnight and noon were two times when ancient people believed destructive influences and

2. A. A. Anderson, *The Book of Psalms, Volume 2, Psalms 73–150*, in Ronald E. Clements and Matthew Black, gen. ed., The New Century Bible Commentary (Paulton, Somerset, England: Marshall, Morgan, & Purnell, 1972), 655.

Homiletical Perspective

sentence the priest offered the blessed assurance that God protects those who willingly live and abide in God's presence. Rather than exploring all the possible meanings locked in the notions of "live" and "abide," the priest went on to indicate what would result for those who live in God's shelter or shadow.

For them, the prospects are very good! The suppliant will be delivered (v. 3a), covered (v. 4a), find refuge and be protected (v. 4b), and be unafraid (v. 5). The metaphors applied to the Deity who does all of those things are mixed. God is imaged as both birdlike and warriorlike, as God "covers" the believer "with his pinions" (the stiff flight feathers of the bird), provides refuge for the believer "under his wings" (v. 4b), and protects the believer with his "shield" and "buckler" (v. 4a). For those unacquainted with the details of battle armor, shields and bucklers are pretty much the same thing, though bucklers tend to be smaller than shields. Notwithstanding, it is worth noting that the metaphors are mixed and God uses defensive and not offensive weaponry to protect the believer.

There is a specific list of dangers from which God provides protection. All of the dangers indicated—"snare of the fowler" and "deadly pestilence" (v. 3), "terror" and "arrow" (v. 5), "pestilence" and "destruction" (v. 6)—should probably be read metaphorically, not literally. Further, the pairs "night" and "day" (v. 5) and "darkness" and "noonday" (v. 6) are a way of saying that God's protection is present twenty-four hours a day, seven days a week. Finally, God protects not only from external threats like traps and pestilence, but also from internal ones like terror. Indeed the confessions made in verse 2—"my refuge," "my fortress," "my God"—form in consciousness in such a way as to provide the believer full spiritual coverage from the Most High, Almighty, self-existing God of Israel (v. 1).

Verses 14–16 put the matter squarely. In these verses God is imaged as speaking to those who have faith, that is, to the worshiping community. These are sublime promises: deliverance for the ones who love God; protection for those who call on God's name; answers for those who make requests; divine presence, rescue from trouble, long life, and salvation in return for loving faithfulness.

The kind of love for God spoken of here has to do with the idea of attachment. Believers who are attached to God will experience the deliverance of God. The psalmist provides no indication of the nature of this attached love or how it occurs. Preachers may want to explore this notion of love as

Psalm 91:1-6, 14-16

Theological Perspective

God, God will answer, be with them in trouble, and rescue and honor them. These divine promises give specificity to the ways in which God's faithfulness is expressed. They encourage prayer, the assurance of the presence of God, and a divine deliverance as ways by which God protects the people of God.

Luther made reference to God's protection in Psalm 91 in relation to the pestilences of his day, the great plagues and dangers he had witnessed. He was afraid the psalm could be used in a superstitious fashion, in a way similar to what he regarded as the superstition in which at the end of the Roman Catholic mass, the prologue to John's Gospel was read and those who heard it were supposed to be safe. Luther recounted: "Three men were riding together, it was said, when a storm arose and a voice was heard to say, 'Strike!' Thereupon one of the men was struck down [by lightning]. A second time the voice was heard saying, 'Strike!' and the second man was struck down. When the voice was heard the third time saying, 'Strike!' there was another voice that replied, 'Don't strike because he heard St. John's Gospel today!' So he escaped with his life."[2]

Positively, Luther could say about verse 15: "See! That is the Christian way to get rid of misfortune and evil, that is, to endure it and to call upon God."[3] Believers are not exempt from "troubles and embarrassments" in life; God does not promise us "a life of ease and luxury" (Calvin, Ps. 91:15). Rather, God protects us in all our troubles because of who God is, the faithful God. So our security and safety is sure. We receive a "long life"—a biblical expression to signify God's pleasure—and ultimately, God will show us "my salvation" (v. 16).

DONALD K. MCKIM

Pastoral Perspective

point, when she "scarcely had the patience to go on living," God gave "comfort and rest for my soul, delight and security so blessed and so powerful that there was no fear, nor sorrow, no pain, physical or spiritual, that one could suffer which might have disturbed me."[3] From the times of slavery to the present, African American Christian worship has witnessed to the reality of God's presence in the face of enslavement, humiliation, and violent subjugation perpetrated by Euro-American oppressors. Song lyrics like "Didn't my Lord deliver Daniel, Daniel, Daniel . . . why can't he deliver me?" affirm confidence in God's constant willingness to act on behalf of God's troubled children. Like the psalmist, these voices refuse to see physical or psychic pain and God's presence as mutually exclusive.

It will not do for Christian worshipers to pretend that faith helps one avoid doubt, fear, or difficulty. Such suggestions risk promoting a talismanic approach to faith professions, rendering the claims of the gospel implausible or alienating those who experience hardship by suggesting they lack sufficient faith to prevent such circumstances. According to Pleins, Psalm 91 "shows us that we will only gain an awareness of God's presence to the extent that we let our worship resolutely seek God, not in spite of, but in light of human suffering." To those who gather for worship longing for a felt sense of God's presence, Psalm 91 offers "a way to reach to God without either drowning in suffering or fancifully imagining that all is well." It assures us that God is available to us in every circumstance.

TIMOTHY HESSEL-ROBINSON

---

2. Martin Luther, *Table Talk*, ed. Theodore G. Tappert, in *Luther's Works* (Philadelphia: Fortress Press, 1967), 54:434.

3. Martin Luther, *The Christian in Society III*, ed. Robert C. Schultz, in *Luther's Works* (Philadelphia: Fortress Press, 1967), 46:34.

3. *The Passion of Ss. Perpetua and Felicitas*, trans. H. R. Musurillo, in *Medieval Women's Visionary Literature*, ed. Elizabeth A. Petroff (New York and Oxford: Oxford University Press, 1986), 75. Julian of Norwich, *Showings*, trans. Edmund Colledge and James Walsh (New York: Paulist Press, 1978), 139–40.

power were especially powerful. Sunstroke and illness occur at noon. Night is the time the demon Lilith was believed by Israel's neighbors to attack human beings. The "pestilence that stalks in darkness" may be a reference to the Babylonian pest demon Namtar.[3]

Verses 11–12 are quoted by the Satan in Jesus' temptation narrative (Matt. 4:6; Luke 4:10, 11). Angels are presented as guardians of the faithful in the Old Testament. In Exodus 23:20, God assures the Israelites, "I am going to send an angel in front of you, to guard you on the way and to bring you to the place that I have prepared." What God promises the people as a whole in Exodus is promised to the individual Israelite in Psalm 91:11–12. "Bear you up" is a metaphor for special care (see Exod. 19:4; Isa. 63:9; Matt. 4:6; Luke 4:10–11) Dashing one's foot expresses the mistakes and troubles one encounters in life. They are a source of satisfaction to one's enemies (Ps. 35:15).

Throughout the Old Testament, the "angel of the Lord" contacts people, most often to bring a saving message from God. Those people include Hagar (Gen. 21:17), Abraham (Gen. 22:11, 15), Moses (Exod. 3:2), Balaam's donkey (and then Balaam) (Num. 22:22).

The one who trusts in God will not have to fear the threats enumerated in verses 3, 5, 6, and 10. More than that, this person will subdue these threats, symbolized by the lion and the adder, two dangerous predators who attack by surprise (v. 13). The lion is a symbol of open, devouring attack and the serpent of cunning, underhanded dealings. Both lions and snakes attack from hidden places.

Verses 14–16 are an oracle of YHWH that closes out the psalm; YHWH speaks to the individual in the first person.

The psalm offers several rich metaphors for the guidance and protection of God throughout life. It also offers several graphic metaphors for life's dangers. We need to preach realism about life alongside a theologically and biblically informed understanding of just what it means to assure people, in terms of verses 14–16, that God will deliver, protect, answer, be with, rescue, honor, satisfy, and save them.

ALYCE M. MCKENZIE

attachment to God. Similarly, preachers may explore what is meant by the phrase "know my name," especially in view of the fact that four names of God are given in verses 1 and 2. Just as verses 3–6 build on the declarations made in verses 1–2, verses 15–16 build on the statements in verse 14. Further, verses 15–16 are a terse restatement of the promises made in verses 3–6.

Preachers may wish to recognize that the one-point or three-point or dialogical or otherwise rationally structured sermon may not be the best medium for communicating what it is to be intimate with or attached to God. This text may require creative genre-bending that offers the experience, or at least an exercise in it, through led meditation or testimony. In the opening words of *The Imitation of Christ*, Thomas á Kempis says, "What good does it do to speak learnedly about the Trinity if, lacking humility, you displease the Trinity?"[1] "How will a leader best communicate the experience of intimacy with the Divine during this worship service?

Several potential preaching themes emerge from Psalm 91. The idea of living and abiding in God's shelter and shadow is powerful. Sermons that focus on this aspect of the psalm will no doubt concentrate on what it means to be in relationship with God by faith. There also exists the possibility of preaching a sermon about the many and complex ways God protects those who intentionally and consciously live in God's presence. The metaphors applied to the nature and person of God in verses 3 and 4, combined with the means God uses to protect and deliver in verse 4 and the fact that God's protection is both internal (psychoemotional) and external (sociophysical) in nature can provide great assurance to contemporary congregations. Loving and knowing God (v. 14), according to the psalmist, positions believers to be recipients of God's promises of protection, answered prayer, deliverance, long life, and salvation.

MARK A. LOMAX

---

3. Terrien, *Psalms*, 656–57.

1. Thomas á Kempis, *Imitation of Christ*, trans. Aloysius Croft and Harold Bolton (Nashville: Thomas Nelson, 1999), 2.

1 Timothy 6:6-19

[6]Of course, there is great gain in godliness combined with contentment; [7]for we brought nothing into the world, so that we can take nothing out of it; [8]but if we have food and clothing, we will be content with these. [9]But those who want to be rich fall into temptation and are trapped by many senseless and harmful desires that plunge people into ruin and destruction. [10]For the love of money is a root of all kinds of evil, and in their eagerness to be rich some have wandered away from the faith and pierced themselves with many pains.

[11]But as for you, man of God, shun all this; pursue righteousness, godliness, faith, love, endurance, gentleness. [12]Fight the good fight of the faith; take hold of the eternal life, to which you were called and for which you made the good confession in the presence of many witnesses. [13]In the presence of God, who gives life to all things, and of Christ Jesus, who in his testimony before Pontius

Theological Perspective

In this essay, I will suggest that the active and courageous choice for true life forms the starting point for Paul's instruction. It is not a passage for moralists, merely meant to condemn the wealthy, or a passage to inspire a futuristic hope in an eternal life to come. Rather, this passage articulates a perspective upon this life that is meant to shape the way humans relate to others and to the material world.

Paul describes this perspective in two phrases: eternal life and true life. Both times he uses these phrases, they are commands that employ words with the Greek root *epilambanomai*. The standard Greek lexicon (Arndt and Gingrich) suggests that this word means "take hold of, grasp, catch, sometimes with violence." Eternal life and true life are the alternative realities to be seized.

First, Paul instructed his readers to take hold of *eternal life* (*aiōniou zōēs*, v. 12). Often we think of eternal life as a futuristic goal, something we get after we have behaved ourselves in this life. Recent scholarship suggests that Paul was talking about something different. Biblical scholar Victor Pfitzner contended that Paul's prize of life is a prize to be seized upon in this life.[1] Modern theological scholarship has also

1. Victor Pfitzner, *Paul and the Agon Motif: Traditional Athletic Imagery in the Pauline Literature* (Leiden: E. J. Brill, 1967), 179f.

Pastoral Perspective

First Timothy here finishes where it began. What opened with a charge to Timothy to follow the writer's instructions, so that he might "fight the good fight" and have "faith and a good conscience" (1:18–19), now closes with the same charge. "Fight the good fight of the faith; take hold of the eternal life to which you were called and for which you made the good confession" (6:12). Scholars speculate that this confession could be from Timothy's ordination or his baptism. The assumption of baptism is strengthened as the writer likens Timothy's confession to the confession Christ Jesus made before Pontius Pilate. Jesus was never ordained, but he was baptized and called "beloved" by God as the water streamed down over his face.

Assuming that this passage reflects Timothy's baptism is more helpful pastorally, because it opens up the instructions in the letter to the entire body of Christ, rather than just those called to be ordained as pastors or deacons. Baptism is the sign and seal that one has given one's life to following the ways of God and has "taken hold of the eternal life" to which God calls every person, the life of faith as one whom God calls "beloved." It is a sign that one is a "God's person" or "a man of God," as Timothy is called (v. 11). "God's person" was an ancient title for a prophet from God. The writer of 1 Timothy charges

Pilate made the good confession, I charge you [14]to keep the commandment without spot or blame until the manifestation of our Lord Jesus Christ, [15]which he will bring about at the right time—he who is the blessed and only Sovereign, the King of kings and Lord of lords. [16]It is he alone who has immortality and dwells in unapproachable light, whom no one has ever seen or can see; to him be honor and eternal dominion. Amen.

[17]As for those who in the present age are rich, command them not to be haughty, or to set their hopes on the uncertainty of riches, but rather on God who richly provides us with everything for our enjoyment. [18]They are to do good, to be rich in good works, generous, and ready to share, [19]thus storing up for themselves the treasure of a good foundation for the future, so that they may take hold of the life that really is life.

Exegetical Perspective

This lectionary reading is a part of the final instructions in 1 Timothy, which begin in 6:2b (or perhaps 6:3). The initial portion of this closing set of exhortations returns to the theme of false teachers, about whom the author has warned earlier in the letter (1:3–11; 4:1–5). One of the accusations leveled against those in the community who are spreading false teaching is that they assume that "godliness is a means of gain" (6:5), that is, that the practice of their faith is the way to financial success. This problem leads the author in verses 6–10 and 17–19 to address the issue of money and wealth. The advice on riches is interrupted by the exhortation addressed to Timothy in verses 11–16.

The author of the Pastorals has earlier stated that indeed godliness is beneficial; it holds "promise for both the present life and the life to come" (4:8). In 6:6 he reasserts that godliness can be rewarding, but not in the materialistic way the false teachers are claiming. Unfortunately, the text does not provide any clues about the exact way in which some people in the community are attempting to profit financially from the Christian faith. Are they religious charlatans? Are they charging for their teaching services? (The author of the Pastorals, as well as Paul himself, did not object to Christian leaders receiving appropriate compensation [see 1 Tim. 5:17–18; 2

Homiletical Perspective

A recent article headed "How to Hide Figure Flaws" described how one can cover up thunder thighs and flabby necks with nifty apparel tricks—a scarf here, bell bottoms and vertical patterns there. It espoused a view that if we do not fit into a certain body shape, we should. If our noses do not measure up, they can be surgically resized—as we can have chins tucked and thighs liposuctioned.

Being "stuck on ourselves" is *idolatry*. Most in our congregations are well acquainted with that term, even if they are vague about how it applies to them. They might need reminding that it is they, not just the heathen others, who are guilty. Some illustration of how easy it is to slip into loving a good thing too much might be in order.

Idolatry's grip is subtle but choking. In most churches we give rightful attention to our physical plant, the gardens, the carpet, the leaky eaves. That is being a good steward of all with which we have been entrusted. Caring too much about those things is idolatry. Putting new carpet in the sanctuary while letting the food pantry for the hungry go empty is dubious at best. Different folk draw the line in different places.

The church in Germany before World War II struggled with such lines, on large scale. In the 1930s, as the German church and the Third Reich

1 Timothy 6:6-19

Theological Perspective

emphasized the present reality of the eternal. Swiss theologian Karl Barth argued that eternity is now, the *nunc aeternum*. Appealing to Jesus' proclamation that the kingdom of God is "at hand," (Mark 1:15 NRSV note), Barth argued that Christ was not looking into the temporal future but describing a reality of the present: the kingdom has arrived now. Christ's coming interrupts present time with the eternal. Building upon this view, Jürgen Moltmann argued that eternity not merely interrupts present time but even converts present time and creates new life: "The eschatology of the coming God calls to life the history of new human becoming, which is a becoming without any passing away, a becoming into lasting being in the coming presence of God."[2] In other words, eternal life is not something we look forward to, it is something that has arrived because Christ has arrived and has brought eternity into our midst. The reality of God's life-giving presence (v. 13) establishes itself in this era and shapes the human perspective on life and on the materials of this world: things are passing; we are not.

Paul's second command to seize is found in verse 19, when he exhorts his reader to seize *real life* (*ontōs zōēs*). The adjective, *ontōs*, is used to describe something or someone that is real or true. Paul builds a contrast between real life and destructive life. For Paul, destructive life is characterized by the pursuit of riches. He explains, "But those who want to be rich fall into temptation and are trapped by many senseless and harmful desires that plunge people into ruin and destruction" (v. 9). The word for "people" is *tous anthrōpous*, which suggests that Paul is referring not only to the damage to those who pursue riches, but also the damage to those whose lives are destroyed by their pursuit.

In our day, human trafficking serves as a poignant example of the destructive pursuit of wealth. In the past fifteen years, as many as two million people have left their homes and entered into human slavery—every year. The trafficking of persons is estimated to net around $10 billion annually; the majority of these persons are forced into sex work, hard labor, or servitude. Many suffer repeated physical and emotional forms of violence that threaten their very existence as humans. While Paul likely was not thinking of human slavery when he detailed the destruction wrought by a pursuit of wealth, the

Pastoral Perspective

Timothy to live into this name just as Christ Jesus did. As an extension of his personal charge, Timothy is to call each person in his community to consider his or her baptism the call to be a prophet in their time. "Prophet" is certainly a fitting title when we remember the baptism of Jesus. It is an eye-opening, shocking title when we consider our own baptism! Are we all called by our baptisms to be God's prophets in our own time?

If so, to what kind of life does our baptism, our "confession," call us? We are called to a life of "godliness combined with contentment" (v. 6). This way of life does not guarantee worldly success. In fact, Timothy is soundly warned to flee from "the love of money [that] is a root of all kinds of evil" (v. 10)—not to flee from money itself, but from the love or desire of riches, because this temptation leads to discontent and is a deep distraction from a life lived with God. The instruction does not exclude the monied among us. Those who are financially rich "in the present age" are called to "be rich in good works, generous, and ready to share" (vv. 17–18) so that they might stay focused on God's ways.

We are also called by our baptisms to "fight the good fight of the faith" (v. 12). The Greek phrase "fight the good fight" is broader in its implications than we might first imagine. It more accurately reads "contest the good contest." As one commentator has put it, "Maintaining the faith and living the faith require the energy of a good athlete."[1] A life that enduringly pursues such qualities as "righteousness, godliness, faith, love, endurance, gentleness" (v. 11) is an athletic life of faith, a life of wholeness and total commitment to the ways of God.

Recently I attended the seventh-degree testing of a black-belt tae kwon do master. The master had studied thirty-five years, almost 90 percent of his life, to reach the level of competency and discipline he demonstrated that day. The physical athleticism was astounding. Even more admirable was the "confession" of the way the master lived his life in order to fund his body's physical performance. At his testing event, the master spoke of seven qualities necessary for the achievement of black-belt excellence: "vision, belief in action, integrity, persistence, expansion, compassion, acceptance, and surrender."[2] These qualities are the "right ways" he is called to follow in

---

2. Karl Barth, *The Epistle to the Romans*, trans. from 6th German edition by E. C. Hoskyns (London: Oxford University Press, 1933), 497–500. Jürgen Moltmann, *The Coming of God*, trans. Margaret Kohl (Minneapolis: Fortress Press, 1996), 24.

1. James D. G. Dunn, "1 Timothy 6:3–2, Putting Wealth in Its Place," in *New Interpreter's Bible*, ed. Leander Keck (Nashville: Abingdon Press, 2000), 11:829.
2. Christopher Natzke, "The Seven Qualities of Black Belt Excellence," essay presented at Master Christopher Natzke's seventh-degree black-belt testing, May 17, 2008, at Cherokee Trail High School, Aurora, CO, 1–4.

Exegetical Perspective

Tim. 2:6; 1 Cor. 9:3–18; 1 Thess. 2:7–9]. Perhaps these false teachers' primary purpose is to make money, rather than promote the gospel.) Are they proponents of a first-century (or early second-century) version of the "prosperity gospel"?

Whatever the context, the situation provided the opportunity for the author to deal with the topic of material wealth. Contentment with the basic necessities of life ("food and clothing," v. 8) is put forward as the proper approach to life. The word translated as "contentment" (*autarkeias*) also means "self-sufficiency." This term, and the attitude it represents, was considered a virtue and was much discussed by the Stoics and the Cynics, two of the most popular philosophical groups in the Hellenistic/Roman world. Paul also used a form of this word in Philippians 4:11 when he said, "I have learned to be content with whatever I have." In Philippians, Paul credits his ability to be satisfied, regardless of the situation, to Christ, "who strengthens me" (4:13). The rationale given by the author of the Pastorals is one found in Jewish wisdom traditions—one comes into the world with nothing, and one leaves with nothing (see Job 1:21; Eccl. 5:15; Wis. 7:6).

The comments on contentment then lead the author to issue warnings about its opposite. Material wealth is dangerous; rather, the greed and love of money that drive the accumulation of riches are dangerous. Those who are caught up in the inordinate desire for wealth risk becoming ensnared by their own greed and ultimately sink into destruction. The warning is that they will eventually face not financial ruin, but eschatological ruin. Jesus made the same point in the parable of the Rich Fool (Luke 12:13–21). To reinforce his words about the dangers of avarice, the writer quotes what was likely a well-known saying, "For the love of money is a root of all kinds of evil" (1 Tim. 6:10). Similar sayings are found in various ancient writings.

Before completing his instructions about wealth, the author pauses to issue an exhortation to Timothy, advising him to "shun all this" (v. 11), referring not just to wealth, but to all the false teaching and errant behavior that have been described in the letter. Instead of "shun," a better translation of *pheuge* would be the more active verb "flee." The author sets up a contrast: Timothy is to flee the wrong and pursue the right, the latter illustrated by a list of virtues. This fleeing/pursuing imagery, along with the instruction to "fight the good fight," conveys the idea that faithful living before God is not easy. It requires dedication and hard work, like that of an athlete

Homiletical Perspective

became increasingly cozy, Christians who agreed with and supported the government were rewarded. If Christians chose to express views contrary to the government's point of view, they were called "unpatriotic," and those "so-called" Christians could be jailed without a trial.

As the 1930s wore on, being patriotic began to take an increasingly radical turn: from a "pure" Germany, to a "pure race," to the extermination of Jews as the "final solution."

Arguably, what started out as a movement summarized by the slogan "God and Country" became more and more about "Country and God." This was no subtle shift.

As some Christians saw the strands of Christianity, militarism, and nationalism being woven into a noose, they fought against it. In 1933 Martin Niemöller established the Pastor's Emergency League. In May 1934, they convened a synod meeting in Barmen, out of which came what we now call the Barmen Declaration.[1]

In this Declaration, the word "idolatry" is never mentioned, but that is what this Declaration is about. Hitler is not God's miracle for the world; Jesus Christ is. God's claim upon us is complete; the government's claim on us is *not*. Christian allegiance is to God and to God alone as revealed in Jesus Christ. Nothing comes before God.

This notion of idolatry is a theological peg on which we can hang what Paul says here about money. It is imperative to note what Paul does *not* say, that money is the root of all evil. It is *not* money that is either good or bad; it is the *love* of money that is bad. In fact, "the love of money is a root of all kinds of evil" (v. 10a).

Those who love money fall into the lot of those who, in their eagerness to be rich, "have wandered away from the faith and pierced themselves with many pains" (v. 10b). This is a pain Paul wants believers to avoid, but this is more easily said than done. At what point does our desire to earn, spend, and save money become idolatrous? When does our patriotism blind us to our kinship with brothers and sisters of other nations? At what point does our family commitment to the traveling soccer team compromise our service of God through Christ's church?

Our congregations are assailed with pressure to do more, to be more, to collect more. This hypercaffeinated accumulation of this kind of so-called

---

1. Jack Rogers, "The Theological Declaration of Barmen," in *Presbyterian Creeds* (Philadelphia: Westminster Press, 1985), 175–201.

1 Timothy 6:6-19

Theological Perspective

problem of human trafficking illustrates his point clearly: the love of money is a root of all kinds of evil (v. 10). By contrast, the love of the God "who gives life to all things" should affirm the *real* life of ourselves and of others.

According to Paul, this *real* life is one of generosity and good works (v. 18). Why is such a life considered *real*? In the experience of life, especially in capitalist societies that are driven by competition and self-interest, acts of self-sacrifice appear to limit one's life. How is it possible that one lays hold of life through an act of self-giving? The work of theologian Paul Tillich moves us toward an answer to that dilemma.[3]

For Tillich, faith is the integrating factor for all of human life; faith provides unity for life and enables persons to function. People can orient their lives around any variety of concerns—wealth, social status, politics, God, or a religious institution. Some of these concerns are ultimate and lasting, and some of them are not; some persons have faith in that which is ultimate, while others orient their lives around that which is temporary or that which disintegrates and destroys. Tillich, like Paul, claims that wealth and power are unreliable objects of faith, for they are fleeting and provide little hope in the face of death. In contrast, generosity and good works affirm real life, because they arise from faith in the ultimate. Such generosity becomes real life because it is an authentic act based on faith in the eternality of life. Thus the self-giving life is not a negation of life but an affirmation of the eternality of life: by God life was given, is being given, and will be given. With this new orientation, persons can make active and courageous choices to affirm the existence of their lives and the lives of those around them.

STEPHANIE MAR SMITH

Pastoral Perspective

his life as an athlete, a martial-arts master, and a teacher. However, it was clear that his athletic life is not separate from the rest of his life. These seven qualities encompass and fund the "confession" of this man's entire life.

The tae kwon do master's list is remarkably parallel to the list given by the writer of 1 Timothy. Each requires that the body, mind, spirit, and heart be fully engaged and working interdependently. Striving for "righteousness and godliness," seeking "vision," and finding "belief in action" demand more than an intellectual assent to certain ideas. They require more than a disciplined commitment to a set of rules just to achieve certain goals or skills or even healthful living. Righteousness, godliness, vision, and belief in action are qualities of life that demand the entirety of ourselves—body, mind, spirit, and heart—if they are to lead us in the ways of "faith, love, endurance, gentleness" or the ways of "integrity, persistence, expansion, compassion, acceptance, and surrender."

Perhaps this whole-life picture of gospel living is the good news of our passage. If so, the pastor's challenge here is to portray the interdependent nature of engaging our full selves in following the right ways of our God. Intellectual assent without an open heart or the introspection of spirit produces empty words and deeds. Any bodily skill without the direction of thought or the fire of our spirit's will or the feeling of our hearts can be aimlessly narcissistic at best and destructive at worst. Acting on the feelings of the heart without mindful intent and awareness can smother relationship with overcontrol. The spirit's intuition is useless without the mind's direction and the heart's compass. To make "the good confession" and live into the life we are called to by baptism, to "take hold of the eternal life," "to fight the good fight of the faith" (v. 12), we must be fully engaged—body, mind, spirit, and heart—in following the ways of God.

JANE ANNE FERGUSON

3. Paul Tillich, *The Courage to Be* (London: Collins, 1952), 173ff.

engaged in an athletic competition (likely the imagery behind the words translated as "fight the good fight"). The reward for such persistence and devotion is invaluable—eternal life.

The reminder to Timothy (v. 12) that he has previously "made the good confession in the presence of many witnesses" (at his baptism? at his ordination [4:14]?) serves both as a word of encouragement and as a reminder to live up to that previous confession. The mention of Timothy's confession before many witnesses provides the occasion for the author to remind Timothy of Christ, who himself made "the good confession" before Pilate. He issues to Timothy a solemn charge to keep "the commandment" (v. 14), without specifying what the commandment is. It likely refers to the entirety of his Christian calling, and especially his calling to be a minister. The exhortation to Timothy concludes with a doxology (vv. 15–16), similar to the one in 1:17, which stresses the uniqueness and sovereignty of God.

In verses 17–19, the author returns to the topic of wealth, this time offering instructions for those in the community who are already rich. That these instructions are included indicates that the audience to whom the Pastorals were addressed includes people of financial means. Whereas verses 6–10 paint a strongly negative picture of the desire for wealth, verses 17–19 are more moderate. Wealth itself is not condemned, but rather the improper attitude toward wealth. Wealth is still seen as possessing inherent danger; one can wrongly place ultimate value on material goods, rather than on God, who is the source of all things. Those who have riches are to make proper use of them, which means they are to use their wealth "to do good, to be rich in good works, generous, and ready to share" (v. 18).

This lectionary text abounds with sound insight about the proper attitude toward wealth. With the exception of sexual misconduct, nothing discredits the work of the church in the eyes of the world more than financial greed and corruption. The advice of the author of the Pastorals is as pertinent to the church today as it was to its original audience.

MITCHELL G. REDDISH

wealth has become synonymous with the American dream. Just as a Barbie doll–proportioned woman could never actually walk, it is impossible to be on this driving, burn-the-candle-at-both-ends track and experience the "gain in godliness combined with contentment" (v. 6) about which Paul writes. Sheryl Crow suggests that "It's not having what you want / It's wanting what you've got" ("Soak Up the Sun"). While we sing that catchy song when it comes on the radio, we do not believe the words. Paul wants us to, because *we have a lot*—"a good measure, pressed down, shaken together, running over" (Luke 6:38), has been put into our lap. We have every reason to rejoice!

There are echoes of Jesus here—when he reminds his disciples, "Those who love me will keep my word, and my Father will love them, and we will come to them and make our home with them" (John 14:23). This is a home not built with human hands. Shalom lives here. Serving others is part of the daily pattern. Worship punctuates each day and evening. This home with God-on-earth offers but a glimpse of that eternal home in which we will join Christ in "unapproachable light" (1 Tim. 6:16). Because of God's grace, we have every reason to be content.

Paul urges his readers *not* "to set their hopes on the uncertainty of riches, but rather on God who richly provides us with everything for our enjoyment" (v. 17). A life with this focus will have to do not with bank accounts and body shape, but with wealth beyond mere *stuff* that rusts and can be eaten up by moths (Matt. 6:19).

This is the full life no idol can replace.

Paul would say that it is vitally important to put wealth (and other potential idols) into proper perspective. Take hold of the life that really *is* life, Paul would say. Do not get stuck on money, or nation, or CNN, or church growth or . . . anything else. "Pursue righteousness, godliness, faith, love, endurance, gentleness" (1 Tim. 6:11).

Not even the quest for perfect thighs is more important than this.

WILLIAM P. "MATT" MATTHEWS

Luke 16:19-31

¹⁹"There was a rich man who was dressed in purple and fine linen and who feasted sumptuously every day. ²⁰And at his gate lay a poor man named Lazarus, covered with sores, ²¹who longed to satisfy his hunger with what fell from the rich man's table; even the dogs would come and lick his sores. ²²The poor man died and was carried away by the angels to be with Abraham. The rich man also died and was buried. ²³In Hades, where he was being tormented, he looked up and saw Abraham far away with Lazarus by his side. ²⁴He called out, 'Father Abraham, have mercy on me, and send Lazarus to dip the tip of his finger in water and cool my tongue; for I am in agony in these flames.' ²⁵But Abraham said, 'Child, remember that during your lifetime you received your good things, and Lazarus in like manner evil things; but now he is comforted here, and you are in agony. ²⁶Besides all this, between you and us a great chasm has been fixed, so that those who might want to pass from here to you cannot do so, and no one can cross from there to us.' ²⁷He said, 'Then, father, I beg you to send him to my father's house—²⁸for I have five brothers—that he may warn them, so that they will not also come into this place of torment.' ²⁹Abraham replied, 'They have Moses and the prophets; they should listen to them.' ³⁰He said, 'No, father Abraham; but if someone goes to them from the dead, they will repent.' ³¹He said to him, 'If they do not listen to Moses and the prophets, neither will they be convinced even if someone rises from the dead.'"

Theological Perspective

The parable of the Rich Man and Lazarus narrates the very reversals of fortune that we find promised in the Magnificat (1:52–53) and the Sermon on the Plain (6:20–26). As such, the parable drives home Luke's relentless concern for the faithful stewardship of goods. Justice is presented as an eschatological balancing of the scales: those who have suffered in need are made full, and those who have reveled in excess are left empty.

What this parable adds to the general injunction to generosity is a narrative in which the very proximity of the rich and poor comes to the foreground. "Rich" and "poor" are not left as vague generalities but are depicted as two men, one inside the gate of abundance and one outside. Their close proximity accentuates the fact that Lazarus seems invisible to the rich man. Even after death, when the rich man gazes across the abyss to see Lazarus in Abraham's bosom, he speaks of the poor man in the third person—as if he were not there.

This text presents us with the great moral challenge of seeing, and then making visible, the invisible suffering of the world. Indeed, this may be one of our most important moral challenges today. Our global network of communication allows us to be more aware of the world's suffering than ever before, but we have become adept at ignoring the suffering

Pastoral Perspective

As parables of Jesus go, this has to be one of the least familiar. It flows from prior dialogue between Jesus and the Pharisees about the love of money and the search for riches and true riches. This parable is not difficult to understand, but perhaps difficult to hear, because its meaning is clear: riches cannot save you. It ends with a deafening silence.

The parable begins in a familiar formula of its time, borrowed from what scholars think is an Egyptian tale. Two worlds within two worlds are clearly set up. The parable first describes two physical worlds: the earthly life and the life beyond this one. These worlds are connected by the experience of death. Curiously woven within each of these are two other worlds: the world of the haves and that of the have-nots, the world of the rich and that of the poor, the world of the comforted and that of the afflicted. This parable is set up with clearly defined boundaries between worlds, and one has to wonder if ever the twain shall meet.

The socioeconomic divisions between the two characters are obvious. Once upon a time there were two men, one rich and one poor. The two players do not interact. This is simply the way things are. There is a clear division of status. The reader can relate and prefers to be related immediately to the rich. Who, after all, would want to be the hungry one lying in

Exegetical Perspective

Money and possessions form a central theme in Luke–Acts.[1] Mary's Magnificat (Luke 1:46–55), the necessity for Jesus' parents to sacrifice the turtledove instead of the lamb when they present him at the temple (Luke 2:22–24), Jesus' stark teaching about rich and poor in the Sermon on the Plain (Luke 6:20–26), the parable of the Rich Fool (Luke 12:16–21), the communal sharing of goods in the earliest Jerusalem church (Acts 2:42–47), the tragedy of Ananaias and Sapphira, who withheld some of their money from that community (Acts 5:1–11)—these are but a few of the many passages that tell the tale of Luke and lucre. Even amid all these vivid and noteworthy texts, Luke's dealing with the problem of wealth may be most directly and clearly treated in the powerful parable of the Rich Man and Lazarus (Luke 16:19–31).

Lazarus is the only character in Jesus' parables who is named. In contrast to him, the rich man has no name, though Christian tradition sometimes calls him Dives, a Latin adjective meaning "rich." The parable begins abruptly, though the theme of money has been prominent throughout the chapter (vv. 9, 11, 14–15). Jesus' story is told in light of "the

1. See Luke Timothy Johnson, *The Literary Function of Possessions in Luke–Acts*, SBL Dissertation Series 39 (Missoula, MT: Scholars Press, 1977).

Homiletical Perspective

Rich man Dives he lived so well.
Dip your finger in the water, come, and cool my
    tongue, 'cause I'm tormented in the flame.
And when he died he went straight to hell.
Dip your finger in the water, come, and cool my
    tongue, 'cause I'm tormented in the flame.

The parable before us is captured in this African American spiritual. The rich man lived so well, yet now he is the one begging, looking up and wanting a handout, desperate for a drop of water to ease his fiery torment. Hearing the melody in our heads only enhances the sense of divine retribution lavishly portrayed in this parable.

The story of Lazarus and the rich man is full of contrasts and reversals. The poor man is named, while the rich man is not. The rich man is dressed in purple, while the poor man is "dressed in" sores. The rich man feasts sumptuously, while Lazarus, looking up, longs to be satisfied with what falls from the table. The rich man has a proper burial, while Lazarus is carried away by the angels. By the end of the story, Lazarus, the poor man, is looking down from heaven, and the rich man is the one looking up, begging.

The contrasts and disparities between the rich and the poor so vividly described here are meant to

Luke 16:19-31

Theological Perspective

that is right at our doorstep. Maybe, in fact, these two things are connected; the more we become voyeurs upon the faraway sufferings of others, the more impotent we feel to do anything about pain and injustice. Despair and cynicism tempt us to close our eyes to suffering and shut down our overloaded sympathies.

In his *Confessions,* Augustine analyzes his own attraction to plays that depict tragic and sorrowful events. He notes that "in the capacity of spectator one welcomes sad feelings; in fact, the sadness itself is the pleasure." Next Augustine asks, "How real is the mercy evoked by fictional dramas? The listener is not moved to offer help, but merely invited to feel sorrow."[1] One might wonder whether our capacities for global communication create a similar result, producing spectators who are invited to feel sorrow but are "not moved to offer help." Instead, with one click we navigate to a new site or a new channel.

As well as anyone, Johann Baptist Metz has called our attention to invisible suffering. For Metz, such attentiveness lies at the heart of Christian spirituality. He invites us into "a God-mysticism with an increased readiness to perceive, a mysticism of open eyes that sees more and not less. It is a mysticism that especially makes visible all invisible and inconvenient suffering, and—convenient or not—pays attention to it and takes responsibility for it, for the sake of a God who is a friend to human beings."[2] This parable challenges us not simply to share wealth but to become attentive to the poor and suffering persons who are before us, who dwell at our doorstep or, more likely, in another part of town where we do not see them if we do not want to. Where is the invisible suffering in our world: the suffering of women and children in sweatshops, who are invisible behind the labels we buy; the suffering of animals in factory farms, who are invisible behind our fast food; the suffering of the suspect who is tortured behind locked doors to calm our cancerous fears? We live within political and economic systems that feed upon the sufferings of others, all the while keeping those sufferings invisible. The call of Christ is to refuse to live any longer by those convenient fabrications.

The latter portion of this parable turns us to a second, though related, theological issue: what motivates change? Not wanting his brothers to suffer his own fate, the rich man begs Abraham to send

1. Augustine, *The Confessions,* trans. Maria Boulding (New York: Vintage Books, 1998), 38.
2. Johann Baptist Metz, *A Passion for God: The Mystical-Political Dimension of Christianity,* trans. J. Matthew Ashley (Mahwah, NJ: Paulist Press, 1998), 163.

Pastoral Perspective

someone's doorway? Most of us would not want to imagine such need and, in truth, cannot. We choose the rich man's perspective.

Robert Frost's poem "Mending Wall" wrestles with the irony of neighbors who long to have clear boundaries on their neighborliness. Frost wonders aloud why it is that we divide ourselves. "On a day we meet to walk the line and set the wall between us once again." There is something about us that likes those clearly defined boundaries of what's my place and what's yours.[1]

In this parable, there is little interaction between the two men. The rich man is not disdainful of Lazarus; he simply does not notice him. What we know about Lazarus is his name and his need. Lazarus's empty stomach and life are gnawing at him, and his gaze is set on the household of the rich man, where he hopes only for the leftovers—or less, the crumbs. He gets nothing. The only ones who notice him are the dogs, who, in a grotesque show of how low a human life can go, lick the oozing wounds of the poor man.

Just when two lives are as far apart as they can possibly be, there is a shift; much like the funnel of an hourglass, all the sand of time is drawn through the narrow sieve of death to be redistributed on the other side. Redistributed it is, again drawing a boundary that this time results in a complete reversal of roles. The one who was afflicted is now comforted, and the one who lived comfortably is now in agony. The division now is more physical than relational; there is a great, impassable chasm between them. On the one side is Lazarus in the arms of Abraham, nestled as a child nestles at the bosom of its mother: fed, safe, warm. Lazarus has never had this experience before. On the other side of the chasm is the rich man, who this time is being tormented in the low place, left to gaze hungrily. Sadly, the man is none the wiser for his death experience, still acting as a little king, though wearing no crown, ordering Abraham to order Lazarus to serve him.

The message is fatal. It is too late. The rich man has had his day. Note how Abraham is curiously compassionate toward this selfish man whom Abraham calls his child. With some measure of sadness, Abraham indicates the gulf between them. It is too late for the man. Abraham takes no delight in this.

Now the man shows the first compassion we have seen, but it is still deceptively mixed with manipulation. "If you cannot help me, help my family. Send

1. Robert Frost, "Mending Wall," in *Robert Frost: Collected Poems, Prose, and Plays* (New York: Library of America, 1995), 39.

Pharisees, who were lovers of money" (v. 14) and who ridiculed Jesus for what he had said about people not being able to serve God and wealth at the same time (v. 13).

The rich man dresses in purple and fine linen clothes, which signifies that he likely comes from royalty. That he lives in a "gated" community indicates social barriers as well. Despite all this, though, the rich man is not depicted as an evil person; he simply does not "see" the man at his gate, though he himself eats "sumptuously every day." The poor man, on the other hand, apparently comes to the gate regularly, desiring to be fed some scraps of this sumptuous food that the rich man ate. He is characterized as a man who is abjectly poor, with sores that the dogs came to lick, no doubt leaving him degraded and also open to infections and slow, if not impossible, healing.

Then both men die, though the reader may notice that only the rich man is buried. Angels carry off the poor man to Abraham's bosom, whereas the rich man dies and ends up in Hades, the abode of the dead. The vision of the other world corresponds to the first-century writing of 2 Esdras 7:36: "The pit of torment shall appear, and opposite it shall be the place of rest; and the furnace of hell shall be disclosed, and opposite it the paradise of delight." There the rich man observes Abraham and Lazarus together. He calls out to father Abraham to have mercy on him and to send Lazarus, still thought of as a servant, with water to cool his thirst. Abraham reminds the rich man that during his lifetime he enjoyed the good things of life and Lazarus had nothing. Furthermore, there is a great gap between where Abraham and Lazarus are and where the rich man is, "and no one can cross from there to us" (v. 26).

The rich man then remembers his five brothers who are still alive and begs Abraham to send someone to warn them, lest they end up in the same predicament as he is. Abraham says, "They have Moses and the prophets; they should listen to them." "No, father Abraham; but if someone goes to them from the dead, they will repent" (vv. 29–30). With this obvious allusion to Jesus' resurrection, father Abraham responds that they will not be convinced even if someone rises from the dead.

The rich man is not pictured as inherently wicked. He does not persecute Lazarus, nor does he refuse him food, nor does he sponsor legislation to rid the gates of poor people like Lazarus. As John Donahue points out, the problem is that all those days on earth the rich never "see" the poor. "One of the prime dangers of wealth is that it causes

evoke an equally vivid reaction. Luke clearly tells us that this parable was given to "lovers of money" (v. 14), so it was a direct message to them. Apparently Jesus wanted to reveal through this story that they loved their money more than people, their possessions more than the poor, their clothes more than compassion, and their extravagant feasts more than sharing food with the hungry. Perhaps Jesus had been a guest at one of his listener's homes and had witnessed a scene similar to the one with which he begins his parable. This surely would have heightened the discomfort created by his words.

There are many uncomfortable questions before us as we surrender to one of the harshest readings in Scripture. Is it possible to preach this parable without the accompanying condemnation? Will our interpretation of this story vary dramatically, depending on our audience? Is it as simple as good news for the poor and bad news for the rich? Can we find a message of redemption anywhere in a parable that shouts out, "Too late, too late"?

The themes presented here stand as powerful indictments of our world today, while at the same time offering the ongoing radical and redemptive ministry we are called to, if we seek to follow the teachings of the teller of this parable.

The Great Chasm. The ever-widening gap between the rich and the poor is one of the most important issues of our day. The intrepid "moral of the story" expressed in this parable is that if you do not cross the gaping chasm between the rich and the poor in this life, you surely will not be able to do it in the next. At least for those who hoard and have more than their share on this earth, there is no respite to be offered in the life to come. Warnings and messages come in every form, but they remain unheeded. In the final day, this chasm cannot be crossed.

There is no escaping this indictment. Those who help create the economic divide by greed and selfishness will not be able to right it for themselves in any other life than this one. This is a parable urging "the haves" to do justice now, for there will be no opportunity later. The saying "Justice delayed is justice denied" extends even further through this teaching of Jesus that seems to imply that *redemption delayed is redemption denied.*

Good News to the Poor. No matter how we exegete it or attempt to soften its message, this parable is a warning to the wealthy and a word of comfort and hope to the poor. Jesus' identity as a prophet who was

Luke 16:19-31

Theological Perspective

Lazarus to warn them. Abraham rebuffs the idea, in part, we might imagine, because the rich man continues to use Lazarus as an object for his own purposes, but also because it simply would not do any good. If the brothers have not listened to Moses and the prophets, why would they listen to a poor nobody who rises from the dead? What the rich man wants is a sign that carries with it no ambiguity, no possibility that it will be treated as just another opinion to take or leave.

As Abraham's answer reminds us, all of our speech, all of our signs function within a realm of indeterminacy and ambiguity. The rich man wants the sign that validates all other signs—an event so miraculous that no one could possibly doubt that this messenger was speaking the truth of God. Abraham tells us that there is no Archimedean point when it comes to truth and language. There is no act of communication that rises above our finitude and our sinful penchant for self-serving misreadings. We are always located in the situation of hearing a word from another and trusting it—or not. We are always in a place of having to have faith. Even if Lazarus returned, the brothers would have to believe that this really was Lazarus, that he really had died, and that he really had a message from their brother. This may well have seemed even less plausible than believing that God had already spoken through Moses and the prophets and that they should listen.

The quest for certitude often becomes an excuse for not acting. This parable suggests that God will not, perhaps cannot, speak to us with a sign that escapes the need to be interpreted and believed. We are left with a call to act based not on an absolute certainty in the divine command, but on the visibility of the suffering face that becomes, for us, the face of Christ himself, shrouded in all the ambiguity of our finitude and fallenness.

SCOTT BADER-SAYE

Pastoral Perspective

Lazarus!" Abraham responds, "They have been given what guidance they need, but they may not listen, even to a voice from the dead."

The end of this parable pushes us back across the chasm into the earthly world. "Break through!" shouts the man, but in fact God has already broken through with his word through the prophets and his Word in his Christ. People have been given what they need to live faithful lives. They will listen, or they will not. They will respond, or they will not.

Perhaps the boundaries and walls we have drawn are not so much between us and others as between us and God. With a mixture of invitation and warning, the angel says to the church in Laodicea, "Listen! I am standing at the door, knocking; if you hear my voice and open the door, I will come in to you and eat with you, and you with me" (Rev. 3:20).

Frost winds down with these thoughts, "Before I built a wall I'd ask to know what I was walling in or walling out."[2]

So consider who is on the other side of that door. Who is this Christ? In Matthew 25, Jesus tells us he is Lazarus: He is that one lying at our door hungry and thirsty. He is that one imprisoned and cut off from "decent" society. He is the marginalized one that you can just as easily walk by. That is God's Christ who stands at our wall, knocking. When we answer, we may not find someone who looks like us, but we may very well find someone who looks like our God, if we are paying attention.

HELEN MONTGOMERY DEBEVOISE

---

2. Ibid.

blindness."[2] In modern times Lazarus corresponds to the person who begs, but one dare not look into his or her eyes, lest a claim is made upon one's compassion. It is acceptable to give aid to the worthy poor, but it is also socially permissible to regard some as not worthy. Perhaps reader and preacher and congregation will find it hard to identify with either the rich man with all his wealth or the poor man with devastation. They both represent people other than us; but perhaps we can identify with the five brothers, those who can be instructed by Moses and the prophets and can come actually to "see" the beggar at our gates. The parable then becomes a word for those left behind to "warn them so that they will not also come into this place of torment" (v. 28).[3] Inherent in Luke's Gospel is the word of reversal that the first become last and the last first (Luke 13:30; 14:9–11; Mark 10:31; Matt. 19:30; 20:16). From Mary's Magnificat (1:46–55) on throughout Luke's Gospel, we read of the God who "has filled the hungry with good things, and sent the rich away empty" (1:53). The parable powerfully calls into question how we handle our money today and raises the question of whether we "see" the poor at our gates.

CHARLES B. COUSAR

anointed to "preach good news to the poor" (Luke 4:18) was manifested in living color as he told this parable. Jesus did not espouse some pie-in-the-sky-by-and-by theology. He spoke out against the real inequities of his day by his stern and unrelenting admonition to the wealthy to share their earthly resources and to cease oppression wherever it existed.

The Hard Work of Transformation. By the parable's end, the rich man is in a place of torment, yet he is still entrenched in his privileged attitude. He still wants to order Lazarus to do something for him. In fact, he does not even speak directly to Lazarus but entreats Abraham to send Lazarus to do his bidding. The rich man, who would not lend a hand to Lazarus, whose only solace was the dogs' tongues, now is asking Lazarus to provide him some relief from pain. He also begs Abraham to send a warning to his brothers, but Abraham replies that even if one were to rise from the dead, that would not be enough. Abraham's words suggest that stepping out of one's privilege is perhaps one of the most difficult journeys of transformation. Two chapters ahead, Jesus will compare it to getting a camel through a needle's eye (18:25).

True Faith. Abraham's words, there is "a great chasm" between you and "us" (v. 26), make Abraham—not God—the judge here. The great teacher puts Abraham, the parent of faith, in the role of judge. Abraham sits with Lazarus, indicating a startling truth about who is faithful and who is not. What we know from the parable is that because of his lack of action and compassion, the rich man cannot cross over to the place of faith, nor does he have a place by Abraham's side. To an impoverished group of people, this parable would offer great comfort that God sees their suffering and is on their side. To most of us, however, steeped in a consumer society and often on the wrong side of the chasm, this parable is one of the hardest to hear . . . if we really hear.

G. PENNY NIXON

2. John Donahue, *The Gospel in Parable; Metaphor, Narrative, and Theology in the Synoptic Gospels* (Philadelphia: Fortress Press, 1988), 171.
3. Arland J. Hultgren, *The Parables of Jesus: A Commentary* (Grand Rapids: Eerdmans, 2000), 116.

Lamentations 1:1-6

¹How lonely sits the city
    that once was full of people!
How like a widow she has become,
    she that was great among the nations!
She that was a princess among the provinces
    has become a vassal.

²She weeps bitterly in the night,
    with tears on her cheeks;
among all her lovers
    she has no one to comfort her;
all her friends have dealt treacherously with her,
    they have become her enemies.

³Judah has gone into exile with suffering
    and hard servitude;
she lives now among the nations,
    and finds no resting place;

Theological Perspective

Theologies of hope, psalms of praise, elations of joy, and the cheery songs of "contemporary" worship are silenced or, at best, reduced to faint whispers in the face of the abject devastation and unthinkable suffering of sixth-century Judah. The nation was in trauma, stripped of all that gave them meaning—their holy city, the promised land, the temple, and the Davidic monarchy. Many of them had been killed; others were exiled. What could be said in the wake of such destruction? How could it be said? Words seemed frail, gratuitous, or utterly useless. A brooding silence hovered over the poet.

The radical suffering near the turn of the twenty-first century resonates hauntingly with the Babylonian captivity of Judah. The global genocides in Europe and Cambodia, the destructive bombings in Oklahoma City and New York City, the massacres at Columbine High School and Virginia Tech beg for theological explanations and moral responses. In addition to these inexplicable public events, many individual congregants must also suffer with their own personal tragedies. The captivity of a silent grief initially shackles the reader and would-be preacher of this text.

I recently spoke at the memorial service of one of my university's students. His death was tragic enough. That he took his own life when his significant other

Pastoral Perspective

She sleeps slumped in a maroon wingback chair, a large-print magazine folded into her lap. The table beside her is piled with third-class mail and a small glass. Beside the chair is a stack of cards and notes, some many years old. Read and reread, they provide a link to her past. They are her memory. A portrait of her husband smiles at her from its place beside the closet door. The television blares, her nap anesthetizing the loneliness.

At the department store where she worked, other clerks had flocked to kibitz about her horde of loyal clientele and glean a trade secret, some insight to increase their own sales. She had developed a skill of building a customer base and kept a file on each woman to whom she sold a dress, noting things like, "She really likes blue." Her arsenal of greetings included, "Have you seen the new stock that just arrived today?" It was a question that started a relationship, not one that ended conversation and led to, "No, thank you. I'm just looking." There are no new customers at Grove Manor, however, and clerks no longer rally for her wisdom.

So she sleeps and reads, still stylish in her jumper and cardigan and designer shoes. Even in her advancing age, she determines to sport chic footwear rather than "sensible shoes." She had reigned as queen of performance and service in the dress

her pursuers have all overtaken her
in the midst of her distress.

⁴The roads to Zion mourn,
for no one comes to the festivals;
all her gates are desolate,
her priests groan;
her young girls grieve,
and her lot is bitter.

⁵Her foes have become the masters,
her enemies prosper,
because the LORD has made her suffer
for the multitude of her transgressions;
her children have gone away,
captives before the foe.

⁶From daughter Zion has departed
all her majesty.
Her princes have become like stags
that find no pasture;
they fled without strength
before the pursuer.

Exegetical Perspective

Lamentations was penned in the wake of the destruction of Jerusalem by the Babylonians in 586 BCE. Many people were killed in the eighteen-month siege of the city, and the lives of survivors were broken and shattered. Lamentations gives voice to those who survived this devastating experience; it is survivors' literature. In more modern terms, post–traumatic stress syndrome was a common reality for those who lived through this horrendous time. The book, traditionally thought to be written by Jeremiah, is authored by a survivor remaining in the land, seeking to address such issues.

One important way of coming to terms with such suffering is to recall as vividly as possible what the community has been through and to honor that memory. Images from Israel's slavery in Egypt pervade the book and help give depth to the depiction of distress (e.g., 1:3). Lamentations brings those suffering voices to the surface, in lyrical poetry, and enables the readers to relive those moments in all of their horrific detail (see the laments over Jerusalem in Jer. 9:17–19; 14:17–19). We will not forget! That the author uses the genre of the lament (addressed to God, vv. 11, 20), so common in the Psalter, to convey these dreadful experiences both signals the gravity of the remembrances and constitutes an invitation to readers to join in these liturgical moments.

Homiletical Perspective

Lamentations' raw pain leaves the preacher with many directions for proclamation, none of them pretty—honest, yes, just not pretty at the start.

Used by Hebrews to mark the temple's destruction and by the Revised Common Lectionary to continue the cries of Jeremiah, these verses anchor their pain in the remembrances of Jerusalem's destruction. Applying Jeremiah's cries to our contemporary world demands that every preacher proclaim good news while confessing pain. Given the reality of that pain to the myriads within and without the church, the preacher should center on the pain these verses convey, without trying to move too quickly beyond it.

C. S. Lewis wrote, "God whispers to us in our pleasures, speaks in our conscience, but shouts in our pains: it is His megaphone to rouse a deaf world."[1] Since pain is ever around us, use this text to proclaim that God's arms are around us too. Many people understand pain to lead to anger. There is anger enough in the text, but it is honest anger that confronts the subjective sense that "the LORD has made [us] suffer for the multitude of [our] transgressions" (v. 5).

In truth, much of our pain is self-inflicted, either directly or indirectly. How often is that honest word

---

1. C. S. Lewis, *The Problem of Pain* (New York: Macmillan, 1962), 93.

Lamentations 1:1-6

Theological Perspective

broke off their relationship on Valentine's Day exacerbated my dilemma: What to say? How to say it? I fumbled for the right words. After appreciatively remarking on his brilliance, personality, and incredible promise, I struggled to find a focus that would bring hope and encouragement. Although the several theodicies from philosophy of religion studies were available to me—providing reasons that could make some sense and bring comfort—I did not proclaim them. They did not seem to "fit," and I refused to engage them before a congregation of broken hearts.

Shortly after that experience, I turned my attention to thinking theologically about our text. I wish I had studied it prior to the memorial service. It provides a marvelous perspective about addressing the unspeakable events of life. At least three foci stand out: brooding in silence, breaking the silence with a message of theological substance, and providing a whisper of solace through protest against God and affirmation of God.

Silence. First, silence seems the obverse of proclamation; yet a rich theology of silence can inform the message and the messenger. Radical suffering initially muffles the usefulness of any rational discourse. As we learn from Job and his friends, not speaking may be the most speakable thing to do. Although Lamentations does not manifest a theology of the absence of God or the dearth of hope, it may be implied that before the poet wrote, he contemplated, silently, before the unspeakable. Victor Turner's notion of "limit situations," in which one comes to a border and senses a suspension of the normal (like being "in limbo") that evokes a sense of the absence of structure and meaning, helps explain the timely silence.[1] Additionally, Rudolf Otto's claim that the most intense encounters with sacred reality are "ineffable," unable to be put into words, becomes existential to the silence. Thus, taking the role of a Cistercian contemplative may be the first step in speaking about the unimaginable.

Breaking the Silence. Second, breaking the silence is a necessary risk for the preacher. You must speak! People long to hear the Word in our words. Mumbling half-hearted clichés will not help. Confessing that you are speechless will provide no healing balm. If we listen to Lamentations in our pondering silence, we may want to rein in our penchant for elo-

1. See Mark Lewis Taylor, "Liminality," in *New and Enlarged Handbook of Christian Theology*, ed. Donald W. Musser and Joseph L. Price (Nashville: Abingdon Press, 2003), 307–10.

Pastoral Perspective

department. Now she sits motionless, finding joy in once-upon-a-time memories prompted by photographs on beige walls.

On the retina of her mind she again sees those scenes of the family together at the Jersey Shore. Those were the wonderful days with cherry snow cones, Coppertone bronzing, and new sandals. She was entertained by the remembrance of caramel-corn evenings on the boardwalk, a respite from the heat of southern Ohio summers.

Eventually the children left home and started their own families. She and her husband still returned to the beach and held hands as they walked on the sand. It was still good. Then came that distressing morning when the medical staff offered them the choice: "Artificial valve or pig valve?" His heart grew weaker. Time edged shorter. The cardiologist said the operation was a success, but soon the resulting infection halted his life.

Her daughters helped her choose the black dress she wore to the funeral. The service filled with friends affirming his significance in their lives and offering her their condolences with hugs and tears. Notes and flowers arrived, but they soon tapered to silence.

Each day includes reading from her *Upper Room* devotional guide. It is routine and comforting, but one day, as the sun comes through, she explodes with the realization that she is a lonely widow. She accepts it. It is less painful. Infrequently kissed, her naps are a reprieve from forced solitude. When awake, she thinks, "If only I had . . ." How lovely! How wonderful! How lonely! How? "How" is a word that initiates introspection as it attempts to embrace the present and search for answers to the question "why?"

"How lonely sits the city! . . . How like a widow she has become!" (v. 1). It is the howl of Jeremiah as he personifies the national tragedy engulfing the kingdom of Judah in 587 BCE. The city of Jerusalem is reduced to ruins, its people deported and scattered. Questions remain: How could God permit the Holy City to be destroyed? How could our powerful God be so impotent in our defense? How can there be justice in this? How could God let this happen?

Grief is expressed in "How." A weeping widow is an apt icon for the weeping prophet, Jeremiah. He recalls in melancholic poetry the nostalgic glory of Judah's past and its current feelings of abandonment. Former glory is diminished. Judah is homeless, her children abused, her wealth and people ravaged. Holidays and feasts have ceased. Even the holy altar has been desecrated and burned.

Together we will remember! There being no vision of future restoration in the book, no all-too-easy focus on "the next life" is allowed to obscure the painful present and the lives so filled with anguish.

It is unfortunate that the text is not extended at least through verse 11, if not verse 12 (a verse made famous by Handel's *Messiah*), so that images of grieving could be more fully experienced by those who hear and read the text. Even more directly, at the end of both verse 9 and verse 11, a shift is made from third person to first person; readers now hear the suffering one with an immediacy that sends them back into the previous verses to catch up on what has been suffered by this "worthless" one.

In Lamentations 1, the city of Jerusalem is personified as a woman (at night, v. 2), a mother, who is mourning the loss of her children and her honor (its citizens and its stature). She is referred to in communal, familial, and affectionate terms: daughter Zion (v. 6), virgin daughter Judah (v. 15), my (God's) people (4:6, 10). Such a personalizing of the city draws the reader more closely into the pain and suffering involved. A city may have fallen, but it is the people who have suffered so deeply. Remember each mother, each father, each son, each daughter, and what they went through! Compare Jesus' use of the lament regarding Jerusalem and its future (Luke 13:34–35; 19:41–44; 23:27–31).

The images for the city/woman are remarkable in their range and intensity, lifting up especially the difference between then and now. How lovely she once was! How horrifying she now is! She is imaged as a lonely widow who has lost her husband and as a princess from the royal palace who has become a vassal, subjected to others' whims and wishes (v. 1); she weeps bitterly, with tears flowing down her cheeks, and she has no lovers left to comfort her, as all her friends and allies have become her enemies (v. 2); she has been exiled, without a home of her own, enslaved to others, and has become a victim of every pursuer, unable to offer any resistance (v. 3); she is deserted by former visitors and supporters, groaning, alone, and bitter (v. 4); her children have been taken captive by enemies, who now prosper (v. 5); her honor and strength have vanished, and her leaders have fled without resources (v. 6). She remembers how good and precious things used to be (v. 7)!

Now, "O LORD, look at my affliction" (v. 9). "Look, O LORD, and see" (vv. 11, 20); take a close look, O God—I am mocked, ravished, despised, without a friend: "how worthless I have become" (v. 11). Even more, "all you who pass by [readers,

spoken? Jeremiah spoke that truth to free God's people. A preacher who is also a pastor knows that the same truth that will set us free may just as truly add pain and frustration. Thus truth has to be spoken carefully, so as to avoid increasing the burden of pain and suffering, but truth must be spoken so that it may be acknowledged. Diseases are caused by bacteria, viruses, and who-knows-what, but behaviors that increase those risks have to be spoken to as well. The Babylonians were aggressors, but Jerusalem and its leaders had not followed God. No effective sermon can sort through the catalog of good vs. bad behavior, but addressing the questions tied to these realities might move a congregation forward into the truth that does set us free. Are all the ills that befall us truly unjust?

Everyone laments in this text because everyone has a reason to. All suffer. Clearly, however, in the eloquence of acrostic poetry reduced to blank verse, some of those who suffer (e.g., the children of v. 5) have not presumably perpetrated any evil that would justify, by human standards, their pain. Clergy invariably address this question of justice throughout their ministry: funerals, lessons, counseling. Seldom will they have a more direct way into the heart of those questions than Jeremiah provides them here. Quoting verse 5, where Jeremiah describes the Lord as having "made [Jerusalem] suffer for the multitude of her transgressions," will demand, in certain contexts, the preacher make a response. Where God is understood to be the "scorekeeper in the sky," the preacher needs to expound on a God who suffers with the covenant people.

Beyond the theodicy issues, however, there are two other approaches that a preacher might want to take. Jeremiah has a corporate understanding of the nature of pain. Since the text discusses the agonies of Jerusalem's people as an aggregate, going from individuals to the entire nation (cf. v. 1 and "Judah" in v. 3), the text introduces the potential for the preacher to address the tensions that exist between individual and group responsibility. Covenant communities hurt when the individuals within them grieve, and individuals can move the broader community to a new life of greater justice and greater righteousness. Confronting her own community, a preacher using this text might well move in the direction of talking about how corporate life and one's own personal life intersect so consistently that you cannot distinguish one from the other. Thus individuals must not act without regard to the consequences of their actions on the body of the whole;

Lamentations 1:1-6

Theological Perspective

quent prose, as though a brilliant turn of a phrase will evoke comfort. Consider the form of proclamation in our text. The poet chooses poetry! Emotive poetry! Poetry embedded with vivid, horrible images. The text itself should have a prominent place in the liturgy of this day. Read it with passion. Let the prelude, anthem, and postlude exude minor keys that mark a dirge or a funeral. Let the ritual suffering expend itself with emotion, as people find their hearts broken together in communal mourning. Like the empty roads to Zion (v. 4a), let the people mourn. Let bitter tears fall (v. 2a), for our loss is great. Pray that the poems become transparent to the aching souls in your pews, allowing them to grieve. We must live in exile before we can be released from its agony (v. 3a).

Solace through Protest. Third, the poet longs for solace, for relief from the pain and suffering. The poet is a survivor, a believing survivor, and protesting survivor. Nothing in his lines borders on unbelief. In fact, he confesses that "the LORD has made her [Judah] suffer" (v. 5) for her rebellions against the sacred covenant with God. This underlying profession of faith, however, is not without protest against the pain and anguish that God has wrought (whether justly or not). How difficult it must have been to confess that God did not just "permit" the destruction or "allow" the devastation, but "made" it happen! Thus, in painful verse after verse, the abject horror of a ravaged city, like a widow (v. 1b) who has also lost her children (v. 5c), is bewailed before God, the cause of it all. Unlike Job, the poet will not be silent before the Awesome One. A powerful theology of protest is thus announced. The pain and horror that have brought death and destruction are too much to bear. No rod and staff can be found in the valley of this shadow!

The poet walks through this vale of tears, as a victim, but also in the emotive tears of anguished verse. The theology of the academy is reduced to ashes, exiled to a strange and silent place. The theology of Proverbs is muted. An end has come. In the very act of addressing God in these poems, however, Lamentations awaits an end to anguish, and a new beginning. A nascent hope tacitly pervades these dark poems.

DONALD W. MUSSER

Pastoral Perspective

City councils in U.S. Rust Belt cities have similar feelings as they huddle in suburban restaurants asking why the stores downtown shiver vacant. Was it the attack of Internet shopping, or inadequate free parking? Grand Gothic churches, their architecture the pride of the urban landscape, now stand empty except for a few faithful. The graying board probes the future and asks, "If we abandon the organ we love and hire a praise band, will people come? If there are PowerPoint-illustrated sermons, will children return? How have we displeased the Lord?"

Walk in nursing-home halls and look into the hollow stares aching for a touch. When you engage the exiles at Grove Manor, you hear groans of despair, to be sure. If you are patiently attentive, however, they tell you how they look forward to visits from family and anticipate breakfast at Perkins instead of the usual institutional fare. Their eyes twinkle as they tell you that a deacon and pastor are coming Sunday afternoon with Communion for them. Their souls are transported to the fellowship they love. They have visions of friends united in praise. So they minister to those who will listen to their anticipation of simple hopes and the future when they will walk the streets of a new Jerusalem.

Jeremiah's elegy of Jerusalem's destruction vividly personified in chapter 1 is a picture of a tormented widow's heart, suffering and pleading for remedy and redress. The prophet lays down a first coat of gloom and despondency on the canvas of these opening lines. They tell us that the Lord intended destruction as discipline and justice for sinful behavior. How we are eager to hear verses like Lamentations 3:21–24! "This I call to mind, and therefore I have hope: The steadfast love of the LORD never ceases." It is hard to change what we are unwilling to acknowledge, and so Jeremiah helps Judah accept consequences in preparation for repentant appeals.

BRUCE G. BOAK

from every generation], look and see if there is any sorrow like my sorrow" (v. 12). Yes, look and see—God and human beings alike: "Is it nothing to you?" Do you have no comfort to offer me? Will you simply pass me by, gapers and gawkers, with no help to offer? Have you no compassion? Take a close look and see!

What are the sources of this suffering? The author begins this train of thought with repeated reference to Israel's enemies (v. 5 and often). Moreover, God has made Jerusalem suffer for her many transgressions (v. 5; vv. 8–9, 12–15 continue in this vein). In other words, God gathers Israel's sins, hands her over to enemies she cannot withstand, and so works judgment through agents (vv. 14–15). Jerusalem forthrightly states: "The LORD is in the right, for I have rebelled" (vv. 18, 22). It is my problem, not God's. Basically, Israel has suffered the consequences of its own sins, not because of a forensic divine decision, but because God has created the moral order and sees to its workings. At the same time, the rippling and random effects of sin will occasion suffering far beyond any simple act-consequence schema. Still, Jerusalem's call goes out to God to see how bad things have become and to wonder about the tragedy of it all. The intent may well be to rouse God to action on their behalf, perhaps even to prompt God to express sorrow (as in Jer. 42:10; Zech. 1:15). The divine agents have exceeded their mandate and inflicted much more harm than was warranted. Perhaps God will express regret and move to heal.

Lamentations will pursue these questions of God, hoping for a response, finally ending on this note: "Why have you forgotten us completely? Why have you forsaken us these many days?" (5:20). God remains silent throughout, but a basic conviction about God lies at the center of things (3:22–33): God's steadfast love endures forever, and "it is good that one should wait quietly for the salvation of the LORD" (3:26).

TERENCE E. FRETHEIM

communities must remember the impact of their actions on individual people.

Finally, however, no fulsome proclamation of this text will allow the preacher to escape the good news implicit throughout this passage of Lamentations. God and God's people are in an ongoing relationship; Jeremiah pours out his heart to God. Neither sin nor failures to be faithful have driven God away. Instead, in their pain, these people discover that God has not forgotten them, but rather is present with them in their pain. Better yet, the God Jeremiah and we address when hurting is a God who proffers supreme concern in the very details of our struggle, attending to the troubles of individuals such as a princess now a vassal (v. 1), children torn away (v. 5), people in grief (v. 4).

This God attends pain not to punish but to console. This God can withstand people's anger. Time and again, as people fear being angry, including angry with God, this text stands to assure people that in the midst of his despair Jeremiah was confident God was listening to his cries, not returning anger for anger. Here the preacher will have to work hard against the tendency to gloss over those times and places in Scripture where God is pictured as reactive and sometimes provoked by people. Better to talk straight on about the God who enters into dialogue and community with us, sharing pain and frustrations.

That is the greatest good news of this text: it points the hurting preacher and God's agonized people to a God who suffers with us and still attends us. Ours is not the God of the quick fix, who comes with an "explanation" of why bad things happen. Our God is the One who is beyond our understanding, yet who stands with us. When the preacher has conveyed that deep reality of pain from this text, every hearer will truly be able to say, "Thanks be to God."

H. GRAY SOUTHERN

Lamentations 3:19-26

¹⁹The thought of my affliction and my homelessness
  is wormwood and gall!
²⁰My soul continually thinks of it
  and is bowed down within me.
²¹But this I call to mind,
  and therefore I have hope:

²²The steadfast love of the LORD never ceases,
  his mercies never come to an end;
²³they are new every morning;
  great is your faithfulness.
²⁴"The LORD is my portion," says my soul,
  "therefore I will hope in him."

²⁵The LORD is good to those who wait for him,
  to the soul that seeks him.
²⁶It is good that one should wait quietly
  for the salvation of the LORD.

Theological Perspective

"Great is your faithfulness" (v. 23), sings this passage, affirming God's abiding goodness throughout all seasons of life. "The steadfast love of the LORD never ceases, his mercies . . . are new every morning" (vv. 22–23a). Alone, these verses portray quiet, persistent confidence in God's mercy; yet the wider context of Lamentations reveals that this remarkable trust in God comes in the midst of bitter agony. Jerusalem has been destroyed, humiliated by its enemies. People lie slaughtered on the ground (2:21); children and babies are starving in the streets (2:11–12). In the midst of such horrific suffering, how can the speaker proclaim hope and trust?

Three theological questions emerge from these verses. How do we understand God's continuing activity in the world (providence)? If God is both powerful and good, why is there suffering and evil (theodicy)? Finally, what is the nature of our hope (eschatology)?

Providence. The writer attests to a strong sense of God's providence, God's continuing care and guidance over the events of history. God's mercies are "new every morning" (v. 23), but not only the good things in life come from the hand of God. Earlier in chapter 3, he said, "[God] has driven and brought me into darkness without any light; against me alone

Pastoral Perspective

So far in Lamentations we have been in a serious drought of hope. Jerusalem is lonely and empty of people. Like a widow she cries all night long. God in (justifiable) anger has laughed at the soldiers of Zion and withdrawn every source of light. The old men sit in dust and ashes, the young women walk around as though lost. Babies are crying and children are starving. How much worse can it get? Mothers are eating the bodies of their dead babies! Enough, O Lord, enough!

Finally, thank God, we get some relief in the reading for this Sunday. Finally we get to the good part in Lamentations. God does still love! There is still hope! God is all there is, and so in God we must put our hope.

What kind of God is this, who destroys unmercifully, punishing the sins of the nation, and still offers mercy to those who are willing to sit and take it? What kind of comfort does this God offer our hurting people in the pew? Too many are too quick to dismiss the first two-thirds of the Christian Bible, assuming that it is about a different God, one who takes delight in the destruction of wayward humans by floods, boils, and wars. Too many want to skip right to the New Testament God of love and forgiveness. But . . . "But this I call to mind, and therefore I have hope: The steadfast love of the LORD never

Exegetical Perspective

The book of Lamentations is an ancient rendition of a great loss. It puts into poetic form the sorrow of the loss of the temple and much of Jerusalem during the Babylonian destruction in 587 BCE. It is a testament to the pain and devastation of war given in five distinct, yet related poems. Few preachers will dare to enter Lamentations, for it is uncomfortable and speaks of despair, sin, war, and death. To make matters worse, this lection text falls on World Communion Sunday. Who wants even to consider the depths of international violence while celebrating peace and community around the Table?

The focus text, Lamentations 3:19–26, is set within the third poem in the book, 3:1–66. The contrast in this poem is striking. Its Hebrew structure is an acrostic, meaning each line begins with a sequential letter of the alphabet. This provides a very regular and regimented structure. The content of the poem, however, is far from controlled. Indeed, the poem is a reflection by an unnamed Israelite on God's punishment for sin (vv. 1–39), followed by an exhortation by the community to return to God (vv. 40–47) and a final individual lament that functions as a call to God (vv. 48–66).

Today's text comes in the middle of the first section. It would be easy to focus only on verses 19–26, which provide a point of hope in the poem, but to do

Homiletical Perspective

Hope among the Ruins. The book of Lamentations bears witness to the voices of unrelenting lament rising from the rubble of a Jerusalem devastated by the Babylonians. How could this unthinkable catastrophe have happened? How could YHWH's temple be destroyed, the city of God's holy habitation be devastated by the hands of infidels?

The anguish and despair screaming from the five poems of Lamentations is almost suffocating. Our text is the testimony of one who has somehow survived the end of the world and sounds an impossible note of hope among the ruins. No such note is sounded elsewhere in Lamentations. Our text is surrounded by voices of despair that would drown it out. In Lamentations 3:1–18, our survivor begins with an unrelenting litany of lament. The weight of despair is cumulative and these verses demand to be read. Only then can our text have its full effect, for it takes us from the depths to the heights; neither is fully visible apart from the other. When they are set against this anguish, the words of our text take flight.

These words actually begin in verses 19–20 with the ending of our survivor's ruminations on his or her wretched and godless state. He has already spoken in verse 8 of the absence—or at least the silence—of God. The fact is that God's voice is absent throughout Lamentations. Even Job finally

Lamentations 3:19-26

Theological Perspective

he turns his hand, again and again, all day long" (vv. 2–3). This claim is hard to hear, suggesting an abusive God prone to violent anger, but this author is convinced that God is directly involved in all events of life, both good and ill. Theologians call this "special providence": God is not just involved in creation in a general way (like the laws of nature), but intervenes directly in specific historical events.

Many classical theologians strongly affirmed such special providence. Augustine interpreted the rise and fall of the Roman Empire in terms of divine providence. Reformed theologian John Calvin insisted that God "so regulates all things that nothing takes place without his deliberation."[1] Calvin reflected Scriptures like Lamentations when he claimed that God directly wills events in history. The events of life are not simply neutral; they tell us something about God's favor or judgment, and we need to respond appropriately, by repenting or by giving thanks.

Some recent theologians have raised serious questions about special providence. First, this view emphasizes God as the real cause of all things, questioning whether humans and other creatures act independently. This can render humanity passive with regard to historical events, leading to a problematic "*que sera, sera*" attitude: whatever will be, will be. A related problem is that this notion of special providence suggests an undifferentiated sense of God's will. Does God will everything in the same way? Does God will, for instance, the children of Jerusalem to starve in the same way that God wills mercy to the covenant people? The biggest challenge to special providence is that it holds God finally responsible for suffering. This leads to the problem of theodicy.

Theodicy. The mammoth destruction of Jerusalem and the mammoth destruction in our own day force us to ask how God can possibly be both all-good and all-powerful. If God causes such suffering, can we really call God all-good? If God did not cause such suffering, can we really call God all-powerful? Theologians have proposed several responses to these questions. Sometimes evil is interpreted as *punishment* of the wicked and chastening of the good. We glimpse this view in Lamentations, but it is hard to apply this to all suffering in our world. Can the Holocaust be understood as punishment of the wicked? Another approach interprets suffering as *divine pedagogy* that moves us toward spiritual

1. John Calvin, *Institutes of the Christian Religion*, ed. John T. McNeill (Philadelphia: Westminster Press, 1960), 1.16.3.

Pastoral Perspective

ceases, his mercies never come to an end; they are new every morning; great is your faithfulness" (vv. 21–23) The Hebrew Scriptures are filled with "buts"!

How we think about God is most important in shaping how we think about ourselves and others. In 586 BCE the people of Judea understood God, or YHWH, to be *their* God, the one with whom they had entered into a covenant. Promises were made on both sides. Consequences of breaking the covenant were spelled out by the prophets—certain destruction of the people if they were the betrayers, and certain destruction of the people if God gave up on them. It seems like a lose/lose situation. However, if the people were faithful to God, God would protect them from harm and provide all the milk and honey they could use. By the way, a definition of God is that God is always faithful, is steadfast, and can never break God's own promises. The prophets were convinced, therefore, that since Jerusalem had been so terribly ruined by the Babylonian armies, Jerusalem must have deserved it.

Old Joe thought the same thing. He had ruined his family, raped his daughters, and threatened to kill them. Now he was dying of cancer and scared. He deserved hell, and he knew it. He had lied to his new wife about everything. She could not understand why his daughters hated him so much and refused to comfort him in his last days, until the truth came out. Now she hated him too. She called the pastor to come and visit. Old Joe hinted at his wasted life, and wondered if it were at all possible that he might sneak into heaven with just a little cabin to live in—he did not need much, and he knew he did not deserve even that. (The pastor knew it too. "You s.o.b., I hope you rot in hell.")

Most of us in mainline churches today would not allow the old prophets to preach fire-and-brimstone effect-therefore-cause sermons in our pulpits. There is terrible suffering in our world, and we can explain the causes in many ways: global climate change, poverty, fanaticism, greed, unbalanced wealth, fear, violence, inept political decisions, evil in human hearts—on and on in an unending circle of blame. We want to offer encouragement and inspiration, and we know better than to think that God is punishing us for our misdeeds. We cannot possibly believe that so-called acts of God are sent to chastise a sinful group of people, can we? Surely we have come to understand that God is indefinable; but at the very least God is good, God is love, God is life.

It is alarming that so many of our church folk still see God as the angry puppet master, pulling this

so would rupture the integrity of the piece itself. The trust and hope reflected here is centered within serious and painful reflection. This poem goes where few are willing to tread, for not only does this author see God as the cause of her or his suffering, but the author thinks God is justified in exacting such a punishment (vv. 34–39). It is a hard pill to swallow, for it requires one to examine one's own culpability in misfortune. This could be a harmful theology if it were twisted into a firm doctrine of retribution, but the context here is one of war and destruction, and like laments from several of the prophets (e.g., Jer. 3:11–20; 8:8–12; Hos. 14:1–9; Amos 2:4–16), it is a reflection on the author's and the nation's culpability in their own destruction. This theology demands that both individual and community examine themselves to determine if their own actions were part of the problem. Jesus also preached a version of this theology when he demanded that we not judge the speck in the eye of another before tending to the board in our own (Matt. 7:5; Luke 6:41). Internal reflection and correction are part of the Christian way of life.

This context is crucial for the remainder of the text, verses 21–26. The hope in God and God's faithfulness is anchored in the expression of loss and personal reflection on sin. God is not just faithful; God is faithful in the toughest of times. First, the poem searches out the problem, even in the midst of suffering, and declares there is hope because God's steadfast love and mercy never end and God's faithfulness is great. These attributes are the same ones Israel has always depended on (Exod. 34:6; Pss. 86:15; 103:8).

The reading opens midway through a reflection on suffering and loss. Indeed, the one who is praying declares that this loss occupies all thoughts. It seems these ancient people also knew about stress and how affliction and homelessness can cause constant worry. The Hebrew reading of verse 20 is even more dire than the translation; the word rendered "soul" literally means the "life" of the person, so the whole life is occupied with this sorrow and "bowed down" from the weight of it all.

The next verse, verse 21, comes as a surprise. In Hebrew, it reads, "This I caused to come back into my heart; therefore I hope." This is more an act of will than the NRSV's English translation indicates. What has caused the change from being bowed down with sorrow to having hope? The poem offers no guidance, so it is up to the one who encounters these words to answer the question. What is clear is that the bridge from sorrow to hope is something

receives a reply, but God is silent in Lamentations. God, if there is a God, is not to be found amid this suffering and desolation. We can hardly be surprised to hear the poet's cry in verses 19–20.

Everything in the experience of the writer flies in the face of the faith once delivered to the saints! Nothing in Lamentations 1:1–3:20 can possibly explain what comes in verse 21. It is totally unexpected, absolutely inexplicable, more than a little unbelievable, when in verse 21, rising up from this slough of despond, we hear a single little word—not a noun, not a verb, but an adversative conjunction: *but*!

But. In spite of everything I have experienced, in spite of everything I have just said, "this I call to mind, and therefore I have hope" (v. 21). The statement is startling, and so it should be in the sermon. What could suggest even the possibility of hope under these circumstances? What force can possibly rescue hope from unyielding lament?

The answer is *memory.* Memory is a powerful thing. It can haunt or heal. It can lead to despair or celebration. The people of Israel lived between memory and hope—the memory of what God had done and the hope that God would do it again. Memory was of critical importance to the people of Israel. They told and retold the stories of God's mighty acts in their history (see, e.g., Jer. 32:20–23 and Samuel's farewell address in 1 Sam. 12). They celebrated multimedia feasts and festivals recalling those mighty acts. They remembered, and in their remembering they found hope. The power and prominence of memory also pervades the Christian tradition. As Jesus celebrated his Last Supper with his disciples, he broke bread and took the cup, instructing them, "Do this in remembrance of me." Paul's commentary explains that "as often as you eat this bread and drink the cup, you proclaim the Lord's death until he comes" (1 Cor. 11:23–26). In Jewish and Christian tradition, the God who has been faithful will be faithful.

So what does our survivor remember? What is the basis of his hope? The appearance of hope in both verse 21 and verse 24b frames the reason for his hope: This nice inclusion offers a fine ABA sermon structure: first, an affirmation of hope (v. 21); next, reasons for hope (vv. 22–23); and then, a return to affirmation of hope (v. 24).

The reason for hope is found in Israel's foundational belief that "the steadfast love of the LORD never ceases, his mercies never come to an end; they are new every morning" (vv. 22–23a). This foundational conviction makes hope among the ruins possible. The shared stories of God's mighty acts in Israel's

Lamentations 3:19-26

Theological Perspective

growth. Suffering then has the positive end of our maturing in faith. How can this make sense of the wholesale demolition of Jerusalem and its people?

Since the Holocaust, several Jewish and Christian theologians have adopted *protest* theodicy, which preserves God's omnipotence, but questions divine goodness. Protest theodicies claim that God has the power to stop suffering and needs to be called to account for senseless destruction in the world. At the other end of the spectrum, *process* theodicy affirms God's goodness, but questions God's omnipotence. Perhaps God does not have all the power, say process theologians, but moves in and through the events of history to lure it to redemption.

This passage affirms that God wills the affliction of the speaker and that God also wills ceaseless mercies. Preachers need to wrestle with this paradox, which includes elements of several theodicies. The writer protests the abusive actions of God through the destruction of Jerusalem, yet trusts in God's goodness. Perhaps God's judging will is temporary, while God's merciful will endures forever. Somehow, in spite of everything, the author affirms that divine mercy trumps judgment—and this gives rise to hope.

Eschatology. This passage ends, "It is good that one should wait quietly for the salvation of the LORD" (v. 26). Though the author looked ahead to the historical moment when Jerusalem would be restored and the people brought home, Christians may also read this statement as eschatology, connected with ultimate "last things." This doctrine has developed a bad reputation among some, who hear it as pointless speculation about future events, having nothing to do with the present. Lamentations shows that eschatology can have imminently practical implications for how we live. In the midst of the ruined city, the writer proclaims that the Lord has been and will be faithful; then he sits down to wait for that salvation to show up. This shows fierce faith that, all appearances to the contrary, God will not abandon God's people. Not affliction, but mercy is the enduring character of God.

Hope for salvation even in the darkest days—is this "pie in the sky, by and by"? Not if it leads to living resistance amid the ruins. Not if it leads to genuine ability to survive and even thrive in the midst of the rubble. Lively eschatological hope is not escape from the troubles of this world, but stubborn insistence that God's mercy will have the last word—and life lived defiantly in light of that hope.

MARTHA L. MOORE-KEISH

Pastoral Perspective

string of catastrophe in order to discipline that string of evil. Even the crying prophet from the sixth century BCE understood that God could not stay angry forever, that God's very nature was one of forgiveness and love.

Every Sunday morning the Joys and Concerns list is lopsided, concerns being the heavier half. My best friend just had a stroke. My sister-in-law has breast cancer. I lost my job. Soon I will lose my house. My nephew was killed in Iraq. My parents were both moved to hospice. In private conversation we hear of the divorce, the drug abuse, the crushing depression. I tell you, pastor, sometimes life is so hard. "The thought of my affliction and my homelessness is wormwood and gall! My soul continually thinks of it and is bowed down within me" (vv. 19–20).

But . . . the joys on the list are followed by exclamation points—the great fall weather! The prayers of my friends in this church! The elk I saw on the way to church this morning! His cancer is in remission! My grandson is coming for a visit! I am thankful for all God's many blessings! "But this I call to mind, and therefore I have hope: The steadfast love of the LORD never ceases, his mercies never come to an end; they are new every morning; great is your faithfulness" (vv. 21–23).

Old Joe was still waiting for an answer, his eyes half closed, his breathing sporadic, his bones and veins prominent. "I'm sorry for the wrong in my life. I'll probably go to hell. Pastor, is there any way God will forgive me?" The pastor had to tell him something. He probably should say something about Jesus Christ, and repentance and forgiveness, and should he throw the cross in there, too?

"Well, Joe, life can be pretty mean, but . . . 'But this I call to mind, and therefore I have hope . . .'"

STEVE D. MILLER

buried under the anxious worry of today's problems and challenges. This ancient author knew that a change in perspective can make all of the difference in one's outlook on life.

Confident in the promises of God on which he or she and all of Israel depend, the author is now more content to hope in the Lord. The Hebrew word for hope is the same word as the one meaning "to wait." We tend to think of "hope" and "waiting" as two different ideas, but the Hebrew demonstrates a basic understanding that waiting is the same as having hope. As with this text, the focus changes from the present-day problems to a firm belief that these things will pass and life will change. Significantly, what clearly does not change is God's love and faithfulness.

World Communion Sunday can become an artificial celebration that does not offer the truth that many Christians struggle in their lives, both as individuals and as communities of faith. We can come to the Table with the cares and sorrows of this world. This passage in Lamentations tells that truth. We praise God, not from a position of strength and power, but from the broken edges of our lives. We long and "wait" and "hope" for the great banquet table at the end of time; only at that table will all of our tears be dried.

The greater context of this text also encourages us to "get real" and to examine our own lives to discover the ways we contribute to our own problems. Even in a context where the historical record sees Israel as a victim, their faith demands introspection and truth telling. Finally, even in the midst of violence and introspection, we can discover the same truth as this poem: even when we are partially responsible for our brokenness, God is still faithful and merciful.

BETH LANEEL TANNER

history are evidence of God's faithfulness. Lamentations proclaims Israel's incredible faith in a God who will not let her go. It is this that our survivor remembers. The writer "does not remain within his immediate, personal situation but lifts his gaze to the infinite horizon of God's rule. He is aware not only that he must delve into the suffering pressing him to the ground and forcing many into despair, but that he must penetrate beyond his own circle into the infinite breadth of God's horizon. Even as he senses the most extreme darkness, as the situation seems hopeless to him, the brightness of God's light shines on him (iii.18–21), inspiring a magnificent vision of God's benevolence and mercy."[1]

Our text concludes with a timely reminder in verses 25–26. Everything about our culture militates against waiting: fast foods, quick fix, express mail, real time. We want things yesterday! Some things, however, we cannot speed up. The corn will grow only so fast. The baby will be born only so fast. The broken bone will mend only so fast. The broken heart? Try as we might to make it otherwise, there are some things for which we will have to wait. It may be for a season, and that season may be long or short. Sometimes we will wait for the Lord. Waiting is a season of the soul.

Here is the good news amid the lament: "The LORD is good to those who wait for him." "It is good that one should wait quietly for the salvation of the LORD" (vv. 25–26). It will not be easy. It will take discipline. Even that waiting is seeking. It is an expression of faith, for, after all, "faith is the assurance of things hoped for, the conviction of things not seen" (Heb. 11:1).

W. HULITT GLOER

1. Joze Krasovec, "The Source of Hope in the Book of Lamentations," *Vetus Testamentum* 42, 2 (1992): 230–31.

2 Timothy 1:1-14

¹Paul, an apostle of Christ Jesus by the will of God, for the sake of the promise of life that is in Christ Jesus,
²To Timothy, my beloved child:
 Grace, mercy, and peace from God the Father and Christ Jesus our Lord.

³I am grateful to God—whom I worship with a clear conscience, as my ancestors did—when I remember you constantly in my prayers night and day. ⁴Recalling your tears, I long to see you so that I may be filled with joy. ⁵I am reminded of your sincere faith, a faith that lived first in your grandmother Lois and your mother Eunice and now, I am sure, lives in you. ⁶For this reason I remind you to rekindle the gift of God that is within you through the laying on of my hands; ⁷for God did not give us a spirit of cowardice, but rather a spirit of power and of love and of self-discipline.

Theological Perspective

Throughout two millennia of their ministry, Christian churches and their leaders have drawn strength and insight from 2 Timothy, finding in its passages clear direction to pursue more enriching lives in service to God. These opening verses of the letter illustrate this value well, addressing themes that are not only consonant with Paul's writings but pertinent to the theological questions of our contemporary church.

Modern biblical scholarship has effectively challenged the authenticity of Pauline authorship of the Pastoral Epistles, based on the letters' linguistic dissimilarities and theological variations. Two primary theological concerns that distinguish 2 Timothy from Paul's undisputed writings are its practical ecclesiology, which focuses on the organization and work of church leaders (among whom is Timothy), and its distinct soteriology, which refers specifically to the appearance of Jesus the Christ as Savior, rather than the typical Pauline emphasis on the sacrifice of Christ on the cross. Consistent with Paul's epistolary concerns, however, the letter addresses issues about doctrinal validity and authority, in this case focusing on the ordination of church leaders and on Christian experience.

Written in part to warn the early church about false teachers, 2 Timothy now raises questions for us

Pastoral Perspective

No doubt parishioners are delighted to hear of a grandmother and mother sharing their faith with their children. Lois and Eunice can bring to mind memories of those who have nurtured our faith too. The recalling of mothers, grandmothers, or ancestors is often a beginning point for preaching this passage. However, what if our congregations are full of baby boomers who tried to pass along their faith, only to have their children go off to college and desert the faith altogether? Faith transmission through families might leave a sense of failure among those who tried but did not succeed. What about those from an older generation who believed religion came in three flavors: Catholic, Protestant, and Jewish? Religion was like DNA—it was permanent. It was not a matter of passing faith along; you just were Presbyterian or Baptist or Methodist, leaving these families to wonder what all the fuss is about. Post-boomer parishioners may feel that their parents, children of the 1960s, defaulted on their charge to teach the faith—that they did not have Timothy's advantages. If your congregation, like most, is filled with a mixture of baby boomers and the Greatest Generation, with some Generation X, then preaching this text with the family responsibility for nurturing faith is going to require careful navigation.

⁸Do not be ashamed, then, of the testimony about our Lord or of me his prisoner, but join with me in suffering for the gospel, relying on the power of God, ⁹who saved us and called us with a holy calling, not according to our works but according to his own purpose and grace. This grace was given to us in Christ Jesus before the ages began, ¹⁰but it has now been revealed through the appearing of our Savior Christ Jesus, who abolished death and brought life and immortality to light through the gospel. ¹¹For this gospel I was appointed a herald and an apostle and a teacher, ¹²and for this reason I suffer as I do. But I am not ashamed, for I know the one in whom I have put my trust, and I am sure that he is able to guard until that day what I have entrusted to him. ¹³Hold to the standard of sound teaching that you have heard from me, in the faith and love that are in Christ Jesus. ¹⁴Guard the good treasure entrusted to you, with the help of the Holy Spirit living in us.

Exegetical Perspective

Of all the Pastoral Epistles (1 Timothy, 2 Timothy, and Titus), 2 Timothy is the most personal. It is animated more by personal relationships than is any other letter in the NT. These relationships are both positive and negative, characterized by both trust and betrayal. This passage, which opens the letter, focuses on the positive. The faithful lives of Timothy's mother and grandmother lead into a discussion of Timothy's own faithfulness. The question is whether Timothy will remain faithful to his calling in spite of the suffering and shameful aspects of the Christian life. The passage will call upon traditional theological images of divine power and grace in order to reaffirm Timothy's loyalty to the tradition. His mother was faithful; Paul was faithful; God is faithful; Timothy must in turn be faithful.

After a fairly standard opening greeting, which includes the nice personal note that Timothy is Paul's "beloved child" (v. 2), the letter invokes a prayer. Most letters in the NT—in fact, nearly all ancient Greek letters of a personal sort—begin with a prayer or blessing. Second Timothy begins with a thanks to God and a recalling of Paul's prayers for Timothy. These remembered prayers lead into a celebration of the faithfulness of Timothy, his mother, and his grandmother. Acts 16:1 states that Timothy was "the son of a Jewish woman who was a believer;

Homiletical Perspective

This reading was written from prison by a father in the faith to his protégé, Timothy, to instill faithful courage at a time when such may have seemed hard to come by. While the Pauline approach seeks joy in the midst of sorrow, it seems clear that the finding is not always going to be easy.

There may have been a temptation to wonder about a leader who ended up in prison. "Do not be ashamed," he writes in verse 8, because "God did not give us a spirit of cowardice" (v. 7). As it was, Jews and Greeks alike were taking offense at the Christian idea of a Savior on a cross (1 Cor. 1:22–24). It was preposterous. If it was true that Christ had conquered death, why was this Christian mentor now suffering? What kind of conqueror would leave his followers in prison? Critics were taking the offensive. Some still are. Richard Dawkins, author of *The God Delusion*, believes that everything about religious faith can be explained away by the Darwinian theory and that religion is bad for the world. Tough questions are being asked of our faith, but here we read that we are not to give in to shame or timidity.

We also read of Timothy's tears (v. 4). These tears seem to have been shed at the time of their separation. Life has such moments in the midst of loss and grief. The mentor encouraged his faith child on the

2 Timothy 1:1-14

Theological Perspective

about its own veracity and authority, since it claims to have been written by Paul. However, the pseudonymous origin of the letter does not categorically restrict the potential truthfulness of its particular theological probing and insight. Nor does the pseudonymous authorship prevent our referencing authentic Pauline passages for illumination of the letter's ideas, since the author certainly wrote the letter with the intent of invoking Pauline authority and tradition.

The opening words of the letter are filled with theological significance. Identifying himself as embedded in God's will, the author asserts security in Christian hope and addresses issues about the nature of suffering, while appealing to Paul's experience. For Paul, the writer attests, suffering is not merely the political and physical oppression that might come from powerful authorities in this world; instead, suffering results from binding one's freedom and fully submitting to the divine commands of ministry. In this regard, E. F. Scott observes that the idea presented here "is that Christ himself has made [Paul] a prisoner for some hidden purpose of his own."[1]

Next, the writer offers a kind of blessing (v. 2b)—a commendation so clearly formulated that ministers throughout the church's history have pronounced it as a benediction. The juxtaposition of this salutation and benedictory blessing generates a sense of urgency, suggesting that a final blessing be given immediately, in case things might end abruptly. The sense of urgency intensifies the focus on a number of theological issues. For example, the preexistence of the Christ is indicated in the reference to grace having been "given to us in Christ Jesus before the ages began" (v. 9; cf. Phil. 2:6–7), but there is no elaboration on this christological theme.

The opening passage in the epistle is also marked by multiple references to several theological concerns ranging from thanksgiving to suffering, and from confidence in the truth to reliance on the Holy Spirit for persevering in the faith. At the very least, the author features Christian experience as a validation of matters of faith—not only the personal suffering that emboldens Paul but also the nurture in piety that Timothy had.

Within the emphasis on the significance of family devotion and personal experience as foundations for religious authority, the act of ordination is identified not merely as a rite of recognition by the church, but

Pastoral Perspective

First of all, your sermon needs the encouragement this pastoral letter offers. Rather than feeling ashamed, humiliated, or guilty about our testimony to Christ Jesus, the author calls upon Timothy and the Christian community to rekindle the gift of God that is within. The author supplies ideas: join in the suffering, rely on God's power, remember your salvation, hold to the standard of sound teaching, and finally "hold to . . . the faith and love that are in Christ Jesus" (v. 13). These admonitions, like signposts on a highway, help us navigate our faith journey. At times we will rely on God's power, at times we will suffer, and at times we will forget our salvation and need a reminder to breathe in the Spirit of God. Meditation in which we take time to breathe in and out, remembering God's presence in our lives, can return us to the center of our beings and our faith in God.

Christianity, when this letter is written, has become a threat to Roman establishment as a new religion. Judaism is familiar, but what is this new Jesus-the-Jew-who-died-and-was-resurrected religion about? The author needs to link the Christ followers with their ancestral roots in Judaism. Once that connection with the past is made, the Pauline author launches into what is specifically Christian—salvation in Christ Jesus. Then, as now, rejection and suffering loom as threats to people of faith. Nonetheless, the author encourages Timothy not to be ashamed of the testimony of Jesus or of Paul's imprisonment, which are according to God's purpose and bring life eternal. This affirms our faith and provides parishioners with sound teaching.

Paul's fear that Timothy will be ashamed and not tell others of his faith reminds us that this good news is always one generation away from extinction. If one generation becomes ashamed of the gospel and does not risk testimony, how will the next generation know? This seems to be the ultimate concern here; at the end of his life, Paul needs Timothy to carry on for him. Parishioners who had grandparents who passed on certain traditions or family treasure before their death can understand Paul's intention. Churches take this responsibility seriously when we provide Christian education classes to pass along knowledge of the Scriptures and faith to all ages. In addition, we hope to transmit a living faith that moves beyond creeds and memorization of Scripture, but how?

In response to this query, in the early 2000s the Pew Forum on Religion and Public Life,[1] seeking an update on today's religious practice, interviewed

---

1. E. F. Scott, *The Pastoral Epistles,* Moffatt New Testament Commentary (New York: Harper & Bros., n.d.), 92.

1. Pew Forum on Religion and Public Life, http://pewforum.org/

but his father was a Greek." This may mean that the faith of Lois and Eunice was that of good Jewish women. This "Jewish" faith models Timothy's "Christian" faith. This recollection of faith and apparent celebration gives way to a reminder. Timothy's own faithfulness is in question.

Although the line in Greek between "faith" and "faithfulness" is often not clear, in this case the question is clearly not whether and what Timothy believes, but whether he can be faithful to his calling. The challenge to "rekindle the gift of God" (v. 6), to "not be ashamed" (v. 8), to "hold to the standard of sound teaching" (v. 13), and to "guard the good treasure" (v. 14), suggests a wavering in the duties of leadership. In the face of this implied wavering by Timothy, the letter offers examples of faithfulness in Timothy's mother and grandmother and especially Paul himself.

This reference to the life and faithfulness of Paul highlights the question of authorship. Most modern commentators, but not all, have concluded that Paul did not write 2 Timothy. If Paul himself wrote the letter, these examples are historical reminders for purposes of exhortation to Timothy. If Paul did not, these examples are generalized for any Christian whose faithfulness is being tested. The wavering of Timothy exemplifies the wavering of all Christian leaders and perhaps of all Christians. The faithfulness of Paul and Timothy's mother and grandmother offers both challenge and hope for such wavering people. These examples demonstrate that it is possible to persevere, that it is possible to remain faithful, even in the face of persecution.

The explicit cause of this wavering appears to be complex. The initial problem is stated in verse 8. Timothy is ashamed of the suffering that Paul, and perhaps he himself, must endure for the sake of the gospel. Paul is under arrest and has endured one "defense," at which "no one came to my support" (4:16). In general, people have abandoned Paul, although Onesiphorus is commended for helping Paul and for not being "ashamed of my chain" (1:16). Timothy's tears that are recalled in verse 4 probably represent anguish over Paul's imprisonment and may be prelude to shame and abandonment. Although there is a powerful tradition of the glory of martyrdom and suffering in Judaism and early Christianity, along with the model of Jesus himself, these traditions do not eliminate the sense of shame that Christians experienced in the abuse that many of them endured.

Second Timothy, like most NT documents, does not specify the details of suffering and shame. Early

journey of faith by focusing on the gifts of God in a spirit of gratitude.

In the face of tearful memories and tough questions, he gave thanks for the gift of Timothy's grandmother Lois and his mother Eunice. He gave thanks for Timothy's faith, and he gave thanks in verse 6 for the opportunity he had to ordain Timothy, through the laying on of hands. In the midst of struggles, there seemed to be no thought of anger or anxiety, but rather gratitude. Amid discouragement or even despondency about the setbacks and the challenges to the faith, the mentor's gratitude helped Timothy to see that he was part of something so much bigger—Christ's ministry. When we face setbacks, pausing to give thanks can make all the difference in the world. Gratitude puts things in perspective.

Not long ago the story surfaced about a sixty-two-year-old man in Britain who was diagnosed with pancreatic cancer and told that it was untreatable and he would be dead within a year. The man decided to live as if there were no tomorrow, buying clothes and cars and cruises and traveling and eating out. In a year he ran out of money and was unofficially bankrupt. The only problem was that he was showing no signs of dying. So he went to his doctor, and a new series of tests overturned the original diagnosis. The man became outraged. He had been given a new lease on life, yet he was contemplating a lawsuit.

The author inspires Timothy to give thanks for the gift, but, second, as he wrote in verse 6, "to rekindle the gift." The greatest gift we have been given is, as indicated in verse 9, the grace that comes "not according to our works but according to his own purpose and grace." To "rekindle the gift" means to stir up the grace and faith and love that we have received, and we stir them up by putting them into practice.

Christians who have become angry with Richard Dawkins and the cohort of neoatheists look and sound like the misdiagnosed cancer patient. In the face of opposition, it is so easy to lose sight of God's gifts. The most important thing to do is to stir up the gifts of grace and mercy and love. Claims that religion is a force for hatred and darkness in the world have trouble contending with the countless examples of Christian love and mercy. Imagine being able to ask the apostle to whom the authorship is attributed, "What are we to do about the likes of Richard Dawkins?" Paul, the past persecutor of Christians, would say that God in grace watches over the church. He would remind us that what transformed him was not an argument but an encounter.

2 Timothy 1:1-14

Theological Perspective

as a bestowing on the ordained of authority to preach the gospel, just as it had been when Paul laid his hands upon Timothy (v. 6). Timothy's ordination represents a fulfillment of calling to Christian ministry, which enjoys the gifts of "a spirit of power and of love and of self-discipline" (v. 7). Although briefly indicated in these verses, this reference to the ritual process and spiritual gifts of ordination has bolstered the church's designation and celebration of the rite as a sacrament.

Several other theological themes emerge in today's passage, which "should not be read, however, as a repository of theological propositions," as Luke Timothy Johnson avers.[2] One of these themes relates to the assurance of new life in Christ (v. 13). Since the writer intended the letter to be read as Pauline, the phrase "in Christ Jesus" purposely calls to mind Paul's customary assertion of reconciliation, as voiced in 2 Corinthians 5:17: "So if anyone is in Christ, there is a new creation: everything old has passed away; see, everything has become new." As a person transformed from old bondage to sin, the Christian newly experiences reconciliation, which mitigates even the apostle's "suffering for the gospel" (v. 8).

A second consistent theological concern is about false teachers. The theme is suggested first in the emphasis on the authority of Paul and Timothy because of Paul's apostolicity and Timothy's ordination, and it is reinforced by insistence that Timothy "guard the good treasure" with "the help of the Holy Spirit" (v. 14). This theme becomes the thread of continuity that connects the entire epistle.

As a culmination to this opening, the author incorporates a stanza of an early church hymn that grows out of the underlying issues of doctrinal authority and personal experience: "I know whom I have believed, and am persuaded that he is able to keep that which I have committed unto him against that day" (v. 12 KJV). Even in translation, the wording is so rhythmic that it is sung today as one of the great traditional hymns. Invoking Pauline authority, the writer proposes that Christian experience serves as the litmus test to verify the salvific work of Christ. He is persuaded by the depth of his belief in Christ as the one who transforms that he will be held in divine acceptance and favor until "that day," the end of time and the judgment of all.

JOSEPH L. PRICE

Pastoral Perspective

35,000 Americans. Pew researchers discovered that 44 percent of all Americans have left the religious traditions in which they grew up and were nurtured by their families. Now, according to research, we shop for our religious or spiritual home, much as we shop for anything else. Most pastors probably already knew this, if new-member classes are an indication of the many denominations and faith traditions through which people have passed on the way into a particular church. The Pew report suggests we leave our religious upbringing frequently as we move from place to place, with an estimated 40 million of us moving each year. One does not need to move in order to change a religious tradition; my brother married a Catholic and converted to Catholicism. He lives in the house in which we all grew up! In fact, none of us siblings practices the faith in our original religious tradition.

In this land of religious freedom and mobility, leaving the religion of our childhood and seeking a faith we can practice—a living faith community where we call one another "brother" and "sister"—seems an advantage. Without realizing it, some families pass along traditions that lack meaning. Therefore, the children leave, seeking a faith that does nurture and give sustenance. Certainly families can pass along prejudices and hatreds just as easily as they can pass along love and the practice of welcoming the stranger.

Jesus offers another choice of family, by calling anyone who does the will of God part of the larger family or community—those called out to serve God. Jesus' ministry presents a balance to transmitting faith only within the family. Jesus asks, "Who are my mother and my brothers?" Looking at those who sat around him, he said, "Here are my mother and my brothers! Whoever does the will of God is my brother and sister and mother" (Matt. 12:49–50; Mark 3:31–35; Luke 8:21). Even amid the physical and spiritual mobility of our time, the images of Lois and Eunice and our own ancestors passing on the faith, alongside the hope of a worldwide "family" of the faithful—such images offer hope that spiritual survival, and even increased faith, is possible.

OLIVE ELAINE HINNANT

---

2. Luke Timothy Johnson, *The First and Second Letters to Timothy*, Anchor Bible (New York: Doubleday, 2001), 324.

Exegetical Perspective

Christian writers assume that their readers understand this experience. Historians have long noted that ancient Mediterranean social hierarchies were based, to a great extent, on the dynamics of glory and shame. While theological traditions might insist that suffering leads to glory, that death leads to life, suffering and abuse in themselves were not occasions for glory. Timothy in this letter embodies the terrors of public shame.

This passage and much of the letter are devoted to overcoming this shame. As noted above, Lois, Eunice, and especially Paul serve as examples of people who remain faithful. However, these personal examples give way to a series of theological affirmations. Paul declares, "I am not ashamed, for I know the one in whom I have put my trust" (v. 12). Timothy is to "rekindle the gift of God" that came from Paul's laying on of hands (v. 6). This gift is "a spirit of power and of love and of self-discipline," not "of cowardice" (v. 7). The grace that has been given to them was revealed in the appearance of Jesus, "who abolished death and brought life and immortality to light" (vv. 9–10). There are, in other words, powerful theological forces that will turn shame to glory and death to life. There are powerful theological forces within Timothy that will enable him, and all Christians, to resist shame and to remain faithful.

This journey from suffering to glory is the heart of the gospel. The challenge here is to hold to this gospel of suffering and glory. Paul was appointed "herald," "apostle," and "teacher" of this gospel (v. 11). Timothy is called to hold fast to this gospel, to "guard the good treasure entrusted to you" and to do so "with the help of the Holy Spirit living in us" (v. 14).

While each theological and personal image in this argument could occasion many different kinds of sermons, the passage as a whole raises the ancient question that haunts many Christians. Do we trust the yet unfulfilled promises of the gospel, when so much evidence in our lives seems to contradict them? Can we live our lives accordingly?

LEWIS R. DONELSON

Homiletical Perspective

Our call is not to win all the arguments but to forgive as we have been forgiven, and to love as we have been loved. We must stir up the gift.

We must also stir up the gift of faith by praying and listening to the word of God. In verse 3, the mentor writes of praying "night and day" for Timothy, and indeed for all of his churches. No doubt he was praying too for his enemies and those who opposed the faith.

All of this leads surely to Paul's third word about the gift: Get in touch with the Giver. Chris Wiman was another terminal cancer patient—thirty-nine, newly married, newly published, and now facing sure death. He and his wife grieved deeply the shared life that would not be. "Then one morning," wrote Wiman, "we found ourselves going to church. *Found ourselves.* That's exactly what it felt like . . . so that we were casting aside the Sunday paper and moving toward the door with barely a word between us; and as if, once inside the church, we were discovering exactly where and who we were meant to be."[1] Long walks talking of God, deep sadness that told them of God's own grief. In the face of death, Wiman found no trite and obvious glories, but rather the quiet scrapings that assured him of a Presence on the other side of a wall.

The gifts God has given call us into relationship with God. As the dear old assurance goes, "I know whom I have believed, and am persuaded that he is able" (v. 12 KJV).

J. PETER HOLMES

---

1. Christian Wiman, "Gazing into the Abyss," *American Scholar* 76, no. 3, June 2007, 64.

Luke 17:5-10

⁵The apostles said to the Lord, "Increase our faith!" ⁶The Lord replied, "If you had faith the size of a mustard seed, you could say to this mulberry tree, 'Be uprooted and planted in the sea,' and it would obey you.

⁷"Who among you would say to your slave who has just come in from plowing or tending sheep in the field, 'Come here at once and take your place at the table'? ⁸Would you not rather say to him, 'Prepare supper for me, put on your apron and serve me while I eat and drink; later you may eat and drink'? ⁹Do you thank the slave for doing what was commanded? ¹⁰So you also, when you have done all that you were ordered to do, say, 'We are worthless slaves; we have done only what we ought to have done!'"

Theological Perspective

For modern ears inside and outside of the Christian family, this passage in Luke seems to characterize a sort of faith that is at best strange and irrelevant, and at worst misleading and dangerous. When the disciples ask Jesus to increase their faith, he speaks to them about a faith that even in its smallest quantity has the power to perform miracles, and then goes on to admonish the disciples to understand themselves as worthless slaves.

Miracles do not happen too often in the sanctuaries of mainstream Protestant churches. How many of us could actually claim the power to transplant trees or to act supernaturally in any other way? The second saying of Jesus in this passage does not make things easier for us—quite the opposite. Individuals and groups in church and society have been busy throughout the last decades with manifold and variously successful efforts to help men and women develop their own healthy sense of self-worth, and for them Jesus' exhortation to see themselves as *worthless slaves* seems to fly into the face of all they have been working for. Especially for women, this passage seems to carry an almost dangerous undertone, something they have heard for only too long: not to boast about their work and achievements, but humbly to accept their manifold duties, just like the slave in Jesus' saying, without expecting any form of

Pastoral Perspective

Who among us does not want more faith? Most of us are not surprised at the disciples' plea that Jesus give them more. There is a guilt-ridden part of us that is not particularly surprised at Jesus' scoffing reply. "If you had even this much faith," he tells them, pinching his thumb and forefinger together, "you would be able to do anything you wished." We hang our heads with the apostles, suffering the scold we know we deserve. If there is one thing we have come to expect from Jesus, it is the constant reminder of how short we fall.

There is a pastoral issue here for preachers. Somewhere along the way we have grown to expect a steady dose of condemnation from Scripture; more often than not, we hear Jesus' words to the disciples—and therefore, to us—as shaming and angry words. It is surprising, in fact, how often congregations, and the people who lead them in worship, assume a punitive tone when reading and hearing biblical texts. This assumed tone will repel many of our worshipers on this October morning. Some bring the scars of a Bible that has been misused on them. Others have always assumed Christianity is all about guilt. These perceptions stand as barriers between themselves and a God who loves them.

We would do well to explore a whole range of tones when reading the words of Scripture. What if

Exegetical Perspective

Luke 17:5–10 consists of two sections: Jesus' response to the disciples' request for more faith (vv. 5–6) and the parable of the Worthless Slaves (vv. 7–10). The first section has a parallel in Matthew 17:20; the second is peculiar to Luke. In addition to addressing elements in each section, exegesis must consider how and why Luke brought them together and placed them in this portion of his Gospel, especially since the context for the first section differs from its setting in Matthew.

In Matthew (17:14–21), Jesus uses a version of the mustard-seed saying to answer the disciples' question about their inability to cast out a demon. They could not cast it out, he says, "because of [their] little faith" (Matt. 17:20). If they had had faith the size of a mustard seed, Jesus continues, they could move mountains (and thus, by extension, cast out demons). By contrast, Luke has Jesus use the mustard-seed saying to address the disciples' request for more faith. Here in Luke, however, there is no story about the disciples' inability to heal, since he had used it earlier (Luke 9:37–43a). Instead, Luke prefaces the mustard-seed saying with two sayings about forgiveness (Luke 17:3–4, which are also in Matt. 18:15 and 21–22). Though most scholars argue that there is no relation between the sayings in verses 3–4 and verses 5–6, because the shift between them is so abrupt, it is

Homiletical Perspective

The two small stories in Luke 17:5–10 remind us of something New Testament scholar Markus Barth used to tell his students: "If you can't find the Word in the text, it isn't the text's fault. Go back and try again. Dig deeper." At first reading, the preacher is inclined to separate the story of the mustard seed and the small parable of the master and his obedient, although underappreciated, slave. A case can be made for focusing on one or the other, but it helps to remember that both stories are Jesus' response to his disciples' request: "Increase our faith." To the preacher digging deeper for the Word, each passage contains obstacles put there by contemporary culture. The wise will proceed with eager caution.

If you had faith the size of a mustard seed, you could do astonishing things such as rearranging the landscape. Matthew makes it even more dramatic by promising the ability to move mountains. It is easy to love this story: the tiny seed, the supernatural power to accomplish great things. When I was a child, a popular item of jewelry was a mustard seed bracelet, a tiny seed embedded in a clear glass sphere that acted as a magnifier. My mother had one, and it symbolizes for me her amazing ability to do big things with very limited resources. Indeed, great things have been done by people who believed in a dream and, in faith, pursued it with everything in

Luke 17:5-10

Theological Perspective

reward. With this history in mind, can you honestly advise women to understand themselves as *worthless*? There is more, yet: Can you without difficulty admonish all of your Christian fellows to understand themselves as *slaves*, in a context where the after-effects of a dehumanizing and deadly system of slavery are still experienced by too many?

Miracles and slaves—nothing that comes to *my* mind immediately when I reflect theologically upon the nature of Christian faith. Yet these two sayings of Christ can lead us, indeed, to some central aspects of the Christian understanding of faith. The contentions I have described above are valid and important reactions, but they should not keep us from probing more deeply into what Scripture wants to tell us here. The most important step to get to the theological core issues of this passage is truly to understand the faith talked about here as *Christian*, not in the sense of the faith of the Christians, but in the sense of the faith *in Christ* that mirrors the faith *of Christ*. Why is that important?

The problems described above come up only if we separate our faith from the One we believe in—if we think about our faith as *our* faith. The disciples at least understood that. In the passage, they ask Jesus to increase their faith, admitting that faith is a gift, that the growth of it is not the result of a ten-steps-to-a-greater-faith program. They understand that faith and its growth are not to be gained by human efforts but are given by God. The true miracle in Jesus' saying is not about overcoming natural laws, but about the presence of *true* faith, a faith that takes hold of the God with whom "nothing [is] impossible," as Luke stated at the beginning of his gospel (1:37). The Heidelberg Catechism characterizes true faith accordingly not only as certain knowledge, but also as a "wholehearted trust which the Holy Spirit creates in me through the gospel."[1] When the disciples ask for greater faith, knowing that difficult times lie ahead of them, Jesus responds by asking for something small: a trusting faith the size of a mustard seed, so that the faithful follower of Jesus might not look at herself, judging her own faith, relying on its strength or being scared by its weakness, but look instead at the One she follows. She knows that her faith is in that sense not *hers*, but the work of the Holy Spirit binding her to Christ. *That* is the true miracle.

This kind of faith is, of course, nothing to be admired, possessed, or stowed away, but a faith to be

1. Heidelberg Catechism, question 21, in *The Book of Confessions* (Louisville, KY: Office of the General Assembly, 1999), 31.

Pastoral Perspective

Jesus is not scolding the apostles at all? What if he is not clucking his tongue and shaking his head over their lack of faith, but speaking these words in a voice of encouragement and love, as one who would give up his life for his friends? For us?

If we listen again to this exchange with these new ears, we hear Jesus answer the disciples with kindness, and maybe even a bit of a smile. "Why, you do not need more faith," he says. "Even this much faith (his thumb and forefinger pinching together again) is enough!" If we hear Jesus speak with the voice of love, we hear him telling the apostles that, in fact, they already have enough faith to do whatever is required of them.

Given the verses that precede this pericope (vv. 1–4), we can understand why the disciples might ask for more faith. Jesus has just told them that discipleship is more demanding than they imagined. They are accountable to one another. In fact, drowning in the sea would be preferable to causing a brother or sister to go astray. If they are wronged, he insists, they are to draw from a bottomless well of forgiveness. It is no wonder that the disciples cry out, "Increase our faith!" They are not sure they are up to this, but Jesus changes the question from "How much faith is enough?" to "What is faith for?" He tells them, through image and story, "You already have the faith you need. Now fulfill its purpose: live it."

After Jesus uses the example of a mustard seed to say that faith is not quantifiable, he tells this parable about a master and a slave to show them what he means. In the contemporary Western world, it is difficult to hear Jesus speak this way about slavery. If, however, we consider the story in the context of a society in which some people work as servants for a period of years before being freed, we see that Jesus is describing a relationship. Does the servant deserve congratulations simply for doing his job, he asks? Should she be rewarded for doing what is expected? "Of course not!" What Jesus describes is a relationship between master and servant that is marked by mutual accountability and expectation. The master expects the servants to perform their duties, and the servants, in turn, expect that when their work is done, they will receive nourishment and rest and protection.

To understand faith in this way, then, is to understand it as a way of life. Those who serve God do so with a sense of duty and delight, living a life according to God's commandments. We live a life of obedience because, as the psalmist sings, "Your decrees are wonderful; therefore my soul keeps them" (119:129). We serve God and one another, not for the bonus

certainly possible that by juxtaposing the request for faith and the requirement to forgive, Luke has linked them, as he links stories elsewhere. (See 8:40–56 for a famous example.)

On this reading, the disciples ask Jesus to increase their faith because they need it to forgive. To extend the link back further: without the faith to forgive, the disciples are in danger of becoming "occasions for stumbling" and thus "thrown into the sea" (vv. 1–2). The resultant meaning is powerful: Luke makes faith as necessary for forgiving as Matthew makes it for healing.

The shift from the sayings about faith to the parable of the Worthless Slaves is also abrupt. There may well be a connection here, too, making the faith·necessary to forgive basic to discipleship. Having forgiven, that is, the disciples are to say, "We have done only what we ought to have done" (v. 10).

The parable turns on the rhetorical question of verse 9: "Do you thank the slave for doing what was commanded?" Everyone in the Greco-Roman world would recognize that the answer to Jesus' question was no. Slaves did what they were commanded; masters were not obligated to thank them. "Enlightened" moralists such as Musonius Rufus and advocates of the more humane laws of the Torah could argue that slaves should be treated well. Masters might even free them for loyal service; but few sought to overturn the system—nor does this parable. Indeed, it makes no comment on the slave system or the master/slave relationship. It simply uses the logic of the system to describe the nature of "what ought to be done."

This notion is set up in a second turning of the parable. We have already seen the link between the saying about faith in verses 5–6 and the preceding sayings about forgiveness in verses 3–4. The link between these sayings and the parable of the Worthless Slaves appears in verse 10, where Jesus addresses his hearers directly and applies the parable to them. "So you also," he says, but whom does he address? The narrative structure leads the reader back to "the apostles" in verse 5 and "disciples" in verse 1. An important shift, however, takes place in the parable itself. Whereas verses 7–9 address the audience in their role as masters, verse 10 addresses them as slaves. What is more, the application of the parable does not direct the hearer to say, "*I* am a worthless slave," but "*We* are worthless slaves." Its concern is with community. This takes the reader back to verses 1–2 with their concern for "the little ones," to verses 3–4 with their concern for rebuking a disciple who sins and forgiving the disciple who repents—as often

them. One thinks of Martin Luther King Jr. and the civil rights movement, grounded in the churches: nonviolent protesters confronting armed police, dogs, water hoses, and crowds threatening violence in defense of racial segregation; of Bishop Desmond Tutu confronting the full power of the state in opposing the terrible racism of apartheid; of crowds streaming out of their churches, holding candles, singing hymns, in Leipzig and Dresden and East Berlin, in defiance of the Communist government as the regime was tottering and falling. Unlikely but profound change happened because people had faith. The landscape of America and South Africa and Europe was altered, fundamentally.

The mustard seed story lends itself to a favorite motif of American culture: "Believe in your goals deeply enough, work toward your goals hard enough, and you will accomplish them." The preacher needs to be cautious here. An enormously popular brand of religion—the prosperity gospel, it is sometimes called—markets the idea, with great sophistication, that an awesome God wants you to be successful, wealthy, healthy, that God can be recruited to the project of helping you accomplish your goals. The preacher needs to be reminded that there are people in the pews who watch prosperity preachers on television, are attracted to the message, want to believe it is true, and wonder why in the world their own minister is not more upbeat.

Most important, however, the preacher needs to remember that in the pews, listening on Sunday morning, are faithful men and women and children for whom things are not going well. Earnest and believing prayer has seemed futile for the twenty-five-year employee whose corporation has downsized him out; for the woman whose lump was malignant; for the boy whose spot on the varsity was supposed to resolve old feelings of inadequacy, insecurity, and unpopularity. There are needy, disappointed, discouraged, grieving people in our pews every Sunday. They hear from the prosperity preacher that there is something wrong with them—they did not pray hard enough, they do not have enough faith. They are not worthy. The preacher needs to be careful not to say that God can be recruited for my project, whatever it is.

If the mustard seed story is pleasant and positive at first reading, the story of the master and underappreciated servant is uncomfortable and perplexing. I'll leave to the scholars the matter of whether he was a slave or a servant. The Greek *doulos* may be translated either way. If we stay with the New Revised

Luke 17:5-10

Theological Perspective

lived out—an efficacious and active faith sustaining the life of the disciple as a life of service to God. Before we can reflect upon the nature of this faithful service, though, it is important to remember yet again that Christian faith is faith in Christ Jesus, who came among us as *the One who serves*, the Lord as Servant, as Karl Barth puts it.[2] Only when we have recognized this can we begin considering Jesus' description of the Christian life using the first-century institution of slavery as an example for the relationship between God and the Christian believer. Jesus does not—and this is crucial—prescribe a social order of slave and master for all times and societies; rather, he uses this example to state his point: The Christian attitude is one of dutiful service and willing obedience, with God owing nothing to the believer. Does that sound like good news to you? Calvin thinks so. He reprimands all human beings for their "wicked arrogance" of trusting in their own merits, but he immediately goes on to explain God's grace in terms of God's pleasure in *becoming willingly* our debtor, something he calls "the height of the divine goodness towards us."[3] This passage in Luke indeed denies all human merits, all human claims upon God, but the worthless slaves whom we meet here are the very same who receive God's grace in Christ as a gift and an extraordinary recognition of their worth.

Summing up the message of the two sections in Luke, Christian faith can now be understood, not as strange or retrogressive, but as hopeful, trusting, strong even in weakness, surprising and cheerfully active—not because of the believer, but because of the One we believe in, and that, indeed, is good news.

MARGIT ERNST-HABIB

Pastoral Perspective

points, and not only because God expects it, but because we know that God has shown us the way to abundant life.

In other words, to question whether one has enough faith is to miss the mark. The issue at stake is how we live together. How do we keep from leading one another into the valley of death? How do we manage to keep forgiving one another, over and over again? We do it not because we have a superhuman reservoir of faith stored up, but because God gives us what we need to flourish abundantly in faithful community. In the economy of faith, we who serve depend on a benevolent master who not only expects us to obey but gives us all that is required to do so.

This view of faith saves the church from all sorts of missteps. In this divine economy, faith is less about personal fortitude and more about mutual forbearance, as we keep on learning that we are all in this together. A community that lives out this sort of faith is not afraid to ask questions or express doubts or show weakness; nor is it afraid to value mercy over fairness, or to forgive one another's failings even when patience wears thin.

In this economy, faith is not stockpiled in a storehouse for the working of spiritual wonders, but is lived out as obedience to a just and loving God. Trusting in the One with whom we are in relationship, we relinquish any illusions of self-reliance, acknowledging that faith cannot be measured, only enacted.

In this economy of faith, we discover more than we dared to imagine about divine blessing. As we walk in God's ways together, we find that the God who expects much from us also promises much and that—wonder of wonders—the rightful master of us all came first and foremost, "not to be served but to serve" us (Matt. 20:28; Mark 10:45).

KIMBERLY BRACKEN LONG

---

2. Karl Barth, *Church Dogmatics*, IV/1, trans. G. W. Bromiley (Edinburgh: T. & T. Clark,1962), 157.
3. John Calvin on Luke 17:7–10, from the *Commentary on Matthew, Mark, Luke*, trans. T. H. L. Parker (Grand Rapids: Eerdmans, 1972), 2:124.

as necessary—and to verses 5–6 with their concern for the faith that makes any discipleship possible.

Within the parable itself there are several difficulties, beginning with the question of how to translate the Greek adjective *achreios* in verse 10. The NRSV renders it "worthless," which is the most common usage, especially when descriptive of slaves. However, a slave who had spent the day plowing or tending sheep and was then told to prepare supper, and then don an apron and serve the meal can hardly be deemed worthless, at least in any normal sense of the word. Thus, many commentators have sought other translations, such as "unworthy," "miserable," or "unprofitable." In the final analysis, however, the alternatives do not seem to change the meaning of the phrase substantively. In one way or another they all reflect the subservient role of a slave. Thus, we should not read too much into the use of *achreios*, for the core logic of the parable points away from any interpretation that suggests debasement or abject humility and toward the question of a slave's duty. In fact, some ancient manuscripts omit the term completely, without changing the meaning of the parable itself.

Even so, the implied description of the relationship between God and humans or between God and believers as one of master/slave is troubling. Many of Jesus' parables and sayings are open to an interpretation along these lines. So we cannot dismiss it outright. (In Luke, see 12:35–43; 14:15–24; and 16:13, for example.) Moreover, sayings in *m. Avot* 1:3 and 2:8 demonstrate that the parable of the Worthless Slave was consonant with Jewish piety: Because we are created to fulfill the commandments of Torah, to do so brings no reward. In keeping with this, some argue that the original purpose of the parable was to condemn false pride in one's relationship to God. Whatever the parable may have meant in its earliest form, however, Luke's placement of it points to a very specific, almost ironic meaning: Just as a slave's duty is to do as ordered, so a disciple's duty is to forgive, an act that in Luke's understanding requires faith.

OLIVER LARRY YARBROUGH

Standard Version's "slave" we need to be sensitive to how deeply and tragically the term resonates in American culture.

The disciples have asked him to increase their faith. Jesus asks them: "If your slave/servant returned from a hard day's labor, would you invite him to join you for dinner? Of course not. A slave is a slave. You would tell him to prepare and serve dinner. He could eat later." It is harsh, perplexing, ungrateful. Then there is an important switch. Having begun in verse 7 by asking them to identify with the master, in verse 10 Jesus asks them to identify with the slave who, after all, was simply doing his duty—"Say, 'We are worthless slaves: we have done only what we ought to have done.'"

Discriminated-against minorities, undocumented workers, people whose ancestors were slaves, women confined to a secondary and subsidiary role—working all day and all evening, putting in eight hours at the office and plant and hurrying home to greet children and prepare an evening meal for their families—read this story in a particular way. The preacher, again, needs to be careful not to use Scripture even to suggest support for the structures of oppression.

Some scholars suggest the "worthless slaves" is a gloss or gross mistranslation. What the preacher needs to remember is that the gospel has been the constant source of personal empowerment and affirmation for oppressed people everywhere. When African American people crowded into a theatre on the south side of Chicago in the 1960s for a rousing worship service/pep rally/political action meeting, the proceedings always began, "I—am—somebody. I am somebody"—a child of God, the object of Christ's love.

The key here is to remember who is telling this story and to compare his own behavior with the conventional, culturally reinforced behavior of the master in this story. "I am among you as one who serves," he said (Luke 22:27). He did not call them "worthless slaves"; he called them his friends. In the most astonishing demonstration of servanthood, he knelt before each one of them on the night of his arrest and washed their feet.

Increase our faith. Try that as a demonstration of faith: a tiny faith that aspires to great things, but that knows how to kneel and serve.

JOHN M. BUCHANAN

Jeremiah 29:1, 4-7

[1]These are the words of the letter that the prophet Jeremiah sent from Jerusalem to the remaining elders among the exiles, and to the priests, the prophets, and all the people, whom Nebuchadnezzar had taken into exile from Jerusalem to Babylon. . . . [4]Thus says the LORD of hosts, the God of Israel, to all the exiles whom I have sent into exile from Jerusalem to Babylon: [5]Build houses and live in them; plant gardens and eat what they produce. [6]Take wives and have sons and daughters; take wives for your sons, and give your daughters in marriage, that they may bear sons and daughters; multiply there, and do not decrease. [7]But seek the welfare of the city where I have sent you into exile, and pray to the LORD on its behalf, for in its welfare you will find your welfare.

Theological Perspective

Ambiguity about the future is the dominant theme of Jeremiah's letter to the first wave of exiles deported from Judah to Babylon in 597 BCE. He advises them to stop expecting an early return to Judah and, rather, to settle down for at least a generation (vv. 5–6). In the larger context of Jeremiah 27–31, we learn that "false" prophets among the exiles have predicted the imminent doom of Babylon, thereby fueling visions of a speedy return to Judah. Jeremiah, the "true" prophet, and the mouthpiece of God, writes that the Lord himself who sent them into exile (vv. 4, 7) desires that they prepare for a long sojourn. This text lends itself to two areas of theological reflection. This essay will address the preacher's "prophetic" role and then designate pertinent theological content in the passage.

Despite a congregation's longing for advice from the preacher, the prophetic spokesperson for God, about how to conduct themselves in the present, in order to live securely into the future, today's preacher must be wary of casually making pronouncements about what people can assuredly expect in their futures. The future is fraught with unforeseen episodes that are unknown to even the most keen and gifted seer. A theological reflection on this passage therefore begins in the proclaimer's self-reflection.

Pastoral Perspective

The president of Grove City College, a small Presbyterian-related school in western Pennsylvania, recounts the changes on Broad Street and why college leadership has made the largest contribution to the borough's main-street revitalization. Improvement to the town's old shopping district was perceived as integral to the college's well-being. He describes the loss of Murphy's Five and Dime and J. C. Penney, the departure of hardware stores, drugstores, and dress shops. He highlights changes in buying habits, a new outlet mall, and the arrival of other stores on the edge of Grove City. He summarizes the outcome this way: "The effect on the downtown (other demographic changes were also ongoing) was the same in Grove City as in other small towns—catastrophic decline. In Grove City, storefronts became empty and the town began to look quite tired and downtrodden."[1]

The demise of this small town's center is being replicated in many villages and cities. Sometimes the adjustment is the result of natural disasters like broken levees and flooding streams. In other places the cause has been the shift of industry to a different location in search of cheaper labor costs or easier

---

1. Dick Jewell, *A Moment for Grove City College*, Grove City, PA, October 2008, retrieved September 28, 2008, http://www.gcc.edu/UserFiles/File/news/moment/October%2008%20Moment.pdf.

Exegetical Perspective

The prophet Jeremiah often contended with false prophets, particularly those who had only positive words to speak about Israel's future (e.g., Jer. 14:13–16; 23:16–22). Too much good news! This text presupposes such a conflict among prophets during the time between the fall of Jerusalem (597 BCE), when many Israelites were exiled to Babylon (see 2 Kgs. 24:10–16), and the destruction of Jerusalem (586 BCE). The immediately prior text, Jeremiah 28, portrays just such a conflict. The prophet Hananiah predicted that the exile would come to an end "within two years" (28:3); for the prophet Jeremiah, the time horizon was more extended (see 29:10). Jeremiah proved to be correct, though it took him time to work it through.

Jeremiah 29 continues in this vein. The chapter consists of three letters from Jeremiah to the exiles in Babylon, with particular concern about the false prophets like Hananiah, who worked among them and promised a quick return home (see v. 21). Notably, while the letters are words written by Jeremiah, he repeatedly reports that he is writing the word of God (vv. 4, 8, 10, 16–17, 19, 21, 23, 25, 31–32). Word of God is both spoken and written (also Jer. 36).

The first letter (29:1–23) is addressed to "all the exiles," not just leaders (and may have been read aloud to them). It is unfortunate that so much of the

Homiletical Perspective

In our text Jeremiah addresses a letter to the exiles in Babylon. His words bring most unexpected news. His message is the last thing they expect or want to hear. No announcement of imminent deliverance. Indeed, no announcement of deliverance at all. Instead, they are instructed to put down roots, build houses, plant gardens, have families, and pray for and seek the welfare of the city. Unexpected news indeed!

Everyone can remember receiving unexpected news. The day the letter came or the e-mail popped up or the cell phone rang and brought good news. A new baby born, a successful surgery completed, acceptance to that college or university, a job offered. We have all been there, and the memory of those moments still brings a smile to our face and maybe even a tear to the eye.

There is also that other kind of unexpected news. The news we dread and hope never to receive. "The baby was born, but . . ." "The surgery was not successful." "Thank you for applying, but . . ." "The President of the United States regrets to inform you . . ." Surely there is some mistake—but there is no mistake, only terrible sadness, deep disappointment, the darkness of despair. Helplessness, even hopelessness.

Back in Jerusalem, the prophet Hananiah has been promising that the exiles will be back home in two years, tops. He is drawing huge crowds with his

Jeremiah 29:1, 4-7

Theological Perspective

First, ask yourself, "Am I Jeremiah or Shemaiah?" Jeremiah, of course, is the true prophet. Shemaiah is revealed in our text as a false prophet. It is very easy for preachers to see themselves, like Jeremiah, as authentic truth speakers for God. Congregations often are more optimistic than preachers about the veracity of pronouncements from the pulpit. We must guard against gilded and glowing tales of what's ahead in what we say and proclaim, remaining self-critical and vigilant. Our fallibility must ever be before us, our prophecies measured.

Second, the text contains a subtle prompt if we compare whom Jeremiah addresses, namely, the exilic leaders (v. 1), and the oracle from God, where God addresses "all the exiles" (v. 4). This suggests that the preacher ask, Whom am I addressing? Am I speaking to the leaders—the decision-making movers and shakers who basically fund and operate the congregation (always a felicitous concern for the "court" prophet)? Or am I addressing all the exiles of my flock, especially the broken, lost, and marginal (the focus of the "true" prophet)?

Third, think about the situation of "exiles" seated before you. To speak prophetic truth, the preacher must know the specific situations of exile embodied in the listeners. What traumas have splintered lives? Who are the lonely outcasts? Whose economic well-being has been shattered? Which family has been fractured? Which home has been divided? Whose future is doubtful, physically, mentally, or emotionally? Deliverance, whether sooner or later, is redemption from concrete conditions.

Fourth, the preacher must stake out a theological turf on which to stand and from which to preach, teach, and act. Jeremiah, as the *nabi* of God, tells the exiles to settle, that it is God's will that they act like settlers and not short-term tourists. After studying, praying, and gutting up the courage, the preacher must, despite fear and risk, stake out positions that bear on how we will live into the future. We must boldly point people in ways that lead to life, that unite the body of Christ, that reconcile and heal, always with humility, recognizing the uncertainty as well as the promise of whatever lies ahead.

Once we have robed ourselves in the garb of the sacred word, what do we say? Our text contains several themes. For one, we are told that the people are in exile because of God's actions ("I have sent you into exile" [v. 7]). The modern pulpit often eschews threatening finger-pointing that claims our sufferings are caused, at least in part, because of our behaviors. There are, however, times and circumstances in

Pastoral Perspective

access to raw materials. Sometimes fear of crime or a collapsing infrastructure ushers in urban decline. Churches in these places look wistfully, if not covetously, toward growing communities, burgeoning with new development, and the congregations wonder, "What should we do?"

Despite exponential growth some places are eager to protect themselves against making mistakes, and they pursue decisions designed to bring them a positive future. They ruminate on the development of parks, transportation systems, and Wi-Fi connections. Suburban communities may sit smugly, grateful that their school buildings are not crumbling and their community budgets are not as stretched. However, to all of these communities—the large, the small, the declining, the growing, the satisfied and secure—the word from Jeremiah comes. Towns and cities change. They are seldom static and to them all the advice of the prophet is, "But seek the welfare of the city where I have sent you into exile, and pray to the LORD on its behalf, for in its welfare you will find your welfare" (v. 7).

When Jeremiah prophesied these words, the people of Judah had been forced to leave their homes in Jerusalem and become refugees in Babylon. They were moving from traditions to change and from the familiar to the new. Many longed for their former life. They wept by the rivers of Babylon, unable to sing or play their harps. They reflected,

> By the rivers of Babylon—
>   there we sat down and there we wept
>   when we remembered Zion.
> On the willows there
>   we hung up our harps.
> For there our captors
>   asked us for songs,
> and our tormentors asked for mirth, saying,
>   "Sing us one of the songs of Zion!"
> How could we sing the LORD's song
>   in a foreign land?
>   (Ps. 137:1–4)

Jeremiah wrote a letter to these homesick exiles. In chapter 28 the prophet gave evidence that he understood their feelings as he paraded around Jerusalem wearing a wooden yoke to depict their captivity and to be in solidarity with them. Jeremiah delivered this word from the Lord: "Build houses and live in them; plant gardens and eat what they produce" (v. 5). Shockingly, this prophet was telling those who moped that God says, "Your old life is dead. Your new life is to be found in Babylon. Deal with it. Settle down. Adjust!" It is a seemingly harsh

letter is removed from the reading. The absence of verses 2–3 from the lectionary text does remove an obscurity (why Zedekiah sent emissaries to Nebuchadnezzar—a tribute payment?), but also some historical specificity. More importantly, the absence of verses 8–9 removes the basic reason for the letter, and the missing verses 10–14 contain the promise that God will bring the exiles home!

The opening of the letter raises issues of divine agency. God is represented as the one who has "sent [Israel] into exile" (v. 4, also v. 20). The introduction to the chapter, on the other hand, ascribes this action to Nebuchadnezzar (29:1; 27:20 and often). This is not a contradiction, however, for often in Jeremiah God works in and through agents such as Nebuchadnezzar, and God is not in control of the agents (they can exceed their mandate, 25:12; 42:10; 50:29; 51:24, 49; see Zech. 1:15).

Jeremiah's basic counsel to the exiles: do not listen to the "good news" prophets, settle in for the long haul, and be patient with respect to the timing of the return. God has promised that they will be returned to their land, so sit back and trust the promise. In effect, Jeremiah makes the exiles privy to the divine strategy at work in this situation. As signs of their acceptance of this strategy, they are to build houses and plant gardens (see Jeremiah's call, 1:10), marry and have children, and plan for the marriages of their children. They will even have grandchildren born in exile! The assumption in this hortatory language is that God will be present and active in their daily lives even in this foreign land, living among people they could call their enemies. Moreover, it is eminently clear that God's concern for Israel is not limited to their spiritual welfare. It includes houses, gardens, and the various dimensions of life that marriage entails.

Remarkably, Jeremiah's letter is concerned not only with the life of the exiles; it also addresses the well-being of the "enemies" among whom they live (v. 7). The exiles are to "seek the welfare [*shalom*] of the city" in which they now live (see Prov. 25:21). Indeed, the word *shalom* is used three times in verse 7 (and for the exiles in v. 11). This repeated language has reference to well-being in every walk of life.

God is here deeply concerned about the welfare of Israel's enemies, indeed, a thoroughly pagan city and people. In seeking the welfare of their enemies, the exiles will "find your welfare" (v. 7). Their work and prayer on behalf of their captors will reverberate back into their own lives and positively affect their own well-being. One might be cynical of such a claim, that

message of unbridled optimism (see 28:1–4, 10–11). As always, Jeremiah's message is filled with "doom and gloom." A letter from the likes of Hananiah would be just fine, but it is a letter from Jeremiah that they get. Helpless and hopeless, they raise their lament,

> By the rivers of Babylon—
>   there we sat down and there we wept
>   when we remembered Zion.
> On the willows there
>   we hung up our harps.
> For there our captors
>   asked us for songs,
> and our tormentors asked us for mirth, saying,
>   "Sing us one of the songs of Zion!"
> How could we sing the LORD's song
>   in a foreign land?
>   (Ps. 137:1–4)

It is Israel's darkest night, and there seems no light in sight.

What are they to make of this unexpected news? They are no longer in the Holy Land but in a pagan land. They no longer have access to Mount Zion and the majestic temple of their God. Instead they are surrounded by temples dedicated to all manner of deities. The Babylonians with their dime-a-dozen deities have defeated the Israelites and their one God. And what are they to do, according to Jeremiah?

They are to do what they would do if they were back home! They are to eat and drink, marry and give in marriage (Matt. 24:38). They are to plant gardens and start businesses. They are to work for their own welfare by working for the welfare of the place where they live, no matter how counterintuitive that must seem. There is still something else they are to do. Did you notice? They are to pray! All the other things they could do—though with gritted teeth, to be sure—but how could they pray to the God whose dwelling place is Mount Zion and to whom the land of Israel belongs?

Jeremiah's letter, which seems on the surface to be so tame and disappointing, so run of the mill and discouraging, is anything but! Jeremiah is calling for a huge paradigm shift. His call to pray is a call to shift from understanding Israel's God as a localized, territorial deity to understanding YHWH as a universal God who rules over all the earth and all the peoples of the earth. He is calling for this at the most inopportune time—when the land of Israel has been overrun by foreign powers who serve other "gods." It is precisely here and now that you are to pray, because even here in Babylon and now as "captives,"

Jeremiah 29:1, 4-7

Theological Perspective

which the "true" preacher challenges the people to take responsibility and accept culpability. On those occasions, the effectiveness of the message will depend on the relationship of preacher to parish. As a young preacher, I well remember assuredly pronouncing godly judgment from the pulpit. What I needed to learn was that in order to be heard, I first had to be pastoral, a wounded fellow traveler who also was walking under judgment, with them, in the dark nights.

A second theme is the difficult matter of accepting the unacceptable circumstance of exile. No "quick fix" is appropriate, according to Jeremiah. The exiles' creative flourishing is possible only if they reconcile themselves to their long-term circumstances. Even though they despise their plight, their future depends on their acceptance of it. The "thorn in their flesh" (see 2 Cor. 12:7–10) is not to be removed. In fact, they have to embrace their captors. Put differently, although exiles cannot control their exilic circumstance, they have some measure of control over their attitudes and behaviors. Like Paul, the confession "[Your] grace is sufficient" exudes faithful courage (2 Cor. 12:9).

A third emphasis of the text is that with condemnation lies hope. Based on an inchoate faith in providence, deeply rooted in the theology of covenant, the exiles are urged to accept bondage in light of the promise of rescue and healing, believing that one day the voice of Isaiah 40 will be heard and their agony will be ended.

Because attitude alone did not suffice, as a fourth theme, action is required of the exiles. In very specific and practical ways of living, Jeremiah advises them to settle into the land of their captors, creating a community of faith there, as unacceptable and impossible as it appears. They are to sing a new song in a strange land (see Ps. 137), transforming the desert of internment into an oasis of fecundity, manifesting hope in their awful plight.

In this passage, the rhythms of covenant resound in the experience of the exiles—in the judgment of God, in the laments and protests, and in the hope of redemption in an unknowable future. Their experience reflects the experience of many parishioners who face unchangeable circumstances, have chronic diseases, suffer unexpected setbacks, and find themselves floundering in the face of an uncertain future. Accepting the unacceptable in courageous hope is Jeremiah's core message.

DONALD W. MUSSER

Pastoral Perspective

and provocative message to all who face the uncertainties and consequences of unintended change. It is a message for those facing loss of employment when the company "downsizes." It is a message for those who become new parents and the familiarity and freedom of private and personal time is eroded by the demands of parenthood. It is a message for those who were able to scrape by on personality and natural intelligence but are now forced to study and prepare in a demanding classroom.

Jeremiah did not want these Israelites to have false optimism. He inserted questions in the minds of those who had cozied up to pundits predicting an early end to their captivity. Jeremiah had a grimly realistic assessment of their situation and foresaw a protracted period of exile. His letter sought to counter the potentially harmful counsel of false prophets. And surely Jeremiah's exhortation to pray for hated heathen who held the people from Judah captive is unique in biblical literature from this period. As yet there had been no New Testament–like advice cascading from the lips of Jesus as when he said, "But I say to you, Love your enemies and pray for those who persecute you" (Matt. 5:44).

Jeremiah's message was radically practical and innovative. He told the Jews that rather than resisting, resenting, or rejecting their circumstances, they should put down roots and become productive. It is a message for all who live in what they believe has become an alien culture, made so by technology, immigration, and new accommodations to politically correct inclusivity. Seemingly gone are the Norman Rockwell scenes of barber-pole streets and postmasters who know our names. Communication has moved from front porches to telephones, from letters to e-mail, from cell phones to text messaging and from text messaging to Facebook postings. Neighbors down the street are no longer Lutheran or Baptist or Catholic. They are Hindu or Muslim or New Age.

Yes, we will miss much of the past, but whining and pining about it will not make it reappear. Instead, Jeremiah challenges the Jews in captivity, and us, to embrace the place where God has us and find ways to be faithful in our living, so that others might inquire about our inspiration, our resolve, and our trust, and thereby be drawn into relationship with God.

BRUCE G. BOAK

this is only a matter of enlightened self-interest. Even if this is the case, there will be positive effects that will redound to the benefit of all, and that is good. God's repeated "plans" for Israel's *shalom* emerges especially in verse 11; God's "plans" (translated "thoughts" in Isa. 55:9) have reference to the divine promise for their return to their homeland.

Even more, the exiles are to "pray to the LORD on its behalf." In effect, they are to pray for their enemies! This theme connects well with certain New Testament emphases (Matt 5:44; 1 Tim. 2:1–2). They are also to pray with reference to their own welfare (v. 12), but their enemies are to get, if you will, equal prayer time. The assumption here is that prayers make a difference with respect to the welfare of all; God is able to be at work more effectively on their behalf and on behalf of others in view of their prayers.

Especially to be remarked in these verses is a relational understanding of creation. The exiles are living among their enemies, and they have the potential of thriving in that context. God is present and active in such a seemingly inhospitable place (cf. Ps. 137)! The hospitality in even such a setting is testimony to the work of God the Creator; such "outsiders" have experienced (if not known) the work of Israel's God, and they manifest that divine activity in ways that can be of benefit to all, including exiles. "Insiders" have often experienced the effects of such divine creative work among outsiders but have seldom acknowledged it!

This creative work of God among the exiles and their enemies is an important time of preparation for God's eventual work of redemption. When God's redemptive work does occur, it will not occur in a vacuum but in a context that has experienced the effective work of the Creator God. God's creational activity among the exiles is an absolutely crucial ingredient for what happens in redemption. Only in and through the growth of this people will God have anyone to redeem!

TERENCE E. FRETHEIM

you can pray to the universal God who rules over all people and all places at all times! You must be faithful to this God, because this God is with you just as much in Babylon as in Jerusalem, in Baghdad as in Boston. This is really *unexpected news*, and it will always require a huge paradigm shift.

Indeed, the recognition that we serve a universal God who is not limited to one nation and people calls us beyond "God Bless America" to "God Bless Everyone!" Jeremiah called the people "to seek the welfare of the city [Babylon!] . . . and pray to the LORD on its behalf" (v. 7). It is the heart of the gospel we proclaim—"good news of great joy for *all* the people" (Luke 2:10–11). "For God so loved *the world* . . ." (John 3:16). There are no exceptions here. This paradigm shift is huge!

There is more. Pray to the Lord for the city of your *enemies*, that is, pray for the welfare of the Babylonians! This is nothing if not counterintuitive. It is unreasonable and unnatural. The closing lines of the psalmist's lament in Psalm 137 are more like it: "O daughter Babylon, you devastator! Happy shall they be who pay you back what you have done to us! Happy shall they be who take your little ones and dash them against the rock!" (Ps. 137:8–9).

Jeremiah's admonition has a familiar ring to Christians. "You have heard that it was said, 'You shall love your neighbor and hate your enemy.' But I say to you, Love your *enemies and pray for those who persecute you, so that you may be children of your Father in heaven*" (Matt. 5:43–45). Centuries before Jesus spoke these revolutionary words, Jeremiah was calling for the paradigm shift that Jesus would flesh out and call his followers to embrace.

Jeremiah's letter of unexpected news reminds us that the God of Abraham, Isaac, and Jacob—indeed the God and Father of our Lord Jesus Christ—is the God of unexpected news. It would be impossible in this short space to tell of all of the unexpected news that fills the biblical narrative, the news that came to Noah, Abraham, Isaiah, Jeremiah himself, Mary and Joseph, and Saul of Tarsus. We have learned to call it "good news," this invitation to the kingdom of God.

W. HULITT GLOER

Psalm 66:1-12

¹Make a joyful noise to God, all the earth;
² sing the glory of his name;
   give to him glorious praise.
³Say to God, "How awesome are your deeds!
   Because of your great power, your enemies cringe before you.
⁴All the earth worships you;
   they sing praises to you,
   sing praises to your name."

Selah

⁵Come and see what God has done:
   he is awesome in his deeds among mortals.
⁶He turned the sea into dry land;
   they passed through the river on foot.
 There we rejoiced in him,
⁷ who rules by his might forever,

Theological Perspective

The NRSV titles this psalm "Praise for God's Goodness to Israel," focusing on God's saving works in Israel's history. Calling all the earth to praise God, Psalm 66 provides an opportunity to reflect on the theological theme of divine *sovereignty*. Its affirmation of God's sustaining care also offers a perspective on *providence*. However, a third, less obvious theological theme arises from the history of interpretation of this psalm; in the fifth century, Augustine reported that it bore the title "a psalm of resurrection."[1] The theme of resurrection is a fruitful place to begin reflection on this psalm, since it raises fundamental issues of Christian interpretation of the psalms in general, and of resurrection and exodus in particular.

Resurrection. "[God] turned the sea into dry land; they passed through the river on foot" (v. 6). The passage from death to life described in verses 6 and 9–12 clearly refers to the exodus, and perhaps also to the Israelites' crossing the Jordan into the promised land. This paradigmatic narrative in Israelite history revealed basic features of God's character: God brought and still brings the covenant people from slavery to freedom, from death to life.

1. Augustine, *Exposition on the Book of Psalms*, in *Nicene and Post-Nicene Fathers*, ed. Philip Schaff (repr., Peabody, MA: Hendrickson, 1999), 8:274.

Pastoral Perspective

Here in ranch country, spacious places are the norm. That is why we live here, in a valley that once was a sea and has been turned into dry land. This valley has been tried and tested many times. Silver miners came and left. A German colony came and left, but many German ranchers stayed, burdened with dry land and heavy winds. Fires have taken homes and forests. In the spring the mud can ride over your head. We live in a spacious place where the majesty of fourteen-thousand-feet-plus peaks dominates every morning. It is impossible to drive to the church early Sunday morning and not shed my performance anxieties as I stare at the pink glow on the snow-capped Sangre de Cristo range (Blood of Christ). How awesome are the Rocky Mountains! How awesome are your creative deeds, O God! How fortunate I am to be assigned to this valley! How I sing your praises for bringing me through the fire and the water and into such a spacious place!

In last week's reading from Lamentations, the prophet spells out the misery of a defeated people in great detail, even saying there was no hope for the people. He interrupts himself with a turnaround "but . . ." and an exclamation point emphasis: *but* still I believe in God's steadfast mercy whose love is new every morning! Now in this Sunday's reading

whose eyes keep watch on the nations—
    let the rebellious not exalt themselves.   *Selah*

[8]Bless our God, O peoples,
    let the sound of his praise be heard,
[9]who has kept us among the living,
    and has not let our feet slip.
[10]For you, O God, have tested us;
    you have tried us as silver is tried.
[11]You brought us into the net;
    you laid burdens on our backs;
[12]you let people ride over our heads;
    we went through fire and through water;
    yet you have brought us out to a spacious place.

Exegetical Perspective

Psalm 66 is a psalm of praise to the great cosmic God (vv. 1–12) and thanksgiving given to God by an individual (vv. 13–20). The complete psalm moves from the cosmic to the particular. The whole prayer resembles a wide-angle portrait of a single act of thanksgiving painted against a picture of God and God's great acts in the history of God's people. Likewise, the focus section (vv. 1–12) also moves from God's acts upon the whole earth to acts on behalf of a particular people. Interestingly, the Gospel text for the week, the story of the ten lepers, also has at its heart thanksgiving to God and could be combined with this lection to demonstrate the same message as the whole of Psalm 66. An individual act of thanksgiving to God is part of a greater thanksgiving for God's acts through all of time. The Jesus who heals the leper is also Lord of the nations and King of creation. This would make the act of the leper a window into the whole of God's saving acts for all of humanity.

Today's text is divided into three sections, verses 1–4, 5–7, and 8–12. The first section is a boisterous call to praise. Verse 1 defines the actor that is called to "make a joyful noise" as "all the earth." This is a psalm with a universal scope. The next two lines continue with more ways to praise. In addition to shouting, the earth is called to "sing" and to give praise.

Homiletical Perspective

Point of view, either as preacher or hearer, determines everything. That reality is never truer than when preaching on Psalm 66:1–12. This hymn of triumph allows that there are troubles: we are refined as silver (v. 10), pushed into a net (v. 11), burdened (v. 11), and brought through suffering caused by others and circumstance (v. 12). However, the psalmist concludes, there is joy, because God delivers us! We are "brought out to a spacious place" (v. 12). A preacher will have to make a decision about which angle or viewpoint, refining or delivering, to adopt when preaching this psalm with its wide view of life and God's activity for us. Regardless of the starting place, the text urges us toward grace.

The text itself is joyous, since God has delivered the people. "Come and see what God has done!" (v. 5). No ambiguity exists as to how God and God's people are to relate. We are to rejoice for what God has done for us. The psalm celebrates the grace of God, who acts preveniently and persistently to accomplish for us what we cannot do for ourselves. That is always good news.

The triumph of God, however, is something that many people neither see nor acknowledge. To engage that community, the preacher will have to begin with all those things that the psalmist declares God to have conquered. That acknowledgment introduces

Psalm 66:1-12

Theological Perspective

Early church interpreters like Augustine, however, did not focus on the exodus in interpreting this psalm, but linked it with Jesus' resurrection as the ultimate event that "kept us among the living" (v. 9). Augustine interpreted verse 6 metaphorically; the sea was the world "bitter with saltness, troubled with tempest, raging with waves of persecutions," now turned by God into dry land. The river was the "mortality of this world" through which those who believe in Christ pass safely.[2] Jesus' resurrection is the event that makes the sea into dry land and guides people through the river of mortality. "There we rejoiced *in him,* who rules by his might forever" (vv. 6b–7a) therefore means that we are called to participate *in Christ,* in whom are light and life.

This raises a question for contemporary preachers: Is it acceptable to interpret the psalms christologically, as Augustine did? Do we read the events in Israelite history explicitly through the lens of Christ? Recent interpreters have shied away from such an approach, because it obscures the particularity of Israel's own theological claims prior to Jesus Christ. However, we may still benefit from the connection of this psalm with resurrection: through the celebration of the exodus event, we can gain new appreciation for the meaning of resurrection itself.

Rather than reading resurrection backwards onto Psalm 66, we might recognize how Psalm 66 and similar texts provide crucial foundation for interpreting resurrection. We might appreciate, for instance, that passage from death to life is not described as an individual event, but an event that includes the whole people. Further, the passage from death to life is not hidden from the world but is precisely the grounds for calling all nations to praise the God who has done this. Christian interpreters, then, may read this psalm as an important source for early church understandings of what it meant to say that Jesus Christ is raised from the dead, and that in him we too are raised from death to life.

Providence. Prominent in this psalm is the conviction that God has cared for the people through hard times, leading them "through fire and water" to a spacious land. A week ago, the lectionary text from Lamentations 3 offered a similar focus on God's providence. In both that Lamentations passage and here, God is responsible not only for the benefits, but also for the trials of life. "You have tried us as silver is tried. . . . you let people ride over our heads;

2. Ibid., 276.

Pastoral Perspective

the psalmist proclaims a similar message—however, from the other side of disaster.

Beginning with joyful noise, with singing, with praise, worship becomes a balm that soothes over the sores of memory and turns those memories into cause for celebration. The worship leader invites all who are present to remember the awesomeness of God and to remember the time the people suffered in captivity, carrying heavy burdens on their backs, building for the pharaohs. Then the people are reminded of their divine rescue led by Moses, passing through fire and water and ending up in a spacious land full of milk and honey.

One can almost see the worshipers dancing in the aisles and hear them clapping their hands and whooping in joy. Their burdens melt away. Broken hearts are mended. Hopes are restored. Hurting souls are healed. Life makes sense once again.

Perhaps in mainline (white) churches we are more likely to catch a mere glimpse of a tapping foot during the choral anthem; we may hear polite applause, and occasionally see a genuine smile followed by a quick wipe at the eyes. Is there any less joy, any less healing, any less restoration of hope? Remember a time when you felt defeated, even persecuted. Where was God? Who was God for you then? How did it feel when you realized you would not be destroyed? How did you feel in that first tingling moment of liberation? Surely praise began bubbling up within you, leaking out your eyes, or your lips, perhaps even your toes.

Let us forget the worship wars. Let us stop seeking to conform to the latest formula for worship success—are we ancient/future or praise or early church or spirit-filled or contemporary or blended or boring—stop! The true pastor's question is different: Are we genuine? Are we allowing our people to find healing in worship? Are we encouraging them to remember their personal encounters with a saving God? Are we leading them to green pastures where they can be restored to hope and health?

Of course, it would hardly be appropriate or helpful to point out the details of any person's failure or sadness from the pulpit. Obviously those stories can be told only with the person's permission and then relayed delicately and compassionately. However, each congregation has its own story of slavery in Egypt, wandering in the wilderness, and arrival in the promised land. Here is one such story.

The pastor had reached burnout, a nervous breakdown, as our mothers might have called it. Rather than quit and disappear, he asked for a move

Exegetical Perspective

Verse 3 gives the reason for all of the loud praise; it is because of God's great works and great power over God's enemies. This mention of enemies may make a modern congregant uncomfortable, but the song is expressing God's supreme power over anything that is working against the will of God, be that persons, nations, or situations. Verse 4 returns to calls for praise, first as worship and then again as sung praises. This is the same verb used in verse 1, providing an ending for this section that is the same as its beginning, that of "making a joyful noise or song." This is the type of praise that is not restrained and is best described in 2 Samuel 6:5: "David and all the house of Israel were dancing before the LORD with all their might."

The next section (vv. 5–7) is a call to experience these acts of God; to come near and see exactly what God has done. Praise and worship is a time to "see" all that God has done. This, of course, is a metaphorical act, for one does not literally peer over the pew to see what God has done. This is a call to engage one's own memory banks to "see" again the acts of God in one's life. The next metaphor, in verse 6, is probably referring to God's salvation at the sea in the exodus and recalls the great salvation event that is the content of Israel's confession (Deut. 6:20–22). This metaphor gathers the congregation together as it moves from the personal to the collective memories of God. Verse 7 completes this section with a return to the universal rule of God. God may act in the particular, but even these acts are part of God's great cosmic rule. This section reminds us that praise is also an act of remembering God's great acts, both as individuals and as a group of gathered believers. Praise, even in its most exuberant, has a content rooted in the real lives of real people.

The final section of this lectionary text again begins with a universal call, this time to "bless our God, O peoples" (v. 8), but the reason is again a particular one. People from all the earth are to bless our God. The exact event here is not clear. In the context of verse 6, it could be referring to the wilderness events where God both kept Israel alive (v. 9) and had issue with their behavior (Exod. 17:7; Deut. 6:16; 33:8; Ps. 95:8). However, this is not the only circumstance that is possible. Both Isaiah 48:10 and Jeremiah 6:27–30 speak of God refining the people like silver, as in verse 10b here. The point of the poetry here is not to identify an exact historical event, but to call to mind all of the times that God has both saved and called us into account. The world is called to praise God both as savior and as one who sets the

Homiletical Perspective

the question of how God's power is at work in the world. Jesus proclaimed that the kingdom had come near, inbreaking but not yet fully realized. This psalm, whose viewpoint stands on "the side" where redemption is realized, is a call of hope. Still, the preacher must be sensitive in using the psalm as a glib proclamation of a better day. Many of the congregation have seen too many bad days readily to accept such an idea.

Faithfulness to the text will require the preacher to move to a strong insistence that not only is God indeed at work in the world, but God is at work to bring about justice and redemption for all those who trust in divine grace. Indeed, the whole earth has reason to praise the Lord (v. 4). That insistence on God's triumph over our troubles is the core witness of the Christian faith. With faith rooted in the exodus and Jordan crossing (v. 6), the psalmist insists on telling of the God who worked through troubles to deliver the covenant people.

The preacher may choose to stay on the theme of God's preemptive activity for us, using this text to bring a message of hope to any people burdened by the realities of everyday life. Psalm 66 echoes the theme of victory: "This is the LORD's doing; it is marvelous in our eyes" (Ps. 118:23). The primacy of God in all activities, whether seen or unseen, demands celebration here; the preacher will sing with the psalmist that because of God's "great power," we, God's creatures, can rest knowing that divine power is at work leading to an ultimate and glorious end for us all.

At this point, the preacher might well move to a discussion of what the church actually means by insisting that there is an end, a "second coming," to all things. Christian faith looks to a day of ultimate fulfillment for all creation. This fulfillment, a dream beyond even the profundity of humanity at peace, has motivated countless listeners to engage with God to share in the inbreaking of the kingdom. Such an eschatological promise is lifted up here, not just as hope, however, but as certainty based on God's prior actions. That sense of connection between the biblical witness (exodus, Jordan crossing, redemption from our enemies) and ourselves can be recalled, leading the listener to trust in the same hope of deliverance that the psalmist conveyed: God has kept us "among the living" (v. 9).

Alternately, the preacher could lead listeners to reconsider human pain and evil. There are indeed those who love to see others cringing (v. 3), enjoying the ride over our heads (v. 12) and rebelling at every

Psalm 66:1-12

Theological Perspective

we went through fire and through water" (vv. 10, 12a).

How are we to interpret the difficulties that we encounter in life? Augustine says, "By applying to us fire, Thou hast not turned us into ashes, but Thou hast washed off uncleanness." The trials of life are not random occurrences but come from God and are intended to correct our behavior. Centuries later, Calvin concurs in his interpretation of this psalm: "When visited with affliction, it is of great importance that we should consider it as coming from God, and as explicitly intended for our good."[3]

God's gracious goodness is at the forefront in this psalm. Though "[God has] let people ride over our heads," God has ultimately led the people into a "spacious place" (v. 12). This refers to events in the past—exodus, entrance into Canaan, perhaps Christ's resurrection—but it is descriptive of God's ways with people all the time. This psalm affirms that, even when fire and flood threaten us, God's mercy is everlasting and God's providential love will prevail.

Sovereignty of God over All the Earth. Because of God's saving work, all of the earth is called to "make a joyful noise" (v. 1). The exodus event was not just for Israel, but for all nations; God's liberation of Israel is to make God's name known in all the earth. As stated earlier, Israel's passage from death to life is not hidden from the world, but is precisely the grounds for calling all nations to praise the God who has done this. This affirmation proclaims that God is sovereign over the whole world and is worthy of praise by all peoples.

Augustine interpreted Psalm 66 as expanding the mercies of God from the people of Israel alone to the Gentile nations. He read "let the rebellious not exalt themselves" (v. 7) as a reference to the Jews rebelling against God's grace to the Gentiles. More recent interpreters have not followed Augustine in his anti-Jewish polemic, but his underlying insight is valuable: this psalm shows that God's mercies are not tribal, not local, but broad, extending even to the Gentiles. So even we, Gentiles that we are, make a joyful noise to God and sing praises to God's name!

MARTHA L. MOORE-KEISH

Pastoral Perspective

from the big city church to the mountains, seeking an easier approach to retirement. The previous pastor was loved by all—she had a nurturing heart and favored no theological confrontation. The new pastor, also preferring no confrontation, brought with him his love of intellectual inquiry and spiritual practice, which, much to his surprise, quickly forced him into defending his faith against attacks claiming he was not even Christian. Excluded by the local ministerial alliance's creed and constantly challenged by a few members of his own church, he finally confronted it all in a sermon, passionately proclaiming the "Open Hearts, Open Minds, Open Doors" policy of his denomination. He was astonished at the intensity of the standing ovation following his sermon. He was not alone. Had the waters parted?

The faithful elders told him the story of thirty years ago. The young pastor and his wife split off and formed a new church in the community, taking several with them. The congregation survived that. Then fifteen years ago another pastor was so terrible that several folks left. They survived that. They will survive this most current loss of several couples. All shall be well. They have come through fire and water and learned to trust in the amazing deeds of God.

This church is now experiencing an influx of intellectual, spiritually grounded Christian exiles. They bring with them a sense of joy at discovering a welcoming church home, especially in such a small community. The choir has rebounded with new voices and instrumentalists (guitars, dulcimers, and autoharps). The midweek classes and Sunday morning classes are full to bursting. The Spirit is crackling the atmosphere every Sunday morning and nearly every day. The pastor is exhausted trying to stay out of the way of this dynamic congregation and trying to understand what happened.

Worship has power to heal. Important stories of redemption need to be remembered and celebrated. Though a few of us may differ with the psalmist about whether God tests us or tries us, intentionally laying burdens upon our backs, we can certainly celebrate with radical gratitude the spacious places in which we now find ourselves, and sing the glory of God's name.

STEVE D. MILLER

---

3. Ibid., 278. John Calvin, *Commentary on the Book of Psalms*, 66:10.

Exegetical Perspective

people back on a straight path. Praise is not reserved for times when God saves the people from others, but is also given when God saves the people from themselves. Again, this may seem odd for a modern congregant, but it tells the truth that we should praise God for all of the times in our own lives when we too needed correction of our actions.

This middle section then represents God's long-standing relationship with the people and God's desire always to bring "us out to a spacious place" (v. 12), whether through salvation or correction. What is clear is that even these acts within the relationship God has with Israel are world events (v. 8). The matter may be between God and God's people, but the whole world is to bless God because of God's acts toward those God has called forth.

There are many ways to connect the psalm and the Gospel lesson. As noted above, the lesson from Luke has a thanksgiving theme much like the psalm, yet the two texts do not fit together seamlessly. In the psalm, the whole earth is called to praise God for God's acts to God's people. In Luke, the one who returns to give praise is an outsider, at least to the people hearing the story. The psalm then can provide a broader view of how God's people and even the whole world should offer exuberant praise to God. In this way, it is a perfect complement to the Gospel lesson.

BETH LANEEL TANNER

Homiletical Perspective

constraint (v. 7), but the psalmist insists that those triumphs are not lasting. God is at work to put wrong to right. That insistence of God's power at work for the last and the least is the source of hope that helps us better understand and cope with this world's troubles. As many preachers have said, "We already know the end of the story." Preachers may lift the note of hope here for their troubled listeners, reminding them that justice will flow down for them and on their troubles. This act of grace, to uphold and console the troubled, is at the heart of Christian assurance. Rooted in God, it gives the listener hope and a deep, abiding ability to endure.

All these gifts—God's triumph, the human ability to surmount pain with God's help, and the comfort that a godly perspective on the human predicament can give—are gifts of grace. Ultimately, this psalm becomes the occasion to celebrate that grace, the unmerited and unconquerable hope of God. (That would be yet another tack to take: a discussion of God's very nature revealed in the exodus event referenced in v. 6.) God is predisposed to be for us—not only predisposed, but rushing to our aid. Conveying that sense of divine initiative will comfort many who see only struggle and demand. The spirit bound up in that initiative will empower others, hearing the word spoken, to act.

The good news of Psalm 66 is that we have been served, challenged, and saved from ourselves. Regardless of the preacher's viewpoint, that is the good news compelling people to hear and rejoice at this song. That will be reason for them to come together, make a joyful noise, and offer praise!

H. GRAY SOUTHERN

2 Timothy 2:8-15

⁸Remember Jesus Christ, raised from the dead, a descendant of David—that is my gospel, ⁹for which I suffer hardship, even to the point of being chained like a criminal. But the word of God is not chained. ¹⁰Therefore I endure everything for the sake of the elect, so that they may also obtain the salvation that is in Christ Jesus, with eternal glory. ¹¹The saying is sure:

If we have died with him, we will also live with him;
¹²if we endure, we will also reign with him;
if we deny him, he will also deny us;
¹³if we are faithless, he remains faithful—
for he cannot deny himself.

¹⁴Remind them of this, and warn them before God that they are to avoid wrangling over words, which does no good but only ruins those who are listening. ¹⁵Do your best to present yourself to God as one approved by him, a worker who has no need to be ashamed, rightly explaining the word of truth.

Theological Perspective

Two recurrent theological themes in 2 Timothy converge in this passage, and in turn they signal additional significant theological concerns. Here and throughout the epistle, the suffering of Paul is featured, not simply as a consequence of the physical constraints and personal restrictions imposed by political powers. Paul's suffering and bondage, the writer proclaims, provide the theological foundation for his perseverance: Paul's suffering is endured "for the sake of the elect, so that they may also obtain the salvation that is in Christ Jesus, with eternal glory" (v. 10). Converging with this recognition that personal suffering might be used for God's glory is the epistle's concern for the core of Christian truth. The passage concludes with sage pedagogical advice to the preacher-teacher, indicating how the truth can most effectively be displayed and communicated.

For Paul, the author attests, the root of suffering lies beyond the physical constraints and political and religious oppression that might come from powerful authorities in this world; instead, his suffering results from his own binding of personal freedom in order to submit fully to the divine commands of ministry. In this way, Paul's endurance of suffering is presented as a model for the building of personal character, especially for the teacher-preacher. Personal suffering thus becomes a sanctifying process for the

Pastoral Perspective

This portion of the epistle sounds a little like Jimmy Stewart's character in the 1965 Civil War movie *Shenandoah*. A pacifist farmer, Stewart is trying to raise seven children without his wife's presence, but with her instructions to help them become good Christians. So he prays over their bountiful dinner, "Lord, we cleared this land; we plowed it, sowed it, and harvested it. We cooked the harvest. It wouldn't be here; we wouldn't be eating it, if we hadn't done it all ourselves. We worked dog-bone for every crumb and morsel, but we thank you just the same anyway, Lord, for this food we are about to eat. Amen."

Imagine a church potluck prayer: "Lord, we cleared this land, we built this church, we gathered the money and the people, and we worshiped. It would not be here; we would not be worshiping you, if we had not done it all ourselves. We are dog-tired and not nearly ready for another program year and stewardship campaign and outreach emphasis, but we thank you just the same anyway, Lord, for this church and the food we are about to eat. Amen."

In 2 Timothy 2:8–15 we read, "This is my gospel, I am suffering for it in prison like a criminal, and I will continue to endure all things for the sake of others' knowing Christ. I will endure hardship and not be ashamed of the gospel." Paul's laundry list of endurance can sound like complaining. He has

Exegetical Perspective

This passage is part of a series of direct exhortations to Timothy that begins in 2:1 with the call to "be strong in the grace that is in Christ Jesus." This call is echoed in the opening challenge of our passage to "remember Jesus Christ." In fact, a particular and rather unusual description of Jesus Christ is the key to this passage. The passage is a recollection and exhortation built upon a christological narrative. The story of Jesus becomes the story of the individual Christian. It is a story of suffering, faithfulness, and salvation.

The literary structure of the passage is typical of the Pastorals in that it does not contain discrete theological and ethical sections but weaves the two together. Theological images are connected to ethical images, and vice versa. The act of remembering Jesus is connected to an account of Paul's suffering and faithfulness (vv. 8–10). This leads to the christological centerpiece of the passage, which is a liturgical interweaving of the behavior of people and that of Christ (vv. 11–13). This christological narrative leads in turn to a challenge to Timothy to explain "the word of truth" while avoiding "wrangling over words" (vv. 14–15).

More puzzling is the question of the proper boundaries of the passage. As noted above, these verses flow naturally out of exhortations in verses

Homiletical Perspective

The writer has been trying to encourage his young protégé from the distance of a prison cell. Seeing one's mentor arrested would tax anyone's hope! There were no great church sanctuaries, or libraries with Christian books, or even the four Gospels, let alone the many other resources we now have to turn to; so the writer begins this section with something to cling to in such times. Perhaps it was a well-known line from a creed or a hymn. It summed things up so well that he was even able to refer to it as "my gospel." He wrote, "Remember Jesus Christ, raised from the dead, a descendant of David" (v. 1). The writer did not have all the answers, yet he believed that if we can get this one thing right, the rest will follow: "Remember Jesus Christ, raised from the dead, a descendant of David." It was like giving his protégé the answer to 1-across and 1-down in the great crossword puzzle of life.

The protégé's ministry was growing more complex. In the verses leading up to this statement the mentor had been trying to convey to his protégé that it was good for him to receive a salary for his ministry. There is also a hint that there may even have been a family to look after. The mentor was probably concerned that this young minister was trying to do everything and to be all things to all people, which is still a temptation, heaven knows. So the advice to the

2 Timothy 2:8-15

Theological Perspective

minister. Never, however, is it a masochistic exercise of merely accepting or celebrating pain; rather, it is transformed into a medium for ministry. This enabling experience grows out of a Christian's identification with the divine suffering that occurred in the crucifixion. In this regard Dorothee Soelle concurs that "the cross of Christ symbolizes an understanding of human suffering in which humans may participate in God's pain that is love's pain."[1]

The passage's concern for truth is introduced with the initial command to "remember Jesus Christ" as the one who has been "raised from the dead" and who was "a descendant of David" (v. 8). While this kerygmatic formula resonates with the Pauline introduction to the Epistle to the Romans (Rom. 1:3–4), it reverses the traditional and chronological sequence by affirming the resurrection before identifying the historical life of Jesus as a Jew in the Davidic lineage. In this way, the author emphasizes the believer's conviction by his or her experience of the risen Christ, which is subsequently corroborated by the recognition of Jesus as the fulfillment of messianic expectations connected with a descendent of David.

The gospel proclamation that Christ has been resurrected is the binding truth, the word of God. Because the truth has the power to set one free to follow Christ in full discipleship (cf. John 8:32), it cannot be "chained" (v. 9). The truth is not subject to constraints that would cause the kind of suffering Paul endures, because his distress results from tension between his human desires and the divine summons to ministry. The power of Christ's resurrection so enables Paul that nothing deters him from his mission to speak the truth of the redeeming love of Christ.

In addition to these theological emphases on suffering and truth, the passage also addresses issues related to discipleship, hope, and Christian instruction. The issues of fidelity and hope are focal in the fragment of the early baptismal hymn quoted in verses 11–13. Its lines attest the Christian's confidence of new life in Christ by noting the beginning of the Christian journey with baptism: "If we have died with him, we will also live with him." Here, the death with Christ is the symbolic death that occurs in baptism (cf. Rom. 6:3–4). When believers have died to their old ways of sin in the world, they will live in the new way of discipleship with Christ. Building upon this joy of living in Christ, the hymn also includes an expression of hope in the

1. Dorothee Soelle, "Suffering," in *New and Enlarged Handbook of Christian Theology*, ed. Donald W. Musser and Joseph L. Price (Nashville: Abingdon Press, 2003), 488.

Pastoral Perspective

suffered for this gospel, built church communities with his own sermons, jumped into the flames for his spiritual children. What part of the load is God carrying? Paul was focused on his own ministry, his gospel, and the results of his work.

Like Paul, at times, we can be self-focused. We worry about our work, the results, our successes or failures. If our work is raising children, we concern ourselves with their abilities in the world, if they will be accepted or rejected. Whether we are the head of a corporation or a teacher in a classroom, some days it feels as though the world rests on our shoulders. At times, we are tempted to list our accomplishments as if we have done them all alone. Complaining is one way we get to the bottom of our humanity, and there we come face to face with our strengths and weaknesses, our abilities and our limitations. It is a way of saying, "God, help me." Even if we cannot recognize that God created the land we cleared, provided the human effort and the materials necessary for building, we are bent toward prayer, wherein proclamation can begin.

Similarly, this Pauline voice of 2 Timothy does more than complain; he proclaims. The Pauline author defined "my gospel" as, "Jesus Christ, raised from the dead, a descendant of David." In this order—the risen Christ, the divine One, and then Jesus, the human one, born of the lineage of David—it gives perspective to our place in the world. It is a briefly put statement, a microcosm of the good news. Paul wants Timothy to know he may suffer for the gospel as well. Paul reminds him and us that the gospel will not be bound, it will not lose its flavor, and it cannot be chained as he is.

Parishioners facing their limitations—be it the death of a near one or a failure in life or just plain stress—need renewal through the proclamation of the good news. We are not alone in this world; in fact, we are saved from this misery of our own humanity. Paul's situation in jail is an example of facing death while proclaiming life through faith in Christ. He refocuses our thoughts on Jesus Christ, who is not bound by worldly standards, our standards, or even our church's standards. Paul's reminder sounds as single-minded as the Barmen Declaration. In 1934 the leaders of the German Confessing Church were facing powers who wanted to use the church in service to the nation of Germany, instead of Christ. In their desire to remind others that Christ would have none of this, that the church should not bow to another authority, they wrote, "Jesus Christ, as he is attested for us in Holy Scripture, is the one Word of God which we

Exegetical Perspective

1–7. Furthermore, the call to avoid "wrangling over words" anticipates the charge in verse 16 to "avoid profane chatter." In fact, most commentators read verses 14–19 or even verses 14–26 as one passage, focused on internal conflict in the community. The lectionary tends to avoid passages that focus on conflict, especially those with personal attacks. This may be why the lectionary ends at verse 15. However, in doing so, it separates the call to faithfulness from the context of community conflict that makes this faithfulness both more important and difficult. The preacher may wish to extend the lection and bring the congregation in on this connection.

This passage, even as clipped in the lectionary, offers rich possibilities for preaching. At the center sits a series of claims about Jesus Christ. The opening affirmation that Jesus is "raised from the dead, a descendant of David" is, of course, traditional (e.g., Rom. 1:3) but comes in this context without warning and without obvious function in the argument. Its role becomes clear in the hymnic piece in verses 11–13. Most commentators think that this series of parallel conditional sentences emerged from early Christian liturgy. It certainly has the rhythms and structures appropriate to worship and to communal composition. However, its images also fit perfectly into the exhortations of this passage and the themes of 2 Timothy.

"If we have died with him, we will also live with him" (v. 11). All four statements follow this pattern, in which "our" behavior elicits a christological response. The first two are positive: if we die, we live; if we endure, we reign. The assertions in verse 8 that Jesus was raised from the dead and was descendant of David find echo here. It is the Davidic king who rules, and the one who is raised from the dead grounds "our" future life. The next two statements are negative. Our denial of Jesus leads to Jesus' denying us. However, our faithfulness cannot make Jesus unfaithful. As the additional clause notes, he cannot deny himself.

This series has struck readers as curious, not because any single affirmation is unusual, but because the combination is. The account of Jesus' attributes seems to be selected not to summarize the Jesus narrative but to address the particular problems in 2 Timothy. The challenge to faithfulness in 2 Timothy emerges from the problem of suffering and the shame that results. In the context of 2 Timothy, it appears that experiences of abuse and shame tempt Timothy (and all Christians) to lose confidence in the Christian story, to reject the Christian

Homiletical Perspective

young protégé becomes God's word to the church here and now: "Remember Jesus Christ, raised from the dead, a descendant of David." In the church we get busy with so many seemingly important things, as we try to balance budgets and programs and personalities, that we forget what is central.

So we are to remember. The word "remember" is rich in biblical meaning. "Remember the sabbath day, and keep it holy" (Exod. 20:8). "Do this in remembrance of me" (1 Cor. 11: 24). Remembering in Scripture is often a call back to the sacred and, ultimately, a call to "re-member" Christ's body and become Christ in this world.

We find the language of remembering again in verse 14: "Remind them of this, and warn them before God that they are to avoid wrangling over words, which does no good but only ruins those who are listening." Some were wasting time and energy arguing and fighting over semantics. So he wrote, "Remember Jesus Christ." When we forget to listen to the living Word, we can be given to wrangling over words. We can lose sight of what matters, which is not simply achieving a goal—be it church growth or better infrastructure, a bigger stewardship draw or a better Web site—but gaining a Christlike character.

When the mentor writes in verse 11, "If we have died with him, we will also live with him," he has upped the linguistic ante, to be sure. Dying and living are the topic, not the color of the pew cushions. The mentor is calling for an end of petty arguments and proud posturing, so that we may come alive to the love and compassion of Jesus.

However, discouragement threatened. The thought of his mentor in chains was upsetting, and the temptation to quit must have been real. Fully aware of the discouraging image of his chains, the mentor wrote, "But the word of God is not chained" (v. 9). The protégé is to remember the risen Christ and, therefore, in the midst of life's setbacks to know that God's love always has the last word. Regardless of circumstances, God is always doing something greater.

In the clarity of this light, even the most passionate rivalries may turn out to have been petty. Canadian missionaries serving in Kenya during the postelection violence of 2008 tell the story of a church that sought to provide refuge and sanctuary in the aftermath of several weeks of terrible violence. They experienced a church that seemed to have no end of compassion, welcoming thousands of refugees, always with room for one more. One woman who had suffered the violence arrived at the church absolutely overwrought by the evil she had

2 Timothy 2:8-15

Theological Perspective

resurrection: "if we endure, we will also reign with him" (v. 12a). If believers persist, they will enjoy the fullness of the reign of Christ in the present and coming kingdom of God.

As the hymn enjoins believers to persevere, it also specifies the penalty for apostasy, for denial of the Christ will provoke his denial of them. When believers might stray, however, Christ cannot deny himself, for faithfulness to the word determines who he is. Thus, while believers are assured of their participation in God's reign, their future depends upon their perseverance (vv. 12–13). This passage is a stark reminder that apostasy, which is the denial of a faith once confessed, remains a threat; this provides a prompt for believers to explore the meaning of "the perseverance of the saints."

While each of the Pastoral Epistles places high value on fidelity to the tradition, 2 Timothy distinguishes itself by directing Timothy in how to be a strong, canonical teacher. Drawing upon the pattern of Paul's sanctification of suffering and the affirmations in the hymnic fragment in verses 11–13, the author exhorts Timothy, as a representative minister, to follow Paul's model and to be "an apt teacher, patient, correcting opponents with gentleness" (vv. 24–25). In the climax of today's passage, Timothy is urged to prepare himself to stand before God as one who, as a worker or teacher, "has no need to be ashamed, rightly explaining the word of truth" (v. 15). By emphasizing the obligation of the teacher to express the truth "with gentleness" (v. 25), the author also reflects the accepted Pauline injunction to speak "the truth in love" (Eph. 4:15).

As part of the specific guidelines offered to Timothy and to all ministers about their instructional role, the author adjures them to avoid "wrangling over words, which does no good but only ruins those who are listening" (v. 14). One of the temptations in talking about matters of faith is to discuss peripheral matters, haggling over word choice rather than focusing on the ground and goal of faith. In sum, the passage advises the teacher to speak the truth with gentle boldness, an instructional style that is both pastoral and prophetic.

JOSEPH L. PRICE

Pastoral Perspective

have to hear and which we have to trust and obey in life and in death."[1]

In addition, the baptismal liturgy included in this portion of the lectionary text offers a rich field from which to harvest. It begins with theology we can grasp. These words are often spoken by ministers at baptism: "For in our baptism we die to Christ and will be raised to live with him." Next comes the mystery. If we endure in this lifetime, the text suggests we will receive closeness with God, the word "reign" indicating future or heavenly life. Then the third line challenges us boldly, "If we deny him, he will also deny us." Quickly our minds recall occasions when we have denied God. Was it at lunch when coworkers were making fun of Christians? Was it when we refused to give to a stranger? Guilt crops up with that feeling that we have denied him. Before we start to exit the practice of faith—the church membership, the prayer we are hearing—the good news comes: "If we are faithless, God remains faithful—for God cannot deny himself." Thankfully, we are swept up in the wondrous love and grace that Christ provides in his resurrection life.

If Paul lived today with cell phones and text messaging, this is a message he would send us, "Remember, remind, and be diligent for the sake of the gospel." An instant message on our computer screen in the cubicle at work or our BlackBerry beeping with a text message while we sit deep in traffic on the way home could be just the thing we need to hear to lift us out of the human predicament and point us toward heavenly hope. When we are faithless, complaining, and self-absorbed, God is faithful.

OLIVE ELAINE HINNANT

---

1. Arthur C. Cochrane, *The Church's Confession under Hitler* (Philadelphia: Westminster Press, 1962), 237–42.

calling, and finally to deny Christ. A Christology is gathered around this. Jesus is raised from the dead and reigns as the son of David. Thus, the sense of failure and loss of social status that haunts the Christian life finds future redemption in sharing Jesus' victories. However, to give in to the temptation to deny Jesus results in Jesus' denying them in return. To turn from the Jesus story and the duties of the Christian life in order to avoid its sufferings means that they will not share in final glories. Their faithlessness to the Christian calling disconnects them from the Jesus story. Jesus, of course, cannot and will not be faithless in return. Jesus remained true to his calling. The readers would certainly hear echoes of the cross.

While the Jesus story hereby becomes the ground of the Christian life and Jesus' own faithfulness models Christian faithfulness, the figure of Paul provides the explicit example of the faithful life (see 1 Cor. 11:1). Paul "suffer[s] hardship, even to the point of being chained like a criminal" for the sake of the gospel (v. 9). The intense shame of arrest and imprisonment does not undo Paul's faithfulness to the gospel. Paul "endures everything" (v. 10) for the sake of the gospel and the salvation of the elect. This is the proper response to suffering and shame. Fittingly the passage concludes with a call to Timothy "to present yourself to God as one approved by him, a worker who has no need to be ashamed, rightly explaining the word of truth" (v. 15).

It is rare for any contemporary Western Christian to suffer the kind of abuse and shaming for her or his faith that early Christians regularly suffered in the Roman world. Certainly for Western Christians to claim that they too suffer for their faith to some extent disregards and underestimates the severity of the early persecutions. However, we do know temptations to faithlessness, and we do waver in our loyalties to the gospel and the Christian life. There are indeed forces in the world that are resistant to the gospel and inhospitable to the Christian life. To these forces, to these temptations, the story of Jesus still speaks, and the examples of Paul and many other faithful people still inspire. In the midst of hardship, we can still "remember Jesus Christ."

LEWIS R. DONELSON

witnessed at the hand of her neighbors of a different tribe. She said, "They didn't love us. They will never love us!" She did not yet know that those who were preparing her meal and a place for her to stay were from her enemy tribe, for this church was multi-tribal. By re-membering the risen Christ, they allowed God's love to prevail over anger and hatred.

Some will recognize the power of the risen Christ but will nonetheless hold themselves back out of humility, recognizing that in our human frailty we can never be Jesus in this world. To those who would hold back for reasons of inadequacy, the mentor writes, "Remember Jesus Christ, raised from the dead, a descendant of David." Some say that Paul included "descendant of David" simply because it was part of the sentence that had been taken from an early creed; but if nothing else, it speaks to the humanity of Jesus. In a longer version, Paul says that Jesus Christ "was descended from David according to the flesh and was declared to be Son of God with power . . . by resurrection from the dead" (Rom. 1:3–4). If nothing else, the mentor reminds Timothy and us that Jesus comes from a long line of humans. He knows what it is to struggle as we do. He was tempted in all manners as we are. His victory over temptation and sin upon the cross was not just his, but somehow also ours. Remember him. He gave his life to free us from sin, and he is with us always to strengthen and encourage.

Nobody knows the trouble I've seen. Nobody knows but Jesus.

J. PETER HOLMES

Luke 17:11-19

[11]On the way to Jerusalem Jesus was going through the region between Samaria and Galilee. [12]As he entered a village, ten lepers approached him. Keeping their distance, [13]they called out, saying, "Jesus, Master, have mercy on us!" [14]When he saw them, he said to them, "Go and show yourselves to the priests." And as they went, they were made clean. [15]Then one of them, when he saw that he was healed, turned back, praising God with a loud voice. [16]He prostrated himself at Jesus' feet and thanked him. And he was a Samaritan. [17]Then Jesus asked, "Were not ten made clean? But the other nine, where are they? [18]Was none of them found to return and give praise to God except this foreigner?" [19]Then he said to him, "Get up and go on your way; your faith has made you well."

Theological Perspective

Let us give thanks to the Lord our God.
It is right to give our thanks and praise.
Eternal God, holy and mighty,
it is truly right and our greatest joy
to give you thanks and praise,
and to worship you in every place where your
glory abides.[1]

Rereading Luke's account of the ten lepers, one is drawn to this eucharistic prayer and central liturgical part of Presbyterian worship (and there is one like it in almost every Christian denomination). It challenges the faithful, when we take the time to contemplate it wholeheartedly, trying to understand it, praying it so that it might become part of us and our self-understanding. These words of the Great Thanksgiving, festive and solemn as they sound, intend to characterize not just some kind of lofty Sunday-morning-worship-service feeling, but every part of Christian living—our mundane, ordinary, trivial, and everyday life. We pray and confess that it is *truly right* and *our greatest joy* to give thanks and praise to God, and, needless to say, we all know that it is certainly right to do so, that we are called to be grateful to God.

After all, is it not our Christian *duty* to show ourselves grateful to God with our whole life for

---

1. "The Great Thanksgiving: B," in *Book of Common Worship* (Louisville, KY: Westminster John Knox Press, 1993), 123.

Pastoral Perspective

"Your faith has made you well" is one of those verses from Scripture that has done as much harm as good. As you enter the pulpit on this Sunday, your congregation is composite. On the one hand, many have given joyful thanks to God after recovering from an illness or an accident. Just as many do not recover, even though they may have prayed just as hard and just as often. Is the problem with their prayer? Some assume their prayers are inferior if they do not "work," but perhaps the problem is with their understanding of faith. Often Christians think of faith as being all about cause and effect—you pray for something, and it either happens or it does not happen.

There is good news for preacher and people: Jesus points to a more profound understanding of faith in this story about the ten lepers who are healed. In this narrative, the actual healing is almost a sideline event. Jesus does it without fanfare. We do not know where nine of the ten go, but we do know that this one—a foreigner, and a despised one at that—comes back to bow down at Jesus' feet, to worship and give thanks. It is difficult to know what tone Jesus uses as he questions the whereabouts of the other nine. Is he sad? angry? flabbergasted? What he does make clear is that this most unlikely one, this double outcast, has been embraced by grace. "Get up and go," he says, "your faith has made you well."

Exegetical Perspective

Luke 17:11–19 is the story of Jesus healing ten lepers, one of whom returns to thank him. It appears only in the Gospel of Luke. The introduction notes that the incident took place when Jesus was "on the way to Jerusalem" (v. 11a). In Luke's Gospel, this journey begins at 9:51 (the Gospel for Proper 8) and continues through 19:27, a section that shows carefully developed narrative structure. Luke has made this journey the occasion for introducing numerous parables and stories he alone relates (e.g., the Good Samaritan, the rich fool, and the Prodigal Son) and for gathering material that Matthew and Mark place in other contexts (e.g., the lawyer's question, the Lord's Prayer, the sign of Jonah, and the treasure in heaven). Luke's primary theme in this section is discipleship.

The first part of the story (vv. 11–14) is structured like most healing narratives. The sick come to Jesus with the request that he heal them. He does and sends them on their way, frequently with an admonition of some kind. A good example to compare to this story is Mark 1:40–45 (= Matt. 8:1–4 and Luke 5:12–16). Here a single leper comes to Jesus, bows down before him, and begs to be healed. Jesus touches the leper and says, "Be made clean," whereupon the leprosy leaves him. Jesus then gives two orders: Do not tell anyone about what has happened, and show yourself to the priest, making an offering

Homiletical Perspective

Karl Barth was fond of saying that the basic human response to God is gratitude—not fear and trembling, not guilt and dread, but thanksgiving. "What else can we say to what God gives us but stammer praise?"[1] C. S. Lewis, as he explored his newfound faith, observed the Bible's, particularly the Psalter's, insistence that we praise and thank God. He also observed the connection between gratitude and personal well-being. "I noticed how the humblest and at the same time most balanced minds praised most: while the cranks, misfits, and malcontents praised least. Praise almost seems to be inner health made audible."[2]

What a wonderful story. What a wonderful gift to the preacher. Luke alone remembers it, perhaps because it features an outsider, a despised minority, a Samaritan, and Jesus touching such is an important theme for Luke.

Jesus and company are walking to Jerusalem in "the region between Samaria and Galilee" (v. 11). The word "Samaria" is itself a red flag, of course. Observant Jews did not go anywhere near Samaria or Samaritans. Samaritans were a despised group, culturally inferior, theological and liturgical heretics. Part of the exegetical task is to relearn how all of that

---

1. Karl Barth, *Church Dogmatics*, III/3 (Edinburgh: T. & T. Clark, 1960), 564.
2. C. S. Lewis, *Reflections on the Psalms* (London: G. Bles, 1958), 78–81.

Luke 17:11-19

Theological Perspective

God's goodness, as the Heidelberg Catechism puts it (Question 86)? Who, however, in our world of independent, self-made men and women would not only call it their duty, but also their greatest *joy* to be grateful, to praise and worship God? Who actually enjoys the thought of owing everything good and worthy in his or her life, indeed life itself, to someone else, to confess that we are definitely not self-made but— quite the opposite—created beings? Who would claim that leading a eucharistic life (in its literal sense, a life of thanksgiving) is the reason for and foundation of personal and communal joy-fullness?

A Samaritan of all people—the foreigner, the social and religious outcast, one who would not be counted under the elected but judged a heretic by most people in his time—epitomizes this kind of godly life and attitude. He demonstrates a faith that lays hold on God, that cannot and will not remain silent in response to what God has done in his life, that publicly, spontaneously, and joyfully directs its thanksgiving to God. Being grateful is not a precondition for being healed by Jesus; all the lepers find themselves cleaned as they show themselves to the priests. However, the Samaritan turns around and comes back. In Luke, as in the New Testament in general, "turning around" as a description for the believer's reaction to Jesus' work is certainly no accidental action, but filled with deep theological meaning. It describes a movement of the whole person, initiated by God's graceful work, a redirection of orientation toward God. Jesus' words, "Your faith has made you well" (v. 19), refer, therefore, not just to the medical healing the Samaritan has experienced, but to the holistic healing of this human being.

Healing and salvation cannot be dissociated here from another. Despite what some exegetes suggest, Luke's account should not be separated into two stories, one of healing and one of salvation, but should be told and interpreted as one story, where salvation and healing are intimately intertwined. Both terms aim to describe the result of God's work in making a human being whole, sound, and well, reconciled with God and people. Luke wants us to see that the healing of the Samaritan is not only a medical cure from a severe disease and restoration of his social status (at least within his Samaritan environment), but also a redirection of his life and faith. With his prostration at Jesus' feet and his giving thanks, the Samaritan demonstrates a faith that is complete because it includes thankfulness. (Interestingly, the Greek term used in verse 16 for the Samaritan's thanksgiving is actually *eucharistō*.) The Samaritan is not grateful

Pastoral Perspective

Jesus offers the grateful leper a wellness that runs beyond the physical. All ten are physically finished with leprosy. Imagine the other nine going on their way. Presumably they head to the priests and are restored to a full and happy life, but what are they thinking? Their failure to thank Jesus reveals a sort of utilitarianism at best ("Well, that worked, didn't it!") or entitlement at worst ("Well, I certainly deserved that"). It is that same utilitarianism that Jesus discourages in his exchange with the disciples about the mustard seed and that sort of entitlement that he condemns in the parable about the master and the servant (17:5–10, treated on pp. 140–45).

Once again, then, we hear Jesus telling us not to be concerned with the quantity of faith—whether we have enough, that is, to make our prayers "work," as if faith were a matter of cause and effect. Rather, Jesus is teaching us about the nature of faith. In short, to "have faith" is to live it, and to live it is to give thanks. It is living a life of gratitude that constitutes living a life of faith—*this* is the grateful sort of faith that has made this man from Samaria truly and deeply well.

One might almost say, in fact, that "faith" and "gratitude" are two words for the same thing: to practice gratitude is to practice faith. If faith is not something we have, but something we do—something we live—then in living we express our complete trust in God. How then can we not practice gratitude, when we know that God, the giver of all good gifts, holds all of life in providential hands? When we practice gratitude, we find that faith is given in abundance, pressed down and overflowing.

These verses, then, complete the sequence that began with Luke 17:1. The demands of the Christian life are great, and sometimes we do not think we are well enough equipped, but Jesus reminds us that living out our faith—by revering God's ways, by honoring one another, and by giving thanks in all things—we are given all the faith that we require.

From a pastoral perspective, this is where the story can reach everyone in the pew—the healed and the still sick, the delivered and the still bound, the successful and the out of work. If prayers of thanks are part of the soul's healing and deliverance and flourish, the physical circumstances of the pray-er become less important. It is the thanking that saves the grateful leper, and such thankfulness is available to all in every circumstance. One can give thanks for his pleasant experience, while another thanks God for bolstering her during hardship. We may even imagine the lepers who were not cleansed (there had

Exegetical Perspective

to mark the cleansing, as prescribed by Moses (Lev. 13:9–17; 14:1–32). Because the story in today's Gospel is so close to this one and because the language is so clearly Lukan, some scholars regard it as Luke's own creation, written to serve as an occasion for the development of the story in verses 15–19. Others regard it as a story Luke found in his special source (a document or carefully preserved oral history that contained the parables and sayings Luke alone recounts) and retold in his own language. Whatever one concludes about the composition of the story, it clearly reflects Lukan concerns, especially in verses 11 and 15–19.

Aside from being in "the region between Samaria and Galilee" (v. 11), the village itself is not identified. Its marginal location and the description of the one who returns to thank Jesus as both a "Samaritan" (v. 16) and a "foreigner" (v. 18) is enough to set the scene. Samaria became "foreign" following Israel's secession from the Davidic monarchy in 1 Kings 12 and the establishment of Samaria as the capital of the northern kingdom under Omri in 1 Kings 16. The Assyrians destroyed the city in 721 BCE, dispersing its citizens and resettling the region with other conquered peoples. In Nehemiah 4, tensions developed between the people of Samaria and the Jews who returned to rebuild Jerusalem after the Babylonian exile. Later, during the Hellenistic period, Jews and Samaritans took differing sides in the various conflicts that unsettled the whole region. In Acts, Luke treats Samaria as one of the first fields of Christian mission (Acts 1:8), a theme which is foreshadowed in Luke 17:11–19 and the parable of the Good Samaritan (10:29–37).

By emphasizing that the leper who returns is a Samaritan and a foreigner, therefore, Luke shows that Jesus' message reaches beyond the borders of Judea, both literally and metaphorically. This, in fact, is one of Luke's primary themes, which he develops by adding material (e.g., 2:32; 4:16–30; and 7:1–9) and by deleting material (e.g., Jesus' stricture against going to Gentiles and Samaritans, found in Matthew's version of the sending of the Twelve [cf. Matt. 9:35–10:6 to Luke 9:1–5 and 10:1–12], and the story of the Syro-Phoenician woman in Mark 7:24–30 and Matt. 15:21–28). The mission to the Gentiles is of course a prominent feature of the book of Acts, especially evident in the pivotal stories of chapters 10 and 15.

The ten who approach Jesus are identified as lepers, who "stood at a distance" (v. 12 NIV). The phrase is telling, if less than clear. In the Hebrew Bible and the New Testament, the term "leprosy" is

Homiletical Perspective

happened and how people so closely related, Jews and Samaritans, could have become so hostile toward one another. One thinks of Protestant-Catholic hostility in Northern Ireland—now abating, thanks be to God—the violent Sunni-Shia conflicts within Islam, and the bitter strife between conservatives and progressives within each mainline denomination. Business people and politicians, accustomed to rough-and-tumble, hard-fought conflict, when introduced to the bitterness between parties within their own church, are astonished at how hateful Christians can be toward one another. We have no reason for smugness as we describe Jewish-Samaritan antipathy.

On the way to Jerusalem, near Samaria, Jesus and his disciples encounter ten men with leprosy. It is difficult to exaggerate the social alienation and isolation of these ten men. People lived in dread of leprosy, a loosely defined term used to describe any skin blemish or eruption that looked suspicious. What we call Hansen's disease is treatable today, but in Jesus' time it was thought to be radically contagious. Skin blemishes could also be an indication of liturgical uncleanness. The result was that people with leprosy lived in total isolation: banished from their homes, from the loving touch of spouses, children, parents, from the faith community—so feared that even to cross the shadow of one with leprosy was to risk infection. They lived alone, away from the community. Sometimes they banded together to become a small company of misery.

"Jesus, Master, have mercy on us!" (v. 13) they call to him, and Jesus does. Luke provides no description of a physical healing, perhaps to suggest a deeper sort. Jesus says, "Go and show yourselves to the priests" (v. 14), the ones who could certify that the leprosy is gone and the person is fit once again for normal human relationships. On the way to the priests for verification, they are made clean. Nine keep right on walking, or run or skip, to show the priests. One, a Samaritan, stops in his tracks, runs back to find Jesus, falls on his face at Jesus' feet, and thanks him.

Jesus inquires about the other nine: "Were not ten made clean? But the other nine, where are they?" (v. 17). Then he says a very interesting thing to the one grateful man at his feet: "Get up and go on your way; your faith has made you well." What does that mean? Was there something about this man that was more well, healthier, than the other nine? Apparently. Does his gratitude have something to do with his faith? Apparently.

The preacher might observe how uninterested Jesus seems to be in the man's religion. We know

Luke 17:11–19   **167**

Luke 17:11-19

Theological Perspective

because it is his duty to be so, but because of his faith in and experience with Christ, because Jesus, his master, had mercy on him (v. 13).

His gratitude is, therefore, the result of a new, a healing and saving, relationship with Christ. In this moment, the Samaritan finds himself in more than one sense *coram Deo*, before God; he understands at this moment with his whole person who his Healer and Savior is and, accordingly, who he himself is. This understanding realization is what changes his attitude from lamenting to thanksgiving. His reaction is a demonstration of what the Westminster Catechism calls the "chief and highest end" of human beings in its first question, and what George Stroup has recently described as follows: "The purpose and end of human existence is gratitude and doxology not because of who human beings are, but because of who God is. The God before whom humans live is a splendor beyond human comprehension, to whom humans respond appropriately only in adoration and praise."[2]

Our task is to call attention to the fact that our human response of thanksgiving is not only the appropriate, but also the most joyful thing to do—at least if we take seriously the eucharistic prayer quoted at the beginning. The Great Thanksgiving calls us to lead eucharistic lives. Luke's account of the healing of the ten lepers grants us a glimpse of what gratitude can look like, and we will have to find out for ourselves what makes our faith a eucharistic one and how it is acted out. Doing so may help us to confess with A Brief Statement of Faith: "In gratitude to God, empowered by the Spirit, we strive . . . to live holy *and* joyful lives."[3]

MARGIT ERNST-HABIB

Pastoral Perspective

to be more than ten by the road, right?) thanking God for being present to them in their infirmity.

To practice gratitude intentionally changes an individual life, to be sure. It also changes the character of a congregation. When Christians practice gratitude, they come to worship not just to "get something out of it," but to give thanks and praise to God. Stewardship is transformed from fundraising to the glad gratitude of joyful givers. The mission of the church changes from ethical duty to the work of grateful hands and hearts. Prayer includes not only our intercessions and supplications, but also our thanksgivings at the table.

There are those who believe that worship—this practice of gratitude—is almost primal, an essential part of being human. John Burkhart once wondered whether "humans can survive as humans without worshiping. To withhold acknowledgment, to avoid celebration, to stifle gratitude, may prove as unnatural as holding one's breath."[1] Worship is certainly at the heart of the Christian life, and the story of the one who returns to give thanks points us to that truth. God promises to be at work in the world, in our church, in our lives; so we cannot but give thanks.

"Go on your way; your faith has made you well" is no longer a problematic saying, even when physical healing does not come. Instead, it is a description of a life of blessing for the church: as we go on our way, we rejoice and give thanks; for in giving thanks in all things, we find that God, indeed, is in all things.

KIMBERLY BRACKEN LONG

2. George Stroup, *Before God* (Grand Rapids: Eerdmans, 2004), 24.
3. A Brief Statement of Faith, in *The Book of Confessions* (Louisville, KY: Office of the General Assembly, 1999), 268.

1. John E. Burkhart, *Worship* (Philadelphia: Westminster Press, 1982); quoted in *A Sourcebook about Liturgy*, ed. Gabe Huck (Chicago: Archdiocese of Chicago, Liturgy Training Publications, 1994), 148.

Exegetical Perspective

loosely used to characterize a host of skin diseases. The Priestly texts of the Hebrew Bible, most notably Leviticus 13–14, describe a variety of such diseases and prescribe their treatment, though less in the medical sense than the ritual sense. While identifiably infected, persons with "leprosy" must be quarantined. They can resume interaction with others only when a priest (not a physician!) determines that the disease is cured and the prescribed sacrifice has been performed. The *ritual* significance of skin diseases explains why varying terms can be used to describe their "cure." In this story, for example, the leprosy is said to be "cleansed" (vv. 14 and 17 NIV; made clean NRSV), "healed" (v. 15), and "made well" (v. 19).

This last phrase draws attention to a tension in the story. In verse 19, Jesus' words to the (former) leper have layered meaning. The NRSV renders them "Your faith has *made you well*," but they can also be translated "Your faith has *saved* you." Both are acceptable translations, though the second has clear theological overtones. Does Luke mean to imply that something other than "healing" happens to the leper who returns? Has he been "saved," in contrast to the nine, who are simply "cleansed/healed"? If so, what is different?

As the story unfolds, the lepers were "cleansed" on their way to the priests (v. 14). Thus the one who returns does so because he recognizes that he *was* "healed"; he does not return *to be* healed (v. 15). He returns, rather, to give thanks and praise God. This is no small act, especially in Luke's eyes. Praising/thanking/blessing/glorifying God is a recurring theme in his writings—from the shepherds in the fields (2:20), to Simeon and Anna at the presentation in the temple (2:28, 38), to witnesses of Jesus' miracles (5:25; 7:16; 18:43, etc.), to the centurion at the foot of the cross (23:47), and to both Jews and Gentiles who witness the growth of the church in Acts (4:21; 11:18; 13:48, etc.). It seems, therefore, that Luke recounts this story not to distinguish one leper from the others but to emphasize the proper response to any act of grace: thanks and praise to God.

OLIVER LARRY YARBROUGH

Homiletical Perspective

only that he is a Samaritan. We do not know what his theology or moral values are—whether he is pro-choice or pro-life, how he votes or spends his Sabbath. All we really know about him is that he recognized a gift when he saw and experienced it, that he returned to say, "Thank you," and that Jesus said to him, "Your faith has made you well." That is surely to say that by Jesus' definition, faith and gratitude are very closely related, that faith without gratitude is not faith at all, and that there is something life giving about gratitude.

The preacher might observe that this man's wellness is more than being rid of his dread disease. Biblical scholars point out the way the Bible uses the concepts of wellness, wholeness, and salvation almost interchangeably. "Your faith has made you well/made you whole/saved you." Being grateful and saying thank you are absolutely at the heart of God's hope for the human race and God's intent for each of us.

There is evidence that Jesus knew exactly what he was talking about. "Boost Your Health with a Dose of Gratitude" was the title of a Web launch by a medical group.[3] The essay cited thousands of years of philosophic and religious teaching urging gratitude and then cited new evidence that grateful people, for whom gratitude is a permanent trait, have a health edge. It may be that grateful people take better care of themselves, but there is evidence that gratitude alone is a stress reducer, that grateful people are more hopeful, and that there are links between gratitude and the immune system. So your mother was right when she made you call your grandmother and thank her for the birthday card.

The basic Christian response to God is gratitude: gratitude for the gift of life, gratitude for the world, gratitude for the dear people God has given us to enrich and grace our lives. The basic Christian experience is gratitude to God for God's love in Jesus Christ and the accompanying gift of hopeful confidence and wholeness and wellness that comes with it, regardless of the worldly circumstances in which we find ourselves.

Writer Anne Lamott says her two favorite prayers are, in the morning, "Help me. Help me. Help me," and at bedtime, "Thank you. Thank you. Thank you." For me, it is that and the weekly ritual of standing and singing, "Praise God from whom all blessings flow."

JOHN M. BUCHANAN

---

3. http://women.webmd.com/features/gratitude-health-boost.

PROPER 24 (SUNDAY BETWEEN OCTOBER 16 AND OCTOBER 22 INCLUSIVE)

Jeremiah 31:27-34

²⁷The days are surely coming, says the LORD, when I will sow the house of Israel and the house of Judah with the seed of humans and the seed of animals. ²⁸And just as I have watched over them to pluck up and break down, to overthrow, destroy, and bring evil, so I will watch over them to build and to plant, says the LORD. ²⁹In those days they shall no longer say:

"The parents have eaten sour grapes,
  and the children's teeth are set on edge."

³⁰But all shall die for their own sins; the teeth of everyone who eats sour grapes shall be set on edge.

Theological Perspective

Two phrases and a "new" idea punctuate the core theology of this famous and favorite text. The repeated phrases are "the days are surely coming" (vv. 27, 31) and "says the LORD" (vv. 27, 31, 32, 33, 34). The former accentuates the eschatology of covenantal theology; the latter identifies the basis for "surety" about the future, at the initiative of the God of the covenant. Both of these phrases create a platform for Jeremiah's announcement of a new, future covenant. This essay, therefore, will emphasize the theology of hope that is coming, the doctrine of God based on the message from the Lord, and the new idea, a covenant unlike, in some respect, any past covenant.

The claim that the future is coming is, at first glance, a banal tautology. Of course it is! That is what the future does. The phrase "the days are surely coming," however, implies something that will rise above the ordinary and the familiar. Like other common words and phrases throughout Scripture—like the haunting question of the psalmist, "How long?" the pregnancy of Paul's series of "Therefore" in Romans, and John's use of everyday notions as "signs"—these words reference time-honored concepts that are potent with meaning and point to a veritable fullness of time. The eschaton is not just any future; it is a future of hope and meaning, brimming with promise.

Pastoral Perspective

Divine amnesia is a blessed gift.

Adolescents yearn for parental amnesia. We are fearful dad vividly remembers the day we crumpled the front fender on the family car. At the time, we had hoped that blame might be lost. We feared that irresponsibility on our part could jeopardize tuition payments. Parental amnesia would be convenient.

Some desire spousal amnesia. We do not want her to keep recalling the day we left the burner on the stove or forgot to put out the garbage. We do not want him to remember that wink toward the handsome man across the room or the day we forgot to pick up our daughter from kindergarten.

Could we wish for "bossal" amnesia? We should not have been a party to water-cooler gossip or expressed our feelings so clearly about management when we did not really have all the facts. We implore pastoral amnesia with prayerful petitions like, "May Rev. Knox forget the day, O Lord, when he walked into my hospital room with that despicable movie playing on the television." Pastors crave congregational amnesia. "May they forget that horrible hymn choice and the day I could not remember her name, dear God."

We are basically biochemical memory. A computer and digital age has made this clear. Our sensory apparatus and body exist to be servants to our

31The days are surely coming, says the LORD, when I will make a new covenant with the house of Israel and the house of Judah. 32It will not be like the covenant that I made with their ancestors when I took them by the hand to bring them out of the land of Egypt—a covenant that they broke, though I was their husband, says the LORD. 33But this is the covenant that I will make with the house of Israel after those days, says the LORD: I will put my law within them, and I will write it on their hearts; and I will be their God, and they shall be my people. 34No longer shall they teach one another, or say to each other, "Know the LORD," for they shall all know me, from the least of them to the greatest, says the LORD; for I will forgive their iniquity, and remember their sin no more.

Exegetical Perspective

This text is embedded in Jeremiah's Book of Consolation (Jer 30:1–33:26 or, possibly, 30:1–31:40), a series of oracles of salvation announcing God's future restoration of Israel. Though their place and time of origin is disputed, these poetic oracles were likely composed around the time of the destruction of Jerusalem in 586 BCE (see 32:1–2), constituting a claim that God's salvific purposes were already at work in the very midst of judgment. The exiles were the intended audience of the present form of the "book" (30:2), which assures them of a bright future in the land promised to the ancestors—an inclusio for this four-chapter volume (30:3; 33:26).

The limits of the pericope (vv. 27–34) are somewhat strange. If verses 27–30 are used, then verses 35–40 should be as well. The phrase "the days are surely coming" would provide an inclusio for the text, as would the very down-to-earth character of the promise—moving from repopulation of both people and animals in verse 27 (see 9:10; 12:4; Ezek. 36:8–11) to the rebuilding of Jerusalem in verses 38–40—forever, for the sake of *God*! Verses 35–37 are especially integral to the larger text, for they make a strong claim regarding the certainty of God's faithfulness to promises—as sure as the "fixed order" of the creation (so also 33:19–26); the focus is not on divine power or sovereignty but commitment. These

Homiletical Perspective

Into the darkest night of the life of Israel and Judah comes the brightest light. Ripped from their holy homeland, forbidden access to their sacred temple by both physical distance and the devastating fact of its destruction, they surely thought their God had abandoned them or, worse still, had been defeated. Into that anguish came Jeremiah's letter instructing them to put down roots in Babylon, build houses to live in, set up shops to practice their trade, seek the welfare of Babylon, and pray for their captors! (29:4–7). Stuck in Babylon and told to carry on. Where is the good news, the promise of a better tomorrow? "Do not be taken in by the so-called prophets and diviners among you. Their proclamation(s) may sound mighty good, just what you want to hear. Do not be fooled; they do not have a clue!" (Jer. 29:7–32)

It is a familiar pattern in history. Dark times come. In personal and corporate lives there seems to be little if any hope. Then into this darkness a voice speaks with news as unforeseen as was the news that sent us into the darkness. This voice of hope suggests that there is light, no matter how deep our darkness may seem. The irony is that it is only in the darkness are we forced to seek out and ultimately able to see that light. So Jeremiah lights a candle of hope in chapters 30 and 31—a bright light that will roll back the exiles' darkness.

Jeremiah 31:27-34

Theological Perspective

Such is the hope promised in our text. The Babylonian exile had drained the present of all meaning and hope. Judgment had befallen Judah. The stages of grief can be tracked in the literature of exile, in the sense that time had stopped, a stultifying ennui had set in, remorse and despair shrouded every day in a strange and alien land, and, assuredly, the future had been severed from the present. Hope had been lost.

In the covenantal theology that presumably rang from the voice and clearly whispered from the pen of Jeremiah, hope would not remain silent. He boldly speaks of the God of the covenant in these verses, using a verbal attention getter that had been silenced under the rubble of destruction and brokenness. "The days" at that time were dark and foreboding, but he resurrects the notion of the "day of the LORD" and proclaims that a new time is coming. "Surely" it is coming, and it will be a sunny and fertile time of building anew and planting anew (v. 28). Both human and animal life will be renewed (v. 27). Thus Jeremiah announces a new future of promise, unlike the judgment of the past, where a disappointed and just God "watched" the destruction (v. 28).

The second theological point of this passage lies in its depictions of God. Numerous sub-points percolate up through the text. First, God assures that a new future is coming. Jeremiah emphasizes four times that a hopeful future will come because of God. Second, Jeremiah affirms the justice of God. Judgment has fallen, not because the exiles are cursed by the sins of previous generations (not because "the parents have eaten sour grapes," (v. 29), but because they themselves have broken the covenant (v. 30). The question of God's fairness is asserted; the projected blame on others is muffled, and the exiles can no longer claim to be "fated" by exile, as in some Greek thinking, as though they are not responsible. Third, although God watches their destruction, God's continued and abiding care is emphasized in the promise of the new covenant. Fourth, not only will God renew the people; God will forgive their sins (iniquity, v. 34), not holding the past against them. God will in fact "remember their sin no more" (v. 34). These affirmations depict the biblical God with clarity and certainty, mirroring the rhythm of the themes of promise and judgment that are central to the biblical narratives.

The third theological emphasis of our text is the new covenant that God will initiate. As "new," it is not in complete discontinuity with the Mosaic covenant given at Sinai, although the passage appears to say that (v. 32), and popular Christian

Pastoral Perspective

minds and memory. Sensory stimuli (eye, ear, nose, and hand) absorb data and transmit it to the brain for storage and retrieval. The calories we consume provide the power our minds need to function. How incredible when decades-old memories surface unexpectedly! We can walk into an old building and recognize that it once housed a dental office because our minds, unknown to us, had cataloged and stored the smell of a dentist's office long ago.

Spousal, parental, bossal, pastoral, or congregational amnesia comfort us with self-serving advantages. These are on the surface. Deep down, we crave the thorough cleansing of divine amnesia.

Unfortunately amnesia is not simple. People undergoing bypass surgery, a life-and-death matter, are directed by doctors to change their eating habits, stop smoking, exercise, and significantly alter their lifestyle. They know they should make those changes, and yet studies indicate that within two years after such major surgery a high percentage of patients have forgotten to alter their behavior. It is behavioral change that God seeks, and God seeks to accomplish this by putting completely new hearts within the faithful.

Today's world so much parallels the Jews' captivity in Babylon. We sometimes feel that we are deeply displaced into a cultural environment that is hostile to Christian faith. Our worship, spiritual discipline, and education seek to help us: practice memory in a world of amnesia; practice grief in a world of denial; practice sacrament in a world of technique; practice generosity in a world of scarcity; practice obedience in a world of indulgence; practice hope in a world of despair.[1]

To make such approaches reality would require most of us to be different. Being different was hard for the divided kingdoms of Israel and Judah. They constantly wanted to be like the nations around them. Even when facing potential exile and destruction, they found it hard consistently to follow God's seemingly contrary directions. In Jeremiah 31 we read how God had provided a covenant at Sinai that contained commands, laws, and declarations. They seemed incapable and powerless to make the lifestyle changes demanded by these laws, so God purposed a new approach. God said, "I will put my law within them, and I will write it on their hearts; and I will be their God, and they shall be my people" (v. 33). This new approach would not require that laws be posted on the wall or carried in a box, but they would be

---

1. Walter Brueggemann, quoted in *News and Views*, Presbytery of Muskingum Valley Newsletter, April 1998.

Exegetical Perspective

verses make clear that God's promises to Israel have not been made obsolete; indeed, the new is grounded in the old! Such claims probably have in mind a dispirited people in exile; they need to hear such strong promissory words.

"The days are surely coming"! This phrase, which introduced the Book of Consolation (30:3), punctuates this text (31:27, 31) and beyond (31:38; 33:14). It is not a precise prediction, but a confident word of assurance that a bright future is in store for the exiles; they can rest back in this promise, for God will be faithful. As certainly as God's word of judgment came to pass, so will God's word of promise (v. 28; language from Jeremiah's call, 1:10). Remarkably, a future event is as certain as a past event! Indeed, all of the exiles from across the ancient Near East (not just those in Babylon), from *both* northern and southern kingdoms (vv. 27, 31), will be caught up in this future of God.

The place of verses 29–30 in this pericope is uncertain. For one thing, sin and death will be a part of God's promised future (evident both in v. 30 and in the forgiveness theme of v. 34; also in Isa. 65:20, but not Isa. 25:8). At the same time, the effects of the sins of the past (=sour grapes; Lam. 5:7; Ezek. 18:2) will not be suffered by this or future generations. They will suffer only for their own sins. We have not yet arrived at this promised day! The moral order (that sins have consequences) has continued to function in an inexact way and does not cut clean with respect to the effects that sins will have.

Verses 31–34 are a classic text. This is the only OT text that refers to a "new covenant" (cf. 32:40; 50:5); the NT picks up on the phrase in several contexts (including Luke 22:20; 1 Cor. 11:25; 2 Cor. 3:5–14; Heb. 8:8–12; 9:15–20; 10:16–17). The text has generated much discussion. Some have thought it to be a new legalism, others a form of supersessionism (see Heb. 8:13)—as if Israel predicts its own demise! Neither of these views will do. It must be stressed that this covenant is given to an existing Israel, indeed *all* Israel (see above), not a people God will create in the future. The context makes it clear that this is a down-to-earth vision, not a heavenly one (see esp. vv. 27, 38–40); it is historical, not beyond this world. To interpret this text in individualistic, universalistic, or narrowly spiritual and Christian terms violates its context.

What is "new" about this new covenant (see Isa. 42:9; 43:19; Ezek. 36:26)? The old covenant in view is the Sinaitic covenant (see Jer. 11:1–17), not the ancestral/Davidic covenant. Jeremiah understands the latter to be still very much in place, and it will

Homiletical Perspective

Our text is preceded by a song of deliverance (Jer. 31:1–25) and ends with the deservedly famous promise of verses 31–34. These verses contain some of the most profound and moving words in the Bible, for many the high point of Jeremiah's theology. They hold before the people the almost unbelievable news that God has not abandoned them, in spite of their disobedience—a word of incredible good news to the many people of every age who despair out of the fear that God has abandoned them. Surely there is a sermon here. The pews are filled with people who carry the backbreaking burden of guilt and despair that somehow they have fallen beyond redemption's reach.

Taken together, these verses form a reminder of God's faithfulness to his people. So chapter 31 begins with this startling affirmation: "At that time, says the LORD, I will be the God of all the families of Israel, and they shall be my people" (v. 1); then we hear, "I have loved you with an everlasting love; therefore I have continued my faithfulness to you" (v. 3b). Despite our unfaithfulness, God remains faithful. Indeed, the whole of the biblical narrative from Genesis to Revelation bears testimony to this fact. Songs celebrating God's faithfulness abound: the songs of Moses (Exod. 15:1–18), Miriam (Exod. 15:21), Hannah (1 Sam. 2:1–10), psalmists (e.g., Ps. 23), Zechariah (Luke 1:68–79), Mary (Luke 1:46–55), and the saints of John's Revelation (e.g., Rev. 4:8, 11; 5:9–10; 19:1–5; 21:3–4). The hymn writer Thomas Chisholm had it right: "Great is thy faithfulness!"

These promises are admitted by all to be unmerited, and so they also remind us of the amazing grace of God. God is the initiator in this new relationship. Notice the proliferation of the first-person-singular pronoun in verses 31–34: "*I* will make a new covenant with the house of Israel and the house of Judah" (v. 31); "this is the covenant that *I* will make" (v. 33a); "*I* will put my law within them, and *I* will write it on their hearts; and *I* will be their God" (v. 33b); "*I* will forgive their iniquity, and remember their sin no more" (v. 34). All the promises in our text result from God's amazing grace. It has, of course, always been so since God called Abraham (Gen. 12:1–2). Then one day God's call (the Word) "became flesh and lived among us, and we have seen his glory, glory as of a father's only son, full of grace and truth" (John 1:14).

The promise consists of a new God-initiated (that is, grace-based) covenant, a new kind of relationship that is possible only because of forgiveness (v. 34b). The Hebrew here suggests that all that precedes it is dependent on this forgiveness. Walter Brueggemann

Jeremiah 31:27–34   173

Jeremiah 31:27-34

Theological Perspective

preaching has emphasized it. The juxtaposition of the law as internal in the new covenant (in the heart, v. 33), as distinct from standing objectively apart from the people in the old covenant, is overdrawn. Several Old Testament texts reference the internalization of the law (see Deut. 30:6, 14). The "new" emphasis here is that in the new covenant the law will not be a yoke or burden, but will be embodied willingly in those committed to it in their behaviors. The Gospels, Paul, and the General Epistles, in reified ways in light of the Christ event, are in significant continuity with Jeremiah (see Luke 22:20; 1 Cor. 11:25; 2 Cor. 3:5–14; and Heb. 8:8–12; 10:16–17).[1] The New Testament is in continuity with the Old Testament; its emphasis is on fulfillment of the Old Testament covenant, not its abrogation.[2]

The theology of this pivotal pericope of the Old Testament exudes hope for the exiled people of Israel and also the citizens of the new covenant in Jesus Christ. Like the God of Jeremiah, the Jesus of the New Testament bespeaks judgment against transgressors of the law. He also promises forgiveness of sins. He further enunciates a new life that is to be lived in the spirit of the law. For Christians, the Christ, as one who walked in union with the will of God, is, in a new place and time, the embodiment of the promises of God to a new people.

DONALD W. MUSSER

Pastoral Perspective

installed in their "hearts." It would be intertwined into their emotions, hopes, and dreams. It was a move from commandments to conversation, from rules to relationship. More than knowing the rules of God, they were to know God with their being. It was a new covenant that would alter their pattern of failure and transform it into a relationship of forgiveness and new life.

It is the kind of change we hope happens. Instead of homes where parents feel confined to write down the rules and set curfews, limits, and chores, how much better to set a tone of conversation and relationship where there is partnership in care for property, encouragement for achievement, and a desire to share in responsibility!

A prominent theological motif in the Old Testament is the concept of covenant. The Hebrew word for it, *berît*, encompasses a vast collection of meanings, yet even this word is not complete to portray the full implications of covenant. In this passage, Jeremiah tells God's intention to make this a covenant of internalized integrity. How can this happen as these exiles shuffle across Babylon with enormous burdens of guilt for having broken covenant with God? Jeremiah declares God's solution with a bold, grace-filled move, "I will forgive their iniquity, and remember their sin no more" (v. 34b). God's strategy is to practice divine amnesia, an amnesia rooted in forgiveness and forgetting, for in forgetting and forgiving God gives optimistic opportunity.

God sees that forgiving allows for mistakes and offense, but forgetting places their remembrance behind, so that they can no longer be a barrier to relationship. God sees that forgiving informs another about the removal of grudges but that forgetting halts the continual negative references. God sees that forgiving accepts sincere regret but forgetting releases harbored anger and hurt. God sees that forgiveness receives apology and accepts blame but forgetting closes wounds and fades scars. God sees that forgiveness soothes disgust and disappointment but forgetting builds determination to deter such distress in the future. God sees that forgiveness is an act of compassion prompting worth and value in another but forgetting is an act of love that reinforces the desire that the relationship not be broken.

So God chose to be amnesiac and mercifully to forgive.

BRUCE G. BOAK

1. On the relationships between old and new covenants, see Terence E. Fretheim, *Jeremiah*, Smith & Helwys Bible Commentary (Macon, GA: Smyth & Helwys, 2002).

2. Pertinent on this point is Gerhard von Rad, *Old Testament Theology*, vol. 2, *The Theology of Israel's Prophetic Traditions* (Louisville, KY: Westminster John Knox Press, 2001), 212–13. See also Walter Brueggemann, *A Commentary on Jeremiah: Exile and Homecoming* (Grand Rapids: Eerdmans, 1998).

last for an eternity (see 33:14–26; 23:5–8; so also, importantly, Heb. 6:13–20, a strike against supersessionism). The new covenant is linked to that one; it will be sheer, unconditional promise, unilaterally made without the people's repentance or agreement (contrast Exod. 24:3–7), and it will be everlasting (Jer. 50:5). Moreover, this new covenant is no longer linked to the exodus (16:14–16; 23:7–8) or to Mount Sinai. The return from exile will be a newly *constitutive* event for the people of Israel, rooted in forgiveness (see Isa. 40:1–2; 43:25), and, in turn, this new covenant will be grounded in that salvific event.

What this newness entails is spelled out in Jeremiah 24:6–7 and 32:38–41 (see Ezek. 11:19–20; 36:26–27; Deut. 30:1–14); God will "give them a heart to know that I am the LORD" (Jer. 24:7). This new heart will replace the "evil will/heart," so characteristic of Israel's prior life (13:10; 18:12; 23:17). The law is a point of continuity between the old and the new, but it will not be an external code any more; it will be written on the heart; moreover, the law will not be identical to the old, but a dynamic law linked to ever new times and places. Even more, this is not a new interiorization of the law (see Deut. 30:6, 14), but it will be so deeply imprinted within them that it will no longer have to be taught. Why? Two reasons are given ("for"): they shall all know God, and God will forgive their sins. Everyone, from "the least of them to the greatest" (31:34), from whatever class or status, from priest to peasant, from king to commoner, from child to adult, will be forgiven their sin and know the Lord, that is, will be in a right relationship with God.[1]

TERENCE E. FRETHEIM

suggests that "all the newness is possible *because* Yahweh has forgiven" and this forgiveness "permits Israel to begin at a new place with new possibility."[1] Forgiveness opens the way for a new freedom to live in relationships once broken, because it welcomes the offending partner(s) whose offenses have become in their minds an insurmountable barrier to relationship.

This new covenant is contrasted with the old covenant in a most unique way (vv. 32–34). The old was an external standard to which we must adhere. The new covenant will be "within," "written on the heart." It will be intrinsic to a relationship, "I will be their God, and they shall be my people" (v. 33b), a relationship we live into, not a standard we live up to, because God will give us a "new heart" and a "new spirit" (Ezek. 36:26).

Universality will be the next trait. The new covenant community will "all . . . know [the LORD], . . . from the least of them to the greatest" (v. 34a). This "knowledge" results from both a present loyalty and faithfulness to God's purposes and the shared memory of God's activity in history. Therefore, this knowledge will be available to all in the community. There is a radical egalitarianism here. "All know the story, all accept the sovereignty, and all embrace the commands."[2]

Here then is the vision of a whole new kind of community: a community that will come to exist by God's grace-full initiative, predicated on God's forgiveness, in which every member knows the Lord on the basis of shared history and present obedience, and in which Torah is incarnate. Here is a new creation (2 Cor. 5:17)!

W. HULITT GLOER

1. See Terence E. Fretheim, *Jeremiah* (Macon, GA: Smyth & Helwys, 2002).

1. Walter Brueggemann, *A Commentary on Jeremiah* (Grand Rapids: Eerdmans, 1998), 294.
2. Ibid.

Psalm 119:97-104

⁹⁷Oh, how I love your law!
　　It is my meditation all day long.
⁹⁸Your commandment makes me wiser than my enemies,
　　for it is always with me.
⁹⁹I have more understanding than all my teachers,
　　for your decrees are my meditation.
¹⁰⁰I understand more than the aged,
　　for I keep your precepts.
¹⁰¹I hold back my feet from every evil way,
　　in order to keep your word.
¹⁰²I do not turn away from your ordinances,
　　for you have taught me.
¹⁰³How sweet are your words to my taste,
　　sweeter than honey to my mouth!
¹⁰⁴Through your precepts I get understanding;
　　therefore I hate every false way.

Theological Perspective

In this central section of Psalm 119, the psalmist extols the virtues of the "law," declaring love for and even physical delight in God's ordinances. Such exclamations may sound odd to contemporary ears and prompt two major questions: (1) What is this celebrated "law"? (2) How are we to relate to this law?

What Is the Law? The psalm portrays the law as not just a set of written precepts, but something to be loved (v. 97), meditated on (vv. 97, 99), kept (vv. 100, 101), and tasted (v. 103). It is divine guidance that is known inwardly as well as studied outwardly (see reference to "teachers," v. 99). This law refers to living instruction given directly from God (v. 102). Thus it is born out of covenant relationship; it is not imposed by distant authority, but given to the people whom God has claimed in steadfast love. This relationship of law and covenant has long been important in classical theology, particularly Reformed theology. The law, in that theological tradition, is not punitive, but is a good gift to guide covenant people in the ways of life.

Though the law is not simply a set of written precepts, there is an integral relationship between law and written Scriptures. Scripture attests to the law and is therefore worthy of study and meditation, as in verses 97 and 99. Within the broad scope of Scripture,

Pastoral Perspective

One hundred seventy-six ways to say the same thing: Sweeter than honey are your laws, O Lord. That honey cuts the bitterness of wormwood that consumed me for a while.

Psalm 119 is an extraordinary exercise in puzzle working, poetry, and praise. It is an acrostic poem with the lines in each stanza beginning with a successive letter of the Hebrew alphabet. What prompted this unusual meditation? How long did it take to complete? What happened to the psalmist during its composition? Was he a changed person after writing it? Sit and read the whole psalm. What happens to you?

The act of writing and reading Psalm 119 seems to be the very thing the psalmist was hoping for—a complete submersion in the presence of God. What one focuses on, shapes who one is. The persons who are absorbed in sports scores and news, or the second-by-second changes of the stock market, will be different in their approaches to life from the ones who read poetry all day, or romance novels, or watch soap operas on TV all day, or Oprah, or reality shows, or PBS. The Benedictines have very little or no television time, but they sing their way through all the Psalms each week, until they have fully chewed, swallowed, and digested them into their souls. Their goal, of course, is to be remade into the image of Christ.

Exegetical Perspective

Psalm 119 is best known as the longest psalm in the Bible, with 176 verses. It is also an acrostic poem, which means there are twenty-two eight-line stanzas, each beginning with a sequential letter of the alphabet. This lengthy poem, however, has a singular central theme: God's torah.

"Torah" is a word that most often is translated as "law" in English ("Oh, how I love your law!" v. 97), but this interpretation is too limiting. In Hebrew, "torah" carries more of a sense of God's teaching or instruction. This understanding of instruction or teaching has a much more dynamic meaning than the classical translation of "law." It is not something old and static. God's instruction is an ongoing function of life as a child of God. As long as we live, we continue to learn and receive instruction from God. In addition, almost all of the 176 lines contain either the word "torah" or one of its synonyms: decrees, precepts, statutes, commandments, ordinances, word. The totality of God's instruction is the single theme of Psalm 119.

The lines of today's reading all begin with the same Hebrew letter, *mem*, and this stanza declares how God's instruction is something precious and provides the way for a good life. It is an important reflection for Christians, who often have the idea that the law has the purpose only of convicting one

Homiletical Perspective

"Oh, how I love your law!" (v. 97). Our juridical culture causes all manner of reaction to the text and to its power, power not to be missed because of our initial reaction. Our initial negative response to the word "law" may incline us to miss the richness of this psalm. Hence the challenge: the preacher must challenge us to love the law.

This stanza, part of a massive ode to the majesty of the divine will, must also be put in the context of the other texts being read today: Jeremiah's new covenant text (31:27–34), Paul's insistence on meeting standards and using Scripture as the basis for that rectitude (2 Tim. 3:14–4:5), and finally Jesus' story about the widow and unjust judge (Luke 18:1–8). These other texts highlight our need to use this portion of Psalm 119 to clarify what God's law offers and asks of us, and what it does not.

The text promotes an understanding that the law is a gift with which we have a dialogue. We are to meditate on it (v. 99), savor it like honey (v. 103). The preacher has to push to communicate an understanding of the law far beyond our congregation's current relationship with it. Our people barely read it, much less recite or even "apply it" in a legal fashion. This psalmist wants much more for us. The law here is something that permeates life—forms us and informs decision making—and thereby is alive itself.

Psalm 119:97-104

Theological Perspective

the Decalogue (Exod. 20:1–17) is a distillation of the law, a symbolic representation of the decrees given by God to the covenant people. A preacher who focuses on the connection of this psalm with the Decalogue might begin by emphasizing that the "first table of the law" (like Ps. 119) focuses on love of God, while the "second table" focuses on love of neighbor, and the two cannot be disentangled. Jesus' summary of the law (Mark 12:28–34) reiterates this point.

How Are We to Relate to the Law? Theologians have long debated how Christians should relate to the law of God, whether identified with the Ten Commandments or with Jesus' summary. Martin Luther proposed two uses of the law: the "civil use" (the law restrains evildoers and maintains social order), and the "convicting use." The convicting use of the law, central for Luther, means that the law shows us our sin. When we encounter the law, we realize that we are utterly unable to keep it. For this reason, the law drives us to Christ, since we are saved only by God's grace in Christ, not by our ability to fulfill the law.

John Calvin agreed with Luther that the law functions in both of these ways. However, the third and "principal use of the law,"[1] according to Calvin, is more positive: God gives law to the covenant people to teach the ways of life. From the beginning, it is a good gift, not something God sends in after human sin. The law shows us that human beings are made not for lawlessness, but for ordered life directed toward worship of God and care for one another.

For centuries, Reformed churches in Zurich, Geneva, and the Netherlands followed an order of worship that pointed to this view of the law as God's good gift for redeemed people. In those places (among others), the Decalogue was read or sung *after* the confession of sin and declaration of forgiveness, thereby proclaiming that those who have been redeemed receive the law as a guide for lives of faithful discipleship.

Of course, even those who are redeemed are still unable to keep the law perfectly. This psalm may sound as if the speaker is wise enough to keep the law on his own: "I understand more than the aged, for I keep your precepts" (v. 100). But closer inspection suggests that the speaker is relying not on himself, but on God's teaching. For instance, "*your commandment makes me* wiser than my enemies" (v. 98), and "*you have taught me*" (v. 102) show that

Pastoral Perspective

Some of us and some of our flock may chafe at the many synonyms in the NRSV for "law"—commandments, ordinances, decrees, statutes, precepts, judgments. These words seem harsh, implying that God is standing just over our shoulder holding a ruler, waiting for us to make a mistake so that we can get our knuckles smacked. However, "your words, your teachings, your promise, your way" are words that are more appealing. Through these words we are able to hear a God who invites us into the divine presence and welcomes us on the path of learning and living spiritual truths.

We do not expect our people to carry their Bibles to church—they are provided in the pew racks. We hope everyone owns one, in addition to the family Bible with personal genealogies listed on the golden pages, the one never read. We hope the other Bible is not an easy-to-read paraphrase produced with a theology and agenda we do not much like. What is it that we want our people to know about the Bible? How do we want them to think about it, to feel about it? What do we want them to do with it?

Do our people even read the Bible? If they do, do they receive it as honey to the mouth, or as gall and wormwood? Some still think of it as magic—God wrote it, and it is too scary to open, so leave it alone—a divine Pandora's box. Some thought they had a science and history book and stopped trusting when it was not so. Some gave up on the book long ago, chased away by the TV bible beaters. Some, thank God, have learned to appreciate the Bible's complexity, contradictions, and beauty and enjoy feasting on its words. Some even who do not see contradictions still come expectant to the feast.

This Sunday may be a good time to introduce your people to *lectio divina*, an ancient practice of meditating on the Bible. Take them through a sitting of it right there in worship. You could share with the congregation your own practice of sermon preparation each week, before you go to the commentaries and sermon helps online or in this publication. Read the selected passage. Then read it again. What word, phrase, or thought jumps out at you? Read it again. Place yourself within the Scripture passage. What do you hear going on around you? What do you see? Who else is there with you? Does God have a particular message for you in this moment?

You might encourage your people to do their own paraphrase of this passage. Here is one example.

My teachers do not understand nearly as well as I, because they do not internalize what they teach. I

---

1. John Calvin, *Institutes of the Christian Religion* 2.7.12, ed. John T. McNeill (Philadelphia: Westminster Press, 1960).

of sin or is something that does not apply because of Christ. This understanding comes from misunderstandings concerning the works of the apostle Paul. Jesus, however, clearly states that he came to fulfill the law or torah (Matt. 5:17–18). This reading informs everyone that God's instruction is a treasure that makes one wise and happy. This psalm, like many others, is written in the first person, making the expressions uttered here personal. The torah is not simply something of importance; it provides a personal way of life—a guiding force for the journey from cradle to grave.

The stanza opens with an exclamation of devotion that is probably surprising for a modern audience: "Oh, how I love your law!" This is not a phrase heard often in the Christian church, but this stanza is a celebration of that very instruction! The psalmist spends days in meditation on God's instruction and teaching. This ancient declaration is exactly in line with life in many Christian communions. God's instruction is a constant, whether one is in church, at a meeting, in the classroom, or in the courtroom. This great God should be part of our daily life. God's instruction should inform our ethical, family, and everyday business decisions, and we should take the time to praise God for the gift of instruction in all aspects of our lives.

At first glance, the next three verses (vv. 98–100) may seem a statement of arrogance. The one praying claims to be smarter than all of the enemies, teachers, and even the elders! The one praying here is not claiming that he or she is smarter than all others. It is God's instruction that provides the way of wisdom. It is the gift of commandments and decrees and precepts that provides guidance and allows for one to show forth wisdom. The psalmist means that God's instruction is better than the teaching of any human. Psalm 146:3–4 echoes this understanding by declaring, "Do not put your trust in princes, in mortals, in whom there is no help. When their breath departs, they return to the earth; on that very day their plans perish." Human wisdom, even the best human wisdom, has its limitations. God's instruction has no such limitations. None, be they friend or foe, knows more than God.

Verses 101 and 102 remind us that God's instruction prevents one from making bad choices. There are real-world decisions to be made everyday, and often it comes down to two choices, the law of love or the law of hate. The world's culture often tells us that we need to look out for number one and to choose things that will enhance us as individuals,

The able preacher might well here use an example of when keeping the letter of the law fails to keep its spirit. Direct attention to times and places where fulfilling the law's spirit leads straight to defying its literal meaning. The last can best be done by example:

> When I worked in my uncle's grocery store, a woman with three children had her food stamps stolen. She stole food from the store. Should we have prosecuted her? Why not? She was guilty, and to subsidize her theft required that everyone's prices be slightly inflated. How would inflating the price you and I pay be fair to us?

Use of this text gives a wonderful pastoral opportunity as well. Many Christian communities struggle to get many of their people involved in spiritual formation beyond worship. Here God tells us through the psalmist that meditating on the law will lead us to true wisdom, understanding "more than the aged" (v. 100). Coming to that wisdom requires the pondering that is an inherent part of the formation process so many contemporary adults need. Invite listeners to enter that dynamic process by moving in the sermon to concrete examples of how that formation takes place in your own community. Invite your hearers to take those steps themselves by offering opportunities to study the living law and gain true wisdom.

The text offers a further dimension of law-keeping. Verse 101 elaborates on one implication of obedience: "I hold back my feet from every evil way, in order to keep your word." God's law requires action and restraint, kept in balance with each other. Again, examples from personal experience or experience appropriate to the congregation may make the point clear: We are commanded to worship, but what of those who work to keep us safe during worship hours? We are directed to pray for the suffering, but is that all we do for those who hurt? At what points do we need to act or to use restraint? How do we find answers to these questions? Responsible preaching acknowledges the inherent tensions of this dichotomy.

What of the times when one Gospel call conflicts with another? We are called to feed the hungry but also to shelter the vulnerable. What do we do when it seems that life is pitted against life? Which value do we honor; what do we do first? Why? What guidance does the law give for conflicting demands? Responsible preaching offers people the truth, trusting in the Spirit's guidance of them. The tension and interpersonal disagreements that can come from diverse forms of law keeping are inevitable in every congregation of people growing as Christian disciples.

Psalm 119:97-104

Theological Perspective

God, not the psalmist, is the primary agent. This is not works righteousness but dependence on divine initiative. Christian theologians similarly acknowledge dependence on God for their ability to live faithfully. Since Augustine, few theologians have claimed that people by themselves can keep the commandments. Rather, God enables people to keep the law—in Christ and by the power of the Spirit. For instance, the Scots Confession (1560) says, "as God the Father beholds us in the body of his Son Christ Jesus, he accepts our imperfect obedience as if it were perfect, and covers our works, which are defiled with many stains, with the righteousness of his Son."[2] Christ alone fulfills the law; we are seen as faithful to the law only because of his faithfulness.

If we follow the law at all, showing genuine love of God and neighbor, Reformed theologians emphasize that this is evidence of the Spirit's work transforming us. Preachers need to attend to the benefit as well as the danger of this teaching. Positively, this affirmation that the Spirit alone enables us to "keep the law" emphasizes that we might live genuinely in accordance with God's will. However, if good works are interpreted as a sign of God's Spirit, this might also lead to judgment that those who do not show the signs of regeneration are bereft of the Spirit.

Christians who meditate on Psalm 119 have a grand opportunity to reclaim a positive view of God's law as truly worthy of praise. Such a view rules out three things:

—antinomianism (teaching that the law no longer applies to those who are redeemed in Christ)
—any view of the law as simply a negative restraint on sinful nature
—a passive approach to Christian discipleship

According to this classic Reformed third use of the law, the whole of life is shaped in thankfulness and praise of God and in love of neighbor. The law shows us who we truly are and enables us to grow more and more into the image of God. How sweet is this word!

MARTHA L. MOORE-KEISH

Pastoral Perspective

internalize what I learn about you. I am wiser than the old ones who do not live out your will for their lives. I may be younger than they, but I actualize what I study. I listen to you and I do it. Your law for life frees me to live with joy. I do not have to worry that I miss the mark and lose your presence in my life.

Then comes the inevitable question—*Is that really true of me?*

The Scriptures have tremendous healing power, when carefully chosen or understood properly. Jim called his pastor three times on Monday, and once on Tuesday. He was quickly weakening from the cancer, and sounded as though he really had to concentrate to make sense. He was worried that Jesus was not listening to his prayers anymore. "Am I praying properly? This is all kind of new to me. I have just been talking to Jesus, and usually I can feel his presence, but not today. Am I doing something wrong? Is there something I can read, a particular Bible passage maybe, that would teach me how to pray?" Several days later Jim's wife, Shirley, called the pastor. Jim had died. After receiving the usual pastoral condolences, Shirley was eager to tell her pastor about her last days and hours with Jim. "He liked it when I read the Bible to him, so I would just get in bed and read to him. It made him feel so much better. He especially liked the Psalms. Could we use the Twenty-third Psalm in his service? He really liked that one." ("Could we?" the pastor thought, "Of course. It is a standard part of the service. This is exactly why.")

STEVE D. MILLER

---

2. Scots Confession 3.15, in *Book of Confessions: Study Edition* (Louisville, KY: Geneva Press, 1996), 40.

even at the cost of damaging another. God's instruction tells a different story. God's law is one of love for God and neighbor. This small section speaks loudly against a world that tells us to protect ourselves and our own over all others.

Verse 103 moves the meditation toward the senses and pleasure, declaring that the love of God's law is like a pleasing taste. The instruction of God is as sweet and precious as honey. Psalm 19 uses very similar language. God's word is as sweet as the sweetest thing known. It is pleasing and delightful. This metaphor reminds us of the preciousness of this gift of torah. It is not just good for you; it is delightful. This broccoli tastes like crème brûlée.

The final verse sets the contrast between following the instruction of God and following the other way of life. It is easy as modern people to look at this contrast and think that life is much more complicated than this stanza suggests. Indeed, all of the torah psalms offer this same perspective of two ways of life. Also, the torah psalms create a feeling that a choice other than God's instruction is the most foolish choice one could ever make; this stanza is no exception. This choice does not imply that one will be easy and the other difficult, just that one would be a fool to choose the path that forgoes God's instruction.

In this way, the psalm text fits well with this week's lection from 2 Timothy, where the recipient is reminded that he should always follow the teachings he has received and know that "all scripture . . . is useful for teaching, for reproof, for correction, and for training in righteousness" (2 Tim. 3:16). God's instruction is still the teacher for all who are wise enough to listen.

BETH LANEEL TANNER

Inviting people to join that process—the very invitation militating against the sin of self-righteousness—strengthens church members' resolve to delve into the law to discover God's truth for themselves.

Apt preaching will lead to that point: here in the law we can begin to understand something of the heart and intentions of God. Here a preacher would move away from consideration of the law's implications for humanity and focus on what the word and its law tell us about the Creator and divine intent for creation. This reversal of the ways in which the law is homiletically considered is legitimated by the text: "Through your precepts I get understanding" (v. 104a). Taking this direction can be a wonderfully pastoral step. People (including regular worshipers) who do not understand that law to liberate, and everyone who has ever chafed at some act of obedience that was difficult, can take heart that the law, and obedience to it, are actually means of grace by which we can draw closer to God. Thus the law provides a revelation of God.

There is hardly another time where the majesty of God is as clearly conveyed as when the law is discussed. Throughout this portion of the psalm, and throughout the psalm in its entirety, we hear God celebrated as the One who alone can speak the law and who ordains what is in the divine will and what is not. An exploration of God as lawgiver calls on the preacher to center thoughts on the intention and desire of God for us, the ones for whom the law was given. That insistence on God tells us something of God's nature: the One who desires us, who created us in the divine image, and who brings us salvation through the gift of Christ. That insistence on God's primacy shows that grace is at the very heart of God. That makes the law a gift and the opportunity to keep it, a gift. That makes preaching about it a gift to God's people and preachers.

H. GRAY SOUTHERN

2 Timothy 3:14–4:5

[14]But as for you, continue in what you have learned and firmly believed, knowing from whom you learned it, [15]and how from childhood you have known the sacred writings that are able to instruct you for salvation through faith in Christ Jesus. [16]All scripture is inspired by God and is useful for teaching, for reproof, for correction, and for training in righteousness, [17]so that everyone who belongs to God may be proficient, equipped for every good work.

[4:1]In the presence of God and of Christ Jesus, who is to judge the living and the dead, and in view of his appearing and his kingdom, I solemnly urge you: [2]proclaim the message; be persistent whether the time is favorable or unfavorable; convince, rebuke, and encourage, with the utmost patience in teaching. [3]For the time is coming when people will not put up with sound doctrine, but having itching ears, they will accumulate for themselves teachers to suit their own desires, [4]and will turn away from listening to the truth and wander away to myths. [5]As for you, always be sober, endure suffering, do the work of an evangelist, carry out your ministry fully.

Theological Perspective

Throughout the Epistle of 2 Timothy, the author repeatedly admonishes the minister to be wary of heresy and false teachers, and he directs Timothy to focus on the truth and to be compassionate in his teaching. The preacher would limit this letter, though, if she or he pigeonholed it as a screed against heterodoxy. The purposes are much more complex. In this passage, the author expands upon these themes by addressing how to discern truthful doctrines, how to use sacred writings, how to recognize faithful teachers, and how to develop pedagogical skills that will improve the minister's communication of the gospel.

As the foundation for his own beliefs and his instruction related to emerging Christian doctrines, Timothy is urged to remember "what you have learned and firmly believed" by "knowing from whom you learned it" (3:14). Authority in matters of truth and doctrine does not come from charismatic speakers who might charm an audience, or from propositions that might ease one's way of living; instead, authentic authority comes from the experience and insights of those who have lived their faith and shared it with the church. It is their instruction, their model of fidelity and insight (especially that of Paul), to which Timothy is urged to turn.

Pastoral Perspective

Like a warning message in small print on the back of a cleaning solution bottle, these verses from the Pastoral Epistle are last-minute instructions for Christians. In case of an emergency, follow these directions: proclaim the message, be persistent, convince, rebuke, and encourage. This portion of 2 Timothy is packed with direct imperatives, succinct Christian theology, and an urgent call to action that not everyone enjoys hearing. It creates a sense that we have not done enough. We have not been vigilantly preaching the gospel 24–7. These statements sound so terse and definitive; they practically squeeze the joy out of preaching and teaching the gospel of Jesus Christ. It is doubtful many parishioners are called to be street-corner preachers or that they consider themselves to be evangelists of any kind. Unfortunately, many in the Christian church do not witness about their faith, and into this vacuum come dazzling messages.

In what could also be called an evangelist's job description, we are reminded of what is central to our faith and our calling as a priesthood of all believers: salvation is through faith in Christ Jesus. This central truth does not need to be reinvented every time we preach. As preachers, we place the gospel in the context in which we minister and let it grow. We proclaim the gospel we know. The Pauline

Exegetical Perspective

Nine verses in this Sunday's lection labor in anonymity while their more famous colleague, 3:16, plays to fanfare. "All scripture is inspired by God," it says, and so it has been widely employed to define the mechanics of inspiration and sometimes to undergird biblical literalism. The wise preacher will recognize this history and help her congregation ask how the tall tree fits within its literary forest.

The context of 3:16 is a series of personal exhortations to Timothy that echoes and restates many of the letter's central themes. The references to childhood, the surety of tradition, future judgment, the appearance of Jesus Christ, bad teachers and bad learners, and the necessity of good works all recall earlier discussions. The exhortations to continue in what you have learned, to proclaim the message, to rebuke and encourage, to be sober, to do the work of the evangelist, and to carry out your ministry also recall earlier exhortations in the letter. In fact, much of this passage functions as summary of the main themes of the letter.

There is a wider context as well. The passage is part of a larger section that runs from 3:10 to 4:8. The force of 3:14–4:5 depends upon the references to the life of Paul in 3:10–13 and 4:6–8. In these passages Paul models the experience and behavior that is exhorted in 3:14–4:5. As was customary among

Homiletical Perspective

"Preach the word . . . in season, out of season" (4:2 KJV). The young pastor to whom this letter was written was reminded in verse 15 that from childhood he had known the Holy Scriptures. His mentor reminded him of this because he was convinced that the Scripture is a primary tool for the ministry of the preacher, pastor, and teacher. He believed that the Scriptures make us wise to the saving ways of God and even that the Scriptures are inspired by God. Unfortunately, most people in today's church have little more than their childhood knowledge of the Bible. Though many would claim to believe that the Bible is God's word, not many read it, let alone heed it. The state of biblical illiteracy within the church is often lamented, yet the Bible is one of the key tools in the ministry to which clergy have been called and in the Christian life to which we have all been called. So often the good book seems to be out of season.

A. J. Jacobs, who describes himself as a secular Jew, conducted a religious experiment and wrote about it in his book, *A Year of Living Biblically*. He lived for a year by the rules and regulations and teachings of the Bible. For example, in accordance with Deuteronomy 22, he engaged the services of a New York *shatnez* tester to ensure that his clothes did not mix wool and linen in them. In accordance with Exodus 23, he removed the names of false gods from

2 Timothy 3:14-4:5

Theological Perspective

Not only is Timothy directed to remember and respect his teachers, he is also instructed to follow "the sacred writings that are able to instruct you for salvation through faith in Christ Jesus" (3:15). Although the designation of these sacred writings is unspecified, the writings certainly would include the Hebrew Scriptures that would have been a part of Timothy's religious nurture; and presumably the letters of Paul would have been considered sacred writings even at the earliest possible dating of 2 Timothy (see 2 Pet. 3:15–16). It is also quite possible that the author would have known of the Gospels, or that Timothy, who represented a ministerial bridge between the Jewish and Greek worlds, might have considered some Greek works of wisdom as sacred writings. Since the notion of the Christian canon was in its very earliest stages of formation during the period of the epistle's composition, it would surely be erroneous to think that reference here to Scripture would include the "New Testament." Even so, the important element in the author's directive about remembering what Timothy has "learned and firmly believed" is that he should know its source—from whom he had learned the teaching or in which writing it had appeared.

As the highlight of the sacred writings that are identified as instructive in Timothy's experience, the epistle's author distinguishes Scripture as inspired by God. Although verse 16 has been used as a proof text for the acceptance of biblical inerrancy, the verse means not that Scripture is God-spoken but that it is God-inspired, that is, having the imprimatur of God's presence in its substance. In that respect, the author recognizes the human element in the writing of Scripture, while noting the divine inspiration that informs the process of writing Scripture. The process of inspiration does not dictate the text but affects its rhetoric or spirit, and its content or vision, by infusing them with a sense of divine wonder and authorization. While the authority of sacred writings might be derived from the tradition of reception that has embraced the writings, the authority of Scriptures, the author attests, is derived from their divine inspiration.

The focus of verse 16, however, is not on the manner of Scripture's composition, but on the use to which Scripture might be put. In that respect the verse resembles and elaborates on Pauline assertions found in 1 Corinthians 10:11, which identifies the purpose of Scripture as instruction, and Romans 15:4, which indicates its use for instruction as well as for emboldening our hope. To these purposes, the

Pastoral Perspective

author does not put a new and fancy twist on the gospel in order to get Timothy's attention, nor is it dressed up or watered down. Here the stress is on the sacred Scriptures, the oral tradition of the gospel, and sound doctrine. There is no argument about baptism or circumcision or dietary laws. The verses place value on the oral tradition while acknowledging the sacred writings—Scripture—are inspired by God for the building up of God's people.

In these postmodern times, there are plenty of inspired teachers writing books and offering seminars on spiritual matters. The gospel gets buried among the "new" messages. Books such as *The Purpose-Driven Life, The Four Agreements, The Secret, The Prayer of Jabez*, and *A New Earth: Awakening Your Life's Potential* create a frenzy of excitement with their promises of a "new" being, a "new" start. In fact, some churches and parishioners study these books alongside the Bible. The desire for something new, like a spiritual fix or wisdom from on high, is part of what makes us human, and it is evident in every generation. As human beings we have a hunger, a thirst, a passion for what will inspire us and lift us out of the mundane, the ordinary.

Is it possible that through these teachers or teachings we are educated, convinced, rebuked, and encouraged in our faith? Is it possible that these books are reaching a group of people who do not attend church and never will? Is it possible that while these books offer a certain spin on the gospel, our job as preachers is to help make the connection between them and faith in Jesus Christ through which our salvation comes? When we place our faith in the latest book on Oprah's list, we will always be waiting for the next "new" message to come along and save us. Even though we seek the new and novel, it is God's grace that satisfies our longings. This is the sound doctrine that is referred to in this letter to Timothy.

The good news is that though we wander, though we turn away from the truth, though we seek other paths, our salvation has been accomplished in the life, death, and resurrection of Jesus. Ultimately, this is a very comforting passage of Scripture when we unravel it in such a way that our hearers accept the warning label for what it is and remember the front of the bottle—the grace of the gospel—"by grace you have been saved" (Eph. 2:5). Despite our faithlessness, God will always be there for us. Presented earlier in 2 Timothy 2:13 is a litany that claimed God cannot deny who God is. As this letter urges, read the sacred writings and find the people of God

first-century popular philosophers, the author of 2 Timothy constantly moves back and forth from personal examples, both positive and negative, to complex and eclectic exhortations of the kind assembled here. This gathering of personal examples, direct imperatives, and theological assurances creates the rhetorical force of the letter. This passage needs the references to Paul in order to make its case.

The opening challenge to "continue in what you have learned . . . knowing from whom you learned it" (3:14) can be read as a rather effective summary of the central purpose of the entire letter. Timothy is presented as wavering in his commitments to the duties and difficulties of his calling. Much of the letter contains imperatives that attempt to counter this wavering. Most are general in tone: "rekindle the gift of God" (1:6), "do not be ashamed" (1:8), "be strong in the grace" (2:1), "remember Jesus Christ" (2:8), and "continue in what you have learned" (3:14). Even the more specific imperatives in 4:2 and 4:5 belong to standard and widespread expectations about Christian life and leadership.

The specifics function to encourage Timothy in the face of suffering, the shame that suffering produces, and the puzzling experience of being abandoned by the people one attempts to lead. The prediction that "the time is coming when people will not put up with sound doctrine" (4:3) articulates this experience of abandonment. While the letter elsewhere addresses the presence of false teachers in the persons of Hymenaeus and Philetus (2:16–17), in the prediction of "distressing times" when these false teachers will gather followers in the community (3:1–9), and in the catalog of people who opposed Paul (1:15; 4:9–16), here the problem is in the community itself. They have "itching ears" and collect teachers who will scratch those ears (4:3–4).

The relationship between Christian communities and their leaders is, more often than not, accompanied by controversy. Nowhere does the letter explain what is at stake in the tensions between Timothy and the community. Communities reject their leaders for all kinds of reasons, some good, some bad. This letter assumes that these people have abandoned Timothy because they themselves are immoral. Such insults rarely further reconciliation. The purpose of such attacks tends to be to intensify the conflict, to get the attention of both the leaders and their communities. This may be the intent here: to shake up both leaders and their communities.

The bulk of the passage is not attack but encouragement. Timothy is challenged to take on the

his vocabulary, which meant that he could not even use the words "Wednesday" and "Thursday," because they honor the false gods Thor and Woden. He allowed the side of his hair to grow uncut in accordance with Leviticus 19 and wore all white garments (Eccl. 9:8). The account is humorous, but from a glance at the publicity photographs, it would seem to suggest that the Bible is hideous.

A few years ago, in an interview on the *Today* show, the brilliant Shakespearian actor Ian McKellen said, "I have often thought the Bible should have a disclaimer in the front saying this is fiction."[1] The Bible is out of season. People do not know it, and at best they do not think it matters. The temptation of the Christian community is to find another book; but Timothy's mentor wrote, "Preach the word . . . in season, out of season." Regardless of the season, the Scriptures will always speak to the heart and soul of who we are as human beings. However, McKellen and Jacobs smother the word with their absolute literalism.

The writer uses the phrase "inspired by God," literally "God-breathed." In the Genesis creation account, God breathes life into humankind; so too God breathes life into his word. We must not smother it. We have to let it breathe. It is the word of God, and it is not only inspired but inspiring—it can breathe new life into us.

A pastor serving in Montreal visited an agitated parishioner in the hospital during the final stages of a terrible disease. Kindly she sat down beside the woman and took her hand and began to read, "The LORD is my light . . ." (Ps. 27:1), but before *she* could finish the sentence, *the patient* did, ". . . and my salvation. Whom shall I fear?" The young minister began to read one comforting Scripture passage after another, only to have the patient take over the reading of each one—except the patient was not reading. The exercise quickly settled the patient like a baby at the mother's breast. As Timothy had learned the Scripture, so too these verses had been instilled in this woman from her earliest days, almost as if they had been given to her for that very purpose on that very day.

Of course few in this day and age learn the Scripture in such a way, but the preacher here may turn to the testimony of someone like the former Princeton scholar Emile Cailliet, who after the horrors of World War I found that his rationalistic upbringing had lost its hold. Nothing made sense until he opened a Bible and came to the Beatitudes and discovered what the preacher knows to be true: when

1. http://www.youtube.com/watch?v=PJcmSMuA_SU

2 Timothy 3:14-4:5

Theological Perspective

author of this Pastoral Epistle adds that "all scripture" is also "useful for reproof, for correction, and for training in righteousness" (3:16).

In addition to his concern for the use of Scripture and the source of beliefs for Timothy as a minister, the author also continues to address issues related to false teachers: How can Timothy distinguish himself from the false teachers who seek "to suit their own desires" and who appeal to "people [who] will not put up with sound doctrine" (4:3)? False teachers deviate from the truth, telling stories that promote personal comfort rather than presenting the hard challenge of the truth that shapes the way to pursue new life in Christ. Even today, enthusiastic biblically oriented preachers are tempted to reduce the gospel to sound bites that pander to the comfort needs and the short attention spans of their congregants, thereby crucifying the truth itself. Indeed, the temptations persist among preachers and teachers today to avoid the sharp edges of truth, to repress its power, or to profane its orientation by turning it toward self-benefit. In contrast to these pursuits of false teachers, the epistle's author promotes the paradigm for a faithful teacher-minister: It is the model of Paul as one who suffers (1:8; 2:9) for the sake of living out the gospel and sharing its truth.

To counter the popularity of false teachers, Timothy is also urged to be consistent and persistent in proclaiming the gospel, regardless of "whether the time is favorable or unfavorable" (4:2). In so doing, he is instructed to exercise "the utmost patience in teaching" (4:2), which should be oriented toward the multiple purposes of building up the body of Christ and enabling its members to manifest their many gifts. The gifts of the faithful teacher include patience, persistence, and consistency; they often do not appear in ministers on the fast track to success and popularity. Instead, they are gifts that must be cultivated in the soil of suffering, in the process of chaining one's desires for the sake of submitting fully to God's demands for ministry (2:9). In this manner the author summarizes the guidance to Timothy as a teacher-preacher with the mandate to "always be sober, endure suffering, do the work of an evangelist, carry out your ministry fully" (4:5).

JOSEPH L. PRICE

Pastoral Perspective

wandering away or rebelling against God, even so boldly as to say, "let us hear no more about the Holy One of Israel" (Isa. 30:11). Stories of wandering and returning are throughout Scripture, and we can see our lives reflected in these biblical characters.

Think of Jacob, the heel grabber and crook who through his dirty deals becomes Israel, the one who struggles with God and prevails. Think of David, when Nathan is sent to confront his adultery. Once David acknowledges his sin, the Lord puts it away and David does not die; there are consequences for his behavior, but he has a second chance. Think of the prodigal son, who is welcomed home after he has spent his inheritance. Think of Zacchaeus, condemned by his community as a greedy tax collector, but recognized by Jesus for his latent generosity. Think of the woman at the well, who has five husbands, but Jesus sees in her a hunger and thirst for living water. Think of Peter, who acts like a brave disciple but later denies Jesus when Jesus faces the cross. Jesus takes a risk. Peter becomes the rock upon which the church is built. Jesus is able to see potential in people that we may not see ourselves.

Along with Scripture we have several hymns in our collective history that offer this story of grace in the face of our wandering hearts and itching ears: "Come, Thou Fount of Every Blessing," "Wherever I May Wander," and a Lenten hymn, "O God, How We Have Wandered." In singing, we confess,

> O to grace how great a debtor
> daily I am called to be!
> Let thy goodness, like a fetter,
> bind my wandering heart to thee.
> Prone to wander, Lord, I feel it,
> prone to leave the God I love;
> here's my heart, O take and seal it,
> seal it for thy courts above.[1]

OLIVE ELAINE HINNANT

---

1. Robert Robinson (1758), "Come, Thou Fount of Every Blessing," in *Hymns of Truth and Light* (First Congregational Church of Houston, Texas, 1998), 407.

burdens and difficulties of leadership. The list of charges is impressive. He is to "be persistent" in good times and bad, to "rebuke and encourage" but to do so "with the utmost patience," to "endure suffering," to "do the work of an evangelist" (4:2–5). One feels the list could go on and on. The virtues and duties of leadership are extensive. The work of evangelist requires the full set of Christian virtues.

The bolstering news of the letter is that Timothy is not in this by himself. Even if his community rejects him, he is surrounded by support. Timothy has memories of his mother and grandmother (1:5) and of Paul himself (3:10–11; 4:6–8). He is surrounded by people.

He is also surrounded by sound tradition. This appeal to tradition and to its soundness is perhaps the distinctive theological move of the Pastoral Epistles. The letter itself is a partial accounting of this tradition. Larger theological narratives are implied. In some ways the letter focuses less on the details of the tradition and more on its status. It is sound, reliable. It comes from reliable people. Thus, Timothy must not abandon it simply because some people will not listen to it. He must continue in what he has learned (3:14).

So we return to the most famous verse in 2 Timothy. In the context of the surety of this tradition, the author adds a comment about the inspiration of Scripture (3:15–17). The meaning of the Greek in 3:16 is not clear. It could be rendered "all scripture is inspired by God and is useful" or "every scripture inspired by God is useful." In any case, the force of the claim is to undergird the tradition with divine presence and authority. The Greek translated "inspired by God" is more literally "God-breathed." Of course, the discussion and debate in Christian tradition about all of this is nearly endless. In context, the passage is not trying to define the nature of inspiration but to show the usefulness of Scripture. Scripture is "useful for teaching, for reproof, for correction, and for training in righteousness." In other words, of all the sound tradition that supports the tasks of leadership, the most important and productive is that of Scripture itself. Many Christian leaders from many different places on the theological spectrum would concur.

LEWIS R. DONELSON

we read the Bible, the Bible reads us. However, as wonderful as the Scripture may be, reading it is not an end in itself. It is given to us to heighten our awareness of ourselves in relation to God.

A. J. Jacobs discovered that he could not interpret the Bible alone. So every day he met with others to discuss its meaning. It drew him into community and into a new way of thinking of others. For the first time he considered the possibility that there is One who created us, and soon he felt a deep connection to the whole human family. It may seem out of season, but it is the word the world needs. By the end, Jacobs referred to himself as a "reverent agnostic" and wrote this: "Studying the Bible is not like studying sumo wrestling in Japan. It's more like wrestling itself. This opponent of mine is sometimes beautiful, sometimes cruel, sometimes ancient, sometimes crazily relevant. I can't get a handle on it. I'm outmatched."[2] God's word does not return unto God void.

The Bible does not need a disclaimer to say it is fiction. Rather, it needs a warning to those who would read it: "It is so true that it will read you. Do not just read it alone. You are outmatched." As we read it, we discover that above all we are outmatched by the love and grace of God who has given us his word and given us his Son, that we might know life eternal here and now and forevermore.

J. PETER HOLMES

2. A. J. Jacobs, *The Year of Living Biblically* (New York: Simon & Schuster, 2007), 119.

Luke 18:1-8

¹Then Jesus told them a parable about their need to pray always and not to lose heart. ²He said, "In a certain city there was a judge who neither feared God nor had respect for people. ³In that city there was a widow who kept coming to him and saying, 'Grant me justice against my opponent.' ⁴For a while he refused; but later he said to himself, 'Though I have no fear of God and no respect for anyone, ⁵yet because this widow keeps bothering me, I will grant her justice, so that she may not wear me out by continually coming.'" ⁶And the Lord said, "Listen to what the unjust judge says. ⁷And will not God grant justice to his chosen ones who cry to him day and night? Will he delay long in helping them? ⁸I tell you, he will quickly grant justice to them. And yet, when the Son of Man comes, will he find faith on earth?"

Theological Perspective

This parable of the Persistent Widow and the Unjust Judge, with its Lukan introductory and its closing sentence, is such a rich resource for theological meditation and consists of so many different layers that finding a starting point is a challenging task. In these eight verses, we find theological key words and topics referring us to an abundance of complex Christian doctrines: prayer and trust, justice and deliverance, judgment and faith, persistence and resistance, the first and second coming of Christ, and the life of believers. Furthermore, exegetical and theological interpretations of this Scripture passage vary to a great degree in determining the focus and perspective of this parable. Is the focus on who God is and how God acts, or on the believers and their call to faithful life? Are conservative interpreters right in emphasizing the need of the devout piety in one's private prayer life, or is a liberal interpretation more sound with its emphasis on communal resistance against injustice?

Reformed theology, John Calvin in particular, has always emphasized that we cannot separate who God is and what God does from who we are and what we are called to do. God's sovereignty over all areas of our life does not allow for a disconnection of private and public faith life. If we use this Reformed guidance principle, we recognize that the structure of Jesus' parable introduced by Luke's summary of it

Pastoral Perspective

Just when you think you have Jesus figured out as a teacher, a healer, and a man of prayer, he goes and tells a story like this. Who knew Jesus was a comedian too? It is not hard to imagine his listeners throwing their heads back and slapping their knees as they laugh at this ridiculous tale. A woman pounds and pounds on the door of a rotten politician who could not care less about her plight, until finally he sticks his head out the window and shouts, "All right, already! Knock it off! I will give you whatever you want if you will just shut up!" They laugh because they know this woman. She always gets a raw deal, because she has nothing—no husband, no inheritance, no social standing. They know this judge too, the one who is only out for himself. No public servant, this one, so they guffaw at the idea of one of their own, this powerless woman, annoying the smarmy guy everyone loves to hate until, finally, he does something good in spite of himself.

Good story! They laugh, and then they sigh, and they remember that Jesus told them that this is what prayer is like. By now Jesus may even have our congregation's attention too. How many of our folks hammer away at God's door, but to no apparent avail? The mother of young children is struck down by cancer, and so we pray and pray and pray, but death comes anyway. We are worn out from praying

Exegetical Perspective

The parable of the Unjust Judge is unique to the Gospel of Luke. As in most parables, the language is highly condensed and the meaning(s) open. The two characters in this parable are a widow and a judge. About the widow we learn only that she sought "justice against [her] opponent" (v. 3) and was persistent in seeking it. The judge, however, is pointedly described as "unjust" (v. 6). This characterization is due either to his delay in responding to the widow's entreaty (v. 4a) or the charge (which he accepts) that he "neither feared God nor had respect for people" (vv. 2 and 4b). Concern for widows (and orphans) is common in Jewish and Christian Scriptures, largely because they needed protection in an economic system that did not provide support outside (extended) family structures. The widow's persistence seems more to the point here, however, since the parable emphasizes it three times in verses 3 and 5. Indeed, the NRSV's alternate translation of verse 5b ("so that she may not finally come and slap me in the face," which is quite literal) shows that this widow could stand her own ground.

If the parable itself focuses on the widow's persistence, Jesus' application in verses 6–8a shift attention from the widow to the judge. The logic of Jesus' comments derives from the literary technique (used by Jewish, Christian, and Greco-Roman writers)

Homiletical Perspective

Ministers know, perhaps more clearly and poignantly than anyone else, that prayers are not always answered, if by answering we mean the fulfillment of the specific request of the one praying. Ministers know the experience of powerlessness standing by the bedside of a critically ill patient whose family members are praying for healing, hoping the minister will pray for a healing miracle, and knowing that healing is, in all probability, not going to happen. Ministers know that the question, "Does prayer really work?" is heavy with emotion and that its answer must be anything but simple.

People seem to want to believe that God will intercede at our urging and do what we want God to do. Annie Dillard calls it "God sticking a finger in, if only now and then."[1] God is regularly given credit for finding a new job, selling a condo for a profit in a buyer's market, a convenient parking place even. Super Bowl champions thank the God who secured their victory (though we hear little from the losers' locker room on the subject). The winner of the lottery, unemployed, down to his last eight dollars, offered up a prayer, "Help me, Lord, . . . just let me win this," and gave God credit for the $295 million jackpot. In 1 Chronicles, a heretofore unmentioned

---

1. Annie Dillard, *For the Time Being* (New York: Knopf, 1999), 168.

Luke 18:1-8

Theological Perspective

resembles an ellipse with two foci; it is about God as much as it is about the believer. All the theological key terms mentioned above, then, would have to be explored and understood with this double perspective in mind. Of these many terms, I have chosen "persistence and resistance," since these two terms seem to emerge rather frequently in conservative and liberal discourse, though with a rather different perception.

Let us first focus on *persistence*—not ours, though, but God's persistence. One way to summarize the biblical message, the good news of the Old and New Testament, would be to speak about God's persistent, unshakable, everlasting love for us, for all of God's creation. Yes, we deserve God's condemnation, as the Brief Statement of Faith puts it,[1] but God is so persistently in love with us, God's love is so sovereign and unshakable, that we can trust in this God to bring about justice. We can be sure that God hears our prayers, our crying day and night, even though we may not see any results yet. God has not forgotten us; God will not delay long in helping. Of course, we grow impatient, losing heart and hope. How could we not? Does the world we are living in come even close to the world Christians have been praying for since Jesus' first coming? As Fred Craddock puts it: "All we know in the life of prayer is asking, seeking, knocking and waiting, trust sometimes fainting, sometimes growing angry."[2]

It is here that the persistence of the faithful enters the picture. Because we know of and have experienced God's persistent love in Christ, we try every day anew to persist in praying "Thy kingdom come." Praying is and always has been hard work in the interim—between God's promise and its fulfillment, in the life of Israel and in the life of the church living between the first and the second coming of Christ—as is keeping hope in our hopeless world. Praying means hopeful trusting in God, not in ourselves.

A perfunctory or even nonexisting prayer life of the believers (communally as well as individually) may have many reasons; often we find at the core of it a faith that has lost trust. The widow kept coming to the judge, hoping against all odds, persistent, determined, and relentless. The believers keep praying, hoping against all odds, persistent, determined, and relentless. Not because they are "good Christians" or because they possess such a great and strong faith, not even because it is "the chief part of

1. A Brief Statement of Faith, in *The Book of Confessions* of the Presbyterian Church (U.S.A.) (Louisville, KY: Office of the General Assembly, 1999), 267–68, esp. lines 33–39.
2. Fred B. Craddock, *Luke* (Louisville, KY: John Knox Press, 1990), 210.

Pastoral Perspective

for comfort and relief in the wake of yet another natural disaster. The radio brings news of more war casualties, even though we continually pray for peace. Is this really the way it is supposed to be?

What hope is Jesus offering? He insists that God is nothing like this unjust judge. If he is pledging even speedier relief to our persistent pray-ers than the widow got from the unjust judge (v. 8a), our people are not feeling relieved. If it is a speedy return of Jesus to earth so that justice is fulfilled (v. 8b), the credibility gap in a twenty-first-century church widens. The pastoral issue of this sermon is that our pews are full of weary or already-gave-up-on-it pray-ers and unexpectant wait-ers. As eye- and ear-catching as it may be, how can this parable land meaningfully when God does not fix things for all who ask persistently, and when most of our people are not exactly waiting on rooftops for Christ's return?

Jesus seems to anticipate our dilemma when he wonders aloud whether, when he comes again, anyone will still have faith. Effectively, he turns the tables. "Stop speculating about when I will return, and start praying faithfully now." Wondering when the Lord will return is a good question, and it is precisely because of this question that Jesus tells this parable about the "need to pray always and not to lose heart" (v. 1). We are reminded, once again, that the life of faith is not only about telling God what is on our wish list but constantly lifting up every joy and concern, every fear and doubt, every lament and plea to the One who hears and answers. The answers may not come when we think they should. "A thousand ages in thy sight are like an evening gone," we sing, echoing the psalmist. The God of Isaiah reminds us, "My thoughts are not your thoughts, nor are your ways my ways" (55:8). It is hard, however, to take the long view when we are praying our hearts out, bruising our hands with our continual pounding on heaven's door.

Jesus says, "God will not delay. God will help. God will grant justice." If the Son of Man is to find faith on earth, we must understand that our prayers do not constitute so many unanswered pleas; rather, they are our participation in the coming reign of God. By praying continually, and not giving up hope, we live in the surety that God has not abandoned this world. Living in hope, we work, in whatever ways we can, for the justice and peace that is coming.

This is the kind of prayer we pray whenever we gather at the Lord's Table: "In union with your church in heaven and on earth, we pray, O God, that you will fulfill your eternal purpose in us and in all

known as "from the lesser to the greater." Though Jesus asks a question (that grammatically requires an affirmative answer, v. 7a), we might paraphrase it something like this: If an unjust judge can grant justice in response to badgering, *how much more* will God grant justice to those who cry out day and night. To avoid the notion that God must be worn out before granting justice, Luke has Jesus state categorically that "he will quickly grant justice to them" (v. 8a). (Like most translations of v. 7, the NRSV hopes to clarify and resolve verb tense issues by dividing one Greek sentence into two. The verb translated "Will he delay long in helping" usually connotes "being patient" [as in 1 Cor. 13:4]. Sirach 35:22 is commonly cited in support of the NRSV and similar translations.)

Luke's editorial introduction to the parable (v. 1) indicates that he understands the parable much as we have laid it out, but his application of it warrants comment, for Luke makes the parable part of Jesus' teaching on prayer. How does Luke understand a widow's persistence and an unjust judge's granting justice to be "about their need to pray always and not to lose heart"? Two explorations will help answer this question: the first into the immediate context of the parable in Luke's narrative, the second into Luke's teaching on prayer.

To examine the context, we must begin with verse 8: "And yet, when the Son of Man comes, will he find faith on earth?" This question adds another dimension to the meaning of the parable, by shifting the focus from the judge/God back to the widow and her perseverance. Luke, that is, makes perseverance in prayer and not losing heart elements of faith. At this point in Luke's narrative, perseverance and courage are not abstract qualities but eschatological necessities.

To see this, we must look to the section of Luke 17 not included in the lectionary cycle for year C: Jesus' teaching about the coming of the kingdom in verses 20–37. This section begins with the Pharisees asking Jesus when the kingdom of God will come. He answers, in language quite different from that in Matthew 24:23 and Mark 13:21, "The kingdom of God is not coming with things that can be observed; nor will they say, 'Look, here it is!' or 'There it is!' For, in fact, the kingdom of God is among [or, within] you" (17:20–21). What follows in verses 22–37 shows that Luke does not dispense with an eschatological understanding of the kingdom of God, as the claim that the kingdom of God is "among/within" you might be construed to mean. (See, for example, *Gospel of Thomas* 3 and 113.) Luke

man by the name of Jabez is remembered as the one who prayed: "Oh that you would bless me and enlarge my border, and that your hand might be with me, and that you would keep me from hurt and harm!" (1 Chr. 4:10). God complied, and on that basis some twenty-first-century Christians are persuaded that God has unclaimed blessings for us, that God wants us to be selfish in our prayers, that it is appropriate to ask God to increase the value of your stock portfolio, and that God will open the storehouse of heaven if you pray persistently.

The pastor, out of daily experience with dear, faithful people who pray heartfelt prayers persistently and whose requests are not fulfilled, knows how theologically wrong and tragically misleading the current prosperity gospel is. Huston Smith observes: "When the consequences of belief are worldly goods, such as health, fixing on these turns religion into a service station for self-gratification and churches into health clubs. This is the opposite of religion's role, which is to decenter the ego, not pander to its desires."[2]

Jesus told a parable once about persistent prayer. The preacher needs to remember that it is a parable, not an anecdote about two people everybody knows. Luke even tells us what the purpose of the parable is: the disciples' need "to pray always and not to lose heart" (v. 1). From the start, Jesus sets out, not to resolve the mystery of answered and unanswered prayer, but to teach his disciples persistence. It is a delightful story about two unforgettable characters: a harsh judge utterly without conscience who "neither feared God nor had respect for people" and a widow who is poor, helpless, defenseless, and in need of justice. It is a parable, not an allegory, even if we might chuckle at Jesus' freedom to picture the petitioned party so negatively; and no details are provided about the widow's case. The scene must be something like a hall of justice, a judge seated on the dais, throngs of petitioners gathered about, some represented by lawyers, others just shouting their requests from the crowd.[3] The woman is in that crowd every day when the court convenes. She wants "vindication" against an unnamed adversary. Every day she asks for justice, shouts for justice. Every day the judge ignores her. Maybe she follows him home and repeats her request nightly and the first thing in the morning. She nags and badgers; she is relentless.

---

2. Huston Smith, *Why Religion Matters* (New York: HarperCollins, 2001), 45.
3. The image is drawn from Kenneth E. Bailey, *"Poet and Peasant" and "Through Peasant Eyes": A Literary and Cultural Approach to the Parables in Luke* (Grand Rapids: Eerdmans, 1983), 134.

Luke 18:1-8

Theological Perspective

the gratitude which God requires of us" (Question 116 of the Heidelberg Catechism), but because the Spirit has given them the courage to do so, to pray without ceasing in a broken and fearful world (A Brief Statement of Faith, lines 65–67). In a way, the widow in Jesus' parable represents not only the need to pray always, as Luke puts it, but also the Spirit's incessant work of encouraging us to pray, the Spirit's nagging persistence and unrelenting perseverance.

This hopeful courage that the believers receive as a gift from the Holy Spirit leads not only to a meditative and introspective life of prayer, but to an active and "extrospective" life of prayer as well, one that includes *resistance* against all forms of injustice. Luise Schottroff underlines this thought emphatically in her interpretation of the parable of the stubborn widow: "Praying and crying to God against injustices describes the whole life of the believers: their efforts, their protests against injustice. It describes also their trust in God, for they know that God acts very differently than the unjust judge."[3]

We can see why and how if we once again look at the God described in Jesus' parable. Twice God is described here as the one who will grant justice, with other words: God's love is not only persistent, but also just. The central event of God's loving justice and just love in Christ's cross and resurrection reveals not only God's resistance against individual sin, but also God's powerful resistance against the unjust powers that be, an act of resistance that has already changed our world, even though it might be hard for us to detect at times. As God's children, the believers are called to join God's resistance, equipped with the special gift of the Holy Spirit: resisting and persisting prayer, of which the stubborn and enduringly hopeful widow is an inspiring example.

MARGIT ERNST-HABIB

Pastoral Perspective

the world. Keep us faithful in your service until Christ comes in final victory, and we shall feast with all your saints in the joy of your eternal realm."[1] Again, "May his coming in glory find us ever watchful in prayer, strong in truth and love, and faithful in the breaking of the bread. Then, at last, all peoples will be free, all divisions healed, and with your whole creation, we will sing your praise, through your Son, Jesus Christ."[2]

We are faithful to Jesus' instruction too whenever we pray, "Your kingdom come. Your will be done, on earth as it is in heaven" (Matt. 6:10). Once again, Jesus makes it clear that faith is actively hoping, eagerly anticipating the coming reign of God, never ceasing in our prayers for others, for the world, even for ourselves.

The pastoral ministry of a church must impart hope to the suffering. In this function, the importance of teaching and preaching about eschatological hope cannot be overstressed. It is necessary continually and actively to pray in this way so that, when tragedies befall us, there is already in place a strong confidence in the unfailing providence of God. It is far more difficult to impart this sense of God's faithfulness when people are face to face with challenges or crises. When, however, there is an active faith at work, faith that is lived as we strive toward the coming reign of God, then hope remains alive, and we can sing, even if voices falter, "Our God, our help in ages past, our hope for years to come, our shelter from the stormy blast and our eternal home."[3]

KIMBERLY BRACKEN LONG

---

1. *Book of Common Worship* (Louisville, KY: Westminster/John Knox Press, 1993), 72–73.
2. From the Great Thanksgiving prepared by the International Committee on English in the Liturgy, in the *Book of Common Worship*, 145.
3. Isaac Watts (1714).

3. Luise Schottroff, *Lydia's Impatient Sisters: A Feminist Social History of Early Christianity* (Louisville, KY: Westminster John Knox Press, 1995), 102.

continues his narrative by placing here much of the material Mark (chap. 13) and Matthew (chap. 24) have in Jesus' discourse on the coming of the kingdom. Most relevant for understanding the parable in Luke 18:1–8 is Jesus' saying to the disciples, "The days are coming when you will long to see one of the days of the Son of Man, and you will not see it" (17:22). In turning his attention from the Pharisees to his disciples and speaking of "longing" for the days of the Son of Man, Luke's Jesus shows concern for the disciples who must endure, who must "pray always" and "not lose heart" (18:1). The final phrase in 18:8, therefore, is not a throwaway line, but in fact draws 18:1–8 within the context of Jesus' eschatological teaching. If the disciples are to be among the faithful when the Son of Man comes, they must persevere in prayer and not lose heart.

Luke makes a similar point in the parable found in 11:5–8 (Proper 12). In this parable, like the one in 18:1–8, there are two characters. Here the "friend" who asks for a loaf of bread at midnight is like the widow who seeks justice; the "friend" who refuses to get up and give it to him is like the judge. Here too, the "lesson" of the parable is persistence (11:8). As he will do in chapter 18, Luke applies the lesson to prayer, for he places this parable between his account of the Lord's Prayer (11:2–4) and his version of the "Ask, and it will be given you" saying (11:9–10). He concludes this section, moreover, with another example of "the lesser to the greater" technique to compare human and divine responses to supplicants: "If you then, who are evil, know how to give good gifts to your children, how much more will the heavenly Father give the Holy Spirit to those who ask him!" (11:13).

The disciples in the Gospel of Luke are taught again and again to persevere in prayer. The widow becomes a sign of this kind of prayerful faithfulness.

OLIVER LARRY YARBROUGH

Finally, realizing that he is encountering some kind of primal force, that she is not going to give up, the judge relents and renders a favorable judgment. "Will not God grant justice to his chosen ones who cry to him day and night?" Jesus asks (v. 7a).

So the preacher must remember that the issue here is justice, not using God to get what one wants or needs—unless, of course, we understand that what God knows we need and what we think we want are not at all the same thing.

I had two good and loving parents. They did not give me everything I wanted. I asked for a horse, a dog, a two-wheel bicycle before I was old enough to ride it. One Christmas I had my heart set on a toy drum set I found in the Sears catalog. My requests were heard and turned down. In retrospect, I understand that I received, not always what I most wanted, but what I most needed.

That is at least part of what Jesus is teaching his disciples, and us, in this parable. The early church, which first read it, certainly prayed for many things it did not receive: safety, protection from persecution, for instance. It did receive what it most needed: a sense of God's loving presence and attentiveness, and the strength and resilience and fortitude it needed to survive.

In retrospect it becomes clear. "Hast thou not seen, how thy desires e'er have been granted in what he ordaineth?" (Joachim Neander [1680]).

Count on God to come down on the side of justice. Count on God to hear the ones who have no power, no influence, no voice. Count on God to hear those who have nowhere else to turn. Count on God not always to grant your requests, but to hear, with loving, parental patience, the persistent prayers of your heart.

JOHN M. BUCHANAN

Joel 2:23-32

[23]O children of Zion, be glad
    and rejoice in the LORD your God;
    for he has given the early rain for your vindication,
    he has poured down for you abundant rain,
    the early and the later rain, as before.
[24]The threshing floors shall be full of grain,
    the vats shall overflow with wine and oil.

[25]I will repay you for the years
    that the swarming locust has eaten,
    the hopper, the destroyer, and the cutter,
    my great army, which I sent against you.

[26]You shall eat in plenty and be satisfied,
    and praise the name of the LORD your God,
    who has dealt wondrously with you.
    And my people shall never again be put to shame.

Theological Perspective

"Therefore that He may raise, the Lord throws down." These words, from the English priest-poet John Donne's "Hymn to God, My God, in My Sickness," are spoken of the work of God in Christ.[1] They also brilliantly encapsulate the message of the prophets, particularly the message of Joel. His message is one of woe in the long shadow of the threat of the Day of the Lord, which is then replaced by a message of hope.

The initial oracles in the book of Joel are concerned with a message of destruction. The land will be invaded and devoured by swarms of locusts, insects that have been aptly named the "incarnation of hunger." To this day, swarms of locusts darken the skies, heralding blight to large parts of the world. A land of plenty is all too swiftly turned into a wilderness. This in turn bequeaths hunger, malnutrition, and death to humankind. In many ways, locusts are like an invading army, destroying land and terrorizing people, leaving devastation in their wake.

Joel's message may have both real and metaphorical locusts in mind; in either case, the invaders become instruments of judgment. Because of the impending disaster, the prophet summons the people to liturgical repentance. In both chapter 1 and

1. https://tspace.library.utoronto.ca/html/1807/4350/poem665.html.

Pastoral Perspective

This text belongs to the genre of *apocalyptic*, in which the prophet speaks a word of hope and salvation to the people in the midst of great suffering. The book of Joel responds in particular to a horrific plague of locusts, which the prophet interprets as a sign of God's judgment, but also as initiating the coming day of vindication for the children of Zion, who are God's own.

There are two pastoral approaches to such texts, depending on the particular context in which the sermon will be preached. The first approach corresponds to events and places where it is easy to identify with the suffering Israelites in the aftermath of disaster—whether at the personal level of individual and familial trauma or at the community level of recovery from a catastrophic event such as a flood, a tornado, or an act of terrorism. The second approach corresponds more to systemic realities of injustice, power, and privilege, in which the task of the preacher may be not only to console his or her hearers, but to call them communally to repentance for unearned privilege and a renewal of courage to work for justice and peace in their communities.

Family therapists Betty Carter and Monica McGoldrick have identified two different types of stressors that cause suffering in the lives of individuals, families, and entire communities: horizontal

²⁷You shall know that I am in the midst of Israel,
and that I, the LORD, am your God and there is no other.
And my people shall never again be put to shame.

²⁸Then afterward
I will pour out my spirit on all flesh;
your sons and your daughters shall prophesy,
your old men shall dream dreams,
and your young men shall see visions.
²⁹Even on the male and female slaves,
in those days, I will pour out my spirit.

³⁰I will show portents in the heavens and on the earth, blood and fire and columns of smoke. ³¹The sun shall be turned to darkness, and the moon to blood, before the great and terrible day of the LORD comes. ³²Then everyone who calls on the name of the LORD shall be saved; for in Mount Zion and in Jerusalem there shall be those who escape, as the LORD has said, and among the survivors shall be those whom the LORD calls.

Exegetical Perspective

Plagues of locusts! Enemy attacks! God to the rescue! These are the themes of the book of Joel. The date of this short prophetic book is unknown, but the national problems it addresses are clear. This particular passage announces God's impending relief of a locust plague and then goes on to describe the wonderful things God will do for the nation.

Joel 2:23–32 should not be read apart from what precedes, since its intricate poetry weaves in images and concepts that appear earlier in the book. Joel opens with a vibrant description of the plague, a natural but devastating occurrence. For nations whose main economic source was agriculture, a locust plague, with its resulting crop devastation, constituted a national disaster, much like the dust bowl years in the United States in the 1930s.

Joel asserts that this plague was sent by God, who is both creator and divine warrior. This imagery may be foreign to some contemporary American audiences, yet it permeates the book. In the first two chapters, God is associated with natural disaster, while in the last chapter YHWH is depicted as a divine warrior. For the ancient audience, these two images are interrelated. Peoples throughout the ancient Near East viewed the forces of nature, which were beyond their control, as a manifestation of the power of the divine realm. In Joel, God's care for the

Homiletical Perspective

Homiletics, according to Webster, is the art of affable, ordinary conversation. Many of us would prefer something more than the ordinary! We wish we could be artists, or at least specially gifted in some way that would raise us above the crowd. We—and many other ordinary people as well—wish we were extraordinary.

A good homily is one in which a preacher puts ordinary conversation into affable form. The words are big, the ideas are small. We are lucky to have Scripture to help us out, because most people are like me. We do not do very well at getting simple. We have an easier time staying above the ordinary. We even have good excuses: we are describing the extraordinary, which is to say, God's actions in the world. However, here is the wonder and the good news of today's text, right at the top: God comes in the ordinary. God comes as plague averted, full vats, and barns full of wheat. God comes via apocalypse, according to the prophet Joel. These are surely contradictory images for most of us. God comes any way God wants to come, in plenty or in fear. God comes, even when we do not understand the meaning, large and small, of God's words. God comes in the ordinary, which includes the varied experience of human beings.

Joel's message is this: bad things were going to happen, but God has intervened. "Apocalypse" is not just a movie title—although the modern world has

Joel 2:23-32

Theological Perspective

chapter 2 there is a summons of the people to fasting and prayer, and to bring their complaint and petition before God—reminding God of past mercy and accepting the divine response.

The immediate divine response, so difficult for Christians to fathom and comprehend (and who can comprehend the mind of God?), is that the locusts come like an army and leave destruction in their wake. So the Lord throws down, but no sooner has God thrown down, than God raises up—for this is indeed the God "whose property is always to have mercy"—or, as Calvin commented, "God offers life to us in death, and light in the darkest grave."[2] So it is that Joel announces a turn of fortune. In place of a wasteland, there is "new creation" in the form of a bumper harvest. The people of Jerusalem and its environs (the usually accepted *Sitz im Leben* of the book of Joel), like most premoderns, saw a rich harvest as a gift of God and a sign of divine benevolence and grace.

Drought gives way to rains. Grain, wine, and oil—those messianic sacramental gifts of creation and redemption—abound; God gives the fruits of the earth in due season. This abundance, however, has a divine purpose. The people will know that I AM is in the midst of them: "I, the LORD, am your God and there is no other. And my people shall never again be put to shame" (v. 27). This is perhaps a liturgical chant. It is certainly a fitting liturgical response of gratitude to the gracious mercy of God. The people are exhorted to praise the name of the Lord who has dealt so wondrously with them.

In Genesis the breath of the Lord brought forth creation and the harvests. Joel now announces a new exhalation of the divine breath, and a fresh fruit of the Spirit. The Spirit of God will be poured out on all human flesh—though here the implication is all Israel's flesh. Prophecy, one of the gifts of the Spirit, will be given to all Israel's sons and daughters, to young and old, who will dream dreams and see visions, and to slaves as well. The divine breath becomes inclusive. Calvin commented: "Then God shall so pour out his Spirits that all the ancient prophecies will appear obscure and of no value, compared with the great and extraordinary light which Christ, the Sun of Righteousness, will bring at his rising."[3]

In light of this prophecy's use in Acts, it is difficult for the church not to see it fulfilled in the events

Pastoral Perspective

stressors and vertical stressors.[1] *Horizontal stressors* are those painful events that occur across a timeline, creating upheaval in the normal developmental processes of growth across the lifespan of persons and groups. Acute events—such as a house fire, the loss of a job, a life-threatening diagnosis, or the death of a loved one— may impact only the intimate circle of family and friends. Other events, including natural disasters (the tsunami in Indonesia), human-caused mass tragedies (9/11), and catastrophes that result from human error in combination with natural forces (Hurricane Katrina), create cohort groups of survivors across communities and even entire nations. When congregations, or members within them, are impacted by such horizontal stressors, Joel's vision of restoration and plenty will be welcome words of hope and healing.

The words "which I sent against you" in verse 25 pose a challenge to the pastoral preacher in terms of classic questions of theodicy and God's involvement in permitting or even (as Joel here suggests) causing evil. Depending on the preacher's own theological perspective and tradition, this text provides an occasion to wrestle with the problem of evil. There are no simple or easy answers to the problem of theodicy (literally, "justifying God"—the tension among the three propositions that God is good, God is all-powerful, and yet evil exists). The preacher needs to ponder and pray in his or her preparation about where she or he stands on the relationship of God to evil in the world, and how his or her tradition has interpreted the reality of human suffering and divine love and power.

The preacher will need to wrestle with the meaning of this verse in relation to Joel's own historical context and theological perspective, in which the emphasis was not philosophical speculation about theodicy but, rather, how God is working to restore relationship with a straying people. The disaster represented by "the hopper, the destroyer, and the cutter" (all references to the swarm of locusts, v. 25b) can further be considered in light of overarching biblical themes of God's goodness, mercy, and ultimate redemption.

The second type of suffering is caused by *vertical stressors*—enduring conditions such as chronic illness, family violence, poverty, lack of education and health care, racism, sexism, heterosexism, and other forms of oppression and deprivation. These stressors

---

2. *Calvin's Commentary on Joel*, http://www.ccel.org/ccel/calvin/calcom27.iii.iii.xxviii.html.
3. *Calvin's Commentary on Joel*, http://www.ccel.org/ccel/calvin/calcom27.iii.iii.xxiv.html.

1. Betty Carter and Monica McGoldrick, *The Expanded Family Life Cycle: Individual, Family, and Social Perspectives*, 3rd ed. (Boston: Allyn & Bacon, 1999), 6.

Exegetical Perspective

nation is manifested in both military victory and agricultural success. In fact, Joel 2:2–11 depicts the locusts as soldiers of God.

Joel 2:23–32 follows immediately on a command from God (vv. 12–17) to assemble the community in prayer and is part of a prophetic assurance that God will indeed hear their prayer (vv. 18–27). Verses 23–25 envision relief from the disaster that they had prayed for. In place of famine and plague, the nation will be rewarded with abundant rain, full granaries, and overflowing vats of wine and oil. Verse 26 states the heart of the matter: they will eat again! When these images are read in light of the devastation of 1:2–2:11, the contrast between want and plenty plays itself out.

Verses 26 and 27 repeat a refrain ("my people shall never again be put to shame") that puts in stark relief the exact nature of the theological problem: this community has been shamed by this natural disaster. For ancient Mediterranean cultures, honor and shame were social commodities that shaped their lives. In both the Psalms and many prophetic texts, "shame" could include a national recognition of Israel's international status as a vassal state or an exiled nation. Enemies taunted and publicly mocked those whom they controlled, often publicly mocking the national god. Joel's assertion that God sent the plague was one way to address the charge that YHWH was not a great enough god to avert the disaster. The dual reference to shame lays bare the degree to which this perceived divine failure had to be addressed theologically.

The problem of communal shame is "solved" by God's pronouncement of what scholars call the "recognition formula": "You shall know that I am in the midst of Israel, and that I, the LORD, am your God and there is no other" (2:27). In the book of Ezekiel, where the problem of communal shame is also prominent, the recognition formula is a statement of God's powerful presence. In Joel, this verse asserts that God exists and is in control.

Joel 2:28–32 forms the heart of this section of the book. Although most Christians read this text through the lens of Peter's sermon during the first Pentecost in Acts 2:14–36, it is also essential to ask what these verses meant to the original Israelite audience. From a literary perspective, this description of a future "spiritual renewal" is the poetic answer to the problems described in verses 26–27, that is, communal shame and the apparent weakness of God.

In the Old Testament, the "spirit" of God endows the human recipient with power that is a manifestation of divine power. In Judges, for example, leaders

Homiletical Perspective

surely given it some good movies and some great press. We speak "apocalyptically" as though we knew what it meant—as though we thought God's revelation were something bad. Humanity acts as if it has its hand in the cookie jar when it approaches apocalypse. We wonder what we did wrong and when we are going to get caught. It is the childish way that people speak to you at cocktail parties once they find out you are a clergyperson. "Oh boy, what did I say?"

In other words, we tend to predict trouble. Joel is trying to convert us to predicting possibility. Our guilt stands in the way of understanding apocalyptic as ordinary. God uses the small and the large to showcase the meaning of history, both the full vats and the scary noises.

Apocalypse uncovers the action of God in the action of the world. In the apocalypse or end time, God destroys the ruling powers of evil. Most often written in the period 200 BCE to 150 CE, by people who did not give their names and who used extraordinary symbols, apocalyptic literature appeared in various forms throughout Scripture, although mostly associated with the books of Daniel and Revelation. The happy apocalypse of Joel fits the bill of apocalypse, in that it is a prophetic revelation. It is a happy ending to a terrible plague and flood, using symbols of wheat, water, and full vats to describe what God is going to do in the world. We see before us "uncovered" the true nature of what is going on. Indeed, bad things have happened, but they will not last, Joel says. We are to be fed, not destroyed, in God's coming time.

One of my favorite minor writers is Henry Bester, who wrote an essay about living for a full year in the outermost house on Cape Cod. When asked what he discovered during this time, he said that we should "learn to reverence night and to put away the vulgar fear of it."[1] He loved the constant shorebird migrations, but even more he loved to go out at night and stare at the cosmos. Apocalypse is a teacher about the vulgar fear of the night. So often we overdo tragic interpretations, when all around us beautiful stars exist in the dark.

When I talk to people who are living in the dark darkly, I often try to retrain their vision. I often try to move their attention to what is good. Someone who had bedbugs throughout her apartment, and could not get either her landlord or her husband to help, said she had just given up thinking she would ever stop itching. Then she spoke of coming to choir

---

1. Henry Bester, *The Outermost House: A Year of Life on the Great Beach of Cape Cod*, seventy-fifth anniversary edition (New York: Henry Holt & Co., 2003), 173.

Joel 2:23-32

Theological Perspective

of Pentecost. Perhaps Pentecost is a further fulfill-ment; it certainly becomes more inclusive, since the church, alongside the continuing Israel, prays and expects the Spirit to be poured out upon, quite liter-ally, all flesh. The whole of humanity is potentially church. Perhaps Paul had Joel in mind in Galatians 3:27–28.

The outpouring of God's Spirit heralds apocalyp-tic signs and the coming of the Day of the Lord. The moon will be bloodred, the sun will be dark, there will be smoke and fire—these signs and portents will herald that day. Those of faith should not fear, for providing they call upon the name of the Lord—the same Lord who is in the midst of them, and who pours forth the Spirit of life and truth upon them—they will be saved.

The name is YHWH, whom Christians know as Father, Son, and Spirit, though none of these are cul-tic magic formulae. To call upon "the name" is to identify with all that the name means and implies. What does it mean to be saved? It implies being saved *from* something and *for* something. Perhaps for Joel and Paul (Rom. 10:12) it is being saved from faithlessness and despair, and being saved for faith and hope. In the case of Joel and his Jerusalem con-text, it is Mount Zion and Jerusalem that become the place of safety and salvation. For Christians, it is the new Jerusalem and the new heaven and earth, where it matters not that the sun is darkened or the moon has turned to blood, for the new Jerusalem has no need of them. The light will come from the sun of righteousness, the Lamb.

BRYAN SPINKS

Pastoral Perspective

rain down continually into the lives of certain groups in society, disproportionately depriving them of equal access to basic human rights, basic sustenance, basic dignity. They are created by ongoing patterns of privilege, power, and domination, whether in the home, or in the society at large, or in both.

With regard to such ongoing suffering, the preacher must decide: Will she or he preach prima-rily to those who are living on the underside of inequality, or to the privileged? Will the sermon pri-marily be a message of consolation and blessing for those who have suffered injustice and lack, or will it be a message of inspiration and a call to use the advantages the people do have in order to work for the coming of the realm of God's peace and justice? The particular location and circumstances of the congregation will in large measure determine the appropriateness of each emphasis.

The Gospel reading with which this passage from Joel is paired reinforces the theme of reversal of pat-terns of privilege and oppression that historically underlies all apocalyptic literature and prophecy. Jesus' insistence on the humbling of the proud and the exalting of the humble in Luke 18:14 amplifies the vision of justice implicit in Joel 2:28–32. These are visions of an end time that would spell disaster to those who were comfortable—in Joel's context, those who had the wealth or the mobility to escape the ravages of the locusts and to manage in spite of agricultural disaster. Blood, fire, smoke, and darkness portend a day of restitution that is "great and terri-ble." As in all apocalyptic visions, such a day would bring joyful vindication for those who had suffered most in the past. It is primarily the hungry who long to "eat in plenty and be satisfied" (v. 26a). They, and all those who were humbled by the disaster, will "never again be put to shame" (v. 26d).

All flesh will receive the spirit, according to Joel, but especially the powerless—the young, the old, and the slaves; male *and* female. This passage does not require that the preacher engage in a potboiling jere-miad of accusation against his or her congregation. "Everyone who calls on the name of the LORD shall be saved" (v. 32a). Like the Gospel passage from Luke, this passage does convey God's special blessing on those who have been historically marginalized, and it offers an opportunity for the preacher to engage the congregation in imagining together what Joel's vision of plenty and salvation means today.

PAMELA COOPER-WHITE

Exegetical Perspective

like Samson become mighty warriors, once the spirit of God possesses them. The spirit of God also comes down on prophets. Sometimes these prophets can do miraculous things while possessed by God's spirit. These manifestations of divine power are meant to convince a doubting community of the legitimacy of the claim of the prophet.

Joel 2:28–32 is truly remarkable in the scope of its vision of prophetic power. In contrast to the story of Elijah's contest with the prophets of Baal in 1 Kings 18, where God's existence is manifested through the miraculous power of a single prophet, Joel 2:28–32 envisions a whole nation possessed by the spirit of God, prophesying. The poet goes out of his way in verses 28–29 to state that this spirit will come down on every single person in their community: young and old, male and female, slave and free. In verse 30, we read that the communal prophetic frenzy will be accompanied by unspecified "signs," often natural miracles such as the sun standing still or salt water becoming fresh. These social and natural signs herald in the "Day of YHWH," which will bring disaster for those who have derided Israel's God. Only those in Jerusalem who still pray to YHWH will be saved. In other words, those who have been shamed will be in a position to scoff at their enemies.

If the problem for Joel's community is shame at their God's failure to save them from a plague of locusts, then this vision of a national prophetic assembly, followed by divine revenge on Israel's enemies, offers hope that the world will one day be convinced that their God exists and is in control. This text merges ecological, military, and prophetic images in its description of Judah's salvation. This interplay of images reflects the larger concerns of the book of Joel.

CORRINE L. CARVALHO

Homiletical Perspective

practice and being able to sing. Singing, she carried on. She lived in the dark darkly and then broke through to an ounce of lightness. She did not resolve her nights of itching, but she had a moment of relief.

Once someone has become the prisoner of darkness—instead of enjoying the night—even ice cream looks bad. It puts on weight or adds to cholesterol or shows that we are undisciplined. This may seem a silly way to talk about apocalypse, but note how the small can assist with the large.

If we do not turn toward hope in ourselves, toward hope in the environment, humans are likely to destroy the earth. If we stay in the dark, we will get hurt. We cannot deny the night. Dark does come, but, as Bester says, is it really all that bad that night turns to day and day to night? What would happen if we were to become reenchanted with the world that God has made, rather than being habitually disenchanted with it and ourselves?

Furthermore, what does it mean when we accuse God of destroying the earth, limiting the wheat, emptying the vats—of being "apocalyptic," in the sense of being scary and judgmental? Who are we to know what God is about to reveal? Who are we to limit God to the dark side of the night rather than the starry side? What if God is about to do something good and we miss it, because we are so scared to look?

I was becoming more deeply afraid about the energy crisis in America. I saw a train wreck everywhere I looked—whether it was the war in Iraq failing or the high prices of gas or the reflex racism of the Gulf Coast disasters. At their heart these interacting disasters threatened my way of life as a middle-class American—as well as embarrassing my reputation as a successful social activist. The president told me to "drive less," and all I could do was laugh cynically. Such individual solutions to systemic problems always amuse me.

One day I awoke a bit early, in order to get on my bicycle and go collect twigs. I do this sort of nature errand as a low-cost form of personal entertainment. I was particularly interested in apple wood, as it gives off a great smell. I would bike along, picking up good pieces of wood, filling up my bike basket. I realized I was ritualizing an act of hope. I was actually doing political liturgy. I was making pictures of the world I wanted. Did my activity resolve the energy crisis or stop the melting of the ice cap? I think not! It did, however, give me a way to touch the prophetic promise of God. That is what matters, as the prophet Joel well knows.

DONNA SCHAPER

Psalm 65

¹Praise is due to you,
     O God, in Zion;
   and to you shall vows be performed,
² O you who answer prayer!
   To you all flesh shall come.
³When deeds of iniquity overwhelm us,
     you forgive our transgressions.
⁴Happy are those whom you choose and bring near
     to live in your courts.
   We shall be satisfied with the goodness of your house,
     your holy temple.

⁵By awesome deeds you answer us with deliverance,
     O God of our salvation;
   you are the hope of all the ends of the earth
     and of the farthest seas.
⁶By your strength you established the mountains;
     you are girded with might.

Theological Perspective

Psalm 65 identifies God in terms of three critical dimensions of God's relation to all that God has made: forgiver, deliverer, provider.

The opening section of the psalm focuses on the gathering of people into God's holy temple. The emphasis is on being chosen and brought to live near God (v. 4). Being chosen and brought near in the courts of God is possible because God is known as the *one who forgives* transgressions (v. 3). Because the Divine One lives in forbearance toward the deeds of iniquity that would otherwise overwhelm humankind, there is a prospect of being brought near, ushered into the courts, indeed into the very house of God.

Despite the fact that the Reformation is sometimes regarded as having registered rights to the trademark of "justification by faith through grace," such a claim is surely a kind of infringement on Psalm 65—not to mention the Old Testament as a whole. However much Christians may find a clarification, or even an intensification, of the "forgiving God" in Jesus' life, death, and destiny, it is the surely the same God to whom this psalmist knows praise is due.

The association of God's forgiving nature with being gathered into God's house or temple summons the faithful of all ages to liturgical clarity. While we might easily be tempted to think of contemporary

Pastoral Perspective

Along Interstate 80 in Iowa, between Newton and Grinnell, is an exquisite place. Driving east through the rolling terrain, one crests an ordinary-looking hill to be greeted by an extraordinary scene of breathtaking beauty. The view encompasses two miles or so. The highway makes a gentle and majestic sweep to the left as it slopes down toward a bridge that crosses a winding stream. On either side of the road, furrows undulate to caress the contours of the land. The place is beautiful in every season, but in the fall, just at the time of harvest, it puts on a show. More than once when captivated by that scene, I have thought to myself, "Tough day for the atheists."

At this time of year, when Christians in many places are beginning to reflect on the meaning of gratitude and its sometimes tenuous relationship to generosity, Psalm 65 comes along as a peculiarly wonderful gift. It describes a movement in the life of the spirit that begins with a dutiful response to God for particular blessings, moves through awe at God's majesty, and culminates in an extravagant eruption of joyous praise. It teaches that to grow in gratitude is to become more and more the fulfillment of what God has created us to be: to move from being dutiful toward becoming truly beautiful.

The psalmist begins (vv. 1–4) in a place of gratitude: "Praise is due to you, O God, in Zion" (v. 1). It

⁷You silence the roaring of the seas,
    the roaring of their waves,
    the tumult of the peoples.
⁸Those who live at earth's farthest bounds are awed by your signs;
    you make the gateways of the morning and the evening shout for joy.

⁹You visit the earth and water it,
    you greatly enrich it;
    the river of God is full of water;
    you provide the people with grain,
    for so you have prepared it.
¹⁰You water its furrows abundantly,
    settling its ridges,
    softening it with showers,
    and blessing its growth.
¹¹You crown the year with your bounty;
    your wagon tracks overflow with richness.
¹²The pastures of the wilderness overflow,
    the hills gird themselves with joy,
¹³the meadows clothe themselves with flocks,
    the valleys deck themselves with grain,
    they shout and sing together for joy.

Exegetical Perspective

In a reflective yet direct manner, the psalmist addresses God, to whom praise is due because of God's compassion, generosity, wonderful works, and life-sustaining care for all creation. A likely occasion for this psalm may have been a time immediately following a drought. A once-parched land is now lush with fauna and flora because God has heard the prayer of a petitioning people now gathered in the temple to fulfill their promises made to God in their time of distress.

Although the poem can be classified as either a hymn or a communal lament, its theme and language suggest that it is a communal song of thanksgiving. Its original setting may have been a ritual for harvest thanksgiving, and its later setting was probably the festival of Tabernacles, otherwise known as Booths and Ingathering (Exod. 23:16; 34:22; Deut. 16:13–15), the feast of the Lord (Lev. 23:39, 41), the "appointed feast" (Lam. 2:6, 7; Hos. 12:9), or Succoth (2 Chr. 8:13).

This festival, celebrated in the early fall, is a joyous event that commemorates the exodus and gives thanks for the harvest of both the threshing floor and the wine press (cf. Deut. 16:13–15). This feast is the greatest feast of the Israelite agricultural year, and is one of three annual pilgrimage festivals (Exod. 23:14–19; 34:22–24; Lev. 23:33–36, 39–43; Num.

Homiletical Perspective

The images in the concluding verses of Psalm 65 are lush and nearly overwhelming. Joyful hills and song-struck valleys, shouting sunsets, and jubilant daybreaks—all are alive with the power of God coursing through them. For this reason this psalm offers preachers a powerful temptation. It is easy to run straight from the psalm's overflowing pastures to an equally florid description of God's presence wherever it was we were last struck dumb by the beauty of this earth: on the beach, or up in the mountains, in a boat out on the bay, or in a cabin in the woods. Unfortunately this method of reading the psalm functions more like a vaguely spiritual trip through a preacher's vacation photos and less like a proclamation of the gospel.

Furthermore, there are other reasons to refrain from preaching this psalm as if celebrating creation in and of itself. I remember standing in our neighbor's cherry orchard all alone when I was nine years old. It was a few days before the harvest. The trees were heavy with the weight of sweetness; some branches brushed the ground and dropped their fruit. The wind came up, and each branch, thousands of branches, began to sway. Hundreds and hundreds of trees in neat rows were all moving, almost dancing, as the orchard came alive for a moment in the rustle of leaves and the whip of the wind, the occasional groan

Psalm 65

Theological Perspective

gatherings for worship as a kind of birthright to which we come as naturally as water flows to the sea, it is worth attending to the psalm's counter testimony. We come, not because of a natural right, but because of the graciousness of a divine choosing that accepts us even when we fail to recognize that our gathering is built upon the foundation of God's forgiveness.

This is why the fourfold worship pattern of Christians—whether traditionally or posttraditionally expressed—often moves from gathering to word (and then on to meal and sending) via the bridge of confession of sin and assurance of pardon. Even if we initially gather as those who are accustomed to a place of worship with familiar faces all around, we are soon invited to acknowledge the genuine basis for our comfort in being there. We stand before the living God, enjoying the goodness of divine nearness and presence, only because God "forgive[s] our transgressions" (v. 3).

The second way in which Psalm 65 identifies God—as *deliverer*—expands the notion of salvation beyond the bounds of forgiveness just celebrated. Whereas some forms of Christianity have limited the delivering work of God to the personal forgiveness that welcomes us into God's holy temple, verses 5–8 declare the "awesome deeds" by which God answers us with deliverance. Rather than deliverance focused in an exclusively personal way, the psalmist speaks of a God of salvation who constitutes "the hope of all the ends of the earth and of the farthest seas" (v. 5). Moreover, the work of salvation is based on God's strength manifest in the creative power that "established the mountains" (v. 6) and by which both the unruly powers of nature and humanity are quelled: "You silence the roaring of the seas, the roaring of their waves, the tumult of the peoples" (v. 7). Whether deliverance is needed from the forces of nature or the threats of nature, God's power is strong to save, making the "gateways of the morning and the evening shout for joy" (v. 8).

God's delivering work is thus never less than, but always more than, personal forgiveness. It is promised in this psalm in the face of hurricanes, earthquakes, and tsunamis. It is promised also in the face of political turmoil, social dislocation, and communal despair. The strength of this deliverance rightly inspires awe and joy to the ends of the earth.

The final identification of God in Psalm 65 is as *provider*. Walter Brueggemann rightly notes that there is no word for "providence" in the Bible, but that God's "sovereign faithfulness and faithful

Pastoral Perspective

is right for God's people to gather, dutifully coming together out of a sense of need for God and performing vows in grateful response to God's goodness. All people, "all flesh" (v. 2), have a need for God. Each of us is in need of forgiveness; all of us are in need of community. The psalmist paints the picture of God as the host to whom the grateful come at God's invitation. We are those whom God chooses and brings near to God's courts, God's house, God's temple. Finding our way to God in gratitude leads us to community and to be "satisfied" (v. 4), a word we do not encounter very often in a world always intent on having more. God's people coming together to God's house with an awareness of our neediness and God's generosity: that is a good starting point for thinking about gratitude.

The next section of the psalm draws a much wider circle. Verses 5–8 point us to God's "awesome deeds." These deeds are manifest in the life of Israel in acts of "deliverance" and "salvation." Abruptly, the psalmist strikes a universal note by extolling God as "the hope of all the ends of the earth and of the farthest seas" (v. 5). All people, whatever the pedigree of their piety, can connect to God through a sense of awe. Then as now, mountains and oceans remind us of our creaturely insignificance before the power and majesty of the divine. To "awesome deeds" is added the imagery of God establishing mountains through strength and silencing the roaring waves (vv. 6–7).

This God of deliverance also calms the "tumult of the peoples" (v. 7). All who are paying attention, even those far from Zion "at earth's farthest bounds" (v. 8), are awestruck. To be in awe of God is to be moved to response; the farthest corners of creation, the "gateways of the morning and the evening" cannot contain their praise and "shout for joy" (v. 8).

So God is known in the lives of individuals, in the salvation history of Israel, and in the awesome signs and wonders of creation, eliciting praise. The final section of the psalm (vv. 9–13) is rhapsodic with the language of love, resplendent with imagery of tenderness and intimacy. God visits the earth and waters it, transforming arid barrenness into flourishing abundance. From images of strength and power we move to the language of delight, with God in the role of lover.

Water is the difference between life and death. The river of God is "full of water" (v. 9). God provides the people with grain, having ordered creation in such a way as to sustain life. This is not mere survival, it is abundance. God waters the earth *abundantly* (v. 10). In preparing the earth for the seed, we

Exegetical Perspective

29:12–38; Deut. 16:16–17; 31:9–13). This festival lasted for seven days and concluded with a special Sabbath that afforded people a time to rest and rejoice (Lev. 23:39–40), and to eat and drink the fruits of their labor (Deut. 14:22–26). The entire law was read every seventh year during this great feast.

Psalm 65, a song of thanksgiving, can be divided into three sections: a description of God's mercy and kindness (vv. 1–4); a description of God's great deeds (vv. 5–8); and a statement about God's graciousness on behalf of all creation (vv. 9–13). Verses 1–4 focus on the community's relationship with God. This God is to be praised because God has heard and answered the people's prayer. The use in verse 1 of a double vocative, "O God" (cf. v. 5) and "O you," followed by subsequent uses of second-person pronouns throughout the psalm creates not only a reverent but also a personal tone.

The exercise of performing vows to God (v. 1b) was common in biblical times and included a variety of expressions such as a tithe (Gen. 28:20, 22) or some other form of sacrifice, that is, holocausts (Lev. 22:18–20) or peace-offerings (Lev. 22:21–22). If the offering were a fellowship offering (cf. Lev. 3; 7:11–36), then portions of it would be eaten by the worshipers (Lev. 7:16; cf. Deut. 12:5–7; 1 Sam. 1:3–4, 9).

Vows were often made in times of need and distress (Jonah 1:16; 2:9), represented a solemn commitment on the part of the one making the vow, and were expected to be fulfilled (Deut. 23:21–23). Transgressions were thought to prevent rainfall (1 Kgs. 8:35–36; cf. Amos 4:7–8), making the divine forgiveness of sins ever more welcomed (v. 3). Verse 4 describes the congregation enjoying a sacrificial meal in the presence of God, their divine and gracious host. Here the word "happy" denotes good fortune because of God's gracious favor.

In verses 5–8 the psalmist declares God's wondrous deeds. The God who answers prayer (v. 1) does so through deeds and not words (cf. 1 Kgs. 18:37–38; Hos. 2:21–23). Such favor leads to the people's acknowledgment of God as their salvation and the hope of all "the ends of the earth and of the farthest seas" (v. 5). In verses 6–8 the psalmist celebrates not only God as the creator of the cosmos but also God as heroic warrior, girded with might, who created matter and then ordered it by working against chaos.

Even the tumult of the peoples (v. 7)—the nations and their potential attack on Israel—are quieted. Here the mountains symbolize the earth's pillars that offer stability over the chaotic seas that God

Homiletical Perspective

or creak of a branch. There was something behind the orchard, or something in it, animating each individual piece of fruit and the trees in their entirety. I could feel it, and I was terribly unnerved, even terrified. I ran straight home.

That experience in the cherry orchard thus pushes me to consider further where an easy read of Psalm 65 as nothing but a celebration of God's might and splendor alive in creation might lead. Indeed, at times the psalm seems to beg a reading in which creation is not distinct from God, but is somehow part and parcel of God's very being. The meadows in verse 13, shouting and singing, sound less like a reflection of God and more like a manifestation of divine presence. This can look beautiful on paper, but as a lived reality it is more than a bit unnerving.

Anyone who has ever felt threatened while camping in a thunderstorm or pitching and rolling on a sailboat knows this truth quite well. Who is to say that the god in nature has good intentions for us? It was, I think, the specter of a panentheistic deity that so rattled me in that cherry orchard. Those trees were alive, and I was not sure of their intentions!

Fortunately we know that "Starry Night" is not van Gogh and the world is not our God. Every creation reflects the character of its creator, but the two are never synonymous. For example, I recently read the collected poetry of the "dirty realist" American author Raymond Carver. In many respects his poetry is a catalog of unvarnished self-examination. Read as a whole, it suggests that Carver spent decades pouring the very best and worst of himself into his work; yet the man never became the product of his efforts. The poet and his poetry remain obviously distinct. God made the world, but the world is most certainly not God.

This may seem like an anxious and orthodox move to distract us from the psalmist's singing waves of grain. However, in an interesting move, Psalm 65 deflates its own celebration of nature by beginning, stubbornly, with a theme less romantic and much more familiar. Indeed, the opening theme is so familiar that on a first reading it gets overwhelmed by the shouting meadows and dancing cornstalks. The psalm opens, "Praise is due to you, O God, in Zion; and to you shall vows be performed, O you who answer prayer! To you all flesh shall come. When deeds of iniquity overwhelm us, you forgive our transgressions" (vv. 1–3).

Sin, forgiveness, and the universal call of God are the opening theme. By starting on these notes, the

Psalm 65

Theological Perspective

sovereignty" are encompassed by the use of the verb "arrange" twice in verse 9.[1] The psalm there speaks of God who "provides" the people with grain by having "prepared" it. The sovereign faithfulness of God is described by a richly layered metaphor of water. The earth is enriched by the gardener God who waters the earth. Grain is produced in the earth because there is a river of God that is "full of water" (v. 9). The heavens dispense showers that water the furrows, settle the ridges, and otherwise soften the parched and brittle earth so that it is fruitful (v. 10). Amazing is the lavish growth that ensues: pastures of the wilderness overflowing, hills girding themselves with joy, meadows clothing themselves with flocks, and valleys decking themselves with grain (vv. 12–13). The earth itself, provided for richly through such abundant watering, produces exuberantly as a virtual shout and song of joy (v. 13).

The use of this layered metaphor of water to speak of God's providence, or faithful sovereignty, is fraught with promise and peril. On the one hand, it vividly depicts the activity of God extending beyond an original act of creation into every present time, sustaining the creation called into being by lavish, overflowing, enriching water. It thus testifies to God present in every moment to support what God has made. On the other hand, although it works as an effective metaphor of God the provider in environments where plentiful water is available to make the earth fruitful, in environments where abundant, clean, nourishing water is a question rather than a certainty, the metaphor may engender more doubt than faith with respect to sovereign faithfulness and faithful sovereignty.

However, the psalm itself overcomes the peril implicit in the metaphor. Water is invoked in the psalm, not only to bespeak the providence of the God who waters the earth to make it fruitful, but also to depict the deliverance of the God who exercises power over tumultuous water (v. 7). Doubtless the psalmist remembers that the God who can silence the roaring of the waves can also bring forth water from a rock (see Exod. 17:6).

D. CAMERON MURCHISON

Pastoral Perspective

gouge deep furrows delineated with sharp edges, but God softens the land again, caressing it with gentle showers, settling its ridges and rounding the contours of the earth to provide for growth.

What growth! The year that culminates in harvest is crowned with bounty. Wagons piled high make deep tracks in the soft earth (v. 11). All creation responds to God not just by growing, but by flourishing! Pastures "overflow," hills "gird themselves with joy," meadows "clothe themselves with flocks," valleys "deck themselves with grain" (vv. 12–13). The natural order is all gussied up for God as for a beloved partner. The whole cosmos—hills and valleys and pastures and woodlands—shouts and sings together for joy.

As God's people, to become truly beautiful for God is also to fulfill the purposes for which we were created, to bear extravagantly the fruits of justice, generosity, and joy. The psalm's imagery speaks of a response to God that holds nothing back, allowing our lives to become effortless and abundant expressions of gratitude to the Holy One from whom we have received the gift of life.

Despite the tidy progression of the psalm—from gratitude that is dutiful, to praise that is awe-inspired, to thanksgiving that is extravagantly beautiful—things do not move along that neatly in the life of faith. Beautiful, radiant extravagance is a place we cannot manage to stay. Awe is a gracious reminder that we are not God, after all, despite our consumer culture's unrelenting invitation to place ourselves at the center of the universe as the arbiters of all things. Duty is often a helpful place to begin, or to begin again. Each of these responses to God has its place. The progression of Psalm 65 is a wonderful reminder of the ultimate outcome of thanksgiving and the invitation to be bountiful and beautiful for God.

DAVID R. RUHE

---

1. Walter Brueggemann, *Theology of the Old Testament: Testimony, Dispute, Advocacy* (Minneapolis: Fortress Press, 1997), 352.

silences (cf. Pss. 18:7; 104:5–6; Job 9:5–6). The psalmist makes clear that such wonders have far-reaching effects (v. 8a). The unit closes on a positive note: each day now begins and ends with joy (v. 8b), thanks to God and God's ways.

In the last part of the poem (vv. 9–13), the psalmist describes God's life-sustaining efforts that bring all creation to life. The central image is water. God is the storm God who comes to "visit" the earth. The language here suggests that God is outside of the created world, residing in the heavenly abode, instead of dwelling in the midst of creation as pictured in Genesis 2:4b–3:24.

This depiction of God typifies the royal theology of the day. Ordinarily seasonal rains that watered the land abundantly fell from late September to early May. The "river of God" in verse 9 is the main water source that irrigates the earth in the form of rain. Although Genesis 2:6 and 10 refer to a river that rises from subterranean waters, and both Psalm 46:4 and Isaiah 33:21 speak about a cosmic river in Zion, this river in verse 9 appears to be a "heavenly" source, originating with God in the realm of God's majestic abode. The gentle rains with which God waters the earth enrich, settle, soften, and bless it, and the earth, in turn, provides the people with grain (vv. 9–10).

The image of God crowning the year with bounty suggests that the earth has reached its full fruitfulness (v. 11). The image of God's wagon tracks overflowing with richness complements the image of God as a storm god who rides in a chariot of rain clouds upon the clouds and pours down rain upon the earth, as rider and chariot course the skies (cf. Ps. 68:4, 33; Deut. 33:26; Hab. 3:8).

The psalm closes with a lush image of the natural world, personified as humanity that has donned its finest attire and now shouts and sings jubilantly (vv. 12–13; cf. Pss. 96:11–12; 98:7–8; 148:1–10; Isa. 55:12). Thus, this psalm celebrates the beneficence of God, who has heard and has responded to the cry of the poor.

CAROL J. DEMPSEY

psalmist seems to insist that before we can go running through nature's splendor, we must first reckon with the God who calls us into worship when the weight of our wrongdoing proves overwhelming.

Before celebrating the God of *everything*, the psalm grounds its reader in the God of *Israel*. By doing so, the psalmist suggests that we cannot begin to understand the One who makes dawn and dusk shout for joy every time the sun rises or sets, without first grappling with the One who calls us, convicts us, and in turn forgives us. Only then, only after we have been redeemed, can we really understand the true nature of the One whose hills gird themselves with joy. Before then, our awe at nature might be sincere, but it will more closely resemble what Paul in Romans 8:26 (my trans.) calls "inarticulate groaning" than worship of the God of Israel and Jesus.

Until, in a very a narrow way, we recognize the God who chose Israel and claims all flesh in Christ, we will never really understand the God of everything. There is no lofty universal perch from which to be religious. The assumption of such a vantage point can lead only to distortion and misunderstanding. As George Lindbeck says so famously, "[One can] no more be religious in general, than one can speak language in general."[1] This means that, if Christians want to get to God, we should not start with nature. Instead, we must begin with the narrow gate that Jesus offers.

Lest this sound unreasonably parochial, we should remember that once we have walked through that gate, we will find ourselves in an incredibly broad and spacious place. This broad and spacious space is one where meadows dance and people are forgiven, one where we are provided with the grain we need for true life, one where cherry orchards speak and sing a word of peace, and one where we discover that we need not fear a thing.

MATTHEW FITZGERALD

---

1. George Lindbeck, *On the Nature of Doctrine* (Philadelphia: Westminster Press, 1984), 23.

2 Timothy 4:6-8, 16-18

[6]As for me, I am already being poured out as a libation, and the time of my departure has come. [7]I have fought the good fight, I have finished the race, I have kept the faith. [8]From now on there is reserved for me the crown of righteousness, which the Lord, the righteous judge, will give me on that day, and not only to me but also to all who have longed for his appearing. . . .

[16]At my first defense no one came to my support, but all deserted me. May it not be counted against them! [17]But the Lord stood by me and gave me strength, so that through me the message might be fully proclaimed and all the Gentiles might hear it. So I was rescued from the lion's mouth. [18]The Lord will rescue me from every evil attack and save me for his heavenly kingdom. To him be the glory forever and ever. Amen.

Theological Perspective

The theological perspective of this passage in the Pastoral Epistles cannot be separated from the intense human struggle for life's meaning that is at its heart. This letter to Timothy is the third of the Pastoral Epistles. We do not know that the historical Paul wrote it; in fact, there is evidence that the theology of the epistle as a whole reflects a later period of Christian history. Be that as it may, the implied author of the letter is Paul (1:1), and for our understanding of this particular passage, authorship is not an issue. The passage picks up some of the themes of Philippians 2:12–18, a passage that we do know to be authentically Pauline. There Paul is dealing with what his absence means to the Philippians. In this passage Timothy, as implied reader, is also surely dealing with Paul's absence, whether that separation is delimited geographically or by the boundary between life and death.

Whether or not the author is the historical Paul, the perspective offered is construed within the narrative framework of Paul's end-of-life reflections. In it, we get to know a Paul who is no longer traveling about the Mediterranean. His adventuring days are done. He is through venturing the seas. He is through walking the city streets and finding the odd job to support his itinerant ministry. Now he whiles away his days sitting in a Roman prison, awaiting the

Pastoral Perspective

In the chancel wall of the United Church of Christ congregation where I grew up, there is a three-part stained-glass window. The window depicts the risen Christ in the center panel and young men in armor on either side panel. A snake winds through the bottom of each panel. The only words in the artwork are taken from the passage at hand: "I have fought the good fight, I have finished the race, I have kept the faith." As a child, I thought this stained glass was the most beautiful thing I had ever seen, particularly during evening services, when its glow when backlit was the only illumination in the darkened sanctuary.

When I was a bit older, I learned that the stained-glass windows in the chancel, so awe-inspiring to me, represented controversy to others. It seems that the long-serving minister my parents revered (and revere to this day, long after his death) had taken a risk when he had led the church to purchase and install the windows. Before the stained glass, the chancel had been adorned with a simple wooden cross, decorated only on Easter with lilies.

Many in the church, including the aunt who told me of the conflict, believed that the stained glass was too ornate for the space. The irony of the Scripture passage depicted in the stained glass now rings out to me when I worship there, as it captures the satisfied but defeated words of a world-weary minister who has

Exegetical Perspective

Unlike 1 Timothy and Titus, which present Paul as a free apostle, 2 Timothy presents Paul as an imprisoned apostle who has been abandoned by friends and coworkers and who is facing an imminent death (2 Tim. 4:6–16; cf. 1:15).[1] Paul is presented as a dying patriarch whose steadfastness in the face of suffering and desertion qualifies him to exhort and encourage Timothy, a cherished coworker, to emulate his example of faithful endurance (3:10–11). The authority of the letter is enhanced by the literary convention of framing it as Paul's "last will and testament." Like Moses passing on advice to Joshua and the fledgling religious community that arose in the wilderness, Paul is presented as a wise aged apostle, passing on precious advice and guidance to his trusted successor, Timothy, and to the fledgling Christian community in Ephesus.

Paul's imprisonment and imminent martyrdom are presented not merely as unfortunate events to which he responded by writing a will; instead the events represent the culmination of a life that had always been moving toward this type of ending.

1. A clear majority of scholars today considers the Pastoral Epistles (1 Timothy, 2 Timothy, and Titus) to have been written by a disciple of Paul in the name of Paul. Throughout this essay, I shall refer to the author as "Paul." I do so preserving the author's desire to attribute Pauline authorship to the correspondence without making a judgment about that authorship.

Homiletical Perspective

Encountering this text is not unlike stumbling across the personal correspondence of a beloved relative, now deceased, written in an earlier time. This is tender, intimate material, infused with the drama of a trial, and it deserves to be preached as such. In a time when instant communication is ubiquitous and every thought is quickly disseminated, one cannot but value the fervent faith, confidence, and hope that lie behind and within these well-crafted words.

The passage at hand concludes a charge to Timothy to be steadfast and faithful, even in the most difficult of circumstances, and its two parts surround the most personal of pleas. This is Paul in a moment of vulnerable humanity, and it might be wise to expand the limits of the assigned text and read all of 4:6–18, so as to let the congregation hear Paul's earnest entreaty to Timothy to come to him before the next winter sets in. Still, within the text limits established by the lectionary there are a couple of rich kernels for preaching.

Concluding the Race. Paul's words in verses 6–8 are often selected by families for use at funeral or memorial services for loved ones whose faithfulness has seemed exemplary. Reset in a Sunday morning service in ordinary time, these same words may afford an opportunity for congregants to reflect on

2 Timothy 4:6-8, 16-18

Theological Perspective

very probably violent end of his life. We are privy to his review of his life's journey and his preparation for the final trek into the unknown.

In his reflection, Paul characterizes the end of his life as a sacrifice, as a drink poured out and offered as a libation. Earlier, in Philippians 2:17, Paul has entertained this concept of martyrdom. He tells the Philippians that even if his life should be poured out for the sake of their faith, he "takes pleasure and great pleasure" (my trans.) in them. His exuberant assurance, however, was still theoretical at that point, despite the suffering that he had endured from time to time. Now he is where he had earlier imagined he might be. As he sits there in that dank Roman prison, a very tough and unjust death almost certainly awaits him. What is he thinking now?

What he is thinking encompasses the broad theological themes of life and death, justice and injustice, betrayal and forgiveness, and finally, good and evil. Interestingly, Paul has few regrets. As he comes to his end, he assesses his vocation and its fulfillment positively with the familiar robust, even athletic, spirituality that we have come to associate with Paul. He writes, "I have fought the good fight, I have finished the race, I have kept the faith" (v. 7). He seems content that the degradation he is presently enduring is not his ultimate reality; his present shame does not define him. Rather, he looks toward an alternative reality.

Part of what is interesting about this passage is what Paul does not do. We know that he had an apocalyptic imagination, as did many people of his time and later. He does not give that imagination free rein here. His mode is not sensationalist; he is not escapist. He imagines that the Lord of justice will crown him and all those who love and look for the appearance of the Lord with justice. The words that we usually translate as righteousness (*dikaiosynē*) and righteous (*dikaios*) can also be translated as "justice" and "just." This is a conceptual leap that is often difficult for North American speakers of English. In this passage, where the situation in which Paul finds himself is so blatantly unjust, "justice" and "just" are likely the better translation. Martyrdom, the highest human acquiescence to injustice for God's sake, becomes doable only in the context of a steady belief that God is the ultimate arbiter of justice.

Paul does not stop there. Paul understands that God's justice is ultimately rooted in God's mercy and that both God's justice and God's mercy entail a human requirement beyond martyrdom and suffering. After some personal comments to Timothy, which are delightfully mundane (Paul reminds

Pastoral Perspective

sought to serve but has faced repeated persecution. The passage also captures, however, the joy one can find in a life of service to others in the name of God, whatever the short-term grudges of those whom one has served.

If the Pastorals were designed as leadership manuals for ministers in the early church, as Wayne Meeks suggests,[1] then the fourth chapter of 2 Timothy offers a compelling lesson on the nature of ministry amid conflict. The tone of this chapter is more personal and passionate than any other section in the Pastoral Epistles,[2] both crying out in the pain of rejection and celebrating a great run. This passage gives insight into the emotion that accompanies reflection near the end of one's life and ministry. The bittersweet quality of the words gives the passage great usefulness pastorally, on both the individual and the communal levels.

First, the passage lifts up the especially joyous nature of succeeding in perseverance, even in the midst of high resistance. Although few scholars still hold on to the claim that Paul himself wrote the letters to Timothy, the letter is built on the assumption that the reader knows of the strong personal bond that existed between Paul and Timothy, as well as some of Timothy's leadership shortcomings.

"Timothy is portrayed as a youthful, inexperienced protégé of Paul," writes John Gillman, "intimidated by strong opposition, requiring the encouragement and instruction of his mentor on both personal and church matters."[3] Standing in for Paul, the author of this letter seeks to demonstrate to Timothy that staying the course in the midst of strife and conflict is inherently virtuous.

Second, the text celebrates God's imminence in the midst of strife. It is impossible to know the historical legal situation in which Paul might have found himself during this writing. The passage suggests that he is undergoing a trial for the second time; although he prevailed in the first instance, he does not expect to do so at this juncture. The writer has been abandoned by those to whom he has ministered and is crying out for help. At the same time, however, he feels completely at peace in God's love and comfort. Thus he is abandoned by the people, but he is not alone.

Third, the passage offers a powerful image of ministry as self-gift through the use of the metaphor

1. Wayne Meeks, ed., *The Writings of St. Paul* (New York: W. W. Norton & Co., 1972).
2. Cf. Clare Drury, "The Pastoral Epistles," in *The Oxford Bible Commentary*, ed. John Barton and John Muddiman (Oxford: Oxford University Press, 2001).
3. John Gillman, "Timothy," in *The Anchor Bible Dictionary*, ed. David Noel Freedman (New York: Doubleday, 1992), 550.

Exegetical Perspective

Paul's life and ministry as a follower of Jesus represented a cultic drink offering that was being "poured out" to the Lord. When one begins the process of pouring out a drink offering, one knows that the drink will eventually be depleted. When Paul began pouring out his life in service to the Lord, he knew that one day his life would eventually be depleted.

While individual drink offerings were always being depleted, drink offerings were continually being presented to the Lord. After one vessel was emptied of its content, another vessel was poured. Drink offerings did not cease with the depletion of one vessel. Paul's words and life are meant to encourage Timothy to live his life as a drink offering to the Lord. Timothy is encouraged to identify with Paul, the exemplar of the faithful believer, whose life is being poured out to the Lord. Because Paul's words function as a final testament, Timothy is being called not only to emulate Paul but also to succeed Paul, both as a drink offering and in the fight against "imposters"—a fight that always results in persecution and divine deliverance (3:10–14).

The author identifies Timothy as a third-generation Christian who stands in the Christian heritage of both his grandmother and his mother (1:5). Since his childhood, Timothy has been the recipient of established Christian teachings and practices (3:14–15); this is why the author speaks of "the faith" as a long tradition of beliefs and practices transmitted from generation to generation, rather than as mere individual belief in Jesus. "The faith" represents a legacy of traditions, practices, and beliefs to which the author has remained committed—he has "kept the faith"—and to which Timothy is exhorted to remain committed.

Keeping the faith is presented as a battle. The author exhorts Timothy to "fight the good fight" (1 Tim. 1:18; 6:12). Paul is presented as fighting such a fight (2 Tim. 4:7a) by contending with opponents who reject the truth and promote a "counterfeit faith" (2 Tim. 3:1–9; 4:14–15). Paul, however, in contending with such opponents, carried out his ministry fully, and he exhorts Timothy to do the same (4:3–5; cf. Titus 1:9; 2:1). He charges Timothy to teach "sound doctrine" consistent with the faith (1 Tim. 1:3–4; 2 Tim. 1:13–14; cf. Titus 2:1), which for the author included female subservience and the submission of slaves to slave masters (1 Tim. 2:11–15; 6:1–4).[2]

2. For the author, "sound doctrine" conforms to many of the ideals of Roman imperial citizenship, which promote the prevailing social norms and cooperation with government and worldly authorities for the sake of peace for the church (cf. 1 Tim. 2:1–4; Titus 3:1).

Homiletical Perspective

their own lives and, perchance, to think about their own mortality. Paul speaks directly here of his coming death, an uncomfortable topic for many, who put off any conversation about death with spouses, families, or friends, even though they long for words of assurance on the matter from the pulpit.

Many people do not know how to speak of death; they employ any number of euphemisms instead of saying the word "die." Newspaper obituaries are particularly telling and display each day the countless ways people choose to say someone has died without actually saying he or she has, well, *died.* Some of the euphemisms are familiar: passed, passed away, passed on, went home to be with the Lord. Some are more creative: completed her mission, closed his eyes and went to be with God, was taken into the arms of the angels, woke up in the arms of Jesus.

In the second of his letters to Timothy, Paul employs not a euphemism, but a metaphor. He knows that his death is coming, and that he will embrace it when it happens—confidently, hopefully, full of trust. He approaches that prospect in the firm belief that he has been faithful to his calling, and the metaphor he chooses to describe such faithfulness is that of a race.

This race has been for Paul not a sprint, but a marathon—indeed, more of a steeplechase, involving multiple hurdles and pitfalls and rigorous opposition. It is a race that will end in his death, which he describes as a form of priestly libation or sacrifice. It is also a race into which he has put forth the greatest effort and in which he has done his unquestionable best, the reward for which will be a crown of righteousness.

On first hearing, Paul's testimony sounds like the declaration of a champion of the faith and may, to some hearers, seem to be much larger than their own experience. His concluding words (v. 8), however, add an inclusive twist: not only those who have run vigorously and successfully will receive the crown; the victor's laurels belong also to all those "who have longed for [Christ's] appearing." Here is a not-so-subtle reminder of the generous and gracious judgment of the One who bestows the crown, the One who waits for *us* when *we* finish our own race.

Standing Trial. Paul is on trial, the underlying context for all that he says to Timothy in this chapter. His complaint (v. 16) that no one stood with him in his first defense is not merely a statement of his own circumstance; it is also a reminder that we sometimes stand alone when we are given opportunity to testify to the truth of the gospel.

2 Timothy 4:6-8, 16-18

Theological Perspective

Timothy to bring the coat he left with Carpus when he comes) but unfortunately do not make it into the lectionary reading, Paul remembers with sadness the desertion he experienced in his first trial. No one took his part, he laments (v. 16), but he forgives them. Using the optative mood, the strongest way the Greeks had to express a prayer or a wish, he hopes that this act of betrayal will not be held against those who thus deserted him.

Paul does not spell out the connection between justice and mercy in this poignant moment, but his naming the betrayal and extending the hope for mercy is not accidental. This act of love, one of his last, grows out of a lifetime of observing the interplay between justice and mercy in the lives of those who follow the just and merciful God. It is at the heart of the Jewish faith into which he was born and to which he remained faithful to his soon-to-come dying day. It is at the heart of the ministry of the Jesus to whom he relinquished his prodigious talents and extraordinary zeal after meeting him, alive, on the road to Damascus.

The reason that Paul is able to let go of the wrongs done to him is the reason he was, so long ago, able to let go of his own violent ways, his enthusiastic persecution of those of his fellow Jews who chose to follow Jesus, in order to join his lot with them and accept the accompanying suffering. It is the reason that Jesus before him was able to let go of the temptation of the sword and accept the cross in Luke 22. In the final analysis, like the author of 1 Peter, Paul trusts the faithfulness of the one "who judges justly" (1 Pet. 2:23). He sees his life story within the larger framework of his trust in the Lord who overcomes evil. The lion's mouth is not the end.

MARY H. SCHERTZ

Pastoral Perspective

of "libation" for Paul's essence being now poured out. Libation carries special significance because it points to the very usefulness of something to drink. Paul does not choose a pouring-out image that suggests wastefulness, but rather one of a saving water or wine. Paul is departing this life, preparing to die, and yet the term he chooses for his poured-out self is one of renewal and refreshment. To drink something in is more intimate and personal than simply to conceptualize or understand it. To offer oneself as a drink for a thirsty people is quite different from fading away.

At first glance, one might see in a passage like this one an excellent text for a farewell sermon, especially a sermon to be delivered after one has been pushed out of a ministry position! It could, passive-aggressively, signal to a congregation that a wronged pastor feels as if she or he was "right" all along, and that, if the price of preaching the gospel is mistreatment, then so be it.

A closer reading of the text, however, indicates that Paul feels intense love for the people to whom he has ministered and that he is not spiteful. Indeed, Paul is able to forgive those who did not come to his aid, in part because he is surrounded by the all-powerful love of God. For this reason, the passage could be of most use pastorally in helping a person who fears conflict, perhaps as Timothy did. The passage can remind that person that saints like Paul poured themselves out so that leaders in our day might find refreshment in the witness of his abiding, unfailing faith.

SARAH BIRMINGHAM DRUMMOND

Exegetical Perspective

While keeping the faith is presented as a battle, Paul assures Timothy of God's faithful delivering presence. Even though Paul's closest friends and associates have abandoned him during his time of persecution, God remains present, providing both strength and deliverance, enabling Paul to carry out his ministry (2 Tim. 4:16–17). Paul wants Timothy to understand that this faithful delivering presence of God will also enable Timothy to "endure suffering, do the work of an evangelist, carry out your ministry fully" (4:5).

God's faithfulness to Paul not only provided Paul with deliverance from suffering, which the author represents by the metaphorical reference to "the lion's mouth" (v. 17b); it also helped secure the "crown of righteousness" that awaits Paul in the "heavenly kingdom" (vv. 8, 18). Typically a crown of laurel, pine, or olive was awarded to ancient competitors in athletic games (2:5). While only one person wins the crown in athletic competitions (cf. 1 Cor. 9:24), the crown of righteousness is not reserved simply for Paul. The crown of righteousness is a prize that awaits all who through fighting the good fight, finishing the race, and keeping the faith demonstrate their desire for the day of the Lord's appearing (2 Tim. 4:8; cf. 1:12, 18).

It is this promise of both the Lord's faithful delivering presence in the face of suffering and the crown of righteousness as the prize for faithful endurance that serves as a source of hope and expectation for Paul. Paul presents this promise as a source of hope for all who await the Lord's return. The message of 2 Timothy is that in the face of opposition, persecution, suffering, and even impending death, the Lord is always present to provide the necessary strength to fight the good fight, to finish the race, and to keep the faith. Therefore, with confidence believers continue in the faith (3:14), knowing that on the day of the Lord's judgment, a crown of righteousness awaits all those who finish the race.

GUY D. NAVE JR.

Homiletical Perspective

Most Christians have considered at one time or another what kind of witnesses they would be in a time of trial, particularly if the stakes were high; wondered how faithful they would be to the faith or how forceful and persuasive their testimony would be. Of course, such pondering misses a key point, which is that such trials occur every day, in countless venues.

At one time or another, we are all called to testify. Who knows when or where, for the trials shift their setting from place to place; they appear in one moment in a dormitory room, the next in an office somewhere, then in a classroom or a store. They pop up in conversations around the family dinner table, in interactions with sales clerks and health-care workers and teachers and counselors. The trials sometimes take the form of a casual conversation, or a debate about investments at a board meeting, or a question in a job interview, or a classroom quiz. The trial goes on, and we will be called as witnesses.

Despite Paul's grievance about being abandoned as he made his defense, he also displays an unwavering confidence in God's accompaniment and strength in his trial and in all circumstances. It is a remarkable juxtaposition—the language of complaint in one breath, the prayer of gratitude and praise in the next. Then again, Paul's honest struggle to be faithful, his need for accompaniment and support, and his faith in God's provision are strivings and needs many Christians can themselves understand and even embrace.

In the end, the gospel in Paul's words to Timothy lies in his assurance that, withstanding the trials of life, those who follow Christ are never ultimately alone, but rather are accompanied by One in whose presence they will find rescue and haven and hope.

ROBERT E. DUNHAM

Luke 18:9-14

[9]He also told this parable to some who trusted in themselves that they were righteous and regarded others with contempt: [10]"Two men went up to the temple to pray, one a Pharisee and the other a tax collector. [11]The Pharisee, standing by himself, was praying thus, 'God, I thank you that I am not like other people: thieves, rogues, adulterers, or even like this tax collector. [12]I fast twice a week; I give a tenth of all my income.' [13]But the tax collector, standing far off, would not even look up to heaven, but was beating his breast and saying, 'God, be merciful to me, a sinner!' [14]I tell you, this man went down to his home justified rather than the other; for all who exalt themselves will be humbled, but all who humble themselves will be exalted."

Theological Perspective

There is no more important question than, "Good Teacher, what must I do to inherit eternal life?" (Luke 18:18). This passage from Luke's Gospel strikes at the heart of the question by contrasting a leading religious authority and a blatant sinner to illustrate how we are justified by God and exalted into heaven (v. 14).

Both of the Old Testament lessons for this Sunday teach us, by contrast, about the goodness of God's steadfast love and the weakness of humanity to sustain ourselves. Twice in Joel the name of the Lord is praised because never again will God's people be put to shame (Joel 2:26–27). God pours out God's spirit on all humanity so that everyone who calls on the name of the Lord shall be saved (2:28, 32).

Likewise, Psalm 65 reminds us that when our sins and misdeeds overcome us with grief, guilt, and shame, God is present to forgive us as the God of our salvation (Ps. 65:3; 5). In Nehemiah 9:6–37 you can find a monumental prayer of confession that absolutely contrasts the insolence of humanity with the persistence of God's mercy and grace.

Complete Depravity. Karl Barth briefly discusses Luke's parable in a section titled "The Sloth and Misery of Man" in his colossal *Church Dogmatics.* For Barth, there is a clear distinction between the

Pastoral Perspective

Who are you, a Pharisee or a tax collector? It is hard to read this parable without placing oneself in one role or the other, or hearing oneself in both people. Which of us has not felt a bit self-satisfied on a Sunday morning? "O Lord, I thank thee that I am not like other people: my next-door neighbor who is enjoying a round of golf right now instead of attending worship; my friend in the other political party who does not understand your will for our nation; or even that scruffy-looking taxi driver sitting two pews over. I am here every Sunday morning and Wednesday evening; I pledge faithfully; I serve on three important church committees."

For some of us, it is only when we mess up in a big way that we gain the humility of the tax collector. Those in recovery programs call it "hitting rock bottom." Major mistakes are sometime required to help us see our need for God's grace and forgiveness. Only then do we echo the tax collector's words, "God, be merciful to me, a sinner!" (v. 13). Church can sometimes be a fairly hostile place for this kind of authentic remorse and humility. Our comfort with the idea that we are all sinful does not translate into the wish to hear in detail about any particular sin, thank you very much.

This parable tells us about ourselves as followers of Christ. If it makes us twinge with remorse at the

Exegetical Perspective

Jesus' parables in Luke frequently serve a moral purpose; they often have a "go and do likewise" quality that exhorts proper Christian behavior as much as they offer a theological disclosure of the realm of God (cf. Luke 10:37). The parable of the Pharisee and the Tax Collector is such a story, although it also says something significant about God.

Luke says Jesus tells this parable to confront arrogance and religious pride. It is addressed "to some who trusted in themselves that they were righteous and regarded others with contempt" (v. 9). Karl Barth identifies pride as the chief sin of the religious person, because it is fundamentally idolatrous: it confuses Creator and creation, Giver and gift.[1] Clearly Luke agrees. Those who are contemptuous of others have come to consider justice a characteristic of themselves, rather than a characteristic that rightly belongs only to God (cf. Luke 18:19, "no one is good except the one God," my trans.). Although the Pharisee in the parable thanks God for his righteousness rather than claiming credit himself, he nevertheless points to his own noble behaviors and so contradicts what humility his prayer may otherwise demonstrate.

1. E.g., Karl Barth, *Church Dogmatics*, IV/1; ed. G. W. Bromiley and T. F. Torrance (Edinburgh: T. & T. Clark, 1956), 358–513.

Homiletical Perspective

Parables are like fishing lures: they are full of attractive features—feathers, bright colors—and they end with a sharp little barb! The parable of the Pharisee and the Tax Collector is just such a parable. On the surface, it is a straightforward and bracing story about the dangers of spiritual pride and the benefits of confession. The careful preacher, though, will craft a message that draws hearers to the bite of truth, just as this parable does. In order to do so, it will be important to bear in mind certain pitfalls that await one who works at an interpretation of this text for contemporary listeners.

Pharisees and tax collectors have become biblical stock figures to us. The self-righteous, rule-bound religious leader, lacking in compassion and insight, is contrasted with the repentant, meek, simple, and humble tax collector. Indeed, the word "Pharisee" has entered common English usage in the adjectival form that means acting with hypocrisy and self-righteousness. So the preacher does well to recall the original significance of these characters to the first hearers of this story.

Pharisees held to a liberal interpretation of Scripture, and the aim of Pharisaic law was to make observance of Torah available to all. Tax collectors, on the other hand, were seen as collaborators with the hated Romans. Far from being seen as humble or

Luke 18:9-14

Theological Perspective

goodness of God the Creator and the sinfulness of the creature. This is clearly the point Jesus wants his audience to comprehend. The Pharisee sees his status before God to be a result of his own actions. His prayer is about what he is doing. The tax collector is ashamed of his actions. His prayer is about what he has done.

Both men are equally "shamed" before God, Barth says, but the difference between the two is that the Pharisee is ignorant of his standing with God.[1] The shame of both men is a result of their sin—or, as Calvin understands it, of their complete and utter depravation. The Pharisee has fallen into the sin of arrogance and pride because he has attempted to exalt himself above others, even God. He gives thanks to God that he is better than the thief, the rogue adulterer, or even the tax collector. He is proud of his religious acts of fasting and giving and therefore justifies himself. The tax collector, on the other hand, is humiliated before God and others. He genuinely recognizes his misdeeds, and his brokenness is evident in his self-mortification (e.g., chest beating).

Although Barth understands the shame of both to be the result of their comparison to the holiness of God, Calvin understands their fallenness to be the result of the original sin committed by Adam and Eve in the garden of Eden (Gen. 3). The doctrine of original sin is the theological view that the sin of Adam was imputed to all humanity. Calvin puts it this way: "[Adam] consigned his race to ruin by his rebellion when he perverted the whole order of nature."[2]

Paul describes human depravity in this manner: "By the one man's disobedience the many were made sinners" (Rom. 5:19). Reformed theologians like Calvin and Barth understand Scripture to teach that the entire person is subject to sin, leaving no one immune to Adam's original sin. This doctrine is most often referred to as total depravity; the idea is that a human being cannot *not* sin. In other words, we are doomed to sin.

The Gift of Justification. Seen through the lens of Reformed systematic theological teaching, the beauty of this parable is that when we acknowledge we are all subject to original sin and completely sinful in our innermost being, we concede two things: (1) we are unable to save ourselves because we are steeped in sin; and (2) we are totally and utterly dependent on God for salvation.

1. Karl Barth, *Church Dogmatics*, IV/2 (Edinburgh: T. & T. Clark, 1958), 385.
2. John Calvin, *Institutes of the Christian Religion*, ed. John T. McNeill, trans. Ford Lewis Battles (Philadelphia: Westminster Press, 1960), 2.1.5.

Pastoral Perspective

thought of acting like the self-righteous Pharisee, it also inspires us with the humility of the tax collector. This parable also tells us about the triune God of mercy—the God who redeems through self-sacrifice. Our justification is not obtained by doing things— even good things like charitable giving. In fact it is not "achieved" at all—at least by us. Justification comes through God's reaching out in mercy to helpless sinners.

Jesus communicates this profound truth in a short story about two men in the temple praying. In typical Jesus fashion, he reminds us that appearances can be deceiving. The one called holy by society walks away from the temple still wrapped up in his grandiose self-righteousness. The one reviled by good church folk "went down to his home justified" (v. 14a). The status quo is reversed in this story, "For all who exalt themselves will be humbled, but all who humble themselves will be exalted" (v.14b and 14:11).

How seductive it is to trust in ourselves that we are righteous and to regard others with contempt (v. 9). We do our good duty and confess our sins each Sunday; we put our envelope in the plate or make that automatic payment online. We serve the church and the world in so many ways. Hooray for us. Boo for those who do not follow the rules as we do—those whose work is detestable, who should not be allowed to sit in the same pew with us. Even if we do not take our judgment upon others to this extreme, it can be difficult to avoid looking on some of them with contempt when they do not conform to our expected standards of behavior, especially in regard to religious practice.

Jesus challenges believers to avoid trusting in our own efforts at fulfilling the law and, rather, to humble ourselves before a merciful and loving God. Trust is called for, but not trust in ourselves or in our ability to keep God's law. What is called for here is trust in God's mercy. In a culture that values individual achievement so highly, this can be a tall order, but even as we are cautioned not to trust in our ability to fulfill the law, nowhere does Jesus say that we may ignore the law. Discipleship is a balancing act.

The Iona Community in Scotland has a gift for articulating through tune and lyrics many of the joys and challenges of discipleship in a complex world. In their song "Sing Hey for the Carpenter!" worshipers are invited by Jesus to "Come with me, come wander," celebrating the liberation that comes through leaving behind false things that were once a source of meaning and comfort. Part of the chorus celebrates the carpenter (namely, Jesus) leaving his tools. It

Exegetical Perspective

Jesus sets the scene in verse 10. "Two men went up to the temple to pray, one a Pharisee and the other a tax collector." This sets the two men both together and apart. They are both Jews (they go to the temple). They are both pious (they go to pray). The one, however, is a Pharisee, someone noted for extraordinary piety. It is curious that he goes to the temple at all, since the Pharisees are the first to promote "the priesthood of all believers," and the locus of their religious lives is the home rather than the temple altar. This one prays in the temple, though. The other is a tax collector. He cannot be a Pharisee, since the Pharisees are particularly contemptuous of tax collectors, who consort with Romans, handle their money, and extort from the populace.

The Pharisee prays, "God, I thank you that I am not like other people: thieves, rogues, adulterers, or even like this tax collector. I fast twice a week; I give a tenth of all my income" (vv. 11–12). Although he properly acknowledges God as the source of his righteousness, he goes on to remind God how fortunate God is to have such a wonderful worshiper. The man obeys the commandments: he does not steal or covet (what the NRSV translates as "thieves" is better rendered "greedy ones"), he is not unjust (what the NRSV calls "rogues"), nor does he commit adultery. He fasts not only on the holy days for which fasting is prescribed, but twice a week. He tithes. Sharon Ringe compares the Pharisee's prayer with Psalm 17:3–5:[2]

> If you try my heart, if you visit me by night,
>   if you test me, you will find no wickedness in me;
>   my mouth does not transgress.
> As for what others do, by the word of your lips
>   I have avoided the ways of the violent.
> My steps have held fast to your paths;
>   my feet have not slipped.

This man is a paragon. What he is not is supremely what the tax collector is.

Ancient Palestinian tax collectors, of course, are not like contemporary Internal Revenue agents paid to enforce the law. They are franchisees of a corrupt and byzantine system that gouges the poor and enriches the wealthy. The tax collector, by definition a wealthy man, pays the empire a set amount for the privilege of gathering whatever he can squeeze from his neighbors. Although he is personally responsible for the money owed by his district, he is free to collect that money any way he wants, and anything he

2. Sharon Ringe, *Luke*, Westminster Bible Companion (Louisville, KY: Westminster John Knox Press, 1995), 225.

Homiletical Perspective

simple, they were seen to be (and sometimes were) venal, unscrupulous, and dishonest. Avoiding falling into these overly familiar stereotypes, helping the hearers of the sermon to get beyond their own assumptions about these characters, is important in order to hear the parable with new ears.

Inviting a fresh hearing of the story may mean providing within the sermon itself some historical background about the social locations of Pharisees and tax collectors in the ancient Near East in the first century. This may mean drawing out parallels or similarities with experiences of the members of your congregation, or disclosing some of your own struggles with spiritual pride and humility, and inviting the worshipers to reflect on their own temptations to brag before God—and who is not so tempted! It may mean helping the congregation confront their own presuppositions and assumptions about other people's piety.

On its face, this seems to be a simple story that encourages humility and condemns spiritual pride. How does one preach on humility without succumbing to spiritual pride? Surely this is one of the greatest spiritual paradoxes. "Be humble!" As soon as we have arrived at a suitable state of humility, we are tempted to take pride in our accomplishment.

A related danger is a liturgical one. "God, be merciful to me, a sinner!" has a familiar sound. Its meaning seems deceptively clear: do not be proud of your spiritual purity; be humble. Confess your sins before God, and you, like the tax collector, will go home justified; but what if the tax collector then cries out, "God, I thank you that I am not like that Pharisee!" How difficult it is to be truly humble, to confront, without flinching, as the tax collector does, our own sins, to beg God's mercy without excuse.

Some attention will need to be given to the use of prayers of confession. If a prayer of confession is normally included in the service, the text must be scrutinized for congruence with the point of this text. If the prayer of confession is a fixed text, it may be helpful to include a reference to it in the sermon itself. Or the text of the prayer may be adjusted to reflect the biblical context and the message of the sermon. Indeed, it would be good to review the entire text of the liturgy of the day for connections with this text and its warning about spiritual pride.

Once one has come to terms with the pitfalls in this story, one can turn to some of the themes and insights the story offers.

The parable provides a vivid example of the dangers of religiosity. The Pharisee is first of all a

Luke 18:9-14

Theological Perspective

The disingenuous Pharisee in our passage justified himself before God by trying to exalt himself. He prayed about who he was, what he had done, and what he had not done to put himself in good standing with God. On the other hand, the tax collector humbled himself, genuinely acknowledging his sinfulness and his desperate need for God's mercy. In the end, the Pharisee was humbled because of his self-exaltation, and the tax collector was exalted because of his humiliation. According to Donald Guthrie, the Pharisee had an overoptimistic understanding of himself and the human condition, and the tax collector had a pessimistic view, which was more in line with our understanding of original sin.[3]

One of the key words in the passage is "justified." After the tax collector humbly prayed for God's mercy, the text says "this man went down to his home justified rather than the other" (v. 14). The doctrine of justification asks the question of how we reach a status of righteousness in God's eyes. The Pharisee trusted in himself for his own righteousness, and the tax collector trusted in God for righteousness. He did nothing to earn or deserve God's mercy. God's mercy was freely given to him. Paul says that "God proves his love for us in that while we still were sinners Christ died for us" (Rom. 5:8).

In Ephesians 2:8 Paul assures us, "For by grace you have been saved through faith, and this is not your own doing; it is the gift of God." Our justification, therefore, is the recognition of our guilt and shame, resulting in the confirmation of our forgiveness and our reception of God's righteousness. One of the hallmarks of the Protestant Reformation is the concept of *sola gratia*, which asserts that we are justified by God's grace alone—the only means by which we inherit the righteousness of Christ. To suggest that we can be justified by any other means is to reject the free grace of God. Paul reiterates this when he writes, "Now to one who works, wages are not reckoned as a gift but as something due" (Rom. 4:4).

ROBERT LEACH

Pastoral Perspective

continues, "Sing hey for the Pharisees leaving their rules! Sing hey for the fishermen leaving their nets! Sing hey for the people who leave their regrets!"[1]

Notice that followers also leave their regrets. This is affirming, since the humility of the tax collector does not require wallowing in self-loathing. The liberation of knowing that God is merciful and loving means that we can leave behind our reliance on our achievements in work or in our faith community. They have their place but not at the center of our relationship with the God of the cross and the Friend of the poor.

How strange that this Gospel reading is joined by 2 Timothy 4:6–8, 16–18 in the Revised Common Lectionary for this Sunday. In verses 6–8, Paul speaks of his confidence that he has "finished the race" and "kept the faith" (v. 7) and that "the crown of righteousness" is reserved for him. This might sound an awful lot like the Pharisee from Jesus' parable, but there are quite a few differences. The Pharisee stood in the comfort of God's temple; Paul writes from prison. The Pharisee heaps scorn on others he deems less righteous than himself; Paul affirms that the crown belongs "not only to [himself] but also to all who have longed for [the Lord's] appearing" (v. 8).

Balance is key. We cannot trust in our ability to fulfill the law to save us, yet we do not abandon the law. We humble ourselves before a merciful God yet are confident in the Lord's promises. Whether Pharisee or tax collector by nature, all find welcome in God's temple. Sing hey!

LAURA S. SUGG

---

3. Donald Guthrie, *New Testament Theology* (Downers Grove, IL: InterVarsity Press, 1981), 190.

1. The Iona Community, "Sing Hey for the Carpenter," in *Heaven Shall Not Wait* (Chicago: GIA Publications, 1989).

collects above what he owes is his profit. The penitent "chief tax collector," Zacchaeus (19:1–10, next Sunday's Gospel lesson), alludes to the practice when he says, "if I have defrauded anyone of anything, I will pay back four times as much" (19:8).

Tax collectors are frequently foreigners, and they often farm out their own responsibilities to others, creating a perfect pyramid scheme of graft. It is no wonder they are roundly despised. This tax collector, however, acknowledges God's judgment of him and throws himself on God's mercy. He too prays with the help of a psalmist. His remorse echoes Psalm 51:1, "Have mercy on me, O God, according to your steadfast love; according to your abundant mercy blot out my transgressions." For that reason, Luke says, he is "justified" (Luke 18:14), that is, made just by God's mercy, while the Pharisee (who considers himself just) is not considered just by God.

On the one hand, the two prayers highlight God's preference for humility over arrogance. "All who exalt themselves will be humbled, but all who humble themselves will be exalted" (v. 14) revises and recasts Jesus' saying that "some are last who will be first, and some are first who will be last" (13:30). On the other hand, though, the prayers of the Pharisee and the tax collector also draw a strong connection between piety and ethics, a theme that also runs throughout Luke–Acts. Ringe considers this parable together with the preceding one (last Sunday's Gospel lesson) and notes that they both concern right living. The unjust judge and the Pharisee both have their verdicts overturned by God's justice. They are "locked into the systems of social and economic competition and the hierarchy of honor and prestige that favor the dominant classes in their society. In both parables, prayer is about the reversal of those systems."[3]

Although this tax collector goes down to his home justified by God, we do not learn the consequences of his repentance. His plea for mercy, in order to be effectual, must issue in right behavior. When Jesus calls Levi, another tax collector, the latter abandons his tax franchise, follows Jesus, and throws a great party to celebrate (Luke 5:27–32). When Zacchaeus accepts Jesus' invitation, he promises to repay what he has stolen (19:1–10, next Sunday's text). It seems likely we are to expect nothing less from this anonymous tax collector.

E. ELIZABETH JOHNSON

religious person, a leader among his fellow Jews, a spiritual guide for those who seek to follow God's law faithfully. He is careful in his religious observance and generous with his money. No doubt he is, in the eyes of the world as well as in his own eyes, a good person and a religious person. The problem here is not his religious observance or his piety, but his inability to see and name his dependence on God.

To most of our congregations, this may be as serious a problem as it was for this Pharisee, to the extent that they are observant and generous. Of course, preachers and pastors are always urging them to these very same things! Prayers of thanksgiving can often go awry at this point. A sermon on this text might draw out the contemporary temptations to couch our spiritual pride in the form of thanksgiving to God, as the Pharisee does.

It may be appropriate to address the prayer of the tax collector. Its candor, simplicity, and absolute trust in God's mercy make it a model prayer. The trick here is that the justification follows the prayer; that is, the one offering this prayer must be willing to stand before God without excuse, without special pleading, without expectations, without a single claim on anything except God's mercy. The difficulty of this prayer, simple as it is, should not be underestimated.

By looking at the tax collector's prayer as a model of prayer, we are drawn to consider the great mercy of God. The sins of the tax collector were undoubtedly real and serious. Tax collectors commonly stole from those they taxed and pocketed the money for themselves; they collaborated with the oppressors of their own people; they accepted bribes as a matter of routine. In other stories we see repentant tax collectors engaging in restitution, but not here. This parable is interested only in his trust in God's mercy. If a tax collector can find mercy before God, who is excluded?

MARJORIE PROCTER-SMITH

3. Ibid.

Daniel 7:1-3, 15-18

¹In the first year of King Belshazzar of Babylon, Daniel had a dream and visions of his head as he lay in bed. Then he wrote down the dream: ²I, Daniel, saw in my vision by night the four winds of heaven stirring up the great sea, ³and four great beasts came up out of the sea, different from one another. . . .

¹⁵As for me, Daniel, my spirit was troubled within me, and the visions of my head terrified me. ¹⁶I approached one of the attendants to ask him the truth concerning all this. So he said that he would disclose to me the interpretation of the matter: ¹⁷"As for these four great beasts, four kings shall arise out of the earth. ¹⁸But the holy ones of the Most High shall receive the kingdom and possess the kingdom forever—forever and ever."

Theological Perspective

While the setting of Daniel is the exile, that time period is too early for the book in its present form. Even if some sections were handed down from tales of court conflict in the exilic period, the final shaping of the book was almost certainly around 169 BCE. Daniel 7, written in Aramaic, borrows the four kingdom motifs found in chapter 2. It is an encouragement to the saints of God to be faithful in all adversity.

The prophet had dreams and visions, and wrote them down. It has been said that a dream is the writing on the plaster of the unconscious, but a vision is the writing on the hidden face of history. Perhaps the writer wanted to avoid the criticism of dreams that is made in Deuteronomy 13:1–5 and Jeremiah 23:25–28, and the dream/vision he records in today's passage has to do with God and the stage of human history.

The vision is of a great sea, churned by the winds of heaven, out of which come four huge beasts. This recalls the opening of Genesis, when a mighty wind swept over the face of the deep, which was part of the abyss, on the verge of chaos. Even when tamed by the creating and ordering word of God, the sea was the home to countless living creatures, including the monsters Leviathan and Rahab. No wonder, therefore, that with the churning of the deep, other monsters are found to lurk within.

Pastoral Perspective

Because this text is chosen as the Hebrew Bible reading for All Saints, our pastoral reading must consider (beyond what the text may have meant in its original time and context, and what it might have to say to us in our current time and context) what it means in relation to this feast and its particular moment in the sweep of our Christian liturgical year. So we will read this text in a special way in light of All Saints, that day in our church calendar when we recognize the manifold gifts of all the faithful, both living and departed.

Originally, this feast was to commemorate a rather exclusive list of spiritual celebrities. In the high Middle Ages, prior to the Reformation, more and more individuals were being officially canonized—sometimes for good deeds and miracles and sometimes for more dubious political or monetary contributions to the church—and the calendar of saints' holy days was getting pretty stuffed! So the Western church invented All Saints' Day as a day to honor all the "minor" saints for whom they could not find room to have a day of their own on the official docket. Of course, the reformers thought this was a dreadful practice. Although they kept many of the principal feasts and fasts of the Western calendar as we do today, they purged the dense thicket of commemorations, and downplayed the feast of All Saints.

Exegetical Perspective

This text contains the beginning and end of a central passage in the book of Daniel. The chapter is better known for the verses that this reading leaves out: the description of the four beasts, the image of God enthroned, and "one like a human being" (or "son of man" RSV, v. 13) receiving dominion. Within Christianity, these images have informed the portrayal of both Jesus and the second coming of Christ.

The shape of this lectionary reading, however, focuses the reader's attention on a different element of the text: the "holy ones" who are promised eternal possession of the kingdom of God. In order to understand the meaning of this verse within its ancient Israelite context, its literary and historical contexts must first be explored.

The book of Daniel is a pseudepigraphical work (meaning that the first-person narrator is actually an assumed persona), dated to the reign of Antiochus IV Epiphanes (175–164 BCE). During this period of Israelite history, the Jewish community suffered persecution and martyrdom at the hands of a Hellenistic despot. Many Jewish texts from this period interpret this suffering, not as a punishment from God, but rather as a test of their righteousness and a sign of a growing conflict between the forces of good and evil.

The vision in chapter 7 is the first of a series of "apocalyptic" visions in the book (from the Greek

Homiletical Perspective

We have a genuinely apocalyptic text in Daniel's seventh chapter, with some very colorful pictures. Imagine beasts churning up the sea. No doubt they would trouble our spirit. This dream of Daniel's is like many silly dreams many of us have. We fantasize horrible things. We have nightmares. We get scared.

Only a fool would say there is more reason to be calm than to be scared. If you do not experience fear, unconsciously or consciously, you are just not paying attention. I know that today you are supposed to speak of troubles as "challenges," and I know that you are supposed to stay upbeat, but every now and then, surely, you look around and see the trouble.

Popular TV shows such as *The Sopranos* remind us of our trouble. Consider Tony Soprano's lament to his psychiatrist, Dr. Melfi. "Lately, I'm getting the feeling that I came in at the end," he says. "The best is over."

Dr. Melfi says to Tony, "Many Americans, I think, feel that way."

"I think about my father," Tony says. "He never reached the heights like me. But in a lotta ways, he had it better. He had his people. They had their standards. They had pride. Today, whadda we got?"

In this session, Tony achieved what David Remnick calls the "menacing rhino plod that would come with time, anxiety and fifteen thousand buttered

Daniel 7:1-3, 15-18

Theological Perspective

The four that rise to make their appearance in this vision are hideous and unnatural in form; for the prophet they represent hideous dynasties that have tried and still try to usurp the kingdom of God. In this case they probably represent the Neo-Babylonian, Median, Persian, and Greek empires and their rulers. Such monsters still arise periodically on the stage of history, always wreaking devastation and destruction in their attempts to become the only kingdom of the whole earth. The devastation of World War II and the Holocaust provides obvious examples, but countless more recent perpetrators of barbarism and wickedness across the globe could easily be listed.

This fact is a reminder also of the monsters and beasts that often lurk within, in the deep psyche of humankind, where they can often lead to disturbed minds and self-destruction. At certain times and under certain circumstances, they tip over, emerging under the guise of political and religious leadership and bringing destruction across the world. In such situations the saints of God are sorely tested, both on account of the general injustices that prevail and because of their own persecution. In the context of World War II, the Confessing Church and Dietrich Bonhoeffer bear witness to what may be needed.

The prophet is unable to understand the vision on his own, and has to appeal for supernatural help to "one of the attendants" (v. 16), a divine representative. Following the dream/vision, in verses omitted from today's reading, the chapter describes a vision of the Ancient One (vv. 9–10), surrounded by myriads of heavenly beings, before whom "the court sat in judgment, and the books were opened" (v. 10b).

The reference to angelic beings became an embarrassment to the later heirs of Enlightenment rationalism, with their preference to demythologize. However, to demythologize the Old Testament vision of heaven runs the risk of demythologizing the whole company of heaven, which includes not only the "council of Yahweh" and the "council of the holy ones" (Jer. 23:18; Ps. 89:6–8) but, more importantly for us, the souls of the righteous of God of all times and places. It is ultimately to demythologize the church (old and new covenant) triumphant, and to call into question the church militant here. Unless God is God of the departed as well as the living, as Paul concluded, our preaching (and all churchly activity) is in vain, and we are pitiful (1 Cor. 15:14, 19).

The heavenly being interprets the hideous beasts as representing four great kingdoms that will arise—though they will arise from the earth, not the sea.

Pastoral Perspective

With the liturgical renewal movement, we have recovered the observance of this feast in many of our traditions, but have given it a rather different emphasis. We now use this day to honor the priesthood of all believers, indeed, the *saint*-hood of all believers! This is empathically not a day to venerate a select number of superstars of the faith, but a time to recognize that all of us as Christians together—both the living and the departed—are saints of God, that "great cloud of witnesses" (Heb. 12:1). This is why this day is a particularly fitting day both for baptisms and for the reverent reading out of the names of the beloved in our communities who have died in the past liturgical year.[1] We welcome new saints of God in baptism, even as we honor the memory of those saints who have entered into the larger life of God but are still with us in remembrance.

So we are *all* saints of God. What does it mean to be a "saint"? In Daniel 7:18, the NRSV translation "holy ones" is a more accurate rendering of what in older translations appeared as "saints": "The holy ones of the Most High shall receive the kingdom and possess the kingdom forever—forever and ever" (v. 18). The Hebrew word gives us a clue to the pastoral meaning of this passage. It is not the word commonly translated as "saints," *hasîd*, which means "pious" or "kind." Such a reading of the text might leave us with the impression that, indeed, it is those (and only those) who are particularly virtuous who will inherit salvation.

On the contrary, the word here is *qadôsh*, which means not "virtuous" per se, but "set apart"—made holy by God's naming and calling them such. It is the same word that we find in Exodus 19:6b, where in the wilderness God commands Moses to tell the Hebrew people, "you shall be for me a priestly kingdom and a *holy nation*." Daniel hearkens back to that moment when the Israelites were made a chosen people, a priesthood of believers, and he recalls God's promise to redeem them, even in the face of persecution, fear, and political turmoil (in Daniel's time, the persecution of the Jews by the emperor Antiochus IV Epiphanes, and political turmoil symbolized by the terrifying dream of the four beast-kings rising out of the sea—for which we may find parallels in our world today).

So "the holy ones" in today's passage does not refer to the perfectly pious, the saint-*ly* among us, but to *all* of us as a holy *people*, through our baptisms

---

1. In the Roman Catholic tradition, the necrology is read the day before, on the observance of the feast of All Souls.

word meaning "revelation"). Apocalyptic literature is marked by some common features, including visions mediated by a divine figure, the belief that historical conflicts are the result of greater cosmic battles between forces of good and evil, a dualistic worldview, the prominence of symbolic images, and the use of a fictive first-person narrator.

The passage starts with a date for the vision, "the first year of King Belshazzar of Babylon." This "date" reveals a common problem in the book of Daniel: the historical information that serves as the setting of the book contains a number of factual errors. For example, Belshazzar was never a king in Babylon, nor was he Nebuchadnezzar's son (5:2). These inaccuracies are not significant for the overall purpose of the book, however, which contrasts pious Daniel with the dangerous but morally and intellectually inferior foreign ruler. In this way, the history-like setting functions as a complex "symbol" of the real threat faced by the audience of the book: the tyranny of Antiochus.

This representation of the foreign ruler is more prominent in the tales of the righteous Daniel that comprise the first six chapters of the book in its Hebrew version. (The Greek version of the text is longer and contains three more tales of Daniel.) In these chapters, Daniel is the wise and pious young man who nonviolently resists persecution. He survives as a member of a foreign court because God rewards his unswerving observance of Jewish law.

The second half of the book, chapters 7–12, contains a series of visions, revelations, and angelic explanations that, while stylistically distinct, should be read in conjunction with the book's first half. These visions, for instance, presume that the reader knows who Daniel is and that the "beasts" represent forces of persecution and martyrdom, as depicted in the story of the men in the fiery furnace (3:19–27) and Daniel in the lions' den (6:16–23). Chapter 7's symbolic representation of four successive kingdoms is also seen in chapter 2, and Daniel's adeptness with visions is demonstrated in his interpretations of the king's dreams (chaps. 2 and 4) and his ability to decipher the "writing on the wall" (chap. 5).

The verses selected in this part of the lectionary provide only a general description of the vision's threat: the announcement that four beasts rise out of the sea. In ancient Semitic thought, the "sea" represented the forces of chaos, which both opposed the creation of an ordered universe and symbolized cosmic evil. The beasts, then, are manifestations of evil.

The use of the number four is significant. The four winds represent the four primary directions,

bialys."[1] Tony used to have a lightness of step. The beasts churned up the waters. Now Tony's favorite phrase is "Whaddya gonna do?" This is a phrase most of us know well. The author of the dramatic series *David Chase* uses a lot of real violence. He also shows the violence underneath the sea: "the exposure of the ordinary disappointments and tragedies . . . addiction, twelve-step recoveries, teenage depression, modern pharmacology, suicides, sexual indulgence, family betrayals, financial manipulation, accidents, heart attacks, strokes, death and dying—and always, afterward the inability to summon a language to equal the emotion."[2]

I just read an agenda from an old meeting in my new church. The first statement on the list was (1) REFRAIN from saying mean things that have already been said or increasing the hurt that exists. I was not at that meeting, but I have been at that meeting!

We like to think that Daniel describes the big stuff, the kind of terrors that peasants used to suffer. It is almost embarrassing to admit what torments us and gives us nightmares! We in modern times have also known the plagues of bad things. We may come to know more. My daughter swears she is going to run a workshop called "Pre-Apocalyptic Training for Post-Apocalyptic Times." She intends to charge.

In July of 1875 the largest recorded swarm of locusts in American history descended upon the Great Plains. It was a swarm about 1,800 miles long and 110 miles wide that extended from Canada down to Texas. North America was home to the Rocky Mountain locust, the most numerous species of locust on earth. At the height of their population, there were an estimated 60 million of them—equivalent to the 60 million bison that had inhabited the West. The Rocky Mountain locust is believed to have been the most common macroscopic creature of any kind ever to inhabit the planet.

Swarms would occur once every seven to twelve years, emerging from river valleys in the Rockies, sweeping east across the country. The size of the swarms tended to grow when there was less rain—and the West had been going through a drought since 1873. Farmers just east of the Rockies began to see a cloud approaching from the west. It was glinting around the edges where the locust wings caught the light of the sun.

1. David Remnick, "Family Guy," *The New Yorker* 83, no. 15, June 4, 2007, 30.
2. Ibid.

Daniel 7:1-3, 15-18

Theological Perspective

Their demise is described later in the chapter. What is pertinent here is the message that ultimately the saints of the Most High—the church triumphant—and the righteous of all ages and places, will receive the kingdom and retain it forever and ever.

The power given to the saints of God is, of course, quite different from the power of the "beasts" of history. The church (when it is really being church and not trying to be a kingdom) does not depend on force, and in fact renounces the sword. It has no iron teeth or metal claws. All it has is a mouth that announces the promise of the gospel and God's reign. In the ebb and flow of human history, with the many outrages that are perpetrated against humankind, it is easy to become disillusioned and give up all hope.

The saints of God are to take heart. The victory of God's kingdom is not in doubt, and this has been sealed and settled in the death and resurrection of the Son of God. That event is God's declaration that there are ultimate standards in the universe of right and wrong, good and bad, justice and injustice. The horrendous evils perpetrated by hideous beasts have no legitimate place in creation and will certainly have no place in the new creation. The resurrection of the Son is God's ultimate stand against all evil and his condemnation of it.

The saints will still experience the testing of faith. There will still be martyrs, but they, and we, shall be part of that whole company of heaven who will forever sing the praises of God, in the thrice holy chant of the seraphim: "Hallelujah! For the Lord our God the Almighty reigns" (Rev. 19:6b). The Bride is clothed with fine linen, which "is the righteous deeds of the saints" (Rev. 19:8b).

BRYAN SPINKS

Pastoral Perspective

named and called by God to faithful living. So on this feast of All Saints, our pastoral emphasis is on relation and remembrance. We remember the riches of our heritage, those women and men whose lives are the complex and colorful textile into which our lives are now woven in our congregations. We may sing the hymn "For all the saints who from their labors rest." In joining the sacred names of our own beloved dead with saints of every time and place, we too are gathered, healed, re-membered (put back together) into God's loving relationship with us and all creation, past, present, and yet to come.

As All Saints is also a day for baptism (or remembrance of baptism), it is again helpful to note that as "saints" we are not superpious, but we are *called*. We do not baptize to make people pure or perfect. Baptism immerses us in the waters of life and death so that we are able to die to loneliness and alienation, to die to the need to rely only on our strength. Out of the water, we rise again to new life—a life of complexity and richness, a life of community, a life now led as a member of the body of Christ—a life of service.

Finally, as we are knit together more closely through remembrance of our faithful departed, we are also re-membered by God—made whole and strengthened for faithful living. Daniel 7:18 is a template for the apocalyptic promise that Jesus later explicitly connects with justice for the poor, in the reading from Luke also appointed for All Saints: "Blessed are you who are poor, for yours is the kingdom of God" (Luke 6:20). So we are strengthened, not just to feel good and at peace within ourselves and one another, but also to work for peace and justice in the wider community and the world. It is we ourselves who are "all saints."

PAMELA COOPER-WHITE

and, therefore, the whole earth. The angelic interpreter tells Daniel that the four beasts represent four nations. Historically these are four kingdoms that subjugated Judah in turn: the Babylonians, the Medes, the Persians, and the Greeks. Symbolically, the use of the number four suggests worldwide opposition to God. No wonder Daniel is "troubled" by this vision.

The "attendant" (v. 16), who is identified in 9:21 as Gabriel, comforts Daniel by stating that they will not succeed. Instead, the "holy ones" will be given royal authority over "the kingdom" for eternity (v. 18). The Hebrew wording of this phrase "holy ones" is used exclusively for divine beings and angels. Even the Dead Sea Scrolls, which were written about 150 years after Daniel, still distinguish between heavenly "holy ones" and the humans who interact with them.

In Daniel 7, the "holy ones" get dominion over the "kingdom" already granted to the "one like a human being" (v. 13). Although Christians read this as a reference to Jesus, the figure is identified later in the book as Michael, the angelic head of God's heavenly army (12:1). In light of the exclusive use of "holy ones" to refer to heavenly beings and the identification of their leader as "like" a human, later identified as Michael, this vision originally referred to the divine armies gaining control over the cosmic forces of evil and chaos. Human history, manifested in tyrannical empires and unjust persecution (beasts), is a manifestation of this cosmic struggle.

Soon, however, the phrase "holy ones" was reinterpreted as a reference to righteous humans sanctified after death. This interpretation takes its cue from the purification of the wise in Daniel 11:35 and 12:10, alongside 12:1–2, which is the clearest reference in the Hebrew Bible to a postmortem judgment between the righteous and the wicked. Reading all of these verses together leads to the conclusion that the "holy ones" in chapter 7 are the wise and pious, who will suffer persecution, be purified, and "awake" to everlasting life, where they will possess God's kingdom. This holistic reading of the book underlies the inclusion of this passage on All Saints' Day.

CORRINE L. CARVALHO

People said the locusts descended like a driving snow in winter. They covered everything in their path. They sounded like thunder or a train and blanketed the ground, nearly a foot deep. Trees bent over with the weight of them. They ate nearly every living piece of vegetation in their path. They ate harnesses off horses, bark off trees, curtains, and clothing hung out on laundry lines. They chewed on the handles of farm tools, fence posts and railings. Some farmers tried to scare away the locusts by running into the swarm, and they had their clothes eaten right off their bodies.

Similar swarms occurred in following years. Farmers became desperate. By the mid-1880s, the rains had returned, and the swarms died down. Within a few decades, Rocky Mountain locusts were believed to be extinct. The last two live specimens, collected in 1902, are now stored at the Smithsonian.

We also have our beasts that rise from the sea: think of 9/11, the Virginia Tech shootings, global warming, the war in Iraq. My college graduate kids are churned up about 401(k)'s, college loans, and the prospect of no more cell phone or health insurance coverage from Mom and Dad. We go from the huge to the insignificant and back as our world turns and our seas churn. We hear the great beat of the monsters rising from the sea, the swarm of the locusts, the things said in psychiatrists' offices—and we become afraid.

What can we do to assuage our fears? We can tell our dreams and nightmares to a friend who will help us make sense of them. We can try not to push the monsters back down in the sea. That just makes them mad.

What else can we do? We can pray and work for a world that will be less absurd and more just. We can stop being innocent or foolishly Pollyannaish. We can listen for the joy of the sea as we ask the monsters why they are churning it up so. What would make them quiet again? Listen deeply for the revelation of God, hidden within the apocalypse.

Then pray for quiet sleep and for the management skills of creation to keep the sea quiet and the monsters abated. Act as if you believe that God will bring a good morning, even if the night be loud.

DONNA SCHAPER

Psalm 149

¹Praise the LORD!
 Sing to the LORD a new song,
  his praise in the assembly of the faithful.
²Let Israel be glad in its Maker;
  let the children of Zion rejoice in their King.
³Let them praise his name with dancing,
  making melody to him with tambourine and lyre.
⁴For the LORD takes pleasure in his people;
  he adorns the humble with victory.
⁵Let the faithful exult in glory;
  let them sing for joy on their couches.
⁶Let the high praises of God be in their throats
  and two-edged swords in their hands,
⁷to execute vengeance on the nations
  and punishment on the peoples,
⁸to bind their kings with fetters
  and their nobles with chains of iron,
⁹to execute on them the judgment decreed.
  This is glory for all his faithful ones.
  Praise the LORD!

Theological Perspective

Psalm 149 might well produce a kind of theological whiplash for the reader. If one is reading happily through this concluding collection of poems in the Psalter, relishing the repeated summons to praise and singing before God, verse 6 seems to fly from nowhere. The transition from "the high praises of God be in their throats" to "and two-edged swords in their hands" is jarring and unexpected. Of course there is a kind of preparation for this shift we can discern retrospectively. Having run into the unexpected in verse 6, we can see that the psalmist has tried to prepare us at the conclusion of verse 4 by speaking of God adorning "the humble with victory."

That is probably too little too late. Especially when we proceed past verse 6 and see the descriptions of what the two-edged swords will bring about: the execution of vengeance on the nations, punishment on the peoples (v. 7), the binding of kings with fetters and their nobles with chains of iron (v. 8). What is ironic is the fact that in the preceding Psalm 148, kings and nobles are arrayed with ordinary people as part of the universal choir that sings praises to God. In this psalm, though, they have quickly become the power to be overthrown as an act of praise to God.

Pastoral Perspective

All Saints' Day can feel like the morning after. With Halloween just behind us, our culture has again indulged in its sugary shudder of nervous laughter at death, whistling past the graveyard and trying much too hard to domesticate deep mysteries; making light of what we do not understand and treating as child's play what we cannot control.

In a more subdued and substantive way All Saints' Day affords us the opportunity to give thanks to God for all the faithful who have gone before us. We utilize the poetry of our faith to talk about the "great cloud of witnesses" who now, "changed from glory into glory," dwell upon "another shore and in a greater light." In some congregations there is a reading of the roll of those who have died during the previous year, sometimes accompanied by the tolling of a bell for each of the departed. It is a somber and solemn occasion that is somehow also filled with joy, offering us a very different view of life and death.

In congregations of the United Church of Christ I have served over the years we have read the following prayer each All Saints' Day, altered through many revisions from a prayer that originated with the Reverend Roger Manners, whose long and loving pastorate in Branford, Connecticut, spanned nearly thirty years:

All Saints

Exegetical Perspective

With a spirit of robust exuberance, the psalmist calls God's people to sing praise with song (vv. 1–4) and sword (vv. 5–9). The phrase "Praise the LORD" in verses 1 and 9, known as an inclusio in biblical Hebrew poetry, sets the tone for the entire psalm and draws it to a joyous close. Seven times, the people are invited to praise God (vv. 1a, 1b, 2, 3, 5, 6, 9b). Central to the psalm is the "faithful (ones)," mentioned at the beginning (v. 1), the middle (v. 5), and the end (v. 9) of the psalm. This poem is a hymn sung in acknowledgment of the God who is "Lord of creation" and "Lord of history." The psalm celebrates God's kingship and sovereignty.

The psalmist begins the hymn with four exhortations to rejoice (vv. 1–4). The call to "praise the LORD" occurs elsewhere in the psalms (e.g., 104:35; 106:1, 48), most notably in the last five psalms of the Psalter, all of which begin and end with "praise the LORD." The faithful are to praise God with a new song (v. 1b; cf. Pss. 33:3; 40:3; 96:1; 98:1; Isa. 42:10). This "new song" is not to be a new hymn with new words but, rather, a new hymn that finds its expression through their lives that joyously tell of, attest to, and embody God's salvation and glory. Hence, the people are not only to *sing* God's praise but also to *be* God's praise. This new song is to be sung "in the

Homiletical Perspective

About ten years ago a group of deep-pocketed fundamentalists spent thousands of dollars on demographic research, trying to determine where in Chicago to plant a church. They decided on the neighborhood I served, launched a church four blocks from the facilities of the church I served, and immediately started bombarding the community with slick advertisements promoting their in-church coffeehouse and their version of fidelity to Scripture.

In an effort to distinguish ourselves from our new neighbors, I changed our church's sign. I took down a bake sale advertisement and put up a quote I have heard attributed to Karl Barth: "We take the Bible too seriously to read it literally." One week after our church had put up our announcement, our neighbors unveiled their new sign. It read, "We take the Bible too seriously to NOT read it literally."

I saw their response, danced back to the church office, and gleefully pulled out the box of letters. I had finished spelling out "hypocrites," and just as I was reaching for the *t* in "fascist," I remembered that Jesus calls us to turn the other cheek. My exultation faded quickly.

There is something intoxicating about religious certainty. It fuels great worship. It made me run four blocks down a busy city street. It helped the psalmist

Psalm 149

Theological Perspective

Theological whiplash should doubtless encourage us to pause and ask questions. Perhaps especially in the light of Christian crusades and Muslim jihads, we do well to ask where the trajectory of this psalm may be taking us, and whether we want to go where it appears to be leading. At its most literal level, Psalm 149 does seem to advocate armed conflict in the name of God. Indeed, the warriors are human agents authorized to execute the judgment of God (v. 9). There are more cases than Christians will wish to recall where this text, or its next of kin, have caused faithful people to try to force the coming of God's kingdom in a manner that resulted in "cruel disaster." Caspar Scloppius used this very psalm to inflame Roman Catholic princes in the Thirty Years' religious war, while Thomas Müntzer used the same means to stir up the War of the Peasants.[1]

So this psalm appears to be one that has to be approached by Christians with the aid of the hermeneutical rule that stresses the centrality of Christ. Such an interpretive approach will juxtapose Psalm 149 to the command of Jesus to his disciple to put away his sword when it had been drawn to protect Jesus from the mob (Matt. 26:51–52). As a consequence, there is a theological-ethical transformation that needs to be employed as we decide how to use this psalm. It will begin with the assumption that in Jesus we see in a new way the power of God to inaugurate the divine reign—not in the power of aggressive warfare, but rather in the power of persistent love; not in wielding a two-edged sword in praise of God, but in wearing the helmet of salvation and wielding the sword of the Spirit (Eph. 6:10–17).

Notwithstanding this interpretive approach to Psalm 149, we also need to be mindful that this psalm does rightly recognize and acknowledge that faithfulness is lived out in a world in which there is genuine conflict between God's reign and the reign of nations, rulers, and other powers. True praise of God does involve standing over against that which resists God's reign, challenging the resistance with persistent love. So we can expect to need at least the sword of Christ's Spirit for the faithfulness to which we are called.

The liturgical context for this psalm is worthy of comment. Psalm 149 is among the readings for All Saints' Day. There is no more pervasive threat to the reign of God than death itself. Death—whether considered in terms of one's personal destiny or in terms

Pastoral Perspective

O God, before whom the generations rise and pass away: we rejoice today in the Communion of Saints, in the remembrance of friends and loved ones who once walked with us in mutual love. We are thankful for every precious memory of their goodness, and sustained by contributions each made to our common life. Our faith that Christ lives brings us the assurance that we are not separate in your boundless mercy. Renew us all in faith, hope, and love; that we may share more deeply the fullness of life with you that is not limited by time, or space, or weakness of any kind. In Christ's name we pray. Amen.

This is a meaningful and comforting tradition that our congregation welcomes each year, but Psalm 149 suggests that a new understanding and another step might be even more appropriate.

Psalm 149 is difficult for interpreters because it seems to take an unexpected turn at verse 6. It resounds at first with comfortable and familiar-sounding imagery, exhorting the faithful to sing a new song to God, to rejoice that God is king, to praise God with dancing and music. It even suggests that God delights in such praise, taking pleasure in the people and lifting up the lowly: "[God] adorns the humble with victory" (v. 4). Since Psalm 149 is the next to last psalm, this note of lofty praise seems a wonderful way to round out the Psalter. Then along comes this jolting imagery: "Let the high praises of God be in their throats and two-edged swords in their hands" (v. 6). Suddenly we are moving from music to mayhem, from victory to vengeance, from celebration to slaughter. What happened here?

Scholars such as J. Clinton McCann sense in this psalm the culmination of a movement that took place after the exile, when the prerogatives and responsibilities of the line of kings descended from David were transferred to the people as a whole. Whereas previously the king had been responsible for executing justice according to God's commands, that responsibility now fell to the whole people of God; hence the appropriateness of this psalm for All Saints' Day.

The problem remains that language calling for "vengeance on the nations" and "punishment on the peoples" (v. 7) sounds bloodthirsty and vindictive. McCann suggests that verse 9a, "to execute on them the judgment decreed," could as well be translated, "to enact among them the justice that is written."[1] Thus the vocation of the faithful becomes the

---

1. James Luther Mays, *Psalms*, Interpretation series (Louisville, KY: John Knox Press, 1994), 449.

1. J. Clinton McCann Jr., "The Book of Psalms," in *The New Interpreter's Bible* (Nashville: Abingdon Press, 1996), 4:1276.

All Saints

assembly of the faithful" (v. 1), most especially when the community is gathered in the temple.

In verse 2 the cultic names for God come to the fore. God is the "Maker," the creator of all, and of Israel especially (cf. Ps. 100:3; Isa. 44:2; 51:13). This God is also the "King" of the "children of Zion," the Israelites (cf. Pss. 5:2; 44:4; 47:6; 68:24; 84:3; 89:18). The people's praise is to be accompanied with dancing and the music of instruments, namely, the tambourine and the lyre (v. 3).

The scene is reminiscent of Exodus 15:20–21, where Miriam and all the women danced and sang with tambourines after crossing the Red Sea. Dancing, a form of praise, was not an uncommon cultic activity (2 Sam. 6:21–23; 1 Chr. 13:8). Tambourines are part of jubilant occasions and celebrations (Gen. 31:27; 1 Sam. 10:5; Job 21:12; Ps. 68:25; Jer. 31:4). Also known as a timbrel, the tambourine was probably a small hand drum that had bells or small pieces of metal around it. The lyre was a triangular instrument that had a sounding box with three to twelve strings, was played with either fingers or a plectrum, and was used for festive occasions (Gen. 31:27; Job 21:12), for praise (Pss. 33:2; 71:22; 81:2; 92:3; 147:7), in public worship (Ps. 98:5). The lyre served also to induce ecstatic prophecy (1 Sam. 10:5; 1 Chr. 25:1). David is said to have played the lyre to relieve Saul of his evil spirit (1 Sam. 16:14–23).

Verse 4 provides the reason why the faithful should make merry before God: Israel's God has taken pleasure in the people and has adorned the humble with victory. As in the days of old (see Exod. 15), Israel, with the help of God, has defeated its enemies. Similarly, God gave victory to David in battle (2 Sam. 8:6, 14). For Israel, God is a victorious warrior God who fights with them and for them. Hence, Israel's salvation is from God and has not been achieved by the people's own strength (2 Sam. 23:10, 12; Pss. 20:5; 48:10; 60:5; 98:1–3; 118:15; 144:10).

The second half of the psalm begins with a double exhortation (vv. 5–6), parallel in form to verses 2–3 but different in content. Here the focus is on praising God, accompanied by brandishing swords instead of melodies accompanied by dancing and musical instruments. In verse 5 the psalmist invites the faithful to "exult in glory." In the OT, "glory" connotes honor, splendor, beauty, magnificence, radiance, and even might (2 Kgs. 14:10) and strength (Prov. 20:29). In Psalm 29, the song of the thunderstorm, God brandishes glory just as a soldier would brandish a sword. Thus the psalmist seems to be calling the faithful to celebrate their God-given strength and

and his people praise God with dancing and tambourines, new songs and ancient glory. With God at our side, anything is possible.

Such certainty can also be a terrible problem—for anyone living after 9/11 also knows that there can be something awful about religious certainty. It can be inseparable from religious violence. This is a claim the war in Iraq proved true. Members of Al-Qaeda found fuel for their attacks in their religious certitude. In response, United States leaders justified an attack on Iraq with an equal amount of religious conviction. In his 2004 State of the Union address, President Bush said, "I believe that God has planted in every human heart the desire to live in freedom." Convinced that God prefers democracy, we went to war in order to expand its sway.

The presumption that God is on our side when we seek revenge is crystallized in verses 6–9 of Psalm 149. In particular, verse 6 begs to be wrestled with: "Let the high praise of God be in their throats and two-edged swords in their hands." I suspect that even churchgoers who are reluctant to explore the ways in which American power and the will of God diverge will be unnerved by the psalm's easy embrace of religious violence.

Oftentimes, when preaching from the Hebrew Bible, the preacher's first challenge is to overcome the great distance between ancient Israel and contemporary America. The practices and beliefs of the psalmist and his people can feel exotic, premodern, and very odd. In the case of Psalm 149, it could be interesting to sit with that distance, to judge ancient Israel for its violent tendencies, to ask whether God really wants to be praised by swinging two-edged swords. A preacher might first exploit our desire to hold the Old Testament at a distance before quickly and powerfully illustrating the fact we too are able to do the unthinkable when we believe that God is on our side.

Of course this move requires a preacher to preach against the psalm rather than alongside or beneath it. But Psalm 149 leaves us no other option. When making this move, it might be helpful to suggest that it is necessary to preach *against* certain portions of Scripture in order to preach *with* the main thrust of the Bible. If we want to take seriously Christ's revelation of God's character, we must reckon with the nonviolent God he discloses on the cross. Rather than triumphing over his enemies by repaying evil for evil, Jesus defeats them by turning the other cheek. This truth sits at the heart of the gospel.

Consider life as a long road trip. You do not have your CD collection or your iPod, just a broken car

Psalm 149

Theological Perspective

of the fate of all things living—calls into question whether God will finally take pleasure in God's people, adorning the humble with victory (v. 4). All Saints' Day marks the Christian calendar with a reminder that the question can never be suppressed. However, it also marks the Christian calendar with the reminder that the question is faithfully answered. All Saints' Day is the day when Christians remember those who have died, in the confidence that their lives are enfolded in the life of God.

While we earlier suggested that the reference in verse 4 to adorning the humble with victory might be a precursor to the vengeful tone of what follows in the psalm, the interpretation offered in the foregoing returns us to verse 4 with a new perspective. The "humble" may now be considered as those who live by persistent love, knowing that when they do so, the forces of the world may indeed destroy them; but the "victory" God promises is the victory of All Saints' Day, the celebration that both the living and the dead abide in God's gracious communion, world without end.

Thus, while we rightly shy away from the temptation the psalm offers to consider ourselves the unalloyed agents of God's vengeance and judgment among peoples and nations, we can be emboldened by this psalm in its broader scriptural context. We can be emboldened to face fearlessly the reality of powers that question the reality of God's reign for creation's well-being, standing with the sword of Christ's Spirit against political, personal, and spiritual threats. If on All Saints' Day we are faced once again with the power of death over the reign of God, our act of praise to the living God will be itself a testimony to the power of God's reign.

D. CAMERON MURCHISON

Pastoral Perspective

expression of praise *and* the enactment of justice. The two are inextricably bound together.

As we sometimes observe it, All Saints' Day tends toward the sentimental. We certainly fall short of dancing or making melody with the tambourine and lyre. We also fall short of renewing our sense of the vocation of all God's people, all the saints, to enact justice. Perhaps we fall short on both praise and justice because the two can never truly be separated; either without the other is incomplete.

Many years ago I attended a gathering of Christians for Justice Action at which William Sloane Coffin Jr., renowned pastor, pundit, and social activist, was to receive an award. The event was a dinner sandwiched between sessions of the General Synod of the United Church of Christ. I went expecting prophetically pointed rhetoric and solemn (if not grim) admonitions to self-sacrifice and political agitation, but the gathering began with the singing of gospel songs. Coffin sat at the piano and pounded them out, one after another, until the place fairly rocked with "songs and hymns and spiritual songs" that one might never have expected to hear from a room full of left-leaning activists! "Amazing Grace" was truly amazing. "Leaning on the Everlasting Arms" had the faithful throwing their heads back and singing with all their might. "There Is a Balm in Gilead" reminded us that the work of justice not only addresses social conditions but also has everything to do with healing sin-sick souls. For a time I was waiting somewhat impatiently for the meeting to begin. Soon enough I caught on that we were already in the heart of it.

Singing to God a "new song" that tells the old, old story goes hand in hand with "enacting the justice that is written." Psalm 149 invites us to elevate All Saints' Day to a rediscovery of the relationship between joy and justice in the life of faith. "This is glory for all [God's] faithful ones" (v. 9). No wonder "the LORD takes pleasure in [the] people" and their songs of praise, even as God "adorns the humble with victory" (v. 4).

DAVID R. RUHE

All Saints

Exegetical Perspective

might, and to "sing for joy on their couches," which mostly likely means their prayer mats.

Having called the faithful to "exult in glory" and "sing for joy," the psalmist now hopes that the high praises of God will be in their throats and two-edged swords in their hands (v. 6). This type of sword had a sharp point designed to penetrate and not slash an enemy. This blow was often more lethal. Those carrying swords in verses 5–9 are to use these weapons against their opponents from other nations. These verses depict Israel as jubilant warriors of God and recall earlier holy-war traditions (Num. 21:21–35; Deut. 2:26–3:7; Joshua 6; 2 Chr. 20:20–30). These verses could be anticipating future victory over enemy nations—their general populace and their leadership.

Those carrying two-edged swords will execute both vengeance on their enemies and the "judgment decreed" (v. 9). In other texts, biblical writers depict God as the one who rules Israel and the world by means of decrees (Deut. 4:45; Job 28:26; Ps. 78:5, 56; Jer. 19:5). The judgment decree that the faithful will execute is God's judgment, namely, deserved punishment for either wickedness or oppression (Pss. 9:17; 68:6; 76:10; 103:6; 135:14).

A parallel to this decree would be "the Day of the Lord" heard throughout the prophets (e.g., Amos 5:18–20). In the last line of verse 9, the psalmist declares that all these warring deeds that the faithful will perform is "glory" for all of them (v. 9ab), for which all should "Praise the LORD!" (v. 9c). Thus, this psalm, reflective of the events of its time and culture, calls the faithful to rejoice in a saving God who will make them victorious in battle. Such victory will attest to God as the King of glory (Ps. 24:7–10) and make the faithful glorious too.

CAROL J. DEMPSEY

Homiletical Perspective

radio. Rush Limbaugh does not come through. Neither does National Public Radio. Instead, the only station you can find is playing the most amazing piece of music you have ever heard. It soars, it ebbs, it reaches crescendos that make you want to floor the pedal and race through the beauty. It affirms you. It convicts you. It makes sense of existence. But your radio is broken. While the music is occasionally clear, there are interludes of ugly grating static. Much of the time you hear both at once: this wonderful piece of music, and hiss and fuzz of a broken receiver.

Consider the stories of Israel and Jesus as this piece of music. The piece is composed by God. Consider the authors of the Bible our broken radio. Sometimes they give us the story in its pure form. Other times God's beauty is hidden in the static of ancient politics or prejudice. Sometimes, as is the case with the last four unfortunate verses of Psalm 149, the signal is lost altogether. All we get is an ugly hiss.

The questions before us are these: Are we going to listen to the Bible carefully, straining to hear the gorgeous music of a nonviolent Lamb who conquers by giving his life for all people? Are we going to listen indiscriminately, confusing the static of ancient nationalism for the symphony itself? I suspect that in most mainline churches these questions may find easy answers and prompt any number of fairly bland sermons. However, things could get quite interesting if we were to consider that the discomfort we feel when witnessing ancient Israel conflate its violent means with divine ends could be put to more appropriate use by exploring the intersection of American violence and the peace of Christ.

MATTHEW FITZGERALD

Ephesians 1:11-23

[11]In Christ we have also obtained an inheritance, having been destined according to the purpose of him who accomplishes all things according to his counsel and will, [12]so that we, who were the first to set our hope on Christ, might live for the praise of his glory. [13]In him you also, when you had heard the word of truth, the gospel of your salvation, and had believed in him, were marked with the seal of the promised Holy Spirit; [14]this is the pledge of our inheritance toward redemption as God's own people, to the praise of his glory.

[15]I have heard of your faith in the Lord Jesus and your love toward all the saints, and for this reason [16]I do not cease to give thanks for you as I remember you in my prayers. [17]I pray that the God of our Lord Jesus Christ, the Father of glory, may give you a spirit of wisdom and revelation as you come to know him,

Theological Perspective

From a literary perspective, the lectionary reading begins somewhat oddly with verse 11, since verses 11–14 round off the extended and extraordinary blessing of God with which this letter begins and verses 15–23 comprise Paul's prayer for the believers at Ephesus. However, in Greek rhetoric, in which this author[1] is obviously well-versed, a section commonly known as a hinge section can function with a dual capacity to finish off one topic and lead into the next. For that reason, we will give the lectionary the benefit of the doubt and understand verses 11–14 as leading into, if not introducing, the prayer in verses 15–23.

Those who come to this text from a Reformed tradition may well focus on the words "destined" and appointed in verse 11 as the theological center of this passage. From a free church theological perspective, what emerges foremost in verses 11–14 is the divine-human partnership that fulfills the purposes of God. There are two sides to this equation that results in the unity of all things in Christ (v. 10). God is the one who accomplishes everything according to the divine will. God is the one who destines and

1. That Paul is the author of Ephesians is in doubt. For the sake of this essay, however, that distinction is not sufficiently pertinent to warrant pedantic use of "the author." The references to Paul should not be understood as taking the position that the historical Paul is the author.

Pastoral Perspective

Most communities of faith that mark All Saints' Day focus their attention on remembering those in the church who have died in the previous year. Such celebrations can provide comfort to those who are still in mourning by reminding them that, in spirit, their loved ones are still present, particularly in the context of Christian worship. The passage at hand offers a reminder that, by broadening the concepts of "saint" and "inheritance," this especially holy day can take on even greater significance, not just to those who mourn, but to those who seek the deeper and broader form of community Christ offers.

In the 350-year-old church of which I am a member, the resident historian (a teacher in the local high school) asks those in the congregation to close their eyes on All Saints' Day and picture generations flowing through the church. He describes what members in different eras might have been wearing, with whom they might have been worshiping, even how they might have been staying warm during long New England winters in an unheated sanctuary. When he calls on those in the congregation to consider how their lives are linked with those of the past, invariably several in the unusually stoic Congregational community are moved to tears as they feel the impact of this broad, new concept of church.

¹⁸so that, with the eyes of your heart enlightened, you may know what is the hope to which he has called you, what are the riches of his glorious inheritance among the saints, ¹⁹and what is the immeasurable greatness of his power for us who believe, according to the working of his great power. ²⁰God put this power to work in Christ when he raised him from the dead and seated him at his right hand in the heavenly places, ²¹far above all rule and authority and power and dominion, and above every name that is named, not only in this age but also in the age to come. ²²And he has put all things under his feet and has made him the head over all things for the church, ²³which is his body, the fullness of him who fills all in all.

Exegetical Perspective

"Praise the Lord, saints."

"Hallelujah."

That was the usual Sunday morning greeting and response, not only at the church we were attending that Sunday, but also at the church that I regularly attended. I could tell, however, that the call-and-response was unfamiliar to the person I had brought to church with me. After service, my friend asked me why everyone greeted each other as "saints." I had never been asked that question before, and was not really sure how to articulate a response. Like others in the service, I had used the word "saints" to address my brothers and sisters in the congregation. We who used the title knew what we meant, but it was difficult to explain the meaning to someone who understood the word "saint" as reserved for people honored and revered for their demonstrations of heroic virtue.

In the New Testament, "saints" (*hagioi*) is the most commonly used title for Christians. It literally means "holy ones," and was used to refer to Jesus-followers because they were considered consecrated to God by the atonement of Christ and the gift of the Holy Spirit (Eph. 1:11–14). As in most of the Pauline letters, Paul addressed the Ephesians as

Homiletical Perspective

This commanding declaration about faith and salvation at the outset of the Letter to the Ephesians underscores the place of the saints in God's purpose and plan. Some congregations will need reminding that in New Testament parlance all Christians are called "saints." Saints are both young and old, both living and departed; they are all who have responded affirmatively to God's call. The observance of All Saints affords an opportunity for the reminder, as well as an occasion to speak the names of those we have known as saints among us.

The Canadian preacher John Gladstone tells the story of a young English clergyman who served a small congregation. It was his custom at evening services to administer the sacrament of the Lord's Supper to any parishioners who remained at the conclusion of the service. One night so few stayed that he questioned whether the sacrament should be observed, but he decided to proceed. In the midst of the liturgy, he read part of the Great Prayer that says, "Therefore, with angels and archangels and all the company of heaven, we laud and magnify thy glorious name." He read it again, "With angels and archangels and all the company of heaven . . ." Then he prayed, "God forgive me. I did not realize I was in such company."[1] The Ephesians text

1. R. Maurice Boyd, *Corridors of Light* (Hamilton, ON, Colonsay House, 1991), 160.

Ephesians 1:11-23

Theological Perspective

appoints, but that destination and appointment are preceded by a human decision to hope rather than despair. God is the one who seals the covenant with humanity with the Holy Spirit, but human response is both necessary and the responsibility of each human being.

The church as Paul knows it is made up of those who chose to hope in Christ; who chose to hear the word of truth, who chose to believe. The result of that unique and powerful and entirely graceful partnership between Creator and created humanity is expressed in the praise of God's glory, as the author reminds us twice in this one short passage, in verses 12 and 14.

This perspective on the divine and human partnership, as we have noted, both brings the blessing of God with which Paul began the letter to a close and segues into the prayer for the Ephesians, which is his next concern. Paul's prayer here is what we commonly term an intercessory prayer. Again, there is a sense of give-and-take, because what compels Paul toward prayer on the Ephesians' behalf is his own awareness of their commitment to be faithful to God and to love the saints.

Certainly Catholic theology has given us a richer sense of saints above and saints below, a sense of the body of Christ reaching far and wide on both sides of the veil that separates us. Paul's prayer for the Ephesians is not a fully developed theology of the communion of the saints, but, especially on this All Saints' Day, let us note that it moves in that direction as he begins with the believers' experience face to face with one another and ends with a cosmic sense of the unity of the body of Christ in time and space.

The theological issue in this passage with which we struggle most is the nature of Christ's dominion over the powers. Paul's own decision not to submit to desperation is evident here; he does not wring his hands over the state of the world and equivocate, as we are apt to do. He declares in ringing tones that Jesus sits at God's right hand in the heavenly realm and that he reigns over every other rule or authority or power or dominion or name. That is a comprehensive list, to be sure.

Thomas Yoder Neufeld suggests that there are three common understandings of these powers: (1) these powers are personal, spiritual, demonic, supernatural; (2) the powers are political, systems of control that are not in themselves necessarily evil or good; (3) the powers language really addresses both supernatural and systemic entities. Yoder Neufeld opts for the third option, because the culture in

Pastoral Perspective

In his letter to the Ephesians (though his authorship is contested by some), Paul proposes a way in which God, through Christ, brings all who believe into unity. That unity takes two forms: unity in time, or in the present moment; and unity across time. J. D. G. Dunn writes, "Jesus himself is the 'place' in which the blessings of heaven and the Spirit are to be known in the here and now, so that the very term 'Christian' denotes a life (and death) bound up with his."[1]

Unity in Christ in Paul's present time came in the form of the eradication of divisions. During Paul's lifetime, the division of most crucial importance would have been between Jews and Gentiles. When Paul turns his attention to the church later in the letter, he does so because he sees the church as the living manifestation of unity in God, through Christ, thus rendering indispensable the unity of Christ's church and all members within it—whether originally Jew or Gentile.

Unity across time receives more attention in the passage, much as it does in the life of most churches around All Saints' Day. Paul writes that through Christ and in Christ believers inherit Christ's resurrection. Much like property passed from generation to generation—which is likely the way a Jewish audience would have received this teaching[2]—the resurrection has been handed down. One way in which Ephesians differs from other Pauline letters is in the absence of claims that Jesus will return; it offers instead the hope that "believers have already been 'saved' and resurrected with Christ."[3] Those who have died and those who are living are one in Christ, as those who have died have been raised, and those who are living are already marked for resurrection.

Upon reading this text closely, one can see that death is not in actuality the central theme. Its focus upon inheritance does not refer primarily to a gift from one who has died to those who are living. Rather, the central theme is unity in God, through Christ, and the broad inheritance to which those who are in Christ are entitled. An inherited resurrection is among the gifts, but the grand nature of the narrative suggests that it is just one of the riches Christ can impart to those who believe.

What are some of the pastoral themes that emerge from this passage and might be of use in the

1. J. D. G. Dunn, "Ephesians," in *The Oxford Bible Commentary*, ed. John Barton and John Muddiman (Oxford: Oxford University Press, 2001), 1168.
2. Ibid.
3. Victor Paul Furnish, "Epistle to the Ephesians," in *The Anchor Bible Dictionary*, ed. David Noel Freedman (New York: Doubleday, 1992), 540.

All Saints

"saints."[1] He informed them that they were all saints because, as he said, "[God] chose us in Christ before the foundation of the world to be holy and blameless" (v. 4). Paul conveyed to the Ephesians a strong belief that it was always God's purpose and plan that all believers—Jews and Gentiles—be numbered among the saints (1:5; 2:14–16). Paul wrote to his Gentile audience informing them that they had been appointed (lit., given a share) in Israel's inheritance (vv. 11, 14).

All Saints' Day (also known as All Hallows Day) is the day after All Hallows Eve (Halloween). Remembering saints and martyrs and dedicating a specific day to them each year has been a Christian tradition since the fourth century CE. In 837 CE, Pope Gregory IV designated November 1 as the day for Christians to remember all saints and martyrs throughout Christian history. Pope John Paul II declared that All Saints' Day "invites us to turn our gaze to the immense multitude of those who have already reached the blessed Homeland, pointing us to the road which leads to that destination."[2]

According to Paul, God has a plan, a "mystery" (vv. 8b–10), that has been active since the dawn of creation but is now being revealed and fulfilled in Christ. The mystery is a plan to gather up all things into one thing, really into one person, Christ. God is gathering all of creation into one harmonious unity in which all share in the divine life of Christ (v. 10). This oneness with all things in Christ is the Christian's inheritance (v. 11) to be accomplished "according to the good pleasure of [God's] will" (vv. 5, 9).

After informing the Ephesians of their blessed status in God, obtained through Christ and enabling them to live "for the praise of [God's] glory" (v. 12), and after identifying the Holy Spirit as the down payment that secured their salvation and "redemption as God's own people," Paul commended the Ephesians for their faith and for the love they demonstrated toward one another (vv. 11–16). Paul then prayed for spiritual wisdom and divine enlightenment, because he realized that the vast richness of God's love for God's people—identified as "the hope to which he has called you . . . the riches of his glorious inheritance among the saints, and . . . the immeasurable greatness of his power for us who

hints at such a gathering of saints and invites our probing in any of several ways.

Concerning the Church. Fundamentally, this passage has to do with the praise of Christ's glory, but the vehicle of Christ's glory in this world is the church. We see such glory in the lives of saints, ordinary people bequeathed the extraordinary grace of redemption (v. 14). There is no question that the church as we know it in its particular forms can sometimes make one wonder what God was thinking in entrusting the gift of salvation to such a beleaguered, befuddled, and often contentious lot. There are also times when the church claims its inheritance, when its capacity for grace and compassion and hope are so enlarged as to point to something far beyond the sum of its members. On All Saints, this text serves as a reminder of the cosmic dimension of the church and of the gift of salvation that forges its unity.

Concerning Hope. All Saints also affords an opportunity for reflection on those in all generations who have lived by hope and faith in God's promises. Many congregations on this day name aloud those who have died in faith in the year now past. It is for some a moment of grief revisited, the marking of painful losses; but it is at the same time a liturgy of gratitude, comfort, and encouragement, as the church draws strength from its memory and from the reminders of God's goodness.

The writer of the Ephesian letter prays for its hearers that their hearts may be enlightened, so that they may know the hope to which Christ calls them (v. 18). When we see only with our eyes or hear only with our ears, we may fail to claim the hope instilled in us. To see with the heart is to imagine the future God is preparing. As Christians we are shaped by more than our own experiences; we are shaped by our hopes, by the future into which we are living, and by the convictions by which we are living. Hope is best perceived with the eyes of the heart. Hope is best lived within the hopeful community, in the company of saints both living and departed.

An old Hasidic tale tells of a disciple who asked his rabbi the meaning of community one evening, when they were all sitting around a fire. The rabbi sat in silence while the fire died down to a pile of glowing coals. Then he got up and took one coal out from the pile and set it apart on the stone hearth. Its fire and warmth soon died out.[2] It is in the company

---

1. The majority of biblical scholars today consider Ephesians to have been written by a disciple of Paul in the name of Paul. Throughout this essay, I shall refer to the author as "Paul." I do so preserving the author's desire to attribute Pauline authorship to the correspondence without making a judgment about that authorship.

2. John Paul II, Angelus (November 1, 2003), http://www.vatican.va/holy_father/john_paul_ii/angelus/2003/documents/hf_jp-ii_ang_20031101_en.html.

2. Heidi B. Neumark, *Breathing Space: A Spiritual Journey in the South Bronx* (Boston: Beacon Press, 1994), 61.

Ephesians 1:11-23

Theological Perspective

which this text is embedded made no sharp distinctions between these different realities. All of life, in whatever sphere, was subject to the supernatural.[2]

The central point of Paul's prayer is as old as the biblical story itself. That God, and Jesus as God's Son, is above every power and therefore takes precedence over every other human attachment to any other power, reaches back theologically to the story of Adam and Eve and historically to Abraham and Sarah. Human resistance to that claim is also as old as the biblical story itself. Ultimate allegiance to God, yes—except when that allegiance interferes with what I perceive to be my own well-being. Ultimate allegiance to God, yes—except when that allegiance interferes with the sovereign right of the state.

The emerging nation of Israel struggled with the call to total allegiance, as did the emerging church. The radical trust in the God who holds the world in hand and heart, for which the biblical witness calls over and over, in every book in the canon, is in essence terrifying for our frail humanity. The paradox of power lies at the heart of the gospel. As Israel learned in the wilderness, and relearned in the exile; as Jesus learned in the wilderness, and relearned the night on Olivet before he was arrested, the victory of God rises from the dead—the way of relinquishment, the way of the cross.

Thus does Christ sit at the right hand of God in victory, and thus do the saints join him there confounding evil. It is an upside-down celebration of victory, a nonsensical win made possible only by the unfathomable love that wrests redemption out of the lowliest incarnation.

MARY H. SCHERTZ

Pastoral Perspective

consideration of All Saints' Day? First, this passage describes a relationship between the Christian and the church of the present moment with those across time. This can serve as a reminder that individual Christians and the church are each part of something greater than themselves, transcending time and space through Christ.

Ironically, the realization that individuals, beloved as they may be, are in a very real way *small* can be immensely comforting to a person who feels the weight of the world on his or her shoulders. The same weight can also be felt in church communities. In this passage, the church is depicted as an entity built on the foundation of prophets and apostles, rather than as an isolated organism. This sense that each church is a small part of something so much bigger than itself can help a community to feel both humble and supported; no one community is the be-all and end-all, and none should feel burdened as though they were on their own.

Second, one might take the further step of emphasizing connectedness with one another in Christ. Paul's message of unity was radical in its day, as it suggested unity across divisions that were woven into the fabric of daily life. This suggests that the early church understood overcoming divisions to be part of its mandate. This text thus could communicate to a congregation that locating and overcoming areas of division within the church and among churches was part of its duty from the earliest days. Being church means overcoming barriers.

The image of the cross takes on new significance when one considers the perspective on time and space proposed in Ephesians. The vertical beam suggests unity with God, above, and ancestors, below. The horizontal beam signifies unity with others in Christ, in the present. As the beams intersect, we recognize that the life in Christ is a life of unity that provides both continuity and community, both awe and humility.

SARAH BIRMINGHAM DRUMMOND

---

2. Thomas R. Yoder Neufeld, *Ephesians*, Believers Church Bible Commentary (Scottdale, PA: Herald Press, 2002), 76.

believe" (vv. 18–19)—goes beyond anything the natural mind can understand. Truly understanding the richness of God's love requires some sort of visionary moment or ecstatic experience bringing humans into an existential awareness of the love of God active in the world. The knowledge of God that Paul desired for the Ephesians was not merely knowledge of facts gained through human teachings but experiential knowledge gained through divine revelation.

Paul's prayer in this section clearly connects with the prayer that comes later in the letter, where the author prays that the Ephesians might "have the power to comprehend, with all the saints" what cannot be known: "the breadth and length and height and depth . . . [of] the love of Christ that surpasses knowledge" (3:18–19). For Paul, knowing and being filled by the incomprehensible love of God is the very definition of what it means to have the "eyes of your heart enlightened [that] you may know what is the hope to which he has called you" (1:18). This enlightenment enabled the Ephesians to recognize God's power, working out the divine mystery, so decisively moved forward by Christ's resurrection (vv. 19–20).

According to Paul, Christ has been granted power and authority over all oppressive forces—present and future, terrestrial and celestial—that obscure and resist the fulfillment of God's mysterious plan (vv. 21–22).[3] For Paul, ultimate power is grounded not in rulers and authorities (v. 21) but in God. Christ's authority is evident in the church, of which Christ is the head and which shares in the fullness of salvation already, even as that fullness is being fulfilled (vv. 13–14, 23).

While the church gratefully acknowledges the authority of Christ in the life of the church and praises God for the power and love of God—manifested through Jesus the Christ—that sets Christians free from oppressive powers, the church must be careful to avoid Christian triumphalism. Such triumphalism may promote the authority and superiority of Christianity and Jesus over all other religions and religious figures and cause Christianity to become for others the same as the oppressive powers from which God through Jesus liberates Christians.

GUY D. NAVE JR.

of saints that we find our life and vitality as we seek to live as faithful bearers of the inheritance we have received. In such company we find comfort in our losses, courage for the daily struggles, and hope as we face the future together.

Concerning Power. The concluding verses of the text underscore the power available to those who believe. They point not to the kinds of power the world so often wields, but to the "immeasurable greatness" of Christ's power, which is "far above all rule and authority and power and dominion" (1:19–21). The language here is apocalyptic, for there is a battle at hand. Preachers may tend to overplay or underplay the dimensions of the struggle, but there is no avoiding the struggle itself.

In the reading of the All Saints necrology, one might well add the names of those who have died as martyrs for their faith. The preacher could take the occasion to remind hearers that the world is ruled by powers hostile to the redemptive power of love and forgiveness, and thus hostile to Christ and to Christ's community of saints, the church. Before the foundations of the world, says Ephesians, God chose saints to be agents of divine power in the struggle. Such election has continued to this day.

We may protest that we are not up to the task, that we lack the courage and the strength necessary to live faithfully in such tumultuous times. To such protests the Ephesian letter serves as a reminder of whose power is at work in the life and witness of the church. Theologian and ethicist Stanley Hauerwas argues that Christians cannot try to become saints. Nor, he says, are saints heroes and heroines of faith. Instead, they are "people like us who have been made more than we are by being engrafted into God's kingdom that is ruled by forgiveness and love."[3]

ROBERT E. DUNHAM

---

3. The authority attributed here to Jesus is an allusion to Pss. 110:1 and 8:6.

3. Stanley Hauerwas, *Unleashing the Scriptures: Freeing the Bible from Captivity to America* (Nashville: Abingdon Press, 1993), 101, 102.

Luke 6:20-31

20 Then he looked up at his disciples and said:
"Blessed are you who are poor,
    for yours is the kingdom of God.
21"Blessed are you who are hungry now,
    for you will be filled.
"Blessed are you who weep now,
    for you will laugh.

22 "Blessed are you when people hate you, and when they exclude you, revile you, and defame you on account of the Son of Man. 23Rejoice in that day and leap for joy, for surely your reward is great in heaven; for that is what their ancestors did to the prophets.

Theological Perspective

This powerful and simply profound passage from the Gospel according to Luke provides tremendous encouragement for all the saints of Jesus Christ to live out their faith in the midst of difficult circumstances. The structure of the passage is four blessings contrasted with four woes that all serve the purpose of encouraging believers to look heavenward during trials and tribulation (cf. Dan. 7:1–3, 15–18). This encouragement is grounded in the life, ministry, and exaltation of Jesus Christ, who provides for us a great hope and an eternal inheritance (cf. Eph. 1:11–23).

The apostles were able to find joy in suffering on account of Jesus and the gospel. Paul wrote, "I want to know Christ and the power of his resurrection and the sharing of his sufferings by becoming like him in his death" (Phil. 3:10). Followers of Jesus can expect to share not only in his ministry but also in his suffering. This theology of suffering simply means that there is eternal meaning in our enduring difficult circumstances for the sake of the kingdom of God. This is the fundamental nature of the first four blessings. To this point, the passage functions to encourage and challenge us not to shrug off being poor, hungry, mournful, or despised because we understand that we have a future inheritance in Christ.

Though we may suffer now, Jesus says, there will come a time in the future when we will be blessed

Pastoral Perspective

In the Gospels, Jesus turns things upside down time and time again. In God's rule, the order of things will be reversed: "All who exalt themselves will be humbled, but all who humble themselves will be exalted" (Luke 18:14). Today's passage from Luke 6 drives home the topsy-turvy good news: "Are you weeping? You are blessed because you will laugh. Do people hate, exclude, and revile you on account of the Son of Man? Jump for joy, for your reward is great in heaven; their grandparents hated and excluded the prophets too" (my paraphrase of vv. 21–23, hereafter by verse). The poor and the hungry are called blessed, for their fortunes will be reversed as well. Good news indeed—if you are poor, hungry, weeping, or excluded for God's sake, but what of us who sit with bellies full, big smiles on our faces, at the nicest seats at the most exclusive restaurants? Good news? Not so much.

The four blessings of verses 20–24 are matched point by point with "woe to you" statements. One might even call them curses, although it seems odd to put a curse in the mouth of the Lord of love. The rich, the full, the laughing, and the well regarded: all of your fortunes will be reversed, he says. If people in the pews (or at least the pews in many of America's congregations) are not squirming a bit when they hear these words, then they are not listening.

All Saints

²⁴"But woe to you who are rich,
    for you have received your consolation.
²⁵"Woe to you who are full now,
    for you will be hungry.
"Woe to you who are laughing now,
    for you will mourn and weep.

²⁶"Woe to you when all speak well of you, for that is what their ancestors did to the false prophets. ²⁷"But I say to you that listen, Love your enemies, do good to those who hate you, ²⁸bless those who curse you, pray for those who abuse you. ²⁹If anyone strikes you on the cheek, offer the other also; and from anyone who takes away your coat do not withhold even your shirt. ³⁰Give to everyone who begs from you; and if anyone takes away your goods, do not ask for them again. ³¹Do to others as you would have them do to you."

Exegetical Perspective

If there is any part of the Gospel tradition almost universally known in Western culture, it is surely the Beatitudes. Many people who never darken the door of a church know, "Blessed are the poor in spirit. . . . Blessed are the meek. . . . Blessed are the peacemakers" (Matt. 5:3, 5, 9). The Beatitudes we know best are generally the nine that begin Matthew's Sermon on the Mount, however, and almost never the four in Luke's Sermon on the Plain (6:17–49).

Matthew's Beatitudes are also more popular because in Luke Jesus' blessings are mixed, and not so comforting in their starkness and directness. "Blessed are you who are poor. . . . Blessed are you who are hungry. . . . Blessed are you who weep. . . . Blessed are you when people hate you" (vv. 20–22). Most disquieting of all is that each of Luke's Beatitudes has a corresponding woe: "Woe to you who are rich. . . . Woe to you who are full. . . . Woe to you who are laughing. . . . Woe to you when all speak well of you" (vv. 24–26). Matthew puts his woes toward the end of his Gospel, and directs them against the hypocrites (Matt. 23:13–36); Luke puts the bad news right next to the good news and directs both, not just to the crowds who follow Jesus, but specifically to the disciples (Luke 6:17), that is, to the church.

What does Luke's Jesus mean when he says, "Blessed are you who are poor"? We think of the

Homiletical Perspective

In traditions that observe All Saints' Day, the liturgy itself, with its thanksgiving and remembrance of the saints of the church, often takes center stage. The naming of the saints is often for communities a cherished ritual and an important personalization of the doctrine of the communion of saints and the continuity of the church beyond the boundaries of death. The sermon can be an important element in that service, especially as it addresses some of the themes found in the Gospel reading in the Beatitudes of the Gospel of Luke, where they form the centerpiece of what is sometimes called the Sermon on the Plain.

The Gospel for All Saints' Day lays out the characteristics of the blessed—the "saints"—alongside the characteristics of the lost, over whom the cry of "woe" rings out. All Saints' Day is an important occasion for remembering and celebrating the blessed of the church's story, both ancient and contemporary, those known to us only by legend and history, as well as those known to us in this life. However, Luke's account of the Beatitudes does not let us rest there, rejoicing in the lives and witness of the saints, but also calls to mind the dangers on the other side of blessedness. Here is where the sermon can make its most important contribution to the liturgical event of All Saints' Day: by reminding the

Luke 6:20-31

<table>
<tr><td>

Theological Perspective

for forgoing the comforts of this life and suffering for the sake of the gospel. There will be an eschatological new life where we will be filled, laugh, enjoy the riches of the kingdom, and experience joy and happiness (cf. Rev 21:2–4). As believers in Christ we are caught between the now and the not yet, between sanctification and glorification. Notice how the blessings admonish us to hold on to the Son of Man indefatigably in this present life, so that we will experience the glory of God in the future (Rom. 8:30).

Sanctification is the theological concept that— through the work of Christ and the Holy Spirit—we are becoming more and more like Christ through faithful obedience (cf. 1 Pet. 1:2). This is not something that happens because of our own power or strength; rather, it is the work of Christ and the Spirit in and through us. Empathically, the four blessings are for Christ's disciples because for Christ they are the ones who live out what it means to be poor, hungry, grief-stricken, and abhorred. We share in his life and ministry by virtue of our baptism into him (Rom. 6:4). Therefore we may expect to experience life *with* Christ. Christ was poor, Christ was hungry, Christ wept, and so shall we. That, however, is not the end of the story.

We are being sanctified unto Christ until our time has come; then we will enter his glory and experience glorification through him (Luke 24:26; 2 Thess. 1:10–12). Glorification is the event in which all the saints who have died in Christ—whose lives are hidden with him—will experience the resurrection of the body at the Parousia (Christ's second coming). "When Christ who is your life is revealed, then you also will be revealed with him in glory" (Col. 3:4). The Apostles' Creed informs us that on that day we will be in communion with all the saints and our bodies will be resurrected like Christ's. In the epistle for All Saints' Day, Ephesians 1:11–23, we are taught that those who are in Christ should live for the "praise of his glory," because we have a pledged eternal inheritance.

Christ's admonishment to each of us about our future glorification is an eternal encouragement like him to endure difficulties, while living in the body. Paul wrote the Corinthian church, reminding them that God's grace was sufficient to sustain them because God's strength is manifest in our weakness (2 Cor. 12:9–10). He went on to persuade the church to endure hardships, insults, and all kinds of calamities for the sake of the gospel, because God chose "what is weak in the world to shame the strong" (1 Cor. 1:27). Christ summarized this thought well

</td><td>

Pastoral Perspective

Of course, it is easy to dismiss the Beatitudes as the vehicle they have sometimes become: a way to placate the oppressed with the promise that injustice now is part of God's plan to redeem them through suffering. In 1911, labor activist Joe Hill wrote parody lyrics to the tune "Sweet By and By." Entitled "The Preacher and the Slave," most people know it as "Pie in the Sky." Hill mocks the tendency of preachers to tell slaves (or anyone who is downtrodden) to work hard and not to complain because their reward is in heaven:

> Long-haired preachers come out every night,
> Try to tell you what's wrong and what's right;
> But when asked how 'bout something to eat
> They will answer with voices so sweet:
> You will eat, by and by,
> In that glorious land above the sky;
> Work and pray, live on hay,
> You'll get pie in the sky when you die.[1]

The irony is that Hill probably came closer to living out the Beatitudes than many a preacher then and now. He certainly went hungry more than a time or two. Perhaps he wept for the plight of others, if not for his own. As a union activist, there can be no doubt that people hated, excluded, reviled, and defamed him, "for that is what their ancestors did to the prophets" (v. 23b). You can be the judge of whether or not their response was on account of the Son of Man.

Preachers might be in danger of falling into the "pie in the sky" trap if they preach only on verses 20–23 or if they preach on the Sermon on the Mount in Matthew's Gospel. It is easier to twist Jesus' words in Matthew, where there are nine beatitudes and no woes and where the blessings are far more "spiritual" virtues. Any preacher who reads and takes seriously the entire lectionary passage cannot maneuver around the voice for the oppressed that shouts through the ages from Luke's Gospel—the gospel where shepherds rather than kings greet the promised Messiah.

If hearers are still sitting in stunned silence and convicted hearts after verses 20–26, Jesus lays lofty expectations on those who would be his disciples. "Love your enemies, do good to those who hate you. . . . If anyone strikes you on the cheek, offer the other also. . . . Do to others as you would have them do to you" (vv. 27b, 29, 31). Here is more bad news for any of us who live in the real world. No wonder

</td></tr>
</table>

---

1. Joe Hill, "The Preacher and the Slave," *Songs to Fan the Flame of Discontent: The Little Red Songbook* (Columbia, SC: Harbinger Publications, 1995), 39.

Exegetical Perspective

people who line up at soup kitchens for dinner because they cannot afford to go to the grocery store, and they do not look all that blessed or happy. Surely Matthew must be right, that it is not the poor but the poor in spirit who are blessed by God. Surely Matthew must be right that it is the poor in spirit, the meek, and the peacemakers who are blessed—not the poor, the hungry, the sad, and the hated.

Luke's Jesus does not say what Matthew's Jesus says, however. By the time we get to Luke 6, it is already clear that in Jesus God makes special claims for the poor, the hungry, the sad, and the outcast. Before Jesus is born, his mother praises God for vindicating the poor (1:50–53); Jesus' first sermon takes its text from Isaiah 61 to say he has been anointed "to bring good news to the poor, . . . to proclaim release to the captives and recovery of sight to the blind, to let the oppressed go free, to proclaim the year of the Lord's favor" (4:18–19).

To be blessed is to have a special place in God's heart, not merely to be happy. If you want anything to do with Jesus or the God who sent him, Luke says, you had better go find the poor, the hungry, the captives, the blind, and the outcast, and join Jesus, as Jesus cares for them. The way we know *who* Jesus is, is to go *where* Jesus is, with the poor, the hungry, and the oppressed.

The poor are blessed because the kingdom of God will belong to them, Jesus says. The hungry will be filled, mourners will rejoice, and outcasts will be exalted. The "year of the Lord's favor," the day of divine jubilee (4:19) that is already being inaugurated in Jesus' ministry (7:22), will bring with it a remarkable reversal of values. The last will be first (13:30), and that means that the food and comfort and happiness to be had on that day will be among those who currently do without. When God's redemption is complete, the poor will be rich and the hungry well fed, the grieving will rejoice, and the outcasts will have the seats of honor at God's banquet (cf. 14:15–24).

The dark side of that coming reversal of values, however, is that not only will the last be first, but the first will be last. "Woe to you who are rich, for you have already received your comfort" (6:24, my trans.). Ironically, this is another part of what blessedness means. A secure financial future, a full stomach, a light heart, and a good reputation are mixed blessings at best, because they are temporary. Not only are they unreliable marks of the good life (cf. 12:22–34); they are also deceptive. Rather than being evidence of God's favor, prosperity can

Homiletical Perspective

worshipers that the life of holiness to which we aspire is challenging and difficult.

Luke's Beatitudes are flatly literal. There is none of the spiritualizing found in Matthew's version. In Luke, Jesus declares that the poor, the hungry, the lamenting, the hated, excluded, and defamed are to rejoice, for their suffering will be reversed and turned into plenty and joy. By contrast, the rich, the privileged, the prominent and comfortable will find themselves outside of the realm of God. "Be-happy-attitudes" these certainly are not! Most of us would be happier with this reading if we gave into a bit of spiritualizing, or at least psychologizing. Many of us would be happier with this reading if we could adapt it a bit: "I am not poor, but I identify with the poor," or even "I work with the poor," or maybe "I send money to the poor, I care about the poor." We might want to quibble about the definition of "poor," or "hungry" or "weeping." Surely we, the faithful, are among the blessed? The preacher will want to challenge such glib assumptions, and this reading assists in the challenge.

The parallels between the structure and content of the Beatitudes and the song of Mary in Luke 1:46–55 are striking. Mary is to be called "blessed"; God has raised up Mary, who is poor and lowly, and brought down the powerful, fed the hungry, and sent the rich away. The radical political message embedded in Mary's song and in the Beatitudes is often missed, hidden behind a romanticized image of Mary and a sanitized version of the Beatitudes that omits the "woes."

Preaching on the woes as well as the blessings in this text will be challenging, but to avoid the challenge is to misrepresent the message of Jesus as Luke presents it. Here all conventional assumptions about religion are overturned: the poor become rich, the rich become poor, the outcast become the blessed of God, the prominent and powerful are cursed. Most of us have a hard time dealing with the idea of curses. The word itself has been trivialized to mean uttering certain words that are considered rude or crude.

Ritually speaking, a curse is simply the reverse side of a blessing. If we believe that blessings are effective (and presumably we do, since blessings are a normal part of church worship), then we must also accept the notion of curses as powerful and effective. If a blessing is a declaration of the holiness and goodness in a person or thing or situation, then a curse, or a woe, is an announcement of the evil and injustice in a person or thing or situation. Jesus does this in this account. He is teaching the large crowds

Luke 6:20-31

Theological Perspective

when he said, "Rejoice in that day and leap for joy, for surely your reward is great in heaven" (Luke 6:23).

In Luke's Beatitudes, the tables turn on those who are rich in this life, who enjoy the comforts this world has to offer, who are not hidden with Christ, and who are not willing to endure suffering with him. They have received their consolation and have nothing more to expect but a reversal in their fortunes. There is no need for the preacher to explore theological perspectives on the final judgment, since Christ does not pursue that line of thought in this passage. These Beatitudes are to strengthen the lives of Christ's followers in this present life (Luke 21:19). What good is it for us to gain the things of this world and yet to forfeit our very souls (Mark 8:36)?

The final section of the passage (vv. 27–31) is an ethical summary listing proactive spiritual disciplines, or ethical imperatives, to help sustain the saints of God until the Parousia. The elementary concept is that since we have been blessed by Christ, we are to bless those who set themselves against us and Christ. We are to pray for our antagonists (v. 28). We are not to retaliate with retribution (v. 29). We are to be willing to give our goods not only for those who seek to take them but to those who plead for them (v. 30). For the whole of Christ's ethical teaching in this section concerning our neighbors is summarized in the statement, "Do to others as you would have them do to you" (v. 31).

ROBERT LEACH

Pastoral Perspective

Jesus says later in the Gospel, "Do you think that I have come to bring peace to the earth? No, I tell you, but rather division!" (12:51).

So if we are not the poor, the hungry, the weeping, or the excluded, what are we to hear from this so-called good news? Luke's Jesus is fulfilling God's compassion for the oppressed. Jesus' first words to people in Luke's Gospel repeat the words from Isaiah: "The Spirit of the Lord is upon me, because he has anointed me to bring good news to the poor" (4:18a). Throughout Luke's Gospel, Jesus lives this out by talking with those on the margins, challenging the status quo, and convicting those who feel certain they are righteous.

When we live in the center rather than the margins and enjoy privilege rather than discrimination, we read Jesus' words and our hearts sink. Any preacher in an affluent congregation should not avoid going to that place, but there is no need to stay there. A sincere reflection on our lives and the power of the gospel can move us from terror and dejection to hope and commitment. People who have been looking for happiness by acquiring that house that is just a bit bigger or who seek the approval of the elite may find release in knowing that those things are hollow. There will always be a house bigger and fancier than one's own, and more and more of the powerful to please.

Perhaps there will be that rare person who makes a radical change and leaves a high-powered corporate job to teach reading in the inner city. For most of us, however, the changes will be more subtle. On All Saints' Day, we cherish the memory of those who have gone before us in the faith. We know that some of the everyday saints struggled as we do to hear this passage as good news. Other more renowned saints lived the gospel in spectacular ways. Their stories inspire us and convict us to do more to claim the blessing and to avoid the woe.

LAURA S. SUGG

actually endanger one's relationship with God, as it does to the rich fool (12:16–21), Dives (16:19–31), and Zacchaeus (19:1–10), all characters unique to Luke's Gospel.

To be blessed is to have a relationship with God that is not in jeopardy. The rich fool, Dives, and Zacchaeus are all perfectly able to take care of themselves, and they do so admirably. It is their very self-sufficiency that traps them and separates them from God. Those who lay up treasures for themselves are not—and cannot be—rich toward God (12:21), because when we can take perfectly good care of ourselves, it is altogether too easy for us not to trust God. It is not only greed that jeopardizes the wealthy Christian's relationship with God, but the simple—and subtle—temptation to think that we can take care of ourselves.

So Luke's Jesus understands blessedness and woe in two closely related ways. On the one hand, the poor and hungry, the sad and the scorned, are blessed because God has special concern for them. The God who sent Jesus is alarmingly partisan: the poor literally have an advantage before God. Without romanticizing poverty or spiritualizing it, Luke also warns that poverty and wealth are more than economic.[1] The poor are blessed because God is on their side and because they are forced by their circumstances to rely solely on the mercy of God, from whom all sustenance comes. Blessedness means not only that God exercises particular concern for one, but also that one relies exclusively on God.

Jesus then issues a series of imperatives to love enemies, resist violence with nonviolence, and give alms, and summarizes them with a version of Hillel's Golden Rule: "Do to others as you would have them do to you" (6:31; cf. Matt 7:12).

E. ELIZABETH JOHNSON

that have followed him through the countryside, seeking healing. He first blesses those whose suffering he must have seen up close during these travels. Then he curses those whose wealth, comfort, and prestige are built upon this same suffering.

The astute preacher will also note the common threads with the words of the prophets. Indeed, in this text Jesus identifies his hearers with the prophets: the blessed ones share in the sufferings and therefore the blessedness of the prophets, while those who are cursed are identified with false prophets. This theme can be expanded to consider modern-day or ancient saints whose lives have embodied the prophetic life imaged here.

In laying out these characteristics of blessedness and accursedness, this reading offers a foundation for the kind of holy living that is celebrated on All Saints' Day. The saints are those whose lives demonstrate life on the margins or under oppressions of various kinds, those who bear witness to suffering and struggle, those who can be identified as prophets.

There is often a temptation to celebrate All Saints' Day in a triumphal tone, where giving thanks to God for the lives and witness of the saints becomes a self-referential celebration of the church. We should guard against this, as it clearly flies in the face of the Gospel message for the day. Therefore, like the sermon itself, the liturgy for the day should also, insofar as this is permitted by local practice or denominational requirements, reflect this radical prophetic challenge to holy living that is grounded in the real suffering and struggle of real people, and the ultimate overthrow of all societies and patterns and relationships that depend on the suffering of many to support the few. It is in this hope that the true celebration of All Saints' Day lies.

MARJORIE PROCTER-SMITH

1. See Luke Timothy Johnson, *The Literary Function of Possessions in Luke–Acts*, SBLDS 39 (Missoula, MT: Scholars Press, 1977).

PROPER 26 (SUNDAY BETWEEN OCTOBER 30 AND NOVEMBER 5 INCLUSIVE)

Habakkuk 1:1-4; 2:1-4

^{1:1} The oracle that the prophet Habakkuk saw.
²O LORD, how long shall I cry for help,
   and you will not listen?
  Or cry to you "Violence!"
   and you will not save?
³Why do you make me see wrongdoing
   and look at trouble?
  Destruction and violence are before me;
   strife and contention arise.
⁴So the law becomes slack
   and justice never prevails.
  The wicked surround the righteous—
   therefore judgment comes forth perverted.

. . . .

Theological Perspective

The name Habakkuk means "to embrace." In his commentary Martin Luther commented that the prophet "comforts and encourages [the people] as one fondles a poor weeping child or other person, quieting and pacifying it with the assurance that, if God wills, conditions will mend."[1] The book has been a favorite with commentators, partly because it is short and succinct. It has been variously dated, but many commentators think that a time just before the invasion of Judah by the Babylonians best suits the content. The text before us is a lament and complaint to God; later the prophet takes the role of a watchman waiting for God to answer the lament, and he makes a declaration of faith that God will indeed give an answer.

Lament is a common theme in prophetic literature. Devastation and violence have broken out across the land, and justice has been replaced by injustice. "O LORD, how long shall I cry for help, and you will not listen? Or cry to you 'Violence!' and you will not save?" (1:2).

The immediate context would seem to be invading armies. The prophet does not blame God for the invasion, but for the lawlessness and destruction that the

---

1. "Lectures on Habakkuk 1526," in *Luther's Works* (St. Louis: Concordia Publishing House, 1974), 19:156.

Pastoral Perspective

"O LORD, how long shall I cry for help, and you will not listen? Or cry to you 'Violence!' and you will not save? Why do you make me see wrongdoing and look at trouble? Destruction and violence are before me; strife and contention arise" (1:2–3). This passage from the prophet Habakkuk speaks powerfully to times of conflict, injustice, and violence—both in our personal lives (whether due to violence in our relationships, our homes, our work settings, or our immediate communities) and in our wider society and world.

The opening of the passage does not flinch from painful realities, but in the biblical tradition of lament and holy argumentation with God, the prophet rails at God and demands an answer! Like the character Tevye in the musical *Fiddler on the Roof*, Habakkuk plants himself squarely where God can see him—at a watchpost high on a rampart wall (2:1)—and has it out with God. Habakkuk's steadfastness—his faithful, watchful waiting—is then rewarded by a vision. In order for Habakkuk to "see" this vision of an end to injustice and a healing of grief, he stations himself in God's sight, suggesting that he is not going anywhere until he receives God's reply!

What gives him the persistence, even the *chutzpah*—the nerve—to confront God? The paradox of lament is that there is no lament without a

²:¹I will stand at my watchpost,
    and station myself on the rampart;
  I will keep watch to see what he will say to me,
    and what he will answer concerning my complaint.
²Then the LORD answered me and said:
  Write the vision;
    make it plain on tablets,
    so that a runner may read it.
³For there is still a vision for the appointed time;
    it speaks of the end, and does not lie.
  If it seems to tarry, wait for it;
    it will surely come, it will not delay.
⁴Look at the proud!
    Their spirit is not right in them,
    but the righteous live by their faith.

Exegetical Perspective

The book of Habakkuk reads like a psalm. In fact, it has so many elements that are found in the biblical psalms that many scholars have wondered whether the author was a member of the temple personnel. The book, dated to the end of the monarchy, gives theological explanations for a rising Babylonian threat. Although different sections of the book reflect slightly different dates within this time frame, the final editor of the book has woven the pieces together into an integrated whole.

In order to understand these particular verses, it is important to see where they are placed within the book. On form-critical grounds, the book can be divided into three general sections: individual laments (1:2–2:5), woe oracles (2:6–20), and a final hymn celebrating God's appearance (3:1–19). The three parts are interconnected. The issue about which the prophet laments in part one is resolved by God's appearance in chapter 3. The woes in the middle contain the oracles against the people who plagued the community in 1:2–2:5.

These verses come from the first part of the book. Verse 1 forms the book's superscription, which may have been added by the final editor of the collection of prophetic books. Although most superscriptions give at least the date of the prophet, this one reveals that little was known about the historical Habakkuk.

Homiletical Perspective

Many of our people think the wicked are winning. How can we even think of talking them out of that pessimism? We can help them stand on watch and wait; we can station ourselves on the ramparts, there writing the vision and making it plain. Though it tarry, it will come. Our words can model patience and persistence, even hope.

I love forceful words of promise. They tell us to wait with patience. I was walking by a Baptist church with a sign out front that said, "Lord, give me patience, and make it snappy." I see in this signboard the message of the text from Habakkuk: promise is a thing for which you have to wait. Like eight-year-olds on their birthdays who have been waiting all year for promised special gifts, many of us find that patience is the hard part.

I also hate these forceful words of clarity and promise. If you are being hurt by the victory of the wicked—say you have cancer and no health insurance or you have gotten old without a pension—then waiting is not so "forceful." Even being snappy does not help. It hurts a lot when the wicked win at your expense. God's promise is what we have to rely on: though it tarry, it will come. Though it linger, it will arrive. How do we find the patience to wait—especially if we are being hurt?

Habakkuk 1:1-4; 2:1-4

Theological Perspective

invaders bring (1:4). Calvin paraphrases the verse, "When all things are in disorder, when there is now no regard for equity and justice, and men abandon themselves, as it were with loose reins, unto all kinds of wickedness, how long, Lord, wilt thou take no notice?"[2] The protest to God of unanswered prayer is a common human complaint. It is found in the cries of Psalms 10, 13, 54 and 55, among others. "Give ear to my prayer, O God; do not hide yourself from my supplication" (Ps. 55:1). Why indeed does God allow suffering? Why does God not answer the prayers of the faithful? Why the apparent divine silence in the face of human misery and earnest devout pleading?

These are difficult concepts for a convincing theodicy—if there is such a thing—to answer adequately. It appears that God is either indifferent or has a profound explanation that is beyond our fathoming, or it suggests that there is, after all, no God. In his book *Night*, Elie Wiesel wrote of a death camp inmate asking, "Where is God? Where is he?" when a youth hanged by the SS was still in agony after thirty minutes. This is what one might call a lost prayer. Jesus prayed such a prayer in John's Gospel, when he prayed that all his followers might be one, and none be lost, even though Judas was already to betray him. God knows what lost prayer is, but Jesus still prayed such a prayer.

More profoundly, though, God in Christ knows what it is like to feel the divine silence. As Wiesel continued his story from the death camp, he said he found himself answering within, "Where is [God]? He is here. He is hanging on the gallows."[3] We hear something similar in the words of Psalm 22: Jesus cried on the cross, "My God, My God, why have you forsaken me?" Here at least, in the incarnation, God experiences that deep human fear that there is no God. Here at least God knows what it is like to pray a prayer that seems to go unanswered.

As the reading continues in chapter 2, the prophet is strenuously objecting to God regarding the treatment of the Judeans. He opts to "stand at my watchpost" (2:1) until an answer is forthcoming. Waiting and patience is always a hard test of faith, but Jesus taught persistence, like the woman who complained to the unjust judge (Luke 18:2–8) or the neighbor at midnight (Luke 11:5–8). God's answer comes in the form of a short oracle, which the prophet is ordered to write down.

Pastoral Perspective

foundation of faith. Grief, sorrow, despair can all exist alongside a void of faith, but argumentative lament presupposes that Someone is listening. Like the psalmist who repeatedly asks, "How long, O LORD?" (e.g., Pss. 13:1, 74:10), Habakkuk's boldness suggests that he is no stranger to this holy disputation. He believes that an answer will come, because he has had such experiences of consolation and clarity before. Ignatius wrote of the rhythm of "consolation" and "desolation" that characterizes the spiritual life. In consolation we are drawn closer to God, while in desolation we find it more difficult to feel God's presence. In times of desolation, however, we are sustained by those times when we felt the movement of the Spirit more clearly.

Catholic spiritual writer Edward Hays recounts a story from the desert fathers and mothers, in which a young man goes to visit a wise hermit.[1] He finds the monk sitting outside his cave, enjoying the sun, his dog lying lazily at his side. The seeker asks, "Why is it, Abba, that some who seek God come to the desert and are zealous in prayer, but leave after a year or so, while others, like you, remain faithful to the quest for a lifetime?"

The old man responds, "One day my dog and I were sitting here quietly in the sun, as we are now. Suddenly, a large white rabbit ran across in front of us. Well, my dog jumped up, barking loudly, and took off after that big rabbit. He chased the rabbit over the hills with a passion. Soon, other dogs joined him, attracted by his barking. What a sight it was, as the pack of dogs ran barking across the creek, up stony embankments, and through thickets and thorns! Gradually, however, one by one, the other dogs dropped out of the pursuit, discouraged by the course and frustrated by the chase. Only my dog continued to hotly pursue the white rabbit."

Confused, the young man asks, "What is the connection between the rabbit chase and the quest for God?"

The hermit replies, "Why didn't the other dogs continue the chase? They had not *seen* the rabbit." They were only attracted by the barking of the dog. But once you see the rabbit, you will never give up the chase. Seeing the rabbit, and not following the commotion, was what kept the old monk in the desert.

Once our heart's eye has seen God, if only for a moment—in the words of one of the previous week's texts, with "the eyes of [our] heart enlightened"

---

2. For this and the second quotation four paragraphs later, see Calvin, *Commentary on Habakkuk*, 2:2, 3.

3. Elie Wiesel, cited in Jürgen Moltmann, *The Crucified God* (London: SCM, 1974), 273–74.

1. Passages in quotations are from Edward Hays, *In Pursuit of the Great White Rabbit: Reflections on a Practical Spirituality* (Leavenworth, KS: Forest of Peace Publishing, 1990), 10–11.

Exegetical Perspective

This verse is followed by the commencement of an individual lament. The phrase "How long, O LORD" is found throughout the Psalter as an introduction to a lament. These laments were sung prayers, and, as in modern church music, the "I" was not simply an individual who suffers. Rather he or she spoke on behalf of the larger community. In other words, this was not just Habakkuk's lament, but rather gave voice to the suffering of his community.

Verses 2–4 use metaphors derived from the legal world. "Destruction and violence" as well as "strife and contention" in verse 3 are legal accusations. In fact, the translation of the word "violence" in verses 2 and 3 can be misleading. This does not mean only physical assault, but also general lawlessness. Verse 4 sums up this message. The word for "law" (*torah*) has a broader meaning that includes ritual instruction and moral teaching. The word translated "slack" originally meant something gone numb from the cold: it is useless, frozen, ineffective. The result is that the community will never see justice, or what they will see will be "perverted" or "crooked." These verses accuse the leaders within Judah of making unjust decisions and failing to provide right teaching. The prophet's community despairs of ever finding relief from this social injustice.

The sections that come between these verses describe the rising Babylonian threat as a punishment sent by God against the evil leaders of Judah (1:6). Even though the Babylonians (Chaldeans, v. 6) are not more righteous than the Judeans, God uses them as an instrument of divine retribution. The Babylonian Empire did, in fact, subjugate and eventually destroy Judah in their imperialist expansion into the Levant. The people of Judah whom Habakkuk addresses feared this rising threat. The book of Habakkuk interprets this threat, not as another instance of God's continued silence, but rather as the answer to problems he describes in 1:2–4.

Habakkuk 2:1–4 finishes off this section of the book, although with no specific reference to the Babylonians. Instead, it picks up on the theme of 1:2, which asks, "How long?" by again asserting that God's help has been delayed. The prophet describes himself as a watcher on a city wall (2:1), a metaphor found in other prophetic books (e.g., Ezek. 3:17 and 33:1–9). Picking up the judicial language of 1:2–4, the prophet is waiting with a rebuttal of God's accusation against him.

Instead, God responds to the prophet a second time in 2:2–4, telling him that a judgment in his favor is pending. As proof of this, God instructs

Homiletical Perspective

When we are hurting, we need a point of focus, something upon which to meditate. People even say you can stand on one leg a long time if you just pick a spot ahead of you and stare at it.

Such a spot can often be found in nature. For example, in June my family's entire backyard lights up like a Christmas tree with a banquet of fireflies. The magic is even more beautiful to me because I watched my three children and the neighbor children chase them and fail, night after night, to catch them. The fireflies blink and then they light; they light and then they blink. They stay close to the ground. They do not come out until it is really dark. When I have been depressed about something—or when I have had to have surgery—I have used these lights in my memory bank to keep me sane. They light up my night.

We can also wear down the wicked with our patience. We can become people who are not afraid of the conflict of not having what we need or knowing that others do not have the justice they need. We can be people comfortable with promise and comfortable with conflict. We can even be glad when conflict arrives, because we know the gospel gives us both the permission and the commandment to enter difficulty with hope.

We know what Jesus went through. We know he came out on the other side. We know that many people—not just we and people we know—go through awful things. We know they manage by standing at the gate and watching. Conflict is omnipresent—at family dinner tables, family reunions, and the United Nations, and in most countries. No person will be far from conflict for long. In our urge to make a difference in the world, we will run smack dab into human pessimism, cynicism, and grief over failed attempts at goodness. Lots of things will be fuzzy, not clear. The majority of people will not want a good person to succeed at anything. They will not know why: they will simply know how important it is for them to sneer at decent objectives.

People like Habakkuk, people who have impatiently learned to be patient, stage and anticipate conflict. We balance our sometimes grandiose hopes with quiet statements thereof. We ask the band to play softly as we walk the high wire. We make our hopes foundational instead of large. Instead of saying we will have peace tomorrow, we ask our friend to make one visit to the local congressional representative next month when he or she is in town. We never think we are the only ones doing this. We ask our friend's companionship from a sense of lightness

Habakkuk 1:1-4; 2:1-4

Theological Perspective

So Calvin says, "This is a remarkable passage; for we are taught here that we are not to deal with God in too limited a manner, but room must be given for hope; for the Lord does not immediately execute what he declares by his mouth; but his purpose is to prove patience, and the obedience of our faith." God's response is that the righteous will live by faithfulness. The verse is of course taken up by Paul in Romans (Rom. 1:17), and Paul in turn by Luther. Whether righteousness is alien righteousness that is imputed to us—and whether Luther can be read as teaching *theosis*, as the Finnish school have argued—is an interesting debate in its own right. Here, though, in Habakkuk, it is perhaps more profitable to consider the implications of faithfulness.

The prophet made his protest at God's apparent silence in the face of woe, and then stood watch in the continued silence. God finally spoke, perhaps in a manner and way that the prophet did not expect. The Father was apparently silent in response to the cry of despair from the Son on the cross. The Son then had no option but to stand watch in the silence of death and the stillness of the grave. Only on the third day did God give an answer, with a resounding vindication and act of love.

Paul remarked of God, "My grace is sufficient for you, for my power is made perfect in weakness" (2 Cor. 12:9). Here is a reminder that God's grace is most effective when we have finished our protest and outrage, and are silent. The God of surprises then acts in ways we could never have imagined. The silence of God in the face of fervent prayer for just causes is always disturbing, but that is part of the trial of faith, and God in Christ has experienced it personally.

BRYAN SPINKS

Pastoral Perspective

(Eph. 1:18)—we are drawn to seek God forever. Something draws us to our place of worship, this gathered assembly of loving, struggling, beautiful, and flawed people, this font of blessing, this table that feeds us with God's love and promise.

Perhaps what draws us is not something we can articulate clearly. Sometimes it feels as if darkness overcomes our vision, and sometimes the "sheer silence" (1 Kgs. 19:12b) of God is drowned out by the sound of the baying hounds of busy-ness, the harsh noise of conflict, or just the clamor of the world around us. Habakkuk counsels patience. Even in the times when we do not sense a vision, a clear path, a way out of present difficulties, "there is still a vision for the appointed time" (2:3a). We will discover how we are being called and what we are to do next with our lives.

What if we, like Habakkuk, would just *station ourselves* at a "watchpost"—a quiet room in our home, outdoors in nature, somewhere at work, a formal place of worship, or even more metaphorically, a "place" inside ourselves, a "rampart" within our hearts—and demand that God clear a way for us, send us a glimpse of healing or wholeness for ourselves and our world? "Here I am, God! I will keep watch and see what you will say to me!" What if we were even to yell at God a little bit about the devastation and the grief we see? What if we refused to turn away, and waited with determination for God's reply?

Habakkuk's promise is that the vision will finally arrive. It will be so plain we can write it down so that a messenger can read it aloud. "If it seems to tarry, wait for it; it will surely come, it will not delay" (2:3b). Finally, Habakkuk knew that God's response was not just for him, but for his whole community who were suffering. This is the promise that also comes from our reading this text together, in community. By our sharing of faith with one another, we stand on the ramparts together, and we never have to cry out to God or to wait for the vision alone.

PAMELA COOPER-WHITE

Exegetical Perspective

Habakkuk to publish the oracle (write it out on tablets, v. 2b). This recording serves two purposes. First, it will act as a warning. The phrase translated as "so that a runner may read it" (v. 2b) inverts the proper order of the Hebrew. It actually means, so that whoever reads it will run, either in terror because of the impending disaster or as a messenger sent to warn others. Second, as implied in 2:3, recording the oracle will later prove that Habakkuk has, in fact, been a true prophet, once the events of the oracle materialize.

Habakkuk 2:4 is both the most difficult verse to translate and the verse that has had the greatest impact on Christian readers. The verse is used by both Paul and the author of Hebrews to explain the role of faith for the Christian. However, these authors focus on only one aspect of the meaning of the word translated here as "faith." The Hebrew word has a much more general meaning, including trustworthiness, reliability, and fidelity. The verse contrasts the wicked person who will suffer from God's actions with the righteous person who will benefit. What is unclear is both the description of the wicked person (various translations have "proud," "puffed up," and "swollen") and who or what is "faithful" or "trustworthy."

Although most Bibles, under the influence of later Christian appropriation, translate the word as a characterization of the righteous person (i.e., this is a person of faith), most commentators agree that, since the issue for Habakkuk is whether God will save them, what is "trustworthy" is either God or the vision that God has sent to the people through the prophet Habakkuk. To be sure, these ideas are interrelated: the person who has faith believes that the vision sent by a trustworthy God is itself trustworthy. Perhaps this verse is deliberately ambiguous, to capture all three meanings.

The book of Habakkuk gives voice to a community that suffers injustice and wonders why God does not do something. It provides visions of God's impending judgment against the wicked, which will come in the form of an invasion by the Babylonians. The book ends by marking this as a manifestation of God as the divine warrior, fighting for the righteous, who trust both God and the prophet.

CORRINE L. CARVALHO

Homiletical Perspective

and joy. We think of our invitation, like the firefly, as beautiful. We think it sparkles. We think it lights the night. When and if our friend says, "No," or "You have to be kidding," or "How dare you invite me to get hurt again?" we listen. We receive. We hear. We make sure our friend knows we have heard. We think of this listening as part of our action and virtue. We act but do not control. We wait with a snappy patience, an active patience, a standing-on-tiptoe kind of patience.

While we wait, we do small things to keep the vision alive within us. Consider the Japanese art of *kazen*, "the small act," from the point of view of the generosity of the widow's mite. Or consider Native American wisdom: it is not the last swing of the ax that fells the tree but all the pressure that has gone before it. Do not think of the hundredth stroke, but of the accumulated force of the previous ninety-nine.

Hope is like that. It comes in small strokes, not big. Big fires conflict with small, beautiful fires. They are not beautiful like a firefly flying. There is a great tension between large and small in the world of keeping a vision and hope alive. Small stuff does not get enough respect, like the firefly. Respecting the small allows us to sustain patience and clarity as well.

The wicked are *not* winning: we give them way too much of their power. Rabbi Michael Lerner calls this the act of "Surplus Powerlessness."[1] We overdo what we cannot do. Some congregations actually do heroic self-marginalization, according to one pundit. We do up our smallness in big ways.

Let small acts take us away from fear of the large—and surprise us with great things.

DONNA SCHAPER

---

1. See Michael Lerner, *Surplus Powerlessness* (Atlantic Highlands, NJ: Humanities Press Int., 1986).

Psalm 119:137-144

[137]You are righteous, O LORD,
and your judgments are right.
[138]You have appointed your decrees in righteousness
and in all faithfulness.
[139]My zeal consumes me
because my foes forget your words.
[140]Your promise is well tried,
and your servant loves it.
[141]I am small and despised,
yet I do not forget your precepts.
[142]Your righteousness is an everlasting righteousness,
and your law is the truth.
[143]Trouble and anguish have come upon me,
but your commandments are my delight.
[144]Your decrees are righteous forever;
give me understanding that I may live.

Theological Perspective

These verses of Psalm 119 are part of an incredibly precise literary structure. They comprise the eighteenth section of twenty-two such sections, each with eight lines. In turn, each of the eight lines draws on a thematic vocabulary of eight terms: law, decrees, statutes, commandments, ordinances, word, precepts, and promise.[1] While some may regard the repetition as an exercise in redundancy, the impact of deploying and redeploying each of eight terms associated with torah in twenty-two different affirmations makes unmistakable the centrality of torah, the law and direction of God, for the life of faith.

Linked by subject matter and by an almost eerie numeric connection to Psalms 1 and 19, Psalm 119 undermines careless attempts, especially among Protestant Christians, to assign the Old Testament to "law" while privileging the New Testament as "gospel." For the torah extolled through Psalm 119, and inevitably also in verses 137–144, is not considered a heavy burden but a life-giving force. Indeed, verse 143 plainly echoes Psalm 1 when it declares, "Your commandments are my delight," while verse 144 speaks of God's decrees as imparting understanding that allows one to live, thus evoking the

1. James Luther Mays, *Psalms*, Interpretation series (Louisville, KY: John Knox Press, 1994), 381.

Pastoral Perspective

Late fall is a busy and demanding time in church life: the program year is well under way, Advent is only a month off, and in many places the annual stewardship campaign is in full swing. It is a time when preachers can feel pressure to perform. We are looking for our "A" material. Hiding right under our noses—the precise opposite of what we are looking for—is exactly what we need to regain perspective for ourselves and our congregations.

Psalm 119 elicits a variety of responses from contemporary readers, not all of which seem positive or promising. At 176 verses—more than 100 verses longer than the next longest psalm in the Bible—Psalm 119 can seem daunting, even overwhelming. Its meticulous structure and devotional character lose a great deal in the translation, not just from Hebrew to English, but also from an ancient culture into fast-paced modernity. Moderns can find Psalm 119 plodding, tedious, or even—dare we say it?—boring.

This psalm has not found much favor with the lectionary. Only 56 of its 176 verses are *ever* scheduled for liturgical reading; most of these texts appear as alternates or in the waning Sundays of Epiphany, weeks that are dropped in years when Easter comes early. It seems that we deliberately shy away from this psalm, but why? Perhaps the most useful pastoral

Exegetical Perspective

Psalm 119 is a sustained reflection on walking in God's ways, according to torah. Reminiscent of Psalm 1 and 19, this psalm is an acrostic that celebrates God's written law. This "law" was seen as an instruction and a teaching, not as a legalistic mandate in a formal sense. Although the psalm reflects a variety of Old Testament traditions, its main focus is on the written Scripture. The overall language of the psalm is personal and intimate. The psalmist talks to God as one would talk with a friend (cf. Exod. 33:11). The psalm serves as a teaching for later generations and is best understood, perhaps, by those who view life as a journey, with God as a companion on the way.

Verses 137–144 focus on God's righteousness (vv. 137, 138, 142, 144). Verse 137 has often been called a "doxology of judgment." In verse 137a, the psalmist not only acknowledges God as "righteous" but also recognizes God's judgments as "right." "Righteousness" or "uprightness" means being "true" or "just" and is characterized by "right relationship" as exemplified in Genesis 1 and Psalms 104:24–30 and 65:1–5, which describe how all creation came into existence and is supported and sustained by the Creator of all. Righteousness, a mandate to the Israelite community (Jer. 22:3), is a quality of leadership and ethical living (Isa. 11:1–5). This wonderful virtue is not reserved for God alone; it is found in various

Homiletical Perspective

While making the rounds during church coffee hour, I occasionally hear parishioners speak harmful words to one another. The harmful words that get repeated most often are these: "Don't worry. God has a plan for you." This is a close cousin to another remark: "God would not give you more than you can handle." These comments are equally pernicious and equally difficult to stamp out.

"Don't worry. God has a plan for you." The saying aims to reassure, and this means that its recipient has probably occasioned the phrase by confessing feelings of aimlessness, dissatisfaction, lack of hope, or what the psalmist calls "trouble and anguish." Unfortunately, the remark, "Don't worry. God has a plan for you," is not so much a theological statement as it is a request to change the subject to the weather, please.

Moreover, such remarks indicate that many people have a caricature of providence that they are very reluctant to let go of. This is the case because the belief that God has planned our lives brings with it the assurance that God *cares about our lives.* With that assurance comes great relief, for with God's plan comes some sense of order. We would rather suffer a cruel divinely ordered plan than a meaningless existence, because we are mired in either/or thinking that admits only two choices:

Psalm 119:137-144

Theological Perspective

poetry of Psalm 19, which regards the law of the Lord as "perfect," reviving the soul" (Ps. 19:7).

Walter Brueggemann observes that this trio of psalms manifests a community resolved to "meditate day and night" on torah. "One may take that as an obsession of exhibitionist legalism, as is often the case in Christian stereotypes of Jews. Or one may understand this commitment to Torah as an acceptance of the reality of Yahweh as the horizon, limit, and center of communal imagination."[2] Clearly anything like a sympathetic reading of these psalms individually and together makes it plain that there is "gospel" in this dedication to the "law," a source of nurture, strength, and life.

The Calvinist strain of Protestantism has sometimes experienced solidarity with Jews accused of "exhibitionist legalism." Sometimes it was surely deserved, as when the Scottish Calvinist James Durham wrote an exposition of the commandments in 1675 that managed to see as clear violations of the Decalogue such things as sleeping in church and talking during the sermon. Similarly, the way in which the Reformers themselves interpreted the commandment to honor one's parents as compelling obedience to the state, or the way in which the Puritans deducted that sobriety and modesty in dress is entailed in the prohibition of adultery, do little to increase confidence in the law as summons to life in its fullness.

In better elements of this tradition, however, a so-called "third use" of the law has meant that the law of God does more than restrain evil (by threat of consequences) or bring forth confession (through recognition of how short of the divine standard all human efforts fall). Beyond both of these "uses" of the law, it also provides a direction, a pattern of life that reflects human wholeness. Whereas both of the first two "uses" of the law are negative in tone (restraining evil, convicting of sin), this one is undoubtedly positive, as the law is experienced as the gift of rightly ordered relationships to God and neighbor.

There is indeed a fine line that ancient and more recent people of faith walk when they walk in the way of Psalm 119. The human condition is such that we always stand under the threat of substituting our achievement for God's gift. Thus, instead of receiving the law as a gift, we may too easily imagine that we are assuring ourselves of God's graciousness by following the law. Psalm 119 insistently affirms that in the gift of the law the power and mercy of God is

Pastoral Perspective

insights from this lectionary reading can be found in the reasons we avoid it.

The psalm's structure is a factor. It is composed of twenty-two sets of eight verses, one set for each letter of the Hebrew alphabet. Within each set of verses, each verse begins with the same letter. Each set of verses also contains eight different words for torah, commonly translated "law" but also sometimes "instruction" or "teaching."

The precision of the structure can make for a mind-numbing march through the psalm. This may be the point. Rather like walking a labyrinth or repeating over and over a familiar prayer, Psalm 119 draws the reader beyond a linear search for meaning into a state of being bathed in blessing, continuously mindful of the myriad ways in which God's law-instruction-teaching informs, guides, and shapes our lives. Indeed, the purpose of the psalm seems to be to shape us, rather than to yield to our dogged search for theological nuggets.

We are not dealing in escapism here. There is an alternation, a genuine dialogue between the psalmist's reflections on torah and reflections on life. Verses 137–138 are addressed to God: "You are righteous . . . your judgments . . . you have appointed." Verses 139–141 focus back on the author: "My zeal consumes me . . . your servant loves [your promise] . . . I am small and despised." The pattern is extended as verse 142 is addressed to God, while verse 143 speaks of the psalmist's "trouble and anguish." The section concludes with an affirmation and a plea: "Your decrees are righteous forever; give me understanding that I may live" (v. 144).

The psalm is about life, asserting that there is no life apart from torah, God's law-instruction-teaching. Clint McCann and others have argued persuasively that the term torah needs to be interpreted broadly, to include not simply written material but also God's ongoing revelation in the natural world and in and through the lives of individuals and nations.[1] This understanding points us to the understanding that God is present and active in and through every aspect of life. When we wander away from that awareness, we need a vehicle of return. Psalm 119 provides a meditative means to refocus our thinking and our very being on the gift of our ongoing relationship with the sacred. We do not do well to dabble in this psalm; better to become immersed in it, embraced by it.

---

2. Walter Brueggemann, *Theology of the Old Testament: Testimony, Dispute, Advocacy* (Minneapolis: Fortress Press, 1997), 445.

1. See J. Clinton McCann Jr., "The Book of Psalms," in *The New Interpreter's Bible* (Nashville: Abingdon Press, 1996), 4:1167.

Exegetical Perspective

biblical characters like Noah (Gen. 6:9) and Job (Job 29:14), and thus human beings are capable of possessing this godly virtue as well.

In verse 137b the psalmist proclaims that God's judgments are right. Here God is acknowledged as a just judge (cf. Ps. 67:4). This God is one who has defended and will defend those in need (Pss. 10:18; 140:12) and who has chastised the guilty (Ps. 94:2). Verse 138 picks up on the imagery and tone in verse 137 and affirms God's ways by asserting that the divine decrees have all been appointed in "righteousness" and "faithfulness."

Historically, as reflected by the biblical text, God has been faithful to covenant and has given Israel victory, redemption, justice, and counsel, with the caveat that the people will be faithful to covenant as well—walking with God, walking in God's ways, and observing God's commands and statutes. For his listeners, the psalmist offers an instruction on the goodness of God as the one who rules the world.

The psalmist becomes self-reflective with God in verse 139. Listeners hear that the poet is consumed by zeal because the poet's foes have forgotten God's words. This consuming zeal provides a window into the psalmist's passion for and great love of God and, accordingly, God's words. Zeal, also understood as "passion," "diligence," and a healthy sense of "jealousy," is related to maintaining the covenantal bond between God and Israel. God is portrayed as a God "jealous" for the people, protecting them and requiring wholehearted commitment (Exod. 20:5; Deut. 5:8; Josh. 24:19).

God's "zeal" for God's own honor or "holy name" (cf. Ezek. 39:25) causes God to rise up to defeat Israel's enemies (Ps. 79:5–13; Isa. 26:11–15) and eventually restore Israel to its own land (cf. Ezek. 36:5–7; Joel 2:18–20; Zech. 1:14–17). Israel, in turn, is expected to be consumed by zeal for God, for God's law, and for God's sanctuary (Pss. 69:9; 119: 139). In verse 139, the psalmist becomes a role model for the rest of his community. Filled with love for God, the psalmist is impassioned against those who forget God's words. Although Israel will not be forgotten by God (Isa. 44:21), Israel often forgets God (Isa. 17:10; Jer. 3:21; Ezek. 22:12; 23:35; Hos. 8:14) as well as God's law (Hos. 4:6), understood here in verse 139 as God's "words" written down.

In verse 140 the psalmist has the self-understanding of a "servant" and comments on God's "promise" that is "well tried" and loved. The promise to which the psalmist refers is obscure in this text, but Israel's history sheds light on this specific reference.

Homiletical Perspective

(1) God's hand must determine every last turn of each individual's course, or (2) life is one random event after another. Either everything happens for a reason, or everything is illogical. We are either flying by the seat of God's pants, or we are the children of an omnipotent nitpicker.

Fortunately, in verse 143, the psalmist draws upon his own suffering to suggest a way out of this kind of dichotomous thinking. The psalmist offers a new way of understanding God's care—or at least an understanding so ancient that it seems new: "Trouble and anguish have come upon me, but your commandments are my delight." In other words, when the psalmist's life begins to come apart, to bleed outside its own boundaries, he finds reassurance in the fact that God has given him a sturdy frame (God's commandments or divine law) in which to live.

In mainline Protestant churches, liberalism gives us an appreciation for each individual's religious freedom. Likewise, according to Luther, the first function of the law is to convict us as sinners. As a result, Protestant liberalism does not appreciate the positive dimensions of God's law, leaving many of us hard pressed to see it as a delight.

The psalmist knows none of this. Instead, the psalmist knows that God cares for him personally, longs for him to live differently, and wants his life to correspond to divine intentions. He believes that God's intentions are best for him. In other words, the psalmist knows that through the law God cares for him, and in the law God has a plan for him. Questions about *why* God has let him suffer "trouble and anguish" do not surface in these verses. Instead, the psalmist celebrates the fact that God has told him *how* to live.

So, how do we discover God's plan for us? How, in the face of life's chaos, do we find the psalmist's "understanding" so that, like the psalmist, we "may live"? A good first step is to admit that our own needs and instincts are not trustworthy guides. If we want to follow God's plan, we must first give up our own. If we want a share of the psalmist's delight, we must trade some of our freedom for it. We must let God tell us how to live.

This last point is forcefully made by Stanley Hauerwas and William Willimon in their reflection on the first commandment:

> Because we live in a culture where submission to any authority other than our own egos is considered unduly authoritarian and unfair, command-obedience is difficult for us. We have freed ourselves from all external authority except servitude to the

Psalm 119:137-144

Theological Perspective

already present, the faithfulness and assistance of God is already available, and no achievement is needed (much less possible) to procure it.[3]

One of the ways in which liturgy has sought to support theology in this respect has been to surround the act of confession with the law. One pattern observed in traditions that have sought to practice the piety of Psalms 1, 19, and 119 has been to call the community to confession by the reading of one form of the law—either the New Testament summary or the Old Testament Decalogue. In either form, the community recognizes its failure to love God and neighbor and so its need to stand before God in honest, freely rendered confession.

Subsequent to the act of confession, the law is recited again in the presence of the community, usually in the form not used at the beginning of the confessional sequence. This place in the sequence is indispensable, because now the law is heard *following* the words of forgiveness and pardon. There is no longer any issue of earning God's favor by dint of virtuous human action. There is instead the receptive community of the forgiven being offered the life-giving gift of life together in ordered relationship to God and neighbor.

Not only in liturgy, but in the composing of theology itself, attempts have been made to reflect the theological current of Psalm 119. The Heidelberg Catechism from sixteenth-century Germany demonstrates a magnificent appreciation of this role of the law of God. The questions in this catechism are divided into three sections. The first section describes the human dilemma of separation from God and other people. The second section describes God's redemptive movement in the people of Israel and Jesus Christ to reconcile us. Then the third section is labeled "Thankfulness"—and here is where the Ten Commandments are discussed. This arrangement expresses the view that living out the commandments is an expression of thankfulness to God for inviting us to enter life in covenant with God and one another.

D. CAMERON MURCHISON

Pastoral Perspective

Of all of the sermons I have preached over the years, the one with the most enduring impact is titled "A Thanksgiving Alphabet." It is exactly what it sounds like: going through the alphabet from A to Z listing things for which I am particularly thankful. As dreadful as it sounds, the idea has remarkable staying power. I have used it so much that I have forgotten where I stole it from. The structure gives the list a predictability that generally proves more pleasing than oppressive. It also allows the listener to anticipate and provide his or her own objects of delight.

If my list includes Ambiguity, Balderdash, and Chocolate, most people quickly discover that they can improve on what they are hearing. Children love to do this as much as adults. The point that stays with people is this: from beginning to end our lives are filled with blessings beyond number and surpassing comprehension. Each trip through the alphabet yields a different dimension of thanksgiving. The overall effect is a mosaic celebrating the gift of life.

Of course this sermon pales before Psalm 119, with its depth of devotion and intensity of focus. Contemplation of torah moves the psalmist to a consideration of God's righteousness, mentioned five times in these eight verses alone. Through God's endless faithfulness we are granted the gift of truth. This boggles the mind—which again is the point.

We have it all backwards. We rush around in search of spiritual insights to fit in around the lives we are living, while the world forms our identity. We accessorize with religion. The church functions like the cut man in a prize fight, patching us up so that we can get back out there one more time, but not really challenging us to change the way we think about ourselves. The perspective of the psalm is precisely the reverse. Faith is what forms us. God's law-teaching-instruction is what tells us who we are. Of course there is plenty of time to contemplate and celebrate this great mystery! What are 176 verses to celebrate the gift of life we have received? To live to the rhythm of this psalm is to be shaped by it as a new creation: "Give me understanding that I may live" (v. 144).

DAVID R. RUHE

---

3. Cf. Karl Barth, *Church Dogmatics*, IV/2 (Edinburgh: T. & T. Clark, 1960), 591.

Exegetical Perspective

Through its patriarchs and matriarchs, the Israelite community has received divine promises of blessing (Gen. 12:2), posterity (Gen. 17:6, 16–17), land for permanent possession (Gen. 17:8), and an ongoing personal relationship with God (Gen. 17:7; Exod. 12:25).

Through David, the community has been promised an everlasting house and kingdom (2 Sam. 7:16; Ps. 89:3–4). Time and again, these promises have been fulfilled, especially God's promise of fidelity and personal relationship to which the psalmist seems to allude in verse 140. Regardless of Israel's transgressions and forgetfulness of God, God has remained faithful to covenant relationship.

Moving from the sense of being a servant, the psalmist shifts the focus to being "small" and "despised" in verse 141a. Although the psalmist gives no indication as to the reason for being despised, one can assume that it was because the psalmist remained faithful to God and God's ways and words (cf. Isa. 52:13–53:12, esp. 53:3; Jer. 11:18–20; 15:10–18; 20:7–18), which becomes clear in verse 141b. The psalmist remembers God's precepts.

The theme of verse 142 recalls verse 137, but with a sharper emphasis. Having stated that God is righteous (v. 137a), the psalmist now declares that God's righteousness is an "everlasting righteousness" (v. 142a). Thus, this righteous God who acts righteously is unchanging with respect to this virtue. Furthermore, the decrees made in righteousness and in all faithfulness (v. 138) are now said to be "the truth" (v. 142b). The psalmist now declares God's law to be a stable set of principles that have faithfully guided the community throughout history, bringing upon those who follow it blessing upon blessing.

The law as a steadfast and guiding principle continues in verse 143, where the psalmist reveals personal challenges and acknowledges consolation found in God's commandments that have become a "delight." A final word of affirmation for God's decrees closes this section (v. 144a) and draws readers back to the psalmist's central theme: the righteousness of God and God's law, of which the psalmist now prays for understanding (v. 144b). In sum, verses 137–144 celebrate the graciousness of God, whose ways and law are life giving.

CAROL J. DEMPSEY

Homiletical Perspective

self. This we hail as freedom, though Israel testifies that slavery (particularly slavery as the necessity to do "what I want to do") comes in many guises. . . . So the issue is not *if* we shall live under some external command, but rather *which* external command will have its way with us.[1]

Instead of embracing the cultural ideology of individualism and its bedrock assumption that individuals should be able to do as we please, let us remember that the Christian doctrine of sin holds that we are flawed creatures who, when "set free," will typically do the wrong thing.

I lead a monthly Bible study at a nursing home. It is a confining place whose residents have sacrificed much of their autonomy in order to live in a sheltered community with expert care. It took about a dozen visits to defeat my assumption that my friends there must be miserable, to realize that the residents are joyful in the face of their restrictions. I am still trying to understand that they might be joyful *because* of them.

In a recent meeting, we took a look at the Ten Commandments. I asked the group which of the ten they thought was the most difficult to follow. One wise woman thought for a moment and then said, "That question doesn't make sense. Given my age and where I live, there are at least five of these commandments I couldn't break if I wanted to." I asked her how this felt.

Without missing a beat, she said, *"It feels wonderful."*

MATTHEW FITZGERALD

---

1. Stanley M. Hauerwas and William H. Willimon, *The Truth about God: The Ten Commandments in Christian Life* (Nashville: Abingdon Press, 1999), 26–27.

2 Thessalonians 1:1-4, 11-12

¹Paul, Silvanus, and Timothy,

To the church of the Thessalonians in God our Father and the Lord Jesus Christ:

²Grace to you and peace from God our Father and the Lord Jesus Christ.

³We must always give thanks to God for you, brothers and sisters, as is right, because your faith is growing abundantly, and the love of everyone of you for one another is increasing. ⁴Therefore we ourselves boast of you among the churches of God for your steadfastness and faith during all your persecutions and the afflictions that you are enduring. . . .

¹¹To this end we always pray for you, asking that our God will make you worthy of his call and will fulfill by his power every good resolve and work of faith, ¹²so that the name of our Lord Jesus may be glorified in you, and you in him, according to the grace of our God and the Lord Jesus Christ.

Theological Perspective

Understanding this passage theologically is made much more difficult, if not impossible, by the lectionary committee's decision to omit verses 5–10. The omission is perfectly predictable, of course, since verses 5–10 contain some of the harshest, least palatable language of the entire New Testament. It is not the kind of language one wants to hear from the pulpit on Sunday morning. Anyone who believes erroneously that the Old Testament is the violent testament and the New Testament is the nonviolent testament, needs only read these verses. In this passage, Paul assures the Christians at Thessalonica that their suffering serves to refine and purify them, while at the same time expressing utter confidence in God's ability and intention not only to punish those who inflict their suffering but to condemn those purveyors of persecution to eternal destruction and banishment from the presence of God.

The material surrounding these troublesome words, the words chosen for the lectionary reading, ring more easily on our ears. In verses 1–4 Paul, speaking also for Timothy and Silvanus, greets the congregation at Thessalonica with considerable affection. His pastoral demeanor toward them is gratitude. He notes that their increasing faith and love for each other, always a mark of spiritual maturity for Paul, are growing stronger and steadier. He

Pastoral Perspective

To say that Paul has had his critics through Christian history would be an exercise in understatement. Critiques of Paul range from minor chafing against the rather bossy tone in some of Paul's letters, to the more extreme view that the churches Paul built ruined the beautiful message of the gospel. One category of critique that deserves attention in light of the passage at hand relates to what one might call Paul's new law. Since this passage lifts up a particular way of striving in faith that one might call, if not a new law, then a guide for the church and for Christians, these critiques shed light on pastoral implications in the text.

Some claim that, even though Paul purported to reject the law, he—perhaps even deviously—built a new one it its place, a new law constructed from a mélange of Judaic code and societal expectations.[1] Others like Schoeps go a step further in another direction and argue that, as Paul reconstructed the law, he misconstrued Jewish law and allowed its elegant logic to be torn apart. Schoeps asserts, "The Pauline theology of law and justification begins with the fateful misunderstanding in consequence of which he tears asunder covenant and

---

1. Adolf von Harnack, "The Founder of Christian Civilization," in *The Writings of St. Paul*, ed. Wayne A. Meeks (New York: W. W. Norton & Co., 1972), 302–8.

Exegetical Perspective

Letters written in the ancient Mediterranean usually began with a prescript that comprised the names of the senders, the addressees, and a brief greeting. While the named senders and addressees are identical in 1 and 2 Thessalonians, most biblical scholars do not believe the writings share the same author(s). First Thessalonians is universally accepted as having been written by Paul. Most scholars, however, reject Pauline authorship of 2 Thessalonians, arguing that it is an imitation of 1 Thessalonians, drawing upon the earlier letter to enhance its authority. (While I share the view of most biblical scholars that 2 Thessalonians was not written by Paul, throughout this essay I shall refer to the author as "Paul." I do so preserving the author's desire to attribute Pauline authorship to the correspondence.)

The identification of three senders—Paul, Silvanus, and Timothy—helps to illustrate the collaborative nature of the early Christian missionary enterprise. Although Paul is often depicted and perceived by many contemporary Christians as having single-handedly founded and nurtured most of the communities he wrote to, there were several evangelists/missionaries who worked with Paul to establish and nurture many of these communities.

While most of the prescript in 1 and 2 Thessalonians is identical, 2 Thessalonians has an extended

Homiletical Perspective

Undoubtedly many preachers will opt this Sunday to work from the more familiar and less problematic story of Zacchaeus in the Gospel lection. The Second Letter to the Thessalonians poses many challenges for exegete and preacher alike; yet one can argue that the church does better when it wrestles earnestly with such challenges rather than ignoring them.

The first counsel to preachers of this text is to read the entirety of 1:1–12, including the verses naming the anger of God that the lectionary framers omit. Many parishioners will be curious enough to read the verses anyway, and they invite substantive interpretation. The second counsel, as New Testament scholar Beverly Roberts Gaventa suggests, is to read the text in worship with "the tremulous voice of rage,"[1] the voice with which it was first penned.

This passage is not for the faint of heart, but it is best heard in its authentic voice. Only then can one faithfully speak to its content; indeed, one will then *have to* speak to its content, cataloged here in four suggested approaches, three of which are from the more limited appointed text:

1. Beverly Roberts Gaventa, *First and Second Thessalonians*, Interpretation series (Louisville, KY: John Knox Press, 1998), 96.

2 Thessalonians 1:1-4, 11-12

Theological Perspective

notes that he holds them up as an example of Christian stability for other groups in other places. In verses 11–12, Paul assures the fledgling church that he, Silvanus, and Timothy will continue to pray for them, that God may continue to sustain their resolve and continue to empower their every intention to fulfill their high calling, to the glory of their Lord Jesus. Thus the lectionary selection, verses 1–4 and 11–12, is nice, but devoid of theological tension, interest, or usefulness.

In the omitted verses, Paul talks about how suffering—not just any suffering but suffering for the kingdom of God—is the way believers become worthy of the kingdom. He goes on, then, to paint a picture of Jesus and God that is terrifying. The Prince of Peace is here portrayed as passing down justice with great flare, accompanied by a fiery army of angels. The enemies of the believers are also the enemies of God and risk not only destruction but exile from the very company of the Lord.

As noted, these are hardly palatable images. The concept of judgment is not a topic we raise often in my congregation. If we do mention it, it is to note that we do not talk about it the way we used to hear it talked about in the congregations in which we were reared. We say that is good—and then we wonder if we may be missing something vital to faith by ignoring it. Certainly bygone emphases on hell and heaven created a culture of fear, on the one hand, and a disregard for the sanctity of the present, on the other.

Perhaps, though, we have too readily tossed out, along with the brimstone and the pie in the sky, a sense that actions have consequences that have an eternal significance. We understand from study of the Greek language that "eternal" has connotations other than an extension of time into infinity—duration of time simply being the easiest way for most humans to understand the beyond-bounds quality that is being referenced. We understood from science that, as the cliché goes, a butterfly flapping its wings on one side of the world can affect climate on the other side of the world.

Morally, however, we want to deny that the decisions we make and actions we take have such consequences for good or ill, and that those consequences extend far beyond what we can see or imagine. Paul's sense here of the cosmic consequences of not obeying the gospel of Jesus resonates with the Iroquois notion of weighing actions in light of how they may affect one's descendants to the seventh generation. Although a theology of fear and escapism has not served us well, neither has a theology of the here

Pastoral Perspective

law, and then represents Christ as the end of the law."[2]

One can hear echoes of these earlier debates in contemporary arguments about the extent to which the church conforms to the laws of society. Many Christians wish to participate in an alternative form of community through their churches. This alternative form of community is to be one that does not exhibit the marks of a culture that is driven by consumption, power, and individual rights. The same Christians, however, want to be a part of an institution that is by design premised upon compliance with certain regulations and standards. Finding an appropriate means for living as a Christian community, in a world where institutions are subject to flawed human laws, has presented a challenge to Christians throughout history.

The passage at hand stands as an argument against those critics of Paul who say that he was unoriginal and captive to the law. Paul had no choice but to present organizing principles for the church. He did so when he offered the image of the body of Christ with Jesus as its head. Again, here, he presents a *telos* for the church that has usefulness today.

The *telos* for the church can be found in Paul's greeting to the church at Thessalonica. Although authorship of 2 Thessalonians is contested, some arguing that it was the product of a member of the Pauline school who mimicked 1 Thessalonians,[3] the message to Christians about what they as individuals and as a church were meant to do is both *clear* and *original*. Paul begins the letter by praising the success of the church in remaining faithful amid persecution. He then offers a specific definition of that success: they are growing in love for each other and in love for God. This is the *telos* for the church: to grow in love for each other and in love for God.

First, Paul's message in this passage is *clear*: In this postmodern era, where institutions are constantly challenged to render more succinct their statements of purpose, this passage provides direction. Churches often bury themselves in flurries of meaningless activity, and over time they become exhausted and confused. By placing love for each other and love for God at True North for church decision making, Christians can find simplicity and fulfillment. Whereas churches often flail for months over the task of creating mission statements, Paul here proposes one that would suit any church at any time.

2. Hans Joachim Schoeps, "Paul's Misunderstanding of the Law," in *The Writings of St. Paul*, 360.
3. Wayne A. Meeks, ed., *The Writings of St. Paul*, 107–12.

Exegetical Perspective

greeting, identifying "God our Father and the Lord Jesus Christ" as the source of the grace and peace pronounced on the Thessalonians. This pairing of God the Father and the Lord Jesus in both 1 and 2 Thessalonians emphasizes the close relationship and collaborative work between the two (1:1, 2, 8, 12; 2:16; 1 Thess. 1:1, 3; 3:11, 13; 4:14; 5:9, 18, 23).

The typical Pauline letter follows the prescript with a thanksgiving, in which Paul gives thanks for the addressees. The thanksgiving in 2 Thessalonians is slightly different from other Pauline thanksgivings in that Paul writes, "we *must* always give thanks to God . . . *as is right*" rather than the typical "we/I thank God always." The construction suggests that Paul was not simply giving thanks, but rather he felt obligated to give thanks for those in Thessalonica. Paul identified the abundant growth in their faith, the love they exhibited toward one another, and their steadfast endurance and fidelity in the face of persecutions and afflictions as the attributes for which he felt obligated to thank God. Unlike the specific reference in 1 Thessalonians 2:14–16, what the author is referring to here as persecutions and afflictions is rather vague.

Whatever the Thessalonians were experiencing, their "steadfastness and faith" in the face of such persecutions and afflictions served as a source of pride and honor for Paul—the founder of the community and a Christian exemplar of faithful endurance in the face of suffering (cf. Phil. 1:12–30; 2 Cor. 12:10). Honor was an important value in the ancient Mediterranean world. The communities that Paul helped establish were often sources of honor for Paul (cf. 1 Thess. 2:19–20; 2 Cor. 9:2–3; Phil. 2:16; 4:1).

Persecutions and afflictions were often perceived as indicative of the end of time (Dan. 12:1; Mark 13:19–27; Rev. 7:14). Belief that the final days had begun could easily lead to fear and anxiety (2 Thess. 2:1–2). This is why Paul commends and praises the Thessalonians for their steadfastness in the face of persecutions and afflictions. Paul's commendation, praise, and thanks for the Thessalonians are interrupted by his attempt to interpret for the community the meaning, purpose, and consequences associated with their suffering (1:5–10; see also 2:1–12).

After interpreting their persecutions and afflictions, Paul offers the first of at least three prayers for the Thessalonians found in this short letter (1:11–12; 2:16–17; 3:5, 16). Paul informs the Thessalonians that he is constantly praying that God will make them worthy (i.e., deserving) of the life and destiny to which God has called them (1:11). Paul's language

Homiletical Perspective

Peace When There Is No Peace. The letter's opening salutation bears within it the familiar prayer that "grace" and "peace" will abide with the hearers (v. 2), which is no small hope, given the letter's subsequent concentration on evil and lawlessness, divine vengeance and holy rage. Is this juxtaposition a cruel joke? The prayer for peace is repeated again at the end of the letter (3:16). The letter writer is not joking, of course, but completely serious. What kind of peace is possible in such a context? The letter describes the peace of God that Christ gives, which is more enduring and substantial than the peace the world settles for most of the time.

The latter is more like the peace of mind insurance companies always advertise, or the peace and quiet parents tell their children they have to have when they are arguing at the dinner table. In contrast, the Christian hope is for peace that is beyond human comprehension, a peace that settles, soothes, and comforts even when the nations rage and the kingdoms totter and the world seems to have gone mad. Such peace is not something one discovers or achieves; it always comes as a gift—priceless and treasured.

Love Born of Common Struggle. The writer to the Thessalonians notes with gratitude that "the love of everyone of you for one another is increasing" (v. 3). It is a singular and remarkable way of emphasizing the way the community has been bound together, even in its suffering under the pain of persecution, by faith and love. The fury of the world toward them has only compounded their mutual love and their regard for one another. There is little warrant in this text for admonishing the faithful to "go and do likewise." There is little chance that such a preaching tack would bear much fruit.

What is worth noting here is the way common struggle often forges an uncommon unity and love for one another. Like the peace that holds the community fast in turmoil, love for one another and congregational unity are best received and celebrated as gifts. Beleaguered communities of faith, in particular, always need the encouragement that comes from such an accounting of gifts.

Suffering for the Faith. The epistle's reference to the congregation's "steadfastness and faith during all your persecutions and the afflictions" (v. 4) not only names the central issue of the letter itself, but also serves as a reminder that the Christian calling is seldom to a vocation of ease and comfort, but to a

2 Thessalonians 1:1-4, 11-12

Theological Perspective

and now that takes no account of this long, or eternal, view.

A theology that dismisses notions of judgment has additional perils besides a distressingly short view. There is also something important to human solidarity missing when we overlook notions of judgment, a concept that privileged folks often find difficult to understand. There is no fighting all the battles if one lives life as a person less privileged. Some battles must be resigned to a higher court—and it is useful to imagine the one who has done wrong standing before the throne of God, compelled to look God in the eye. That unique space before the eye of God, however, is also a completely democratic place. It is where we all belong—and the eye into which we are compelled to look holds for us not only judgment but unfathomable love. That holy space before the eye of God is where we can no longer hide, and it is the place where we need no longer explain ourselves.

Whether or not we find useful the colorful biblical images and rhetoric of judgment, the concept of an accountability that is somehow larger than human time and space is essential to both biblical justice and to biblical theology more generally. Justice and mercy are at the very heart of the biblical understanding of who God is and how God acts in human history. Generations past have sometimes collapsed this central biblical paradox in favor of judgment, to our loss. In North American contexts of privilege, we are in danger of collapsing this paradox in favor of mercy, also to our loss.

Paul understood—as did the psalmist before him, and as we also must understand—that justice and compassion embrace in the being of God. That divine kiss, with both components of the paradox fully and creatively present, is the ground that allows us the freedom and responsibility to be fully human, fully accountable, and fully trusting.

MARY H. SCHERTZ

Pastoral Perspective

Second, Paul's message is *original*: By placing love at the forefront, guiding all human interaction, Paul offers a new form of covenant as defined through Christ. Just as Jesus reinterpreted all the laws into a love commandment, Paul proposes that love is the guiding light for the newly formed institutional church. In this way Paul successfully recasts the law without simply replacing one set of strictures with another.

One way in which the passage must be interpreted carefully, however, before direct hermeneutical application to the life of today's church, relates to the community to whom Paul was writing. It is clear from the passage that the church in Thessalonica is persecuted and vulnerable. The church of today, although by no means without its struggles, occupies a position of privilege and power. Therefore, were the Thessalonians to have taken Paul's message to mean that they should "take care of their own," in order to survive persecution, this is likely to have been a helpful message. Were the church of today to consider Paul's words as license to focus on one's own privileged community to the detriment of others, the interpretation would be misguided.

Paul (or his eponymous follower) writes to boast of the faith of the Thessalonians, and in doing so he highlights their growth. He focuses on their improvement; not unlike an elementary school teacher, he commends not only their performance but their effort. A pastoral reading of Paul's applause for the Thessalonians should today be understood as affirming their love for God and love for the least of these as the basis for a successful institutional church that seeks to be a community of faith.

SARAH BIRMINGHAM DRUMMOND

clearly implies that it is God's grace that makes the faithful worthy of God's call.

Furthermore, it is through the grace of "God and the Lord Jesus Christ" that both Jesus and the Thessalonians are "glorified" (v. 12). Returning to the importance of honor, Paul asserts that the desired outcome of the Thessalonians' persecutions and afflictions is to bring honor (i.e., "glory") to "the name of our Lord Jesus," so that Jesus is glorified in them and they are glorified in him.[1]

In order to understand what Paul might mean by this, it is necessary to understand social relationships in the ancient Mediterranean world. Social relationships consisted primarily of patron-client relationships. In a patron-client relationship, a patron had social, economic, and political resources that were needed by a client. The client in return gave expressions of loyalty and honor that were useful for the patron. Often a broker served as mediator between a patron and a client when direct access between the two was not possible. In such cases, honor was shared among the three.[2]

According to Paul, God is the one who through God's own power and grace makes the Thessalonians worthy of God's call so that the name of Jesus is glorified in the Thessalonians and they are glorified in Jesus. Based on the patron-client relationship, God functions as patron, Jesus as broker, and the Thessalonians as client. In this patron-client relationship, Jesus honors (and is honored in) the Thessalonians and the Thessalonians honor (and are honored in) Jesus, all of which brings honor to God.[3]

GUY D. NAVE JR.

unity with Christ in suffering. Affluent Christians in the developed world find such a suggestion more troubling than do those who live marginally in developing lands, where such an affirmation is a steady source of comfort.

Without trivializing the deep suffering of persecuted Christians in our time, the preacher will want to remind the congregation of the way in which suffering can be a gift in shaping a life of endurance and a deeper reliance on the grace of God. We live in a high-speed, analgesic culture; we do not like pain, and we will do most anything to see our way through the pain quickly and in order to regain a measure of "normalcy."

By its nature, however, endurance is not a quality we can develop in a hurry. Real suffering is not a momentary affliction; for some people suffering is an unwelcome companion for years. Through endurance in such a context we gain an unparalleled opportunity to reflect deeply on our lives, perhaps to see there the imprint of the hand of God, and therein to transcend either despair, on the one hand, or blithe optimism, on the other, on the way to an enduring hope.

The Vengeful God. As noted above, preachers would do well not to ignore verses 5–10, even though they are not part of the assigned lection. They pose a real dilemma for preaching, to be sure, for they present an image of God unfamiliar to many contemporary congregations. If the church does not speak to such matters, however, it tacitly surrenders these words to the purveyors of a gospel of hate and fear. In preaching the wrath of God proclaimed herein, it is essential to note that the text is rooted in a concrete historical situation of persecution and struggle, albeit one that scholars cannot precisely define.

In the midst of such affliction, the writer declares to the Thessalonians that God's justice is dependable, that God will deal harshly with those who treat them harshly, while giving relief to those who have been afflicted. Holding these words in creative tension with the whole canon, the preacher can then focus attention more fully on that promise of relief. In the end, this text encourages faithfulness and offers assurance that God will not forget such steadfastness.

ROBERT E. DUNHAM

1. Note the emphasis placed on "glory" in vv. 9, 10, and 12, as well as 2:14 and 3:1.
2. For a summary of patron-client relationships, see Halvor Moxnes, "Patron-Client Relations and the New Community in Luke–Acts," in J. H. Neyrey, ed., *The Social World of Luke–Acts* (Peabody, MA: Hendrickson, 1991), 241–68.
3. This idea is more fully articulated in Philip Esler, "2 Thessalonians," in *The Oxford Bible Commentary* (Oxford: Oxford University Press, 2001), 1216.

Luke 19:1-10

¹He entered Jericho and was passing through it. ²A man was there named Zacchaeus; he was a chief tax collector and was rich. ³He was trying to see who Jesus was, but on account of the crowd he could not, because he was short in stature. ⁴So he ran ahead and climbed a sycamore tree to see him, because he was going to pass that way. ⁵When Jesus came to the place, he looked up and said to him, "Zacchaeus, hurry and come down; for I must stay at your house today." ⁶So he hurried down and was happy to welcome him. ⁷All who saw it began to grumble and said, "He has gone to be the guest of one who is a sinner." ⁸Zacchaeus stood there and said to the Lord, "Look, half of my possessions, Lord, I will give to the poor; and if I have defrauded anyone of anything, I will pay back four times as much." ⁹Then Jesus said to him, "Today salvation has come to this house, because he too is a son of Abraham. ¹⁰For the Son of Man came to seek out and to save the lost."

Theological Perspective

In today's powerful and moving story from Luke's Gospel, a wealthy tax collector named Zacchaeus responds to the call of Jesus. One must take the wider context of Luke into account in order to appreciate the contrast between the rich ruler who refuses to sell his possessions (18:18–30) and Zacchaeus, who freely offers to give half of his possessions to the poor (v. 8). The pericope parallels Luke's story of the blind beggar who, like Zacchaeus, seeks out Jesus along a road (18:35–43).

Although it is hard not to feel warmhearted toward Zacchaeus, who is "short in stature" and must scamper ahead of the crowd and scurry up a tree to see Jesus, we must not lose sight of the christological concentration of the passage. Luke's narrative illustrates the lordship of Jesus Christ and his missiological objective to "seek out and save the lost" (v. 10). The key theological point is that Jesus, as Son of God, is able to carry out his earthly mission purposefully and effectively. The gospel is the power for salvation (Rom. 1:16).

It is not clear from the text whether Zacchaeus merely wants to observe Jesus (who has a reputation as a friend to sinners and tax collectors) or if he hopes to address Jesus directly. Either way, he encounters obstacles in his pursuit. Some scholars have suggested that the reference to Zacchaeus's

Pastoral Perspective

Wee Zacchaeus is such a peculiar little man. It seems fitting to call him "wee" the way a Scot might, or the way folks in the South sometimes call children named for a parent "Little Walter" or "Little Ann." Even though he was a social outcast at the time, it is fun to think of wee Zacchaeus relaxing with the great saints and apostles of the early church. In a group photo, he would either be sitting in the front of the group, or better yet, still hanging out in a tree with a very big smile on his face. In ten short verses (no pun intended) we learn a lot about this little man from Jericho. Not only is he rich; as the *chief* tax collector, he is particularly despised by his fellow Jews. The chief collectors were known for colluding with Rome and for taking advantage of others to make a good profit for themselves—think corrupt subprime mortgage agents on steroids.

If you were reading the Gospel of Luke from the beginning in one sitting, you would definitely not expect this story to end happily for Zacchaeus. Luke has had quite a few harsh things to say about rich people before this story comes along. Early in the Gospel, Jesus blesses the poor but warns the rich, saying, "But woe to you who are rich, for you have received your consolation" (6:24). In chapter 12, he tells a parable of the rich farmer who hoped to build bigger barns in which to store all his crops, but that

Exegetical Perspective

The story of Zacchaeus demonstrates several important Lukan themes: Jesus' welcome of outsiders, the character of faith and repentance, the right use of money and possessions, and the presence of God's salvation in the world. It also calls to mind the parable of the Pharisee and the Tax Collector (last Sunday's Gospel lesson), suggesting what that penitent tax collector might be expected to do in light of his prayer for mercy. Zacchaeus too experiences the mercy for which that tax collector begs, and he too is justified.

Jesus walks through Jericho on his way to Jerusalem, where he will arrive in 19:28, and meets Zacchaeus, a "chief tax collector" (vv. 1–2). All tax collectors, by definition, are wealthy; they purchase the right to collect taxes and profit from what they charge above what they owe the empire. When some tax collectors ask John the Baptist, "Teacher, what should we do?" he tells them, "Collect no more than the amount prescribed for you" (3:12–13), which effectively puts them out of business. Zacchaeus has been very successful, since Luke says he is well-to-do. Jericho is a big city—Herod had a grand palace there—and is therefore a major center of taxation,[1] so Zacchaeus has numerous underlings collecting on his behalf. His prosperity is to be expected.

1. Joseph A. Fitzmyer, *The Gospel according to Luke X–XXIV*, Anchor Bible 28A (Garden City, NY: Doubleday, 1985), 1223.

Homiletical Perspective

As one who is "short in stature" myself, I have always taken pleasure in this charming and familiar story of Jesus' encounter with the wealthy, short chief tax collector named Zacchaeus. The preacher's challenge is to move the story from folklore to message. At least three possible themes suggest themselves: (1) the extravagance of divine love, which calls forth extravagance from us; (2) God's relentless desire for us; and (3) a relationship between generosity and salvation.

Divine Extravagance. Much of the charm of this story lies in the extremes demonstrated by the characters, and the hyperbolic extravagance of their actions, especially those of Zacchaeus. Zacchaeus is both extremely short and extremely rich. He impetuously runs up a tree to get a look at the passing prophet. Jesus invites himself impulsively to Zacchaeus's house for a visit. In response to that visit, Zacchaeus promises to donate half his possessions to the poor and to repay fourfold anyone he has defrauded. It is in this context of these extravagant gestures that Jesus declares Zacchaeus's salvation. Even in this context, God's offer of salvation to the sinner Zacchaeus stands as the most extravagant gesture of all.

God's Relentless Desire. Jesus does not wait for Zacchaeus to invite him into his home. He invites

Luke 19:1-10

Theological Perspective

stature may have more to do with his profession than his actual height. The crowd may have shunned or barricaded him because of what he did for a living. In any case, Zacchaeus is hindered from seeing Jesus.

This does not prevent Jesus from coming to Zacchaeus's tree, making eye contact with him, calling him down, and inviting himself into the tax collector's home and life. Here is a stark reminder that on our own, apart from God, we are hindered from seeing and experiencing the grace of God. Our sinful condition eclipses the light of God from shining into our lives (Matt. 6:23; John 3:19). However, when God speaks light into our hearts, God gives us knowledge of the glory of God in Jesus Christ (John 1:5; 2 Cor. 4:6; Eph. 5:8).

In the passage at hand, Jesus seeks not only the lost in general but Zacchaeus in particular. Theologically we might refer to this movement as a heavenly initiated divine call. Here as elsewhere, Jesus selects individuals from crowds and extends personal invitations to them to become followers (Matt. 4:18–22; John 1:35–51). Zacchaeus is another case in point.

This divine calling by Jesus is not whimsical; rather, this is the vocation of God to call persons out of sinfulness into his glorious light. Calvin suggests that encountering Jesus in this manner, as the Word of God, is to commune with the light of God and reflect the glory of God.[1] Although the text does not use the word "call," Jesus does *call out* to Zacchaeus, and in doing so he initiates salvation.

When God calls us, we respond with faith and obedience. When Jesus calls out the name "Zacchaeus," we can see a theological concept at work— namely, that in our divine call God names us as his own children (Gal. 3:26). This is the missiological objective of the Son of Man (Luke 19:9), who is Lord of salvation. The divinely providential initiative of Jesus illustrates that the salvation of God always begins with God. Jesus is God with us, Immanuel, who saves us because we are impotent to save ourselves (Rom. 7:19).

Karl Barth writes that Jesus, the "One," is the initiator and sustainer of our calling and vocation. It is only in and through the being of Christ that we are called.[2] Jesus pronounces the call and salvation of Zacchaeus by affirming that salvation has come to his house. Zacchaeus is truly a "son of Abraham" (v. 9). We agree with Paul that the gifts and calling of God are irrevocable (Rom. 11:29).

1. T. F. Torrance, *Calvin's Doctrine of Man* (London: Lutterworth, 1949), 31.
2. Karl Barth, *Church Dogmatics*, IV/3.2, (Edinburgh: T. & T. Clark, 1962), 520.

Pastoral Perspective

very night he was called to account by God. A few chapters later, he tells another parable, about Lazarus in heaven and the rich man in hell. In chapter 18, just before today's reading, the rich young ruler walks away from Jesus sad.

Jesus is on the way to Jerusalem to face his death when he encounters this man whom we might rightly expect him to rebuke. Jesus is always welcoming the wrong people and confounding the good righteous people. If wee Zacchaeus had been like the Pharisee in the parable from last week's reading (18:9–14), self-righteous and pompous, then Jesus probably would have walked right by him. However, this important and disliked community businessman did something extraordinary. He had obviously heard a bit about this man Jesus who was coming through town. He wanted to get a look for himself, but those crowds got in the way. I guess he got tired of looking at the backs and bottoms of tunics, and put pride aside to get a good view. He dashed ahead of Jesus and climbed a sycamore tree, whose low branches made a good climbing tree for a little man.

"Ah, now I can see him." What a shock for Jesus to stop and give Zacchaeus the honor of staying at his house that night. The social outcast responds to this with great joy! When the good church folk grumble that Jesus is staying with a sinner, Zacchaeus stands up on his little feet, stretches up as tall as he can, and declares that he will give half his possessions to the poor. What is more, he will repay any fraud fourfold. This goes far beyond what Jewish law demands. Furthermore, Zacchaeus makes this commitment not with a frown on his face, but with a light heart and a smile. Jesus confirms what the reader has already guessed when he declares that "salvation has come to this house" (v. 9), because Zacchaeus is indeed a child of Abraham just like the grumblers.

The story of Zacchaeus tells us that the gospel is about serious commitment to God, but it is also about joy. We good church folk do not always do joy very well. Zacchaeus's little stand and big smile convict us to do better. Communion is serious business, but it is also a celebration. The word "Eucharist" means thanksgiving. As we share the elements with each other and say words like "bread of heaven" and "cup of salvation," a good response is, "Thanks be to God!" We respond to Jesus' invitation to the table with joy because we are included in God's family.

The story of Zacchaeus also tells us something about looking for Jesus, even as he is looking for each one of us. It is comforting to remember the last words Jesus says in this story: "For the Son of Man

Zacchaeus is great with respect to wealth, but small with respect to height. His infamous "short stature" causes him to seek a seat in the balcony of a tree along the way, in order to catch a glimpse over the crowd of the wandering preacher (vv. 3–4). Is he merely curious? Does he sense something in Jesus that touches him? Luke says he runs ahead of the crowd to catch a glimpse (v. 4), which suggests eagerness. Rather than just watching Jesus unnoticed up in the tree, though, Zacchaeus attracts the latter's attention. "Zacchaeus, hurry and come down; for I must stay at your house today" (v. 5), and Zacchaeus "welcome[s] him joyfully" (v. 6, my trans.).

Jesus invites himself to the tax collector's home—a startling breach of etiquette, and also a brazen demonstration of his reputation for associating with outsiders. The religious purists have already asked him, "Why do you eat and drink with tax collectors and sinners?" (5:30) and Jesus quotes them as saying, "Look, a glutton and a drunkard, a friend of tax collectors and sinners!" (7:34). As they were drawn to John the Baptist (3:12), the "tax collectors and sinners" are attracted to Jesus, and he welcomes them (5:29; 7:29; 15:1).

Rather than being defiled by their company, Jesus instead communicates wholeness and welcome. The bystanders echo the Pharisees' shock: "He has gone to be the guest of one who is a sinner" (v. 7). Table fellowship, by Pharisaic standards, denotes not merely friendliness but parity and acceptance. To sit at table with someone indicates approval of that person, and Jesus seems to be approving of Zacchaeus's sinful life. In addition, in Luke's view, Zacchaeus here approves of Jesus, and that changes his life.

The character of faith and repentance in Luke is emphatically ethical. It is not sufficient to understand that Jesus is God's Messiah and to believe in him. One's life must reflect one's confession. Zacchaeus clearly understands and demonstrates this. He says to Jesus, "Look, half of my possessions, Lord, I will give to the poor; and if I have defrauded anyone of anything, I will pay back four times as much" (v. 8). While the proud Pharisee in last Sunday's parable reminds God of his faithful tithing (18:12), Zacchaeus offers half of his substantial wealth to the poor. Then he makes the restitution the Bible requires: "the thief shall pay five oxen for an ox, and four sheep for a sheep" (Exod. 22:1). Zacchaeus thus identifies his shakedown of his neighbors as theft rather than taxation, and he repents of it. After he gives half his money to the poor and he refunds four

himself in. Zacchaeus is, at least initially, apparently motivated by curiosity, but Jesus is motivated by love. Jesus meets Zacchaeus's curiosity with invitation and ultimately with the declaration of salvation to his house. Importantly, Jesus' desire for Zacchaeus's salvation flies in the face of the normal expectations of the crowd. They grumble that Jesus is the guest of a notorious sinner like Zacchaeus. Jesus' action, however, is consistent with a frequent theme in Luke's Gospel. Jesus time and time again acts against social expectation and religious decorum, by associating with those regarded as outcast or unclean in some sense. In seeking out Zacchaeus, Jesus demonstrates the extravagant desire of God for the salvation of the lost, that is, for our salvation.

Generosity and Salvation. That Zacchaeus is the very model of generous restitution seems evident in the story. He stands before Jesus and says that he is giving half of his possessions to the poor and repaying fourfold those he has cheated. This goes beyond generosity to extravagance. This act of restitution seems to form the basis for Jesus' announcement of salvation. Whereas the tax collector in Luke 18:9–14 by offering his humble prayer in the temple "goes down justified" on the basis of his simple trust in God's mercy, Zacchaeus's salvation lies in his good deeds and his eagerness to amend his life.

The preacher may also want to consider the interpretation of some biblical scholars that the NRSV translation of Zacchaeus's proclamation of his generous acts is misleading in implying that he is making a promise about *future* actions. Some argue, rather, that the verb suggests that Zacchaeus says he is already doing these things: giving half his goods to the poor and paying restitution. If one takes seriously this reading of the text, a different sermon emerges. If we draw upon this reading, the issue is not Zacchaeus's conversion at all, but the unfair and harsh judgment of the observers, who see Zacchaeus as a sinner. In this light, then, Jesus' statement that Zacchaeus too is a "son of Abraham," that he is a good Jew, is a defense of Zacchaeus against those who judge him to be a sinner and therefore outside the faith. This offers another approach to the theme of generosity and salvation, but here the lack of generosity of the self-righteous observers serves as a foil against which to see the generosity of Zacchaeus.

Once again, as throughout Luke's presentation of Jesus, expectations about religious roles are overturned, and the outsiders are presented as those whom God accepts. The twist in this story can be

Luke 19:1-10

Theological Perspective

Our Lord, even in his humanity, exhibits divine foreknowledge that enables him to carry out his missiological objective. Divine foreknowledge is the ability to know people or events before they happen, as Jesus knows Zacchaeus's location and name without ever having met him before. Paul spoke of this when he wrote, "For those God foreknew he also predestined to be conformed to the image of his Son" (Rom 8:29; 11:2).

God calls us into a salvific relationship with himself, and we respond. The passage clearly portrays Zacchaeus's response to the call of the Messiah. Very simply, he comes down out of his safe haven in the tree and stands with Jesus, who "happily welcomes him" (v. 6, my trans.). His actions should not be overlooked by the theologian/preacher, for they teach us that there is always a human response to the gracious word of our Lord. This response is due to the refashioning of one's inner being by the grace of God, resulting in further illumination and ethical redirection (i.e., repentance).

This redirection is evident in Zacchaeus as his attitude toward his fellow human beings changes. Without being prompted or coerced, he entrusts half of his estate to the poor and commits himself to making fourfold restitution to those against whom he has sinned (v. 8). Thus Calvin says that Zacchaeus is "changed from a wolf not only into a sheep, but even into shepherd."[3] Zacchaeus is coming into alignment with the word of God as a new creation. The theological beauty of the passage is the narrative breadth of the salvific experience of Zacchaeus as he goes from being a distant observer of Jesus to being a faithful disciple of Christ.

ROBERT LEACH

Pastoral Perspective

came to seek out and to save the lost" (v. 10). Our salvation is *not* contingent on our efforts—thanks be to God! This reassurance does not mean that we may remain totally passive, going about life without a thought how we can take a step toward Jesus as he walks miles to find us time and again.

The stories of how each of us looks for God are going to be more varied than the Aaron-to-Zacchaeus stories in the Bible, but we can take a few tips from wee Zacchaeus. He humbles himself by running and climbing a tree. Zacchaeus was not thinking of appearances. He was thinking about Jesus. He was not trying to be anyone but himself. He just wanted to see Jesus. The crowds were getting in the way, so he climbed a tree.

As we try to follow Christ in worship, in our work lives, or in the marketplace, we can remember a happy saint of the church: wee Zacchaeus. We may not *have* to climb a tree to see Jesus above the crowd—Jesus will find us anyway. If, however, you are finding yourself tired of staring at the backs of the crowd, look for your tree to climb. If graced with a memorable encounter with God, perhaps your response will be as joyous as Zacchaeus's and it will lead to your own kind of cheerful commitment to justice. "For the Son of Man came to seek out and to save the lost."

LAURA S. SUGG

---

3. John Calvin, *Commentary on the Harmony of the Gospels* (Rio, WI: Ages Digital Library, 1997), 2:325.

times what he has taken in tolls, Zacchaeus is no longer quite the wealthy man he was.

Luke's concern for the proper use of wealth is no mere indictment of rich people or an ascetic preference for poverty. It is a matter of distributive justice. Before Jesus is born, his mother praises God for filling the hungry with good things and sending the rich away empty-handed (1:53). Jesus' blessing of the poor with the promise that they will be rich has a corresponding woe to those who are wealthy, because they have already received their consolation (6:24). The parables of the Rich Fool (12:13–21), the Dishonest Manager (16:1–13), and the Rich Man and Lazarus (16:19–31) all highlight the danger that personal wealth (a) easily becomes an idol and (b) can deprive others of what they need.

The story of the Sabbath banquet ends with Jesus' saying, "When you give a luncheon or a dinner, do not invite your friends or your brothers or your relatives or rich neighbors, in case they may invite you in return, and you would be repaid. But when you give a banquet, invite the poor, the crippled, the lame, and the blind. And you will be blessed" (14:12–14). God has designed wealth to be shared, something the ruler in 18:18–23 learns to his great sorrow. This is why Jesus says, "Indeed, it is easier for a camel to go through the eye of a needle than for someone who is rich to enter the kingdom of God" (18:25).

Finally, Zacchaeus's repentance demonstrates the presence of God's salvation in the world. Jesus says to the crowds who have criticized him for associating with the (now former) tax collector, "Today salvation has come to this house, because he too is a son of Abraham. For the Son of Man came to seek out and to save the lost" (19:9–10). Zacchaeus (whose name derives from the Hebrew for "clean" or "innocent"[2]) is in the end declared saved. Salvation has come to "his house" because he has repented, changed his ways, and come to follow Jesus. This is the very purpose of Jesus' life and ministry, "to save the lost" (v. 10).

E. ELIZABETH JOHNSON

seen in comparison with a similar outsider story, the woman bent double, whom Jesus heals on the Sabbath (13:10–17). She is called "daughter of Abraham" by Jesus (13:16), who thereby removes her from her marginalized position due to her infirmity and places her within the community of the saved. As a woman with a serious physical deformity, she was doubly outcast.

Zacchaeus, by contrast, is outcast by reason of his occupation. Although he apparently has considerable wealth and, presumably, considerable power as chief tax collector, he too is treated as an outcast, a sinner, by the same religious leaders who condemn Jesus for healing a woman on the Sabbath and going home with a notorious tax collector. The preacher might wish to give some thought to contemporary examples of ways that these different forms of rejection play out in our world and in the world of the hearers.

In thinking about the performance of the sermon and its place in the larger context of the liturgy, it will be well to keep in mind the great physicality of this story. Zacchaeus runs ahead, climbs a tree, hurries down out of the tree, and stands in front of Jesus. The sermon, then, in its performance aspect will be most effective if it embodies this energy. Indeed, this should be true of the whole liturgical context. This story emphasizes bodies to a high degree. Zacchaeus's short stature, his running and climbing up and down, and, ultimately and dramatically, his standing before Jesus (and his detractors?) to declare his just acts, make clear the embodied character of faith. The sermon and the liturgy might provide the congregation with the opportunity to engage physically with this story, with energetic music and movement, with physical action, and with embodied declaration of our own faith, in forms that would be appropriate to the community and tradition and consistent with the character of this story.

MARJORIE PROCTER-SMITH

2. Ibid.

Haggai 1:15b–2:9

^{1:15b}In the second year of King Darius, ^{2:1}in the seventh month, on the twenty-first day of the month, the word of the LORD came by the prophet Haggai, saying: ²Speak now to Zerubbabel son of Shealtiel, governor of Judah, and to Joshua son of Jehozadak, the high priest, and to the remnant of the people, and say, ³Who is left among you that saw this house in its former glory? How does it look to you now? Is it not in your sight as nothing? ⁴Yet now take courage, O Zerubbabel, says the LORD; take courage, O Joshua, son of Jehozadak, the high priest; take courage, all you people of the land, says the LORD; work, for I am with you, says the LORD of hosts, ⁵according to the promise that I made you when you came out of Egypt. My spirit abides among you; do not fear. ⁶For thus says the LORD of hosts: Once again, in a little while, I will shake the heavens and the earth and the sea and the dry land; ⁷and I will shake all the nations, so that the treasure of all nations shall come, and I will fill this house with splendor, says the LORD of hosts. ⁸The silver is mine, and the gold is mine, says the LORD of hosts. ⁹The latter splendor of this house shall be greater than the former, says the LORD of hosts; and in this place I will give prosperity, says the LORD of hosts.

Theological Perspective

To think of the past as a better and maybe more glorious time than the present seems to be a common human tendency. A few centuries ago, the Spanish poet Jorge Amado declared, "Always to our view, time now past was just better to us" (my trans.). Prophet Haggai and his contemporaries apparently believed this too.

The outcome of the work of restoring the temple in Jesuralem was quite disappointing, when not frustrating, to those of the small nation of Judah. Back in their land after decades in Babylon, the people were trying hard to bring back the presumed glories of their preexilic past, but nothing had gone as expected with the restoration work.

For Haggai's contemporaries, a less-than-perfect temple was nothing in comparison with their image of what the temple had looked like during those better times in the past. That "nothingness," the result of their current efforts, was acknowledged by the prophet himself, but not without a bit of irony and surprise. "Who is left among you that saw this house in its former glory?" Haggai asked. (The expected answer was, of course, "Nobody.") "How does it look to you now? Is it not in your sight as nothing?" (2:3)

Humans generally look for someone to be responsible for a failure, someone to carry the blame for the rest of the group. In this regard, we are no

Pastoral Perspective

In this text, we find Haggai speaking to Judah on God's behalf. The listeners include the remnant living before the temple's destruction and those too young to have experienced the horror. All have returned from exile. Cyrus, emperor of Persia, has permitted the Jews to come home and rebuild the temple. The temple restoration has languished. The Jews' commitment to temple reconstruction has waned. The people have lost their priorities and have focused more on their own homes and personal security than on establishing the center of their faith community.

As the center of the community, the gathering place of the people to worship God, and thereby the locus by which the Jews would rightly orient their lives, the temple was essential. Haggai has asked those aging members of the community who remember the details of the old temple to comment on the progress. They inform the community that the work does not approach the level of stateliness and quality of handiwork found in the former temple. It is likely that the goal of rebuilding the temple to an even higher state seems unattainable to them and thereby pointless.

Both in this passage and in the context of the postmodern world, the temple is not merely a building but a community of faith living in response to

Exegetical Perspective

Haggai was one of three postexilic prophets who arose in Judah after Persia became the dominant power in the ancient Near East (539 BCE), and Jews were permitted to return to their homeland. The other two were Zechariah and Malachi. Haggai's oracles can be narrowed down to the three-to-four-month period between August and December, 520 BCE, making him a contemporary of Zechariah, who prophesied from 520 to 518 BCE. Malachi was active a century later.

Haggai and Zechariah are associated in the book of Ezra (Ezra 5:1; 6:14), and the LXX ascribes Psalms 145–148 to the two of them (the Vulgate ascribes only Psalms 145 and 146). According to rabbinic tradition, these were the last of the Hebrew prophets, as it was believed that prophecy in Israel had come to an end (1 Macc. 9:27). Only after a silence of four centuries or more was the prophetic voice heard again in John the Baptist (Matt. 11:9–10).

Darius I became king in Persia in 522 BCE, and soon after sent Zerubbabel, a grandson of exiled King Jehoiachin (Hag. 1:1; 1 Chr. 3:16–19), to Judah as governor of the territory (Ezra 2:1–2). It is generally believed that Haggai (and Zechariah) came to Judah with Zerubbabel, but some have argued that Haggai was never exiled to Babylon but was, rather, a farmer residing in Judah.

Homiletical Perspective

The slightly jumbled dates that begin this reading serve to remind the preacher/witness and the congregation that we proclaim a God who acts through human history and who is understood through human voices in community. The prophet Haggai is such a voice. Many scholars say he provided much of the energy for the rebuilding of the temple when the children of Israel returned from Babylon. Haggai looked around at the people rebuilding their own homes and not doing anything about rebuilding the temple, and he called them on it. It is well worth the preacher's time to read the two chapters of this prophetic book in its entirety (especially if you are getting ready to launch a building campaign!).

Haggai directs his words to the power brokers of the community—Zerubbabel and Jehozadak—as well as to "the remnant of the people" (v. 2), and his first question to them is this: "Who is left among you that saw this house in its former glory?" (v. 3). This question is certainly evocative.

Many congregations have a Camelot memory. Perhaps memories of Camelot are annoying to the newly arrived occupants of the kingdom, but unleashing the energy in them in a nondefensive, interested but nonthreatening manner could be a shot in the arm to an overly nostalgic or complaining community. In a congregation who experience

Haggai 1:15b-2:9

Theological Perspective

better than our biblical predecessors. If we cannot find someone among us, then the next obvious candidate is God, as happens so often in the Scripture. After all, should not God know or fare better than us? If God does not do better than us, then what does it mean to be God? Surely God knows well the people's frustration as well as their complaint.

During the short period of prophetic activity for which we know Haggai, the prophet addresses some of these concerns. First of all, he declares that, even if it is not quite obvious, God is with them, working with and through them (v. 4). This affirmation of God's presence and support alone should give them courage. In addition, the prophet insists that God remembers the promises made to the people's ancestors in the past (v. 5). "My spirit abides among you," says the Lord of hosts; "do not fear" (v. 5).

This is God's promise to the people. Not even the most difficult circumstances for the most arduous task will persuade God to stay away. Actually, staying away or being unconcerned is not in the nature of this God. Whatever it takes to help the people out, God is able and willing, even if it means shaking "the heavens and the earth . . . the sea and the dry land; and . . . all the nations" (vv. 6–7).

Most importantly, God will provide what the people need for the task at hand. The resources they need to rebuild and restore the temple will come from other lands. This is another sign that God is God above all nations. The treasures of the earth, as well as the accumulated goods of other nations, fall under God's active rule. The spirit of God moves and goes anywhere, abiding where God wants it to. This abiding spirit is the promise of divine presence and initiative among the people.

This last point brings us to one of the basic tenets of Haggai's theological thinking: the presence of God is evident in the glory of *God*, which is where the real glory of Haggai's people lies as well (not in former glory of the *temple*). Without the glory of the divine presence, all attempts at national rebuilding will come to naught. Never mind about how things look or do not look, Haggai says. Concern yourselves instead about whether God has decided to make God's presence felt among you. Either the spirit abides, or the spirit does not abide. The spirit dwells where God decides it will.

This prophetic word neither precludes nor distracts from the tasks that lie ahead for the people of God. No one needs to feel dismayed. The people are actually encouraged by the prophetic utterance to move ahead in confidence that God is working with

Pastoral Perspective

God. Just as a family may look at an old farm and relish the heydays of yesteryear without putting effort into tilling the soil and planting the seed, so the present community may be unwilling to do the work necessary for a rich harvest. YHWH calls God's people into relationship with God and one another. Sustaining both of these relationships is key to building and supporting the community of faith. So is constant assessment of our expectations.

The church cannot live on what was in the past. Take, for example, an intercity church struggling to make ends meet. The membership has grown old, and the building has become dilapidated. Young folks who might otherwise join are overwhelmed by the expectation that they are the ones to turn the congregation around, restore the building, and bring in new members. The task may seem too great for young adults who are also struggling to juggle work, family, and other various responsibilities. They may find it easier to start fresh without a building or simply to join a well-established church in the suburbs than to face the monster expectation of turning the church back into what it once was.

At the same time, some of the older members look back to the time when the church was in its heyday. The building was in miraculous shape, the pews were full, and the building buzzed with activity. When the church was built, their parents and others mortgaged their homes to make the church edifice possible. Some may expect younger members to do the same, mortgaging their family homes to keep up the church building.

This only leads to dismay. It is easy to make the actual building the focus of a congregation's expectation, rather than to hear the call of God to be the church—the kingdom of God—here and now in this place. Like the field that needed to be tilled, such a church calls for the full intentionality of its members as they build a community of faith that worships, prays, and plays together.

A variety of questions about "being the church" can be stirred out of this text. What does it mean to put God first, creating a space for the congregation to gather to worship God together, to study Scripture together, and to seek to live out our lives together as the people of God? Does this always entail a building? Does God call us to provide a gorgeous sanctuary, or to discover a sustainable way of living out our faith together?

The great assurance Haggai offers the people is that God is truly present with them as they struggle with their past and with their future. "Take courage, all you

Haggai is credited with spurring the people on to get the temple rebuilt, receiving support for the enterprise from Zechariah. Sheshbazzar, Judah's first governor, in eighteen years was unable to get beyond a laying of the foundations (Ezra 5:14–16). The book of Ezra reports tensions between the Judeans and Samaritans over rebuilding the Jerusalem temple (Ezra 4:1–5), but Haggai's word was heeded, and the rebuilding began. In five years or less work was completed, and in about 515 BCE the temple was dedicated (Ezra 6:14), fulfilling Ezekiel's prophecy (Ezek. 40–48).

Now in the second year of Darius, that is, 520 BCE, in the seventh month of Tishri (September / October), YHWH told Haggai to speak to Zerubbabel, Joshua the high priest, and all the people, asking who among them had seen the glory of the First Temple. Early Jewish and Christian writers argued on the basis of verse 3 that Haggai was an old man who had himself seen the First Temple, but of this we cannot be sure.

Were any in his audience able to remember the former temple? Again we cannot know, but it is possible that someone of seventy-five years or older could remember having seen it. The First Temple was destroyed by the Babylonians in 586 BCE, and now in 520 it was only sixty-six years later. Haggai's question, of course, may be rhetorical; perhaps he and others knew only what had been reported about the glory of Solomon's temple. What everybody did know, however, was how the temple looked now, with only foundations and a course or two of stones in place. Compared with the First Temple, it was nothing, but Haggai told the assembled to take courage and get on with the work. YHWH of hosts had given them his great "I am with you" promise.

"Glory" (kabôd) here may refer more broadly to the splendor of the temple in its entirety or perhaps to its splendid interior. The oracle goes on to say that silver and gold treasures would be returned from Babylon; this temple, filled with glory, would surpass the former temple and its glory (vv. 7–9). An inventory of temple treasures taken to Babylon is given in 2 Kings 25:13–17 and Jeremiah 52:17–23. Besides all the bronze broken in pieces or taken away intact, there were the small bowls, fire pans, sprinkling bowls, pots, lampstands, incense dishes, and libation bowls of gold and silver. It was said that whatever was gold was taken for its gold, and whatever was silver was taken for its silver. Jeremiah promised that one day these treasures would be brought home (Jer. 29:14; 30:3, 18; 31:23; etc.), and at some point in the return they were (Ezra 1:7–11).

their best days behind them, the preacher could do some good work in allowing people to claim those memories—not just in clandestine parking-lot conversations about the good old days, but in public worship. A real gift to a stuck community could be to raise the whispered question in public worship.

For example, what if a new pastor acknowledged the grief that some might feel at the passing of the old? Of course, change in the vitality of a particular congregation is a mirror reflecting the changes upon changes in every person, family, workplace, school, neighborhood, town, city, nation, and world. "Who is left among you that saw this house in its former glory?" This question is not the end of our faith journey, nor should it provide the only energy in a sermon, but the question of who remembers the glories of old, used evocatively, could be a rich beginning.

The next question Haggai asks the leaders of the community and their diminished flock is, "How does it look to you now?" (v. 3). This is the prophetic thrust; it is the calling forth of clear-eyed, unsentimental communal seeing of the present reality. In this question, the preacher can invite the congregation to live in the present and to see the present beyond the misty allure of nostalgia, wishful thinking, and all manner of other illusions. "How does it look to you now?" This is a loaded question.

The preacher might be tempted to tell the congregation what they *ought* to be seeing. The wisdom of humility comes in handy at this time. The preacher is certainly allowed to say how things look to her or to him, but much of the real work of this question goes on between the ears of the listener. "How does it look to me now?" leads to "How does it look to us now?" A shared comprehension of what the reality is today can become the beginning of a new vision for tomorrow.

The final question that Haggai asks in this text is this: "Is it not in your sight as nothing?" (v. 3). The preacher and the congregation may hear this question as a challenge, if not a scathing indictment of the values of the community. Either way, that seems a pretty accurate reading of the text.

Remember the context in which Haggai prophesied. The people have come back from captivity, enslavement, and exile. They have been set free to rebuild their community on their own turf. What happens? They scatter each to his or her own project, each to care for me and mine. Meanwhile, they all forget about the temple and the core values the temple stands for: praise and worship of the God who set them (and us) free; and care for the neighbor

Haggai 1:15b-2:9

Theological Perspective

them and through them. The task ahead might be truly uphill, but God through the spirit will be with and for the rebuilders. The spirit will abide with the people, so that the temple's—and hence the nation's—"latter splendor . . . shall be greater than the former" (v. 9). Within this concrete place, God will show what only God can do and wishes to accomplish. Divine presence is the glory of the people.

For a people who have been downtrodden for a long time, and whose hopes have all but disappeared, the assurance of such divine presence is quite uplifting, to say the least. Here we have a small remnant of a nation, a people with almost no resources except for themselves and their faith. In the midst of utter despair, they can hear a gracious word of affirmation as a people from the one who matters the most: their God, the Lord of hosts. Now they have not only God's spirit but also God's word to go with them.

A little-known prophet named Haggai delivers the word of God to them. Although his prophetic activity is said to have been short, probably a season of no more than three months, it is significant enough to be recorded in the Scripture. Thus one of the lessons from Haggai's story is clear: God calls and uses whomever God wants to send with the word. Moreover, everything has its season in God's time. Wherever God through the Spirit makes a dwelling, God is there to guide and stay, even though it may not be obvious to anybody besides the prophet.

NELSON RIVERA

Pastoral Perspective

people of the land, says the LORD; work, for I am with you, says the LORD of hosts, according to the promise that I made you when you came out of Egypt. My spirit abides among you; do not fear" (vv. 4b–5).

The divine call to build the temple is a call to relationship and commitment with God. Whatever may befall us, whatever the quandary of the day, we have YHWH's promise, "I will be with you" (Gen. 26:3; 31:3; Exod. 3:12; Josh. 1:5; Isa. 43:2), which is echoed throughout the whole Old Testament.

This promise is given again by Jesus in all four of the Gospels, but perhaps most poignantly in the Gospel according to John, when he says to his disciples on the night before he dies, "And I will ask the Father, and he will give you another Advocate, to be with you forever. This is the Spirit of truth, whom the world cannot receive, because it neither sees him nor knows him. You know him, because he abides in you, and he will be in you. I will not leave you orphaned; I am coming to you" (John 14:16–18).

Here, as elsewhere, Jesus uses the second-person-plural pronoun when he says "you." He is speaking not to one individual but to the whole community of faith. The blessing of the church comes through God's joyous interaction with the people (and theirs with one another). It is precisely the relationship of the three persons of the Trinity that demonstrates authentic community and its possibility for all humanity. In his own time and place, Haggai calls us to hear and rely on the facts: that God is truly present with the people, that the relationship between God and humanity is real, and that the community will flourish in ways pleasing to God.

MARY ELEANOR JOHNS

Exegetical Perspective

Restorations of a similar nature have occurred in modern times. During the Second World War, for example, the high altar at St. Mary's Basilica in Cracow, Poland, was dismantled and hidden in August 1939. The invading Germans found it, and transported it the next year to Germany. After the war, it was discovered in the Nuremberg Castle and returned to Cracow in 1946.

Centuries after the rebuilding of the temple in the late sixth century, when Herod had made the Lord's house into an even grander structure, a disciple remarked to Jesus as he came out of the temple, "Look, Teacher, what large stones and what large buildings!" Jesus said, "Do you see these great buildings? Not one stone will be left here upon another; all will be thrown down" (Mark 13:1–2). So it happened when the Romans destroyed the Second Temple in 70 CE. Jesus also told the Samaritan woman at Jacob's well that the day would come when the true worship of God would be neither at the Jerusalem temple nor at the Samaritan temple, but "in spirit and truth," for that is the way God wants it (John 4:23).

John reported in his vision of the new Jerusalem that there would be no need for a temple, building on the words of Jesus in the Gospel and moving away even further from the prophecy of Haggai:

> I saw no temple in the city, for its temple is the Lord God the Almighty and the Lamb. And the city has no need of sun or moon to shine on it, for the glory of God is its light, and its lamp is the Lamb. The nations will walk by its light, and the kings of the earth will bring their glory into it. Its gates will never be shut by day—and there will be no night there. People will bring into it the glory and the honor of the nations. (Rev. 21:22–26)

JACK R. LUNDBOM

Homiletical Perspective

with heart, mind, and soul, as one cares for oneself. These core values of the children of Israel are being neglected.

So when Haggai asks the question "Is it not in your sight as nothing?" he is not simply condemning people for failing to rebuild the worship space. He is calling them to account for not rebuilding the community of the children of God. For Christians, this echoes in New Testament language about building a temple not made with hands (Mark 14:58) and building up the body of Christ (1 Cor. 3:9–15; Eph. 4:12). We are not to repeat this language in triumphalist terms but in terms of a gathered community of prayer, healing, almsgiving, and sacrificial love.

Finally, God reminds us through Haggai of two realities that are timely in any congregation at any hour. First, we are not in this alone. We do not need to self-produce all of the resources to build the house of God in the kingdom of heaven, for our God is a God of abundance who "will shake the heavens and the earth and the sea and the dry land; and . . . all the nations" (vv. 6–7). Our God will fill this house with splendor. The promises of God are promises of abundance in the past, in the present, and in the future. Second, the move into the future is not just a repeat of the past and a faint echo of former glory. In God's future we are moving toward and cocreating a surge of wonder, grace, beauty, power, and love. The Lord declares through his prophet Haggai that "the latter splendor of this house shall be greater than the former" (v. 9). Isn't that something?

MARTHA STERNE

Psalm 145:1-5, 17-21

¹I will extol you, my God and King,
   and bless your name forever and ever.
²Every day I will bless you,
   and praise your name forever and ever.
³Great is the LORD, and greatly to be praised;
   his greatness is unsearchable.

⁴One generation shall laud your works to another,
   and shall declare your mighty acts.
⁵On the glorious splendor of your majesty,
   and on your wondrous works, I will meditate.

. . . .

Theological Perspective

Psalm 145 focuses on the vast creative power of God in creation, a power that compels the singer to acknowledge God's providential bounty, strength, and justice. The verses lifted out for this lectionary selection form the opening and closing of the psalm. Standing alone they are a bit like bookends without books, especially given the rich content of the twelve verses between the lectionary selections, which include one of the most beloved lines of the Bible, repeated from Exodus 34:6 and Psalm 86:15, that God is slow to anger, abounding in love (v. 8).

Overall, the psalm praises God's plenitude and justice. It presents a vision of divine rule over a kingdom in which the faithful are rewarded with plenty and peace, where welfare is abundant, where all "who are falling" and who are "bowed down" are raised up, and where justice is effective, such that the "wicked" are destroyed. This is a political vision that "works," under a ruler who inspires confidence.

From the opening lines, this psalm focuses its praise through the frame of divine royalty. Indeed, Barnabas Lindars writes, "conceptually the kingship of Yahweh is the apex of the meaning of the poem."[1] The psalmist is doing nothing radical here. Depicting

---

1. Barnabas Lindars, "The Structure of Psalm CXLV," in *Vetus Testamentum* 29, 1 (1980): 26.

Pastoral Perspective

The superscription of this psalm (not printed above) is "Praise. Of David," making this the only psalm with the word "praise" in the superscription. The Psalter as a whole is entitled *tehillîm*, or "songs of praise," indicating that the primary topic of the Psalter is the praise of God. This psalm, emphasizing praise from the outset, thus expresses in a concentrated way the Psalter's chief purpose and message. The importance of this psalm has been recognized by the church, which appoints it for use several times in the Revised Common Lectionary.

This psalm is also the last in the Psalter that has a superscription, implying that the superscription applies to the remaining psalms, Psalms 145–150, all of which are songs of praise. In the Psalter as a whole, there is a continual oscillation between lament and praise, the two movements of the human spirit in response to God often occurring in the same psalm. However, there is a distinct trajectory of this oscillation, and that is toward praise, since the final six psalms of the psalter contain almost no notes of lament, or even mention of enemies, but are wholly focused on praising God. Psalm 145 sets this final movement of praise in motion, and with its closing words, "all flesh will bless his holy name forever and ever," invites the paean of praise to continue. The rest of the Psalter takes up that invitation,

17The Lord is just in all his ways,
    and kind in all his doings.
18The Lord is near to all who call on him,
    to all who call on him in truth.
19He fulfills the desire of all who fear him;
    he also hears their cry, and saves them.
20The Lord watches over all who love him,
    but all the wicked he will destroy.

21My mouth will speak the praise of the Lord,
    and all flesh will bless his holy name forever and ever.

Exegetical Perspective

The final psalm bearing the superscription "of David," this is the only one titled "Praise" (superscription not printed above). The lectionary reading selects the first five and last five verses of this psalm of jubilant praise. It is often preferable to use the entirety of a psalm in worship, and in fact, the most familiar portions of this psalm are in the missing middle, verses 8–9, which are often quoted along with verses 18–19 as an assurance of pardon after confession, and verses 15–16, which have been used for centuries among both Jews and Christians as a table blessing. However, if a shortened form is called for, this particular psalm reads smoothly in the abbreviated version suggested by the lectionary. In fact, some of the same words and thoughts introduced in the beginning are repeated toward the end. Verse 2 vows, "Every day I will bless you, and praise your name forever and ever," while verse 21 expands the same thought to a universal level: "All flesh will bless [God's] holy name forever and ever."

The psalm is shaped as an acrostic: after the superscription, the first word of the first verse begins with *aleph*, the first word of the second verse begins with *bet*, and so on all the way to the last letter of the Hebrew alphabet, *tav*. The only exception seems to be a copyist's error: the verse that should begin with *nun* is missing in the Hebrew Masoretic Text. The

Homiletical Perspective

The Westminster Shorter Catechism (ca. 1640), a standard in many Reformed churches, begins with these well-known lines,

> Q. What is the chief end of man?
> A. Man's chief end is to glorify God, and to enjoy him forever.[1]

While many of us might wish for more inclusive language in the catechism, the truth that is contained within its opening lines endures. Humanity's chief end in life is to glorify and enjoy God. Psalm 145 is an example of such an approach to a life of faith. The psalm entices us, urges us, to glorify and enjoy God forever. Several preaching themes emerge. Themes centering around glorifying and enjoying God, and around an eternal relationship with God are particularly evident in this scriptural text.

Glorifying and Enjoying God. In the English translation of this passage, there are nine different references to proclamation. The psalmist announces that he or she will extol (v. 1), bless (v. 1, 2), praise (v. 2), laud (v. 4), declare (v. 4), speak the praise (v. 21), and join with all flesh to bless (v. 21). This glorifying is not a

---

1. *The Book of Confessions* (Louisville, KY: Office of the General Assembly, Presbyterian Church (U.S.A.), 1999), 175.

Psalm 145:1-5, 17-21

Theological Perspective

God in easily recognized political terms of king and ruler served as a kind of shorthand that the psalmists and other biblical writers used to convey the greatness and power of God. Hymns and poetry depend on metaphors. Such images allowed the psalmist to avoid the philosophical difficulties that an otherwise unnamable and iconoclastic God requires of Israel's theologians (and later of the theologians of Christianity and Islam).

One of the theological challenges of verses such as these is the authoritative legitimacy they bestow upon the metaphors of monarchy and kingdom, not only as a frame for praise of God's abundant providence, but as a frame for right relation in general. A contemporary, post-Reformation theological approach to this psalm begs the question of whether the cultural shorthand of kinghood deployed by the psalmist is the ultimate meaning of the Scripture (as Lindars seems to suggest) or if the goodness and justice for which God is praised is the meaning that kinghood was intended to serve. If it is the latter, and if monarchical metaphors no longer automatically presume a meaning of goodness and justice, then the problem is how best to articulate that goodness and justice in the spirit of the psalmist without losing the poetry.

Writing in the late Roman imperial period of fifth century CE, Augustine did not question the political imagery of this psalm at all. He focused instead on the problem of eternal praise, quipping that if "you are going to praise God for eternity, you may as well begin now."[2]

However, since the Reformation and the rise of postmonarchical cultures, the "holy character of kinghood" has been under suspicion, and for many it no longer works as shorthand for divine goodness or power. Indeed, most modern theologians have to grapple with the fact that contemporary people are less and less able to imagine monarchy in such positive terms, and so must exert themselves in interpretive calisthenics to make the association of monarchy with goodness work at all. The challenge is whether divine monarchy is in fact the meaning of the psalm, and so must be managed, or whether the image is shorthand for something more complicated.

Calvin addressed this challenge by managing the image. In the sixteenth century, in the midst of political upheaval and violent Protestant emergence in Europe, he meditated on this psalm and surmised that the song reflected a flourishing Davidic political

Pastoral Perspective

the words of praise becoming ever more exuberant until the closing line of Psalm 150, "Let everything that breathes praise the Lord!" which echoes the end of Psalm 145.

Psalm 145 is an acrostic, meaning that the lines begin with successive letters of the Hebrew alphabet. Acrostic psalms aim for comprehensiveness, and this psalm thoroughly canvasses all the reasons for giving praise to God. God is described as the king whose reign is universal in both space and time. God's kingship is defined by both power and goodness; God does "mighty acts," both in creating the world and in delivering God's people from harm, and God also provides food and protection to those in need.

God is awesome in power, but also "gracious and merciful, slow to anger and abounding in steadfast love" (v. 8). God is splendid and glorious, but also kind, watching over those who love God. All of these attributes of God make God worthy to be praised; but in addition, God is praiseworthy simply for being God, just as a beautiful flower is praiseworthy simply for being itself. "God's greatness is unsearchable" (v. 3), declares the psalmist, suggesting that there is a praiseworthiness in God that cannot be reduced to God's acts on our behalf, but resides simply in God's being God.

With all these reasons to praise God, the psalmist simply cannot resist bursting into speech: "I will extol you. . . . I will bless you. . . . I will declare your greatness" (vv. 1, 2, 6). This impulse to praise God is so strong that the psalmist imagines it spilling out to all others, being passed from generation to generation. Not only humans, but indeed "all [God's] works" (v. 10) will give praise to God. The universality of praise corresponds to the universality of God's beneficent and glorious reign. There will be an unbroken chain of praise continuing forever, throughout all time and space.

When we pray this psalm, we enter into this chain of praise that the psalmist envisions extending to all living beings of every time and place. We enter the movement of praise that is the final word of the Psalter. By doing this, we are encouraged to claim the movement of praise of God as the first and last word of our own lives. There are certainly times in our lives when praising God is far from what we feel inclined to do. There may be times of hardship when the words of lament seem closer to the truth of our experience. However, the words of Psalm 145 are given to us to pray so as to reshape us toward a different orientation, one in which praise is fundamental, no matter what may be going on in our lives. In

---

2. Augustine, *Expositions on the Psalms*, part 3, vol. 20, trans. Maria Boulding, OSB, in *Works of St. Augustine: A Translation for the 21st Century*, ed. Boniface Ramsay (Hyde Park, NY: New City Press, 2004), 380.

Exegetical Perspective

NRSV supplies it (second half of v. 13) on the basis of four ancient witnesses: not only an alternate Masoretic manuscript, but a Qumran manuscript, the Greek, and the Syriac.

Acrostic poems in the Bible, especially in the Psalms, sometimes lack the dramatic movement of other poetry and instead convey the feel of a list or catalog whose order is determined more by the alphabetic form than logical or narrative development. For other acrostics, see Psalms 34, 111, 112, 119; Proverbs 31:10–31; and most chapters of Lamentations. This form often conveys the sense of having covered the subject "from A to Z."

The psalm's fullness comes not only from the acrostic form but also from the large number of times the word "all" is used (seventeen times; no other psalm uses the word so often). The universal scope is particularly apparent in the last several verses, where God is just in *all* ways and kind in *all* deeds, near to *all* who call on God, *all* who call on God in truth; the keeper of *all* who love God, who will destroy *all* who do evil. Finally, *all* flesh will bless God's holy name, forever and ever. A temporal fullness also shines through, the sense of God's greatness being reflected "forever and ever," a concept that is repeated six times in various ways, and rings out in the conclusion.

In this psalm's universe, the role of humans is to speak. Worshipers describe themselves as extolling, blessing, praising, lauding, telling, meditating, proclaiming, declaring, celebrating, singing, giving thanks, speaking, and making known. The role of God is to act. Frequent references to God's deeds, might, actions, wonders, awesome deeds, and power keep this role front and center. Even if God's greatness is declared unsearchable (v. 3), worshipers still try their best to search it out and shine light upon it. In verse 14, worshipers begin to specify God's awesome deeds. God's reign is characterized by justice and plenty: God upholds all who are falling and raises those bowed down. God gives all creatures their food and satisfies all desires. God acts with righteousness and kindness, hearing cries, and saving all who call. God preserves the faithful, but destroys the evil ones.

It is this discordant note toward the end of an otherwise dazzlingly kindly psalm that draws attention to itself. Throughout the psalm, God's mercy is described. Using, as so many psalms and prophets do, the words so well known from Exodus 34:6–7, the worshipers describe God as "gracious and merciful, slow to anger and abounding in steadfast love."

Homiletical Perspective

quiet act; it is not a private act. It is loud and ebullient, shared with others, contagious. In fact, the psalm is an acrostic—a veritable A–Z of glory and praise. This kind of expansive praise spawns great hymns of all genres, and the delivery and content of the sermon should evoke such praise from its hearers.

One way to think about how the sermon can evoke such praise is consistent with American Sign Language for the word "preach" or "testify." It is the sign for faith, initially held close to one's head, then moving forward. The idea is that testifying is taking faith out of one's own head (self) and moving it forward to others—giving faith, giving witness. How does the hearing community do the same? How do we take faith from inside our own experiences and give it forward?

It is important to note that the glory given to God is "every day" (v. 2), not just on special occasions. What does this mean for the believer? Most of us can remember or imagine glorifying God during times of celebration. How do we proclaim God's magnificence when times are arid? How do we "sing the Lord's song in a foreign land?" (Ps. 137:4).

An answer to these questions is perhaps found in the way that God is described in Psalm 145: God is an active God. God is not sitting on some mountaintop passing judgment, but is deeply engaged in the lives of followers. This God is just (v. 17), kind (v. 17), and near (v. 18). God hears, saves, and fulfills (v. 19), watches and even destroys (v. 20). This God is a vivid, life-giving force.

The lectionary committee has cut out the middle of this psalm, leaving just the first and last verses. These smaller segments fall neatly into two categories: verses *to* God (vv. 1–5) and verses *about* God (vv. 17–21). The verses about God exemplify this active God, one who intercedes on the part of humans. This is a God with whom one can be in relationship—who is "near to all who call on" God (v. 18). This God is one whose actions should cause us to rejoice!

Eternal Relationship with God. The psalmist repeats the phrase "forever and ever" three times within the psalm. Our enjoyment and glorification of God is not to be a temporal experience, pulled out for special occasions like the good china for guests. It is for every day, forever.

Verse 4, "One generation shall laud your works to another, and shall declare your mighty acts," speaks to this eternal relationship. We are not called to enjoy and glorify God and God's works only for our

Psalm 145:1-5, 17-21

Theological Perspective

reality. Referring to David as the putative author of the psalm, he argued that "in calling God *his king,* he gives both himself and other earthly princes their proper place, and does not allow any earthly distinctions to interfere with the glory due to God."[3]

Calvin's negative use of the psalm's metaphor to elevate God via the humiliation of human kings (an interpretative move that Barth would carry to its extreme in the twentieth century) is closer to rabbinic readings of the psalms than to earlier Christian commentaries like that of Augustine, for whom the monarchical metaphor perfectly reflects his construction of an eschatological empire of Christ in the city of God. Calvin accepts the metaphor as apt, that divinity is describable in the political terms of monarchy.

The psalm's closing presses the question of the metaphor most poignantly. The final verses form a series of assurances of divine provision and proximity to those who call upon God to such an extent that one wonders if anxiety about impending threats to the Davidic monarchy may actually simmer below the surface. Indeed, the ultimate assurance of the closing series is that the wicked will be destroyed. From within the frame of political rule, military and penal associations are nearly impossible to avoid, casting "destruction of the wicked" into juridical or bellicose terms. Without the political image of monarchy, it is difficult to measure providence in terms of favor or justice in terms of retribution. Theologically, then, the challenge of this psalm lies in separating the dream of a perfect kingdom—in which bestowal of favors and execution of criminals make for praise—from the God behind the praise, whose slowness to anger undermines the wicked, and whose abundance of love shames monarchies.

LAUREL C. SCHNEIDER

Pastoral Perspective

fact, it may be by speaking these words of praise that we discover that they are true.

The words change our awareness, so that we begin to notice the power and the goodness of God in our lives—the ways in which God has provided for us, has been close to us, has fulfilled our desires and our needs. In this way we begin to discover the truth that in our own lives too, praise necessarily has the first and last word. Not only because of all that God has done for us, but also simply because God is God, there are no truer words we can speak than the words of praise.

To orient ourselves primarily toward the praise of God is a political act. By describing God as a king whose kingship cannot be equaled anywhere in time and space, the psalm makes a political statement. It is a declaration that the God of Israel, and none other, is indeed the king of the universe and the only one worthy of praise. To give praise and worship to this God is to refuse to give praise or allegiance to lesser kings and rulers, since these do not have the perfections of God so fully described here. The praise of God as king is a movement against idolatry and toward the worship of the one who alone is God.

As we orient our lives toward praise of God, making praise our first and last word, we affirm the political statement made by this psalm. We declare that we believe God is indeed the only ruler of the universe, the only one capable of protecting and providing for us, and thus the only one ultimately worthy of praise. By committing ourselves to the praise of God, we reject the claims of ultimacy offered by the powers of this world. In embracing the praise of God as our truest word and work, we not only reject a false destiny, but orient ourselves toward our own true eschatological destiny, since at the end of all things, our sole occupation will be the praise of God in eternity.

RUTHANNA HOOKE

---

3. Jean Calvin, "Psalm CXLV," in *Commentary on the Book of Psalms,* vol. 5, trans. James Anderson (Grand Rapids: Eerdmans, 1949), 272.

Exegetical Perspective

Moreover, God's compassion reigns, not just over Israel, but over the entire creation, who all give thanks to God. God is declared faithful, just, and kind. God's grace seems to long to extend itself fully over all that God has made.

As the psalm unfolds, however, a quality of moral accountability emerges. God's deeds are not simply wonders to impress; rather, righteousness and justice drive them. The order within which the worshipers live is a realm where God reigns as majestic sovereign, whose dominion extends over the whole world and throughout all generations. Those who call on God "in truth" are heard and kept close. Those who are excluded from this all-encompassing realm are not enemy nations, not the Canaanites, not the Babylonians. Nor are they any class of people: they are not the wealthy, nor are they society's usual outcasts. They are not women or men, old or young. They are not even Gentiles outside the Israelite covenant. They are simply evildoers.

Other psalms define more closely what it means to be evildoers. Psalm 5 describes them as boastful, lying, bloodthirsty, deceitful. Psalm 10 characterizes them as persecutors of the poor, greedy for gain, renouncers of God, ambushing and murdering the innocent, lurking to seize the poor and drag them off in nets, believing that God will never see or rebuke their deeds. In other words, evildoers are not just people we do not like or approve of, but rather those who cause significant harm to vulnerable people, mayhem disruptive to an equitable society. These and other psalms sometimes envision punishments to fit the crimes, poetic justice, such as falling by their own counsels or into the traps they have prepared. Other psalms, like Psalm 145, devote to evildoers no more words than absolutely necessary to assure the faithful that in the realm of God's justice they will be free from oppression, free to bless God's name forever and ever.

PATRICIA TULL

Homiletical Perspective

own time, but also to pass that knowledge, that attitude of praise, to other generations. The psalm calls for our *proclamation,* our sharing of the good news with our children and our children's children, with our elders, with our peers.

In many ways, this particular verse calls modern Christians to be accountable, giving the preacher opportunity to remind the church communally and individually to be faithful witnesses to God's greatness. Campus ministries and college chaplaincies are often the first things cut from judicatory budgets. Vacation Bible schools are challenging to sustain. Locating volunteers to teach Sunday school taxes religious education committees. When soccer games compete with Sunday school or worship, soccer is often the victor. How are we doing at lauding God's works to the generation that follows us? How will our children know of God's glorious deeds if we do not share this news? Outside of formal programming for younger members, how are we sharing our witness? Is the faith that is inside of us finding its way forward through conversations, family prayers, example? Are our children really hearing the word of God's mighty acts from our lips?

Further, while the phrase "generation to generation" is traditionally understood as referring to elders passing knowledge to younger generations, there is a way in which younger generations can pass knowledge to their elders as well. Do we let our children teach us? Do we allow them to teach us to praise (in the inimitable gleeful way of children)? Have we heard the testimony of our teenagers? Do we allow young adults to teach us, or are we writing off their generation and its attendant culture wholesale? Technology has changed culture at a breathtaking pace. The culture of the youngest Christians is different from that of the oldest. While we need to be ever vigilant about proclaiming God's works from eldest to youngest, we must also be mindful of the new songs being sung by our youngest members, and open our hearts to their new ways of bringing glory and praise to God's name.

Nestled into Proper 27, when many experience November's shorter days and elusive sun, this extremely preachable text calls us not just to remember but to proclaim God's glory in all days and all times and for all generations—those behind us and those before. Indeed, Psalm 145 calls us to glorify God and enjoy the creator forever.

SUSAN K. OLSON

2 Thessalonians 2:1-5, 13-17

¹As to the coming of our Lord Jesus Christ and our being gathered together to him, we beg you, brothers and sisters, ²not to be quickly shaken in mind or alarmed, either by spirit or by word or by letter, as though from us, to the effect that the day of the Lord is already here. ³Let no one deceive you in any way; for that day will not come unless the rebellion comes first and the lawless one is revealed, the one destined for destruction. ⁴He opposes and exalts himself above every so-called god or object of worship, so that he takes his seat in the temple of God, declaring himself to be God. ⁵Do you not remember that I told you these things when I was still with you? . . .

¹³But we must always give thanks to God for you, brothers and sisters beloved by the Lord, because God chose you as the first fruits for salvation through sanctification by the Spirit and through belief in the truth. ¹⁴For this purpose he called you through our proclamation of the good news, so that you may obtain the glory of our Lord Jesus Christ. ¹⁵So then, brothers and sisters, stand firm and hold fast to the traditions that you were taught by us, either by word of mouth or by our letter.

¹⁶Now may our Lord Jesus Christ himself and God our Father, who loved us and through grace gave us eternal comfort and good hope, ¹⁷comfort your hearts and strengthen them in every good work and word.

Theological Perspective

In 2 Thessalonians 2:1–17, Paul (or someone so closely familiar with Paul and his letters as to assume his name) continues the message of comfort and assurance with which the letter began. Specifically, the writer addresses a false teaching the Thessalonians had apparently received from another source that had greatly agitated them. This source, purporting to be Paul himself, had led many in the community to believe that the "Day of the Lord" was already occurring. This apparently referred to the day when all righteous believers would be judged worthy and gathered up to meet the Lord upon his coming again. In his first letter to the Thessalonian community, Paul had stressed the nearness of the Day of the Lord and the nearness of the Thessalonians' salvation, so as to keep hope alive, given the hardships and persecutions they were facing. In this second letter, however, the emphasis is reversed and now they are reminded that, though still very near, the Day of the Lord has not yet arrived. The Thessalonians lived in a time of heightened expectation that the end of the world would be coming soon, so they were apparently worked up into an apocalyptic frenzy. The writer's insistence that the Day of the Lord had *not* yet arrived would have been reassuring.

Ironically, reassurance comes in the form of reminding them of impending evil: the coming of

Pastoral Perspective

My husband once asked a particular congregation to identify one of their hardest times. Since the church is located in a port city, he expected them to talk about the changes in the church as various immigrant groups arrived and changed the nature of the town. Perhaps they would go back to their early history and talk about their Revolutionary War experiences. The British had burned the church and shot and killed the minister's wife. No, none of those topped the list. The congregation said that the hardest time came in 1843, when a Millerite pastor persuaded members of the congregation to give away their homes and farms, to put on their white robes, and to wait on the hilltop for Jesus. They waited, but then they had to come back home and, shamefaced, ask for their property to be returned.

We may laugh at their naiveté, but there is something about the idea that God will step in to end the world that continues to draw us. Witness the popularity of the *Left Behind* series or the earlier *Late Great Planet Earth*. Today such folk see signs of the end in global warming, in the mess of the Middle East. Earlier generations found it in Soviet empire. If you are determined, signs are not hard to find.

What is the appeal? Surely it varies. For some, there is that one-upmanship that comes from knowing things that others do not. For others, the idea

Exegetical Perspective

Readers of today's lectionary selections (2:1–5, 13–17) will find in 2 Thessalonians altogether a litany of interpretive hurdles. Compared to 1 Thessalonians, 2 Thessalonians is peculiarly distinctive, if not somewhat puzzling, in its reflections on love, God, Christ, and the end time. It speaks of a love directed only toward the believers (2 Thess. 1:3) and not toward all, as was the case with 1 Thessalonians (3:12; cf. 5:15). It portrays a God who will seek eternal vengeance against enemies (2 Thess. 1:6–9). It depicts a Christ who is not identified by his death/resurrection, but virtually only by his Parousia or return (2:1, 8). It describes Jesus' Parousia as occurring at an unspecified time in the future (2 Thess. 2:1–12), not imminently, as in 1 Thessalonians (4:13–18).

The end time is featured, moreover, with an enigmatic apocalyptic drama of vindication (2:3–12). That is, the letter's basic story of good winning out over evil and of God and Satan set in opposition includes a forthcoming and decisive confrontation littered with enigmatic persons or forces. Thus, at that confrontation and with only his breath (2:8; cf. Isa. 11:4; 2 Esd. 13:10), God's agent (Jesus) will summarily destroy Satan's agent, the so-called lawless one, but this tyrannical usurper's identity (2 Thess. 2:4) remains for us a mystery, as does the identity of

Homiletical Perspective

The pastor encountering this text might take consolation from the fact that congregational divisions and rumors are nothing new. Any time people of faith gather, there is likely to be some confusion, misinterpretation, and differing speculation about how best to live together as God's people. This passage also requires the preacher to spend some time pondering the theological importance of the second coming for her congregation, since it is a central theme of this passage.

While most scholars agree that Paul penned the first letter to the church at Thessalonica, there is some dispute over the authenticity of Paul's authorship of this second letter. While the first letter is one of pastoral concern and compassion, this one has a much sterner tone. It is parental, like a letter to a son or daughter away at college who is getting involved with the wrong crowd. The author wants to remind the Thessalonians about the truth they know. He seeks to clarify some misconceptions about the return of Christ and the way in which they should wait for that return.

Paul is not our only authority here. We have Jesus to thank for the expectation of the second coming and its link with the end of the world as we have known it. Chapter 13 of Mark's Gospel gives us a passionate oration by Jesus describing the signs of

2 Thessalonians 2:1-5, 13-17

Theological Perspective

the Lord Jesus Christ will be preceded by specific apocalyptic events and a struggle between good and bad entities. The original readers of this letter likely knew what historical events and entities the writer referred to, though today's readers do not. Most interpreters of this text agree that the specific references are shrouded in mystery. In any event, verses 3–4 refer to an evil "rebellion" against God that will occur and a "lawless one" who will be revealed, enthroning itself in God's seat and claiming to be God. Subsequent verses explain that ultimately the lawless one will be restrained by a good force, destroyed by Christ, and the faithful will be vindicated.

In the history of interpretation of this letter, some have been tempted to scrutinize intensely the particulars of the events and characters being depicted. These readers have attempted to figure out precisely the identity of the lawless one and the nature of the apocalyptic struggle; some have even tried to correlate the verses with certain contemporary events so as to identify the forces in their lifetime predicting the second coming of Christ. They effectively attempt to decode what the text says about the end times to help believers get ready.

The majority of interpreters, however, argue that to attempt to decipher the precise events described in this letter is to miss its point. Despite the high drama, they contend, the letter does not actually delineate events very carefully, and therefore one can conclude that the Thessalonians are not being given serious theological instruction about the end time. Instead, the writer is trying to calm them down and refocus their attention. As Abraham Malherbe puts it, "Paul lays out an apocalyptic schema, the didactic elements of which are not offered for their own sake, but rather to support his practical purpose of exhorting them to live calmly and faithfully."[1]

Still, in assigning only modest weight to the details, in favor of reaching the correct overall interpretation, we would not want to downplay the potential theological significance of the specific cosmic forces alluded to in the text. Walter Wink has persuasively argued that because most of us no longer believe in creatures like Satan or the lawless one, we tend to dismiss them as unimportant. Yet these creatures remind us that catastrophe and evil are real, even if we no longer personify them. The worldview of people in New Testament times included a host of principalities and powers they

Pastoral Perspective

that the world will end and they will be among the elect is a wonderful escape from a difficult situation. It may be bad here, but just wait! "I'm gonna put on my long white robe and walk the golden streets."

Whatever draws us to contemplate the end of the world, the Day of the Lord, the second coming of Christ—call it any of those—that theme is consistent throughout the Bible. The Old Testament prophets looked forward to the Day of the Lord. Jesus saw his own ministry as leading toward that day, and his followers eagerly awaited his return.

Think about the logic of it. God is in charge of the world, yet God's people are so often the target of injustice, derision, and persecution—which does not speak well for God. How can this happen? Should there not be a time for payback? Is there not a time when God will rise up and say, "Enough!" Yes. Someday it will happen. Evil will lose its power in the world. Sin and injustice, sickness and despair—even death itself—will come to an end. That is the promise.

How do you live for that tomorrow? Do you put on your long white robe and sit on the hill to wait? Apparently that was the thinking of the early church in Thessalonica. Folk were so sure that the big event was just around the corner that they quit working and moved to full-time waiting. Paul has to tell them it could be a long wait.

At this point the lectionary skips over the specifics of Paul's warning—which is probably just as well, because it lends itself to wild speculation. We should instead listen to Jesus' warning that even he does not know when the Day of the Lord will arrive.

The one thing that is clear from Paul's description is that there will be an accounting for those who rebel against God. Deep inside, each of us knows that there are times when, despite our best efforts, we do deny God's rightful place in our lives. Rather than speculate about the who and the when of Christ's return, we need to tend our own souls. Rather than try to identify the lawless one, we need to recognize our own tendency to play that role.

There is also another way: to live as if the Day of the Lord has already come. My seminary theology professor used to say, "If heaven is like that, what are we doing in a mess like this? We need to roll up our sleeves and get to work." Knowing that God will triumph and the work of God's people will be vindicated is a powerful motive to work for justice and peace even in times of discouragement.

Too often the promise of Christ's return and the defeat of evil have been used as weapons to send the message, "If you do not do . . . whatever . . . you will

---

1. Abraham Malherbe, *The Letters to the Thessalonians*, Anchor Bible 32B (New York: Doubleday, 2000), 414.

the force or person presently constraining him (vv. 6–7).

Even the style and literary logic of 2 Thessalonians seem lacking. Whether one considers its simple letter-opening (2 Thess. 1:2; cf. 1 Thess. 1:1), its repeated thanksgivings (2 Thess. 1:3; 2:13; cf. 1 Thess. 1:2; 2:13), or one of its intercessory prayers (2 Thess. 2:16–17; cf. 1 Thess. 3:11–13), many of its forms seem excessively dependent on 1 Thessalonians. What is worse, many scholars deem the whole of 2 Thessalonians to be disparate, with hardly a unifying thread running through it.

When faced with these interpretive hurdles, readers usually ask two questions. Could this letter really have come from Paul? Does the letter's puzzling theology and strange figures relegate it to the dustbins of pragmatic irrelevancy? Oddly enough, if one does not envision Paul as the letter's writer and considers some of the common threads in today's lectionary selections, one finds an important degree of intelligibility in this otherwise distinctive and puzzling letter.

Second Thessalonians' Authorship. Scholars usually have taken two routes on the question of the letter's authorship. For some, the letter's similarities with 1 Thessalonians confer upon the work a Pauline stamp, with the assumption that Paul wrote 2 Thessalonians shortly after writing 1 Thessalonians, with the differences explained as an evolution in Paul's thought. For others, however, the same similarities represent an attempt by a later figure (perhaps one of Paul's followers) to imitate him.

They especially consider it hard to reckon that Paul would espouse an imminent Parousia in 1 Thessalonians, assume a delayed one in 2 Thessalonians, and then resume the idea of an imminent one in his later letters (cf. Rom. 13:11; 1 Cor. 7:29; Phil. 4:5). That 2 Thessalonians also presupposes an overall Pauline epistolary style (3:17) likewise raises questions, for a Pauline style would hardly have been available shortly after 1 Thessalonians was written.

Second Thessalonians' Pragmatic Relevance. If we accept the letter to have been written at a period after the death of the apostle, the letter's writer may have asked a critical practical question, a question that actually brings a measure of coherence to the entire letter: "How can the assembly control what may be deemed errant thought or irresponsible behavior in a postapostolic period?" As we shall see, the answer to this question appears to lie in the common threads between the two selections of today's lectionary reading.

the end of the age: "There will be suffering, such as has not been from the beginning of the creation that God created until now" (Mark 13:19). "Then they will see 'the Son of Man coming in clouds' with great power and glory. Then he will send out the angels, and gather his elect from the four winds" (Mark 13:26).

Ever since Christ's arrival, his followers and curious onlookers have wondered about his return and the consequences for creation. We encounter the church at Thessalonica struggling with some rumors that the day of Christ is at hand. Understandably, panic set in and anxiety rose for those not grounded in love and compassion as Christ encourages.

Police logs across the country in October 1938 chronicle the chaos of the people who had heard the Orson Welles radio program *War of the Worlds* and thought it was a true news story. A tremendous amount of energy and damage control had to go into getting folks calmed down and back on track. The same spirit is in this paraphrase from the passage: "Do not become easily unsettled or alarmed by some prophecy, report, or letter supposed to have come from us, saying that the Day of the Lord has already come" (v. 2). Imagine the anxiety early believers at Thessalonica must have felt when the rumor of the end times spread through their city. Daily life and worship were disrupted with concerns over how to wait, how to prepare, who would be "taken up" and who would be left behind.

In some way, this sense of anticipation of the end times brings to mind the old Southern business of exploiting the poor with something called funeral insurance. Frightened to be found lacking when the time for a proper funeral came, the poorest members of the community would fall prey to schemes whereby the dishonest insurance salesperson would guarantee a proper funeral for those who paid regularly on their policy. Those selling insurance often exaggerated both the unpredictability and the imminence of someone's death in order to make the sale.

While the writer of today's letter does not indicate any such exploitation, there is an air of disorientation and confusion that he tries to quell, assuring the congregation that they will know for certain of the return of Christ and that the return will be victorious. The author seeks to soothe them with a mysterious reference to the man of lawlessness. Scholars are unclear about this reference but agree that its purpose is to calm the anxious congregation with an indication that evil must yet be overthrown prior to the return of Christ.

2 Thessalonians 2:1-5, 13-17

Theological Perspective

took to be quite real. "What the ancients called 'spirits' or 'angels' or 'demons' were actual entities, only they were not hovering in the air. They were incarnate in cellulose, or cement, or skin and bones, or an empire, or its mercenary armies."[2] Wink suggests that we might reinterpret the biblical principalities and powers for today as symbolic projections of spiritualities inhabiting institutions, nation-states, regimes, economic systems, and other entities that exercise power over our lives. Accordingly, we might interpret the lawless one as a spirit of extreme arrogance, embodied in anyone or anything that claims to be godlike but is really anti-God.

According to the lectionary, this text is to be read in late autumn, a time when thoughts may be turning to supernatural spirits and their mysterious realm. The holidays we observe at this time—All Hallows Eve (Halloween) and the feasts of All Saints and All Souls—may help us overcome some of our skepticism and unease with what is mysterious and unseen. Perhaps there is wisdom in granting the existence of nefarious forces whose appearance signifies the end of the world as we know it, if only to take more seriously the very real evils we know *do* exist. Beverly Gaventa suggests that 2 Thessalonians may "place before us the obligation to rage against evil."[3] Finally, granting the reality of the powers allows us to take all the more comfort in the One who saves us from them. Only those who appreciate the true depth and intractability of evil will, after all, be able to receive the love of God who "through grace [gives] us eternal comfort and good hope" (v. 16).

BARBARA J. BLODGETT

Pastoral Perspective

burn in hell." I do not hear Jesus trying to scare people into the kingdom, and that is not what I hear here. The promise is that evil will be defeated. Evil will not rule the world. That is a promise that is comforting, hopeful, and challenging. The work for justice and peace is too often slow and discouraging. There are times when evil seems to hold far too much power. If we can hang on to the promise that its power is limited, that it will not have the final say, then we can continue the struggle. Knowing that God's favor will fall on those who do feed the hungry, visit the sick and imprisoned, clothe the naked, can sustain us in the hard times.

The story is told that one day back in early Puritan New England there was a major eclipse. The sun was blotted out, the day turned dark, and people were terrified. "The world is going to end. What shall we do?" One insightful man replied, "Let us be found doing our duty."

Think about it. As a parent, was it not wonderful to leave the kids alone for a few hours and come home to find things in order? You took pride in the fact that all was well. I think God is like that. When the Day of the Lord does come, when God no longer limits God's power in the world, when evil is finally banished, God wants to find us at work for those things that are dear to the heart of God. Our task is to keep on keeping on.

NETA PRINGLE

2. Walter Wink, *Unmasking the Powers: The Invisible Forces That Determine Human Existence* (Philadelphia: Fortress Press, 1986), 5.
3. Beverly Roberts Gaventa, *First and Second Thessalonians*, Interpretation series (Louisville, KY: John Knox Press, 1998), 96.

Exegetical Perspective

One common thread is the use of complementary requests near the beginning and end of 2:1–17. That is, the writer's initial entreaty (v. 1) for the assembly "not to be quickly shaken" from their "understanding" (*nous*, v. 2a, my trans.) "nor to be disturbed" (v. 2b, my trans.) is likely the counterweight to the writer's later positively stated request for the assembly "to stand firm" and "to hold on to the traditions" (v. 15, my trans.) which they were taught. If so, the writer suggests that there is a standard by which the assembly can govern its thought/speech and actions, a standard that lies in an understanding already available to the believers. This standard, moreover, is embedded in a specific set of traditions (v. 15; cf. 3:6) from which the assembly is not to part or be shaken.

Another common thread between verses 1–5 and verses 13–17 is the writer's allusion to the apostolic past. In 2:1–5, shortly after introducing the "lawless" one, the writer asks: "Do you not remember that I told you these things when I was still with you?" (v. 5). This question ostensibly certifies the writer's rendering of what has to take place before the Day of the Lord occurs, by means of an appeal to the assembly's memory of the apostolic past. In 2:13–17, virtually in the middle of a prayer collection (vv. 13–14, 16–17), the writer also alludes to the apostolic past with the words "the traditions that you were taught" (v. 15).

Thus, for this writer, the solution for controlling errant thought and irresponsible behavior lies in a specific set of traditions associated with the apostle's past. Understandably, then, the writer draws repeatedly on the forms and apocalyptic tradition of 1 Thessalonians. The strange remark about Paul's style in "every letter of mine" (3:17) rhetorically is yet another way for the writer to link his own letter to the Pauline tradition. Even the letter's inner-directed love and harsh view toward outsiders may have been designed as a rhetoric of solidarity to create a degree of unity in a context in which differences of opinion about appropriate speech/thought and action likely abounded.

The letter altogether then is not bizarre. Beyond its group-solidifying introductory and closing verses (1:1–12: 3:16–18), it speaks vividly against errant thought (2:1–17) and irresponsible behavior (3:1–15), both of which apparently are to be critiqued by a perceived standard from the apostolic past. Thus, long before the production of widely acceptable creeds, biblical canons, and ecclesiastical councils, this letter writer found his own standard by which to provide intragroup critique for a struggling community.

ABRAHAM SMITH

Homiletical Perspective

In addition to pondering the question of the return of Christ, there is perhaps another invitation for the preacher in this first segment of the passage. There is a creative opportunity for preachers to imagine what other end-time scenarios congregations often fall prey to. In what way does anxiety steal the energy and prevent the healthy flow of life in a congregation? What situations real or imagined threaten to undermine the faith and centered belief of the people of God in your community? Does a sudden change in the economy shake the foundations? What about a failed capital campaign or a slow and steady loss of membership in the church? Some have said that 9/11 was the beginning of the end. The harbingers of doom are all around us, telling us that the end is near. What do we, as leaders of our congregations, say to them?

Gratitude and encouragement are the antidotes to this fear-based hysteria. The letter takes a decidedly sharp turn in verse 13, when the author offers up thanksgiving for the faith of the people and their receptivity to the good news preached among them. There is an intentional shift on the writer's part to take inventory of what is right in the life of the community. He reminds them of their calling and their inheritance in the glory of Christ. We are not called to run in fear that the sky is falling. We are called to be the sons and daughters of Christ.

There is also a grounding admonition here to "stand firm and hold fast to the traditions that you were taught" (v. 15). This rich phrase is rooted in texts all the way back to Exodus 14:13, at the very pivotal moment of the exodus. Our God is a God who makes a way where there is no way. We need not fear, only believe and let our hearts be strengthened "in every good work and word" (v. 17).

ELIZABETH BARRINGTON FORNEY

Luke 20:27-38

²⁷Some Sadducees, those who say there is no resurrection, came to him ²⁸and asked him a question, "Teacher, Moses wrote for us that if a man's brother dies, leaving a wife but no children, the man shall marry the widow and raise up children for his brother. ²⁹Now there were seven brothers; the first married, and died childless; ³⁰then the second ³¹and the third married her, and so in the same way all seven died childless. ³²Finally the woman also died. ³³In the resurrection, therefore, whose wife will the woman be? For the seven had married her."

³⁴Jesus said to them, "Those who belong to this age marry and are given in marriage; ³⁵but those who are considered worthy of a place in that age and in the resurrection from the dead neither marry nor are given in marriage. ³⁶Indeed they cannot die anymore, because they are like angels and are children of God, being children of the resurrection. ³⁷And the fact that the dead are raised Moses himself showed, in the story about the bush, where he speaks of the Lord as the God of Abraham, the God of Isaac, and the God of Jacob. ³⁸Now he is God not of the dead, but of the living; for to him all of them are alive."

Theological Perspective

"God is not a God of the dead." This does not mean that God is indifferent toward humans who are already dead. God has not forgotten them. On the contrary, in relation to God, death is an enemy, and overcoming death is for God as important as defeating sin.

"Where, O death, is your victory? Where, O death, is your sting?" (1 Cor. 15:55) With these words, Paul rejoices with gratitude for the victory of God in Jesus Christ over the powers of death. However, Paul's statement is not meant to support the idea that death does not really exist or that there is a continuation of our lives after our deaths. Rather, we have to take seriously what the living Lord says in Revelation 1:18: "[I am] the living one. I was dead, and see, I am alive forever and ever; and I have the keys of Death and of Hades." These keys are only in the Lord's hands and never in our hands. If we are his followers, then we follow the one who has these keys in his hands.

It is this living Lord who is encountered in today's text by some Sadducees, a group of modern intellectuals of that time. The Sadducees refused the idea of a continuation of life after death. According to them, everything comes to an end with death; therefore, life is to be lived as fully as possible within the boundaries of earthly time. Because their belief is in

Pastoral Perspective

Luke's passage opens with intrigue as the Sadducees, who have a clear understanding that there is no resurrection, are asking Jesus questions about the resurrection. Questions have many functions in conversations. Questions are posed to gain knowledge and comprehension, analyze and assess a situation, challenge authority, shame an opponent, or win an argument or debate. Questions often give an opponent the advantage, as the question sets or reframes the conversation. The one who asks the question has the power. The Sadducees are questioning Jesus about a mystery that they have already considered and rejected. Their questions are not for the purpose of genuine dialogue, but for the purpose of prompting debate, with the hopes of showing up Jesus and showing onlookers that Jesus is not trustworthy or knowledgeable. Jesus seizes this moment of questioning as a teachable moment about the nature of heaven. Rather than taking the questioning as a personal attack, Jesus uses this moment as a time to teach about the love and mercy of God.

Jesus answers the questions by describing how heaven and earth are not the same. The ways of God are not the ways of humanity. God's judgments are not our judgments. Things do not work in heaven the way they work on earth—thank God! Jesus answers the question by saying that in heaven even

Exegetical Perspective

Question concerning Resurrection. Between 200 and 100 BCE, Pharisees and Sadducees disagreed over belief in resurrection when they emerged as opposed divisions within early Judaism. According to Sadducees, there was neither a doctrine of resurrection of the dead nor belief in angels in the written Torah (Genesis, Exodus, Leviticus, Numbers, Deuteronomy). Pharisees, emphasizing that written Torah must be kept up to date with oral Torah, namely, ongoing streams of interpretation handed down by word of mouth, coordinated with written Torah new beliefs that emerged in prophetic literature and the Psalms.

Of special importance was acceptance by Pharisees of the book of Daniel, which blended traditions of wisdom and prophecy with the new tradition of apocalyptic belief that emerged around 200 BCE. Daniel not only features the angels Gabriel (Dan. 8:15–17; 9:20–27; 10:4–9) and Michael (10:13–21; 12:1) but also presents the earliest clear biblical reference to resurrection of the dead in the context of a final judgment to everlasting life or everlasting contempt (12:2–3). Jesus adopted updated apocalyptic beliefs characteristic of Pharisees and participated in their debates about oral interpretation of written Torah.

By the time of the Gospel of Luke (80–90 CE), Christians and Pharisees had become major competitors. When Paul, a Pharisee, joined the Christian

Homiletical Perspective

Preachers interpreting the Scriptures for their congregations discover Jesus doing the same thing in Luke 20:27–38. As he teaches in the temple, a variety of challenges confronts Jesus, questioning his authority and attempting to entrap him in a net of his own words. Amazed by his unanticipated response to a question about paying taxes to the emperor (v. 25), the scribes and chief priests fall silent, while the Sadducees step forward. With the destruction of the temple the Sadducees almost disappeared into the dust of history, but Josephus described them as people from an elite upper crust who were "able to persuade none but the rich,"[1] and received small confidence from ordinary folk.

Perhaps the question they ask Jesus evidences their scorn of the common citizenry. Careful readers can almost hear their snickering as they cite Moses's teaching about levirate marriage (Deut. 25:5–6; Gen. 38:6–11) and propose an absurd scenario of a woman consecutively marrying seven brothers before asking, "In the resurrection . . . whose wife will the woman be?" (v. 33). In earlier days in a rural society levirate marriage may have provided a compassionate social arrangement to secure the posterity of deceased men

---

1. Josephus, *The Life and Works of Flavius Josephus*, trans. William Whiston (Philadelphia: John C. Winston, 1957), 397.

Luke 20:27-38

Theological Perspective

stark contrast with what Jesus teaches about survival after death, the Sadducees set an intellectual trap for him, thus hoping his answer will show that his teaching about the resurrection of the dead is absurd.

They say, let us imagine the case of seven brothers who marry their brother's widow as prescribed by the law of the time. If there is eternal life, upon the death of all the brothers and the woman, to whom will the woman be married? This imaginary scenario is meant to make fun of Jesus. Nevertheless Jesus takes them seriously, and he makes this one basic point: After their death they will no longer marry or be given in marriage, for they are now like angels, children of God, and will remain so forever (vv. 34–36).

What Jesus points out to the Sadducees is that eternal life is not simply the continuation of mortal life beyond death. Whatever the reality is on the other side of earthly life, we should not think of it as a continuation of this life that affords us an opportunity to complete still imperfect works. Indeed, we humans have to do *now* what we can do for the good, such as help the needy, work for the improvement of the human situation, resist egoistic threats to fellow humans and other creatures. "But exhort one another every day, as long as it is called 'today'" (Heb. 3:13a).

Certainly the decisive point that Jesus makes to the Sadducees is this: Death is the end of many things, but it is not the end of everything. Our death is not the end of God. In a German hymn Paul Gerhardt writes, "Everything passes away / but God stands / without faltering; / his thoughts, / his word and his will have eternal ground." We are living in a certain time, but God "alone is immortal" (1 Tim. 6:16 NIV).

When this is quite clear for us, then we are allowed to make a further step. This God is not a mere god. This God does not release his creatures. In his compassion God puts them in his heart, and they will not ever be excluded from it. We humans are not eternal, but God's love for us humans is eternal. Our life does not continue constantly, but God's mercy is unending toward those to whom he is merciful. As they *were*, so they *are* now in God. Because they are in God, this means that they are now healed from their illnesses and cleansed from their evils.

In the hours of the last evening of his life, the theologian Karl Barth was working on a lecture. In that last lecture, he wrote of God as the God of the living in these words: "All live to him, from the Apostles to the forebears of yesterday and the day

Pastoral Perspective

the lowliest of the society would be considered "like angels and are children of God, being children of the resurrection" (v. 36) This *radical* statement of the gospel, that in heaven there are no sociopolitical strata, is good news even today. The mystery of the resurrection revealed by Jesus is that heaven is a place where those who have been dehumanized will be restored; those who have been oppressed will be set free; and those who have been treated as inferior will be raised up and called beloved. Women will no longer be the property of men, treated as chattel— passed from man to man at will and whim. Women will be children of God, able to give love and receive love as they see fit. In heaven, those who are children of the resurrection will know the joy and peace that was kept from them on earth.

Jesus says in verse 38 that God is the God of the living—the God of newness, forgiveness, and liberation. Oppression on earth does not dictate the rewards of heaven. The bondage and slavery of human life does not inscribe how life will be in heaven. Persons suffering under oppression and those who are victims of the dehumanizing systems of racism, sexism, classism, and heterosexism often struggle to look beyond the day-to-day reality that would keep their backs bent and their minds unable to see an alternative, unable to see even the promise of freedom. Victims of oppression tend to believe "how it is" determines "how it will always be." Suffering keeps people from imaging new possibilities, but faith provides hope. The suffering and hope of enslaved African people in North America portrays the transformation of suffering through faith.

Slavery in North America is considered one of the most inhumane and dehumanizing systems of oppression ever foisted upon a people by others. During this time of forced labor and exploitation, enslaved African people were forbidden to read or write, by penalty of disfigurement or death. If persons were caught with a book, especially a Bible, severe penalties would be exacted. Slave owners would cut off hands, gouge out eyes, or give severe lashings with a bullwhip. This time of brutality and violence would have brought genocide to the people, had it not been for their faith that "[God] is God not of the dead, but of the living" (v. 38). In other words, the faith of the enslaved Africans told them that things in heaven would be different than on earth. This steadfast belief is captured and articulated clearly throughout the spirituals.

The spirituals, songs written during slavery, provide a glimpse into the faith of the enslaved

Exegetical Perspective

movement and presented a Christian interpretation of God's resurrection of Jesus from the dead in 1 Corinthians 15 (ca. 55 CE), he assured a type of Christianity that participated more in beliefs of Pharisees than beliefs of Sadducees. In addition, the destruction of the Jerusalem temple in 70 CE abolished the special network of priests, money, and power the Sadducees used to perpetuate their beliefs (Acts 4:1–2; 23:6–10). The Gospel of Luke, by tradition written by Luke the companion of Paul (Phlm. 24; Col. 4:14), presents Jesus as a skillful Pharisee-like interpreter who can show that written Torah does present belief in God's resurrection of the dead. Thus, in ways perhaps curious to us today, by the end of the first century, even though Christians were opposing Pharisees, the two were allied against beliefs of Sadducees.

Of special interest are ways in which the Lukan version differs from Matthew 22:23–33 and Mark 12:18–27. The Lukan version contains an opening, middle, and closing that focus on the Sadducees' question (vv. 27–33), Jesus' response (vv. 34–38), and the response of some scribes along with a statement by the narrator (vv. 39–40).

Whose Wife Will the Woman Be (vv. 27–33)? Sadducees, whom the narrator describes as not believing in resurrection, open with a question (v. 27). Their reference to what Moses wrote (v. 28) reveals their special focus on written Torah. They challenge Jesus about belief in resurrection from the dead by reciting teaching attributed to Moses in Deuteronomy 25:5–10, about levirate marriage (cf. Gen. 38:8). According to this commandment, a brother-in-law was required to perpetuate his brother's name by marrying his brother's widow, if his brother died leaving his widow childless. The creation of a fictional situation where a woman married seven brothers in sequence, and they all left her childless, provides the Sadducees an opportunity to humiliate Jesus in public about belief in resurrection, since it will be difficult for him to find a passage in written Torah that indicates to which brother the woman had "really" been married.

The God of the Living (vv. 34–38). Jesus' response in the middle also has an opening, middle, and closing. The opening (vv. 34–35) introduces the distinction in apocalyptic thinking between "this age" and "the coming age," here referred to as "that age." The key to Jesus' response is the apocalyptic belief that a person's earthly body will be transformed into an

Homiletical Perspective

and provide homes for their widows and children, but it is difficult to imagine that it shaped the wedding plans of the well-heeled Sadducees of urban Jerusalem. Still, Moses said it, so what will the rustic rabbi from Nazareth say about that?

Jesus responds by teaching the Sadducees what Moses meant and interpreting their Scriptures. For the Sadducees, the Scriptures were limited to Torah, the five books of Moses. "Moses wrote for us," they begin their interrogation. Jesus honors their tradition by responding, "Moses himself showed" (v. 37), and interprets Exodus 3:6, when the voice from the burning bush announces, "I am the God of your father, the God of Abraham, the God of Isaac, and the God of Jacob."

Jesus' interpretation is fluid and imaginative. He scores his points on the Sadducees' home field of Torah, using their ball and playing by their rules, and if that interpretation does not exactly spell out the resurrection of the dead, it at least hints of mysteries of which the Sadducees dare not dream. In this dazzling interpretation, Abraham, Isaac, and Jacob are not denizens of a richly remembered heritage but citizens of a new age characterized by the resurrection of the dead. God does not say, "Once upon a time long ago I used to be the God of Abraham, the God of Isaac, and the God of Jacob, but now they are dead and gone, though I remember them with great fondness."

No, God speaks in present tense to announce that God was, is, and continues to be the God of Abraham, Isaac, and Jacob; and Jesus concludes, "For to [God] all of them are alive" (v. 38b). Jesus reads Moses with a resurrection hermeneutic in which our name and identity are not limited by membership in a particular family but infinitely expanded in bold descriptions such as "children of God" and "children of the resurrection" (v. 36). Abraham, Isaac, and Jacob participate in this new age and new life, not because of their obedience or faithfulness, but as heirs of the promise of God—which is also the inheritance of those of us who hear this story so many years later.

This episode with the Sadducees gives us enough hope to live in and enough hope to face death. It does not answer our many questions about the resurrection, nor does it provide a road map of the new creation. That "to [God] all of them"—and all of us—"are alive" (v. 38) proposes a hope that hints more than we can directly speak. We have questions— God knows we have questions—but we are invited to trust that in God all our questions come to rest.

Luke 20:27-38

Theological Perspective

before yesterday. They do not have only the right, [but also relevance in the present] to be heard also today."[1] These sentences call our attention back to the text, to the sentence about the God of Abraham, of Isaac, of Jacob (v. 37b) and the assertion that to God all of these ancestors are alive (v. 38).

What does it mean to say, "to him all . . . are alive"? This means that all the humans who lived before us and who are now not among us are living "to God." Because of that connection with God, they are also not dead to us. They have not only spoken in their former times; they still speak today. We do not live without them. The members of the first elected people of Israel, the members of the Christian church who were loved by God before our birth—none of them has passed away. We are today, together with them, the complete people of God.

We cannot know fully all members of the people of God, but again and again several of them are revealed to us. They come close to us by the God of the living, if we understand that today they still have a say in what *we* have to say. Such communion with those who precede us belongs to the praise of this God who is "God not of the dead, but of the living" (v. 38).

EBERHARD BUSCH

Pastoral Perspective

ancestors of African Americans. In these songs we hear the profound hope of a people who knew personally and passionately the good news of Jesus' resurrection and who understood themselves to be children of God, even while the world told them they were two-thirds human. The song "I've Got a Robe" is an extraordinary example of the slaves' theological imagination, in that they saw themselves in a different situation regardless of the current horror. This song echoes Jesus' response to the Sadducees by proclaiming that God loves and cares for the disenfranchised, the widows, those persons considered disposable, discardable, and exploitable by law and the will of the oppressor. The song, written by persons who were forbidden to own land and whose children and loved ones were often sold away from them, boldly describes a heaven where their worth and dignity are restored. The song, in defiance of dehumanization and hatred, says:

> I've got a robe, you've got a robe,
> All of God's children got a robe.
> When I get to heaven
> goin' to put on my robe,
> Goin' to shout all over God's heaven.[1]

As if this courageous faith statement is not extraordinary in and of itself, in the next stanza, the writer/singer takes a swipe at his/her captors and proclaims God's judgment on the unjust by singing,

> Everybody talking 'bout heaven ain't goin' there,
> Heaven, heaven,
> Goin' to shout all over God's heav'n . . . Goin' to
> shout all over God's heav'n.

The good news of Jesus Christ is that God is the God of the oppressed, and the children of God will not be forsaken even in death. We have this wisdom from Jesus, we have examples of this faith and belief in our tradition, and we are strengthened for our own lives here on earth as we walk this Christian journey. Resurrection is, especially for the least, the lost, and the left out, a place of honor and respect as we experience the joy of God's love in the resurrection: "All God's children got a robe."

NANCY LYNNE WESTFIELD

---

1. Karl Barth, "Starting Out, Turning Round, Confessing," in *Final Testimonies* (Grand Rapids: Eerdmans, 1977), 60.

1. *Songs of Zion* (Nashville: Abingdon Press, 1981), 82.

eternal "heavenly" body to dwell in "that" age. In verses 34–35, Jesus presents the thesis that sexual procreation, which God intended for a created, earthly body (Gen. 2:24; 3:16), God did not intend for an eternal heavenly body.

The middle (v. 36) presents one of the explicit apocalyptic Jewish beliefs about the resurrected body, namely, that it acquires the eternal nature of an angel. In this statement lies the key to the argument in the Lukan account. According to 1 Enoch, an apocalyptic Jewish writing not in the Old Testament but as old as the book of Daniel, God did not give wives to angels, because they are eternal and do not need to procreate (1 Enoch 15:3–7). Understanding the phrase "sons of God" in Genesis 6:2–4 as referring to angels, apocalyptic writers believed that some of the angels who were "watchers" over people on earth procreated with beautiful daughters of men on earth. Thus, angelic beings can procreate with human beings, but they should not do so. According to this reasoning, if the husbands of the woman had become like eternal angelic beings, God would not give them their former wife as a wife in heaven. The Lukan account emphasizes this belief with its unique wording among the Gospels (v. 36) that the former husbands "cannot die anymore, because they are like angels and are children of God, being children of the resurrection" (i.e., they have the nature of eternal angelic beings).

Jesus' response in the closing (vv. 37–38) presupposes that humans who are with God in heaven have been given the nature of eternal angelic beings. They could have this nature only if God raised them from the dead into "living beings." Repetition of the words "God," "living," and "alive" in verses 37–38 presupposes that the Lord God would make only true claims in the Torah. If the Lord claims to be the God of Abraham, Isaac, and Jacob in Exodus 3:6, this means, Jesus argues, that these humans are at present "alive to God."

Teacher, You Have Spoken Well (vv. 39–40). Only in Luke do the scribes call Jesus "teacher" a second time (cf. v. 28) and say he has spoken well. Matthew 22:33 says the crowds were amazed at Jesus' teaching. In contrast, Luke asserts that many of the scribes accepted the truth of his argument and did not want to risk public humiliation by asking more challenging questions. For Luke, this is only one of Jesus' arguments that brought him public honor in Jerusalem before his dishonorable and innocent death.

VERNON K. ROBBINS

The question the Sadducees ask is a joke. Who would have ever guessed what funny, laugh-a-minute guys the Sadducees are? They can afford to chuckle. Their wealth, power, and prestige insulate them from the real pain implied in this tawdry tale of a woman passed from one brother to another, never finding the security of home.

The Sadducees joke about it, but we all have to live with dilemmas hinted at in their joke. We have questions, even if we do not speak them aloud. We live and we die, and we have questions about that, serious questions. We joke about it too, and the good jokes help us bear the weight of loss and the tears of grief, and a chuckle eases the load so we can do what we have to do.

Every pastor deals with these questions. A child comes shyly asking about the beloved old kitty who did not wake one morning, whom Daddy buried in the backyard. Older members outlive their spouses and remarry and even remarry again—maybe not seven times, but enough to make them wonder and ponder the question. The questions the Sadducees pose have to do with ownership and marital rights, but we ponder the question on our own terms.

Faith commands us to love one another. We promise to love one another, and in marriage we try our very hardest to love one another, whether or not we are very good at it. The apostle Paul announces triumphantly that "love never ends" (1 Cor. 13:8). We are acquainted with the poignancy of love that lives on after the loved one dies. What does such love mean or matter in the grand scheme of living and dying? Whatever else dies, love does not die. We recognize this as we read the story of our lives through a resurrection hermeneutic.

Jesus does not answer all our questions, though one of our fondest illusions is that he should. What he does is point us to a God whose faithfulness to those whom God has called is immeasurable and inexhaustible, and in that faithfulness we find enough to endure all that life and death will ask of us.

PATRICK J. WILLSON

PROPER 28 (SUNDAY BETWEEN NOVEMBER 13 AND NOVEMBER 19 INCLUSIVE)

Isaiah 65:17-25

> ¹⁷For I am about to create new heavens
>   and a new earth;
>   the former things shall not be remembered
>   or come to mind.
> ¹⁸But be glad and rejoice forever
>   in what I am creating;
>   for I am about to create Jerusalem as a joy,
>   and its people as a delight.
> ¹⁹I will rejoice in Jerusalem,
>   and delight in my people;
>   no more shall the sound of weeping be heard in it,
>   or the cry of distress.
> ²⁰No more shall there be in it
>   an infant that lives but a few days,
>   or an old person who does not live out a lifetime;
> for one who dies at a hundred years will be considered a youth,
>   and one who falls short of a hundred will be considered accursed.

Theological Perspective

In this text the prophet has a vision of new heavens and a new earth, giving us a picture—like a work of art—of the prophet's conception of newness, born of his own creative imagination. The result is a quite vivid and concrete representation of a transformed environment: peoples, habitations, and nature all woven into a complex relationship of wholeness. This indeed is a new creation, where the heavens and the earth are no longer alienated from one another.

What moves the prophet in this way? Where does the visionary get his or her picture? The straightforward answer is: from the word of God. "For I am about to create new heavens and a new earth," says YHWH, the great I am. When that happens, the past will be past. Actually, there may not even be a past, since "the former things shall not be remembered or come to mind" (v. 17). This is a total envisioning of new things. Remarkably, though, the prophet's vision itself does depend on memory of things known, even though their common functions and interrelations have all been altered in the new picture.

The prophet's vision also comes within a given context. The context is a people who have for the most part turned their backs on God and have followed their own way according to their own devices. This makes the prophet's vision difficult for them to embrace. If they are to start anew, then present

Pastoral Perspective

This passage speaks of hope through the prophecy that God will create new heavens and a new earth. At a quick glance, we might see this passage as laying out a utopia of sorts that can never be achieved, but the vision of new heavens and a new earth does not imply utter destruction of the present world and creation of a whole new one. Rather, it is about building upon the original creation that the Divine called good. It is about transforming that creation into something new.

To understand this vision of a transformed world, it may be helpful for Christians to look at it through the lens of the incarnation of God. The totality of Jesus' life provides a whole new framework for understanding Isaiah's prophecy. Jesus' radical inclusivity, his model of claiming power through nonviolent action, and his ministry of presence reveal an unexpected model of messianic attributes. Jesus' life, death, and resurrection provide a new set of lenses for the world to engage in the new creation, not as a goal to be looked for off in the distance, but one to be realized here and now.

The text describes radical transformation of living conditions in the new Jerusalem, including low infant mortality, housing and food for all citizens, and sustainable employment. Such details push us to focus on the manner in which Jesus' church

²¹They shall build houses and inhabit them;
  they shall plant vineyards and eat their fruit.
²²They shall not build and another inhabit;
  they shall not plant and another eat;
  for like the days of a tree shall the days of my people be,
  and my chosen shall long enjoy the work of their hands.
²³They shall not labor in vain,
  or bear children for calamity;
  for they shall be offspring blessed by the Lord—
  and their descendants as well.
²⁴Before they call I will answer,
  while they are yet speaking I will hear.
²⁵The wolf and the lamb shall feed together,
  the lion shall eat straw like the ox;
  but the serpent—its food shall be dust!
  They shall not hurt or destroy
  on all my holy mountain,

                                    says the Lord.

Exegetical Perspective

The buoyant optimism in Second Isaiah (chaps. 40–55) gives way in Third Isaiah (chaps. 56–66) to a more realistic picture of restored life in Jerusalem after 538 BCE, when the first wave of exiles, who returned under Sheshbazzar, are faced with the monumental task of rebuilding a ruined city, a ruined temple, and a ruined Judah. The temple, as yet, has not been rebuilt (66:1), putting a terminus ad quem of 515 BCE on the present oracles, perhaps even 520 BCE, when Haggai is urging the temple rebuilding.

A mood of pessimism pervades the oracles in chapters 56–59, dealing as they do with down-to-earth problems of wickedness (57:20–21), bloodshed (59:3), miscarriages of justice (59:4–8), syncretistic worship (57:3–10; 66:3–4, 17), fasting while oppression continues (58:1–9), profaning the Sabbath (56:1–8; 58:13–14), and leaders who are blind, greedy, and perpetually drunk on wine (56:9–12). Interspersed are words of penitence and confession (59:9–15a), some of which occur in an extended prayer for YHWH's mercy and help (64:5–7).

The prophet then becomes almost lyrical in describing Zion's coming glory, a time when prosperity and peace will reign, when city inhabitants will be righteous, when good tidings will lift up the poor and brokenhearted, and when nations of the world will come to see Zion's renewal (chaps.

Homiletical Perspective

What are the capacities of God? In our mystery-stripped world, we tend to focus on human capacities. Isaiah lifts our eyes and hearts to contemplate the capacities of God.

God has the capacity to create. Well, we know that; however, Isaiah reminds us that God creates on an unimaginable scale—new heavens and a new earth. In other words, there is nothing in all of creation, or in all that we imagine beyond creation, that is beyond the capacity of God to change. For people mired in regret or loss or sin, and for people ground down by oppression and the pain of living in bondage, what a message! Nothing is final; everything is up for grabs in the mystery of the creative capacity of God.

At the heart of the Judeo-Christian faith is this Creator who emerges even in the bleakest hour of human history to create anew. No wonder these words of Isaiah are remembered and beloved by individuals and communities of faith in all seasons of the human journey. No matter what the circumstance, the preacher/witness reminds the people that God has the capacity to create new heavens and a new earth.

Not only will there be new creation, but the former things shall not be remembered or come to mind. There is an ambiguity about this half-verse

Isaiah 65:17-25

Theological Perspective

things will have to end. As the new reality breaks in, it will turn the world and all of its known dynamics upside down.

The announcement that everything will pass is a word of judgment. However, judgment is never God's last, or definitive, word. The word as promise is what has come to stay. The promise is the possibility of everything becoming new. The word as promise creates the vision and its realization, as well as the very faith that is needed in order to believe it in the first place. The word of God is very powerful indeed. It is capable of doing the most difficult thing of all: creating anew out of what is very old. This is not creation out of nothing; this is creation out of the chaos of human endeavors, of spoiled nature, and of everything in between.

Although sometimes mundane, the images in the prophet's vision could not be more concrete. There are houses to live in, vineyards to plant, and fruit to eat. There are infants and old people, wolves and lambs, serpents and humans, all living together peacefully. This new earth would be anybody's dream world.

This is the very stuff of a new reality as conceived within the prophet's vision of God's willful ability to create new things. This is what God intends for all things and all relationships to be. According to this prophet's vision, the very stuff of life as we know it needs to be changed for good.

The prophet knows about change, restoration, and new things. The people of God have been brought from exile to enjoy the land once more. All that happens to them matters to God. The way that they conduct their lives and business now matters too, yet even God's people fall short of divine will and expectation.

The chapters of Third Isaiah, including today's text, thus reflect a time when the people of Judah are divided and somewhat cynical about their prospects. There is hardship in the land all around them; their lives are difficult. Their resentment of other nations is strong because of their experience of exile. The people are pursuing new venues of comfort and help.

Therefore, the writing in Third Isaiah contains warnings and admonitions concerning the need to stop the ways of evildoers, to practice justice, and to pursue peace for the sake of all, including other nations. Hence the promises of God are given to Israel through a word of both judgment and salvation.

Nevertheless, it is through the very promise of God, who is doing and will still do a new thing as described in today's text, that hope is kept alive.

Pastoral Perspective

participates in his messianic rule. We may not know how God means to transform the universe, but we can confess that we know it is in God's power to do this. What remains possible for the single believer, the single congregation, is to do the work involved in such transformation by following the patterns of mercy that Christ has laid out for us.

We are able to give one drink of cold water at a time. We are able to bring comfort to the poor and the wretched, one act of mercy or change at a time. One book given, one friendship claimed, one covenant of love, one can of beans, one moment of commendation, one confession of God's presence but for the asking, one moment in which another person is humanized rather than objectified, one challenge to the set order that maintains injustice, one declaration of the evil that is hiding in plain sight, one declaration that every person is a child of God: these acts accumulate within God's grace.

The whole of Isaiah rests on the messianic activity of God. The church's job is not to cloister itself proclaiming the resurrection just in the everlasting. The proclamation is for the resurrection of life in this world as well. In theological terms, it concerns realized eschatology. How does God call us in the modern world to live as stewards of the biosphere, if we rest only in the idea of the life to come? How shall we engage the fact that the world's species are dying, not only as global warming takes place in the world's natural rhythm, but also as the predatory habits of humanity hasten their death? How do we understand our call to respond and participate in the new creation that Isaiah prophesies?

This message of hope is more perceivable than ever with God breaking into the world in the person of Christ in order to restore humanity's relationship with the Divine. We respond to God's grace not simply as a means one day to claim Isaiah's vision for ourselves, but in order to experience relationship with God. By that we are able to actively engage in God's reordering of creation. We step out with hope in the God who creates, reconciles, and sustains us.

There is no denying that elements of radical suffering still exist in the world. However, we are given a foretaste of the new heavens and earth through the life, death, and resurrection of Jesus. Created by God, we are given gifts and abilities and invited in to participate in the ongoing formation of the new Jerusalem for all children of God whereby we can work to diminish suffering. The question is, how do we get in on what God is already doing? Are we identifying our God-given gifts to figure out how it

60–62). These spirited words reach a climax in our prophecy of a new heaven and a new earth, a divine oracle delivered in classic style, that is, it concludes with "oracle of YHWH" (*ne'um YHWH*) in v. 25b. Nothing like it is to be found anywhere else in the OT. "The new heavens and the new earth" are mentioned again in 66:22.

YHWH is the speaker throughout, employing the verb *bara'* ("create") three times in vv. 17–18 to emphasize the creation YHWH intends to bring about. In the OT this verb occurs only with God as subject. "Former things" will not be remembered, which are the "former troubles" mentioned at the end of the prior oracle (v. 16b). People are called upon to be glad and rejoice in the new creation, for YHWH will create a Jerusalem rejoicing (cf. Isa. 35:10), and YHWH will be glad and rejoice in the people inhabiting the city.

In this felicitous time there will no more be sounds of weeping (cf. Isa. 25:8), infants dying a few days after birth, and men not living into old age—some of the more grievous sorrows of the former age. In a flight of imagination the prophet says that the child shall live to be a hundred, and even the sinner will not be accursed until he reaches a hundred years of age (cf. Zech. 8:4). Covenant curses on house and vineyard (Deut. 28:30, 39; Amos 5:11; Mic. 6:15; Zeph. 1:13) will be reversed: the builders of houses will be able to inhabit them, and the planters of vineyards will now be able to enjoy their fruit (62:8–9). Earlier prophets promised the same on the other side of divine judgment (Jer. 31:5; Ezek. 28:25–26; Amos 9:13–14). Whereas previously YHWH did not answer because people failed to call upon him (65:1–2a; cf. 64:12b), now YHWH will do them one better by answering even before they call (v. 24).

The oracle's final verse (v. 25), which some believe to be an abridged add-on from Isaiah 11:6–9, speaks of the peace and restored harmony in YHWH's new creation. The wolf and the lamb shall feed together, and the lion shall eat straw like the ox. This is Isaiah of Jerusalem's eschatology, where the future is seen as a return to primeval time when creation was in perfect harmony (Gunkel: *Endzeit gleicht Urzeit*, "end time is like primeval time"). It was in Eden, after all, that peace and harmony prevailed before sin intervened (Gen. 2–3). Mention of the serpent eating dust, which the prophet adds to Isaiah's prophecy, belongs rather to the garden curse after sin was committed (Gen. 3:14).

The LXX and Targum translate "tree of life" for "tree" in verse 22, showing that they too have the

that is worth exploring. Many in the congregation will puzzle as to the wisdom of forgetting even the most painful episodes of life. As the saying goes, those who forget history are doomed to repeat it. Why would Isaiah's God offer to erase memories that may in fact save us from repeating terrible mistakes?

A newly ordained person was troubled by her occasional forgetfulness of the issues that parishioners brought to her. She could not remember the congregational quarrels and gossip that people described to her, nor did she remember the specific content of some heartrending pastoral sessions and confessions. An experienced pastor suggested to her that perhaps some forgetfulness is a gift from God. Perhaps there is such a thing as "holy amnesia."

Isaiah offers holy amnesia as a gift from God. Perhaps some memories are best lost, so that people can begin anew. The preacher/witness might offer the possibilities of intentional, prayerful forgetting as the kind of creative stuff from which God's gifts of healing and forgiveness can emerge.

Individuals can certainly find personal solace and hope in the power of this passage; however, as in so many of Isaiah's words, the focus is on communal salvation and new life. Isaiah is not talking about good fortune coming to a person here or a family there. God's joy is in creating the new and beautiful city, and this holy joy will be reflected in the lives of all people. Jerusalem also stands in for all human communities everywhere, even—and maybe especially—those who have turned away from God, love of neighbor, and justice for everyone.

There is some interesting work to be done in this passage to line out the tension between God's infinite capacity to create newness and the finite consequences for human sin and brokenness. Isaiah is writing to a community that has turned away from God and for whom the consequences of unfaithfulness are real, even unto exile. Yet even the deserved consequences of exile and ruin for the city are finally going to be swept up in the holy surge toward joy for Godself and for the people of God. In spite of Israel's unfaithfulness, Isaiah declares that God will rejoice and delight in God's people and in the holy and ruined city. Human sin is no match for God's joy. No more shall weeping be heard in Jerusalem, or the cry of distress.

What would human community look like with no one weeping? People would not die before they had "live[d] out a lifetime" (v. 20). How would such a community spend its resources? How would the common good be embraced when all people had the

Isaiah 65:17-25

Theological Perspective

Through the prophet's utterance and by the picture that the prophet is able to draw, the people of God are called back to trust and hope in the God who restored them to the land in the first place. This is equally an invitation to the people to get involved and act.

As we said before, the vision is very concrete, almost mundane at points. This is the case because it is as much a vision about the possibilities of the present as it is about the hopes for the future. In one of the most remarkable passages of Scripture, one that generations of Christians have referred to often, a reign of peaceful cohabitation on the holy mountain of God is promised to all who hear and heed God's will and word. "For I am about to create Jerusalem as a joy," God says, "and its people as a delight. . . . no more shall the sound of weeping be heard in it, or the cry of distress" (vv. 18–19).

Christians have taken this word as a promise of redemption meant to be extensive beyond the confines of the Jewish people and into the realms of all nations around the world. It is also an invitation to hear God's word and be part of God's people. That God's word comes to us in judgment and salvation only adds relevance to the message. Through this announcement of what passes away and the new thing that comes after that, we hear God speaking to real people in real time, so to speak. The stuff of Isaiah's vision is the stuff that makes belief in God a living faith.

NELSON RIVERA

Pastoral Perspective

is we can participate in the kingdom of God here and now? Think of the little things that can be done to show signs of God's new creation.

Taken collectively with those of other believers, single acts of serving God and neighbor illustrate God's kingdom breaking into the world today. Examples of such signs include the work of the Carter Center out of Atlanta, Georgia, and Samaritan Patrol in Tucson, Arizona.

The Carter Center focuses on advancing human rights and alleviating unnecessary suffering in the world. One of their health programs works with agencies to eradicate river blindness, caused by a parasite. This disease affects the poorest of the poor. Elimination of this threat is not difficult with the administration of a drug to prevent and treat the disease. With Merck offering the drug to those in need at no cost, the key is having people work together to educate the afflicted population and distribute the medicine.

The Samaritan Patrol, an interfaith organization made up of volunteers in Tucson, navigates the Sonoran Desert along the U.S./Mexico border, looking for migrants in distress. With a jeep full of water, food, and medical supplies, ordinary human beings (including at least one translator and one medical professional) provide emergency care and aid to those in need. As they do so, they exemplify God's call to claim those who are our neighbors and to do justice, love kindness, and walk humbly with God. In response to the grace of God extended to them, individuals and groups respond to needs in the midst of God's creation and thus participate in the new Jerusalem.

Again, we seek to participate in God's new creation not as a means of earning it but as a way of responding to God's grace extended to us. Through our restored relationship with God and our relationship with all of God's creation, we are given new lenses of hope by which can experience a foretaste of the new creation that Isaiah prophesies.

MARY ELEANOR JOHNS

Exegetical Perspective

Yahwistic account of creation in the back of their mind (Gen. 2:9; 3:22, 24). In biblical thought, however, eschatology does not exactly reproduce protology; that is, the end time is not a complete return to beginning time, for what is envisioned here is not a new garden of Eden, but a new Jerusalem. YHWH says the coming peace and harmony will exist on "my holy mountain," which is Jerusalem (v. 25b; cf. Zech. 8:3). The city has replaced the garden in the prophet's eschatology.

This oracle becomes the prototype for the NT prophecy of a new heaven and a new earth (Rev. 21:1–22:5; cf. 2 Pet. 3:13). John writes in the Apocalypse:

> Then I saw a new heaven and a new earth; for the first heaven and the first earth had passed away, and the sea was no more. And I saw the holy city, the new Jerusalem, coming down out of heaven from God, prepared as a bride adorned for her husband. (Rev. 21:1–2)

Here the old creation is destroyed, and a completely new creation will come into being, again, not a new garden of Eden but a new Jerusalem, adorned in bridal attire of gold, pearls, and an array of precious jewels (Rev. 21:9–21). Nothing so grand is envisioned in our prophecy, where former things may be put out of mind, but the old creation itself is not destroyed. The prophet is speaking about a transformation of the world as he knows it—as in 51:6—where creation provides the background for history in the new age. Jeremiah's moving vision of the heavens and earth returning to primeval chaos (Jer. 4:23–26) is of similar scope, pointing not to a real return to primeval chaos, but to a destruction of YHWH's created order on an enormous scale—people dead from sword, famine, and disease, the land made an uninhabitable ruin, and a nation tumbling headlong into inglorious demise.

Our oracle here speaks of Jerusalem transformed, from a city of wickedness, injustice, false worship, and ruin heaps, into a glorious new city that will make Israel glad and will bring within its walls nations of the world to witness YHWH's creation.

JACK R. LUNDBOM

Homiletical Perspective

opportunity to live in the fullness of time? Health care, education, safe neighborhoods, plentiful good water, environmental stewardship—what if all these human goods are not just the pipe dreams of social idealists but the will and future of God? Our mission as preachers is simply to point toward the sure future that God has already announced.

Economic justice is never far from Isaiah's vision. In a human community created for the joy of God, labor is not done for the rich and the few. The land is God's gift to all; as all join in the work of building and planting, they shall all inhabit the dwellings and eat the fruits of their labor. To labor in vain and not to see an escape for one's children is the scourge of exile and captivity. God rejoices in and blesses lives of justice with prosperity.

The sustenance of true community is in deep and active relationship with God. God's promise in Isaiah is to be listening so closely to the people that before they call, God will answer, and before they get their concern out of their mouth, God will hear. Such an intimacy is perhaps already and always available, if we simply have ears to hear the loving and constant invitation.

The passage ends with the beloved metaphor of the wolf and the lamb—the predator and the prey—feeding together. The most fierce animal Isaiah can think of, the lion, munches on straw like an ox. The lowly, wily serpent no longer bites people and their livestock, but its food is dust. Thus we circle back to the mystery of the creation of new heavens and new earth where no creature shall hurt or destroy on God's holy mountain.

Most of us, slogging through complicated and often difficult days, find it impossible to move beyond an understanding of the world as a survival-of-the-fittest kind of place. This is what we see and what we fear we will always be up against. Through this metaphor, the preacher/witness can offer an invitation to imagine a world of tenderness and plenty on God's peaceable mountain, a mysterious, evocative reality fully within God's capacity to create new heavens and a new earth.

MARTHA STERNE

Isaiah 12

¹You will say in that day:
 I will give thanks to you, O Lord,
  for though you were angry with me,
 your anger turned away,
  and you comforted me.

²Surely God is my salvation;
 I will trust, and will not be afraid,
 for the Lord God is my strength and my might;
 he has become my salvation.

Theological Perspective

This hymn of praise forms the ending to a dramatic set of prophecies in the chapters leading up to it. Those passages swing from utter destruction to hope for a messianic reimagining of the world. As a conclusion, Isaiah 12 cannot be meaningfully excised from that context.

The first ten chapters of Isaiah contain a litany of harsh and bitter biblical predictions of divine wrath against Israel. The prophet, who bemoans his own unclean lips, describes massive, even genocidal, judgment against the Israelites and those who collude with their greed, injustice, and apostasy. He outlines their destruction in almost cinematic detail, concluding with the survival of only a tenth of the people, and then the burning of that tenth until only a stump, a "holy seed," is left (6:13).

It is not the purpose here to address directly Isaiah's brutal warning to Jerusalem in Isaiah 1–10. However, any theological treatment of Isaiah 12 is facile and misleading if it does not keep in mind the holocaust that comes before. Both the story and the God whose anger appears literally to decimate the people should not be forgotten in the relief and praise that flood this brief conclusion.

Destruction, however, is not the only prelude to this hymn. Praise is nonsensical in the context of destruction if some sort of restoration does not

Pastoral Perspective

Isaiah 12 concludes the first section of the book of Isaiah, during which Isaiah prophesies God's judgment on the people of Judah for their breaking of covenant with God, and for their acts of injustice toward the weakest members of their society. Jerusalem, God's chosen dwelling place, has been defiled, and has to be purged by judgment in order to make it fit for God to dwell there. God chooses Assyria to punish Judah, but then promises the Judeans that Assyria itself will be punished, and that God will preserve a remnant of Israel. In addition, God will raise up a Davidic monarch under whose rule the remnant will return to the land, and both peace and justice will prevail there.

By the time we reach Isaiah 12, the people of God have been through the wringer: severely punished, defeated, brought low—and then miraculously promised restoration, a new beginning, a new leader who will bring about a reign of peace. Isaiah 12 envisions what the community will say to God once this transformation occurs. The use of the future tense suggests that, in relation to the historical circumstances of Isaiah 1–11, this "day" of restoration is still in the future. As such, this chapter might point forward to the postexilic times of Second Isaiah or even beyond, to an eschatological fulfillment of these promises of a glorious homecoming into a reign of

³With joy you will draw water from the wells of salvation. ⁴And you will say in
    that day:
  Give thanks to the LORD,
  call on his name;
  make known his deeds among the nations;
  proclaim that his name is exalted.

⁵Sing praises to the LORD, for he has done gloriously;
  let this be known in all the earth.
⁶Shout aloud and sing for joy, O royal Zion,
  for great in your midst is the Holy One of Israel.

Exegetical Perspective

Isaiah 12 is positioned in the book of Isaiah as a
thankful closing to the drama of chapters 1–11, in
which the prophet denounces the sins of Judah and
Israel, decrees the Assyrian invasions of the eighth
century BCE, and finally, in chapters 10 and 11, fore-
sees the end of the Assyrian threat and the beginning
of deliverance and peace. This deliverance, the
prophet says, is like the deliverance from Egypt so
many centuries before (11:16). Just as Moses and
Miriam led the people in a song of celebration
(Exod. 15), the prophet teaches the people of Judah a
hymn of praise to sing on the day of their salvation.
By providing in advance the words of thanksgiving
that will celebrate this day, the prophet offers a hope
to hold them through the dark times in between.

The hymn, in fact, echoes the Song of the Sea,
repeating the unusual phrase from Exodus 15:2: "The
LORD is my strength and my might, and . . . has
become my salvation." Almost the entire chapter is
woven from phrases and lines from related psalms.
The line cited above is also found as Psalm 118:14,
one of the Hallel Psalms that came to be associated in
ancient Jewish worship with the joyful harvest festival
of Sukkot (Booths). Other language from the same
psalm (118:21) is echoed in Isaiah 12:1's opening.

"God is my salvation" in verse 2 echoes a common psalmic theme, perhaps most clearly seen in

Homiletical Perspective

"Surely God is my salvation. I will trust and will not
be afraid" (v. 2). While many writers have embroi-
dered this single line from Isaiah 12 into sermons,
liturgies, and prayers, sermons on the text in its
entirety are relatively rare. This often-neglected
chapter is a treasure trove for the homiletician.
When viewed in light of Isaiah 5–11, it becomes
clear that this is a responsive psalm, reacting to all
the good things that God has promised. Several
preaching possibilities follow below.

Anger and Comfort. The first verse references
thanksgiving for God's comfort. Specific thanksgiving is given for the ways in which God is present
even when God has been angered by the human's
behavior. If you spend any time at all with young
children, you notice their fear of adult anger. While
parenting experts and child psychologists train
adults to couch corrections in the language of behaviors ("I am angry at your decision to color on the
walls") rather than persons ("I am angry at *you*"),
the truth is that many—if not most—children *and*
adults fear loss of love in the face of anger.

It is difficult for us to separate rejection of our
behaviors from rejection of our persons. If we fear
loss of love from our parents, partners, and friends,
how much more do we fear it from God? This text

Isaiah 12

Theological Perspective

follow it. Isaiah predicts that the tiny remnant will finally stop straying and will "lean on the LORD, the Holy One of Israel" (10:20). An ethos of peace and equity will govern the earth. Chapter 11's poetic and intensely messianic description of the peaceable society, led not by a warrior but by a child, comes hard on the heels of horror and, perhaps in part because of that sequence, leads naturally to the anticipatory praise in this chapter's opening, "You will say in that day . . . "

It is tempting to read Isaiah 12 only in connection with the beauty of Isaiah 11, to resist the divine bloodlust and vengeance that pile up, stanza after stanza, for ten chapters before the wolf finally lies down with the lamb. It is also tempting to read this hymn as a generic praise psalm in an attempt to avoid the complex mirroring of Moses's relief for making it through the Red Sea on the one hand, and the clear indication from the use of the future tense that trouble is not yet over, on the other. Isaiah 12 is written in the future tense; it contains praise for a rescue that has not yet occurred, for a survival the cost of which has not yet fully been borne. This is a song sung by slaves who are singing now the songs of their great-grandchildren, far in advance of freedom.

What do people who proclaim a God of unending love and mercy do with a praise song that is embedded in predictions of brutal divine wrath, followed by promises of "nevermore"? This looks like a pattern of abuse in which the violence of the abuser's rage is followed by gifts and tenderness. This pattern binds abused to abuser, distorting the meaning of love. Such patterns, too common in families, risk repeating themselves here if the preacher focuses on the morning-after gifts of chapter 11, ignoring the rage before. Many of us reject such violence in God and believe that holocausts, Middle Passages, and other genocides constitute apostasy and evil, not divine will.

One way to approach these challenges is to recognize the metaphoric character of prophecy while pursuing the truth that metaphors labor to illuminate. In this sense, the story that Isaiah tells here is metaphoric, meaning that it reveals a truth by telling it "otherwise," as in a parable. The truths to which this story points, however, are not metaphoric. The people's suffering and dying under godless powers are not metaphoric. Their collusion in oppression and injustice is not metaphoric. The fact that the suffering, dying, and collusion are still going on is not metaphoric. The link of faithfulness to accountability is not metaphoric.

Pastoral Perspective

justice and peace. In any case, God's promise of restoration is so sure that, for the faithful remnant, it is as though it has already happened, and they are compelled to offer thanks in response.

This song of thanksgiving represents the people's first words uttered in response to all that has happened, and in a sense sums up what they have learned from all they have been through. The first thing they have learned is that God's anger always gives way to "comfort," a word that in Hebrew literally means the removal of a burden so that a person can breathe freely again. God does lay upon God's people the burden of judgment when their deeds mock the demands of justice and compassion that God sets forth in the covenant. However, once this judgment has served its purpose, the grace of God always releases the burden and allows for new life, new breath, and a new beginning. God's judgment is always part of God's grace, so that out of that refining fire may come a purer way of living.

Verse 2b quotes the song the Israelites sang after their deliverance from the Egyptians at the Red Sea (Exod. 15:2). The use of this quote suggests that Isaiah's remnant has learned that the God who saved them is the same God who delivered their ancestors from oppression. It is the same God who continues to be faithful to God's people, and now brings them home in a second exodus. Because this is the same God, who is always their savior, they know that they can "trust and . . . not be afraid" (v. 2).

The choice to trust God was the same one Isaiah urged on King Ahaz in Isaiah 7. Ahaz, however, refused to trust God and gave way to fear instead, with disastrous results. Now, having been through the judgment and the restoration, the people know that trust in God is warranted, and that with that trust comes a freedom from fear. Finally, the people learn that the experience of being saved by God leads to a desire and even a compulsion to testify to God's greatness and to spread this testimony throughout the whole earth. At the heart of their testimony is the astonishing fact that God, who is so holy that even angels cannot look upon God (6:3), has chosen to live in the midst of God's people, to be Immanuel (7:14).

What can today's communities of faith, today's faithful remnant, learn from reading Isaiah 12? We can learn, first of all, that just as this song of thanksgiving points back to the exodus and forward to the restoration in Second Isaiah, so too the promises of salvation point forward to our own lives. The same God who was active in Israel's past is active in our lives, and is our salvation. The prophecies of return

Exegetical Perspective

Psalm 68:19. The following phrase plays with the similar sounds and contrasting meanings of the words ʾevtah ("I will trust") and ʾefhad ("I will fear"), echoing the account of the exodus in Psalm 78:53: "He led them in safety [or "in trust"], so that they were not afraid." Verse 3's lines, "Give thanks to the LORD, call on his name; make known his deeds among the nations," are identical to the opening words of Psalm 105, which likewise retells the exodus story in detail. Verse 5 continues to echo themes and wording from Psalm 105.

While most of the chapter sticks very closely to language from the psalms, a unique metaphorical image in verse 3 ("you will draw water with joy from the springs of salvation," my trans.) is not psalmic, but rather recalls the crucial contrast, so central to Isaiah 8, between the "mighty flood waters of the River, the king of Assyria," which would flood the land of Judah "up to the neck" (8:7–8), and the gentle, life-giving waters of Shiloah in Jerusalem that signaled God's provision (8:6). Shiloah, or Siloam, is the place from which, according to the Talmud, priests would draw water every day during Sukkot; they then processed with it to the temple to the sound of the trumpet blast, and poured it as an offering on the altar. This water libation, based on the wording of Isaiah 12:3, was accompanied by such jubilation that, as the Talmud described: "Whoever has not seen the rejoicing at the Place of the Water-Drawing has never seen rejoicing."[1]

A cascade of voices proclaims salvation. The prophet offers hearers words of praise for their use. The prophet's words call others to *call others still* to offer praise and to pass the word along to an even larger audience: to proclaim "among the nations" (v. 4) that God's name is exalted, with the expectation that not only Israel but the surrounding nations as well will recognize God's saving deeds and give praise. Back in Isaiah 6:3 in the divine throne room Isaiah heard the seraphim proclaiming proleptically that "the whole earth is full of God's glory," even though the prophet himself knew that he lived "among a people of unclean lips" (v. 5). Now, what the seraphim alone said is to be echoed not only by the prophet and his hearers, but by his hearers' hearers as well, until the whole world is indeed filled with God's glory.

As a psalm associated in Jewish tradition with Sukkot, the feast of ingathering at the fall harvest season, Isaiah 12 is particularly appropriate for

1. Babylonian Talmud *Sukkah* 51a-b.

Homiletical Perspective

offers the opportunity to explore the tender tangle between love and anger, for here we find God's willingness to love and comfort us *in spite of* all that we have done to anger God. Where human relationships may falter on this front, God, who is all-knowing and righteous, will not withhold God's love and comfort, even when justifiably angry. The preacher might draw into the sermon narrative biblical examples of God's persistent comfort in spite of anger (Jonah and Noah come to mind, to name two), as well as stories from present human experience.

Wells of Salvation. The image in verse 3 of drawing from the wells of salvation is a lovely one. While most contemporary readers are far removed from the business of drawing water from a well, it is a practice worth recalling. The wells referred to here would, most likely, have been little more than simple holes in the earth, dug by hand. People would have drawn water for themselves, their animals, and their crops by lowering a pot on a rope and hoisting it back up again. The practice would have been imprecise, tedious, and messy—but necessary for life. Even the more modern hand pump wells still in use on farms and in campgrounds are similarly messy—and physically exhausting—to use.

What a provocative metaphor! This salvation is ours—a gift of the creator. We shall draw deeply from the "wells of salvation" with joy, but not without some effort. It will tire us, tax us, spill all over our dry clothes, and muddy our feet. So, what does it mean to do all this with joy? How might we describe salvation that can be drawn from wells? Is it a once-in-a-lifetime event or a continuous stream? Does this saving water emerge gleaming in a stone pot, or splatter out of a lopsided pitcher? Can we even begin to keep it for ourselves, or does it, by definition, splash onto everything and everyone in our midst?

Verse 2 also makes use of the word "salvation." This salvation is described as a protective force—"my strength and my might," the source of trust in God. What do we make of this rock-solid image juxtaposed with the more limber, fluid image of water? Is salvation the font or the water that fills it—or both?

You Will Say in That Day. The passage contains two parts, each set off by the repeated phrase translated, "You will say in that day" (vv. 1, 4). The entire chapter is translated into the future tense for good reason. This is not a psalm of praise, extolling God for what is. It is a poem of hope, praising God for what *will be* in the future.

Isaiah 12

Theological Perspective

Perhaps we can even say that divine wrath is not metaphoric *insofar* as it represents the actual distance of Divinity from oppressive social and genocidal violence. The only way to get to this conclusion, however, is through a deeply apophatic, or metaphoric, reading of this story. Only then can the preacher say that the persistence of such violence in Isaiah's world and in ours is godlessness, regardless of who perpetrates it or who suffers it.

So, in conclusion, what is this future-oriented hymn of praise? Willem Beuken calls it the "first prayer in the book of Isaiah that we are invited to join."[1] Perhaps then it is more than wishful thinking, and very different from the relief that survivors feel when the rage of their abuser temporarily passes. Instead, we can view this praise prayer as intentional "futuring," as Quaker sociologist Elise Boulding has called it.[2]

We can sing such songs, not in denial of the "wrath" that is divine distance from our violence and not in denial of the fact that we are still caught in its midst. We can sing such songs as the naming of, and protest against, the injustices and genocides that national fervor demands. We can sing such songs as the work of intentionally bringing into view another possibility, a future filled with "the knowledge of God" to which the metaphor of the peaceable society points, making the relief and praise of Isaiah 12 both metaphoric and real. Such futuring is the first and most audacious of theological tasks. To sing the perfect future brings it into view, making our responsibility for the present, and our capacity to choose God instead, actually imaginable.

LAUREL C. SCHNEIDER

Pastoral Perspective

and restoration, of a reign of justice and peace, are for us to claim as our own inheritance and hope as well.

Living in this hope, we can view even the judgment of God as part of our salvation. God's judgment on us is real when we, like the Israelites of Isaiah's time, mock our covenant with God by abusing the weak and making our peace with injustice. This judgment is meant to purify us so that we can return to God and recommit ourselves to live in accordance with God's ways. This text teaches us, then, to consider where in our own lives we may have fallen out of covenant with God, especially in our treatment of the poor, and how we may be under God's judgment because of this. This judgment may manifest itself in subtle ways: in a loss of joy, purpose, or vitality—the sense of a burden that makes us unable to breathe freely. The text further calls us to give thanks even for this judgment itself, because it wakes us up to the wrongness of our way of living, and hence makes a new life possible.

This text also reminds us of the fundamental choice that is always before us, the same choice Ahaz faced: to trust God or to fall back into fear. There are plenty of reasons to be afraid, but Isaiah 12 reminds us that there is one overpowering reason to trust, and that reason is that God is with us. The Holy One of Israel, the one who is incomparable in beauty, power, and goodness, has made the astonishing choice to dwell with us, and to save us again and again. If we can trust this God, fear departs and is replaced by a joyous partaking in God's abundance. This joy will naturally overflow in our own lives into testimony—wanting to tell others about the God who is with us and continues to save us.

RUTHANNA HOOKE

---

1. Willem A. M. Beuken, "A Prayer for the Readers of the Book of Isaiah: A Meditation on Isaiah 12," in *Calvin Theological Journal* 39 (2004): 381.
2. Elise Boulding, "A Journey into the Future: Imagining a Non-Violent World," in *Peace and Conflict Studies* 9, no. 1 (2002): 51–56.

Exegetical Perspective

November, the culmination both of the growing season and of the liturgical year. The Old Testament lesson for the day comes from the same book as this psalm. Isaiah 65:17–25 anticipates rejoicing, security, long life, fruitfulness, and blessedness, in which the inhabitants of the land can count on enjoying the fruit of their own labors of building, planting, and bearing children. Together the prophecy and the psalmic response of praise provide a portrait of well-being, a hope with which to steady the hearts of those suffering tribulation, and a glimpse of the joy that will surely come.

Most lectionary readings from Isaiah occur during Advent, Christmas, Lent, and Easter, when their own sense is overshadowed by the constellation of readings centered on the life of Christ. It is more unusual to find a reading from Isaiah (or even two!) in "ordinary time." This one occurs near the end of a series of selections from the prophets that began back in July with the book of Amos, and included Jeremiah, Hosea, Joel, Habbakuk, and Haggai, as well as Lamentations and Daniel. It is a good opportunity to explore these messages from the biblical prophets, which conclude on such a high note in Isaiah.

Remarkably, the Old Testament readings for this Sunday are allowed the role often reserved in the lectionary for the New Testament readings, that of proclaiming unbounded eschatological hope, whereas the New Testament readings instruct and warn in sober tones. This is an excellent opportunity to invite consideration of the joyful hope the prophets voiced for the future of life on this side of eternity—the side on which all living persons now find ourselves. It is an opportunity to offer communal thanks for all the springs from which we draw our sustenance for daily life, both literal and spiritual, and for whatever peace and prosperity we have enjoyed in the season that has passed. For worshipers enduring painful seasons, it is an opportunity to pray with anticipation for the day when spontaneous and heartfelt joy returns, the day of salvation.

PATRICIA TULL

Homiletical Perspective

The first "you will say" (v. 1) is in the singular, speaking to an individual person. These are words of consolation to an individual who has angered God. The individual does not yet know the comfort of God's "turning away," but he or she will. Here is the kind of hope that one believer has on behalf of another believer, a fervent trust that all will be well, even when the sufferer cannot see that for him or herself. The preacher might remind the congregation of times when the particular community of faith has held hope for those in its midst who could not hold that hope for themselves.

The language shifts at verse 3 to a plural form of "you." At this point, the writer holds hope not just for the individual but for the community at large. Once again, the individual holds hope for the group until such time as the group can carry hope for itself. The praise that is described here—proclamation, singing, shouting—is robust and exuberant. The individual holds hope for a future that is not merely better; it shines.

This great joy and thanksgiving is not just for the group but for the nations. It is the task of those within the circle of thanksgiving to make these deeds known to the nations. The experience of thanksgiving is not an individual one, or even one kept within the safety of one's faith community. It must be shared.

The psalm offers a hopeful word to the people of God. Shared in sermon, it reminds us of the certitude of God's love, even when we have angered God. It points us toward a joyful response to God, to wells of salvation and shouts of thanksgiving that we may proclaim to all with whom we share this earth.

SUSAN K. OLSON

2 Thessalonians 3:6-13

[6]Now we command you, beloved, in the name of our Lord Jesus Christ, to keep away from believers who are living in idleness and not according to the tradition that they received from us. [7]For you yourselves know how you ought to imitate us; we were not idle when we were with you, [8]and we did not eat anyone's bread without paying for it; but with toil and labor we worked night and day, so that we might not burden any of you. [9]This was not because we do not have that right, but in order to give you an example to imitate. [10]For even when we were with you, we gave you this command: Anyone unwilling to work should not eat. [11]For we hear that some of you are living in idleness, mere busybodies, not doing any work. [12]Now such persons we command and exhort in the Lord Jesus Christ to do their work quietly and to earn their own living. [13]Brothers and sisters, do not be weary in doing what is right.

Theological Perspective

Some of the Thessalonians are letting the others down by refusing to contribute to the community by working. Paul has had to address this problem before (see 1 Thess. 5:14) but apparently now the situation has become even worse. So Paul (or someone so closely familiar with Paul and his letters as to assume his name) admonishes them again. The writer does not mince words: he tells the responsible ones to keep their distance from the slackers and tells the slackers to either get back to work or expect not to eat!

It is important immediately to clarify three potential misinterpretations of the theological intent of this passage. First, the writer does not counsel the community to shun completely its idle members. All believers, even obstructive ones, are considered worthy of inclusion and concern. Second, the writer is not addressing individuals who were unable to work for some reason. There is no suggestion that dependents are being criticized for their dependency alone; such an interpretation would contradict the entire thrust of New Testament teaching on caring for all regardless of ability. Finally, the writer is not expressing "an early form of the Protestant work ethic."[1] To early Christians, work and prosperity were not signs of individual grace

---

1. Beverly Roberts Gaventa, *First and Second Thessalonians*, Interpretation series (Louisville, KY: John Knox Press, 1998), 128.

Pastoral Perspective

Like those who come after them, the early Christians are generous folk who tried to alleviate the needs around them. However, human beings being what they are, there are those who try to take advantage of this generosity.

My favorite illustration concerns an elder in a former church. John had grown up poor. "We weren't just poor. 'We was poaw.' When Mama said there was pork chop for dinner, that's what she meant. One chop and everyone got a bite." He was one of the fortunate ones. People had helped him along the way. He had gone to college and was now a grade-school principal. He was eternally grateful for what had come his way, so he always tried to help others when he could.

We lived in a poor town, so there was always ample opportunity for that. One day a man approached John with a great tale of woe. He had not eaten in days. John was street smart enough to temper his desire to help with some cynicism. "I'm not going to give you money, but I will buy you a sandwich. What do you want? Roast beef?" "Sure." "With mayo?" It was a good sandwich. John felt he had done the right thing, until he heard behind him a voice calling out to passersby, "What will you give me for this good roast beef sandwich?"

There obviously are some folk like that in Paul's congregation. They know how to play on good

Exegetical Perspective

Readers who regard 2 Thessalonians as primarily about the future are, perhaps, unduly influenced by the vivid future imagery featured in the letter's early chapters. Second Thessalonians 1:5–10 certainly presents Jesus as a future avenging Lord. At his revelation (1:7–8), Jesus will come with "mighty angels" and a "flaming fire," images of power drawn respectively from either Zechariah 14:5 or *1 Enoch* 1:9 on the one hand, and from Isaiah 66:15–16 on the other. Jesus will also be glorified "on that day" (1:10), a shorthand for "the Day of the Lord," which was once associated with God's deliverance of justice to the alienated and the oppressed (e.g., Isa. 13:6; Jer. 46:10; Zech. 14:4, 6, 8, 13, 20, 21). In 2 Thessalonians 2:1–12, moreover, Jesus remains God's agent of justice, but the fated recipients of his vengeance also include Satan and the so-called lawless one whose razzle-dazzle of deception will meet a decisive end.

A case could be argued, however, that the letter writer's gaze toward both the past and the future is rhetorically positioned to respond to specific needs in his present. A close reading of the problem addressed by the letter writer in today's lectionary selection and its larger literary context, moreover, makes emphatically clear the writer's primary orientation to the present.

Homiletical Perspective

Upon first reading, this passage sounds like the antithesis of the mission statement of any church's feeding ministry. A casual reading might close the doors of soup kitchens across the country. Its jarring message is in seeming contrast to the delightful and generous invitation of Isaiah for everyone to "come to the waters; and you that have no money, come, buy and eat!" (Isa. 55:1). It even seems to contradict Jesus' own directions to his disciples at the feeding of the five thousand. When they wanted to dismiss the hungry masses, Jesus gave them a clear mandate of hospitality and compassion by saying, "You give them something to eat" (Mark 6:37). How are we to reconcile these messages of grace with the stern command from this third chapter in 2 Thessalonians that "anyone unwilling to work should not eat" (v. 10)?

The preacher's response will include making the significant distinction between the disciplined life among a community of believers and the ancient imperative of the people of God to offer hospitality to strangers. Hospitality to strangers is an essential aspect of both the Jewish and Christian faiths. Hospitality customs in the biblical world are concerned with two distinct classes of people: the resident alien and the traveler. In most cases, the two are not distinguished. The word used to delineate these people

2 Thessalonians 3:6-13

Theological Perspective

but, rather, evidence of supporting oneself and thereby the whole community. To refuse to work was therefore to rebel and take unfair advantage of others, and *this* was the problem, not mere idleness.

In fact, in the history of interpretation of this text, many have suggested reading "idleness" as "disorderliness." It is legitimate, therefore, to go beyond the specific issues of laziness and labor and consider more generally the problem of disorderly conduct within communities of faith like the Thessalonians. This will help us better to appreciate the strict disciplinary tone of the text.

Churches order themselves not so much by way of regulations and constitutions but rather through *practices*. Practices are informal means of molding and shaping both individuals and communities into the kind of people they are. Practices both convey and constitute morality. They embody a way of life. As Craig Dykstra defines practices, they are

> those cooperative human activities through which we, as individuals and communities, grow and develop in moral character and substance. They have built up over time and, through experience and testing, have developed patterns of reciprocal expectations among participants. They are ways of doing things together in which and through which human life is given direction, meaning, and significance, and through which our very capacities to do good things well are increased. And because they are shared, patterned, and ongoing, they can be taught. We teach one another how to participate in them. We can pass them on from one generation to the next.[2]

Some commonly recognized theological practices of the church are hospitality, tithing, confession, communal worship, keeping Sabbath, and, for our purposes, supporting one another materially. It would have been a "reciprocal expectation" of the Thessalonians that each should shoulder the burden of labor for the sake of the common good.

Practices are taught in several ways. Teaching by example is primary; after all, one does not learn something like hospitality by memorizing a set of rules but, rather, by watching and absorbing the way a seasoned host welcomes guests. Hence, the writer reminds the Thessalonians of how he himself pulled his own weight while he was living among them by working "night and day" (v. 8) instead of accepting

2. Craig Dykstra, *Growing in the Life of Faith: Education and Christian Practices* (Louisville, KY: Geneva Press, 1999), 69–70. Attention to practices has enjoyed a revival of late, especially since philosopher Alasdair MacIntyre's work to retrieve Aristotelian tradition. See Alasdair MacIntyre, *After Virtue* (Notre Dame, IN: University of Notre Dame Press, 1981).

Pastoral Perspective

intentions, so he advises, "If you will not work, you cannot eat."

At this point I want to make very clear that Paul and I are not talking about folk who want to work and, for one reason or another, cannot. The rule is aimed at the "moochers," those folk who put their energy into working the system rather than working the job.

Anytime we give, there will be someone who tries to take advantage of that. We need to be realistic about that and put in place whatever safeguards we can. Paul's advice, no work, no dinner, gives us permission to set some boundaries. We are not called upon to have folk take advantage of us. Nevertheless, we still need to risk the giving. If sometimes we get taken, so be it.

Paul deals with the moochers. Then he takes on the busybodies. Every organization has them, and churches are no exception. There is a fine line between being helpful and butting in, but we all know people who are much too interested in another's business. They assume ownership of issues that are not theirs. They speak with great authority about things that are none of their business—and about which they often have information that is limited or just plain wrong. They second-guess the decisions of others: "It should have been done this way, not that." They are very good at keeping things stirred up.

Moochers and busybodies. In many ways they are two expressions of the same ill: What is thine is mine. Such folk do not have good boundaries. They think they are entitled to whatever comes their way—money, food, recognition, or information. Furthermore, neither the moocher nor the busybody contributes to the general well-being of the community.

Is Paul just trying to settle down a disruptive situation, or is there something more at work here? This text raises two significant spiritual issues.

The first has to do with the individual. Each of us needs to take responsibility for our own life—our physical life and our spiritual life. Remember the line from 1 Corinthians 13:11? "When I was a child, I spoke like a child, I thought like a child, I reasoned like a child; when I became an adult, I put an end to childish ways."

When grandson Matthew was two, if he wanted something he would grab it and demand, "Share!" At four he has already started to grow out of that childish way, but some people never do. To become mature Christians means that we do give up childish ways. We learn that we are not the center of the

Exegetical Perspective

The Problem Addressed. Although scholars debate the exact nature of the behavior addressed by the writer in 2 Thessalonians 3:6–13, many now think the "errant" behavior was not "idleness," as the NRSV (v. 6) suggests, but a type of disorderliness. The writer describes the problem as that of any person (v. 6) or persons (v. 11) walking/living *ataktōs*, literally "without order." With a pun on the word "working," the writer also notes that such persons are not "working" (*ergazomenous*) but "working around" (*periergazomenous*, v. 11), with "working around" being the opposite of "working [*ergazomenoi*] quietly" (v. 12), which the writer lauds as an ideal. The pun, though, is an extended one, for the writer earlier insists that the "disorderly" actions are incommensurate with his own paradigm of "working" (*ergazomenoi*) constantly (v. 8) or his own command, "Anyone unwilling to work [*ergazesthai*] should not eat" (v. 10).

The writer insists, moreover, that he did not act *disorderly* (*ētaktēsamen*, v. 7) but modeled a willingness to work. The pun and the paradigm, thus, critique an *unwillingness* to work, not anyone's *inability* to work. Furthermore, the problem addressed in 3:6–13 is actually a part of the writer's second set of hortatory appeals (3:1–15). The first set (2:1–17) treated errant speech/thought. The second set, featuring a perceived errant behavior, initially offers words of assurance framed by prayer notices (vv. 1–5) before giving specific instructions for correcting the behavior (vv. 6–15).

If 2 Thessalonians was written in a postapostolic period (see the exegetical commentary on Proper 27, pp. 279–83), the writer's most critical problem was the absence of a standard for settling intragroup disputes. To create a standard, the writer makes two appeals. He appeals to the apostolic past within which he perceives an acceptable ideal. He also appeals to the dualistic ledger of an apocalyptic future through which he can cast the "errant" behavior as negative.

Appeal to the Apostolic Past. In verses 1–15, the writer's appeal to the apostolic past includes allusions to 1 Thessalonians. Accordingly, in 2 Thessalonians 3:1–5, for example, the adverb "finally" (*loipon*, v. 1a); the request for prayer (v. 1b); the declaration that "the Lord is faithful" and "will strengthen you" (v. 3); and the closing wish-prayer (v. 5) respectively are variations of 1 Thessalonians 4:1; 5:25; 5:24, 3:13; and 3:11–13. With respect to 2 Thessalonians 3:6–12, moreover, the expression "in the . . . Lord" (v. 6); the imitation diction (vv. 7, 9); the disorderliness notices (vv. 6–7, 11); and the request for quiet living (v. 12)

Homiletical Perspective

means, in essence, one who does not belong to a community or group.

Survival in ancient times required that travelers or strangers be offered water, food, and protection. These strict codes extend as far even as offering hospitality to enemies. You can hear a powerful reference to this life-giving hospitality code in the Twenty-third Psalm: "You prepare a table before me in the presence of my enemies" (Ps. 23:5). There was no fee expected for this service, and the one receiving such mercy incurred no debt. It was offered out of compassion and an understanding that all humanity is vulnerable. Later, in the book of Hebrews, a reference to this code appears in the warning, "Do not neglect to show hospitality to strangers, for thereby some have entertained angels unawares" (Heb. 13:2 RSV).

While the vulnerability of the resident alien and the stranger creates the necessity for codes of hospitality, providing for this hospitality requires that anyone in the community who is able to work should do so. The situation in the church at Thessalonica had arisen out of an eschatological expectation that Jesus was coming soon. This expectation must have led some to assume there was no longer a reason to tend the fields or the shop, since all would be gathered in the Lord any day. The community may also have fallen prey to the common occurrence of some members being less motivated to serve and toil than others.

From the time the first disciples gathered into a community and discerned how they might live peaceably together, regulations have been needed to help balance the workload. Perhaps the most well known is the Rule of St. Benedict, which dates to the sixth century. Hoping to alleviate some of the inevitable tensions among Christians sharing a common life that involved cooking, eating, working, living, and praying together, Benedict created his Rule. In it, he acknowledges differences in ability and accommodates every person's skill. All are to work as they are able. In his marvelous modern translation of St. Benedict's Rule, John McQuiston writes this of the necessity of service: "No one is excused from rendering personal service to others. No one is exempted from performing the mundane tasks of daily life. Rendering service to others is necessary to our own fitness. Exempting someone from commonplace chores endangers them to vanity."[1]

Life in community requires that everyone be enabled and encouraged to work. This commonality

1. John McQuiston II, *Always We Begin Again: The Benedictine Way of Living* (Harrisburg, PA: Morehouse Publishing, 1996), 55.

2 Thessalonians 3:6-13

Theological Perspective

handouts. (He even points out that he had a right to help himself to their bread, but did not.) Practices are also learned by doing. The Thessalonians should learn proper conduct by imitating the writer's attitude and behavior. Practices are also taught by invoking tradition; in this way they can be transmitted to new generations who did not participate in their initial development. Practical wisdom gets passed on through the repetition of stories and sayings like "Anyone unwilling to work should not eat" (v. 10).[3] Hence the writer makes reference to the tradition the Thessalonians would have already received and should have known (v. 6). By issuing his command in the name of Jesus Christ, the writer also implies that he is passing on traditions about daily life in Christian community that he himself once received.

Sometimes a practice needs to be taught by explicit instruction and even command, especially when its patterns have broken down. So the writer plainly admonishes the idle Thessalonians to earn a living: "such persons we command and exhort" (v. 12). Discipline is not incompatible with the development of practices. In fact, Dykstra argues for the interchangeability of the terms "practice" and "discipline," especially insofar as the latter connotes spiritual or church discipline.

Disciplining rebellious and disorderly members, as strict as it may seem, is actually one way to sustain mutual trust within a community. When the bar for orderly conduct is set high and clearly articulated, all members of a community are assured that their life together has "direction, meaning, and significance" and that the ultimate ends for which they formed themselves together as a community in the first place are still being sought. Practices require disciplined effort but help people continually to grow in the life of faith.

Churches today, like the Thessalonians, are sometimes plagued by forms of misconduct. In response, they might do well to remember that discipline and community formation are not necessarily contradictory. As individuals and as communities, brothers and sisters need to be encouraged gently but firmly not to become "weary in doing what is right" (v. 13), for each other's sake.

BARBARA J. BLODGETT

Pastoral Perspective

universe. We learn that sharing goes both ways. We learn to respect the needs and rights of others.

There are those who do not mooch just sandwiches. They want to mooch spiritually as well. They may sit in the pew Sunday after Sunday, but they do not do any work themselves. "The preacher will tell me what the Bible says. The congregation will do my praying for me." At that point Paul's admonition— "If you will not work, you cannot eat"—becomes descriptive rather than prescriptive. If you do not read the Bible for yourself, if you do not have your own prayer time, no one else can do it for you. You will not be fed. You will not grow. You will not mature as a Christian.

The second issue Paul focuses on concerns the life of the community. It is not enough to have an individual commitment to Christ. That commitment must be lived out in the context of a community of faith. Read Paul's letters and see just how much his writings focus on building a community that is caring, supportive, and joyful. Moochers and busybodies disrupt the community. They build resentment and distrust. They shame us in the eyes of the world. Who wants to be part of a group that is always fighting? Moochers and busybodies tarnish our witness and keep us from being Christ's body in the world.

How then do we live together? That is Paul's concern. Do the folk outside the church look at us and say, "That is not any place I want to be!" Does the face that we present to the world embarrass our Lord? Do we create a place that makes folk stop and look: "Maybe there is something happening there that I want to be part of. Might this be a place where I can grow in my faith"? Does the face that we present to the world do honor to our Lord?

NETA PRINGLE

---

3. See Abraham Malherbe, *The Letters to the Thessalonians*, Anchor Bible 32B (New York: Doubleday, 2000), 452.

respectively emanate from 1 Thessalonians 4:1; 1:6; 5:14; 4:11.

Likewise, in 3:1–15, the writer's appeal to the apostolic past includes direct notices of the apostle's former presence with the assembly. For example, the apostle connects the command to stay away from the "disorderly" to the "*tradition* [*paradosin*, v. 6; cf. *paradoseis*, 2:15] . . . *received* from us." Furthermore, the paradigm and the past command about work (v. 6–10) were given when the apostle was present with the assembly. Thus the writer makes the apostolic past the standard for correct action in the present, though the specifics of that standard are defined solely by the writer.

Appeal to an Apocalyptic Future. The writer's imagery of the future in 1:5–10 largely distinguishes the believers from the unbelievers in the present. That is, with a dualistic apocalyptic ledger, all persons are lined up on one of *only* two sides: either the side of good, which entails future relief (1:7) and the opportunity to glorify Jesus (1:10); or the side of evil, which entails retributive vengeance (1:6–9).

Three aspects of this apocalyptic ledger also bleed beyond 1:5–10 to affect the diction and ideas used to address the "disorderly" in 3:1–15. First, the *rhetoric of space* is crucial to both units. In 1:5–10, those not obeying the gospel will be separated forever *from* (*apo*) the Lord (1:8–9). In 3:1–15, although the writer regards the "disorderly" as brothers (and sisters), the assembly is warned to stay away *from* (*apo*) and not associate with them (3:6, 14) to ensure their reform. Second, the *rhetoric of (proclamatory) agency* adheres in both units. In 1:5–10, persons fated for rest initially became believers because "*our* testimony . . . was believed" by them (1:10). This rhetoric continues as the writer speaks of "*our* proclamation" (2:14); "the traditions . . . taught by *us*" (2:15); and, within 3:1–15, "the tradition . . . received from *us*" (3:6b). Third, the *rhetoric of obedience* is crucial to both units. In 1:5–10, persons fated for destruction are those who did not *obey* (*hypakouousin*) the gospel of the Lord Jesus Christ (1:8). In 3:1–15, the "disorderly" are those who "do not *obey* [*hypakouei*] what we say in this letter" (3:14).

With such an apocalyptic ledger, the writer thus positions the "disorderly" as persons dangerously close to the enemy side of the ledger, though they are not to be viewed as enemies (3:15). Ultimately, then, the imagery of the future in 1:5–10 serves as a matrix from which the writer in his own present positions himself positively and the "disorderly" ones negatively.

ABRAHAM SMITH

is essential for the cultivation of both dignity and humility. Leaving someone out of the work life of the community can be demeaning. Just ask the stroke victims or the senior citizens in your congregation if they do not wish there were more they could do to feel part of the life of the church. By the same token, allowing anyone who is able to work to be dismissed from work creates disparity in the community.

Modern monastic communities know this as well. Pilgrims to the Iona Community in Scotland and the Taizé Community in France are given the opportunity to serve in the working life of the community. Simple jobs such as assisting in preparation of meals or tending a common garden not only deepen pilgrims' appreciation of the ministry of the place; such tasks also allow participants to join in communion with others whom they might not otherwise encounter. Opportunities to work are invitations into the inner workings of the Christian body in these places, deepening relationships with others on the same journey as well. Not to work would render one a "tourist" and truncate the experience of the Christian life. The depth of hospitality is shown in this community as those who are differently abled are invited in and presented with opportunities for service that match their skill.

These thoughts bear important implications for much of our congregational life. The preacher whose church participates in a feeding ministry might wonder if the guests who are willing and able are being given ample opportunity to serve alongside church members in preparation and serving of the meals. Is a disparity being created that makes guests dependent on being served?

Are there members in the church community who do not participate in any way in the work of the church? What of them? Can opportunities be created to suit their needs and skills so that they too can enjoy the blessing of being necessary to the life of the community? There is ample opportunity in this text both for instruction about compassion and for a prophetic call to partnership in ministry.

ELIZABETH BARRINGTON FORNEY

Luke 21:5-19

⁵When some were speaking about the temple, how it was adorned with beautiful stones and gifts dedicated to God, he said, ⁶"As for these things that you see, the days will come when not one stone will be left upon another; all will be thrown down."

⁷They asked him, "Teacher, when will this be, and what will be the sign that this is about to take place?" ⁸And he said, "Beware that you are not led astray; for many will come in my name and say, 'I am he!' and, 'The time is near!' Do not go after them.

⁹"When you hear of wars and insurrections, do not be terrified; for these things must take place first, but the end will not follow immediately." ¹⁰Then he said to them, "Nation will rise against nation, and kingdom against kingdom;

Theological Perspective

Here we are invited not to be terrified (v. 9). This is possible because of the promises of God in Christ that "not a hair of your head will perish" (v. 18) and "by your endurance you will gain your souls" (v. 19). Thus we are allowed to be quietly and confidently safe in a hand that carries us. Still, it is certainly astonishing that these words are found in the biblical text for today; it is a text that is full of bad news, full of reasons that could make us timid and hopeless.

What is described in this text is similar to what happens in the windstorm that is reported to us in Matthew 8:24–26. The disciples of Jesus, together with their Master, run into the deadly danger of tempestuous waves upon the sea. As the disciples panic, Jesus lies in the boat sleeping, a sign of the heavenly peace that cannot be destroyed by any fear. Likewise, in this text, the Savior gives the same assurance to us that he gave his disciples: Be not terrified! There shall not be a hair of your head that perishes!

Indeed, even today we cannot ignore Jesus' encouragement, because it is spoken to us in an equally dangerous situation. The ground upon which we live is tottering. Securities of which we thought highly are breaking all around us. Are the words of Jesus only for the ancient world of long ago? If we think about it, we discover that Jesus' words are as relevant now as they were 2,000 years ago.

Pastoral Perspective

Every generation, at some time in its history, has thought its time was the end of time—and the dawn of the twenty-first century has been no exception. The current generation can reflect upon experiences of war, natural disaster, and political chaos as fodder for apocalyptic possibility.

Most people remember where they were and what they were doing on September 11, 2001, when nineteen terrorists associated with Al-Qaeda hijacked four commercial airline jets. The sight of hundreds of military tanks streaming across the desert toward Baghdad as part of the "shock and awe" campaign is emblazoned on the American imagination. On December 26, 2004, the world was startled by a tsunami in Indonesia, one of the deadliest natural disasters in history. Many people have vivid memories of news footage from New Orleans during and after Hurricane Katrina. While it is not clear that these and other phenomena are in any way apocalyptic (only God knows the end time), Jesus' directions to the disciples concerning what they ought to do in times of chaos and destruction were quite challenging then, and are equally challenging for us today.

In Luke 21:5–6 Jesus speaks of the destruction of the temple, prompting the disciples to ask two questions: When? What will be the sign? Jesus goes on to describe three things that will happen in the future

¹¹there will be great earthquakes, and in various places famines and plagues; and there will be dreadful portents and great signs from heaven.

¹²"But before all this occurs, they will arrest you and persecute you; they will hand you over to synagogues and prisons, and you will be brought before kings and governors because of my name. ¹³This will give you an opportunity to testify. ¹⁴So make up your minds not to prepare your defense in advance; ¹⁵for I will give you words and a wisdom that none of your opponents will be able to withstand or contradict. ¹⁶You will be betrayed even by parents and brothers, by relatives and friends; and they will put some of you to death. ¹⁷You will be hated by all because of my name. ¹⁸But not a hair of your head will perish. ¹⁹By your endurance you will gain your souls."

Exegetical Perspective

The Jerusalem Temple, Worldly Turmoil, and Persecution. As the scene opens, Jesus engages in public dialogue with people about the beautiful Jerusalem temple (vv. 5–7). As it continues, Jesus presents a monologue about future times of false leadership, violence, and suffering (vv. 8–11), about arrest, persecution, and endurance (vv. 12–19), and about destruction of Jerusalem that signals the eventual coming of the Son of Man (vv. 20–36).

Future Destruction of the Temple (vv. 5–6). The magnificent temple in Jerusalem during the lifetime of Jesus was the result of a rebuilding project started by King Herod in 19 BCE. Herod more than doubled the size of the Temple Mount. People could gather in large colonnades or porches around the Temple Mount for various purposes, including speech making and healing (see Acts 3:11; 5:12). While the temple itself was completed in eighteen months, work on the outer courts and decorations continued throughout Jesus' lifetime until 62–64 CE.

Less than a decade after everything was completed on the Herodian temple, it was destroyed by the Romans in 70 CE. The descriptive language in Luke 21:5 exhibits widespread knowledge of its beauty and magnificence. After its destruction, people knew about its magnificence all the way to Rome, as a

Homiletical Perspective

As was the case in last week's text, Jesus continues to teach in the temple. Luke's account of Jesus' teaching in 21:5–19 provides a cluttered text full of disorientation, dismaying ideas, and distractions aplenty.

The disciples begin distracted. They marvel at the beauty of the temple, the enormous stones of its walls, and the wealthy worshipers coming to dedicate their gifts. Small wonder they are distracted. The public exhibition of fabulous wealth has a way of distracting us, whether we see it in *Town and Country* or *People* magazine, and the temple was Herod's temple, the jewel in his architectural crown. The New Testament remembers Herod as a paranoid despot, but history and archaeologists remember him as a builder. In the church library there is probably a volume that includes an artist's rendering of Herod's temple. Look it up: you will be impressed too. Everyone was.

Perhaps not everyone. Jesus interrupts his disciples' distraction by hanging out a sign naming everything that so dazzles them as "Condemned Property." The enormous stones, beautiful, smooth, and apparently indestructible: "not one stone will be left upon another"; the glorious temple dedicated to a glorious God (but also filled with graft [20:47]): "all will be thrown down" (v. 8).

Writing sometime after the destruction of the temple, Luke characterizes Jesus as a reliable prophet

Luke 21:5-19

Theological Perspective

Many wars have happened since the Second World War with its millions of dead! As armies continue to be extravagantly funded, there are always new reasons to feel threatened. "Revolutions" today are called terrorism. There are "earthquakes" on the stock exchange. The polar region is melting. We are plagued by pandemics—will humans die of a virus against which we are defenseless? There are famines—great numbers of humans cannot be supplied with bread and water; do not the requirements of rich countries deprive poor countries of the possibilities for feeding themselves? Even with all the progress in 2,000 years, there are disadvantages, and do not these disadvantages have more and more of a global effect?

What can we do? An old and always new answer in such a situation says, "Let us eat and drink, for tomorrow we die" (Isa. 22:13; 1 Cor. 15:32). Do not a majority of privileged humans speak in this way today, even with the dangers of a global collapse? Such thinking is an egoistic flight from reality. Jesus shows us quite another approach in our biblical text. He says, "Not a hair of your head will perish."

In this sentence he says with cheerful confidence that our salvation lies always in good hands, in God's hands. Where there is such confidence, we are given the endurance by which we gain our souls. Such endurance requires patience, not the laziness of persons who do nothing more than "eat and drink." As legend has it, when Martin Luther was asked what he would do if he learned the world were coming to an end, he said, "If tomorrow is the Day of Judgment, then today I want to plant an apple tree."

The most evil danger is still to be highlighted. Worse than wars and earthquakes is what Jesus warns in verse 8: "Many will come in my name and say, 'I am he!' and, 'The time is near!' Do not go after them." A couple of images come to mind to illustrate Jesus' warning. A man who follows a false prophet is like a man in a plunge holding on to a seemingly secure rope, but it tears. It is like a beggar dying of starvation who receives bread, but discovers that it is in fact stone. In other words, there are persons who can tell others persuasively about Christ, but we must heed the urgent warning of the real Jesus Christ, who says, "Do not listen to those so-called preachers in my name. Do not follow them. They seem to save from ruin, but in fact they lead to it."

The Russian writer Dostoevsky has written a dismaying story with the title "The Grand Inquisitor." It concerns an old cardinal of the Christian church who hears that the real Jesus has come suddenly to

Pastoral Perspective

(vv. 8–11): imposters will come and try to trick the faithful; war and conflict will rage on; and natural disasters will be prevalent. Jesus assures the disciples that the end times are in the future and that they will not happen all at once. Then Jesus says a rather peculiar thing in verse 13: "This will give you an opportunity to testify."

He goes on to tell the disciples that their testimony must not be rehearsed or "canned." Instead, they should rely on the incontestable wisdom that will be given them in the moment. Jesus says that the reward for their testimony and their endurance of these catastrophic times will be the gaining of their very souls. Let us reflect on Jesus' peculiar statement about suffering as opportunity for testimony.

What kind of testimony does a faithful person give in the face of death, betrayal, and the execution of loved ones? Most of us are accustomed to testimonies that praise God for good times, good things, blessings of redemption, healing, rescue, and salvation. Testimony is usually reserved for the stories that declare how God brought the faithful out of slavery into freedom, how God made a way when there was no way; how God acted to save a distressed people. The peculiar words of Jesus in this passage, however, tell us that when we experience destruction, betrayal, and loss, we are to see these times as opportunities to testify. What kind of testimony does one give in the face of great suffering and great hatred?

"Suffering always means pain, disruption, separation, and incompleteness," writes Shawn Copeland. "It can render us powerless and mute, push us to the borders of hopelessness and despair."[1] The opportunity to testify during times of destruction is, in part, the audacity to muster courage in the face of fear, the boldness to speak in the face of suffering. Great suffering changes some people and defeats others, but for those who endure—their very souls are gained.

Suffering provides an opportunity for those who have been changed to tell of their hope. For some, the change brought about by suffering is tangible, literal, physical. Howard Thurman, brilliant African American theologian, has seen suffering change people: "Into their faces come a subtle radiance and a settled serenity; into their relationships a vital generosity that opens the sealed doors of the heart in all who are encountered along the way."[2]

---

1. M. Shawn Copeland, "Wading through Many Sorrows: Toward a Theology of Suffering in Womanist Perspective," in *A Troubling in My Soul: Womanist Perspectives on Evil and Suffering* (Maryknoll, NY: Orbis, 1993), 109.
2. Howard Thurman, *Disciplines of the Spirit* (1963; Richmond, IN: Friends United Press, 1977), 76.

Exegetical Perspective

result of the exhibition of the plundered furnishings and the large paintings of the events of the Roman siege and burning of Jerusalem that were paraded on wagons in a triumphal procession in Rome in 71 CE (Josephus, *Wars* 7.3–5). In the Gospels, the destruction is described as "not one stone will be left upon another; all will be thrown down" (v. 6). When Jerusalem and its temple were destroyed in 70 CE, Christians considered this a confirmation of a prediction Jesus had made during his lifetime.

False Leadership (vv. 7–8). During the time leading up to the destruction of Jerusalem, many people either took action to defy the governing powers or were suspected of doing so and were destroyed by Herodian or Roman soldiers. A current Web site lists fifteen leaders between 4 BCE and 70 CE who were perceived to have defied the Romans and were destroyed.[1] Verse 8 quotes Jesus as saying that the appearance of various leaders, some claiming to be Jesus or at least divine ("I am he!") and some predicting the end of time, will be the first sign that the destruction of the Jerusalem temple will soon take place (v. 7). Luke's Gospel presupposes that the appearance of various leaders who were captured, imprisoned, and/or killed confirmed Jesus' view of events that would happen before the destruction of Jerusalem and its temple.

War and World Turbulence (vv. 9–11). After Jesus warns about people who will come to lead them astray, he describes terrible events that grow ever greater in magnitude. In the Lukan account, these are not "the beginnings of the birth pangs" (Matt. 24:8; Mark 13:8). Rather, these events represent the turmoil that will increase until the destruction of Jerusalem and its temple. First there will be wars and insurrections (v. 9). This may refer to the rapid succession of four Roman emperors in 69 CE prior to the siege and destruction of Jerusalem. Second, nations and kingdoms will rise up against one another (v. 10). Instead of making this warfare a transition to end-time events (cf. Matt. 24:7; Mark 13:8), the Lukan account makes it the next step in the process that leads to the attack on Jerusalem. Third, there will be great earthquakes, and in some places famines and plagues (v. 11a). Luke's own account of the time between Jesus and the destruction of Jerusalem presents a famine in the time of

1. http://www.livius.org/men-mh/messiah/messianic_claimants00.html. The list of fifteen includes Jesus.

Homiletical Perspective

whose words were proven true by historical events. Those who listen to him discover that all of Jesus' words are true, and therefore listeners can trust these words that threaten such dismaying dislocations.

Theologically Luke means to distinguish the end time of all things from particular historical events. The temple may have come to an end, but that is not *the* end; peace will come to an end and be swallowed by war, but war is not the way the world ends; security will end, shaken in earthquakes, but fear and uncertainty are not the end either. People will try to mimic Jesus and misuse his name attempting to prophesy as he did, but the world does not end with truth's impersonators. "Dreadful portents and great signs from heaven" (v. 11) may tempt you to play prophet yourself, reading the concealed meanings of mysterious happenings, but knowing the end does not belong to you (cf. Acts 1:7; 1 Thess. 5:1–11). Theologically Luke no doubt has an important point to make, but rhetorically he frightens his readers to their wits' ends.

Wars, insurrections, earthquakes, famine, plagues, and, just when it seems it cannot possibly get any worse, it gets personal: *You* will be arrested, *you* will be persecuted, *you* will be thrown into prison and hauled before the authorities. Then, Jesus says, then you will have them right where you want them. They will have to listen to you. Just when everything looks so dark, when falsehood appears so persuasive, when war seems everlasting and inevitable, when the earth trembles beneath you, when you are forced to account for yourself, you have "an opportunity to testify" (v. 13).

This rambling, discombobulated directory of events—wars, earthquakes, famine—these are not random happenings, nor are they reliable signs of the end, but they are things that *must* first happen in the grand design of God's redemption (v. 9, the divine imperative *dei*: "these things *must* take place first"). We had not noticed the plan. The sheer immensity of wars, earthquakes, famine, and plagues so completely arrests our attention that we seldom look for something even more overwhelming. In Jesus' vision, however, these dramatic historical events are simply a required stage setting for the great drama of speaking God's truth.

Given the towering backdrop of wars, earthquakes, and famine, we might assume we do not have much to say. Moreover, arrest, persecution, and arraignment notoriously intimidate and silence people. Everything, however, is working according to plan, God's plan: "This will give you an opportunity to testify" (v. 13). If we must speak we should like

Luke 21:5-19

Theological Perspective

his town, where he has healed a blind man and raised a young girl from the dead. When the cardinal sees this, he asks him: "Why, then, have you come to interfere with us?" The cardinal would like to burn him at a funeral pyre as the most evil of all heretics, because what he did long ago is done far better by the church today. The church does not need him, even if it is called by his name. However, the cardinal does say: "'Go and do not come again . . . do not come at all . . . never, never!'" And he lets him out into the dark 'square of the city.'"[1] Dostoevsky illustrates this sentence of Jesus: "Many will come in my name, claiming, 'I am he!' . . . Do not go after them" (v. 8).

What can help us in the face of such an earnest threat? It is important that we live by what is said at the beginning of this essay. In the face of such threat, there is no technique that we may learn from Jesus and put into practice by ourselves. Our help is from the Helper himself. Jesus gives us the promise that he watches over us so that "not a hair of [our] head will perish" (v. 18). Without him holding our hands, we would be lost or like that apparently pious cardinal. While our Lord holds us, we are able to cling to him and to his word: "So make up your minds not to prepare your defense in advance; for I will give you words and a wisdom that none of your opponents will be able to withstand or contradict" (vv. 14–15).

EBERHARD BUSCH

Pastoral Perspective

An opportunity for testimony born out of a time of loss, grief, and chaos is recorded in the song "Precious Lord," written by Thomas Dorsey. Thomas Dorsey, born in 1889 in rural Georgia, was a prolific songwriter and an excellent gospel and blues musician. While a young man, Dorsey moved to Chicago and found work as a piano player in the churches as well as in clubs and playing in theatres. Struggling to support his family, Dorsey divided his time between playing in the clubs and playing in the church. After some time of turbulence, Dorsey devoted his artistry exclusively to the church.

In August of 1932, Dorsey left his pregnant wife in Chicago and traveled to be the featured soloist at a large revival meeting in St. Louis. After the first night of the revival, Dorsey received a telegram that simply said, "Your wife just died." Dorsey raced home and learned that his wife had given birth to a son before dying in childbirth. The next day his son died as well. Dorsey buried his wife and son in the same casket and withdrew in sorrow and agony from his family and friends. He refused to compose or play any music for quite some time.

While still in the midst of despair, Dorsey said that as he sat in front of a piano, a feeling of peace washed through him. He heard a melody in his head that he had never heard before and began to play it on the piano. That night, Dorsey recorded this testimony while in the midst of suffering:

> Precious Lord, take my hand,
> Lead me on, let me stand;
> I am tired, I am weak, I am worn;
> Through the storm, through the night,
> Lead me on to the light;
> Take my hand, precious Lord,
> Lead me home.[3]

NANCY LYNNE WESTFIELD

---

1. Fyodor Dostoevsky, *The Brothers Karamazov*, trans. Richard Pevear and Larissa Volokhonsky (New York: Alfred A. Knopf Everyone's Library, 1992), 250 and 262.

3. Thomas A. Dorsey, "Precious Lord, Take My Hand," in *The Presbyterian Hymnal* (Louisville, KY: Westminster/John Knox Press, 1990), 404. See also http://www.pbs.org/thisfarbyfaith/people/thomas_dorsey.html (pbs—*This Far by Faith: Series on People of Faith—Thomas Dorsey*).

Exegetical Perspective

Claudius (Acts 11:28; ca. 47 CE) and an earthquake in Philippi (Acts 16:26; ca. 50 CE). Fourth, "there will be dreadful portents and great signs from heaven" (v. 11b). Scholars have noticed that Josephus's account of a star resembling a sword and a comet at the burning of the Jerusalem temple (*War* 6.289) is similar to the conclusion of the Lukan sequence of events. Jesus' speech in Luke, then, focuses first on the destruction of Jerusalem and its temple, rather than on the end of time.

Arrest, Persecution, Hatred, and Endurance (vv. 12–19).
In Luke's account, Jesus does not present suffering and persecution as part of the tribulations that lead up to the end time (cf. Matt. 24:9–14; Mark 13:9–13). Rather, Jesus says that arrests, persecution, trials, betrayal by family members, and hatred against them will all occur before the sequence of turmoil that leads to the destruction of Jerusalem and the temple (v. 12), which the author knows occurred in 70 CE, about twenty years before he wrote his Gospel. This means that verses 12–19 refer to events like those one reads about in the Acts of the Apostles, which is the second volume Luke wrote sometime after completing the Gospel of Luke.

In Luke's historical theology, the time of the church is a time when people who endure will "gain [their] souls" (v. 19). Matthew 24:13 and Mark 13:13, in contrast, feature Jesus saying that those who endure to the end will be saved. The Lukan account has Jesus describe the destruction of Jerusalem in terms close to the way it happened, namely, being "surrounded by armies" (v. 20) as Rome enacted "days of vengeance" against a rebellious population (v. 22). In a similar way, it has Jesus describe the sufferings and hardships of his followers in terms Luke uses in Acts. Jesus' followers will be arrested (v. 12a; cf. Acts 4:3; 5:18; 12:1; 21:27). They also will be "handed over" to authorities (v. 12b; cf. Acts 21:11; 28:17). They will testify before kings and governors (vv. 12–13; cf. Acts 24–26) and present wisdom that others will not be able to withstand (v. 15; cf. Stephen in Acts 6:10). In Luke's account of Jesus' speech, then, the emphasis in the initial part is not on the coming of the end time but on events that happened in the lives of followers of Jesus through the time of the destruction of Jerusalem and its temple.

VERNON K. ROBBINS

Homiletical Perspective

some time to prepare, to consult perhaps a volume like this and to arrange our thoughts, but Jesus dismisses our anxiety as unnecessary. Our powerlessness to speak may be our most essential qualification.

For those who do not know what to say at a crucial moment, conventional wisdom provides maxims like "Don't worry, it will come to you!" and "You'll be just fine; you'll think of something at the last moment!" Those folk anodynes are precisely what Jesus does not offer those compelled to speak. Instead, he promises them, "I will give you words." The words we have to say we receive as a gift. Christ possesses a wisdom our troubled world and his troubling opponents cannot calculate or comprehend. Although they have rejected his words before, once again Christ will speak the word of the kingdom through his church.

Christ promises to speak the word, which is to say we do not have to create these words. The word we are given is the word that created all things in the beginning (Gen. 1:3, John 1:1–3) and continues to create in its speaking. We do not speak with confidence but rather out of our speaking and hearing ourselves bear testimony we receive the gift of faith: "Faith comes from what is heard, and what is heard comes through the word of Christ" (Rom. 10:17). Such is the power of Jesus' words that they not only describe a kingdom but fashion a habitable place. The disclosures of Luke 21:5–19 take their own opportunity to testify to this.

Just as the destruction of the temple testified to the truthfulness of Jesus' words when the Gospel of Luke was written, so do these words spoken in the worship of Christian communities bear witness to Christ's unshakable promise. They are only words, small breaths of air spoken millennia ago, but these words endure with power, even power to "gain your souls" (v. 19). The temple is destroyed, not one stone left on another. The Roman Empire collapsed into history. These words endure, and their promise is not diminished by earthquake, war, or famine—or even by the passing of years.

PATRICK J. WILLSON

Jeremiah 23:1-6

¹Woe to the shepherds who destroy and scatter the sheep of my pasture! says the LORD. ²Therefore thus says the LORD, the God of Israel, concerning the shepherds who shepherd my people: It is you who have scattered my flock, and have driven them away, and you have not attended to them. So I will attend to you for your evil doings, says the LORD. ³Then I myself will gather the remnant of my flock out of all the lands where I have driven them, and I will bring them back to their fold, and they shall be fruitful and multiply. ⁴I will raise up shepherds over them who will shepherd them, and they shall not fear any longer, or be dismayed, nor shall any be missing, says the LORD.

⁵The days are surely coming, says the LORD, when I will raise up for David a righteous Branch, and he shall reign as king and deal wisely, and shall execute justice and righteousness in the land. ⁶In his days Judah will be saved and Israel will live in safety. And this is the name by which he will be called: "The LORD is our righteousness."

Theological Perspective

Bringing people together is never an easy task, despite all our best efforts. This is not to say that we should not try to gather people together. It only means that we are better served by keeping our expectations grounded—not necessarily low, but realistic. Still, bringing people together, especially people scattered over many places, or people who actually come from many places, seems to be what God is doing, according to the text that occupies us this Sunday.

The task of bringing together is not necessarily doomed to failure. This assurance lies in the promise that God is giving in the passage, especially in the words "I will bring them back" (v. 3), which surely sounds like "I will do the job myself." It is reassuring to hear such a promise, because it means that God is the one who is control and who will bring the promise to fruition. The word here is that God will ultimately do the much-needed job.

How did the people spoken of in these verses get to be so scattered in the first place? It is a long story of invasions and exiles, but the blame, says God through Jeremiah, finally lands on the leaders of this people, the nation of Judah. Thus we are confronted here by a situation that seems to repeat itself at other times and in other places: leaders taking advantage of their positions and serving their own narrow interests, rather

Pastoral Perspective

In five weeks, some of us will be singing William Chatterton Dix's "What Child Is This?" with jubilation and verve. Three times we will proclaim through the refrain, "This, this is Christ the King, whom shepherds guard and angels sing; haste, haste to bring him laud, the babe, the son of Mary!"[1] The time has not quite arrived, however, for us to sing about the babe in the manger, as the Muzak in public places and Christmas sales in every shop lure us to believe. We are just coming to the end of the Christian year. It is, however, a perfect time to sing with great energy and vigor the whole story of the kingship of Christ with Dix's "Alleluia, Sing to Jesus" on Christ the King Sunday.

A modern-day rendering of the story can be found in "Christmas Song," by the Dave Matthews Band. This song points to the radical nature of a king who hung out with the poor and marginalized and then hung on a cross for the sake of God's love for the world. Whether the narrative of his life comes from one of the Gospels or from a contemporary songwriter, Jesus is not the kind of king most people expect. He is not a military ruler.

During the time this text from Jeremiah was being written, the term "shepherd" connoted "king." In the

1. William Chatterton Dix, "What Child Is This" (1865).

Exegetical Perspective

These verses, part of a literary unit consisting of Jeremiah 23:1–8, divide into two distinct units as indicated by section markings in the Hebrew Bible: (1) three prose oracles on the shepherds in Judah, two indicting and judging them for having scattered YHWH's flock, and a third that promises new shepherds YHWH will raise up to shepherd the people properly (vv. 1–4); and (2) a fourth, "Look, days are coming," oracle in poetry, announcing a righteous Shoot for David that YHWH promises to raise up (vv. 5–6). All the oracles contain "oracle of YHWH" messenger formulas. Another "Look, days are coming" oracle (vv. 7–8) concludes the King Collection of oracles that takes in all of 21:11–23:8.

The "shepherds" here are doubtless Judah's kings (commentators Rashi and Kimchi), although "shepherd" is a general term in the ancient Near East denoting any high-ranking leader. The indictment in verse 1 and judgment in verses 2–3 are general, but speak indirectly to the royal houses of Jehoiakim (609–598 BCE) and Zedekiah (597–586 BCE), Judah's last two kings. Jeremiah says that neither shepherd called the sheep to account, for which reason YHWH is calling them to account.

Oracle I (v. 1) opens with "Woe," which is not a lament, but a prophetic invective (cf. Jer. 22:13). The shepherds are indicted for scattering sheep in what is

Homiletical Perspective

The "woe to the shepherds" passage from Jeremiah is a cry of outrage against those who have abused God-given power. On Christ the King Sunday, there is clear opportunity to talk about human power, abuse of power, and the power of God. Few people in the twenty-first century live in a small, clearly marked arena in which one person wears a crown and has unquestioned authority. We do not know much about ancient kings or shepherds, and we really are not clear about the dynamics of power—our own power or the power of others. We just know that we are scattered and driven by forces, and that many aspects of our individual lives, as well as our communal lives, seem out of our control. Perhaps Christ the King (who is also our Shepherd) Sunday, celebrating the most paradoxical wielder of power in the history of the world, would be a good time to reflect on realities of power in the lives of individuals and cultures.

Who are our kings? Who are our shepherds? How does somebody get power over us? Power by position or formal role is not new, of course. The boss, the parent, the cop, and the teacher all hold such power, to name just a few. However, power by expertise or information seems to be a huge and growing kind of power. The abdication of power to experts could be a fascinating thing to explore with a congregation whose members feel inept in areas that people once

Jeremiah 23:1-6

Theological Perspective

than the best interests of their own people, whether in ancient Israel or in the modern world.

Of course there are some added dimensions to the biblical story. The leaders of Judah were seen as shepherds to the people. We can say that their role as leaders had a religious dimension, since these leaders represented God (YHWH) to the people. They were considered God's anointed ones, called to lead in God's name and on God's behalf, although God was the one true Shepherd of the people.

Because God is the one true Shepherd, God cares so much about present conditions, and has decided to do something about them. Thus the harsh word of warning that God will do the reckoning from now on, pushing out of the way those who have caused the problem in the first place, is actually a reassuring word. A people scattered by the action (or inaction) of their leaders will be brought back under the sole oversight of God as Shepherd. Once they have been gathered together like a flock, God will see that new shepherds, who will lead in accordance with God's heart, will be put in place to lead the people of God securely once more. Order will be reestablished. Fear will dissipate. Most importantly, the people will trust again fully in their God.

Under the new order, all of the people of God will be served well. They will prosper and increase. God will see to it. Moreover, it is clear from the text that those formerly of Israel, to the north of the land of Judah, have not been forgotten. God will "gather the remnant of my flock out of all the lands where I have driven them, and I will bring them back to their fold, and they shall be fruitful and multiply" (v. 3). In a way, this serves as a warning about things to come for those in the south if God does not again become their true leader. Either God is in charge, or their situation is doomed to get badly out of control.

Most importantly, the promise of God does not stop at the effort to bring back the scattered ones, and to put in place new leaders who will serve the people. The promise goes beyond the present to another time—a time that is not necessarily lost in infinite possibility. The word is that God will raise for the people a true heir of David's lineage, "a righteous Branch, and he shall reign as king and deal wisely, and shall execute justice and righteousness in the land" (v. 5). This is clearly a word of restoration, but one that does not limit itself to things past. It is a word that looks forward to the future, a different future, that belongs to God, since God is the only one with an ever-open and secured future.

Pastoral Perspective

chapters preceding today's passage, one can see that Jeremiah's use of the term "shepherd" is directed specifically to the kings living during his lifetime. Jeremiah makes clear that the demise of Israel is directly connected to the poor leadership of the kings, including evasion of their duties to uphold justice for the poor, widowed, and oppressed. Context is everything. We glean a better understanding of Jeremiah 23:1–6 through looking at Jeremiah 21:11–22:30. In his oracles about the house of David, Jeremiah names the failure of kings Jehoahaz, Jehoiakim, and Jehoiachin as the ultimate cause of Judah's downfall. Again and again Jeremiah admonishes these kings for failing to execute justice. Their greed for power and prosperity leads them away from the justice they are called to provide for the people.

Looking back through Jeremiah, we are able to see his expectations for a righteous king, a king Christians find fully realized in Christ Jesus. This king does not exhibit the behaviors of a grand military ruler, but models ultimate leadership by being present with the people, all the people. This king reached out beyond the margin with a model of radical inclusivity. This king's ethic modeled what Micah's call to the people was all about: "to do justice, and to love kindness, and to walk humbly with your God" (Mic. 6:8b). This is the model we are called to emulate.

As we look to Christ as the model shepherd or king, what can we learn for living in and engaging the world? As our world struggles with war, famine, and fuel shortages, how do we consider our call to live as God's people? Are there really shortages, or is God's abundance simply unevenly distributed? What are useful responses to the underlying issues of poverty, health care, hunger, clean water, violence, and power? How do we get in on God's restorative justice?

The reign of Christ is the reign of peace. The perennial question for the church is, how do we live faithfully under this reign? As Christians, do we stand by and let national leaders direct us into war, or do we stand up, moving the prism around until we discover a just and equitable approach to handling the impasse at hand? Whether the crisis in our region, nation, or world is war, natural disaster, young people dying violently, lack of work, racism, sexism, trade policies, or migration, we are called to look to the underlying issues that play into the brokenness. At times, we are even called to upset the applecart in order to empower all people as children of God.

YHWH's pasture, not their own (Pss. 95:7; 100:3; Ezek. 34:31). Shepherds are in the employ of YHWH, who is the landowner. In the background of the present oracles lie royal injustices warned about in Jeremiah 22:3–4 and said in 22:13–17 to have been committed by Jehoiakim. Oracles I and II reflect the social unrest and exodus from Judah before and after the calamity of 597 BCE, when Nebuchadnezzar forced the surrender of Jerusalem and many Judahites were carried off to Babylon (2 Kgs. 24:10–16; Jer. 52:28). The dispersion, however, was also because people fled the homeland on their own in the hopes of finding sanctuary in Egypt (24:8), Ammon (41:15), and other neighboring countries. When Jeremiah arrives later in Egypt, Judahite communities already exist at the frontier towns of Migdol and Tahpanhes, at historic Memphis, and at Pathros in Upper Egypt (44:1).

Oracle III (vv. 3–4) opens with an emphatic divine "I," where YHWH says he will gather the remnant from their places of dispersion, restore them to their pasture, where they will be fruitful and multiply, and will raise over them shepherds who will do the job right. The God who scattered will be the God who gathers (31:10). This new people will no longer be afraid, no longer be broken in body and spirit, and no longer require painful visitations from YHWH resulting in punishment.

Oracle IV (vv. 5–6) says that in YHWH's future the pastoral number will be reduced to a single Shoot (NRSV "Branch") of Davidic stock, whose reign shall succeed as the reigns of Judah's present kings have not, doing justice and righteousness in the land. The "Look, days are coming" phrase is not eschatological, that is, it does not look ahead to the end of world history, at which time God will reward the righteous and punish the wicked. It simply points ahead, as do other occurrences of the phrase in the book, to an indefinite future after national collapse, when kingship will be reinstated. Then a "righteous Shoot" will sprout for David (cf. Luke 1:69). The Hebrew can also be translated "rightful Shoot," that is, legitimate offspring, which is supported now by readings in Phoenician and Ugaritic.

If this is the correct translation, then the expression betrays uncertainty in Judah after 597 BCE about who was the rightful king, the exiled Jehoiachin or the enthroned Zedekiah. Jeremiah could be saying that neither king is legitimate; for a legitimate king, the people must wait until YHWH raises one up in the future, but a "righteous Shoot" also suits the context, for the verse states that this

tried to figure out. The power of annoyance or nuisance is also a growing variety of power. We are sometimes scattered and driven simply by our desire to avoid further contact with a nuisance.

The illusive power coursing through all sorts of human systems and institutions is nothing new; Paul nailed powers and principalities in the first century. However, we live in a time when the systems are so huge and often anonymous that we are like fish swimming in a little corner of the sea trying to tell each other about the oceans of the world. This is worth exploring, particularly since the water that we swim in and the air we breathe are both endangered by the very systems in which we live and move and have our being. What if the king is just lost in the machinery of the systems of the world? What if there is no shepherd who can shepherd us toward our safe home fold? What if there is no fold anymore, but just the windswept wildernesses of postmodern existence?

One thing is for sure: human power—our own power or the power of others—is not wise enough or strong enough or good enough to direct the universe, even small patches of the universe. Adam and Eve learned this original lesson in the garden that used to be called paradise. Perhaps the lesson of human limits is the PowerPoint lesson for every human being on the road to spiritual maturity.

It could be illuminating for a preacher to ask people to look at themselves and their personal power. What power do I have? How did I get this power? Whose interest am I serving? To whom am I accountable?

Another homiletical approach might be to remind the congregation that there are significant moments in human history when a renewed and powerful cry for justice does in fact serve as a vehicle for the power of God to change the course of human events. Certainly this reading has been and will be helpful in rallying a community that has been weakened and scattered through bad leadership. A prophetic voice speaking truth to power is surely the heart of the liberation of God's oppressed people down through the ages. Perhaps it is the same prophetic cry that reverberates century after century.

One way to invigorate the prophetic witness of truth to power in the present day would be to remind people of the prophets/preachers/witnesses of other ages: Moses, David, the Hebrew prophets, John the Baptist, Peter, Catherine of Siena, Martin Luther, Teresa of Avila, Frederick Denison Maurice, Martin Luther King Jr., Dietrich Bonhoeffer, and Archbishop Desmond Tutu to name a few, along with the voices

Jeremiah 23:1-6

Theological Perspective

The movement in the text takes us from judgment to promise; from the description of the situation to its solution; and from what humans have messed up to what God is still able and willing to accomplish. The promise of God comes in the midst of a bad situation. We could even say that this word of promise creates the very condition of salvation, as it re-creates the people's trust in God. The word is the word of God's promises, a word of assurance, a vision in the present of new things to come.

It is no wonder that these verses have been cherished by generations of believers for their messianic utterance, particularly on Reign of Christ Sunday. No doubt this passage (especially vv. 5–6) has messianic implications, but this should not be understood merely as end-of-the-world indictment, or exclusively as future eschatology. The truth is that, at one and the same time, this passage speaks powerfully both to what God will do in the future and to what God is doing in the here and now. Such is the dynamic life of the word of God wherever it is uttered. It speaks to the possibilities of the present, as well as to the hopes of the future. God is able to do all of that under one and the same word of promise.

NELSON RIVERA

Pastoral Perspective

Living under Christ's reign means we are called to stand behind those who model Christ's example to love God and neighbor. We are called to see the value God has bestowed on every human being and thereby work toward justice and God's restoration for all people.

Elias Chacour, archbishop of Galilee for the Melkite Greek Catholic Church, stands out as an authentic model of Christ's leadership in the world. Archbishop Chacour shows a different way as he works with his own people and with those in opposition, amid controversy between Palestinians and the state of Israel. Grounded in the understanding that all human beings are children of God, and therefore sisters and brothers of one another, he works for justice and peace building for all involved.

Preaching before the 218th General Assembly of the Presbyterian Church (U.S.A.), the archbishop said that he did not need our help if we were going to take sides, one or the other. Rather, he charged folks of the PC(USA) to come to Galilee, to experience the place where Christ was resurrected, and to help encourage a new model of living in peace for Jews, Muslims, and Christians. Archbishop Chacour is one of many models of Christians living as Christ our King lived and lives. It is not by brute force but by caring for those who are oppressed that he communicates leadership and thereby the power and love of God for all people.

As God continually calls us back into relationship, how is it that we claim God as ruler of our lives? We are called to look to the righteous branch of David, manifest in the life, death, and resurrection of Christ, and we are constantly to reorient our lives, proclaiming to all whom we encounter the justice and love of the triune God.

MARY ELEANOR JOHNS

king will "do justice and righteousness in the land" (v. 5, my trans.; cf. Isa. 32:1). David was remembered as doing both (2 Sam. 8:15—partially lost in RSV and NRSV). Then the phrase would be an indirect condemnation of Jehoiakim, who was the most unrighteous of kings (22:13–17).

In the days of this future king, a united Judah and Israel, such as existed under David, will experience deliverance (from enemies) and a secure existence. Babylonian and Assyrian texts from Nineveh and Assur (ca. 650 BCE) have turned up predicting the rise of unnamed rulers, how long the new king will reign, and whether a country will experience well-being or major unrest.

The concluding line of Oracle IV (v. 6b) states that the future Davidic king will be named "YHWH is our righteousness," a wordplay with reversal on the name of Judah's reigning king, Zedekiah, which means "My righteousness is YHWH." This future king will be a complete turnaround from the present king—what Zedekiah should have been, but was not. If verse 5 is alluding to Jehoiakim, then the oracle as a whole is taking aim at both kings, for the concluding line clearly alludes to Zedekiah. The words "I will raise up for David a righteous Shoot" are given messianic interpretation in Targum Jonathan, in certain medieval Jewish commentators (Kimchi; Abarbanel), and in Calvin, but these are all later elucidations. The seeds of later messianism are nevertheless here, as they are also in Isaiah 9:6–7; 11:1–9; Amos 9:11; Micah 5:2.

In Jeremiah 33:14–16 this same prophecy repeats with minor changes. Here YHWH will make sprout for David a "Shoot of righteousness," supporting the "righteous Shoot" interpretation in 23:5. Also, in chapter 33 it is not the future Davidic king but the city of Jerusalem that shall be called "YHWH is our righteousness" (cf. Isa. 1:26b). The prophecy then no longer censures Zedekiah, but both versions, especially the one in 23:5–6, fit well into Advent, because they announce a future Davidic king that the church has confessed to be Jesus the Christ.

JACK R. LUNDBOM

to be found in the history of every local community. Quoting prophets of other days is a powerful way to remind people of our own day of the prophetic call that has always and everywhere shepherded the people of God toward their deepest home.

No matter where one wanders, one needs eventually to come home. In Christian tradition, home is found by following the Shepherd King who knows the way in and through the grace and power of God. The power of God "attends" (v. 2) to those leaders who do evil. The power of God gathers "the remnant of [the] flock" (v. 3) out of all the lands where the holy I AM has driven them. (Does God scatter sometimes in order to gather?)

Finally, the power of God brings them back to their fold and declares that the flock will be fruitful and multiply in a new time of abundance. The power of God raises up new shepherds who will—in fact and not just in title—shepherd the sheep so that the people of God will no longer be afraid or dismayed, nor shall any be missing. The days are coming for this new Shepherd/King in the mode of David who will reign and shepherd, executing justice and righteousness in the land. The power of the people will be secure in the power of God, for the Lord will be the righteousness of the people (v. 6).

How will we know the righteous Shepherd King? We have so often been blind to righteous power before. The anonymous Advent hymn below might be a graceful hint as the Advent season approaches.

> Thou shalt know him when he comes,
> Not by any din of drums,
> Nor his manners, nor his airs,
> Nor by any thing he wears.'
>
> Thou shalt know him when he comes,
> Not by crown or by gown,
> But his coming known shall be,
> By the holy harmony
> Which his coming makes in thee.
> Thou shalt know him when he comes. Amen.

MARTHA STERNE

Psalm 46

¹God is our refuge and strength,
  a very present help in trouble.
²Therefore we will not fear, though the earth should change,
  though the mountains shake in the heart of the sea;
³though its waters roar and foam,
  though the mountains tremble with its tumult.   *Selah*

⁴There is a river whose streams make glad the city of God,
  the holy habitation of the Most High.
⁵God is in the midst of the city; it shall not be moved;
  God will help it when the morning dawns.
⁶The nations are in an uproar, the kingdoms totter;
  he utters his voice, the earth melts.

Theological Perspective

The opening themes of divine refuge and help in this psalm seem to address one of the thorniest theological problems of every age: where is God in times of real trouble? The answer, that God is an ever-present help in trouble, is not perfectly self-evident in human experience. So theologians through the centuries have sought to interpret the psalm's meaning in ways that make sense in spite of suffering and desolation.

The theological challenge, of course, does not lie in the declaration of God's strength and help but in its persuasiveness, in the question of its evidence in the face of so much contradiction. The good die young, wars persist, and innocents are slaughtered; suffering does not abate, whether from individual, political, or meteorological sources. In such circumstances, how can we possibly understand God to be refuge and strength, a very present help in trouble? For more than fifteen centuries since Augustine, theological interpretations of the psalm's confidence have tended in one of two directions: toward the individual, or toward politics.

Writing in the early fifth century, as Rome rotted from within, Augustine approached the opening lines of Psalm 46 with the poignant claim that refuges are sometimes not places of strength, but instead weaken those who would flee to them. A keen psychological interpreter, the North African

Pastoral Perspective

Psalm 46 is a particularly beloved psalm, famously turned into the hymn "A Mighty Fortress Is Our God" by Martin Luther. Perhaps one reason why Luther and others have loved this psalm is that it steadfastly proclaims faith in God's protection and presence, even while being highly realistic about the ways things actually are in the world. It moves in a counterpoint between the realities of chaos, both natural and political, and the serene confidence that the life of faith allows, even in the midst of troubles. The psalm offers a vision of the faithful life that frankly acknowledges the dangers and difficulties that surround us, but maintains an attitude of trust in God even in the midst of these challenges.

God as refuge and strength is proclaimed first in relationship to natural tumult: "the mountains shake in the heart of the sea . . . waters roar and foam" (vv. 2–3). It is as though the earth itself were reverting to the watery chaos that the book of Genesis attests as existing before God created the world. This chaos, then, is an attempt to undo God's creation and ordering of the world. In recent times many peoples of the world have lived through such terrifying events of natural tumult and destruction: tsunamis, hurricanes, earthquakes, tornadoes. When such calamities overtake us, we may well wonder whether the God who created the earth and called it good is

^{7}The Lᴏʀᴅ of hosts is with us;
  the God of Jacob is our refuge.   *Selah*

^{8}Come, behold the works of the Lᴏʀᴅ;
  see what desolations he has brought on the earth.
^{9}He makes wars cease to the end of the earth;
  he breaks the bow, and shatters the spear;
  he burns the shields with fire.
^{10}"Be still, and know that I am God!
  I am exalted among the nations,
  I am exalted in the earth."
^{11}The Lᴏʀᴅ of hosts is with us;
  the God of Jacob is our refuge.   *Selah*

Exegetical Perspective

An affirmation of faith spoken in the plural voice of
"we," Psalm 46 well deserves its reputation as one of
Scripture's most beloved hymns. Its roots lie deep in
ancient Near Eastern concepts of the relationships
among humans, God, and the natural world. At the
same time, its treatment of war, peace, danger, and
security speaks with reassurance to contemporary
anxieties. The psalm underlies Martin Luther's great
hymn of confidence, "A Mighty Fortress Is Our God."
It proclaims God's presence with God's people,
steadying the faithful in the midst of all in this world
that can, in Luther's words, "threaten to undo us."

Its central theme is the presence of God in
Jerusalem, the "city of God." It reflects what scholars
often call "royal Zion theology." This theology held
that God had chosen both Jerusalem as God's holy
city and the family of David to rule as God's regents,
and had pledged steadfast loyalty to both. The visible
sign of God's presence in the city was Solomon's
magnificent temple on Mount Zion, and within the
temple the "ark of God, which is called by the name
of the Lᴏʀᴅ of hosts who is enthroned on the cheru-
bim" (2 Sam. 6:2). Whether the psalm's creation preceded or followed the dramas of 734 and 701 BCE,
when Jerusalem twice escaped enemy threats (Isa. 7;
36–37), it is closely connected with Isaiah's affirmation, "Immanu El," "God is with us" (Isa. 7:14).

Homiletical Perspective

In the dizzying weeks after September 11, 2001,
many of us turned to the words of Psalm 46. Martin
Luther's hymn "A Mighty Fortress Is Our God,"
inspired by this psalm, rang out in churches sprin-
kled across the expanse of the country. It was read
responsively as a call to worship. Knock-kneed new
ordinands preached on it in their first calls, as did
Billy Graham in the National Cathedral. Psalm 46
was on our lips.

For good reason. Psalm 46 is a great psalm of comfort, appropriately used in the event of national
tragedy, as well as in personal or community tragedies
of smaller but no less potent scale. It has been pulled
out for a variety of such occasions with some regular-
ity. The text is, however, more than a spiritual defibril-
lator and is appropriate for preaching on Sundays
when things are, if not calm, at least not as chaotic as
the Sunday after that tragic Tuesday in 2001.

Christ the King Sunday is one such week. The
preacher will find several textual themes that lend
themselves to preaching on this final Sunday of the
liturgical year. In particular, Reign of Christ themes of
sovereignty and lordship found in this psalm describe
the kind of Lord in whom we should place our trust.

*God Provides Refuge from the Chaos of the Natural
World.* Verses 2 and 3 deal with God's protection

Psalm 46

Theological Perspective

bishop consistently read the Bible through the lens of individual struggles with faith, despair, and hope. The whole of his approach to Psalm 46 focuses on the inner state of the believer, whose only hope of finding refuge in the city of God lies in acknowledgment of divine power, creation, and victory. He makes no attempt to explain divine help in military, social, or political terms, none of which pan out in actual historical experience enough to make such claims about God plausible anyway. Instead, Augustine argues that God's refuge is available only upon the individual's realization that there is no refuge in the self, or in the world, and so it is fruitless and misleading to fight—or pray—for it.

> But the contentious uproar in the human mind is oblivious, so to this uproar the command is given, "*Be still:* clear your minds of their disputatious noise. Do not argue with God, as though to take up arms against him. . . . *Be still,* because you no longer have anything to fight with. If you are still and empty within yourselves, you who formerly presumed on yourselves may entreat me for all you need. *Be still,* and you will see *that I am God*."[1]

Placed in the context of Roman political dissolution, the Augustinian insights—that refuges are not always strengthening and that struggle against God is ultimately fruitless—may best reflect his own search for solid ground in an uncertain time. For him, the answer to theodicy lies in the human heart and mind, in an interior, even Stoic, posture of surrender that stills the tumult and does not engage in the hoax of battle any more than the impotence of shaking a fist at hurricanes.

God is inexorable and constitutes the sort of refuge that does not weaken the sheltered. This is because God is not a refuge *from* the world and its excesses, but a refuge *in it,* in the sense of a reorientation away from self-protection and its errors. God's present help is of the sort that undoes self-delusion, which one might reasonably say alters the meaning of refuge entirely. Perhaps, therefore, refuge has nothing to do with protection.

The influence of Augustine's personalistic and challenging approach shifted after Martin Luther wrote his wildly popular hymn based on the psalm and Protestants sang of God in military terms as *ein feste Burg,* a mighty fortress that never fails. Sometimes referred to as the battle hymn of the Reformation, Luther's hymn

1. Augustine, *Expositions of the Psalms,* trans. Maria Boulding, OSB, in *Works of St. Augustine,* part 3, vol. 16, ed. John E. Rotelle, OSA (Hyde Park, NY: New City Press, 2000), 311 and 322–23.

Pastoral Perspective

still in charge. However, the psalmist does not waver in insisting that God is with us and is our refuge, even in such circumstances.

God's strength and protection are next offered in relationship to political chaos, which, if anything, would have been even more terrifying to the beleaguered peoples of Israel. Such chaos is likewise well known to us in our own era, when wars ravage many peoples of the earth, causing nations to totter and fail. The same verbs are used in Hebrew for the political chaos that were used for the natural tumult in earlier verses: the nations roar just as the waters do, and the kingdoms totter just as the mountains do. The repetition of these verbs emphasizes that the political uproar is like the natural tumult in being an effort to undo God's good creation. The repetition also highlights the contrast between all that roars and totters, whether natural forces or nations, and that which does not move—God's holy city.

In contrast to the upheaval all around, the city of God is presented as a place of peace and protection. The stream flowing through it brings gladness and nourishment, in contrast to the roaring waters without, which can only destroy. This psalm is categorized as one of the "songs of Zion," psalms that celebrate Jerusalem as the place of God's habitation, and thus a place of beauty and abundance, a safe refuge from the destructive forces of nature and history. In our own lives, given natural threats and disasters, and the prevalence of war and political tumult, we may well long for a place of delight and protection such as is presented in this psalm.

The psalm speaks to this longing, but also goes beyond it, as the key source of protection is not the city itself but God's presence in the city. The psalmist presents the city in an idealized light; there is no stream running through the actual Jerusalem, for instance. In other psalms, Jerusalem is described as being on a high mountain, whereas in fact it is on a rather low hill. The point of these idealized portrayals is to highlight the fact that it is not the city itself that protects and gives delight, but God's dwelling in the city. Fundamentally it is God who is the refuge, the safe and secure place, more than any earthly city can be. The psalm thus reminds us not to place our trust in any earthly place, person, or thing for our ultimate security amid the storms of life: "Did we in our own strength confide, our striving would be losing," says Luther. Rather, the psalm calls us to place our trust in God alone.

With this trust, we are able to affirm the most audacious part of the psalmist's vision: that God

Water imagery suffuses the psalm. The world beyond the city wall is envisioned as a chaotic place where the earth itself is unstable, filled with earthquakes and roaring floods, a world from which the faithful find refuge in God alone. The use of floods to signify international threat and political havoc is widespread, especially in the prophecies of Isaiah and Jeremiah. Isaiah describes attacking nations as "the thundering of the sea" and "the roaring of mighty waters" (Isa. 17:12) that will flee away at God's rebuke (see also Isa. 5:30; Jer. 6:23; 50:42; 51:55). Such images partake of the ancient Near Eastern notion of the sea as a personified force of chaos, more powerful than humans, but put in its place by divine might, whether by combat (as in Job 26:12; Ps. 89:9–10; Isa. 51:9–10) or by command (as in Gen. 1:9–10; Ps. 107:28–29).

In contrast to the roaring waters without, the river within the walls, "whose streams make glad the city of God" (v. 4), gives life and inspires joy. Since no river actually flows through Jerusalem, some see here a symbolic reflex, much like Ezekiel's envisioned river flowing from the temple (Ezek. 47:1–12) to water and fructify the surrounding countryside, and even to sweeten the salty Dead Sea. The wording also calls to mind the Gihon spring to Jerusalem's east, the spring from which Hezekiah dug a tunnel, bringing water inside the city walls to Shiloah, or Siloam. Isaiah 8:6–8 contrasts "the waters of Shiloah that flow gently" with "the mighty flood waters of the River," the Euphrates. Isaiah's contrast between Jerusalem's own spring and the powerful Assyrian river articulated the choice between reliance on Jerusalem's God and reliance on imperial forces that would ultimately threaten to overrun the city. The psalm affirms that those who trust in God will enjoy the life-giving waters and find refuge from the "flood" of invaders.

Three divine names are found in the psalm. The most frequent is *Elohim*, God, also called "the God of Jacob." Closely connected in the refrain found in verses 7 and 11 is *YHWH Sabaoth*, "the Lord of hosts," the name associated with the ark that once traveled with Israel and now stood in the Holy of Holies. A third name, in verse 4, *Elyon*, "Most High," was associated with Jerusalem since pre-Israelite days (Gen. 14:18–22), signaling God's abiding presence over the centuries of cultural change. These names, drawn from different corners of tradition, deliberately signifying one God, remind contemporary worshipers that all Earth's tribes, who remember God by diverse names and stories, are one creation under

from chaos in the natural world. When mountains and waters no longer behave as humans expect, fear is a natural response, yet the psalmist urges us to recognize God's presence in the midst of that and to replace fear with trust in God.

The choice of mountains and waters as descriptors of chaos is not accidental. To the psalmist, those mountains would have been the foundations of the earth, and the waters its life source. The shaking of the mountains would have held huge significance to the first readers of this psalm. Contemporary readers may be far enough removed from natural life that these nuances would not be caught. We tend to rely on our safety systems (even when evidence proves that they are fallible). In a world without evacuation shelters, air bags, and emergency announcement systems, a shaking mountain and roaring ocean would be terrifying. Most of us are not as afraid of hurricanes as we are of a lack of hurricane shelters. Removing a layer of insulation doubles the panic. Though we may be one step removed from the source of terror, we still need and have a refuge in God.

God Provides a River Whose Streams Make Glad the City of God. Verse 4 contains the elegant transition line, "There is a river whose streams make glad the city of God." This is an interesting play on the ideas of rivers and streams. While school science classes teach us that, technically, all bodies of moving water are streams, most people understand rivers to be larger bodies of moving water—progressing toward an ocean, lake, or larger river. Streams, on the other hand, tend (in common usage) to lead to—and from—rivers. Not all streams are viable. Some dry up in harsh weather, returning in the spring rains. Some meander about, not taking the direct or obvious route from their source. Still others overflow, drenching fragile banks. Yet such tiny, imperfect, but immutable streams "make glad the city of God." God, it seems, dwells with joy in the minutiae of this world.

Water is a powerful image both biblically and in our common life. Biblical references to water abound (more than 150 references to rivers alone; see Gen. 2:10; Mark 1:5; Rev. 22:1 as a sampling). In this psalm, water is seen both as violent and uncontrollable (v. 3) and as the path to the city of God (v. 4). Water in all its forms shapes and molds us, feeds us, makes life possible. Both our physical life and our Christian life begins with it.

God Is in the Midst of the City. Verses 4–7 give us a vision of God in the midst of a city in turmoil.

Psalm 46

Theological Perspective

was sung by his followers as they squared off against Rome under the banner of this image of divine might, in the middle of what Calvin saw as the disintegration of the whole world. The fact that Luther sang the song to a lute suggests that he, like Augustine, may have been thinking of something more paradoxical and interesting in his interpretation of the psalm, but that detail is seldom noted. The idea of a military fortress for the faithful against the chaos of the world has prevailed, metaphorically.

In recent years, commentators have shied away from triumphalist readings of the psalm, but still affirm political over personal, or epistemological, interpretations. For instance, Eberhard Jüngel argues that (presumably despite its monarchical context) the psalm originates with oppressed people, and is directed toward them: "Not in order to make them *self-confident!* By no means! *Release* is announced."[2]

Psalm 46 expresses confidence that God cannot be undone by the worst calamities the singer can imagine. The promises of presence and refuge, which repeat after every stanza, cannot mean that God will insulate the people from such calamity. That conclusion does not bear out, as everywhere the good and innocent are felled. Perhaps instead, as Calvin suggests, the point to take from this song is one of courage over against the acidic dissolution that fear creates. He writes that no matter what happens, terror does not win out. Rather, the people gather strength and courage enough to allay all fear.[3] Or perhaps it is reasonable to suggest that the singer is in fact afraid, and rightfully so, as kingdoms totter and angry waters rise. Perhaps then the song is a midnight prayer alone at a kitchen table in a time of trouble, the kind that lays open the heart's fragile hope and stills the mind, the kind best sung with a single lute.

LAUREL C. SCHNEIDER

Pastoral Perspective

will, that God *does*, make war to cease throughout the whole earth. Given the prevalence of war throughout the earth, it is hard to imagine this happening in the future, much less that it is happening *now*. However, with eyes of faith, we are enabled to see the various places on earth where God is indeed bringing an end to war. Wherever this happens, we can, with the psalmist, interpret this as a statement of God's sovereignty—for it is in destroying the weapons of war that God calls us to "be still, and know that I am God" (v. 10).

God's ultimate assertion of power occurs in God's destruction of those tools by which we seek to impose our power over others. The destruction of this weaponry shows God to be the true power, the true ruler of the universe. We are to cease and desist from taking up weapons of violence, and to acknowledge God's sovereignty—a particularly apt message on the Sunday of the liturgical year when the church celebrates the reign of Christ.

Psalm 46 was most likely sung in a liturgical setting, perhaps in an annual ritual that celebrated the enthronement of YHWH as lord of Zion. Through this ritual, the people of Jerusalem affirmed God's protection and sovereignty, which brought delight and peace even in the midst of chaos threatening on all sides. The psalm can have the same effect on today's worshipers. In worship we as a community reaffirm our faith in God's unfailing protection. Out of this liturgical reaffirmation we derive strength to live as people of faith. This faith does not mean shutting our eyes to tumult, wars, and suffering; it means knowing that in the midst of all that threatens us, God is also there, and God ultimately reigns. As Luther says, "And though this world, with devils filled, should threaten to undo us; we will not fear, for God hath willed [God's] truth to triumph through us. . . . [God's] kingdom is forever."

RUTHANNA HOOKE

2. Eberhard Jüngel, "Sermon on Psalm 46," trans. Allen G. Jorgenson, in *Consensus* 30, no. 1 (2005): 92.
3. Jean Calvin, "Psalm XLVI," in *Commentary on the Book of Psalms*, vol. 2, trans. James Anderson (Grand Rapids: Eerdmans, 1949), 196.

Exegetical Perspective

God's sovereign rule. Just as the stories of Jacob, Moses, and Jerusalem were woven into a greater whole, so the diverse accounts of God from many nations carry the potential to be woven into the greater fabric of human awareness of God.

God's role as "help," introduced at the beginning, is reiterated more specifically in verse 5: "God will be her [Zion's] help when dawn arrives" (my trans.). The temporal phrase recalls precisely dawn's arrival at the Red Sea in Exodus 14:27, after the Israelites had crossed, when the sea returned to its normal depth, when God turned the mighty waters, which yesterday had seemed a lethal barrier between the fleeing slaves and their freedom, into a barrier protecting them from enemies, a mighty force drowning the oppressing foe.

This echo portends the nations' actual introduction in verse 6, their verbs paralleling those that already characterized the natural elements: just as the waters roared, so the nations roar; just as the mountains shook, so the kingdoms shake. The general statement is followed by an invitation: "Come, behold the works of the LORD, who has brought desolations on the earth" (my trans.). Upon closer inspection, however, the "desolations" prove anything but violent. They are sheer disarmament: God "breaks the bow, . . . shatters the spear, . . . burns shields [or chariots] with fire" (v. 9), destroying not armies but armaments.

At that heightened moment, the divine voice breaks in, the voice that melts the earth. The words are familiar; the setting, however, demands attention. "Be still, and know that I am God" can hardly be heard today without instantaneous association with robed choral voices concluding Sunday worship with a final plea for reverent contemplation as the pastor strides toward the greeting door and the parishioners furtively gather coats and purses, sippy cups and crayons. In their psalmic setting, however, the divine voice roars at warring nations: "Stop!" As the Jewish Publication Society Tanakh puts it: "Desist! Realize that I am God! I dominate the nations; I dominate the earth." We affirm with the psalmists: "The LORD of hosts is with us; the God of Jacob is our refuge" (v. 11).

PATRICIA TULL

Homiletical Perspective

Contemporary readers, particularly those familiar with urban life, will have no trouble placing these words in the current context. For most, they could have been written last week. As kingdoms totter and nations rage, God's children will seek refuge. God is that place of refuge, that safety belt. Preachers will take care to note that God is in *the midst of* the city, not running from it. Where God is, there shall the people of God be found as well.

God Calls Us to Alert Stillness. Among the most quoted portions of this psalm is verse 10a, "Be still, and know that I am God." Most usages of this phrase are pulled outside the context of the psalm and refer to stillness in the vein of relaxing or quiet meditation. That is not the kind of stillness to which this psalm refers. The phrase is more like the sound of a parent sharply correcting her or his fidgeting child: "Be still!" This is not a stillness of mauves and quiet music. It is a stillness of snapping to attention, of hyperattentiveness, of dropping whatever is in your hands or distracting you, and attending carefully to God's word.

God Is with Us. The psalm closes with the line, "the LORD of hosts is with us" (v. 11a), repeated from verse 7a. The repetition is more than just a liturgical move. It reinforces the central theme of the psalm. The Lord of hosts is *with* us, in the midst of the city, in the midst of the roaring waters and shaking mountains, in the midst of all—real or imagined—that frightens us. The Lord is with (*immanû*) us, a small prepositional phrase that, in fact, defines the larger point of the psalm.

The psalm takes the reader through many of the themes common in Christ the King readings and liturgies: sovereignty, protection, power. It calls readers to attentiveness. Perhaps most importantly, it reminds readers that this sovereign, powerful God is *with* us, in the midst of the city, in the midst of the chaotic natural world, in the midst of our lives. God is perpetually with us—*immanû*. This omnipresent God is one king worth following.

SUSAN K. OLSON

Colossians 1:11-20

¹¹May you be made strong with all the strength that comes from his glorious power, and may you be prepared to endure everything with patience, while joyfully ¹²giving thanks to the Father, who has enabled you to share in the inheritance of the saints in the light. ¹³He has rescued us from the power of darkness and transferred us into the kingdom of his beloved Son, ¹⁴in whom we have redemption, the forgiveness of sins.

¹⁵He is the image of the invisible God, the firstborn of all creation; ¹⁶for in him all things in heaven and on earth were created, things visible and invisible, whether thrones or dominions or rulers or powers—all things have been created through him and for him. ¹⁷He himself is before all things, and in him all things hold together. ¹⁸He is the head of the body, the church; he is the beginning, the firstborn from the dead, so that he might come to have first place in everything. ¹⁹For in him all the fullness of God was pleased to dwell, ²⁰and through him God was pleased to reconcile to himself all things, whether on earth or in heaven, by making peace through the blood of his cross.

Theological Perspective

These verses in the letter to the Colossians represent the writer's intercessory prayer for the community and thanksgiving for their redemption in Christ. The writer employs a preexisting hymn or poem (vv. 15–20) to declare God's revelation through Christ and assert the reign of Christ throughout the entire world.

The hymn is a statement of what today we call "high Christology," a view of Christ that emphasizes his divinity. The hymn's Christology unfolds in three parts, describing him as one who participates in creation, holds all things together, and reconciles all things in heaven and on earth through his death on the cross. The hymn's inclusion in this letter serves to underscore the sufficiency of Christ over and against all other cosmic powers, for in the second chapter the writer goes on to warn the community against rival teachings that were apparently encouraging religious practices and pieties that competed with the gospel.

This text is thus fittingly assigned in the lectionary to the Sunday of the Christian year known as the Reign of Christ (or Christ the King). On this Sunday, worshipers are reminded that, as Christians, they are subjects of Christ and Christ alone. Christ's power transcends all other powers. Moreover, salvation in Christ has been achieved for all.

Pastoral Perspective

Paul's letters are not just an academic treatise, but words and ideas spoken to the problems of real churches with real people struggling to understand a faith newly embraced. When confronted with new ideas and new world constructs, the temptation is to take the unfamiliar and fit it into an existing worldview. For many of Paul's fledgling churches, that means fitting Jesus into a gnostic understanding of the world—something that is not hard to do if you begin with Gnosticism. It can make room for all kinds of ideas, prophets, and gods.

That is if you *start* with Gnosticism.

Paul will have none of it. His worldview begins with and is shaped by Jesus Christ, "the firstborn of all creation" (v. 15). This is a radical shift that utterly changes the way in which we look at the world. To help his congregation understand just how radical it is, Paul speaks of our being transferred from one kingdom to another. His image conjures up pictures of refugees, rounded up after battle and taken to the victor's land, of Israelites marched far from home to live in Babylon—a kingdom so different, so far from home in both geography and style. Here the rules are different, the ruler is different. All the assumptions about the way in which life goes on—indeed about its very meaning—are different.

Exegetical Perspective

Readers who move too swiftly to the latter portion of Colossians 1:11–20, where weighty truths about Christ are cast in a paean of praise (vv. 15–20), may actually miss the letter writer's pastoral concern, for which all of 1:11–20 and its larger literary context play a critical role. Thus, to capture that pastoral concern, we need to understand (a) the overall rhetorical drive of the letter, (b) the larger literary context of 1:11–20, namely, 1:3–23a, and (c) the contribution that the larger literary context makes to the letter's overall drive.

Colossians was written to encourage believers in the Lycus River Valley (modern-day Turkey) to "continue securely established and steadfast in the faith, without shifting from the hope promised by the gospel that [they] heard" (v. 23). The letter recipients first heard this gospel (v. 5) from Epaphras, the founder of their assembly (vv. 7–8). The letter writer himself was a servant or minister for this same gospel (v. 23).

With repetitive expressions, moreover, the letter writer clarifies both the hope promised by the gospel and the only source of wisdom through which that hope can be realized. Accordingly, with repeated expressions of *growth*, the writer makes clear the nature of the promised hope (v. 23; cf. v. 5), that is, the believers' full maturity before God or a "holy and

Homiletical Perspective

There are many preachable gems in this text. It is filled with blessings, testimony, early church doctrine, and a refutation of gnostic heresies. Paul is writing to a congregation he has not met in person and is seeking to set straight the heart of the Christian message to a community of mostly Gentile people. A clearly enumerated set of statements about the person and power of Christ is presented most likely as a refutation of the gnostic Gospels that had become a source of much confusion in the region. The energy and passion in this particular piece of writing fits well with the notable celebration of the Reign of Christ for this Sunday in the church calendar.

An exquisite blessing opens this pericope that identifies the source of the Christian's power, namely, Christ. We are not strong in ourselves but only as children of God. The King's might is that which keeps the people strong. Another reference to the sovereignty of Christ comes in the phrase, "He has rescued us from the power of darkness and transferred us into the kingdom of his beloved Son, in whom we have redemption, the forgiveness of sins" (vv. 13–14). The word "transferred" is of special note.

The Greek verb here is *methistēmi*, a word with special significance in relationship to the spoils of battle. As William Barclay notes, "In the ancient world, when one empire won a victory over another,

Colossians 1:11-20

Theological Perspective

This is the last Sunday of the church year and as such represents a transition point in the calendar. It is like a new year's eve, a time when observers look back and reflect on the meanings of the past year and look ahead with hope to the future and its meanings yet to be revealed. Reign of Christ Sunday shares theological themes with Palm/Passion Sunday, also a transition point in the Christian calendar and also a day on which Jesus Christ is hailed as a king. Of course, the specter of Jesus' death hovers over Palm Sunday. On Reign of Christ Sunday, it is the advent of Jesus' nativity that in one week's time will be on the mind of Christians. Both days thus celebrate the multiple meanings of Christ's identity: the same Christ who is hailed as king also suffers a cruel death at the hands of the state, and the same Christ who rules over all creation also enters the world as a vulnerable baby. The timing of the reading of this Colossians text, therefore, works subtly to juxtapose a high Christology with a low one.

Such a theological juxtaposition may strike even some who regularly follow the lectionary as bizarre and even bewildering. How can the same God be so many things? Why are different meanings of divinity presented in such rapid succession? The paradox, however, is important theologically. Christ's reign takes on special meaning when understood within the context of the whole narrative of his birth, life, suffering, death, and resurrection. Christ is no ordinary king. Returning to the Colossians hymn, the text yields several clues as to what kind of king he is.

First, the text emphasizes Christ's rule over all people and, indeed, even over the nonhuman realm. Normally, a king connotes one who rules only over certain subjects, especially citizens of a geographical or political region. Many commentators have pointed out how frequently the word "all" appears in these verses, lending weight to a theology of universal salvation. Christ is ruler not just of some but of all.

Second, Christ is described as "the firstborn of all creation," existent even before humans were created. Actual kings usually ascend to their thrones by genetic inheritance. They are normally descendants of a particular line of people. The reference to being "firstborn" appears twice (vv. 15, 18), underscoring that Christ belongs not to a particular people but rather to all peoples.

Finally, Christ's reign is established in a paradoxical way: through crucifixion. The text refers first implicitly (v. 14) and then explicitly (v. 20) to a reign whose freedom and peace are achieved through the saving power of death on a cross. He does not rule

Pastoral Perspective

Some years ago a young couple in a church I was then serving adopted children, two and five years old, from Russia. As the congregation watched them come into our midst, I was continually struck by just how greatly the childrens' lives had changed. It was not simply a matter of moving from institutional living to a home and a family with people they did not know, or of English words crooned to them at night instead of Russian. Everything was different: the food, the smells, the sounds. They were forced to make an incredible adjustment.

Paul says that becoming a Christian is like that. It is not simply a matter of fitting Jesus into our present way of thinking. We are transferred, moved, deported, from one kingdom to another, from one way of living into another. Nothing is as we have known it.

What does that old struggle with Gnosticism have to do with us today? How do Paul's concerns speak to our time? Have you never heard someone say, "All religions lead to God. This is my path. Someone else has another path. Both paths are equally good"? Words to that effect are common, even among the folk who sit Sunday after Sunday in the very churches that proclaim, "Jesus is Lord."

The tolerance that makes this country work, and rescues us from sectarian violence, often becomes the uncritical worldview into which we then "fit" Jesus. Paul, however, says it needs to be the other way around; Jesus himself must become the worldview into which we then fit all the rest. How do we do that?

Paul gives us a good example. He proclaims this radical new message in words that are already known and familiar to the Colossian church. In essence, he says the creed. It is a solution that lives in the story told of a young monk who went to his Abba, "Father, what am I to do? I cannot believe."

"Say the creed, my son."

"But how can I say what I do not believe?"

"Say the Creed, my son. Even when you do not believe, say the creed."

While there are difficulties with that approach, the reality is that words do shape us, even as they are spoken into the formless void that shaped the world. Words "create" us, they shape our belief. Rather than an exercise in hypocrisy, this approach is more akin to what my therapist friend calls, the "fake it 'til you make it" approach of modern-day cognitive-behavioral therapy. To continue to say the creed is to allow those words to shape us and become our own.

The creedal hymn to which Paul turns speaks to another issue that faced both his pagan world and

Exegetical Perspective

blameless and irreproachable" state (v. 22). The writer's intercessory prayer report, for example, speaks of the assembly "[bearing] fruit in every good work" and growing "in the knowledge of God" (v. 10). Later, with a rich "body" metaphor, he insists that the assembly hold onto Christ, "the head, from whom the whole body, nourished and held together by its ligaments and sinews, grows with a growth that is from God" (2:19). Furthermore, the writer also acknowledges his role and that of Epaphras as persons seeking or praying to bring other believers to maturity (1:28; 4:12).

Likewise, with repeated expressions about *wisdom*, the writer makes clear that the only source of wisdom through which the aforementioned hope can be realized is the wisdom already available for those who are in the body of Christ. On the one hand, the writer emphasizes this source with a contrast between a "spiritual wisdom" (1:9) and a teaching that has only the "appearance of wisdom" (2:23). Thus, true wisdom is found sufficiently in Christ (2:3; cf. 3:16), and it stands in contrast to the deceptive and unprofitable teaching (2:4, 8, 22–23) against which the letter recipients seem to be contending.

Furthermore, the letter writer has taught this true wisdom (v. 28) toward the goal of presenting everyone as mature in Christ, which is also the goal of Christ's reconciliation (v. 22). This true wisdom also provides a mode for any action conducted toward outsiders (4:5). On the other hand, the writer emphasizes this source of wisdom in the implicit assertion that Christ is wisdom itself, as highlighted by the writer's depiction of Christ on the order of Personified Wisdom (vv. 15–18a; cf. Prov. 8:22–31; Sir. 24:9). The source of wisdom by which the promised hope is assuredly realized then is found only and sufficiently in Christ, on to whom the letter recipients are holding firm, despite the threatening presence of a sham "philosophy" (2:8).

Colossians 1:11–20 is a part of a larger literary context (1:3–23a) that is preceded by the letter's opening (vv. 1–2), followed first by the writer's reflections on his own commitment to the gospel (1:23b–2:5) and then by larger remarks on what the assembly's commitment to the gospel would entail (2:6–4:6), along with an epistolary closing (4:7–18). More specifically, 1:3–23a may be adumbrated as follows. Initially, a thanksgiving notice (vv. 3–8) reveals the assembly's commendable faith and love, and "the hope laid up for [them] in heaven" (v. 5), a hope communicated in Epaphras's gospel (v. 7). Next, the writer reports his intercessory prayer for the audience's right

Homiletical Perspective

it was the custom to take the population of the defeated country and transfer it . . . to the conqueror's land."[1] Christ is the conqueror of darkness, sin, and death, and we are taken to dwell as a whole people in the kingdom of God. No longer are we subject to the powers of darkness, but we become God's beloved people and citizens in the kingdom of heaven through Christ's sacrifice.

In verses 15–20 we are offered a beautiful weaving of testimony and doctrine. We hear an echo of Jesus' declaration in the Gospel of John, "If you know me, you will know my Father also. From now on you do know him and have seen him" (John 14:7). In this passage Paul asserts that Christ is the one who makes the invisible God visible. Paul's choice of the word "image" is significant. Here is it used, not just in the sense of a representation of God, but as an actual manifestation of God. Jesus is not *like* God, not *an exemplary* follower of God, but in fact God. This assertion is a clear refutation of the gnostic belief that Christ could not be God, since God could not take on a material form.

One can almost hear the trumpets begin to sound as the list of entities over which Christ is sovereign is enumerated. It lends itself to a liturgical reading and might serve well as a call to worship or declaration of faith in the worship service for the Reign of Christ. There are echoes here of the litany in Romans of things that cannot separate us from the love of God (Rom. 8:38–39). It is almost as though the lawyers have gotten down to the fine print, so that we make no mistake, finding no loophole in the complete and total lordship of Christ.

New Testament scholar Walter Wink has made great study of this passage and its reference to "things visible and invisible, whether thrones or dominions or rulers or powers" (v. 16). In the epilogue to Wink's seminal work *The Powers That Be*, he suggests that this passage is one in which we hear clearly that the work of Christ seeks not only to reconcile the people to God and free them from the powers of this world, but, "to reconcile the Powers themselves to God."[2] It is not enough simply to disengage from the hierarchies and idolatries to which we often find ourselves subject. The call of the Christian life is to seek to transform those systems so that they emulate the grace, mercy, and compassion we experience in the kingdom of God.

1. William Barclay, *The Letters to the Philippians, Colossians, and Thessalonians* (Louisville, KY: Westminster Press, 1975), 111.
2. Walter Wink, *The Powers That Be: Theology for a New Millennium* (New York: Galilee Doubleday, 1988), 199.

Colossians 1:11-20

Theological Perspective

by threat or military domination or acquisition. His authority is not sustained by asking homage from others. He does not subject people to himself. His "kingdom," therefore, stands in stark contrast to other imperial rules. His is an entirely different sort of empire than, say, that of Rome.

One symbol Christians use to represent the theological paradox of a crucified king is the crown of thorns. It is employed in art and literature to depict Christ's redemptive suffering for others. An example is Peter De Vries's 1961 novel *The Blood of the Lamb*. A desolate and desperate character named Don Wanderhope, who has just lost his daughter to cancer, has defaced a statue of Christ by throwing a cake at it. The pastry lands squarely on the face, just below the crown of thorns. But Wanderhope experiences the power of redemption offered in this symbol of sacrifice:

> Then through scalded eyes I seemed to see the hands free themselves of the nails and move slowly toward the soiled face. Very slowly, very deliberately, with infinite patience, the icing was wiped from the eyes and flung away. I could see it fall in clumps to the porch steps. Then the cheeks were wiped down with the same sense of grave and gentle ritual, with all the kind sobriety of one whose voice could be heard saying, 'Suffer the little children to come unto me . . . for of such is the kingdom of heaven.'[1]

Like the Colossians hymn, images such as this affirm that in the reign of Christ, God is "pleased to reconcile to [God]self all things, whether on earth or in heaven, by making peace through the blood of his cross" (v. 20).

BARBARA J. BLODGETT

Pastoral Perspective

ours: How do we understand God's role in the creation of the world? Certainly in our own day that question is tearing at communities and school boards, creating anger and division. While there is little similarity between the gnostic understanding of creation and that of modern science, the way in which Paul deals with the question is helpful. Today's preacher does not need to go into the intricacies of the gnostic views, because Paul himself avoids them. Rather than becoming bogged down in questions of how; Paul addresses the questions of who and why.

The answer, as with so much of Paul's thinking, lies in Jesus the Christ: "All things have been created through him and for him" (v. 16). It is here, in Jesus, that the means and the meaning of creation are found.

It is also here, in Jesus, that the redemption of creation is possible—a redemption not just for human beings but for all of creation. How does this help us as we struggle to make sense of the complexities of human social constructs—politics, philosophies, family? What does Paul say to the "green" concerns of ecology and diet and fuel consumption? Does that feel like a far reach in thinking? If we do indeed proclaim that Jesus is the way in which God "rescued us from the power of darkness" (v. 13), does he not offer a way out of our human dilemmas?

Does that sound overstated or simplistic? Consider this: Paul says that to follow Jesus is to orient one's life in a new way. Paul's insistence that in Christ all things hold together is another way to say that. Our faith in Christ gives us a worldview that is both large enough and consistent enough to address the myriad questions and problems that confront human life. To proclaim Christ as King is to acknowledge his lordship over all of life, all of creation.

NETA PRINGLE

1. Peter De Vries, *The Blood of the Lamb* (Boston: Little, Brown, & Co., 1961), 237.

walking (that is, their bearing fruit, growing in knowledge, being empowered for endurance and long-suffering, and giving thanks to God, vv. 9–11). Then the letter reveals God's role (vv. 12–14) and Christ's role (vv. 15–20) in making the aforementioned growth possible.

To God, thanks is offered for the initial incorporation of believers into the dominion of Christ, through which the believers were granted both a new status as saints and the inheritance or benefits that accrue to that new status (vv. 12–14; cf. 1:2; 3:10). In a powerful creed or hymn (vv. 15–20), moreover, Christ's singular role is emphasized, not only as the agent or representative according to which *all* of creation (vv. 15–18a) came into being, but also as the conduit by which *all* of creation is reconciled to God (vv. 18b–20). Within that reconciliation process, Christ overcomes the once-estranged relations between the believers and God (v. 22) and makes possible the continuing maturation of believers, until eventually they are presented fully mature before God (v. 22), again, as long they do not shift from the gospel they have heard (v. 23a).

Given the letter's overall emphasis on the letter recipients' remaining committed to the gospel, 1:3–23a functions in at least four ways. First, the diction associated with the gospel (bearing fruit and growing, v. 6) anticipates the same diction that describes the potential maturation of believers (v. 10). Second, the "hope laid up . . . in heaven" (v. 5) is linked to the gospel that the letter recipients have heard (vv. 5–6) in anticipation of a similar linking given later (cf. v. 23). Third, the writer's prayer that the believers "lead/[walk, (*peripatēsai*)] lives worthy of God" (v. 10) resounds throughout the letter, for the believers are admonished to continue walking/living (*peripateite*) in Jesus, just as they received him (2:6), and to conduct/live (*peripateite*) before outsiders wisely (4:5).

Likewise, the believers are reminded of how they once walked/lived (*periepatēsate*, 3:7). Fourth, the writer's declaration that Christ, the head of the church, brings peace (vv. 18–20) becomes the orientation or mode by which the church lives out its own life, with believers allowing the peace of Christ to rule in their hearts (3:15). Thus, all of 1:3–23a, including verses 11–20, both anticipates and is ingredient to the writer's emphasis on the hope for full maturity as acknowledged in the gospel that the assembly has already heard.

ABRAHAM SMITH

This passage goes on to amplify further the lordship of Christ, offering the preacher fabulous images to explore. The declaration that "in him all things hold together" (v. 17) lends itself to wondering what some of those things are that might feel as if they are falling apart or are not held together. Budget battles for mission and music versus expenses for education and outreach have left many a parishioner feeling as though church leadership were something less than holy. Here we are given a summons to unified vision and ministry. While there are separate parts of congregational life and activities, celebrating Christ and sharing his message of reconciliation and forgiveness is our supreme task. While there are as many different views of God as different denominations, it is love for Christ and Christ's love for us that ultimately trumps any one doctrine or theological dispute. The "one bread, one body, one cup" language from the communion liturgy is powerfully evoked in these words.

Lest we get lost in bickering about priorities either personal or communal, Paul offers us this clarifying nugget of wisdom: Christ "is the beginning, the firstborn from the dead, so that he might come to have first place in everything" (v. 18). How many church arguments, mission statements, or personal dilemmas might be resolved by simply asking the question, "Does this allow Christ to have first place?" What else could anyone offer as a higher priority than the one who conquered the grave and opened the doors to heaven for us? There is a fabulous invitation here to take stock of our personal lives and our common life to see what else might have edged into first place, and to ask that God reorder our lives to suit God's holy purpose.

ELIZABETH BARRINGTON FORNEY

Luke 23:33-43

³³When they came to the place that is called The Skull, they crucified Jesus there with the criminals, one on his right and one on his left. [³⁴Then Jesus said, "Father, forgive them; for they do not know what they are doing."] And they cast lots to divide his clothing. ³⁵And the people stood by, watching; but the leaders scoffed at him, saying, "He saved others; let him save himself if he is the Messiah of God, his chosen one!" ³⁶The soldiers also mocked him, coming up and offering him sour wine, ³⁷and saying, "If you are the King of the Jews, save yourself!" ³⁸There was also an inscription over him, "This is the King of the Jews."

³⁹One of the criminals who were hanged there kept deriding him and saying, "Are you not the Messiah? Save yourself and us!" ⁴⁰But the other rebuked him, saying, "Do you not fear God, since you are under the same sentence of condemnation? ⁴¹And we indeed have been condemned justly, for we are getting what we deserve for our deeds, but this man has done nothing wrong." ⁴²Then he said, "Jesus, remember me when you come into your kingdom." ⁴³He replied, "Truly I tell you, today you will be with me in Paradise."

Theological Perspective

What might we consider when we celebrate the festival of the Reign of Christ today? Perhaps the words "Reign of Christ" suggest to us the high and magnificent power and pomp of a glorious king whose rule contrasts with others above whom he is to be exalted. This lectionary text makes clear to us something quite different. The majesty of this king is revealed, not when we look up, but when we look down.

Here we find someone who is deeply humiliated. We see here a man who has to suffer injustice that harms him. What is revealed in this text is miserable, deeply moving, even shocking. We would prefer to hide our face as we watch someone who is truly honorable tortured, because even our compassion is not able to help him. To say to this helpless man, "Help yourself!" is to mock him. To call him "the King of the Jews" is to ridicule him.

These last moments of Jesus' life all seem to be in contrast to what is valued as great in our world. The world presented to us in newspapers or on television is not poor, but is a world of glamour. In this world, the ideal is to be rich and beautiful and influential. The pressure of this ideal is like an infection that overtakes us as we strive for it. In this world, one has to be successful. In this world, the slogan is "Help yourself!" and with this slogan you may survive.

Pastoral Perspective

Here is an elegant statement, unfettered by embellishment of prose or exaggeration, glistening with empathy and compassion. The statement is profoundly poignant because of its context and circumstance, and it is known to be true simply because of the reputation and identity of the man who spoke it: "Truly, I tell you, today you will be with me in Paradise" (v. 43). For a dying man, a convicted and confessed thief, these words uttered by the crucified Christ must have caused sheer unadulterated ecstasy—unspeakable joy.

Jesus' last words to another human being before his death and resurrection were words of forgiveness congruent with the ministry of his short life. Jesus had spent his life teaching about the kingdom of God, preaching liberation to the captives, and healing those who were sick and lame. Jesus' miracles and teachings had so confounded the status quo of the elders, priests, and politicians that he was deemed a threat to their religion and their way of life. Jesus had challenged the unjust treatment of women, preached the need for patience with children, and accused the Pharisees and Sadducees of lacking good faith. His ministry had been controversial, powerful, and world altering, to the point that those whom he threatened condemned him to death by crucifixion.

Exegetical Perspective

Jesus' Virtuous Composure on the Cross. In Luke, Jesus' words to the women following the procession (vv. 28–31), to those crucifying him (vv. 34, 43), and to God as he dies (v. 46) present Jesus as a virtuous, innocent man. Indeed, in Luke, when the centurion at the foot of the cross speaks after seeing Jesus die, he praises God and declares, "Certainly this man was innocent" (v. 47), rather than declaring, "Truly this man was God's Son [or "a son of God"]" (Matt. 27:54; Mark 15:39). The issue in Luke is Jesus' innocence (vv. 15, 41), his lack of any action of insurrection (vv. 5, 19, 22, 25), murder (vv. 19, 25), or "perversion of the people" (vv. 2, 13). In turn, Jesus' speech in Luke while he is hanging on the cross exhibits a deep, personal relationship to God, continually nurtured through a life of prayer (3:21; 5:16; 6:12; 9:18, 29; 10:21–22; 11:1; 22:32, 41).

Father, Forgive Them (v. 34) The earliest manuscripts do not contain Jesus' prayer in verse 34, which expresses the motif of ignorance expressed in Stephen's prayer in Acts 7:60. Throughout time, the motif of ignorance from Luke's second volume was inserted into manuscripts of his first volume, and Jesus' prayer for those who crucified him has become widely known and treasured as an additional exhibition of Jesus' compassion and concern for others.

Homiletical Perspective

"There is a fountain filled with blood drawn from Emmanuel's veins,"[1] goes the old hymn, whose popularity has waned with the passing years. The hymn goes on, "The dying thief rejoiced to see that fountain in his day," but what was it that the dying thief saw? Luke's story makes it clear that he was witnessing the crucifixion and death of Jesus, but why would the thief "rejoice" to see that? Why, beholding this grim scene, so choreographed by the Romans as to deter insurrections by providing such vivid visual instruction, might this thief ask so boldly, "Jesus, remember me when you come into your kingdom"? No simple reason for the thief's request floats to the surface of Luke's narrative.

Luke's story so grinds on our sense of narrative that interpreters have felt compelled to provide midrashic elaborations that supply reasonable motives for this man's request: he knew Jesus back in Nazareth, but they went their separate ways, this man into a life of crime, Jesus into the work of a Messiah; or they had met the night before in Pilate's prison, they had talked, and one thing had led to another. No reasonable explanation, however, will diminish the abruptness of the man's request. This

---

1. William Cowper, "There Is a Fountain," *Evening Light Songs*, rev. ed. (Guthrie, OK: Faith Publishing House, 1987), 183.

Luke 23:33-43

Theological Perspective

Those who cannot survive this way do not make a big thing out of it.

Is Christ just in the world as a shining example for such people? If Christ is the ruler, is he then not necessarily a figure high above the rest of the people?

This passage of the Bible takes us by the hand and gives us the surprising news: Christ is the highest, and he has to suffer awfully. Both fit together in the event of the Savior. The Lord above all lords is exactly the same one who was humbled on the cross; no other is the Lord. This is the Lord. Conversely, this man who is beaten and driven into death has more power than all those who sit in positions of authority and who have forced down so many men and women. That this Lord is hanging helpless on the cross does not stand in contrast to our confession of him. We have to confess of him: "Yours is the power."

The cruel joke that this maltreated human is the "King of the Jews" expresses pure truth because of God's wonderful intervention. The miserably suffering one we see on Golgotha is at the same time the man of whom Pilate says, according to John 19:14, "Here is your King!" We cannot see this king differently from the one who is crucified. In Bach's *St. John Passion*, when the Christian congregation looks to him, they join in a hymn, "O mighty king, great for ever."[1]

That hymn is sung in this context as a commentary on Jesus' answer to Pilate's question, "Are you the King of the Jews?" (John 18:33). Jesus answers, "My kingdom is not from this world. If my kingdom were from this world, my followers would be fighting to keep me from being handed over to the Jews. But as it is, my kingdom is not from here" (John 18:36).

This means he truly is a real ruler and conductor, but in a way that is quite different from what is typical for all other leaders in this world. This kingdom is still hidden behind the noise of the still pompously ruling empires of our time, but the kingdom of God is not simply beyond our world. It overcomes those empires. That it is not from this world is shown in the cross of Christ as the crowning of his life.

That his kingdom is not of this world is proved in what this ruler wants to happen and makes happen that other powerful rulers are not willing or able to do. The ruler of this kingdom does not help himself, but he helps others who need his help (Luke 23:35). Still more: he does not meet evil with evil, but repays evil with good. Indeed, he forgives the people who do not know the evil things they arrange by asking

1. Johann Heermann, "Herzliebster Jesu, was hast du verbrochen," 1630 (Fischer-Tümpel, I, #334).

Pastoral Perspective

Who among us is worthy of grace? We are more like the thieves who hung next to Jesus than we are like Jesus. We do not know what happened to the thief who hung on the other side of Jesus' cross—the one who, rather than asking for mercy, spoke chiding words, challenging Jesus to show his might and power by saving himself and the criminals who surrounded him. Yet the grace of God as revealed in the incarnate Jesus is a word of forgiveness and deep, abiding love. It is hard for us to believe in the gracious God, in the forgiving God, in the God who would love us even when we disappoint and sin.

Jesus' stories of forgiveness are legendary. Jesus spent much of his ministry describing the kingdom of God as having different rules and different expectations from the rules and laws and penalties of humanity. He said that the kingdom of God is like the love freely given when a son foolishly asks his father for his inheritance, takes it, goes to a foreign land, and squanders all he has. Then, when the son comes to his senses and returns, hoping his father will forgive him, he is met with celebration, rejoicing, and jubilation because of the father's great love and ability to forgive him (Luke 15:11–23).

Jesus said that the kingdom of God is like a shepherd who cares so deeply for all his sheep that when one is lost, the shepherd goes in search of the lost and does not give up until the sheep is found (Luke 15:1–7). Jesus said the kingdom of God is like a rich man who gives a party and when the other rich people are too busy for the party, the rich man throws open the invitation and invites the poor, the blind, and the lame to be part of the feast (Luke 14:16–23). Jesus spent more time talking about the kingdom of God than any other topic or issue. Jesus' act of forgiveness while dying on the cross resounds with his teachings that forgiveness is given to all who repent and believe, even condemned thieves during their own executions.

This kind of forgiveness is a challenging notion for many of us. Part of our inability to believe and trust the forgiving power of God's grace and mercy is our inability to believe that other people deserve mercy. *We* want to judge whom God lets into heaven. Many of us are more comfortable not knowing what happened to the thief who scoffed at Jesus than knowing that an undeserving thief was let into paradise. We would rather have had Jesus say that God loves the people we like and the people we say we are like, and that God does not love the people we do not like and the people we say are not like us. We would prefer if God did not love the crackheads

This verse presents Jesus addressing God in his customary way as "Father" (10:21–22; 11:2; 22:42; 23:46; cf. 2:49; 6:36; 9:26; 11:13; 12:30, 32; 22:29; 24:49). In it, he enacts the principle he taught in the Sermon on the Plain, to pray "for those who abuse you" (6:28). Even though the verse probably is an addition to early manuscripts, it is easily understood and welcomed within the Lukan portrait of Jesus.

Verse 34 presents Jesus praying a petitionary prayer that asks God to grant a particular benefit. Jesus taught his disciples in the Lord's Prayer to petition God for benefits (11:3–4; see also 11:9–13), and he himself petitions his heavenly Father prior to his arrest (22:42). Jesus' request participates in an emphasis in Luke on forgiveness, which often focuses on sin (1:77; 3:3; 5:20–24; 7:47–49; 11:4; 24:47). Jesus does not, however, ask God to forgive the sin of those who are crucifying him, as Stephen does in Acts 7:60. Rather, he requests that God forgive actions that come out of ignorance, without calling such actions sin. This absence of defining ignorance as sin gives Jesus' prayer a natural coherence with the Lukan portrayal of Jesus. Various people throughout Luke's Gospel exhibit ignorance, perhaps without malice (cf. 5:30; 6:2; 7:39; 11:38). Jesus addresses ignorance sometimes through skillful teaching (e.g., 10:25–37) and sometimes through sharp prophetic language (e.g., 11:37–52). While hanging on the cross, Jesus speaks priestly language, namely, prayer that petitions God to forgive those engaging in ignorant action.

Let Him Save Himself and Us (vv. 35–39). Luke's account limits the scoffing of Jesus to one group, "leaders" (v. 35), followed by an abbreviated scene of soldiers mocking Jesus (vv. 36–37). In Matthew and Mark, in contrast, soldiers mock Jesus before the procession to the cross (Matt. 27:27–31; Mark 15:16–20), and then multiple groups scoff at Jesus while he is hanging on the cross (Matt. 27:39–43; Mark 15:29–32). The rearrangement and abbreviation in Luke features one of the criminals (Gk. *kakourgoi,* evil-workers) hanging alongside Jesus (v. 39) making the third and climactic act of scoffing and mocking. In contrast, Matthew and Mark only say that the bandits (Gk. *lēstai,* brigands) crucified alongside Jesus "taunted him in the same way" others did (Matt. 27:44; Mark 15:32b).

The reader experiences the depravity of the criminal who speaks out against Jesus through a sequence that builds from the leaders' "making fun" (NRSV "scoffed at") of Jesus (*ekmyktērizō,* v. 35) to the soldiers' "ridiculing" (NRSV "mocked") of Jesus

dying thief has seen something, recognized something in this moment, that others will come to understand only by being taught by the risen Christ.

Three days later a pair of bewildered disciples on the Emmaus road will listen to Christ interpret the Scriptures with the hermeneutical key, "Was it not necessary [*edei*] that the Messiah should suffer these things and then enter into his glory?" (24:26). Later, a second time Jesus will interpret "the law of Moses, the prophets, and the psalms" so that they may understand the divine necessity that "the Messiah is to suffer and to rise from the dead on the third day" (24:44, 46). Jesus' disciples have the same advantage we are given in worship to hear the voice of Christ interpreting the Scriptures, but the dying thief stretched out on a cross lacks this benefit. All he can know is the brutal gore and stench of crucifixion.

His astonishing, out-of-the-blue request raises the question of how we discern the work of God when it irrupts in our midst and how we are to recognize the presence of God's authorized prophet. In Luke's telling of the crucifixion of Jesus, quite a conversation takes place. Jesus' words begin and end the conversation, but in between, three challenges are voiced that echo the three challenges with which Satan tempted Jesus at the beginning of the story (4:3, 6–7, 9). Jesus' identity and integrity are called into question in the hope of provoking him to provide a stunning and utterly compelling demonstration of his character as God's chosen prophet. After all, how can we ever receive a Messiah who does not act like a Messiah? How can you see salvation if no one is being saved?

Talk of salvation hangs thick in the air in these few verses. Jesus is taunted, "let him save himself" (v. 35), then twice dared, "save yourself" (vv. 37, 39), each time with the implication that by doing so he might prove himself and thereby verify the titles—Messiah, King of the Jews—they have pinned upon him. Jesus remains silent. Moments before, he had prayed for their forgiveness. Early in Luke's Gospel, Zechariah's song connected "knowledge of salvation" to "the forgiveness of their sins" (1:77). The dying thief does not preface his request with either of the royal titles that were being tossed around that afternoon, but addresses him only as "Jesus" in the simple, ordinary way one person might address another.

The speaking of that name, however, evokes a world of meaning and of hope. Luke does not spell this out, as Matthew does, "You are to name him Jesus, for he will save his people from their sins" (Matt. 1:21), but it cannot be otherwise than that the name Jesus means "God will save," and that is the

Luke 23:33-43

Theological Perspective

his Father in heaven to forgive them (v. 34). Still more: he allows someone condemned to hell to implore him, "Jesus, remember me when you come into your kingdom" (v. 42).

Apparently we may pray for this, because the coming kingdom of God is the great help and rescue for common people. In this kingdom they are no longer forgotten, but come to light. And still more: this kingdom of God will not come in a remote future; it dawns already, now, "today." This is true because the ruler of the kingdom of God is already with you, in your life and in your dying, and with you even in damnation by sin. Indeed, he is close to you even in your distance from God.

This man is the king in the lowlands, because he does not want us to die and suffer in that dark and sad region. Maybe you are "today" in a sort of darkness, but because the Holy One is with you today and for you today in that darkness, you will be with him today in paradise. Thank God!

EBERHARD BUSCH

Pastoral Perspective

and addicts, the adulterers, the thieves, the prostitutes, the rebellious teenagers, and the disgruntled employees. We would prefer it if paradise were exclusively for the nice people, the clean people, the polite people, the well-behaved people, the right people.

As Christians, we have a confessional faith, not because we are weak, but because God is strong and God is love. We have a confessional faith because the grace of God is sufficient for all. There is grace for us *and* for the people we do not like. We have a confessional faith because God is our refuge and our strength. We confess because God will hear and forgive our sins and their sins too. Our salvation is not dependent upon the preacher, the bishop, or each other, but on a loving, grace-giving God. We confess because God's saving grace will heal, restore, redeem, and forgive those whom God has created and whom God loves fiercely. All have sinned and fallen short; all have angered, frustrated, and disappointed God. God so loved the entire world that whosoever, whosoever, whosoever believes shall get all the grace that God has to give. Thank God that God gives grace and that we do not.

Jesus spent his entire ministry teaching and preaching about the kingdom of God. One of Jesus' last forgiving acts on earth was to proclaim that a repentant sinner would be with him that day in heaven. Oh, praise God!

NANCY LYNNE WESTFIELD

(*empaizō*, v. 36) to the criminal's "blaspheming against" (NRSV "deriding") Jesus (*blasphēmeo*, v. 39). The criminal's blasphemy denies Jesus' identity as the Messiah (cf. v. 35) as it taunts him not only to save himself (cf. 23:35, 37) but the two criminals as well. The criminal's speech continues the scoffing of the leaders, who made fun of the possibility that Jesus was God's Messiah, the "chosen one" (vv. 35; cf. Isa. 42:1), and expands the language about "saving" to include the criminals. When the criminal speaks, he denies both the messianic status of Jesus and Jesus' ability to save life.

Today You Will Be with Me in Paradise (vv. 39–43). The blasphemous statements of the one criminal set the stage for virtuous statements by the other. Instead of blaspheming against Jesus, the second criminal rebukes the other criminal. Rebuking is the language authors of the Gospels use for Jesus' casting out of demons (cf. Luke 4:35, 41; 9:42), but it appears in other contexts in Luke as well (4:39; 8:24; 9:21, 55; 18:15, 39; 19:39). From the perspective of Luke's Gospel, the second criminal's rebuke of the first criminal enacts Jesus' directive: "If another disciple sins, you must rebuke the offender" (17:3). The second criminal, then, exhibits attributes of a disciple when he rebukes the first one, telling him that they themselves are getting what they deserve for their deeds, while Jesus has done nothing wrong (v. 41).

Instead of petitioning for God's kingdom to come (11:2), the second criminal petitions for Jesus to remember him when his own kingdom comes (v. 42). This presupposes a kingdom for Jesus himself (cf. 23:2, 3, 38) and has a direct relation to Jesus' statement to his disciples in 22:29–30 (cf. 1 Cor. 15:24). Instead, Jesus grants him a place "that very day" in paradise, a Persian term for the king's hunting grounds, adopted by Jews and Christians for the eternal, heavenly garden of Eden (Gen. 2:8–10; Rev. 2:7; 22:1–2; *1 Enoch* 60:8; *2 Enoch* 8–9; 2 Esd. 7:36, 123; 8:52). "Today," which occurs emphatically in Jesus' statement (v. 43), does not refer to the day of Jesus' crucifixion, but to the day of messianic salvation inaugurated by Jesus. For Luke, Jesus' coming inaugurates a special day of salvation (cf. 2:11; 4:21; 5:26; 13:32–33; 19:9; 22:34, 61) that continues forever.

VERNON K. ROBBINS

name, and therefore the hope, the dying thief speaks. It is the last gasp of a dying man, perhaps a deathbed confession; it seems so little, so pitiful.

It is sufficient. He does not ask to be saved, to be rescued, but asks only, " Jesus, remember me when you come into your kingdom." Perhaps his plea is meant to echo these words: "Do not remember the sins of my youth or my transgressions; according to your steadfast love remember me, for your goodness' sake, O LORD!" (Ps. 25:7), which is to say, do not remember me according to my wickedness, but remember me according to your goodness.

The thief asks Jesus to be remembered in his kingdom. Surveying the scene at "the place that is called The Skull" (v. 33), we find not the slightest shred of evidence that such a kingdom exists, ever has existed, or ever will exist. The thief asks nonetheless. Somehow he has found the hermeneutical lens that permits him to recognize salvation that intrudes into the absolutely hopeless moment where no one is saved from suffering and death, which is also exactly the moment when salvation breaks through.

"Today you will be with me in Paradise," Jesus promises the thief, but "today" in Luke's Gospel is not merely a twenty-four-hour interval, but the moment when God's salvation fractures time (cf. 2:11; 4:21; 5:26; 19:9).

Here, at the end of the Christian year, we might say of this final reading from Luke that the leaders, soldiers, and first thief all live in ordinary time, where the powers of violence determine events and death is the last word; but the second thief lives already in the reign of Christ. If we can see this, we might also see—as thick darkness falls over this sad scene (v. 44)—a far, faint light rising from the dawning of this realm, a place as calm and refreshing as the garden called paradise.

PATRICK J. WILLSON

Contributors

David R. Adams, Assisting Priest, The Episcopal Church of St. Luke in the Fields, New York, New York

Ellen T. Armour, E. Rhodes and Leona B. Carpenter Associate Professor of Theology, Vanderbilt Divinity School, Nashville, Tennessee

Scott Bader-Saye, Associate Professor, University of Scranton, Scranton, Pennsylvania

Jon L. Berquist, Executive Editor for Biblical Studies, Westminster John Knox Press, Louisville, Kentucky

Bruce C. Birch, Dean Emeritus, Wesley Theological Seminary, Washington, D.C.

Barbara J. Blodgett, Minister for Vocation and Formation, Parish Life and Leadership, Local Church Ministries, United Church of Christ, Cleveland, Ohio

Bruce G. Boak, Pastor, First Presbyterian Church, Pittsford, New York

Frederick Borsch, Professor of New Testament and Chair of Anglican Studies, Lutheran Theological Seminary at Philadelphia, Philadelphia, Pennsylvania

Sally A. Brown, Elizabeth M. Engle Associate Professor of Preaching and Worship, Princeton Theological Seminary, Princeton, New Jersey

John M. Buchanan, Pastor, Fourth Presbyterian Church, and Editor/Publisher of *The Christian Century*, Chicago, Illinois

Sharon Peebles Burch, Retired American Baptist minister, San Rafael, California

Eberhard Busch, Professor for Reformed Theology, University of Göttingen, Germany

Ronald P. Byars, Professor Emeritus of Preaching and Worship, Union Theological Seminary and Presbyterian School of Christian Education, Richmond, Virginia

Corrine L. Carvalho, Professor of Theology, University of St. Thomas, St. Paul, Minnesota

Pamela Cooper-White, Ben G. and Nancye Clapp Gautier Professor of Pastoral Theology, Care and Counseling, Columbia Theological Seminary, Decatur, Georgia

Charles B. Cousar, Professor Emeritus, Columbia Theological Seminary, Decatur, Georgia

Helen Montgomery DeBevoise, Co-Pastor, Park Lake Presbyterian Church, Orlando, Florida

John T. DeBevoise, Pastor, Palma Ceia Presbyterian Church, Tampa, Florida

Carol J. Dempsey, Professor of Theology (Biblical Studies), University of Portland, Portland, Oregon

Lewis R. Donelson, Professor of New Testament, Austin Presbyterian Theological Seminary, Austin, Texas

Sarah Birmingham Drummond, Associate Dean and Assistant Professor of Ministerial Leadership, Andover Newton Theological School, Newton Center, Massachusetts

Robert E. Dunham, Pastor, University Presbyterian Church, Chapel Hill, North Carolina

Margit Ernst-Habib, Reformed theologian, Ubstadt-Weiber, Germany

Jane Anne Ferguson, Associate Minister, First Plymouth Congregational Church, United Church of Christ, Englewood, Colorado

Matthew Fitzgerald, Senior Minister, Wellesley Hills Congregational Church, United Church of Christ, Wellesley, Massachusetts

Elizabeth Barrington Forney, Minister of Word and Sacrament, Presbyterian Church (U.S.A.), Clarksville, Tennessee

Terence E. Fretheim, Professor of Old Testament, Luther Seminary, St. Paul, Minnesota

W. Hulitt Gloer, Professor of Preaching, George W. Truett Theological Seminary, Waco, Texas

Timothy Hessel-Robinson, Lunger Assistant Professor of Spiritual Resources and Disciplines, Brite Divinity School, Fort Worth, Texas

Olive Elaine Hinnant, Adjunct Professor, College of Santa Fe, Santa Fe, New Mexico

J. Peter Holmes, Minister of the Congregation, Yorkminster Park Baptist Church, Toronto, Ontario, Canada

Ruthanna Hooke, Assistant Professor of Homiletics, Virginia Theological Seminary, Alexandria, Virginia

Mary Eleanor Johns, Director of the Summer Youth Institute and Admissions Associate, Pittsburgh Theological Seminary, Pittsburgh, Pennsylvannia

E. Elizabeth Johnson, J. Davison Philips Professor of New Testament Language, Literature, and Exegesis, Columbia Theological Seminary, Decatur, Georgia

Henry F. Knight, Director, Cohen Center for Holocaust Studies, Keene State College, Keene, New Hampshire

Robert Leach, Pastor, Ogden Dunes Community Church, Ogden Dunes, Indiana

Mark A. Lomax, Interim Dean, Johnson C. Smith Theological Seminary, Atlanta, Georgia

Kimberly Bracken Long, Assistant Professor of Worship and Coordinator of Worship Resources for Congregations, Columbia Theological Seminary, Decatur, Georgia

Jack R. Lundbom, Visiting Professor of Old Testament, Lutheran Theological Seminary, Hong Kong, China

Dwight M. Lundgren, Coordinator of Intercultural Ministries, American Baptist Churches USA, Valley Forge, Pensylvania

William P. "Matt" Matthews, Pastor, St. Giles Presbyterian Church, Greenville, South Carolina

Alyce M. McKenzie, Professor of Homiletics, Perkins School of Theology, Southern Methodist University, Dallas, Texas

Donald K. McKim, Executive Editor for Theology and Reference, Westminster John Knox Press, Germantown, Tennessee

Steve D. Miller, Minister, Community United Methodist Church, Westcliffe, Colorado

Martha L. Moore-Keish, Assistant Professor of Theology, Columbia Theological Seminary, Decatur, Georgia

D. Cameron Murchison, Dean of the Faculty, Executive Vice President, and Professor of

Ministry, Columbia Theological Seminary, Decatur, Georgia

Donald W. Musser, Senior Professor of Religious Studies, Stetson University, DeLand, Florida

Guy D. Nave Jr., Associate Professor of Religion, Luther College, Decorah, Iowa

G. Penny Nixon, Senior Minister, Congregational Church of San Mateo, United Church of Christ, San Mateo, California

Susan K. Olson, Director, Career Counseling, Yale Divinity School, New Haven, Connecticut

Lanny Peters, Pastor, Oakhurst Baptist Church, Decatur, Georgia

Joseph L. Price, C. Milo Connick Professor of Religious Studies, Whittier College, Whittier, California

Neta Pringle, Minister of Word and Sacrament, Presbyterian Church (U.S.A.), Wilmington, Delaware

Marjorie Procter-Smith, LeVan Professor of Christian Worship, Perkins School of Theology, Southern Methodist University, Dallas, Texas

George W. Ramsey, Herrington Professor of Bible Emeritus, Presbyterian College, Clinton, South Carolina

Charles E. Raynal, Associate Professor Emeritus of Theology, Columbia Theological Seminary, Decatur, Georgia

Mitchell G. Reddish, O. L. Walker Professor of Christian Studies, Stetson University, DeLand, Florida

Stephen Breck Reid, Professor of Christian Scriptures, George W. Truett Theological Seminary, Waco, Texas

Nelson Rivera, Associate Professor of Systematic Theology, The Lutheran Theological Seminary at Philadelphia, Pennsylvania

Vernon K. Robbins, Professor of New Testament, Emory University, Atlanta, Georgia

Arthur (Art) Ross III, Pastor, White Memorial Presbyterian Church, Raleigh, North Carolina

David R. Ruhe, Senior Minister, Plymouth Congregational United Church of Christ, Des Moines, Iowa

Rodney S. Sadler Jr., Associate Professor of Bible, Union Theological Seminary and Presbyterian School of Christian Education at Charlotte, Charlotte, North Carolina

Donna Schaper, Senior Minister, Judson Memorial Church, New York, New York

Mary H. Schertz, Professor of New Testament and Director, Institute of Mennonite Studies, Associated Mennonite Bible Seminary, Elkhart, Indiana

Laurel C. Schneider, Professor of Theology, Ethics, and Culture, Chicago Theological Seminary, Chicago, Illinois

Abraham Smith, Professor of New Testament, Perkins School of Theology, Southern Methodist University, Dallas, Texas

Stephanie Mar Smith, Visiting Assistant Professor of Theology, Whitworth University, Spokane, Washington

H. Gray Southern, District Superintendent of the North Carolina Conference of the United Methodist Church, Durham, North Carolina

Bryan Spinks, Goddard Professor of Liturgical Studies and Pastoral Theology, Yale Divinity School, New Haven, Connecticut

Thomas R. Steagald, Pastor, LaFayette Street United Methodist Church, Shelby, North Carolina

Martha Sterne, Associate Rector, Holy Innocents' Episcopal Church, Atlanta, Georgia

Laura S. Sugg, Associate Pastor, Westminster Presbyterian Church, Charlottesville, Virginia

Beth LaNeel Tanner, Associate Professor of Old Testament, New Brunswick Theological Seminary, New Brunswick, New Jersey

Gray Temple, Episcopal priest, retired, Duluth, Georgia

Emilie M. Townes, Andrew W. Mellon Professor of African American Religion and Theology, Yale Divinity School, New Haven, Connecticut

Patricia Tull, A. B. Rhodes Professor of Hebrew Scriptures, Louisville Presbyterian Theological Seminary, Louisville, Kentucky

Nancy Lynne Westfield, Associate Professor of Religion Education, Drew University, Madison, New Jersey

Patrick J. Willson, Pastor, Williamsburg Presbyterian Church, Williamsburg, Virginia

Oliver Larry Yarbrough, Tillinghast Professor of Religion, Middlebury College, Middlebury, Vermont

Scripture Index

Author Index

Marjorie Procter-Smith	Proper 25 G HP, All Saints G HP, Proper 26 G HP	Stephanie Mar Smith	Proper 19 E TP, Proper 20 E TP, Proper 21 E TP
George W. Ramsey	Proper 19 OT EP, Proper 20 OT EP, Proper 21 OT EP	H. Gray Southern	Proper 22 OT HP, Proper 23 PS HP, Proper 24 PS HP
Charles E. Raynal	Proper 17 G PP, Proper 18 G PP	Bryan Spinks	Proper 25 OT TP, All Saints OT TP, Proper 26 OT TP
Mitchell G. Reddish	Proper 19 E EP, Proper 20 E EP, Proper 21 E EP	Thomas R. Steagald	Proper 17 OT TP, Proper 18 OT TP
Stephen Breck Reid	Proper 19 OT TP, Proper 20 OT TP, Proper 21 OT TP	Martha Sterne	Proper 27 OT HP, Proper 28 OT HP, Proper 29 OT HP
Nelson Rivera	Proper 27 OT TP, Proper 28 OT TP, Proper 29 OT TP	Laura S. Sugg	Proper 25 G PP, All Saints G PP, Proper 26 G PP
Vernon K. Robbins	Proper 27 G EP, Proper 28 G EP, Proper 29 G EP	Beth LaNeel Tanner	Proper 22 OT EP, Proper 23 PS EP, Proper 24 PS EP
Arthur (Art) Ross III	Proper 17 PS PP, Proper 18 PS PP	Gray Temple	Proper 17 E TP, Proper 18 E TP
David R. Ruhe	Proper 25 PS PP, All Saints PS PP, Proper 26 PS PP	Emilie M. Townes	Proper 17 G TP, Proper 18 G TP
Rodney S. Sadler Jr.	Proper 17 G EP, Proper 18 G EP	Patricia Tull	Proper 27 PS EP, Proper 28 OT EP, Proper 29 PS EP
Donna Schaper	Proper 25 OT HP, All Saints OT HP, Proper 26 OT HP	Nancy Lynne Westfield	Proper 27 G PP, Proper 28 G PP, Proper 29 G PP
Mary H. Schertz	Proper 25 E TP, All Saints E TP, Proper 26 E TP	Patrick J. Willson	Proper 27 G HP, Proper 28 G HP, Proper 29 G HP
Laurel C. Schneider	Proper 27 PS TP, Proper 28 OT TP, Proper 29 PS TP	Oliver Larry Yarbrough	Proper 22 G EP, Proper 23 G EP, Proper 24 G EP
Abraham Smith	Proper 27 E EP, Proper 28 E EP, Proper 29 E EP		